THE ARTHUR

OF THE ENGLISH

ARTHURIAN LITERATURE IN THE MIDDLE AGES
II

THE
ARTHUR
OF THE
ENGLISH

THE ARTHURIAN LEGEND IN MEDIEVAL ENGLISH LIFE AND LITERATURE

edited by

W. R. J. Barron

CARDIFF
UNIVERSITY OF WALES PRESS
1999

British Library Cataloguing-in-Publication Data

A catalogue record for this book
is available from the British Library

ISBN 0-7083-1477-5

Typeset by the Editor
Printed in Great Britain by Bookcraft Ltd., Avon

ARTHURIAN LITERATURE IN THE MIDDLE AGES

Series Editor

W. R. J. Barron

Further volumes in preparation

The ALMA series is a cooperation between
the University of Wales Press and the Vinaver Trust

Acknowledgements

My thanks are due to my colleagues of the Vinaver Trust for their encouragement and support in the planning and execution of this project, to the University of Exeter for its hospitality, to its Research Fund for a grant in aid of production, and to its Pallas Computing Centre – in particular Mike Dobson, Gary Singer and Katherine Fenton – for technical advice and assistance in the production of this volume. **W.R.J.B.**

CONTENTS

PREFACE

When, some years ago, the Vinaver Trust considered revising the standard history of its academic field, *Arthurian Literature in the Middle Ages* (ed. R.S. Loomis, Oxford, 1959), the authors of the opening chapters on Celtic texts were the first to be approached. Their feeling was that the passage of time and the advance of scholarship made necessary a more fundamental revision than was possible within the original single-volume format. The book had served several generations of students well, but the Trustees were persuaded that the time had come for a more fundamental approach to Arthurian literary history.

ALMA, as it appeared in the Abbreviations to a hundred volumes, had reflected its editor's professional interests closely and, even within the limitations of a single volume, given a rather narrow picture of Arthurian studies. Changing perspectives, the accumulation of scholarship and the more flexible technology of publishing now make possible a fuller record. The basis of the volumes listed on the facing page is cultural rather than purely linguistic, as more appropriate to a period when modern nationalism, and in many cases modern nation states, had not yet evolved. Each takes into account extraneous influences and includes some texts which the influence of the mother culture carried into the wider world.

Each volume in the series is primarily addressed to students of the individual culture in question, but also to those of other cultures who, for the appreciation of their own Arthurian literature, need to be aware of the manifold forms it took in the wider world and of interactions between various expressions of the legend. With this dual readership in mind, the text has been confined to a statement of current received opinion as individual contributors see it, concisely expressed and structured in a way which, it is hoped, will help readers to appreciate the development of Arthurian themes within the particular culture. Tangential issues, academic controversy, and matters of documentation, more likely to be of scholarly interest, are confined to the notes.

Within this remit, the editors have had complete control over their individual volumes. They themselves would admit that they have not ensnared that rare bird, the Whole Truth of the Arthurian legend, and that in time a new survey will be needed, perhaps on a different basis. But if, for the moment, they have allowed others to catch a glimpse of that universal phoenix, the Arthurian myth, through the thickets of academic speculation, they will feel that they have done what was presently necessary.

W. R. J. Barron

THE CONTRIBUTORS

FLORA ALEXANDER is a Senior Lecturer in English at the University of Aberdeen. A regular contributor to *BBIAS*, she has written on various Arthurian topics as well as on Canadian fiction and the teaching of Women's Studies

ROSAMUND ALLEN teaches Old and Middle English literature at Queen Mary and Westfield College, University of London. She has published on the medieval English mystics, on Arthurian texts, including Layamon's *Brut*, and on Gower.

RAY BARRON was a student at St Andrews, Yale and Strasbourg, taught at Aberdeen, Manchester and Shiraz, and is currently a Senior Research Fellow of the University of Exeter, a Past President of IAS, and a Vinaver Trustee.

CATHERINE BATT is Lecturer in Medieval Literature, University of Leeds. Her research includes comparative literature, and she has published on Anglo-Norman and Middle English hagiography, the *Gawain*-poet, Malory and Caxton.

CHRIS BROOKS is Reader in Victorian Culture in the University of Exeter and Chair of the Victorian Society. He has published extensively on the history of the Gothic Revival, Victorian architecture and arts, and the literature of the period.

INGA BRYDEN, Senior Lecturer in English at King Alfred's College, Winchester, will shortly publish a four-volume collection of Pre-Raphaelite writings and is finishing a book on the reinvention of the Arthurian legends in Victorian culture.

DAVID BURNLEY is Chairman of the School of English at Sheffield University. He has written books on the language of Chaucer and the history of English and courtly culture, as well as material on medieval French, and English lexicology.

JAMES CARLEY, a professor of English at York University, Toronto, has written extensively on Glastonbury Abbey and the Arthurian legend. He is presently completing books on the libraries of Henry VIII, and the Tudor antiquary Leland.

PETER FIELD is a professor of English at the University of Wales, Bangor. He has published extensively on authors from Nennius in the ninth century to Anthony Burgess, but the focus of his interests has always been Malory.

ROSALIND FIELD is Senior Lecturer in the Department of English, Royal Holloway College, University of London, with research interests and numerous publications in Middle English and Anglo-Norman romance, and in Chaucer.

DAVID GRIFFITH gained his doctorate from Exeter in 1991 and now teaches Old and Middle English at the University of Birmingham. His research interests are in medieval romance and late medieval art.

KAREN HODDER teaches in the Department of English and Related Literature and the Centre for Medieval Studies at the University of York, and has written articles on medieval and Victorian Arthurian subjects.

LESLEY JOHNSON, formerly Senior Lecturer in the School of English, University of Leeds, now lives and works in Frankfurt, and has published widely in the field of medieval English historiography and in feminist studies.

FRANÇOISE LE SAUX, graduate of the University of Wales and of the University of Lausanne, Switzerland, has taught in the universities of Lausanne, Geneva and Freiburg-im-Breisgau, and is now a Lecturer at Reading University.

CERIDWEN LLOYD-MORGAN has published widely in the field of Welsh Arthurian literature. She is currently Senior Assistant Archivist in the Department of Manuscripts and Records at the National Library of Wales, Aberystwyth.

MALDWYN MILLS is an Emeritus professor of English in the University of Wales, Aberystwyth. Educated at University of Wales Cardiff, and Jesus College, Oxford, his chief research interests are the Middle English romances and Chaucer

GILLIAN ROGERS, a doctoral graduate of the University of Wales, is English Faculty Librarian in the University of Cambridge. Her main research interests are in the Middle English *Gawain*-romances and in the Percy Folio manuscript.

DIANE SPEED is a Senior Lecturer in English in the University of Sydney. Her research interests include medieval romance, Biblical literature and *exemplum*. She is currently working on the Anglo-Latin *Gesta Romanorum* and Gower.

CAROLE WEINBERG is a Senior Lecturer in the Department of English and American Studies at the University of Manchester, where she teaches medieval literature. Her present area of research is medieval Arthurian literature.

ELIZABETH WILLIAMS taught medieval English at the University of Leeds where she also pioneered a course in children's literature. Since early retirement in 1991 she has continued research in medieval romance, folk-tale and ballad.

JOHN WITHRINGTON is currently Director of the International Office of the University of Lancaster and Honorary Lecturer in English there. He publishes on medieval and modern Arthurian literature, particularly Malory.

JULIET VALE studied at Lady Margaret Hall, Oxford, and the Centre for Medieval Studies, University of York. She is currently an independent scholar whose work focuses on medieval chivalric and courtly culture.

INTRODUCTION

The English think of Arthur as their own. His name has been borne by their princes down the ages – all too often an ill-omened cradle-gift. It is written across the map from Edinburgh to Tintagel, Caerleon to Camboglanna, and in a dozen places where the Hope of the British lies sleeping until the hour of national need – but on no authentic gravestone anywhere. Fifteen centuries of celebration in myth, legend, chronicle, epic, romance, drama, opera and film have engraved it upon the national consciousness as if England and Arthur were one, a secular St George emblematic of nationhood.

Yet the myth and legend belong to another culture which struggled for centuries to protect its national identity from the encroaching hegemony of the English. And in the vernacular literature of that culture Arthur figures merely as a charismatic folk-hero, leading a rumbustious brotherhood in casual adventures ranging across the Celtic west – no hint of a national cause or a dynastic destiny. Only in the Latin chronicles of the Celts can be detected the shadowy outline of a military career, battles against Saxon foes widely scattered across the map, a death made mysterious by hints of internecine conflict – all vague and fragmentary. But enough to half-convince respectable historians of the existence, once long ago, of a great national champion, without apparent consideration of ethnic identity.

From an early twelfth-century perspective the wish was perhaps father to the thought: a hybrid society of many races – Celtic, Anglo-Saxon, Norwegian, Danish, Norman, Breton – in search of an identity needed a sense of dynastic continuity from an honourable antiquity, however improbable. With all the ornaments of history, but in the spirit of romance, Geoffrey of Monmouth supplied what was needed. Once he had placed Arthur at the apogee of his two-thousand-year arc of British history, and his book had swept Europe, the identity of man and island was fixed for all time.

There are signs that the age was ripe for the association: even before Geoffrey's *Historia* appeared, other historians had – reluctantly, dubiously – extrapolated from the missing grave the possibility of survival and return, already an article of faith with lesser men, as the doubting canons of Laon, mobbed at Bodmin in 1113, found to their cost. Local tradition and popular conviction extended and vivified what the *Historia* had made authentic and coherent. Each of the island races added its own gloss. Geoffrey's politic silence on Arthur's fate prompted Wace's discreet acknowledgement of the

Hope of the British without confirmation, tacitly implying that his Norman patrons had succeeded to the dynastic inheritance. And they, who called themselves English even before they spoke the language, assumed its imperial claims, which rivalled those their French contemporaries had inherited from Charlemagne. Laʒamon in turn appropriated it for his own people: at the moment of Arthur's passing, having reiterated that 'the Britons still await the time when Arthur will come again,' he ends the epoch with a new gloss on Merlin's prophecy, 'þat an Arður sculde ʒete cum Anglen to fulste' (*Brut*, 14297; *that an Arthur should again come to aid the people of England*).

The sleight-of-mind by which Arthur becomes the Messianic hope of the Saxons who were his bitterest enemies, who inherit it as they inherit the land and the dynastic succession, sets the pattern for the future. Hereafter the Arthurian epoch, however vague, features as a golden age, a focus for patriotism in which all races could associate themselves with the victorious Britons and identify any invader as the perennial enemy. Arthur becomes all things to all men: to the Welsh a future liberator; to the Angevins and Plantagenets an eminent predecessor whose dynastic inheritance could be legitimized and at the same time neutralized by a conveniently-discovered grave; to the Tudors a Celtic forebear to whose succession they could assert a double claim; to the Scots an old enemy honourably remembered, and a surrogate for the English in Scotland's persistent struggle for national independence. The tragic ending to his reign, since it prefigured the eventual downfall of invading dynasties, Saxon and perhaps, eventually, Norman, was no bar to Arthur becoming a symbol of national identity to all the island races. Out of their multiple ambivalences grew the concept of Britain, englobing England yet greater than England, a convenient fiction of national unity sporadically undermined by nascent nationalism. Arthur was to remain for centuries an active force in island politics and his Round Table company a model for manifold forms of social idealism.

To the end of the Middle Ages and even beyond, the history of the island in all its languages, Latin included, is rooted in Geoffrey's dynastic chronicle. Numerous chronicles in verse and prose link past and present in an unbroken continuum, using Merlin's prophecies to imply a national destiny, projecting Arthur as the archetypal ancestor, embodiment of strong rule, a model for contemporary kings and a measure of their achievement. The variety of versions and the multiple manuscripts in English – always a majority medium and a literary language since the seventh century, inevitably returned to national dominance – demonstrate the form in which Englishmen of all classes absorbed the sense of their nationhood. Though vastly influential, such chronicle material is inadequately represented in this survey; neglected by historians as factually suspect, by literary analysts as lacking in art, it still awaits scholarly attention. The tinge of romance which rendered Geoffrey's *Historia* suspect to serious historians prompted Wace's indication of intervals in Arthur's reign when the fabulous adventures linked to his name in popular tradition might have taken place and occasional echoes of literary romance in the later chronicles. The association of history and romance lent a gloss of idealism to the patriotic sentiment inherent in the chronicles, making their dynastic theme particularly attractive to the authors of English romance.

It was perhaps a natural consequence of the cultural shock of the Norman Conquest that the earliest romances produced in England thereafter, in Anglo-Norman as well as English, dealt with heroes and episodes from the native past of the island, Norse or Anglo-Saxon rather than Celtic, as if seeking ancestral roots beyond the revolutionary present. Though the Matter of Britain was present in multiple forms of French romance, its Arthurian court made a testing-ground for complementary and conflicting idealisms of love and chivalry, English redactors were highly selective in what they took from such sources. Their judgement of the interests of English readers favoured those elements which could be most closely related to national figures and themes: Arthur as an embodiment of national aspirations, Merlin as abettor of his imperial ambitions, Josph of Arimathea in his association with the Grail and Glastonbury. Where they reproduced any extensive section of the French structure, their tone was dutiful rather than inspired, exploiting patriotic consciousness to inform as well as entertain. Most characteristically they concentrated on the triumph of Arthurian civilization and on its downfall, interpreted in one case in epic terms as treason from within, in another in a modified version of the *roman courtois* conflict of love and duty. The two versions of the death of Arthur, alliterative and stanzaic, are perhaps the most characteristic of all Arthurian texts in English. In both the choice of medium roots them in native tradition, while the contrast between them demonstrates the range of expressive means available to English poets. Both explore the dynastic theme, though deriving from very different versions of it, the alliterative imperial and martial in emphasis, the stanzaic, narrower in focus, domestic and personal. The situations, relationships, values, ideals involved in both have close counterparts in contemporary life; readers are invited to reflect upon the nature of kingship, the moral basis of governance, conflicts of public duty and personal feeling, loyalty and love. Both poets provide a variety of perspectives upon the action and passionate undercurrents of emotion, but do not arbitrate in the judgement they invite. Except, perhaps, through the atmosphere they evoke of regret for the passing of a golden age, for human idealism undermined by the very nature of humanity.

The same ambivalence underlies those romances which focus on various aspects of chivalric idealism, exemplified by individual knights, implicitly in the service of king and country, but presented in personal rather than dynastic terms. Inevitably, Arthur drops into the background, still the embodiment of truth and justice, occasionally dynamic and decisive, but often passive to the point of feebleness. For some of those who assume his central role, the adventures through which they demonstrate valour, wit, fidelity, seem an end in themselves. Much of the material composing them derives from the French tradition, often so freely treated as to obscure the textual relationship. In the process, the codes of *roman courtois* are either largely ignored – notably courtly love – or expressed in terms of such basic human values as 'trawþe' (*truth/troth/fidelity*). Personified most frequently in Gawain, the embodiment of English concepts of manliness, moderation and good sense, renowned as Arthur's loyal lieutenant in dynastic struggles, the social appeal of such chivalric romances seems to have been wider than that of their French counterparts. Though the corpus is small, its range is wide. At one extreme, in *Sir Gawain and the Green Knight*, it rivals the most subtle and sophisticated of *romans courtois*; at the other, in *The Jeaste of Syr Gawayne*, compiled from episodes of French romance rejected by a more idealistic Scots redactor, it resembles folk-tale in the dominance of incident over ideals.

An even more pronounced shift in the balance between values and adventures marks the texts grouped here as folk romances. The features which distinguish them from the chivalric romances, though blurred in some examples, are so clear-cut in others as to defy common classification. Comparatively brief, late in date and popular in tone, their plots revolve around the un-ideological tests, vows, quests of folk-tale. Here too Gawain is the most characteristic protagonist, Arthur is further degraded by his ineptitude, irresponsibility and heartlessness, and the ideals of the Round Table are undermined by cynicism and burlesque. It is as if the wheel has come full circle and Arthur has shrunk to the parody figure of the early Celtic texts, playing a marginal role in the adventures of some questing folk-hero.

Any easy assumption that the distinctive features of folk romance reflect a difference of authors and audiences is queried by the possibility that one of them, *The Weddynge of Sir Gawen and Dame Ragnell*, was written by Sir Thomas Malory. Yet Malory's *Morte Darthur* reads like a summation of the noblest elements in the Arthurian tradition, French and English. However it evolved, the existing structure of the *Morte* presents the wide-ranging adventures of individual knights within the dynastic framework of the rise and fall of Arthur's kingdom. The effect is to associate chivalric aspiration and achievement with the past of that society with which England had come to identify itself – an effect increased by Malory's repeated evocation of its geography. Chivalric idealism is given greater relevance by the association; England's past is dignified as the scene of such exalted aspiration.

In the centuries which followed, Arthur's giant reputation was to dwindle still further, his former greatness mocked and parodied by a society which had found more rational bases for its perspective on the past, different forms of social idealism. But, across centuries of neglect, Malory provided a bridge to a new romantic age whose confident nationalism valued a dynastic figurehead, and which incorporated Arthurian chivalry in its ideal of the English gentleman. With the *Morte Darthur* in the van, Arthur was to go round the English-speaking world and figure in new forms, new cultures, fulfilling the prediction which Laȝamon put into the mouth of Merlin, even before Arthur's conception, that he was to be a Messianic saviour who, down the ages, would be meat and drink to the tellers of tales:

> 'Longe beoð æuere, dæd ne bið he næuere;
> þe wile þe þis world stænt, ilæsten scal is worðmunt; . . .
> Of him scullen gleomen godliche singen;
> of his breosten scullen æten aðele scopes;
> scullen of his blode beornes beon drunke. (*Brut*, 9406-7, 9410-12)

> (*'As long as time lasts, he shall never die; while this world lasts, his fame shall endure; . . . Of him shall minstrels splendidly sing; of his breast noble bards shall eat; heroes shall be drunk upon his blood.'*)

THE CELTIC TRADITION

Ceridwen Lloyd-Morgan

The study of Celtic traditions of Arthur was once dominated by attempts to establish that Arthurian literature in France and England had its roots in 'Celtic' sources. Only rarely, however, is it possible to find unambiguous textual or documentary evidence of direct connections between romances from the twelfth century onwards and texts in one of the Celtic languages predating the composition of French or English works. In fact, it is far easier to trace influence in the opposite direction, in the later Middle Ages and beyond, when both Irish and Welsh translators and compilers made use of established French and English Arthurian texts. Moreover, to refer to 'Celtic traditions' of Arthur is misleading, as it implies a degree of cultural unity that did not exist. Such Arthurian traditions as have been preserved in the written literature of the Celtic languages are mainly in Welsh. Arthurian material in Irish is rare, late and derivative. The first, very brief, reference to Arthur in Irish is found in a praise-poem by Gofraidh Fionn O Dálaigh who died in 1387,[1] and the only full-length medieval Arthurian text in Irish is the incomplete fifteenth-century *Lorgaireacht an tSoidhigh Naomhtha* ('The Quest of the Holy Grail'),[2] which is ultimately derived from the early thirteenth-century French Grail romance *La Queste del Saint Graal*. Four other Irish Arthurian tales are known, composed between the fifteenth and seventeenth centuries, all of them combining native material with Arthurian elements of English or continental origin. It has been argued, for example, that *Eachtra an Mhadra Mhaoil* ('The Story of the Crop-eared Dog') may be related to *Arthur and Gorlagon*; similarly *Eachtra Mhacaoimh-an-Iolair* ('The Story of the Eagle-Boy') has Arthurian elements, but these may well be later accretions. Whatever their precise status, however, it is clear that there was no early, indigenous Irish Arthurian tradition.[3] Since Scottish Gaelic presented a cultural and linguistic continuum with Irish until at least the seventeenth century, it is not surprising to find that in Scotland also Arthurian literature never achieved the popularity it enjoyed elsewhere during the Middle Ages.[4] In this, as in so many respects, the Brythonic countries – Wales, Cornwall and Brittany – have more in common with each other than with Gaelic culture.

There is strong evidence of Arthurian tradition in both Cornwall and Brittany, whose languages and traditions are closer to each other than to those of Wales. Unfortunately, the surviving written literary evidence is patchy and late and thus could have been influenced by material from other cultures. Nonetheless, taken together with other kinds of evidence, it reveals the existence of a rich vein of popular traditions of Arthur and his entourage in those countries.[5] But it is only in Welsh that we find a substantial body of literary material preserved in the medieval vernacular and from which some evidence can be deduced of the development of an Arthurian tradition. Despite the comparatively late date of extant vernacular manuscripts from Wales, there can be no doubt that a number of the older texts, especially poetry, predate Geoffrey of Monmouth by several centuries and are thus important witnesses to the earliest strata of Welsh tradition. Latin sources from Celtic Britain, such as the *Annales Cambriae* and *Historia Brittonum*, may well reflect early tales circulating in the vernacular, of course, but in their present form they clearly represent a different strand of tradition, and it is on the vernacular sources alone that this chapter will focus. It should be stressed that these are not historical but literary texts and thus cannot be taken as evidence for the existence of a putative historical Arthur.

The development of Arthurian tradition in Welsh is inextricably linked with places and events outside Wales. The earliest surviving references are in Old Welsh poetry whose locus is generally in northern Britain, on the borders of England and Scotland, a region which was not Goidelic but Brythonic-speaking, and remained so even after the advancing Saxons drove a wedge between it and Wales in the early seventh century. Hence the Welsh poem *Y Gododdin*, attributed to the poet Aneirin and preserved in *Llyfr Aneirin* (The Book of Aneirin), which provides an early but tantalizing reference to Arthur, has been described as 'the oldest *Scottish* poem'.[6] It contains a series of elegies which, in their present form, may go back to the ninth century. In one of them a warrior called Gwawrddwr is compared with Arthur: he is praised for his generosity and his success in killing enemies.[7] Poetry was an exclusively non-narrative genre in Welsh, so here, typically, although parallel narrative traditions are evoked, there is no elaboration, since the audience is assumed to be familiar with them. But even this first enigmatic reference shows that by the time of the composition of *Y Gododdin* Arthur was known as a figure from a historical or legendary past, and that he was seen above all as a warrior, a model hero against whom contemporary fighting men could be measured.

A similar image is evoked in an Old Welsh poem in the Book of Taliesin. Again the provenance is ultimately north British, for the semi-legendary poet Taliesin, who is mentioned in the *Historia Brittonum*, was associated later in his career with the court of Urien in the north British kingdom of Rheged, although he is also said to have been a court poet in Wales. *Preiddeu Annwn* ('The Spoils of Annwfn'), which may have been in existence by the tenth century, reflects what was perhaps one of the original stories about Arthur in Brythonic tradition.[8]

Arthur and his men make a series of disastrous expeditions to Annwn, usually an otherworld, but here presented as a land across the water from Wales. Their purpose is a quest for a magical sword and cauldron, and thus *Preiddeu Annwn* provides our earliest example of a theme which is paralleled much later in the development of the Grail story in France and England. Furthermore, whilst Arthur is presented as an active, heroic leader, sharing danger with his men, their adventures involve the supernatural – specifically a non-Christian magic – which is emphasized by the mysterious nature of the fortresses they visit.

One of the dialogue poems in the Black Book of Carmarthen, beginning 'Pa gur yv y porthaur' (*Who is the gatekeeper?*), creates a similar mood.[9] Here Arthur stands outside the court asking admittance from the gatekeeper Glewlwyd Gafaelfawr, and boasting of the exploits of the warriors in his retinue. The supernatural figures prominently in the list, for those they have vanquished include wizards, witches and various monsters. In *Pa gur* for the first time we have a clear picture of Arthur's retinue, and it is worth noting that some of the names, such as Manawydan fab Llyr, are not normally associated with Arthurian tradition, although they are familiar to us from other Welsh sources. The two who were to remain attached to Arthur throughout later developments are Bedwyr and especially Cai, perhaps the most prominent of Arthur's associates in the earliest Welsh sources. In this poem he already has his traditional epithet: he is 'Cei Gwyn' (*Fair Cai*), and is presented as an attractive, heroic figure. It is only in later texts, which have been influenced by non-native sources, that he comes to be depicted as a surly, sulky seneschal. In this dialogue poem he is said to have fought nine witches, perhaps recalling the nine maidens associated with the cauldron in *Preiddeu Annwn*, and also the monstrous 'cath palug', Palug's cat, which might be related to the *chapalu* of later French tradition. Cai is also linked here with a more shadowy character, Llacheu, Arthur's son, with whose murder Cai was to be credited in later traditions, French as well as Welsh.[10] *Pa gur* thus provides some of the earliest references in any language to characters and events which appear in much later texts and popular traditions. Divorced from their original full narrative context, however, many remain enigmatic. The reference to Arthur in the *Beddau englynion* ('The Stanzas of the Graves'), also preserved in the Black Book of Carmarthen, poses similar problems of interpretation.[11] In its list of the burial-places of warriors, many of them with recognizably Arthurian names, such as Bedwyr and Owain, for Arthur's grave alone no precise location is given. The ambiguous statement 'anoeth bit bed i Arthur' (*the world's wonder is the grave of Arthur*), could be read as a hint at some unusual circumstances surrounding his departure from this life, perhaps even as a forerunner of the story that Arthur did not die but temporarily withdrew from the world. Another theme which comes to prominence elsewhere is that of the abduction of Arthur's queen. In a poem preserved only in later manuscripts but apparently belonging to the same tradition as *Pa gur*, a dialogue between Gwenhwyfar and, probably, Melwas seems to be connected with an account of the abduction of the queen by the latter in the early twelfth-century Latin *Life* of St Gildas by Caradoc of Llancarfan.[12]

Although the earliest Arthurian texts in Welsh are non-narrative, they nonetheless contain what could be regarded as the bare bones of what was to become a rich and complex tradition in Wales and especially beyond. Arthur was already identified with a heroic ideal, was building up a retinue of followers, involving himself in quests for symbolic objects; he had married and fathered a son, but his queen was already involved, willingly or not, with another man.

By the twelfth century important changes had occurred within this tradition. There had been a geographical shift and Cornwall had become a more important locus for Arthur's activities; perhaps many tales were already current in the south-west and simply came to the fore in Welsh tradition at a particular time. But now too Arthur's originally heroic image seems to be questioned. A key text here is *Ymddiddan Arthur a'r Eryr* ('Dialogue of Arthur and the Eagle'), where the eagle is identified with the soul of Arthur's dead nephew, Eliwlad mab Madog mab Uthr.[13] At one point he addresses Arthur as 'chief of the battalions of Cornwall', reflecting a change of focus from the old kingdoms of north Britain to the south-west. But also Arthur is presented throughout as foolish and uneducated, for when catechized by the eagle he reveals appalling ignorance of the basic tenets of Christianity. Although in other poems Eliwlad is presented as an ideal of bravery and manhood, here he is used to contrast that heroic ideal with Christian values, curiously prefiguring a theme of the grail romances of the thirteenth century and later.

Cornwall is again an important setting in *Culhwch ac Olwen*, which is not only the earliest Welsh Arthurian prose tale but the only one predating the *Historia Regum Britanniae*, for the text in its present form may date from the late eleventh or early twelfth century.[14] In *Culhwch ac Olwen* Arthur's chief court is at Celli Wig in Cornwall, although most of the events take place in Wales. In this text, the common folk-tale of the young man wooing the giant's daughter, and being set a series of apparently impossible tasks to win her, has been recast in an Arthurian context, suggesting that by this stage the figure of Arthur had become sufficiently popular in Wales for characters and narratives from other strands of native tradition to be drawn into his ambit. The hero, Culhwch, has now become Arthur's nephew, and enlists the help of the king and his men. We are still to some extent in the world of the *Pa gur* poem, for the dialogues between Culhwch and Arthur's doorkeeper, Glewlwyd, and between Cai and an unnamed doorkeeper at the castle of Wrnach Gawr, are closely related to that between Arthur and Glewlwyd. Cai, too, is still presented in positive terms as one of Arthur's chief warriors, whose magical characteristics make him a useful leader on campaign.[15] But Arthur himself, in a foretaste of later developments, is now less of an active warrior, moving instead towards the role of the king whose court provides the focus for knights and their adventures. For the young Culhwch, his admittance to Arthur's court is an initiation into adult life and warrior status, but Arthur, having promised him his help, remains rather passive. It is perhaps significant that the only task he actually undertakes himself is the killing of a witch by slicing her in two. In view of the presumed early date of *Culhwch ac Olwen*, the shift of Arthur away from active participation in combat is an important – and significantly early – development in the tradition.

In addition to poetry and prose narrative, the Triads provide another essential source for establishing the nature of the earlier strata of Welsh Arthurian material, for the oldest ones in the extant corpus can be shown to predate Geoffrey of Monmouth and reflect a much earlier body of narratives,[16] sometimes at odds with the *Historia Regum Britanniae* and indeed other, earlier Latin sources. In the oldest triads, for example, references to Arthur's battles ignore Badon, named in the *Historia Brittonum*, and give prominence instead to the battle of Camlan, mentioned in the 'three unfortunate counsels of the Island of Britain' (Bromwich no.59). Here, however, the theme of Arthur's downfall is linked with Medrawd, echoing the reference in the *Annales Cambriae* to the Battle of Camlann 'where Arthur and Medrawd fell'.[17] Another Triad (Bromwich no.53) gives the cause of that final battle as one of the Three Harmful Blows of the Island of Britain, struck by Gwenhwyfach upon Gwenhwyfar. Here Gwenhwyfach, a doublet of Gwenhwyfar, may bring to mind a similar duality in the early thirteenth-century French *Prose Lancelot*, where a 'false Guinevere' rivals the queen, but it is possible that Medrawd (or even the earlier Melwas) was originally the one who dealt the blow and that the story of the adultery or abduction of Gwenhwyfar lies behind this triad.[18] Other earlier Triads name the major figures at Arthur's court, providing more detailed evidence than Old Welsh poetry about which heroes figured in the pre-Geoffrey Arthurian circle. Most of these characters, who include Owain ab Urien, Geraint fab Erbin, Peredur fab Efrawg, Gwalchmai and Cai, had already appeared in the earliest surviving poetry and accordingly their home territories, or those of their fathers, are located in the north of England or Lowland Scotland. Despite the separation of Wales from those northern kingdoms since the early seventh century, and the focus of some Arthurian activity moving to Cornwall, the tradition that those major heroes came from the north, not from Wales itself, was unshakeable.

For all its massive impact in Welsh literature, Geoffrey of Monmouth's

Historia Regum Britanniae did not completely overshadow the older traditions. Whatever the precise sources of the *Historia* and the status of the putative 'ancient British (or Breton?) book', it contained material compatible with certain strands of native tradition and it was not difficult to incorporate Geoffrey's new Arthurian history into the existing body of Welsh material. Geoffrey's *Historia* was translated or adapted into Welsh a number of times from the mid-twelfth century onwards.[19] Some changes were made for the benefit of the new audience; some redactors removed certain elements or added details from native Welsh tradition here and there. In its original Latin and in the vernacular versions, the *Historia* had enormous influence on the development of Welsh literary tradition. At first that influence is perceptible in details: the addition of a few adventitious references in *Culhwch ac Olwen* after the tale had achieved its present form, a number of Triads adapted or even created by borrowing from the *Historia*,[20] and the relocalization of Arthur's chief court at Caerleon. More importantly, it marked the beginning of a chapter in the development of Welsh Arthurian tradition. From now on Welsh story-tellers would draw on an increasingly wide variety of new sources which they might use selectively and creatively to form new traditions. This procedure was not in itself unprecedented. Throughout the Middle Ages Welsh tradition followed a process of continuing development through linking in new ways originally disparate stories and characters. Just as characters of mythical origin, such as Mabon, Manawydan, and Lleu, the humanized descendants of gods, were linked at one stage with Arthurian tradition, as the *Pa gur* poem shows, so too other tales were brought into the Arthurian ambit: Culhwch's wooing of Olwen came to be linked with Arthur's court, whilst Myrddin, presented in poems in the Black Book of Carmarthen as a poet from north Britain who went mad in battle and took to the trees,[21] was similarly drawn into the same circle. Now, however, tales which had evolved within the Welsh culture were often combined with material borrowed from sources in other languages or which derived from other cultures. If there had been a specifically 'Welsh' cultural tradition – and that tradition was never completely insulated from the mainstream of European culture – by now it was becoming increasingly hybrid in terms of the literature produced.[22] Thus the Middle Welsh Arthurian tale *Breuddwyd Rhonabwy* ('The Dream of Rhonabwy'), perhaps composed in the thirteenth century, combines proper names and other details taken from Geoffrey of Monmouth with elements from early Welsh sources, all within the context of a new story which is a consciously literary, individual creation referring to the recent historical past and commenting on contemporary life.[23]

But Geoffrey was not the only new influence. By the early thirteenth century Arthurian traditions which had developed in France began to find their way to

Wales, a country by now increasingly aware of continental literature and culture generally. The first clear signs of French influence are found in the tales of *Peredur*, *Geraint* and *Owain*, which correspond to the romances of *Perceval*, *Erec* and *Yvain* by Chrétien de Troyes.[24] Even though the heroes of the three Welsh texts were still associated with their old northern territories, in their broad outlines the narrative of each has obvious similarities with the corresponding French romance. The exact relationship between the French and Welsh texts has been controversial; it is difficult to establish with any certainty and is different in each case. The problem is exacerbated by the apparent instability of the Welsh texts, for the manuscript witnesses of *Peredur* in particular differ from each other so much as to suggest that we should not think in terms of a definitive version, but rather of a series of retellings where choices and selections were made by different individuals in different times and places. In this respect these later tales present a parallel with earlier ones like *Culhwch ac Olwen*, where a similar process seems to have been at work. In other words, the concept of a stable text, deliberately composed, was not yet the norm in Welsh tradition, where oral transmission was still crucial, despite the increasing importance of the written word.

In other respects too, notably style and narrative techniques, each of these three texts has much in common with earlier Welsh prose tales, and each contains material not found in the corresponding French romance. *Peredur*, *Owain* and *Geraint* thus appear to represent a transitional phase. Welsh redactors had become familiar with continental romances and were able to adapt them – or parts of them – for a new audience by combining them with indigenous material, retelling the resulting composite narrative according to the norms of native storytelling. They recognized in French knights such as Perceval and Yvain their own Peredur, Owain and so on, and realized the potential of these new stories about familiar heroes to enrich and widen the scope of the existing stock of Welsh narrative tradition.

The next step in this process was to translate or adapt complete romances into Welsh. *Y Seint Greal* or *Ystoryaeu Seint Greal* (*c.* 1400) is a translation of two early thirteenth-century Grail romances, *La Queste del Saint Graal* and *Perlesvaus*.[25] And although the earlier *Peredur* had included a description of a procession approximating to that in Chrétien's *Perceval*, including lance and vessel, it had not used the term 'grail'; significantly it is in *Y Seint Greal*, an avowed translation, that the Welsh word 'greal' is first attested with this meaning. If the potential raw material of the grail legend – quest, spear, vessel – was present in native Welsh tradition, the concept of the grail itself must have formed elsewhere.

By this stage the cultural hegemony of France had extended throughout

Europe and French romances were being translated into a number of different languages, including Irish, as we have seen. In Wales interest was unabated in the later Middle Ages, when antiquarian scribes continued the process of combining material from French, Welsh, Latin and, increasingly, English sources. The last major Arthurian text of this kind in Welsh is undoubtedly Elis Gruffydd's *Chronicle*, written in Calais *c*. 1548-52.[26] This vast work, tracing the history of the world from the Creation to the chronicler's own day, includes a section devoted to a biography of Arthur, as well as prophecies of Merlin and other related material. The biographical section draws principally on written sources such as Geoffrey of Monmouth's *Historia*, the English Chronicles of William Caxton and Robert Fabian, and the French *Prose Lancelot*, but also incorporates folk-tales and other Arthurian material drawn from both English and Welsh popular tradition, apparently collected by Elis Gruffydd himself.[27]

In his Chronicle we find for the first time in Welsh a response to Polydore Vergil's critique of Galfridian history. Based as he was in Calais, Elis Gruffydd had access to new texts and ideas, and his own writing was influenced by recent, more critical approaches to history and the use of sources. Yet even though he acknowledged the power of the arguments against the validity of Geoffrey's history, he could not completely reject it. Like his countrymen Sir John Prys and David Powel in their ripostes, Elis Gruffydd preserved a strong emotional attachment to the *Historia Regum Britanniae*. It was the model of British history presented in the *Historia* which commanded such loyalty, for it had become deeply imbedded in the Welsh psyche. After the final conquest of Wales by Edward I in the late thirteenth century, the Arthurian legend, or rather the Galfridian history of Britain, took on a special meaning for the Welsh, for it presented the ideal of a united Britain under the rule, in England, of a native British king. This, together with the theme of loss and decline after Arthur's reign, touched a deep chord, and under the influence of the *Historia Regum Britanniae* the Saxons became ever more explicitly identified with the contemporary English as the oppressors of the Welsh and stealers of their inheritance, a process facilitated by the obvious derivation of *Saeson*, the Welsh word for the English. Life mirrored art as political poetry and prose drew heavily on these ideas and on the terminology of the *Brut*, which became virtually the only alternative model of governance that could be imagined. Not surprisingly, this view was actively encouraged by the Tudors, who, in their campaign to win the English crown, made much of their Welsh blood in the years leading to Bosworth Field. So deeply was this myth rooted in Wales that it was still influential in the eighteenth century, as witness Theophilus Evans's *Drych y Prif Oesoedd* ('The Mirror of the Chief Ages', 1716, revised 1740), a history of Wales much indebted to Geoffrey and including a section devoted to Arthur.[28]

In popular tradition, however, Arthur is not such a dominant figure as might be expected. In the earliest poetry he is one among many warrior heroes, and it is tempting to speculate that without the advent of Geoffrey of Monmouth he would be a less prominent figure in the written records of Welsh literature. There is no hint in the earliest vernacular sources of Arthur's role as a national hero, not dead but sleeping until the hour when he will return as redeemer.[29] In Wales throughout the Middle Ages and beyond that role was associated far more with Owain, especially in the popular tradition.[30] Even in the fourteenth and fifteenth centuries, when Arthurian literature was at the height of its popularity, contemporary individuals were identified with that redeemer Owain, within both indigenous nationalist and Tudor propaganda. Perhaps Elis Gruffydd was correct in his assertion that, in his day at least, the English paid far more attention to Arthur than did the Welsh. The seeds of much of later continental and English Arthurian tradition were implicit in the earliest Welsh sources, but outside Wales that tradition developed autonomously and in a very different fashion, influenced by different social and political circumstances. The Arthur of the English was not the Arthur of the Welsh.

2

DYNASTIC CHRONICLES

The distinctive Arthurian tradition in English is rooted, not in the folk-tale of Welsh tradition nor in the romance which dominates the French corpus, but in chronicle format embodying a dynastic theme with every appearance of historical conviction. The concept that those who held the island of Britain were heirs to a dynastic succession which linked them with the heroic civilization of Troy and bridged the centuries between, passing from conqueror to conqueror whatever their race or origin, was the work of three remarkable men. It was conceived by Geoffrey of Monmouth, scholar, historian, romantic, who knew how to present the British past not as it was but as his Norman patrons might wish it to have been. Its historical formality was modified by Wace, court poet and stylist, who gave it a gloss of contemporaneity which allowed Anglo-Norman rulers to imagine themselves the rightful heirs to Arthurian power and chivalry. And modified again by Laȝamon, provincial cleric and antiquarian in an age when English was a provincial medium, to reclaim the heroic values of British resistance to foreign conquest for his own race, imaginative association rooted in recent experience of invasion obliterating the role of their Anglo-Saxon ancestors as alien aggressors. Variations of language and medium spanned the three component cultures of twelfth-century Britain, implying the common interest of different audiences in the common past of their country. Each author ignored the reality of Celtic Britain to propagate a myth which seized the imagination of contemporaries and was woven into the historical fabric of the island by a host of lesser men, chroniclers and poets, over the centuries to come.

Geoffrey of Monmouth's *Historia Regum Britanniae*[1]

In January 1139, the chronicler Henry of Huntingdon, visiting the Abbey of Bec, was shown a new book which surprised and delighted him. His own work had been frustrated by lack of information on British history before the coming of the Romans, whose imperial era was documented in a respectable learned language.[2] Now he held in his hands a Latin volume which purported to cover the history of Britain from the arrival of the founding father, Brutus, great-grandson of Aeneas, to the departure of Cadwallader, last of the native rulers of the land, into voluntary exile in the year AD 689. It was to prove one of the most seminal books of the Middle Ages. Not, however, in the sense which Henry of Huntingdon might have wished; on closer reading some elements of the new history, particularly its account of King Arthur, became suspect, fascinating but scarcely credible.[3] But for writers of imaginative literature, for centuries to come, fascination outweighed cynicism. Manuscripts multiplied, versions proliferated, translations and adaptations spread all over western Europe.[4]

The new book, the *Historia Regum Britanniae*, was the work of Geoffrey of Monmouth, a provincial cleric ambitious to rise in the world but never, as far as we know, directly associated with the court. His cognomen, presumably derived from his birthplace, suggests that he came from a region of the Welsh borders where many immigrants, particularly Bretons, had settled after the Conquest.[5] A number of documents witnessed by him between 1129 and 1151 show him in association with Walter, Archdeacon of Oxford and provost of the secular College of St George. Geoffrey, who occasionally styled himself *magister*, may well have been a teacher there, though the University of Oxford had not yet been formally constituted. The various dedications to his writings suggest a man in search of patronage, but though he was eventually rewarded with the bishopric of St Asaph in 1151, Welsh rebellion against central rule probably prevented him entering his see before his death in 1154/5.[6]

The Arthurian legends may have been a personal obsession with Geoffrey, sometimes referred to by contemporaries as Galfridus Arturus; his three known works all deal with them. In his *Prophetie Merlini* he wove a collection of political prophecies, supposedly translated from early Welsh verse, round Myrddin, the half-crazed seer whom legend credited with asserting that the British would ultimately drive the Anglo-Saxon invaders from their land.[7] Though apparently begun by 1135, and in independent circulation thereafter, they were also incorporated in the *Historia* (§§111-17)[8] with the original dedication to his clerical superior, Alexander, Bishop of Lincoln, and an introduction (§109) explaining that friends had urged him to release material of whose importance rumours had reached them. The prophecies, relating to events included in the *Historia*, to Geoffrey's own age and onwards – with increasing vagueness allowing the maximum of interpretative ingenuity – to doomsday, were cleverly calculated to appeal to a society which knew little of the past, and viewed the future with an apprehension fired by its troubled present. Within a few months of their appearance, they were being cited by serious historians; and they were still in circulation centuries later, each age seeing in them something relevant to its own circumstances. Geoffrey later capitalized upon their success with a verse life of Merlin, the *Vita Merlini* (*c.* 1150), dedicated to another canon of the College of St George, Alexander's successor as Bishop of Lincoln.

The same sound instinct for useful patrons and contemporary tastes marked his *History of the Kings of Britain*, completed by 1138 and variously dedicated to King Stephen (1135-54) and to two great nobles representing rival factions in the civil war of his reign, as if to catch the shifting currents of favour in a troubled age.[9] To an age in need of historical precedents which might resolve current constitutional issues, yet conscious of the darkness cutting it off from the past – particularly that remote past which lay beyond the increasingly incomprehensible and neglected record of the *Anglo-Saxon Chronicle* and Bede's specialized account of ecclesiastical history – Geoffrey's *Historia* furnished a link with the ancient, honourable, seemingly stable world of its schoolroom texts. The founding father Brutus, giving his name to the colony he plants in the island of Albion, whose capital city on the Thames is to be Trinovantum, 'New Troy', brings an inheritance of heroic values from fallen Troy to which later ages were to look as the source of their social idealism and national identity. Among the kings said to be his successors are Bladud, founder of Bath, Leir and Cymbeline, later to be Shakespeare's heroes, and Belin who, with his brother Brenne, is said to have sacked Rome.

This is fantasy; with the coming of Julius Caesar it is challenged by a reality which Geoffrey only reluctantly admits, the eventual success of the Roman conquest in the face of stubborn British resistance. The epoch ends when the half-British senator Maximian, hoping to use his native backing to seize imperial power, undertakes the conquest of Gaul, leaving the now Christian island vulnerable to attack by the barbarian Picts and Huns. When the Romans finally abandon Britain, the royal line established from among followers of Maximian settled in Brittany is displaced by the usurper Vortigern, who enlists the help of the pagan Saxons Hengist and Horsa against the incursions of the Picts. His new allies, seeing the vulnerability of the kingdom, invite their Germanic kinsmen to join them; they treacherously massacre many of the leading Britons, and Vortigern takes refuge in Snowdonia.

Summoned to his aid, Merlin prophesies Britain's long-term future, Vortigern's imminent fate, and the return of the royal line he had displaced. The brothers Aurelius and Uther, returning from Brittany, defeat and kill Hengist. Both in turn are poisoned by their Saxon enemies, but not before Uther has fathered the greatest of British heroes, illicitly upon another man's wife. Seized with a passion for Ygerne, wife of Gorlois, Duke of Cornwall, he is transformed by Merlin into the likeness of the duke, enters his fortress of Tintagel, and sires the future King Arthur at the moment when Gorlois falls in battle, allowing the boy to be born in wedlock.

On Uther's death, Arthur succeeds him at the age of fifteen, immediately marches against the Saxons under Colgrim, besieges them in York and eventually, with the help of Howel, King of Brittany, defeats them at Bath. Turning upon their allies the Picts and Scots, he corners them at Loch Lomond and starves them into submission. Having restored his northern allies to their Scottish fiefdoms and rebuilt the ruined churches of York, he marries Guinevere, descendant of a noble Roman family. To punish the Irish for their aid to the Scots, he conquers their country, then Iceland, the Orkneys and Norway. Invading Gaul, he kills the Roman Tribune Frolle in single combat and captures Paris. While he is celebrating at a plenary court in the City of the Legions (Caerleon-upon-Usk), envoys arrive from Lucius, Procurator of the Roman Republic, summoning him to Rome to be tried for crimes against the state; Arthur sends a message of defiance and gathers his forces. Leaving Britain in the care of his nephew Modred, he crosses to Barfleur, kills the giant of Mont St Michel single-handed, defeats the Roman army at Saussy, subdues Burgundy, and is about to march on Rome when news comes that Modred has seized the throne and taken the queen adulterously. Returning in haste to Britain, Arthur drives Modred into Cornwall, kills him in a final battle on the river Camlann, is himself mortally wounded and carried off to the isle of Avalon, leaving the kingdom to the care of his cousin Constantin.

After Arthur's departure, the twin forces of foreign enmity and domestic treason combine to overwhelm the nation; Modred's two sons join in revolt with the Saxons recruited as allies by their father. Constantin corners and kills the two young men, but the Saxons continue to harass his successors, allying themselves with Gormund, King of the Africans, who has established himself in Ireland. Together they drive the Britons to the west, into Wales and Cornwall, where they maintain their Christian faith until Augustine is sent by Pope Gregory to convert the pagan invaders. Eventually a friendship grows up between the British ruler and the King of the Northumbrians whose son, Edwin, is brought up in Brittany with Cadwallo, heir to the British throne. When Cadwallo succeeds, Edwin asks for a crown of his own, but the British king, reminded of the repeated treachery of the Saxons, refuses and, in the ensuing war, is driven out of his kingdom. Returning, with the help of his Breton kinsmen, he kills Edwin and is widely successful against the Saxons and the ever-troublesome Scots. But under his son Cadwallader God turns against the Britons, famine and plague overwhelm the country, and the king takes refuge in Brittany. When he thinks of returning to his kingdom, an angelic voice forbids it, though prophesying that, at the appointed time, the faithful British should once again hold the island as their own. Cadwallader goes as a penitent to Rome and dies there in the year AD 689.

This closing date, one of only three in the whole *Historia*, is uncharacteristic in its preciseness; but the air of historical precision is intentional. Elsewhere Geoffrey maintains the historical fiction by relating events in Britain to others in world history: the reigns of native kings are correlated with those of Old Testament kings and prophets; Cordelia's brief reign after the death of Leir is followed by the founding of Rome by Romulus and Remus; that of Cymbeline falls during the long reign of the Emperor Augustus. This synchronic dating – underscored in some, particularly early, manuscripts of the *Historia* by scribal emphasis or marginal rubrics[10] – contributes to structure as well as verisimilitude, marking the passage of time over almost two thousand years.

History requires authentication by learned, preferably Latin, sources. Geoffrey makes his claim for respectability by the statement (§2) that he is merely translating 'a certain very ancient book written in the British language', given him by Walter, Archdeacon of Oxford, who, he adds in a final paragraph (§208), brought it '*ex Britannia*'. It is not clear whether the reference is to a Welsh book brought from Wales or a Breton book from Brittany – though Geoffrey's usage throughout the *Historia* suggests that *Britannia* can only mean the latter. The present consensus of scholarly opinion, however, dismisses the ancient book as the kind of fabulous source commonly claimed by medieval authors in search of authority for their own inventions.[11] Had it existed, it would have been a highly unusual text since the *Historia*, wide-ranging and complex in its components, nonetheless gives a strong impression of homogeneity, authorial control and relevance to the interests of the age for which it was written.

Our understanding of the compositional process is still at a fairly rudimentary stage. But Geoffrey's scholastic education and rhetorical training would have given him both materials and method for filling the lacuna in British history. As general models for what a dynastic chronicle, the history of a race in search of its identity as a nation, should be, he had the Old Testament, Livy and other Roman historians; as a personal model of charismatic leadership engaged in imperial conquest, the career of Alexander the Great, widely disseminated in both learned and popular forms (Tatlock, 312-20); and, for the heroic manner in which such a subject should be treated, Virgil's *Aeneid*. Among the earlier historians of the island he acknowledges (§1) Gildas (*c*. 516-70) whose lament for the internecine strife and moral decline among the British, *De Excidio et Conquestu Britanniae*, provided the dark undercurrent of his national epic, and Bede (673-735) whose *Historia Ecclesiastica* supplied details of the Anglo-Saxon invaders and their eventual conversion by the Augustine mission. Geoffrey's treatment of Gildas is highly selective: modifying the superiority of the Saxon invaders by transferring their sack of British cities to the army of the African king Gormund summoned by them from Ireland (§§184-6); postponing a characteristic lamentation for the moral decline of the British until he can put it into the mouth of Cadwallo as the final collapse approaches (§195); conflating a plague and a famine in the catastrophe which ultimately overwhelms the nation (§203). These alterations bring Gildas's tragic view of British history to bear upon Geoffrey's vision of national greatness with all the greater effect after the glory of Arthur's reign.[12]

The compositional process is less apparent in the Arthurian section, about a fifth of the whole, since Geoffrey's sources for a figure unknown to history are less clear. The Arthur of legend is a warrior whose shadowy career may reflect that of some British war-leader who, for a period towards the end of the fifth century, temporarily delayed the Anglo-Saxon conquest.[13] One form in which the material relevant to Geoffrey's purpose might have reached him with some gloss of historical respectability is exemplified by a manuscript in the British Library, Harley 3859, containing texts of the Welsh Annals, medieval Welsh king-lists and genealogies, and the ninth-century *Historia Brittonum* traditionally attributed to the Welsh historian Nennius. From some version of 'Nennius' he could have taken the historical framework of the Saxon advance, the list of battles which constitute Arthur's first campaign against them, culminating in the triumph of Mount Badon (Bath). The tenth-century Welsh Annals confirm his victory at Badon and his fall, together with Medraut, at the battle of Camlann. But it was apparently Geoffrey who made Modred his opponent there, an embodiment of the discord and treachery among the Britons lamented by Gildas. From the lists of British cities given in 'Nennius', Geoffrey contrived both a concrete setting and a sense of national history, often accounting for a place-name by inventing a story about the supposed founder.

The concept of a court of faithful companions gathered about a warrior king is already present in the wonder-working companions, heroes of lost epics and gods of dead religions, surrounding Arthur in Welsh folk-tales, as are the names of many of his weapons. The material surveyed in the previous chapter probably represents no more than haphazard fragments of what once existed, no doubt largely in oral form, and we cannot tell what access Geoffrey may have had to it.[14] But within the 'historical' framework of

Arthur's reign there are shadowy romantic figures: a king identified with a heroic ideal, defending his people by personal prowess; a seer prognosticating greatness; a brotherhood of charismatic companions engaged in folklore quests; a queen involved, willingly or not, with another man; an epic end in mystery and ambiguity.

The romantic potential of this material, of which later ages were to make so much, is barely discernible beneath the dominant pattern of national destiny, 'the rise to greatness of a favoured people and their decline and loss of sovereignty' (B.F. Roberts in Bromwich, 102):

> . . . Britones olim ante ceteros a mari usque ad mare insederunt donec ultione diuina propter ipsorum superueniente superbiam Pictis et Saxonibus cesserunt. (§5)

> (. . . *the Britons once occupied the land from sea to sea, before the others came. Then the vengeance of God overtook them because of their arrogance and they submitted to the Picts and the Saxons.*)[15]

The apex of Britain's greatness is the reign of Arthur, foretold in the Prophecies of Merlin as the Boar of Cornwall (§112.2), his coming signalled by portent (§133), his heroic status predicted at his mysterious begetting (§137); but at the zenith of his power, Arthur's absorption in imperial conquest and the treachery of Modred begin the nation's decline towards loss of sovereignty. Only the ambiguity of his passing leaves a faint hope of renewal and the restoration of British nationhood.[16]

The lingering hope, like Arthur's imaginary triumphs, was no doubt consoling to the humiliated spirit of a defeated people; but the dispossessed Welsh were not Geoffrey's primary audience. To his English contemporaries the *Historia* offered sublimation of their own recent humiliation through identification with ancient national tradition rather than Anglo-Saxon history, with land rather than race, repeating the process by which the Celts they once defeated had turned that brutal fact into romantic fiction. For Geoffrey's Norman patrons it provided legitimization of their conquest by putting it into historical perspective, showing Brutus as an invader bringing a superior culture, Cadwallader accepting the end of British rule as God-ordained, the Saxons as perfidious and brutal, unfit to rule.[17]

Geoffrey's appreciation of the frustrations of various races, native and immigrant, victors and vanquished, striving to become a nation, to trace a dynastic link with a past in which they could take mutual pride, was to give the *Historia* enduring appeal to their descendants in the centuries ahead. His skill as a story-teller, in the synthesis of disparate materials, in weaving together unconnected but evocative elements, was to attract the interest of other cultures, other ages. As far afield as Poland its format was imitated, its material incorporated in national chronicles. Vernacular versions quickly made it available to popular audiences; Wales alone produced at least five, of which some sixty texts still survive.[18] It remained current there up to the eighteenth century, but elsewhere the rational cynicism of the Renaissance rapidly undermined its historical status. Long before then, however, the poets of western Europe had begun to mine the vein of romance in the story of Arthur which was to give it currency around the world.[19]   **W. R. J. Barron**

Wace's *Roman de Brut*

The demand for vernacular versions of Geoffrey of Monmouth's *Historia Regum Britanniae* was felt soon after its appearance. The respectable, historiographical format given by Geoffrey to his work, together with the inherent interest of his material for a non-clerical audience, made his *Historia* an ideal candidate for literary reappropriation. In 1155 a translation into French verse was completed by Wace, a Norman cleric living at Caen.[20] Wace's work became an instant success on both sides of the Channel: twelfth-century Normandy and England shared the same ruler, their élites spoke the same language, and Caen was at the time an important intellectual and political centre which had many links with England, notably through land ownership.[21]

Most of what we know of Wace we learn from the poet himself, in his unfinished verse history of the Dukes of Normandy, the *Roman de Rou*. Born in Jersey, some time about 1100, Wace was taken to Caen as a child; he completed his education in the Ile de France (probably at Paris), then returned to Caen, where he began to write poems in French. Five of these are extant: his *Geste des Bretuns*, now known as the *Roman de Brut* (finished in 1155), the *Roman de Rou* (begun in 1160), and three religious works. The *Roman de Brut*, his translation of Geoffrey's *Historia,* was made under the patronage of Henry II, who later rewarded Wace with a prebend at the Norman abbey of Bayeux. His name appears on a number of Bayeux charters, the latest dated 1174; the date of his death is unknown.[22]

Wace was well-travelled – he had visited Brittany and was acquainted with south-western England[23] – and socially experienced. He had lived at court and, according to the later English poet Laʒamon, presented a copy of his *Roman de Brut* to Eleanor of Aquitaine, then Queen of England. No copy of the *Roman de Brut* dedicated to Eleanor is extant, but we know that he later undertook the *Roman de Rou* at the request of Henry II. So, despite his clerical status, Wace was familiar with the world of aristocracy. This accounts for the dual drive evident in the *Roman de Brut*, which is both fashion-conscious and intent on the betterment of the mind of the reader. The Latin prose of his source is recast into jaunty octosyllabic rhyming couplets, colourful descriptive vignettes enliven accounts of sea-journeys, battles or state events, and, wherever his narrative permits, Wace introduces a flavour of chivalry designed to please his noble patrons. But he also cultivates the pose of the critical author, interspersing his narrative with such characteristic comments as 'Ne sai . . .' (*I don't know, I couldn't say whether this was really so*). The status of his work as 'serious' history is thereby enhanced, while it is made more attractive to the non-clerical audience implicitly targeted by any translation from Latin.[24]

When Wace set to work there were two versions of the *Historia* in circulation: that written by Geoffrey himself (the Vulgate version), and a Variant version of unknown authorship, which rephrases and condenses Geoffrey's narrative. Wace used both; he appears to have had access only to the Variant for much of his project, then, approximately half-way through the composition of his work, he seems to have come across Geoffrey's original version. From this point onwards, coinciding roughly with the appearance of Merlin, Wace regularly merges the two Latin accounts, not consistently corresponding to either.[25] Whole sections of the *Roman*, particularly at the beginning of the poem, can be read in parallel with the Variant version of the *Historia*, without material additions or modifications. But as Wace proceeds in his work, he gradually becomes more daring in his presentation of the successive episodes. In the second half of the poem, he regularly omits material he thinks uncongenial, abridging detailed accounts of ecclesiastical history, for example. Most strikingly, he excludes the entire Book of the *Historia* containing the Prophecies of Merlin, with the excuse that he could not understand the prophecies well enough to translate them. Moreover, particularly in his account of the reign of Arthur, he weaves into his narrative elements of a more openly fictional nature, including oral tales. The Arthurian section of the *Roman de Brut* thus contains the first reference in writing to the Round Table:

> Pur les nobles baruns qu'il out,
> Dunt chescuns mieldre estre quidout,
> Chescuns se teneit al meillur,
> Ne nuls n'en saveit le peiur,
> Fist Artur la Roünde Table
> Dunt Bretun dient mainte fable.
> Illuec seeient li vassal
> Tuit chevalment e tuit egal;
> A la table egalment seeient
> E egalment servi esteient;
> Nul d'els ne se poeit vanter
> Qu'il seïst plus halt de sun per. (9747-58)[26]

(Because of the noble lords that he had around him, each of whom considered himself the best and of whom none could have said who was the least good, Arthur created the Round Table, about which the Britons/Bretons tell many stories. The noblemen used to sit at it, all at favoured places, and all equal. They were seated at the table as equals, and were served their food as equals; none of them could boast that he had a seat of higher dignity than his companion.)

Wace also expands – somewhat wryly – Geoffrey's cryptic reference to the 'Breton hope' of Arthur's return (13279-93)[27], and generally shows awareness that his audience shared an alternative, non-historical image of the great king. The narrative content of this extra-textual tradition is not outlined in the *Brut* but, in his *Roman de Rou*, Wace makes clear that it was a highly fanciful one, and that he shared the fascination of his contemporaries with these stories. He describes how he went to the forest of Brocéliande (later to attain literary fame in the work of Chrétien de Troyes) in the hope of encountering fays and other 'merveilles', and his disappointment at not having met with any: 'Fol i alai, fol m'en reuinc' (*Rou*, III, 6397; *A fool I went there, a fool I returned*).

Wace's attitude to the stories surrounding King Arthur is one of qualified scepticism. He does not doubt that the king existed – Arthur's reign is one of a sequence, attested by his reputable main source, and firmly confined within specific dates – but he suggests that his exploits have been exaggerated by successive generations of story-tellers:

> En cele grant pais ke jo di,
> Ne sai si vus l'avez oï,
> Furent les merveilles pruvees
> E les aventures truvees
> Ki d'Artur sunt tant recuntees
> Ke a fable sunt aturnees.
> Ne tut mençunge, ne tut veir,
> Tut folie ne tut saveir.
> Tant unt li cunteür cunté
> E li fableür tant fablé
> Pur lur cuntes enbeleter,
> Que tut unt fait fable sembler. (9787-98)

(It was during the long peace I have just told you about (I don't know if you heard about it), that the wonders and adventures attributed to Arthur were proven and revealed. They are not entirely false, nor entirely true, neither complete folly nor total wisdom. The story-tellers have told their stories so often, the tellers of fables have told their fables so often, that in order to embellish their stories they have made everything seem imagined.)

In effect, Wace is validating these *cuntes* and *fables*: however fantastic they may seem, they are explicitly endowed with a kernel of truth. He places them at specific stages of Arthur's reign: the twelve-year period of peace following Arthur's conquest of Scandinavia, and the nine years spent by the king in France after his conquest of that country. With the *Roman de Brut*, Arthurian stories gain additional authority, and are implicitly located on both sides of the Channel, not just in Britain. So Wace paves the way for the romances of Chrétien de Troyes, some fifteen to twenty years later.

It must, however, be stressed that Wace's Arthur has little in common with the shadowy figure of Arthurian romance. The *Roman de Brut* not only retains Geoffrey's historiographical format, it also depicts Arthur in essentially the same manner as the *Historia Regum Britanniae*, as a great warrior-king. The legendary material integrated by Wace into his narrative is of marginal importance, the emphasis being on Arthur as conqueror: his glorious campaigns against Scandinavia and France are given particular prominence, and the descriptions of the pomp and splendour of Arthur's court following these two major triumphs function primarily as indicators of the heroic status of the king. Arthur as epic hero also comes to the fore at the beginning of the fateful Roman campaign, when he overcomes in single combat the monstrous giant on Mont St Michel. Wace's Arthur, like Geoffrey's, is a latter-day Alexander the Great. Moreover, the valour of members of the Round Table serves to equate Arthur with Charlemagne and his twelve peers.[28] Gawain's qualities as a fighting man are given special emphasis during the Roman campaign, as is the prowess of Bedevere and Kay, whose battles are recounted with great gusto in a vein frequently akin to that of the *chanson de geste*.

In the main, therefore, Wace's depiction of Arthur does not vary significantly from that of the *Historia*; but the importance of the Arthurian section, as compared with the other reigns in the work, is underlined by the greater space allotted to it in the *Roman de Brut* – over 4,000 lines out of a total of some 15,000, as opposed to approximately one sixth of the total length of the *Historia*.[29] Moreover, Wace modifies the balance between the different phases of Arthur's reign. The king's earlier exploits, predominantly defensive and on English soil, are somewhat overshadowed by the enthusiastic account of his later conquests outside England: in Scotland, and especially in Scandinavia and France, where he is depicted as invincible and universally feared. The immediate consequence of this reshaping of the Arthurian section in the *Roman de Brut* is a subtle relocalization of the story: Britain remains important, but what is really interesting is what Arthur does elsewhere.

Another consequence of this shift in emphasis is a defusing of the political undercurrent present in Geoffrey's work, part of a general trend in the *Roman de*

Brut. Many of the speeches condensed or omitted by Wace are among the most ideologically charged in the *Historia*, and one suspects that the true reason for his omission of the Prophecies of Merlin was Wace's desire to produce as uncontroversial a work as possible: the 'predictions' were politically sensitive stuff which could have cost the poet his royal patronage.[30] The overall effect is that Wace's poem is better suited to a mixed audience: more so than the *Historia*, the *Roman de Brut* can be read as a collection of individual stories. Moreover, Wace appears to have taken pains to make these stories attractive to the aristocratic reader/listener. The amateur of the *chanson de geste* would have relished the heightened epic resonances of Arthur's Roman campaign; later in the work, the devout would have enjoyed the lively account of St Augustine's adventures while preaching to the English. Though it would be difficult to find many of the themes connected with 'courtly love' in the poem, some gestures are made in that direction: for example when Gawain, defending the virtues of peace, praises the benefits of love for society as a whole, and for the behaviour of knights in particular.[31] Yet, all the while, the *Roman de Brut* retains the authority of a work of history based on the best possible sources.

As a result, Wace's work proved particularly suitable for later rewriting. He had not merely translated Geoffrey's material; he had successfully transposed a long Latin prose narrative into elegant French verse, and unobtrusively adapted it for a wider audience. Moreover, from his relatively apolitical stance resulted a narrative which could easily be reshaped to correspond to the vision of the past that best suited the ideology of future English historians. The first and greatest of these was the poet-historian Laȝamon.   **Françoise Le Saux**

Laȝamon's *Brut*

The appearance at some time during the early decades of the thirteenth century of a translation of Wace's *Roman de Brut* by the English poet Laȝamon is a milestone in the development and transmission of Geoffrey's dynastic chronicle in England. Written in English, at a time when the literary idiom of the island was overwhelmingly French, Laȝamon's *Brut* is one of the first major pieces of literature to have come down to us in Middle English; its loosely alliterative verse form, at times strongly reminiscent of Old English poetry, may be said to prefigure the alliterative revival of the fourteenth century;[32] and, most crucially for our present concern, it is the earliest surviving work in the English language to deal with the figure of Arthur.

The poem is extant in two manuscripts, both dating from the second half of the thirteenth century, both in the British Library, London: MS Cotton Caligula A ix, and the fire-damaged MS Cotton Otho C xiii, a slightly abbreviated and 'modernized' version of the work.[33] The date of composition cannot be determined with any precision, beyond the fact that it must have been started after 1185 and was probably completed by 1225.[34] The poem comprises 16,095 long lines; each long line is divided into two half-lines of varying length and featuring varying patterns of rhyme and alliteration, a metre apparently derived from Old English metrical prose.[35] The language of the *Brut* has a markedly archaic flavour, with remarkably few French loan-words, despite its derivation from Wace's *Roman de Brut*;[36] internal evidence suggests that the English poem was written for a broader spectrum of society than was its French source – possibly 'the mixed household group of a moderately prosperous manor house'.[37]

The little we know of Laȝamon is what he tells us in the Prologue to the *Brut*, his only known work: he was a priest, his father's name was Leovenath, and he 'bock radde' (*read books*) at 'Ernleȝe' on the banks of the river Severn (1-5). 'Ernleȝe' is now identified with Areley Kings, a village some ten miles from Worcester, an important ecclesiastical centre with a well-endowed cathedral library, which Laȝamon certainly used. Despite the fact that Areley was a relatively unimportant village, the church where the poet officiated (if that is indeed what his expression 'bock radde' implies) was built of stone, at a time when many churches would still have been made of wood.[38] Whatever his duties there, he clearly benefited from generous patronage, both in terms of the time he was able to devote to a work that must have taken many years to complete, and the expense implied by his travels in search of sources. Who his patron was can only be guessed at, however.[39]

The Prologue to the *Brut* announces a piece of serious historical writing for which the author has secured all possible sources:

> Laȝamon gon liðen   wide ȝond þas leode,
> and biwon þa æðela boc   þa he to bisne nom. (14-15)

> (*Laȝamon travelled far and wide throughout this land, and obtained the excellent books which he took as a model.*)[40]

The *Brut* is explicitly said to combine three authoritative works: Bede's *Ecclesiastical History of the English Nation*, Wace's *Roman de Brut* and a mysterious 'book of St Albin and Austin'.[41] This choice of authorities is revealing. All three books are recognizably historiographical works, but they also represent three literary traditions: Latin, the language of science and learning; French, the language of the aristocracy; and English, the language of the dispossessed. Laȝamon is thereby placing himself on the cultural map of England, advertising himself as educated and well-bred, yet also claiming his Anglo-Saxon heritage.

The reality of the text is somewhat different: Laȝamon barely used Bede, and the 'book of St Albin and Austin' is something of a red herring; Wace's *Roman de Brut* is unmistakably the main source of the *Brut*, with only incidental additions from other works. The second most important literary influence on Laȝamon's poem after Wace would appear to be Geoffrey of Monmouth himself: there are indications in the *Brut* that the English poet was not only familiar with the Vulgate version of the *Historia Regum Britanniae*, but that he espoused much of Geoffrey's view of history.[42] In particular, Laȝamon restores the focus on Britain, to the extent that it has been said the true hero of the *Brut* is the land itself.[43] This has far-reaching consequences for his account of the reign of Arthur.

We have seen that in his reworking of the *Historia*, Wace is most responsive to those features of Arthur which Geoffrey apparently modelled on Alexander the Great, and gives corresponding emphasis to the king's conquests beyond the boundaries of England. Laȝamon's interests lay in the opposite direction. The most ornate passages in the Arthurian section of the poem all relate to the initial struggle against the Saxons on British soil. By contrast, the campaigns abroad are only rarely expanded, and where expansion occurs (during Arthur's campaign against Rome), the focus is on Gawain rather than on the king himself.[44] This emphasis on Arthur as a specifically British king serves to strengthen the political, dynastic thread in his material. Laȝamon's poem is much closer to Geoffrey than to Wace both in outlook and in general thematic structure: while the successive reigns he depicts can be read individually with pleasure (one thinks especially of the King Leir section), the true import of any one episode can only be assessed in conjunction with the totality of the work.

Laȝamon's account of Arthur's reign covers some 4,400 lines out of a total of just under 16,100; in purely arithmetical terms, therefore, the episode does not appear to have been given additional prominence by the English poet.[45] On the rhetorical and stylistic level, however, the Arthurian section contains some of the more memorable passages of the work, predominantly at the beginning of Arthur's reign. The issues thus highlighted are recurrent in the poem, and give it an underlying structure which is quite distinct from that of the *Roman de Brut*.

A noteworthy feature of Laȝamon's work is the poet's disapproval of non-defensive warfare, despite his obvious relish for spirited battle scenes.[46] It is therefore appropriate that the high point of the Arthurian section is the 'just war' in which the young king defends both his homeland and Christendom against the Saxons. Arthur's early exploits involve three major battles, all victorious, and all displaying a striking rhetorical feature known as the long-tailed simile. Epic similes such as 'he rushed upon his enemy like a wild boar' are to be found throughout the *Brut*, but in the early Arthurian section these similes are turned into elaborate vignettes. Arthur's first battle, at the river Douglas, describes the young king as 'swa þe runie wulf / þenne he cumeð of holte bihonged mid snawe,

/ and þencheð to biten swulc deor swa him likeð' (10041-3; *like the frost-grey wolf when he comes from the snow-hung wood, bent on devouring whatever prey he pleases*); and the defeated Saxons are likened to

> . . . þe wilde cron
> i þan moruenne   þenne his floc is awemmed
> and him haldeð after   hauekes swifte,
> hundes in þan reode   mid reouðe hine imeteð.
> Þenne nis him neouðer god,   no þat lond no þat flod:
> hauekes hine smiteð,   hundes hine biteð.
> Þenne bið þe kinewurðe foȝel   fæie on his siðe. (10061-7)

(*. . . the wild crane in the moorland fen when his flock is scattered and swift hawks pursue him, hounds ruthlessly attack him in the reeds. Neither the land nor the water is safe for him then: hawks strike him, hounds bite him. Then the royal bird is doomed in his tracks.*)

Even more elaborate is the simile put in the mouth of Arthur when he accepts the Saxons' unconditional surrender after their defeat at Lincoln. Their leader Childric, he says, had planned to seize the kingdom:

> 'Ah of him bið iwurðen   swa bið of þan voxe
> Þenne he bið baldest   ufen an þan walde,
> and hafeð his fulle ploȝe   and fuȝeles inoȝe.
> For wildscipe climbið   and cluden isecheð,
> i þan wilderne   holȝes him wurcheð;
> faren whaswa auere fare   naueð he næuere nænne kare.
> He weneð to beon of duȝeðe   baldest alre deoren.
> Þenne siȝeð him to   segges vnder beorȝen
> mid hornen, mid hunden,   mid haȝere stefenen.
> Hunten þar talieð,   hundes þer galieð,
> þene vox driueð   ȝeond dales and ȝeond dunes.
> He ulih to þan holme   and his hol isecheð,
> i þan uirste ænde   i þan holle wendeð.
> Þenne is þe balde uox   blissen al bideled,
> and mon him todelueð   on ælchere heluen;
> þenne beoð þer forcuðest   deoren alre pruttest.' (10398-413)

(*'But it has befallen him as it does the fox when he is at his boldest up in the woods, and has his fill of sport and birds in plenty. From mere wantonness he climbs and seeks the hilltops, digs holes for himself in the waste places; wheresoever he may roam he has never a care. He considers himself to be the boldest of all animals in valour. Then beneath the hills men come after him with horns, with hounds, with loud clamour. There hunters shout, hounds bay, driving the fox over hills and dales. He flees to the hilltop and makes for his earth, goes into the den at the nearest place. Then the bold fox is robbed of all his pleasure, and men dig him out from every side; then the proudest of all animals is there the most wretched.'*)

Similarly, in Arthur's battle-speech before his decisive victory near Bath, the king compares himself to a wolf and Colgrim, the Saxon leader, to a goat about to be savaged (10629-36); and he likens the enemy dead floating in the river Avon to 'stelene fisces',

> 'mid sweorde bigeorede   heore sund is awemmed;
> heore scalen wleoteð   swulc gold-faȝe sceldes;
> þer fleoteð heore spiten   swulc hit spæren weoren.' (10641-3)

(*'steel fish trammelled with swords, their swimming impaired; their scales gleam as if they were gilded shields; their fins drift in the water like spears floating there.'*)

These strikingly elaborate similes, which occur nowhere else in the *Brut*, clearly mark out the struggle against the Saxons as not only the high point of Arthur's reign, but of the history of Britain as a whole.[47]

The subordination of 'Arthur the Conqueror' to 'Arthur the Defender' brings about a renewed emphasis on the king as ruler rather than warrior. The aspect stressed by Laȝamon in this connection is that of the monarch as law-giver, already a recurrent theme in Geoffrey, but given especial prominence by the English poet. Arthur is described as a just king: 'woh him wes wunder lað and þat rihte a leof' (9950; *wrong was most hateful to him and the right was always dear*). His treatment of wrong-doers is depicted at some length in Laȝamon's account of the foundation of the Round Table (an anecdote found in none of his extant sources). A brawl breaks out at Arthur's court during a meal, and becomes so serious that the King has to retire to fetch his guards. This breaking of the King's peace in his very presence would have been considered an aggravated act of treason, and the punishment meted out by Arthur is correspondingly severe.[48] A craftsman from Cornwall, hearing of the incident, offers to make a round table at which sixteen hundred may be seated but which Arthur can nonetheless take with him on his travels (11422-43). The Round Table is therefore closely related to Arthur's duties as enforcer of justice and peace; and while his way of dealing with wrong-doers seems to a modern reader exaggeratedly brutal (for example, he kills all the inhabitants of Winchester and destroys the city as punishment for their support of Modred), this indication of the king's firm hand could well have appeared a positive trait to a thirteenth-century English audience.[49]

More so even than in Wace, Laȝamon's Arthur is the ideal king. The English poet follows his French source in acknowledging that not all that is related about Arthur is truthful; but he ascribes these falsehoods to the great love of the Britons for Arthur, rather than to the desire of story-tellers to 'improve' on facts, commenting:

> Swa deð aueralc mon   þe oðer luuien con;
> ȝif he is him to leof   þenne wule he liȝen
> and suggen on him wurðscipe   mare þenne he beon wurðe;
> ne beo he no swa luðer mon   þat his freond him wel ne on.
>
> (11456-9)

(*Each and every man who feels love for another does the same; if he is dear to him then he will lie and say more in praise of him that he is worthy of; there is no man so base that his friend will not wish him well.*)

The exaggerated stories are thus traced back to a nobler impulse; moreover, stresses Laȝamon, 'Inoh he mai suggen þe soð wule uremmen / seolcuðe þinges bi Arðure kinge' (11474-5; *He who is willing to speak the truth can tell many marvellous things about King Arthur*).

One such 'teller of truth' is of course Laȝamon himself; and, unsurprisingly perhaps considering his attitude towards his material, much of what he has to say of Arthur is indeed marvellous. His Arthur is endowed at birth with gifts from fairy godmothers:

> Ygærne wes mid childe   bi Vðer kinge,
> al þurh Merlines wiȝel,   ær heo biwedded weore.
> Þe time com þe wes icoren;   þa wes Arður iboren.
> Sone swa he com an eorðc,   aluen hine iuengen;
> heo bigolen þat child   mid galdere swiðe stronge:
> heo ȝeuen him mihte   to beon bezst alre cnihten;
> heo ȝeuen him anoðer þing,   þat he scolde beon riche king;
> heo ȝiuen him þat þridde,   þat he scolde longe libben;
> heo ȝifen him, þat kinebern,   custen swiðe gode
> þat he wes mete-custi   of alle quike monnen;
> þis þe alue him ȝef,   and al swa þat child iþæh. (9605-15)

(*Ygerne was with child by King Uther before she was married, all through the magic of Merlin. The time predestined came; then Arthur was born. As soon as he came upon earth, fairies took charge of him; they enchanted the child with magic most potent: they gave him strength to be the best of all knights; they gave him another gift, that he should be a mighty king; they gave him a third, that he should live long; they gave him, that royal child, such good qualities that he was the most liberal of*

*all living men; these gifts the fairies gave him, and the child thrived
accordingly.)*

Arthur is therefore not only connected with magic through the circumstances
surrounding his conception, as in Geoffrey and Wace, but is himself literally
'magic'. His connection with fays is further emphasized in the *Brut* at the
moment of Arthur's departure for Avalon: the fairy-queen Argante, he tells his
followers, will tend his wounds and cure him; then he will return to his kingdom.
The supernatural connections of Arthur are also hinted at in the scene where the
young king puts on his armour before the all-important last battle against the
Saxons, at Bath: his corslet was made by 'an aluisc smið' (10544; *an elvish
smith*), and his sword Calibeorne was crafted in Avalon 'mid wiȝelefulle craften'
(10548; *by magic arts*).[50]

But this is only one facet of Arthur. Laȝamon's ideal king may well benefit
from fairy powers, but his ultimate protection in battle comes from the Virgin
Mary, whose image is engraved in gold on his shield Pridwen: Arthur is an
emphatically Christian king, fighting most of the time against pagans (or powers
allied to pagans), frequently appealing to God at moments of crisis, upholding the
Church and ensuring that religious duties are not neglected. He has psalms sung
all night before his single combat with Frolle, the 'king' of France, and on several
occasions is seen praying;[51] some of these prayers put one in mind of Old English
poetry, such as when Arthur wakes up after his dream during the crossing to
France:

> 'Lauerd Drihten, Crist,   domes Waldende,
> midelarde Mund,   monnen Froure,
> þurh þine aðmode wil,   Walden ænglen,
> let þu mi sweuen   to selþen iturnen!' (12760-3)

*('Christ, our Lord and Master, Lord of destinies, Guardian of the world,
Comforter of men, Ruler of angels, let my dream, through your gracious
will, lead to a good outcome!')*

Moreover, Arthur is no shadowy romance character. In the same passage where
he is depicted as wearing both fairy armour and a Christian image, his helmet is
specifically said to have belonged to his father Uther, thus firmly placing him in a
dynastic perspective. For all this wealth of supernatural protection, Arthur is
fundamentally a British king, like Uther, like all the monarchs who succeeded
Brutus on the throne of Britain before him, and like those who are to follow him.

The glorious reign of Arthur can thus be seen as representative of the
greatness and valour of the Britons, who, at the end of the poem, may yet hope
that God will restore the land He has taken away from them.[52] Whereas Wace
states unequivocally that the Britons, in the shape of the Welsh remnant, are too

degenerate ever to aspire again to dominion over Britain, in the *Brut* the same angelic voice that makes Cadwallader renounce his claims to the British throne predicts the return to power of his people:

> 'Ah Alemainisce men Ænglen scullen aȝen,
> and næuermære Bruttisce men bruken hit ne moten
> ær cume þe time þe iqueðen wes while,
> þat Merlin þe witeȝe bodede mid worde.
> Þenne sculle Bruttes sone buȝen to Rome
> and draȝen ut þine banes alle of þene marme-stane,
> and mid blissen heom uerien uorð mid heomseoluen
> in seoluere and in golde into Brutlonde.
> Þenne sculle Bruttes anan balde iwurðen;
> al þat heo biginneð to done iwurðeð after heore wille.
> Þenne scullen i Bruttene blissen wurðen riue,
> wastmes and wederes sele, after heore iwille.' (16018-29)

('But men from Germany shall possess England, and the Britons shall never again have it in their keeping until the time comes which has been foretold, which Merlin the seer prophesied. Then the Britons shall go at once to Rome and remove all your bones from the marble tomb, and joyously bear them away with them to Britain, enclosed in silver and gold. Then the Britons shall soon grow bold; everything they undertake shall turn out as they desire. Then there shall be widespread prosperity in Britain, the crops shall be good and the weather fine, all just as they wish.')

This passage is strongly reminiscent of the medieval Welsh prophetic tradition. This is not particularly surprising; Wales was literally on Laȝamon's doorstep, and it was the logical place to look for additional, 'genuine' sources relating to the Britons.[53] The Welsh, who for Wace were a distant and alien people, are for Laȝamon respected neighbours and informants; and he consequently flatly contradicts his French source in his description of them. Wace's lines

> Tuit sunt mué e tuit changié,
> Tuit sunt divers e forslignié
> De noblesce, d'onur, de murs
> E de la vie as anceisurs. (14851-4)[54]

(They are all changed and different, they have completely deviated and degenerated from the nobility, the honour, the customs and the life of their ancestors.)

become

> Þæs Bruttes on ælc ende foren to Walisce londe,

and heore laȝen leofeden   and heore leodene þæuwen;
and ȝet wunieð þære,   swa heo doð, aueremære. (16088-90)

(The Britons flocked from every region to Wales, and lived according to their laws and according to the customs of that nation; and, what is more, will live there, as they now do, for evermore.)

This stress on institutional continuity is particularly revealing, coming as it does from a poet who rates a firmly established legal framework among the major achievements of human society.   The laws upheld by the Welsh Britons constitute in the *Brut* a link with Laȝamon's native Anglo-Saxon culture, in that the Mercian laws are explicitly said to be of British origin: King Alfred 'wrat þa laȝen on Englis ase heo wes ær on Bruttisc, / and whærfde hire nome on his dæȝe and cleopede heo Mærcene laȝe' (3149-50; *Alfred framed the law in English where it had previously been in British, and in his time changed its name and called it the Marcene law*). The cultural boundaries between the Britons and the English become blurred; Laȝamon appears to have appropriated the Celtic history of the island, and merged it with the more recent Anglo-Saxon past.[55] Even Arthur, the most bitter enemy of the Saxons, is somehow coopted into the English cultural sphere. His helmet is given an English name, Goswhit ('goose-white'), and his 'return' is to profit England, rather than Britain:

Bute while wes an witeȝe   Mærlin ihate;
he bodede mid worde   – his quiðes weoren soðe –
þat an Arður sculde ȝete   cum Anglen to fulste. (14295-7)

(But there was once a seer called Merlin who prophesied – his sayings were true – that an Arthur should come again to aid the people of England.)

The key element in this process is the character of Merlin, presented in greater detail than in either Geoffrey or Wace. We are thus given the description of Merlin in a trance, trembling and writhing 'swulc hit a wurem weore' (8938; *like a serpent*);[56] the foreknowledge of the prophet is also stressed, in that, contrary to what we find in Wace, Merlin never needs to be told anything. He knows exactly what the different kings want of him, and is repeatedly shown awaiting their unannounced messengers.[57] As in Geoffrey of Monmouth's *Vita Merlini*, there is a price to pay for these powers; he cannot accept gifts, because '"ȝif ich wilne æhte þenne wursede ich on crafte"' (9446; *were I to covet possessions then I would diminish in skill*).[58] More so than in Wace, Laȝamon's Merlin is directly responsible for the conception of Arthur; he knows that Uther will never be able to win Ygerne – '"bute þurh mine ginne"' (9401; *save by my magic skill*). It is fully in Merlin's power at this stage to prevent the coming into being of Arthur, and he is aware of it.

The Merlin of the *Brut* not only makes the birth of the hero possible, he also shapes the narrative through his prophecies. Laȝamon does not provide the full text of the Prophecies of Merlin omitted by Wace, but he quotes or echoes specific sayings which he thinks relate directly to the material at hand. Before Merlin sets out to help love-sick Uther, he prophesies that Arthur will rule the princes in Rome,[59] and that he is to be the subject of songs:

> 'Of him scullen gleomen   godliche singen;
> of his breosten scullen æten   aðele scopes;
> scullen of his blode   beornes beon drunke.' (9410-12)

> (*'Of him shall minstrels splendidly sing; of his breast noble bards shall eat; heroes shall be drunk upon his blood.'*)

This quasi-messianic description of the future king, which closely parallels chapters 112-15 of Geoffrey's *Historia*, also recurs later in the narrative (11494-9).[60] The repetition of these prophecies throughout the Arthurian section, together with the constant affirmation of the truthfulness of Merlin's sayings (as opposed to Wace's wry detachment), underline the tragic irony of Arthur's life.

The king's future downfall is hinted at on two occasions, through cryptic dreams which increase the tension and suspense of the account of the campaign against Rome. The first of these occurs during the crossing to France: in his sleep, Arthur sees a bear in the eastern part of the sky, which savagely fights with, and is killed by, a dragon coming from the west. In Wace, the dream is explained by the King's retainers as announcing a victory over a giant (and indeed, Arthur does later defeat the Mont St Michel giant). But no one interpretation is given by Laȝamon, who hints at the possibility of a more sinister meaning: 'Ne durste þer na cniht to ufele ræcchen na wiht' (12792; *No one there dared interpret it as in any way ill-omened*). The ensuing fight with the giant on Mont St Michel reintroduces the idea of fate – the giant knows that only Arthur can defeat him.[61] The second dream, which occurs after Arthur's victory at Saussy, is clearly emblematic of the future course of events. Arthur dreams that he is sitting on the roof of a great hall, with Gawain. Modred comes and hacks down the hall with a battle-axe with the help of Wenhauer, causing Gawain to break both his arms in the fall; Arthur breaks his right arm, but seizes his sword in the left hand, cuts off Modred's head and chops the Queen to pieces. Then he himself is seized by a golden lioness, and dragged into the sea. A fish eventually brings him to the shore, cold, wet and sad. A British envoy confirms the truthfulness of this bad omen, and Arthur and his men return to Britain where they meet their end at Camelford.[62]

However, according to the *Brut*, Arthur's destiny has already been fulfilled by his victory over the Roman emperor at Saussy:

Þa wes hit itimed þere   þat Merlin saide while,
þat Rom-walles sculden   aȝein Arður touallen.
Þat was agan þære   bi þan kaisere
þa ueol þerinne fehte   mid fifti þusund monne;
ruren þer to grunde   riche Rom-leoden. (13964-8)

(Then there had come to pass there what Merlin had once said, that the walls of Rome should fall before Arthur. That had been fulfilled by the fall in battle there of the emperor and fifty thousand men; the might of Rome was there brought low.)[63]

The Arthurian episode, in Laȝamon's terms, is therefore a totally glorious one. Arthur has fulfilled Merlin's prophecies, and leaves the final battlefield victorious (even if it is a somewhat pyrrhic victory). He is badly wounded, but not dead; the king who succeeds him is technically only a regent, and the return of 'an' Arthur is apparently assured by God Himself. Moreover, Merlin has announced that the 'new' Arthur is to help the people of England as a whole, not just the Britons. In effect, Laȝamon creates a distinct myth which makes allies of the hereditary enemies whose struggles are depicted in his *Brut*: from this point, Arthur is truly 'of the English'. **Françoise Le Saux**

Prose Chronicles

The narrative independence, the poetic vigour, the sheer mass of Laȝamon's *Brut* promised a tradition of national history, of a land peopled by several nations successively dominant, successively displaced, in a native idiom slowly regaining national status. A line of continuity from Laȝamon to the alliterative *Morte Arthure* and through it to Malory would be logical, but cannot, in the present state of research, be established.[64] Whatever localized success his *Brut* may have had in the West Midlands, it represents a blind alley; the high road of English historiography ran from Geoffrey of Monmouth, through Wace to multiple forms of national chronicle, in verse and prose, in Latin, French and English.

Even before Wace, the present was connected to the legendary past by the tripartite structure adopted by the Anglo-Norman Geffrei Gaimar, who combined his verse translation of Geoffrey's *Historia* (made in the 1140s and now lost) with a sequel, *L'Estorie des Engleis*, largely based on the Anglo-Saxon Chronicle, and a brief sketch of the reign of Henry I (1100-35). In this attempt to bring the history of the country right down to his own time he set the pattern for popular history for the next three centuries (Legge, 28-9). Wace's version of the *Historia*, which displaced Gaimar's, became a popular component of such tripartite structures, both in its original form and in prose paraphrases. Composite chronicles exist in Latin and English as well as Anglo-Norman. An Anglo-Norman prose version, beginning with the legendary settling of Albion by exiled daughters of an eastern king, who give birth to the race of giants discovered by Brutus on his arrival in the island,[65] followed by a version of Wace, and ending originally with the death of Henry III in 1272, compiled shortly after that date, was the primary source of the most popular of the English prose chronicles. The earliest English manuscripts date from about 1400, the estimated date of composition.[66]

It is, however, misleading to speak of the prose *Brut* as uniform and static, or even as a single chronicle. It survives in more than 170 manuscripts, many varying in content, scale, component sources, even in the basic translation of the Anglo-Norman text incorporated,[67] and in the continuations added from time to time. The original Anglo-Norman continuation to 1333 may already have been supplemented from English sources; there follow continuations to the death of Edward III (1377), Henry V's taking of Rouen (1419) and the accession of Edward IV (1461), individual manuscripts ending with other events and dates.[68] Despite the general adoption of prose as a serious and appropriate medium for history throughout fourteenth-century Europe, no absolute distinction was made in England, and sections of the prose *Brut* were incorporated in some manuscripts of metrical chronicles, while a version in Latin seems to have had something like official status.[69] Caxton recognized its national standing by publishing a version under the title *Chronicles of England* in 1480 and again in 1482; a dozen more editions followed, from various presses, before 1530, and for the rest of the sixteenth century most English histories began with the coming of Brutus and his Trojans.

Following the outline of Geoffrey, Wace and Laȝamon, the prose *Brut*, radically abbreviated, covers the reign of Arthur at proportionate length (§§71-89), except that the Prophecies of Merlin, in a version adapting the animal imagery of Geoffrey's *Historia* to predict the characters and deeds of late medieval monarchs, bulk unduly large (§75).[70] The reign ends with a notably ambiguous statement of the Hope of the British:

> Arthure himself was wondede to þe deth. But he lete him bene born in a liter to Auyoun, to bene helede of his wondes; and ȝitte þe Britons supposen þat he Leueþ in a-noþere lande, and þat he shal come ȝit and conquere al Britaigne; but certes þis is þe prophecie of Merlyn: he saide þat his deþ shulde bene dotous; and he saide sothe, for men þerof ȝitte hauen doute, and shal for euermore, as me saiþ, for men weten nouȝt wheþer þat he leueþ or is dede. (§88)[71]

And indeed it is as if Arthur lives on throughout the prose *Brut* as a potent memory, even though Britain has long been lost to his race and its name changed by Saxon Hengist (as here interpreted (§96)) to 'Engistes lande'. Mementoes of him, tangible and symbolic, crop up across the ages. Edward II's arrogant favourite, Piers Gaveston, 'made so grete maistries, þat he went into þe Kyngus tresorie in þe Abbay of Westminster, and toke þe table of golde, wiþ þe tresteles of þe same, and meny oþere riche gewelles þat some tyme wer þe noble Kyng Arthures' (§187). In the ninth year of his reign, Edward III instituted the Round Table 'to be holde þer at Wyndissore in Whitesen-wike euermore after erly' (§226). The ambitious Mortimer, as if in emulation, 'was so ful of pride and of wrecchednesse, þat he helde a rounde table in Walys to alle men þat þider wolde come, and countrefetede þe maner & doyng of Kyng Arthureʒ table' (§220). And a great nobleman, on his way to execution for treason, was mocked for his fall from power as ' "O Kyng Arthur, most dredeful!" ' (§198). The memories of Arthur, the commentaries of Merlin link past and present, implying the linear succession of English kings from Brutus, of national heroes such as Richard I, Edward III and Henry V from the archetypal British monarch.[72] As, over the course of two centuries, the prose *Brut*, more widely diffused than any vernacular text other than the Wycliffite Bible, became the nearest equivalent to a national chronicle. It must have played a major role in establishing Arthur as the focus of patriotic sentiment, the embodiment of a concept of nationhood, an amalgam of many cultures, evolved over centuries.

We do not know where, by whom, or for whom it was written. Such evidence as there is suggests a London origin: the continuations after 1377 draw upon London chronicles and reflect their mercantile point of view, and the dissemination of the *Brut* in numerous copies over several centuries implies the support of some institution, perhaps an office of clerks forming part of the central administration.[73] As for the audience, the indications are that it widened and diversified from age to age. The Anglo-Norman original, with its interest in heraldry and genealogy, its narrative coloured by the literature of chivalry, seems designed to appeal to nobility and gentry; yet it was indebted to monastic sources as well as London chronicles (Taylor, 112). The preponderance of manuscripts in English reflects the expanding literacy of the fifteenth century: 'That the English prose *Brut* was owned all over the country by nobility, gentry, merchants, clerics, and academics, can be documented from ownership marks and wills.'[74] Widely disseminated, it became the standard vernacular history textbook of late medieval England, its account of Arthur's reign the authoritative and authentic one for all except a few suspicious scholars. Throughout the sixteenth century most compilers of English chronicles began with the coming of the Trojans, Tudor antiquaries accepted the substance of the *Brut*, playwrights dramatized episodes from it. Shakespeare, whose *Lear* and *Cymbeline* inherited (by devious routes) elements of Geoffrey's *Historia*, might have given us a play on Arthur. The *Brut* was not likely to be the immediate source, but it prepared the audience to accept their contemporary rulers as dynastic successors of Brutus and Arthur. Spenser condensed the reigns from Brutus to Uther in the second book of the *Faerie Queen* to provide a fitting ancestry for the hero, Prince Arthur; but his allegorical adventures in quest of Gloriana, embodiment of Tudor restoration of the glory of England, focus on her rather than him. Ben Jonson, Milton and Dryden all considered and abandoned plans to write an Arthurian epic. Conviction of Arthur's place in our dynastic inheritance was slowly waning.

The decline is already apparent in the *Polychronicon* of Ranulf Higden, despite the influential status of his work. Higden was a Benedictine monk of St Werburgh's abbey, Chester, who died in 1363 aged 64. He was, like Laȝamon, a provincial cleric working in comparative isolation. But his circumstances, some century and a half later, were very different: working with the resources of a monastic library and in Latin prose, Higden wrote at great length a universal history ranging – with later additions – from the Creation to the Treaty of Bretigny in 1360. History is preceded by topography, the chronicle opening with a description of the structure of the universe, the location, climate, natural resources, roads, rivers and cities of England, its laws, marvels, dialects and the characteristics of its peoples. There follow accounts of a succession of world empires, Assyrian, Persian, Greek and Roman; the modern world, British, English and Norman, is reached late in the work and entries become briefer as the fourteenth century approaches.

In an age of reviving interest in classical studies, Higden's detailed treatment of the ancient world, the width of his reading in Roman authors and the works of medieval humanists, fascinated his contemporaries.[75] The impulse which had led medieval societies to produce fictitious and legendary histories, such as the *Brut*, connecting their origins with the ancient world, lent interest to a reconstruction of antiquity associating the history of modern England with that of Troy. In this respect his is a monastic chronicle, extending Geoffrey's synchronic technique to interrelate events in Roman and papal history with events in Britain. Higden himself expanded his original, completed in the 1320s, producing two further versions before his death. The surviving texts represent short, intermediate and long versions; monastic communities and individual clerics extended their own copies with

brief accounts of contemporary history, and several of the major chronicles
of late fourteenth-century England were written as continuations of Higden's
work (Taylor, 101-3). Among laymen, the zest of his writing, his sense of
significant detail – Caesar dictating to four secretaries simultaneously, the
thickness of Chester's city walls, and the excellence of salmon fishing in the
Dee – made his work widely popular in English translation just when its
influence on the writing of history was beginning to wane.

Its popular influence began in the 1380s with the translation by John
Trevisa, student of one Oxford college and fellow of another, later vicar of
Berkeley in Cornwall, scholar and translator of many learned and sacred
works. He had theories of his own on the art of translation and on the
validity of English as a literary medium that colour his version of the
Polychronicon, in which he comments upon and contradicts Higden.[76] The
Latin original survives in at least 118 manuscripts and nine fragments, the
English in fourteen complete texts and five excerpts.[77] Caxton published it in
1482, with an updating conclusion of his own compilation, and two further
editions followed from other presses. Signs of the *Polychronicon*'s influence
are apparent in vernacular literature both sacred and secular, including the
work of Chaucer, Lydgate and Usk.[78]

In Higden's vast scheme, the age of Arthur comes late, in the fifth of his
seven books, Geoffrey's *Historia* supplying the framework of early British
history but the account of Arthur coming mainly from Henry of Huntingdon
and the *Gesta Regum Anglorum* of William of Malmesbury. He seems to
have absorbed some of their academic doubts about Arthur, since his
treatment is brief and partial. Having paraphrased Vortigern's introduction of
the Saxons under Hengist and Horsa, he omits the mysterious birth of Merlin
and his obscure prophecies of Britain's future, because they are found only in
Geoffrey's British book – 'and I wolde putte it to þis storie ȝif I trowed þat it
be i-holpe by soþenesse' (V, §1).[79] Arthur 'þe werriour', is introduced, aged
eighteen, in the reign of Cerdic, King of the West Saxons, against whom he
fought twelve times, ending in the battle of mount Badon where he slew nine
hundred with his own hand. Weary of the long struggle, he leaves the Saxons
in possession of Wessex, while his ambitious nephew Mordred, treacherously
complicit with the invaders, is crowned king of the Britons.

> But þe storie of Britons telleþ þat Arthur fauȝt afterward wiþ Mordredus, and
> slouȝ hym, and was i-slawe, and i-buried in þe vale of Avalon bysides
> Glastonbury. Aftirward his body and þe body [of his wif] Gwenvere were i-
> founde in þe secounde kyng Henries tyme, and i-translated into þe chirche,
> aboute þe ȝere of oure Lord enlevene hondred and foure score. (V, §6)

But, despite the evidence of Giraldus Cambrensis, who 'handelede Arthur his bones', doubts of Arthur's historicity delay him longer than the history itself. Why, Higden wonders, have Roman, French and Anglo-Saxon historians nothing to say of his conquest of thirty kingdoms, his victorious campaigns in Europe and the defiant march upon Rome with which Geoffrey credits him, his defeat of Frolle, King of France, and the Roman procurator Lucius Hiberius, both unknown to history as Arthur is unknown to Gildas and Bede. The analytical mind of the scientific historian looks for textual confirmation and does not find it. Yet, for all his doubts, he cannot help echoing, in the second, intermediate version of the *Polychronicon*, William of Malmesbury's ambivalent comment on Arthur's worthiness to be celebrated, not in the false fables of the Britons, but in truthful histories as the support and inspiration of his fatherland.[80]

Trevisa, eager to be convinced, answers his doubts with textual rationalization, pointing out that Saint John includes in his gospel many details not mentioned by the other evangelists.

> So þey Gaufridus speke of Arthur his dedes, þat oþer writers of stories spekeþ of derkliche, oþer makeþ of non mynde, þat dispreveþ nouȝt Gaufrede his storie and his sawe, and specialliche of som writers of stories were Arthur his enemyes. (V, §6)

True, Arthur may well have been over-praised – the belief that he will return to rule the Britons again is for madmen only – but even the ancient Greeks were more famed for their deeds than the facts warrant: 'and þat was for þere were writers of clere witte, and hadde ioye and likynge to torne here witte and here tonge to greet, hiȝe, and huge preysinge'. Even Higden undermines his own rigorous argument by concluding rather lamely that it is only natural the British should praise Arthur extravagantly, just as the Greeks praise Alexander, the Romans Octavian, the English Richard I, and the French Charlemagne. Despite the ambivalence of both author and translator, Arthur's place among the Nine Worthies seems assured.[81]

But that status, as an international icon of a giant reputation petrified for all time, marks a decline in Arthur's historical significance.[82] Even the prose *Brut*, more convinced of his dynastic role, gives pride of place to personal attributes in summarizing Arthur's reputation:

> ffor þe noble Knyȝt Arthure was þe moste worþi lord of renoun þat was in al þe worlde in his tyme, and ȝitte come neuer non soche after him, for alle þe noble knyȝtes þrouȝ Cristendome of dede of Armes alosede, duellede wiþ Kyng Arthure, and helde him for her lord; and þat was wele sene, for he conquerede a Romayn þat me callede Frolle, & gete of him þe reaume of France, and quellede him wiþ his owen hande. And also he fauȝt wiþ a

Geaunt þat me callede Dynabus and quellede him, þat hade rauisshede Elyne, þat was Kyng Hoeles nece, Kyng of Litil Britaign; and afterward he quellede in bataile þe Emperour of Rome, þat me callede Lucye, þat had assemblede aȝeyns Kyng Arthur forto feiȝt wiþ him so miche peple of Romayns and of Peiȝtes and of Sarasynus, þat no man couþ ham nombre; and he descomfitede ham alle, as þe story of him more pleynloker telleþ. (§220)

Here Arthur is seen as a once-great conqueror whose personal prowess is equally devoted to the defence of ladies in distress, drawing to him a warrior brotherhood among whom he is first and foremost a knight, leader of a chivalric company, much as Malory was to see him at the end of the Middle Ages.   **W. R. J. Barron**

Metrical Chronicles

En gestes aunciens trovoums-nous escrit
Quels rays et quels realmes ly rays Arthur conquist,
Et coment sun purchace largement partyst.
Roys suz ly n'avoit ke ly countredist,
[Counte, duc, e baron, qe unqes le faillist],
En guere n'e[n] bataille ke chescun ne suyst.

(*In ancient histories we find written*
What kings and what kingdoms king Arthur conquered
And how he shared largely his gain.
There was not a king under him who contradicted him
Earl, duke, or baron, who ever failed him
In war or in battle, but each followed him.)[83]

These approving remarks about King Arthur's qualities as king and conqueror occur in the early fourteenth-century verse chronicle composed by Pierre de Langtoft, an Augustinian canon from Bridlington, Yorkshire, but not in the section of the narrative which describes the major events of Arthur's reign; instead they occur much later, in the section which deals with the reign of Edward I. Having reminded his audience of the achievements of King Arthur and his exemplary relationship with the leading men of the realm, the narrator goes on to compare the practices of King Edward unfavourably:

Ly rays sir Eduuard ad done trop petyt;
Par quai a sun aler, quant en mer se myst
Vers ly roys de Fraunce, fet ly fu despit,
Ke nes un ses countes of ly le aler emprist. (II, 296)

(The king sir Edward has given too little;
Whereby at his departure, when he put to sea
Against the king of France, the affront was shown him
That not one of his earls undertook the expedition.)

Langtoft's comment suggests some preliminary observations about the defining features of the group of texts, the Middle English metrical chronicles, with which this section is concerned.[84]

Most obviously, in terms of subject matter, these are narratives which are not only concerned with recounting the story of the foundation of Britain and its sequences of rulers, but also with tracing the making of England and its sequences of pre- and post-Conquest kings. These narratives, like others before them in Latin, appropriate the alluring vision of an imperial British history provided by Geoffrey of Monmouth within a historical frame orientated towards the history of England.[85] But just as the Arthurian period has a larger contextual significance in Geoffrey of Monmouth's history (and in the adaptations by Wace and Laȝamon), so too, the Arthurian sections of these metrical chronicles are best understood and read with reference to the larger narratives of which they form part. The British Arthurian period may be set up, as it is in Langtoft's chronicle for example, to serve as a model and measure for the regnal achievements of a contemporary king (Edward I in Langtoft's case), though it may not always serve this function, as we shall see in the case of the Auchinleck version of the so-called *Short Metrical Chronicle* (*Zettl*) in which a more 'convenient' model of an ideal king is constructed out of the figure of Hengist, rather than King Arthur.[86]

Similarly, although I will be concerned with chronicles written in Middle English which attempt, in varying degrees of detail, to span the period from the foundation of Britain to the reigns of post-Conquest English rulers, these are by no means the only vernacular narratives circulating in post-Conquest England which address this subject: Anglo-Norman verse and prose are important, indeed, precocious media, for historical narration in England. An 'Arthur of the English' may equally well be represented in an Anglo-Norman historigraphical narrative, such as that recounted by Langtoft, as in narratives composed in English or in Latin in England. Anglo-Norman verse is the medium, in Gaimar's *Estoire des Engleis*, for the first vernacular narrative which attempts to provide a continuous account of the discontinuous rulers of Britain and England; to use Anglo-Norman prose as a historiographical medium seems to have been an option for writers in England some time before it was an option to write historical narratives in Middle English prose.[87] The texts which make up the category of Middle English metrical chronicles – that is Robert of Gloucester's *Chronicle* (*Wright*), the *Short*

English Metrical Chronicle (*Zettl*), Robert Mannyng's *Chronicle* (*Sullens*), and Thomas Castleford's *Chronicle* (*Eckhardt*) – form part of a much wider spectrum of vernacular historiographical writing with which they interact, as we will see, in varying degrees.[88]

What, then, is the significance of writers choosing to use English verse as their medium for historical narrative in the thirteenth and fourteenth centuries? It is tempting to conclude that such writers were composing for an audience of the 'lewd' (or unlearned) rather than the educated, Latinate, élite – as Robert Mannyng claims in the prologue to his *Chronicle* (*Sullens*, 1-10).[89] However, this rather oversimplifies the situation and the factors involved in determining the relationship between the choice of literary language and the actual audience of texts circulating in England during this time. English was available as a literary medium throughout the medieval period (despite the impression given in some literary histories of it having somehow 'gone underground' until the fourteenth century) and, in choosing to write in English, writers were choosing to compose in, potentially, an 'inclusive' language which would allow their work to circulate in a variety of contexts (not necessarily monolingual contexts, as one copy of the *Short Metrical Chronicle* demonstrates).[90] It may also be that some composers/redactors of the metrical chronicles were trying to exploit the potential of the language to function as a category of identification (to identify, that is, the national community of 'the English' via those who use English), and thus to provide a history of the land in its distinctive language (Turville-Petre 1996, 22). Though, again, we must be careful not to overgeneralize about the intentions of the composers of these narratives, nor the possible significance of these narratives for their varied audiences.

We can more confidently characterise the effect of the decision to write historical narratives in Middle English verse on the modern reception of these metrical narratives: it has been quite calamitous and these works are only now beginning to recover from their status as the 'poor relations' of medieval historiography and to attract more sustained research and analysis – some fruits of which are to be seen in the new edition of the *Chronicle* of Robert Mannyng and the first edition of the *Chronicle* of Thomas Castleford. One problem for modern readers has been that the use of English verse as a historiographical medium has set up expectations of 'artfulness' which are not necessarily appropriate to the functional aspects of using this medium. Modern responses to, for example, the extraordinarily well-organized narrative known as Robert of Gloucester's *Chronicle* have been overshadowed by some very influential derogatory comments about the poetic quality of his work (*Wright*, xl). But full appreciation of the Middle

English metrical chronicles has also been inhibited by the patronizing attitude of modern readers to medieval historiographical enterprises in general, although these, too, are in the process of revision: we are at least beginning to realise now something of the potential sophistication of 'medieval' senses of the past. What follows here, then, is a discussion of some large texts squeezed into the space available. These are texts of the future, to some extent, which are going to attract a great deal more attention and be more sympathetically understood in the years to come.

Whether there is sufficient evidence to prove that a Robert of Gloucester was responsible for the chronicle attributed to him by John Stow in 1570 is a matter of some debate.[91] The work is extant in two recensions, the most significant divergences occurring long after the Arthurian section and, on the evidence of some internal topical references, its composition would appear to date from the late thirteenth or early fourteenth century; the earliest manuscript dates from *c.* 1325.[92] This is the most widely circulated and, in this sense, most influential and important of the Middle English metrical chronicles: in addition to the fourteen manuscript copies which survive (taking both recensions together), there are two prose adaptations of the material which date from the fifteenth century and a number of references to, and citations of, material from this chronicle in the work of later historians from the sixteenth century onwards, as well as three late seventeenth-, early eighteenth-century copies of extant manuscript texts.[93] Yet modern assessments of Robert of Gloucester's *Chronicle* have tended to be rather disparaging.

Although lack of poetic art is the frequently cited reason for its poor modern reputation, it may be that the particular narrative strategies employed by its composer have also affected modern responses to the narrative. In contrast with the historical narratives composed by Laȝamon and Robert Mannyng, for example, the audience of Robert of Gloucester's *Chronicle* is not given any developed self-portrait of the originator of the work, nor is any intertextual frame of reference for its sources developed in the text: the impression of a self-conscious artist at work is not cultivated in this *Chronicle* as in theirs.[94] And yet, in practice, as has been recently observed (Turville-Petre 1996, 76), considerable art was required to produce a narrative history out of a range of sometimes conflicting sources (predominantly in Latin); moreover an impression of a set of controlling interests and themes cumulatively develops throughout the work – in the relationship between the 'might' or power of a leader and his right to rule; in the relationship between the quality of rulers, their piety, and the welfare of their subjects; in the relationship between the history of the institutional development of church and realm.[95]

What readers interested in King Arthur find in Robert of Gloucester's *Chronicle* is an account of Arthur's reign which follows Geoffrey of Monmouth's version quite closely (unlike the abbreviated accounts of some of the other kings of Britain in Robert of Gloucester's narrative) but with some shift in emphasis (Arthur's piety and exemplary chivalric behaviour are particularly stressed);[96] with some abbreviation of material (particularly in the details of the military campaigns and battle scenes);[97] but also with some important additional details. The great assembly at Caerleon is described as being a gathering of the 'rounde table' (*Wright*, 3881-2, 3901-2, 3915-6) and the references here imply membership of a chivalric group that apparently needs no further explanation or justification.[98] In the final phase of Arthurian history in Robert of Gloucester's *Chronicle*, Arthur kills Mordred in a personal confrontation, described as his last act of 'chiualerye' (4574-9), a detail which reflects the influence of Henry of Huntingdon's account of this scene.[99] Arthur, having handed over the crown to Cador's son, then dies from his wounds, and the narrator notes how his bones were later discovered at Glastonbury, the oldest church in the land, as we learn later in the narrative (4776-97), where Arthur's tomb is to be found in the choir (4592-4).[100]

So no credibility is given in this narrative to the possibility of Arthur returning to be 'a king of the future': there is no equivocation about the fact of his death, although the mistaken hopes of the British and Cornish about Arthur's return are acknowledged (4589-91).[101] However the audience is also left in no doubt of Arthur's status: the cumulative impression built up through the narrative is of an exemplary king, a taker of counsel, a man of personal might, the 'beste kni3t' ever (4588), whose noble qualities both magnetically attract and positively affect those in his milieu. Arthur's death is a great loss to the land and its people, as the narrator later reminds his audience (4653-54).

Robert of Gloucester's version of Arthurian history (indeed the scale of his narrative as a whole) contrasts with that offered in the *Short Metrical Chronicle* – the modern name of which does little to attract the interest of readers, although there is much of interest here, not only for enthusiasts of variations on Arthurian themes, but also for those interested in female foundation stories.[102] The single title actually refers to a group of texts: from the five complete, or near complete, copies extant (which include two strikingly variant versions of the text) the editor, Zettl, posits an original, composed sometime after the death of Edward I in 1307, which provided an epitomised history of the kings of Britain and England from the occupation of the island up to the new reign of Edward II, in around 900 lines.[103] The attraction and utility of this kind of historical narrative (of which there are many other examples in Latin and Anglo-Norman) obviously resides in its brevity.[104] It is designed to offer an overview of British/English regnal history; a very much simplified, abbreviated and more portable overview compared with that provided by the other, much longer, metrical chronicles in English by Robert of Gloucester, Robert Mannyng and Thomas Bek.[105]

In just over two hundred and seventy lines the *Short Metrical Chronicle* moves from an account of the foundation of Britain by the Trojan Brutus, to the foundation of England by maid Inge of the Saxons, who combines the roles played by Hengist and Rowena in the Galfredian version of British history, and perhaps distantly recalls Queen Dido. Arthur's is the thirteenth and penultimate reign in this sequence and is narrated in varying degrees of detail, depending on the particular version of the text. In London MS BL Additional 19677 (Zettl's base text) Arthur's reign is described in just six lines (*Zettl*, 243-8). Arthur, we are told, was 'a man of gret fauor . . . þe best knyȝt at nede', who reigned twenty-two years and is buried at Glastonbury.[106] The version in BL MS Royal 12.C. XII offers an account of Arthur's reign (and British history in general) which bears more resemblance to the Galfridian frame, in that Arthur's conquests in Italy and France are briefly recounted (R. 281-8), as is his betrayal by Mordred (here his 'cosyn') (R. 289-96). In this account, however, Arthur is able to deal with Mordred's threat successfully and reigns for another ten years before being buried at Glastonbury (R. 297-308).

This view of Arthur as an exemplary, outstanding figure which is especially promoted in the Royal version (R. 267-70) could not be more different from the impression given in the version of the *Short Metrical Chronicle* found in the so-called Auchinleck manuscript, which contains many surprises for modern readers familiar with the outlines of Arthur's reign.[107] The Auchinleck does not open with an account of Brutus's foundation of Britain, but with an account of the prior foundation of the island by a group of unruly royal sisters from Greece, led by the eldest, Albin, after whom the island is named.[108] Familiar figures from the Galfridian sequence of British history are given new historical location and functions in this sequence, none more so than Hengist who appears in the pre-Arthurian sequence of kings of Britain (*Zettl*, A. 651-872). In this text Hengist, an exemplary king and conqueror of 'Jnglond Wales & Scotland' who rules for 250 years, plays the most important role in organizing the government and civilizing the whole land. His extraordinary technological approach to conquering France achieves results without bloodshed and as a figure he seems designed to offer a idealised 'historical' role model for the contemporary king of England, Edward III (Turville-Petre 1996, 109-10).

Arthur appears later in the sequence as a King of Wales who is requested to help mobilise an opposition to King Vortigern (A. 1029-42). Following Arthur's victory, he is crowned king at Glastonbury in 560 in a chair of gold (A. 1051-60); yet his reign is no golden age, but one beset by internal personal and political problems. Launcelot de Lac holds Arthur's wife Gwinore in a set of specially designed underground caves in Nottingham Castle (A. 1071-98).[109] Once this problem is peacefully resolved, a magic cloak that appears to be able to detect adulterous wives is brought by Cradoc to Arthur's court at Glastonbury, where it can still be seen according to the narrator (A. 1099-1109). Here, it seems, we not only have echoes of contemporary romances and *lais* about Arthur, or associated with his court, incorporated into the narrative, but also echoes of events from more recent history, 'a memory of Roger Mortimer and Queen Isabella in 1330 barricading themselves into Nottingham Castle' (Turville-Petre 1996, 111).[110]

If the *Short Metrical Chronicle* (in whatever version) offers very much an epitomised account of the history of the kings of Britain and England, Robert Mannyng's *Chronicle*, which was completed in 1338 and survives in the form of two copies and a small fragmentary text, offers in contrast a much more encyclopaedic account of the ruling figures of British and English history up to 1307. This 'story of Inglande' (*Furnivall*, 3) endeavours to fill out any narrative gaps in the sequence by incorporating material from a wide variety of narrative and historiographical sources in Latin and in the vernacular.[111] Robert Mannyng, probably a canon of the Gilbertine order (*Sullens*, p.13), is a sophisticated and self-conscious historical writer and it is entirely characteristic of the way he positions his work within a broader historical, literary and linguistic context that his account of the reign of Arthur should contain two interesting passages on the wider circulation of narratives about Arthurian adventures and how they can be fitted into the chronology of Arthur's reign.[112]

Mannyng's most important sources are, as he tells us himself, the *Roman de Brut* of Wace and Pierre de Langtoft's *Chronicle*, but he prefers Wace's version of British history to that offered by Langtoft because it provides the fuller account of these times. In the Arthurian sections Mannyng follows Wace's version fairly closely, though sometimes incorporating distinctive details from Langtoft's narrative, such as the allusion to how far Arthur travels to Rome (*Sullens*, 13467-8), and the account of Mordred's and

Arthur's wounding at each other's hands (13693-700).[113] The important passages of commentary on the circulation of Arthurian narratives function as ways of filling in what may seem to be narrative gaps in Wace's and Geoffrey's account of Arthur's reign: in the account of Arthur's twelve-year period of peaceful rule in Britain after he has unified the land and returned from his successful Northern Isles campaign (10391-420); and in the account of the nine-year period of Arthurian rule in France which follows the defeat of Frolle (10765-74).

On the first occasion Mannyng develops Wace's asides on the British fables in circulation about Arthur (*Brut*, ed. Arnold (1938-40), 9787-99) into a passage which begins by identifying this twelve-year period of peace as the time when many adventures occurred that now are read about in verse narratives (*Sullens*, 10391-404). But Mannyng then continues with a discussion of the textual evidence for Arthurian history, its value (which he defends), and its accessibility, commenting that French writers seem to have produced more on the subject of Arthur than those in 'here' (10418).[114] The circulation of Arthurian material in France is the central topic of Mannyng's second commentary passage for, he suggests, it was during the nine-year period of Arthurian rule in France that the adventures occurred which French writers subsequently preserved in their prose narratives, the 'grete bokes' of 'so faire langage' (10419-21). The nine-year period of Arthurian rule in France gives Mannyng both 'a chance to explain away the puzzling fact that the Arthurian prose so avidly read in England – presumably Mannyng had the Vulgate Cycle in mind – was produced in France' (Putter, 8), and the opportunity to give this body of Arthurian prose material, like the body of verse material Mannyng referred to earlier, a historical location.[115]

That Arthur's achievements will always excite narrative interest is clear for Mannyng: 'Til Domesday men schalle spelle / & of Arthures dedes talke & telle' (10419-20), but he is equally clear about the reality of Arthur's death. Unlike Langtoft and Wace, Mannyng is not prepared to countenance any equivocation on this subject and firmly denounces the hopes of the Britons that Arthur is still alive (13717-24).[116]

We know a reasonable amount about the context in which Mannying was writing, mostly because this is a writer who seems to want his audience, present and future, to know about him: he includes biographical information in both his *Chronicle* and his earlier work, *Handlyng Synne*. We know very little by contrast about the writer responsible for the work known as Thomas of Castleford's *Chronicle*.[117] The name appears on the first folio of the single extant manuscript of the work (Göttingen, Niedersächsische Staats- und Universitäts-bibliothek MS 2 Cod. hist. 740 Cim.) and could well be a record of an owner rather than its compiler. As the editor of the first complete edition has observed, 'it may be preferable to regard the work as anonymous' (*Eckhardt,* xi). This 'Boke of the Brute', as the narrator refers to the narrative (*Eckhardt,* 229), charts the rulers of Britain and England up to the accession of Edward III and follows the Galfridian frame for its account of British history, although material on the early saints of the island has been amplified and the narrative opens with a version of Britain's foundation by 'Dame Albine'.[118]

Thomas of Castleford's *Chronicle* seems to have been designed as a functional manual on the subject of British and Arthurian history: the narrative is divided up into clearly indicated books and chapters which would facilitate ease of reference. It is the first English verse translation of the *Historia Regum Britanniae* to offer its readers a version of the prophecies of Merlin in their original context, and this is perhaps its most distinctive feature for a modern audience interested in Arthurian matters.[119] However there are some small details in the Arthurian section itself which appear to represent a departure from the material of the *Historia*: the device of the Round Table is mentioned (21104-17) in ways which suggest some influence of the *Roman de Brut*; Arthur himself kills Mordred (23914-23) and is later buried at Glastonbury (23976-89).[120]

More information about Thomas of Castleford's *Chronicle*, its sources and perhaps its reception, may come to light with the appearance of the third volume of the new edition. This 'Boke of the Brute' awaits more detailed research, as do all the other texts discussed here. Alongside the chronicles of Britain and England in Latin and Anglo-Norman, the Middle English metrical chronicles represent an important conduit for the transmission (and modification to some extent) of the Galfridian tradition of Arthurian history and for its integration into the wider sweep of the history of England. This awareness of King Arthur as a historical figure imbricated in a larger national narrative is one that the composers of Middle English Arthurian romances are able to exploit in various ways in their work and is a distinctive feature of it. However, the Middle English metrical chronicles themselves also offer some interesting insights into the contemporary circulation of a wider spectrum of narratives about King Arthur in the vernaculars of England, as I have indicated at several points in my discussion and especially with reference to Robert Mannyng of Brunne: in his 'story of England' Mannyng attempts to give the 'grete bokes' in circulation about King Arthur a more secure historical foundation and to rationalise the interest of French vernacular writers in the marvels of this British king.   **Lesley Johnson**

A

ARTHUR IN ENGLISH HISTORY

James P. Carley

There is an important distinction to be made between the Arthur *of* History and Arthur *in* English History. In recent years the former topic has formed the focus for a number of studies and it is covered elsewhere in this volume.[1] The general movement has been towards scepticism: most critics now consider that a historical Arthur is not necessary to explain the legendary phenomenon, and that if there ever were such a person, he is not now recoverable from the later legends. The legendary aspect appears to predominate from the very beginning;[2] even in the first so-called 'historical' text, the *Historia Brittonum*, the dual nature of Arthur is evident. In the early historical writings he is portrayed as a British hero and not an English one: indeed the English are seen as oppressors.[3] Up to Geoffrey of Monmouth's *Historia Regum Britanniae* Arthur retains his Britishness and aspects of his mythic quality, although he does share some characteristics with the Norman kings.[4]

The unresolved tension between the fabulous and the historical Arthur came into sharp focus in the twelfth century when we see a real disjunction between the Arthur of the vernacular romances and the Arthur of Geoffrey of Monmouth and his contemporaries.[5] The Latin tradition celebrated the heroic Arthur most memorably delineated by William of Malmesbury in the 1120s:

> Hic est Arthur de quo Britonum nugae hodieque delirant; dignus plane quem non fallaces somniarent fabulae, sed ueraces praedicarent historiae, quippe qui labantem patriam diu sustinuerit, infractasque ciuium mentes ad bellum acuerit.
>
> (*This is that Arthur of whom the trifling of the Britons talks such nonsense even today: a man clearly worthy not to be dreamed of in fallacious fables, but to be proclaimed in veracious histories, as one who long sustained his tottering country and gave the shattered minds of his fellow citizens an edge for war.*)[6]

But on the Continent, presumably basing himself in part on the 'Britonum nugae', Chrétien de Troyes introduced a different Arthur: the *roi faineant* hovering in the background while his knights dominate the action.[7] Chrétien's work was succeeded by a number of vernacular Arthurian romances and romance cycles, many of which were later disseminated in

England as well as on the Continent. Nevertheless, relatively little of this *matière de Bretagne* was translated into English.[8] In England, therefore, the version of Arthur which prevailed, in the romance tradition as well as the chronicles, was basically that of Geoffrey of Monmouth.[9] Only at the very end of the Middle Ages, did Thomas Malory supplement Geoffrey's whole account of the rise and fall of the kingdom with materials from the French romances.[10]

A turning point in the historicizing and anglicizing of Arthur was the exhumation of his relics at Glastonbury Abbey in 1191. In that year his body, and according to some accounts that of Guenevere too, was 'discovered' in a sarcophagus buried at great depth between two ancient pyramids in the monks' cemetery, a leaden cross revealing the identity of the remains. Much of the remainder of this essay will be concerned with Glastonbury as focus for the portrayal of Arthur by English medieval historians and as he appears in English political propaganda.[11] Concerning the discovery J.-C. Cassard has observed: 'cette stratégie de captation de la gloire antique de la Bretagne devait contribuer de façon efficace à désarmer psychologiquement les Bretons de l'île. Elle présentait également l'avantage de faire des rois angevins les héritiers légitimes d'Arthur: dès 1192 on voit Richard d'Angleterre offrir à Tancrède, roi de Sicile, la célèbre épée d'Arthur, Calibur.'[12] There are various explanations of why Arthur came to be associated with Glastonbury, but most scholars have accepted Caradog of Llancarvan's *Vita Gildae*, written for the monks of Glastonbury in the 1120s or 1130s, as the precipitating factor.[13] In this *Life* Arthur is firmly associated with Glastonbury and an etymological link is made between Glastonbury and the Isle of Glass. This link once having been established, moreover, it was inevitable that there would be a further conflation of the otherworldly Isle of Glass and the mythical Isle of Apples to which Arthur had been transported for the healing of his wounds, according to Geoffrey's account.[14]

Why the discovery of Arthur's body took place precisely when it did appears to have been the result of several factors.[15] The devastating fire at Glastonbury in 1184 created a financial crisis and the community would have been highly sympathetic to the kind of publicity Arthur's discovery would generate. According to Giraldus Cambrensis, Henry II suggested the dig and in the 1180s Henry II would have had good reason for reminding the Welsh that Arthur was dead and buried (and in English territory at that).[16] He might also have wished, in the aftermath of the Becket fiasco, to have promoted Glastonbury as an alternative site to Canterbury for the origins of English Christianity.[17] Cooperation in this matter would thus have been beneficial both to king and community. Before the stage was finally set for the great event, however, Henry died and was succeeded by Richard the Lionheart, who shared none of his father's concern for Glastonbury; his energy and surplus revenue were devoted to crusading.[18] Nevertheless, Richard's naming of his nephew Arthur as heir in 1190 may have encouraged the Glastonbury community to revive its earlier schemes. As Wood postulates:

> to inform Richard the Lionheart that the bones of the man after whom his heir had been named – indeed, of the king on whom at least some of the Plantagenet claims to legitimacy were seen to rest – had been rediscovered at Glastonbury only thanks to the bardic intervention of his own father was none too subtly to remind the crusading king that the time had come for the generosity of the king to be renewed by the son.

Like the descriptions of the motivating forces behind the excavation, the accounts of the wording on the cross vary in significant detail. According to Giraldus's *De principis instructione* (*c.* 1193), the inscription ran 'Hic iacet sepultus inclitus rex Arthurus cum Wenneuereia uxore sua secunda in insula Auallonia' (*Here lies buried the famous king Arthur with his second wife Guenevere in the Isle of Avalon*). Ralph of Coggeshall (*c.* 1194) read it as 'Hic iacet inclitus rex Arturius, in insula Auallonis sepultus' (*Here lies the famous king Arthur, buried in the Isle of Avalon*). Writing some half a century later, the Glastonbury chronicler Adam of Damerham maintained that it read 'Hic iacet sepultus inclitus rex Arturius in insula Aualonia'. At the time of the dissolution, John Leland, who claimed actually to have handled the cross, gave the reading as 'Hic iacet sepultus inclytus rex Arturius in insula avallonia'. It is this version which is known to posterity through William Camden's engraving of 1607.

The variations, and in particular Giraldus's reference to Guenevere (and as second wife at that), have provoked scholarly discussion. In Wood's opinion Henry of Sully (abbot 1189-93) gathered together the 'props' for the 1191 discovery. For this enterprise his chief written guide was, quite naturally, Geoffrey of Monmouth and he was unaware of the adulterous Guenevere celebrated by Chrétien. Even more unfortunately, he did not think about the parallels between Mordred and Richard, Guenevere and Eleanor of Aquitaine. The moment that Richard the Lionheart became associated with the event, therefore, Guenevere needed to be expunged and so she does not feature in the later descriptions of the cross.[19]

Richard Barber has postulated that Giraldus was not, in fact, an eyewitness to the exhumation, as scholars have tended to portray him.[20] Originally, by Barber's reckoning, three bodies were discovered in the cemetery and the monks associated these with Arthur, Guenevere and

Mordred (who is not necessarily a villain in Celtic tradition). Soon afterwards they realized the unfortunate implications of including Mordred in the identifications and excised him from subsequent versions. In this scenario Giraldus became the first purveyor of the new account, but remnants of the older form remain embedded in the description of the coffin as divided into three parts.

Over the next centuries the historical Arthur must be seen very much in the context of English imperial policy and the need of its rulers to impose themselves on their nearest neighbours.[21] Geoffrey's Arthur stands as an emblem of a unified kingdom;[22] by analogy the kings of England needed only to show that they were the legitimate successors of Arthur, both literally in terms of their genealogies (and there were many genealogies constructed showing the descent of the English monarchs from Arthur) and also metaphorically as *Arthur redivivus,* in order to assert their sovereignty over the whole island.[23] Almost inevitably, therefore, the evidence of Arthur's grave seems to have been invoked when tensions between England and its Celtic neighbours were most acute, marked on two occasions by a royal visitation to Glastonbury.[24] Although Arthur is a standard feature in medieval histories, his role is highlighted in periods of 'national' crisis.[25]

In 1277 Edward I defeated the Welsh and forced Llywelyn ap Gruffydd, prince of Wales, to submit to him. To justify their domination of the Welsh, the English represented themselves as the legitimate successors of Brutus and Arthur, both of whom held sovereignty over Scotland and Wales. By the spring of 1278 Edward faced the danger of renewed Welsh opposition, rallying under the banner of the prophesied return of Arthur, the sleeping king. This, then, is the subtext of the 1278 Easter visit to Glastonbury by Edward and Eleanor, the highlight of which was Arthur's 'second' exhumation – 'one of the few great set performances of his reign'.[26] Adam of Damerham, himself presumably an eyewitness, provides a description of the occasion. According to this account Edward found in the tomb:

> . . . in duabus cistis, imaginibus et armis eorum depictis, ossa dicti regis mirae grossitudinis, et Gwunnarae reginae mirae pulcritudinis . . . In crastino uero . . . dominus rex ossa regis, regina ossa reginae, in singulis palliis preciosis inuoluta, in suis cistis recludentes, et sigilla sua opponentes, praeceperunt idem sepulcrum ante maius altare celeriter collocari, retentis exterius capitibus et genis utriusque propter populi deuocionem, apposita interius scriptura huiusmodi: Haec sunt ossa nobilissimi regis Arturi, quae anno incarnacionis dominicae millesimo ducentesimo septuagesimo octauo, terciodecimo Kalend Maii, per dominum Edwardum, regem Angliae illustrem, hic fuerunt sic locata . . .

> (. . . *in two separate chests, decorated with their portraits and arms, the king's bones of wonderful size, and those of Queen Guenevere of great beauty . . . On the following day . . . the king again enclosed the king's bones in their chest, wrapped in a precious pall, while the queen did the same for the queen's bones. They marked them with their seals and directed the tomb to be placed speedily before the high altar, while the heads and knee-joints of both were kept out for the people's devotion. This was the inscription put on the inside: 'These are the bones of the most noble King Arthur which were placed here on 19 April in the year of the Lord's Incarnation 1278 by the illustrious Lord Edward, king of England, . . .)*[27]

This was clearly the secular equivalent of the translation of saints' relics with the attendant identification of the king with the revivified saint:

> The exhumation of 1278 was, then, an assertion that Edward I as king of England was a legitimate successor to the Arthurian imperium – albeit not by lineal descent – and a hint that the restoration of the imperium was not far from his thoughts.[28]

The intended conflation of Edward with Arthur seems to have been accepted and later in the reign Pierre de Langtoft (d. 1307), for example, made explicit comparisons between Arthur and Edward in his chronicle.[29] More importantly, as Riddy has argued:

> . . . the production of the [Anglo-Norman] *Brut* should be seen in the context of the self-conscious Arthurianizing of Edward I's reign: the reburial of Arthur and Guinevere in 1278, the presentation of Arthur's Welsh crown at the high altar of Westminster Abbey in 1284, the Arthurian style Feast of the Swan in 1306, the Arthurian tournaments, and so on.[30]

Edward himself believed that his coronation oath gave him authority over the whole imperium and that he was entitled to exercise his control in both Wales and Scotland. As in the case of Wales, Arthurian precedents were used in Edward's confrontations with the Scots – most notably after the Scottish crisis of 1290 when Edward was called upon to adjudicate the succession question.[31] Unsure of his own constitutional position, Edward launched a historical inquest, sending circular letters to the monasteries in 1291 and again in 1300, in which each community was instructed to search its chronicles and archives for evidence concerning the status of the two realms. When he came to write his letter in 1301 to Boniface VIII outlining his position on the Scottish question, Edward – presumably basing himself on the findings of certain of the returns[32] – included Arthur as an important piece of evidence:

Item Arturus rex Britonum princeps famosissimus Scociam sibi rebellem subiecit, et pene totam gentem deleuit et postea quemdam nomine Anguselum in regem Scocie prefecit et cum postea idem rex Arturus apud ciuitatem Legionum festum faceret celeberimum, interfuerunt ibidem omnes reges sibi subiecti inter quos Anguselus rex Scocie seruicium pro regno Scocie exhibens debitum gladium regis Arturi detulit ante ipsum et successiue omnes reges Scocie omnibus regibus Britonum fuere subiecti

(Arthur, king of the Britons, that most famous leader, made subject to his authority rebellious Scotland, and destroyed nearly all its people and then appointed as king of Scotland one Anguselus. When later the same King Arthur had a celebrated feast at Caerleon, all the kings subject to him attended, among whom Anguselus, king of Scotland, displaying his service for the kingdom of Scotland, bore King Arthur's sword before him and subsequently all kings of Scotland have been subject to all kings of the Britons.)[33]

The Scots, not surprisingly, quickly retaliated in kind; conceding that Arthur may well have conquered Scotland, they maintained nevertheless that since he died without issue Scotland automatically returned to its previous independent status.[34]

Scottish problems continued to plague the English in the first decades of the fourteenth century. In particular, after Edward III's repudiation of the treaty of Northampton in 1330 there was a renewal of hostility on the northern border.[35] Not long afterwards, just before Christmas 1331, Edward and Philippa paid a visit to Glastonbury, thus publicly reaffirming Edward's Arthurian connections in the same manner as Edward's grandfather had done in 1278.[36] It was at roughly the period of Edward's visit, too, that the prophecy of Melkin the Bard was concocted at Glastonbury. In this cryptic text the mysterious Holy Grail of Arthurian romance tradition has been transformed into a wholly respectable Holy Blood relic, historically unimpeachable, brought to England by Joseph of Arimathea.[37] Glastonbury thus took on apostolic status. The story must have spread quickly, since in 1345 a Londoner, John Blome, was granted the right to search for Joseph's remains in Glastonbury's ancient cemetery. Apart from its local interest, moreover, the affirmation of Joseph's mission to Glastonbury served Edward's needs on the Scottish front admirably.[38] In *Scimus, fili*, Boniface VIII had cited the special relationship between the Scots and St Andrew, and the Declaration of Arbroath stated that the Scots were converted by Andrew.[39] Joseph at Glastonbury undermined, of course, the force of the Andrew story; and the genealogical chain from Joseph to Arthur which the Glastonbury writers formulated added even more potency to Edward's claims as monarch and overlord. Apostle and monarch became part of the same sanctified chain.[40]

Apart from Melkin's prophecy, there were two other documents relating to origins and the Arthurian past composed at Glastonbury soon after Edward's visit in 1331 – *Quedam narracio de nobili rege Arthuro* and *De origine gigantum*.[41] Both translations from Old French, they are found together in a Glastonbury copy of Geoffrey of Monmouth's *Historia Regum Britanniae* (now Oxford, Bodleian Library, Bodley 622), the script of which can be dated to the first half of the fourteenth century. Stylistic and other considerations suggest that they are the work of the same translator.[42] In both cases the author has taken a romance text and has translated it to show its applicability to a historical/political context.[43] *De origine gigantum* is a translation of the Anglo-Norman *Des Grantz Geanz* (mid-thirteenth to early fourteenth century), which gives an account of the first inhabitants of Albion and the establishment of English sovereignty over the island. In essence, *De origine gigantum* forms a preface to Geoffrey's *Historia Regum Britanniae*. Apart from Bodley 622, an early copy of *De origine gigantum* is found amongst prefatory documents to the Great Cartulary of Glastonbury in close juxtaposition with Scottish materials, on which it provides an implicit commentary. *Quedam narracio de nobili rege Arthuro* derives from the Old French Grail romance *Perlesvaus*, itself a work with strong Glastonbury resonances. The translator of *Quedam narracio* adapted the opening sequence of *Perlesvaus* in order to show why Arthur changed his coat of arms and why he had a particular devotion to the Church of Our Lady at Glastonbury. In its Latin form the episode, moreover, provides an explanation of Arthur's patronage for Glastonbury and forms one aspect of a coherent narrative which ultimately leads up to the 1191 discovery. It is thus a particularly interesting example of the use of romance in the construction of historical narrative, especially when it came to be embedded in John of Glastonbury's chronicle account of the history of the monastery.

In the years after his visit to Glastonbury Edward's fascination with his illustrious ancestor intensified, culminating in his pledge of 1344 to re-establish a fellowship of the Round Table.[44] Soon afterwards his interests shifted and in 1348 he substituted the Order of the Garter for the proposed Round Table.[45] More generally, his ambitions in France lessened his concern with the Scottish question and by 1357, when David II was released from the imprisonment which had begun with his capture at Neville's Cross in 1346, peace was effectively established. The need to rebut Scottish foundation claims became less pressing, therefore, and the *De origine* story, having lost its *raison d'être*, never seems to have been used politically at a national and international level as originally intended.

John Hardyng's fifteenth-century verse chronicle may, however, provide a hint of how this text was designed for an Arthurian context as evidence for England's sovereignty over Scotland.[46] Hardyng, who quoted Melkin (in the forms Mewynus, Mewinus and Mewyn) as his source for various points concerning Joseph of Arimathea, the Round Table and Galahad, claimed to have found in Melkin's writings evidence which would refute Scottish claims to independence.[47] Nevertheless, although Hardyng's sources in the sections where Melkin is evoked are various, surprisingly they do not correspond neatly with John of Glastonbury, who is our only surviving primary witness to Melkin's writings.[48] When Hardyng described Scota as 'Doughter and bastard of kynge Parao', whose exploits are juxtaposed with Joseph's mission, he gave Melkin as his source. Melkin is also the authority for the description of Galahad's creation of the Order of the Grail after he became king of Sarras. In this section – on f.78ʳ of the Long Version – there is a gloss which states: 'What the Reule of ordour of Saynt Graal was her is expressed and notifyed as is conteyned in þe book of Josep of arymathie and as it is specified in a dialoge þat Gildas made de gestis Arthur.' In John of Glastonbury's chronicle the Joseph section opens with a *Tractatus de Sancto Ioseph ab Arimathea*. This is succeeded by material found 'in gestis incliti regis Arthuri', describing Galahad, Lancelot and the Round Table.[49] The two titles in John (*Tractatus de Sancto Ioseph ab Arimathea* and *Liber de gestis incliti regis Arthuri*) correspond very closely to those invoked in the Long Version of Hardyng's chronicle ('þe book of Josep of arymathie' and 'de gestis Arthur') and both John and Hardyng are dealing with the same individuals and adventures at this point. Indeed, the parallel is so close that it would seem to indicate that there may have been some sort of compendium concocted at Glastonbury separate from John's chronicle (but into which it was partially incorporated) which contained the book of Joseph of Arimathea, a dialogue *de gestis Arthuri*, Melkin's prophecy and other materials, some attributed to Melkin.[50] The compendium presumably had an independent circulation and some form of it, or excerpts from it, may have been available to Hardyng. In this case the citation of Melkin as a source for the Scota story in the context of Joseph of Arimathea may not derive from Hardyng's own 'fertile imagination' but from developments which took place at Glastonbury almost a century earlier.[51]

The cult of Joseph of Arimathea at Glastonbury derives ultimately from Joseph's role as Grail guardian in the French Arthurian Grail romances; and from the mid-fourteenth century onwards, according to English tradition,

Arthur and Joseph were linked together in a genealogical chain. In the fifteenth century Joseph was invoked by the English in conciliar settings at a period when councils were growing in importance within the Church hierarchy: his English connection was exploited by English delegates at the Council of Pisa in 1409, at Constance in 1417, at Pavia-Siena in 1424, and at Basel in 1434. In 1417, in particular, the English delegate Thomas Polton dwelt at some length on Joseph's mission in an attempt to show England's right to stand as an independent nation. Joseph's evangelization of Britain thus became a crux for the English and, as in the case of Arthur over two centuries earlier, relics must have seemed desirable. Most surviving accounts, nevertheless, suggest that the Glastonbury community never managed to unearth Joseph's remains. Recently, however, there has come to light a copy of a letter written in 1421 by Abbot Nicholas Frome to Henry V, in response to what must have been an emphatic request that the body be found.[52] As a result, some sort of excavation did occur, and it seems that the stage was set for a royal visitation by Henry V to Glastonbury, similar to that of Edward I and Edward III, which would culminate in a public unveiling of the desired relics. Like his earlier namesake Henry II, however, Henry V died before his plan could come to fruition. On this occasion there was no later precipitating factor, no equivalent to Richard the Lionheart, and indeed conciliar issues became less pressing as the century went on. It is not surprising, therefore, that Joseph's remains were left unidentified.[53] Although Joseph's cult continued to be fostered, his burial place was never revealed; the fulfilment of Melkin's prophecy remained something safely *in futuris*, a variant on the *rex quondam rexque futurus* theme surrounding Arthur himself.[54]

There is no evidence that Arthur was systematically invoked by either side in the Wars of the Roses, although his name crops up in contemporary chronicles,[55] and Edward IV did renew the Order of the Garter and emulate the Burgundian court in general.[56] Slightly later, when Henry VII managed to unite the houses of Lancaster and York, he envisaged Arthur as a unifying and legitimizing symbol, naming his first born son after England's most illustrious king and his own remote ancestor.[57] Just one year earlier, in 1485, Caxton published Malory's *Morte Darthur*, which can be seen as a kind of encyclopaedia of the Arthurian legend as it circulated in England at the end of the Middle Ages. Malory himself, writing in the unsettled 1460s, accepted the essential truth of the basic story, although this does not seem to be an issue with which he concerned himself. Caxton, on the other hand, noted the existence of doubters, those who would maintain that 'alle suche bookes as been maad of hym ben but fayned and fables by cause that somme cronycles make of hym no mencyon ne remembre hym noo thynge ne of his knyghtes'.[58] In his version, therefore, he tried to reconcile Malory with canonical history (as represented in the use of the *Chronicles of England* to revise Book V). In the preface, moreover, he pointed out that the sheer quantity of 'archaeological' evidence should convince – Arthur's seal at Westminster, Gawain's skull at Dover Castle, the Round Table at Winchester and the tomb at Glastonbury Abbey *inter alia*. In Levine's words:

> Caxton had stumbled onto a question of fact and had done what he could to fathom the issue. The criticism of Arthur was most unusual in raising the question; the defense was even more unusual in attempting to meet the challenge by systematically assembling the evidence. It failed, of course, because the evidence was counted, not weighed. But what else could Caxton do? There was nothing in his training, nothing in all his culture, that could help him to evaluate the motley assortment of objects and testimonies, words and things, that had accumulated over the centuries. Perhaps, if the issue had mattered more to Caxton and his friends, they might have done better. But here, as elsewhere, the distinction between history and fiction did not really make much difference.[59]

By this time, too, humanism and the new historiography were beginning to make themselves felt in England and in some quarters the Arthurian myth was seen as old-fashioned and inaccurate as well.[60] A more fully articulated sense of anachronism came into play and scholars realized that one could indeed discriminate between different kinds of evidence. By the beginning of the sixteenth century there were those, the Italian humanist Polydore Vergil (1470?-1555) in particular, who wished to jettison the bulk of the story.[61] Vergil himself, so he alleged, was willing to grant that Arthur reigned after Uther and that he might have reunited Britain for a time if he had lived longer.[62] But, that he was buried at Glastonbury was, in Vergil's opinion, an indefensible piece of anachronism since the monastery was not even founded until after Arthur's death.

In response, the English antiquary John Leland (1503?-52) mounted a spirited defence of Arthur, concluding confidently that 'I can prove Arthur to have existed with as certain, clear, true and indeed numerous arguments as Vergil can prove Caesar to have existed.'[63] But in spite of his confident assertions, Leland failed in his enterprise, as Levine observes, precisely because like his opponents he went back to sources, and

> agreed to play the same historiographical game: to collect all the original sources archaeological and literary, and to date and sift and compare them . . Put to the test, it became gradually clear that all the evidence for the historicity of the British story – not only Geoffrey of Monmouth and the

medieval romances but Arthur's seal, floating traditions, gravestones at Glastonbury, even the Round Table itself – were equally untenable.[64]

When the Duke of Norfolk approached the imperial ambassador Eustace Chapuys in 1531 with evidence concerning England's status as an empire, he followed the example of Edward I and Edward III's advisers and cited Arthur as a trump card, producing what Chapuys took to be the inscription on Arthur's tomb: ARTHUR THE PATRICIAN, EMPEROR OF BRITAIN, GAUL, GERMANY AND DENMARK.[65] The ironic response was very different from what it would have been in the past (Chapuys claiming that he did not know at first which Arthur was in question):

> . . . my answer was that I was sorry to see that he was not also entitled Emperor of Asia, as he might have left the present King Henry for his successor in such vast dominions; but that as all things in this world were so subject to change, it was reasonable that an English monarch of our days should conquer a portion of the provinces above named, since in those very countries men had been found who had conquered and held for a long time this very kingdom of England, where the succession of William of Normandy still lasted. If by showing me the inscription the duke meant that the present King Henry might be such a conqueror as King Arthur, I could not help observing that the Assyrians, Persians, Macedonians, and Romans had also made great conquests, and everyone knew what had become of their empires.[66]

Leland's heroic efforts notwithstanding, the medieval Arthur was indeed dead and buried. Henry VIII's concept of imperium and the uses to which he wished to put it paralleled and even exceeded those of Edward I and Edward III, but Arthur no longer represented a viable historical exemplum. Although Joseph of Arimathea would resurface in the context of the justification of the Church of England, Arthur retreated into the land of faerie, only to re-emerge quite transformed in the next generation as Prince Arthur, the ostensible hero of Spenser's great epic poem.[67]

3

THE ROMANCE TRADITION

Catherine Batt and *Rosalind Field*

'Ne tut mençunge, ne tut veir'
(Neither all lies, nor all true)[1]

Romance, to the twentieth-century reader, may suggest fantasy, love and escapism, but the origins of medieval Arthurian romance are culturally and historically specific and we need to relocate it in its time and place in order to appreciate its cultural frame of reference (Brownlee, 1-16). In order to understand the relation between French and English romance, we need to be aware of how different are the geographical and cultural conditions of medieval northern Europe from those of the twentieth century and so rethink to some extent our categories of both nation and literature. The territories of France in the twelfth and thirteenth centuries do not correspond to its modern boundaries. The use of the French language does not define a homogeneous court culture on the Continent, and in the extraordinary conditions obtaining in post-Conquest England, several different languages – English, French, Latin, Anglo-Norman – serve the varying cultural needs of insular communities (Clanchy; Turville-Petre 1996, 181-221). That the Matter of Britain should spread from the Celtic lands of Wales and Brittany to appear in French rather than English is a consequence of the political and linguistic history of twelfth-century Britain. On the accession, in 1154, of Henry II, recently married to Eleanor of Aquitaine, the Angevin realm stretched from the Pyrenees to Scotland with Wales and Brittany in significant proximity at its borders. Moreover, there had been a sizeable Breton element in the Conqueror's original army and it was at the courts of the Norman marcher lords and amongst the Breton diaspora that the tales of the Celts would have become available to the Anglo-Normans (Bromwich, 273-98; Bullock-Davies). The Latin writings of clerics such as Walter Map and Gerald of Wales bear witness to the interest in Celtic material a generation after Geoffrey of Monmouth,[2] but it is with Geoffrey's translator, Wace and other vernacular writers associated with the Anglo-Norman and continental French courts of the second half of the twelfth century that Arthurian romance begins to take shape.

At the same time, tastes in narrative literature were changing and a new public emerging. The change in sensibility in the twelfth century indicates a newly leisured courtly public, receptive to fresh material from the western or the eastern borders of Europe, preferring tales of individual adventure and emotional crisis to those of imperial legend. Critical opinion has long expressed the development and definition of romance in terms of contrast with epic,[3] in particular, to the Old French *chansons de geste*. Thus epic can be seen to deal in wars, romance in quests. Epic promulgates loyalty to the masculine group or the nation, romance to the lady or the integrity of the individual. Epic is redolent of the oral, romance is self-consciously literary. Romance seems more intent on exploring literary possibilities than on defining absolutes: the 'dogmatic principles' of epic contrast with the 'inductive' lines of romance.[4] But recent work on the *chansons de geste* demonstrates the extent to which such distinctions may themselves be the product of a critical over-eagerness both to categorize and to privilege one form over another.[5] We need to bear in mind that 'epic' and 'romance' are two modes, even moods, not sequential literary forms, and that Arthurian romance, with its historical shading, is one literary area where the two interpenetrate.

The adventures of the quasi-historical Arthur and his traditional companions may have had a challenging political relevance for Geoffrey's readers in Norman Britain, but viewed from across the Channel the same material would evoke the distant and the exotic, infused with the additional fascination of the Celtic supernatural to provide an alternative to the serious matter of the history of France. For an insular public, however, Arthurian material, even in the romance mode, could rarely be detached from its historic or geographic origins to be entirely ahistorical or exotic, as it could be for the public for the romances of Chrétien and his followers in French, German, Italian, Spanish or any of the other languages of medieval Europe (Lacy 1991, 160-2; 182-8; 254-7; 425-8). This is not to exclude the possibility of a continuing mediation of political and social concerns in Arthurian romance in French as well as in Middle English, but for insular readers and writers of romance, its underlying historicization, sanctioned by Geoffrey's *Historia*, influences both the selection and interpretation of material.[6]

For these reasons to describe a work in French or in English, as an 'Arthurian romance', is not only to identify certain themes and motifs, but also to raise questions about its nature and function. In an influential, because rare, contemporary analysis of medieval vernacular writing, Jean Bodel (1165-1209) claims that while the Matter of Rome is conducive to wisdom and the Matter of France is authentic, the Matter of Britain is 'vain et plaisant' (1-11). While he may have had a professional interest in denying Arthur historical relevance, as his own work concerns Charlemagne's campaign against Arthur's old enemies, the Saxons, the terms 'vain et plaisant' are not necessarily pejorative,[7] and Bodel's ambivalent formulation suggests a larger potential for Arthurian romance. For in the blending of 'mençunge' and 'veir' around the figure of the quasi-historical Arthur, whose realm may have resonances for a contemporary social order, romance writing finds a fitting subject for an investigation of literary authoritativeness, a concern of the major vernacular writers of the twelfth century. So, from its inception, a self-consciousness about the status and effects of vernacular composition characterizes romance narrative, which defines itself against other forms of literature but also appropriates developments in twelfth-century literary culture, such as the language of religion and Scripture, of history and of subjectivity.[8]

The authors of what were probably the first romances had claimed Latin antecedents as their authority in retelling in the vernacular the classical stories of the Matter of Rome. In these *romans antiques*, the *Roman d'Eneas*, the *Roman de Thèbes*, the *Roman de Troie*, all written between *c.*1150 and 1170, narrative presentations of the past invite moral interpretation and, although they do describe their characters' emotional engagements, they also locate Ovidian love within historical, social and political contexts.[9] But the Arthurian world, provided by Wace's *Roman de Brut*, gave a broader literary horizon, an imaginative freedom from clerical Latin, and figures able to adopt the modern mind-set of Christian Europe without undue anachronism. Arthurian romance, set as it was in a post-Trojan and pre-Anglo-Saxon world, could take advantage of the intervals Gaufridian history opens up to interpolate other, more fantastic, narratives.[10] This is evident in the developing versions of Arthurian material in Wace and Chrétien: Wace presents Arthur's reign as a locus of idealized British history, Chrétien as a heightened version of contemporary courtly society. So the quintessential romance hero becomes a knight of Arthur's court: defined by deeds of arms and love, his adventures lead him through the forests of Logres, in quest of his lady, or of the Grail, and his temporal context, indistinct as it may be, is the reign of Arthur (Auerbach, 123-42).

Versions of the ancient tale of Tristan provide another formative ingredient in the twelfth-century development of the Matter of Britain. Written, like Wace's *Brut*, for the Anglo-Norman courts, they further exemplify the search for an authoritative version and the attraction of the accumulating Arthurian cycle. The antiquity of the primitive tale is evident in its un-medieval (un-courtly and un-Christian) concept of an illicit, irrational love conferred by a fatalistic potion.[11] The love triangle in which Tristan of Cornwall loves Isolde, the bride of his uncle, King Mark, subverts the very bases of feudal society, providing a pattern to be echoed in the other great Arthurian theme of tragic passion, the love of Lancelot and Guinevere. In the version of Thomas 'd'Angleterre', the potion-induced passion leads to an intense, introspective adventure, exploring the emotions of love and hate, the frustrations and exigencies of sexual desire, and demonstrating the power of love to subvert social values and confuse rationality. His account displays the cool analysis of the schools, suspending ultimate judgement while inviting his readers to address the riddle of which character suffers the most for love. It may well be that it was Thomas's poem that established the tale of Tristan as the archetype of passionate tragedy, certainly it is his version that Gottfried von Strasbourg prefers in the next century. Even so, Gottfried, like Thomas before him, invokes the shadowy figure of 'Bleheris', a semi-mythical Breton jongleur (Michel Zink in Lacy 1987, 23), evidencing the need to establish an ancient authority in British narrative.[12] Beroul's version is both more entertaining and less disturbing than Thomas's, giving an episodic treatment of the complex tale with a preference for violent, even shocking action over emotional analysis. Beroul is unflinchingly partisan, castigating the courtiers who alert Mark to his wife's adultery as traitors. In his version the ancient tale approaches the safety of the carnival world of fabliau. It also begins to be drawn into the Arthurian cycle, as Mark's rule in Cornwall is here contemporary with Arthur's in Britain.

The appeal of these treatments of the full Tristan story is attested by the number of short, allusive works dependent on the frame of reference they provide. Lyrics from the troubadours to Chaucer use Tristan as the epitome of the suffering lover. Short narratives dwelling on a single episode in the tale include the Anglo-Norman *Folie Tristan d'Oxford* and Marie de France's lai of *Chevrefoil*. The *Folie Tristan* relates the episode of Tristan's return to court disguised as a madman and his riddling testing of Iseult, a performance through which runs a vein of misogynistic cruelty. The madman's obscure references to past events recapitulate the story for those who already know it, while recreating the danger to the lovers should the disguise be penetrated by anyone else. The provocative contribution of the Tristan story to the romance tradition gives rise to an immediate reaction, evidence of which is to be found in the group of identifiable 'anti-Tristan' romances, including the *Cligés* of Chrétien.[13]

Marie de France also assumes familiarity with the Tristan and Arthurian material amongst her courtly audience. Her identity remains uncertain, although the possibility that she was the Abbess of Shaftesbury, half-sister to Henry II, is intriguing. Her situation as the only known female writer of Arthurian romance has led to a minute inquisition of gender attitudes in her tales,[14] and most readers find an original perspective in her handling of traditional material. Her *lai* of *Chevrefoil* is a lyrical and allusive episode in which the lovers are briefly re-united in the forest on the edge of Mark's kingdom. The poem focuses on an emblematic object, the symbiotic honeysuckle and hazel tree, which conveys the message that separation would, indeed will, mean death. Like Thomas, Marie does not locate her Tristan material in the Arthurian world, which does, however, provide the setting for her lai of *Lanval*. Here she constructs Arthur's court in terms derived from Wace, but portrays it as a courtly world of false values, sexual corruption and injustice, and her evocation of Arthur and his queen, of the select band of knights to which the hero aspires but never belongs, is astute and interrogative. In the melancholic figure of Lanval she explores the individual cost of the celebrated international attraction of Arthurian chivalry; in opposition to it she sets the world of the Fee, which rescues and ultimately absorbs the hero. Enigmatic and opaque, *Lanval* has left its readers and adaptors at odds, but it is a significant witness to the vitality of Arthurian literature in the French-speaking courtly milieu of the twelfth century. ·

Already in the work of Marie and in the Anglo-Norman *Tristans* we can discern important elements in the Arthurian tradition: the dualistic topography of court and forest, the quizzical view of court life, the tensions between feudal king and knight – exacerbated in the primitive pattern of the uncle–nephew relationship – the conflicting demands of the public persona versus the private, or the masculine versus the feminine, the integration of which may be possible only in death or its alternative, the otherworld of Avalon. Marie de France's *Lais* illuminate the beginnings of the Francophone enthusiasm for Arthurian material. Only one *lai*, *Lanval*, is clearly 'Arthurian', the other eleven are 'Breton', broadly Celtic, rather than Arthurian, providing a distinct body of tradition which was still recognized in the fourteenth century. But the gravitational pull of the Arthurian centre came to dominate.

The focal point of any discussion of French Arthurian romance must be the work attributed to Chrétien de Troyes (fl. *c.* 1160-90),[15] about whom we know only what he tells us in his romances, that is, where he comes from (*Erec*, 9), that Marie de Champagne is a patron (*Lancelot*, 1-29), and Philippe, Count of Flanders, a dedicatee (*Perceval*, 7-15). The narrator of the stories, however, supplies a strong authorial presence, one claiming an authoritative permanence for his writings to supersede the unreliable fictions of minstrels (*Erec*, 18-26). Chrétien seems to be the first to identify 'romans' as genre, and he methodically outlines the literary process by which he produces his authoritative *livre* (*Lancelot*, 24-5).[16] It is important to his sense of cultural continuity that he does not 'invent' Arthurian subject matter, but extends it by drawing on Celtic as well as classical sources (Bromwich, 273-98). His ambiguously phrased prologues emphasize the need for active readerly engagement with his work,[17] and the romances themselves are carefully structured so as to open up for debate the very bases, narrative and ethical, upon which he founds them.

We can interpret Chrétien's five extant Arthurian romances, *Erec et Enide*, *Cligés*, *Lancelot* or *Le Chevalier de la Charrete*, *Yvain* or *Le Chevalier au Lion*, and *Perceval* or *Le Conte du Graal*, as experiments in working through the effects of the internal contradictions of romance. His works show a concern with the relation between love and masculine martial valour which is chivalric romance's central dynamic, but which is also the source of ideological and narrative tension. The young protagonists of *Erec et Enide* resolve this tension only through their mutual quest, undertaken after Erec believes himself betrayed by his wife Enide for revealing to him what others say about his neglect of chivalric duty in favour of love. One might read this text as consolidating social, individual, feudal and monarchical interests in the eventual coronation of the protagonists. But there is also room for a darker interpretation that sees gender relations unsatisfactorily resolved, or finds in its classical allusions a critique of current narrative practices.[18]

The plot of *Yvain* may appear to provide a more comfortable romance of wish-fulfilment for landless young knights, and an easier solution than in *Erec* to the dilemma of how to achieve a balance between arms and love, with its story of prowess rewarded with the provision of lands and sexual satisfaction through marriage to an heiress, both lost and regained in the course of the narrative (Knight 1983, 73). But it also implicitly asks whether Yvain's bipartite history really represents a re-education of the hero or ultimately gratifies male desire, while the coercive treatment of the heroine does not invite too close an examination.[19]

Cligés is a studiously metatextual romance: its prologue, invoking the great translation of power, military and scholarly, from east to west, from past to present civilizations, raises questions about the relation of learning to chivalry, while the narrative also uses material from Wace to suggest the complexity of Arthurian history itself.[20] The tale of the young lovers is, conceptually and narratively, self-consciously patterned on the Tristan legend, even as it articulates resistance to it, as for example in the happy resolution to the dilemma of the heroine Fenice who explicitly resists identification with Iseult (3105-24). Yet Chrétien's mention of his own (lost) work 'of King Mark and the fair-haired Iseut' (6), signals a complex intertextuality in which past narratives, and past narrations, form the subtexts to subsequent retellings.

In *Lancelot*, the earliest extant romance to feature this hero, both protagonist and author are caught up in male–female relations. Lancelot's very identity is contingent on manifestations of a female desire itself never fully defined,[21] while Chrétien is similarly in service to his patron, Marie de Champagne. But the assertion of male textual control, in Godefroi de Leigni's claims at the end of the romance to have finished the task Chrétien left incomplete (7098-112) redefines the power relations of patron and author, male and female.[22] It prompts a revision of the gender relationships within the text itself, and in terms of historical experience, when it explores the question of who is best served by a religion of love. Chrétien's romance plot presents Lancelot with continual detours and obstacles to his reaching and rescuing the object of his desire, Guenievre.[23] Yet the queen, in her puzzling initial rejection of her lover, seems less a representation of female power than a plot device, deferring further the satisfaction of the hero's desire, and obfuscating the very terms of *fin amours* that have defined him as hero.

It is clear that in Chrétien's hands, romance can provide for the scrutiny as well as the celebration of chivalric action, especially where it defines masculine identity in relation to women, or, more exactly, to an idea of the feminine. For if women are adored by men who define themselves in relation to them, they are also subject to a brutal plot mechanism in the 'custom of Logres' (important because it features in many romances, and of which Guenievre, snatched away by Meleagant, is herself a potential victim) according to which a woman travelling alone depends for her physical safety on a knight's sense of honour, but should she be in another knight's company she may be fought over and 'won' legitimately, and her consent is no longer an issue (*Lancelot*, 1302-21).[24] The paradoxical positions women occupy as initiators of narrative, the measure of masculine honour and instruments of male desire, raise difficult and endlessly debatable questions about the nature and function of *fin amours*.

The unfinished state of Chrétien's last romance, *Perceval*, together with the enigmatic nature of the Grail that it introduces into Arthurian romance, offer fine opportunities, as its several continuations demonstrate, for amplification and sequelization by other romance writers. The simpleton Perceval, initiated by Gornemanz into the ways of knighthood, finds a disjunction between the terms of chivalric ideology and the wisdom that comes with experience as, mindful of prescriptive advice, he fails to ask about the Grail the question that he later learns would have saved the Waste Land. Specific historical crusading reference may inform this text; Philippe, Count of Flanders, in his failure to take positive action in the Holy Land, may be likened to Perceval.[25] Aesthetically, however, the strangeness of Perceval's adventures, the contrast between the reputation and the reality of chivalry and the Arthurian court, and the questions of structural integration posed by the intercalation of Gawain's adventures, serve to extend the possibilities of the quest motif. The inscrutable Grail, religious gloss notwithstanding, offers the reader who has somehow to interpret it, a marker of the desire for and unattainability of, an ultimate meaning. The non-ending may be fortuitous or deliberate, but it invites others to continue the narrative. Its lack of conclusion is eloquent of the romance's open-endedness and infinite rewritability.

Chrétien's romances construct new spaces for the hero, internal and reflective as well as topographical, with the Arthurian court as reference point in the romance (although it may feature little in the narrative proper), so that the circular form of the quest romance, beginning and ending at Arthur's court, achieves classic status in these works. But while establishing the genre, they open up lines of inquiry about the nature and scope of romance itself. Rather than offering idyllic versions of an Arthurian past, these works present a society the constituent elements of which lie in uneasy relation to one another, and to the worlds of their readers. Arthur himself may feature little, and there is potential for friction between the interests of a centralized monarchy and individual chivalric volition; the terms of masculine heroic identity may be apparently ill co-ordinated; the declared relationship between deeds of arms, the inspiration love offers, and respect for ladies often occludes violence about and towards women; and the language of love and chivalry, especially as various characters articulate it through internal monologue, may demand critical scrutiny viewed against the nature of chivalric action.

Although Chrétien obviously exercises a strong formal and thematic influence on Arthurian romance in general, only a small group of English texts (for example, *Ywain and Gawain*, *Percyvell*) directly rework aspects of Chrétien's oeuvre, rather than record an oblique debt. But we cannot tell whether the paucity of surviving texts indicates English writers' lack of interest in, or distaste for, Chrétien's themes and treatment, or whether important material witness has simply been lost: it is pertinent to note that one of the masterpieces of English Arthurian romance, *Sir Gawain and the Green Knight*, exists only in one undistinguished-looking manuscript.[26] Even where we cannot find indisputable direct links between English writings and French works, we need to be aware of Chrétien's innovativeness with regard to romance structure and motif and the influence he exercises over later French writers whose work English authors such as Malory take up. To recognize Chrétien's play with intertextuality also helps us appreciate the method of writers in English who draw on a range of Arthurian allusion in their own production of romance.

The possibility of correspondence between secular and sacred, the courtly and religious worlds, that Chrétien begins to explore in *Perceval*, is especially fruitful ground for later French writers, whose enthusiasm for a quasi-spiritual narrative context for Arthur appears to lie behind the continental trend for extended Arthurian material in prose, which by the late twelfth century claims ascendancy over verse as the medium of authoritative truth.[27] Robert de Boron's verse Grail cycle, which constructs a version of sacred history (in an account of *Joseph d'Arimathie*, *Merlin* and a *Perceval*), soon appears in prose. These continental prose works contextualize Arthurian time within various historical models, fabulous, Scriptural or apocalyptic, whereas English adaptors will set Arthur in localized historical contexts, just as their treatments of Joseph of Arimathea reflect the saint's established cult at Glastonbury Abbey.

The Vulgate Cycle, composed by author(s) unknown, *c.* 1215-35, both appropriates the spirit of Robert de Boron's Grail narratives and, in its huge sprawl of prose, accommodates Arthurian time within an overarching world-historical design encompassing both sacred and secular reference.[28] Chrétien inspires the account of Lancelot's career as knight and lover of Guenievre which is central to the cycle. (There is also the non-cyclic *Lancelot do Lac* (*c.* 1215-20), which does not intercalate Lancelot's career with Grail material.) Books of sacred and secular history (apparently written after the other books, but made proleptic of them) precede the cyclic *Lancelot*; the *Estoire del Saint Graal*, telling of Joseph of Arimathea as guardian of the Grail, which ultimately arrives in Britain to await the 'good knight' at Corbenic castle, and the *Estoire de Merlin*, a 'historical' account of the prophet Merlin's management of Arthur's rise to power. Subsequent to the *Lancelot* is the *Queste del Saint Graal*, which rewrites chivalric heroism in the language and morality of Scripture as Galahad wins the Grail, and *La Mort le Roi Artu*, which shows the apocalyptic collapse of Arthur's society, and his death at his son's hand.

The Vulgate Cycle, in its concern with naming authors and scribes who contribute to the work, shares Chrétien's self-consciousness about the authoritativeness of romance writing, and in its poising of the Arthurian world between 'truth' and 'fiction' it also partakes of thirteenth-century interests in historical narrative.[29] The Cycle both elaborates on a historiographical context for Arthur and clears more narrative space for individual heroes, and so invites readers and (re)writers to concentrate in varying degrees on aspects of historical accountability and individual agency. The Post-Vulgate *Roman du Graal* (1230-40) takes up the former invitation and produces from the stories of the Grail and of Arthur an uncompromising perspective on Arthurian history, emphasizing both 'Misfortune' and human culpability and the urgent need for the expiation of sin.[30] The hugely popular *Prose Tristan* (c. 1225-75), surviving in over fifty manuscripts, which intercalates the hero's achievements with those of Lancelot, is just one example of the appetite for the endless configurations of adventure the Cycle's multiple chivalric genealogies suggest.[31] The long prose romances seem less concerned to endorse a particular model of history than to exploit the self-declared authority of romance narrative to generate ever more extravagant adventures and all-encompassing fictional worlds. Malory's *Morte Darthur*, the prose work in English closest to these French productions in structure, differs significantly from them in that its vision of the Arthurian world is mediated by the reading of English responses to French romance, as well as itself constituting a fresh reading of the continental material. Malory is typically English in redrawing for himself the boundaries of Arthurian meaning and influence.

Chrétien's verse narratives had opened up the field of reference for Arthurian romance in general and constitute a significant element of the vernacular romance writer's intertextual inheritance: one can trace Chrétien's influence in expansive prose romance and verse composition alike in thirteenth- and fourteenth-century France. It seems Chrétien's legacy that Arthurian romance should concern a particular world rather than Arthur himself, a locus of individual adventures that raise questions about ethical issues and the nature of romance form. In verse romance, the debt may range from playful allusiveness – as in Payen de Maisières's compression of Chrétien-like romance motifs in *La mule sans frein* – to more considered expositions of (for instance) the problems inherent in romance constructions of heroic masculine identity. Gawain emerges as the focal figure of a number of problematic romances. The early thirteenth-century fabliauesque *Le Chevalier à l'épée* has Gawain worrying over both his courtesy and his reputation for sexual prowess when he finds himself enduring an inhospitable custom which links sex and death in the suspension of a protective sword above the bed of his host's daughter. But when the wife he thus wins chooses another partner, the deeper questions of the fissures in what constitutes Gawain's masculine chivalric honour are replaced by a disingenuous antifeminism that declares women inconstant, a rhetorical fall-back which the author of *Sir Gawain and the Green Knight* will later explore relentlessly and shrewdly. In *L'Atre Périlleux*, Gawain is thrown into an episodic series of adventures by the surprising news that three rogues have killed him. The romance neatly deploys the false Gawain's body as a marker of the depredations of counter-chivalric forces and eventually the hero literally reconstructs the body, forcing its murderer to revive it, as final proof that he – and chivalry – are not dead after all.

From the modern perspective it may seem odd that England did not itself produce Arthurian romance in line with developments on the continent. In part this is due to the linguistic situation in England in the thirteenth century which meant that audience demand for courtly romance could be met by imported French works. But the existence of a sizeable corpus of insular romance – Anglo-Norman to begin with, then translated into English in the fourteenth century – suggests a different attitude to romance in general and Arthurian romance in particular. In Anglo-Norman England the interest in history and the credibility offered by historical narratives had taken another direction – towards the Anglo-Saxon or Norse, rather than the Celtic, resulting in a series of lengthy, localized romances, exploring issues of feudal ideology and in some cases commissioned by baronial patrons. The tales of heroes such as Horn, Havelok, Guy of Warwick and Beves of Hamptoun in their various forms indicate a taste for 'ancestral' romances, in which lands are won by the returning exile, marital love supports the hero's ambitions, and local lordship may successfully challenge the claims of the monarch. Many of these romances – Hue de Roteland's *Ipomedon* and the later and highly derivative *Gui de Warewic* in particular – exploited the motifs and techniques of continental romance, displaying an awareness of Chrétien's work and sharing his distrust of the Tristan theme. Yet while the writers of history and chronicle kept Arthur's name alive as a great British king,[32] the romance writers of Anglo-Norman England avoided the Matter of Britain.[33] What we know of the patronage and audience of insular romance suggests that this was a response to the use of Arthurian symbolism to bolster the claims of the Plantagenet monarchy. It seems that provincial Anglo-Norman narrative left little room for the production of insular Arthurian romance, partly because of differing attitudes to kingship, and while it was to modify later romance into recognizably English patterns, it never grew to equal Arthurian romance in scope or achievement, lacking as it did both royal patronage and Celtic glamour.

But there was an audience for continental romances. In thirteenth-century England Arthurian romance was available as a fashionable import, a literary enthusiasm shared between the Francophone court of England and the continental sources of Arthurian material (Alison Stones in Baswell, 52-86). Evidence for the knowledge of French Arthurian romance in England at this time comes from anecdote and legacy. There are numerous casual references, of which the most famous is Chaucer's teasing remark about the *Lancelot*.[34] Otherwise, our sense of the availability and accessibility of French romance evinced in the intertextuality of later English versions, can only be supported by the evidence of ownership. Wills provide non-specific reports of numerous romances owned by the aristocracy of England,[35] and a royal interest in Arthurian romance is apparent in copies of French romances passed down from one generation to another.[36] But for the most part we cannot distinguish one version of an Arthur, Lancelot or Tristan romance from another, although it seems likely that most such titles represent some version of the Vulgate cycle. There is one manuscript collection containing Chrétien's romances apparently made for an English patron, MS B.N.f.fr.1450,[37] but otherwise Chrétien's name, while revered in France,[38] seems unknown in England and two other extant pieces of manuscript evidence suggest that his works may have been valued for extra-literary reasons.[39] Other evidence of an active familiarity with romance fails to identify texts, as with the lending library in the Tower from which the court of Edward I and Edward II borrowed a number of romances (Vale 1982, 49). It may be amongst such unidentifiable volumes that the independent romances whose influence has been detected in later English versions are to be traced.

It can be no coincidence that the appearance of English Arthurian literature accompanies the gathering strength of English as a literary language and the growing sense of national identity most sharply felt in relation to France. From the fourteenth century onwards French romance is re-interpreted for an English audience for whom Arthurian material is inescapably historic and iconic. The legendary locations of French romance – Camelot, Logres, Astolat – become recognizable English places – Carlisle, Winchester, London, Guildford – the lone knights of preference are local heroes – Perceval of Wales, Gawain of Galloway or Orkney, Tristram of Cornwall. As with place, so with time; there is a continual undertow towards the exemplary, the minatory, the political, which may explain the resurgence of Arthurian writing in times of civil war.[40]

In any account of medieval Arthurian romance, French romance will dominate, because of its scale and quantity and the essential contribution to the formation of the genre by Chrétien and his successors. It lends itself to critical analysis with an identifiable taxonomy of motif and a clear sense of narrative structure that enables a description of the typology of French Arthurian romance such as evades critics dealing with the later, disparate examples in English.[41] But these in their turn are to be seen as deliberate acts of literary reception that have to be understood and appreciated in their historical and ideological contexts.[42] Authors and audiences of English romance as well as French, recognize a 'horizon of expectation'[43] which enables the elaborate play of allusiveness and intertextuality, but it may be used to quite different ends. The continental tradition offered later English adaptors openings for debate, satire and experiment. In this production of experimental works, independent of the encyclopaedic structures of the prose cycles, the insular response to Arthur remains closer to that of the twelfth century. The historically charged treatment of Arthur and the localization of many of the central figures and events may appear to undermine the generic markers of French romance; the landscape of English medieval romance will be one through which Auerbach's knight might not find his way.

4

DYNASTIC ROMANCE

The chronicle context of the Arthurian legend which, with its dynastic implications, had such significance for English audiences, as a unifying account of national origins and a focus for patriotic spirit, naturally meant little to the French. Though they inherited the complete span of Geoffrey's *Historia* through Wace, only the Arthurian era had much significance for them, and then only as the shadowy, temporally and geographically vague, setting of a legendary kingdom. What interested them was the court at the heart of that kingdom, developed by Chrétien and his contemporaries as a locus for chivalric adventures and a crucible for the proving of courtly values (see above, pp.62-8). Their thirteenth-century successors, with the passion of the age for order and completeness, elaborated round the Galfridian core a world history at many levels, legendary, biblical, mystical, chivalric. The most characteristic and influential form of this new historical perspective was the vast prose Vulgate Cycle.[1] There the empire of Arthur provides a continuum for endless adventures in which dynastic significance is submerged in manifold forms of romance. But the dominant figure is now Lancelot whose knightly qualities, exalted by the love of Guinevere, make him supreme in chivalric achievement even while their adultery bars him from spiritual supremacy in the *Queste del Saint Graal*, a quest destined to be achieved by his son Galahad embodying the ideal fusion of chivalry and spirituality. The roots of that spirituality are traced in an elaborate prologue, the *Estoire del Saint Graal*, where the mystic vessel of Chrétien's romance is identified with the cup of the Last Supper in which Christ's blood is caught at the Crucifixion by Joseph of Arimathea, whom legend associated with Glastonbury, site of an early Christian community. The secular counterpart to this sacred pre-history is supplied in the following section, the *Merlin*, in which devils, furious at Christ's rescue of the righteous Jews from hell, plot to mislead mankind through a prophet, half human half devil, who contrives the siring of Arthur and his accession to the throne of Britain. The ambivalence of that inheritance emerges in the final section, *La Mort le Roi Artu*, in which Lancelot's adultery ultimately brings a breach with Arthur, civil war, and the downfall of Britain.

Dynastic history has become little more than the background to endless variations on a romantic ideal of personal achievement, given wider significance by associating it with the rise and fall of a society, and a gloss of spirituality by exalting the Grail quest as a mission of mystic self-fulfilment and spiritual service for a messianic hero in the course of which the inadequacy of worldly chivalry is repeatedly demonstrated. From this mass of narrative material English authors selected a limited range of elements, those most likely to appeal to the historical preconceptions of English audiences or to their familiarity with local legends not originally associated with Arthur.

Arthur, The Legend of King Arthur, King Arthur's Death

Arthur was probably written in the last part of the fourteenth or the early fifteenth century.[2] A unique copy is preserved in the *Liber Rubeus Bathoniae* (the 'Red Book of Bath'), Longleat House 62 MS 55, No.28, ff.42b-46a, dated 1412-28 (Guddat-Figge, 232-5). The MS is a miscellany of items in English, Latin and French, in verse and prose, some of which share *Arthur's* interest in genealogy, chronology and kingship, and is very unusual, having been compiled for the use of the Magistrate of Bath. Despite the generally utilitarian character of the MS, it contains some illuminations and *Arthur*, in particular, is embellished on ff.43b and 44a by four coats of arms, including King Arthur's. *Arthur's* 642 lines of English verse are uniquely squeezed into double columns between two portions of a Latin Prose *Brut*, continuing the chronicle account between references to Uther Pendragon's and Arthur's conquests and the succession of Constantine.

 Arthur's existence has been attributed to a brief surge of spontaneous patriotic feeling inspired by the subject matter.[3] However, it is worth noting that, as in the case of the expanded Arthurian section of Laȝamon's *Brut*, there must have been English models of heroic verse for the author to draw upon and, if the chronicler were a cleric, as is usually supposed, he must have been prepared, like Laȝamon, to borrow from a popular secular genre. The special decoration of this portion of the MS and its unusually cramped copy might also suggest something added later from an alternative source, and cast doubt on the idea that the Bath scribe invented *Arthur*.

 The dialect is southern with some northern and Kentish characteristics (*Furnivall*, vi) and its metrical form is the four-stress couplet. It is possibly the work of one of a class of 'translator-versifiers, poor hacks one notch above the scribes who also earned their bread in the manuscript shops' (R.W. Ackerman in Loomis 1959, 482). *Arthur* concludes with a conventional exhortation to 'Reed on þe frensch boke' in order to discover more 'gestes' of Arthur's heirs (*Furnivall*, 634-42); and it seems probable that the poet's source was a version of Wace's *Roman de Brut* sharing features with Laȝamon's *Brut* and with the alliterative *Morte Arthure*.[4]

The poem opens with a conventional minstrel call, 'Herkneþ' and then proceeds to remind the audience of other Arthurian stories that 'we in bokis do rede' (4). Its poet is interested in the names of Arthurian locations such as 'Euerwyk' (York) (557), Carlyon (584) and Camelford (604) and he refers to prophecies of Arthur's return made by 'Bretons and Cornysch' (618), as well as to Arthur's burial at Glastonbury and the inscription on his tomb, dated as AD524 (627). He also has a fondness for catalogues like those of Arthur's guests at Carlyon (141-64), his allies in his campaign in France (301-28) and the weaponry used in the battle against Lucius (458-63); and he relishes gory detail: 'Þere men were wetschode / All of brayne and of blode' (469-70).

Arthur is characterized as egalitarian (44-54), courteous (236-40) and devout (495-502), and is more simply and unambiguously virtuous than his counterpart in the alliterative *Morte Arthure*. His chief adventure as an individual champion, the slaying of the Spanish giant who has raped Elaine of Brittany, suffers by comparison with the similar incident as described in that poem. *Arthur*'s weak transition – 'Now ys an ende of þis þynge / And Artour haþ nyw tydynde' (403-4) – is stylistically typical of its poet's recourse to trite formulaic phrases and tags. The single combat between Arthur and Frollo, however, does justice to a similarly stirring event in Wace's poem; the fact that this incident is treated with greater metrical freedom than any other part of the poetic fragment may be a significant feature of this relative success.[5]

A similarly synoptic approach to material ultimately derived from a French exemplar (in this case, the Vulgate *Mort Artu*), but with less artistic and historical pretension than *Arthur*, is represented by the ballads *King Arthur's Death* and *The Legend of King Arthur*, preserved on ff.179[r]-182[r] of the Percy Folio MS (1650), that repository of so many popular versions of more sophisticated Arthurian romances. Separated into two ballads by Percy in his *Reliques*, according to a practice that has now become standard, *The Death* and *The Legend* are more appropriately described as a single, composite text.[6]

The Legend occupies 100 of the 255 lines with a first person narrative in which the king recounts his history, ending with the disastrous consequences of the last battle. The 155 lines of *King Arthur's Death* (the original title for the whole) are concerned with the battle itself and with the passing of Arthur. That *The Legend* was, at some time, an independent ballad, seems indisputable and this is confirmed by the discovery of a couplet version in an Elizabethan account by Lloyd of the Nine Worthies.[7] The composite ballad, therefore, seems to be an example of the most characteristic type of the sixteenth-century ballad genre, the abridgement of a famous medieval romance.[8] Despite the challenge they represent to modern notions of artistic unity, the two blended ballads deserve to be considered as a not entirely unsuccessful attempt to integrate inherited romance material by someone who wrote the version preserved in the Percy Folio using both *The Legend* and Malory's *Morte Darthur*. A close textual comparison between *The Death of King Arthur* and the final book of *Morte Darthur* shows that the former is certainly derived from Malory's work and that similarities with the stanzaic *Morte Arthur* may be merely coincidental, given Malory's own use of that romance.

Popular ballad treatment of Arthur's monologue in *The Legend* ensures that the major incidents of his downfall, such as his campaign in France and betrayal by Mordred, the death of Gawain and the destruction of the chivalric fellowship, are all transmitted minus the implicit complexities of the longer romance version. Mordred, although alluded to in *The Legend* as 'my sonne' (*Hales and Furnivall*, 62), is pursued and killed as a rebel and a traitor, without any reference to the context of Arthur's fateful incest; and the part played by Lancelot's adultery is likewise excluded from the tragic denouement. The use of prosopopeia follows a tradition according to which the Nine Worthies speak directly to the audience (as they do, for example, in Arthur's dream of Fortune's Wheel in the alliterative *Morte Arthure* (*Benson*, 3272-7)). It looks as though *The Legend* has retained this stylistic feature, although the context for it has vanished.

King Arthur's Death shows some skill in the process of abridgement: two examples are its reduction to single incidents of Arthur's two dreams and of the two encounters with Mordred, and its adaptation of Malory's account of the poignant death of Lucan the Butler in such a way that it motivates Arthur more strongly in his fatal attack on Mordred.[9] Most notable is the independent treatment of the passing of Arthur: there are no references to Avalon or to Arthur's tomb, the king simply vanishes 'from vnder the tree' (231) where Lukin has left him and may, or may not, be on the mysterious barge with the wailing queens (232-7). The effect of romantic strangeness that we associate with the supernatural in the best ballads, or in a successful popular romance like *Sir Orfeo*, is potently evoked.

Another late Arthurian survival is the fragment *King Ryence's Challenge* which was sung before Queen Elizabeth at Kenilworth in 1575.[10] Its forty-two lines are divided into rime royal stanzas and tell how Ryence, King of North Wales, demands Arthur's beard to add to those of the kings which already trim his mantle. The source is probably a romance based on the *Estoire*[11] and the minstrel improvised freely, including a speaking part for a courteous Sir Kay and casting a 'doughty dwarf' in the starring role of messenger. Such examples of medieval stories used for entertainment seem to spring from the sixteenth-century Arthurian revival,[12] and show that some of the least serious and unhistorical material could be aimed at a socially elevated audience.　　　　　**Karen Hodder**

Joseph of Arimathie

Returning to an earlier period of high Arthurianism, we find the legendary figures of Arthur and Joseph of Arimathea traditionally linked by English romances from the mid-fourteenth century onwards, sometimes according to a strongly nationalist agenda. The processes by which Joseph's story was appropriated, together with the historical, political and ecclesiastical considerations contributing to this situation, are more fully accounted for above (pp.54-7). The conception of Joseph of Arimathea as the apostolic evangelist of Britain is added to the existing Arthurian pretensions of Glastonbury around 1250 and that tradition, embellished during the late fourteenth century, appears to have influenced both Lovelich's and Malory's conceptions of Joseph. However, the earliest English romance treatment of the legend, *Joseph of Arimathie*, like the ballad *King Arthur's Death* (though unlike *Arthur*), represents a tradition unaffected by Glastonbury propaganda (*Lawton*, xi).

Joseph of Arimathie is an untypical alliterative poem of 705 lines which survives in a unique acephalous copy in the famous Vernon MS, Bodleian Library MS Eng. Poetry A.1, ff.403^r-404^v, where it is set out as prose. It has been suggested that *Joseph* may owe its inclusion in this collection to the connection of its subject matter with the Legend of the True Cross and with Marian devotion, as well as to popular interest in Joseph manifested by several other items in the MS (*Lawton*, xv-xvi, xli).[13] Popular apocryphal gospels such as the *Evangelium Nicodemi* and the *Narratio Josephi* had fostered the growth of Joseph's supposed role in Christian history, and there were a number of secular romances featuring Joseph in the late Middle Ages which testified to an increased interest in him, as well as other cults relating to the preservation of the Precious Blood, such as the Holy Blood of Hayles.[14]

The Vernon MS was probably produced close to 1400, providing the only secure evidence of *Joseph*'s date, or its potential medieval audience (Meale 1994, 209-10; *Lawton*, xxv, n.12). The dialect of the Vernon scribe has been identified as that of North Worcestershire,[15] but the authorial dialect of *Joseph of Arimathie* is unidentifiable, beyond the presence of some northernisms, acquired along with the poem's traditional alliterative style (*Lawton*, xxvi). This style has been subjected to intensive scrutiny by Lawton, from which he concludes that *Joseph* defies over-rigid modern categorization, being 'a median form of rhythmical composition' (xxi). He asserts that the main interest of *Joseph* lies in its form and the insight this gives into compositional method, as well as its status within the canon of alliterative poetry (xli). However, like Lovelich's romances and the Prose *Merlin*, *Joseph of Arimathie* is also significant for its handling of its source and what it reveals about the possible attitudes of its author and audience to this inherited 'historical' material, inseparable, in this case, from devotional ends and not at all preoccupied with Arthurian romance.

The nature of the adaptation has inevitably dominated most critical studies of English translations of the Vulgate romances. It is generally agreed that *Joseph*'s author had a single source, consisting of the opening section of the *Estoire del Saint Graal*.[16] An alternative theory, that the *Joseph*-poet worked also from a passage in the *Queste del Saint Graal*, has not yet won acceptance as an essential means of accounting for his drastic adaptation of the *Estoire*.[17] *Joseph*, like a number of other English translations, radically abridges what, in this case, was most probably a version of the longer redaction of the *Estoire*.[18] This was the source also used by Lovelich, and is the version of the Joseph legend which includes the evangelization of Britain, though this element is omitted by *Joseph of Arimathie*. Cistercian influence has been associated with the forces behind the propagation of Joseph's legend in Britain and also with the MS in which *Joseph* survives.[19] The Vernon MS was the product of a major religious scriptorium (*Lawton*, xiv) and may have been commissioned for a secular or religious community of women of 'gentle status' (Meale 1994, 222).

This putative social context is quite compatible with the apparently didactic and devotional objectives of the English adaptor. The genre to which *Joseph* belongs has variously been defined as 'a religious story in which certain romantic elements have been incorporated', 'both saint's life and romance', and 'a didactic saint's legend'.[20] Its message is a straightforward one on the rewards of accepting the Christian faith and the dire consequences of rejecting it.[21] The conversion of unbelievers, especially pagan royalty, is the chief theme, and *Joseph* and *The Siege of Jerusalem* and *Titus and Vespasian* have been linked as types of story which 'illustrate a rather crude concept of the Christian faith . . . best expressed by slaughtering as many infidels as possible' (Mehl 1994, 277, n.50). If the audience of *Joseph of Arimathie* were female, it seems they may have shared some antisemitic bloodthirstiness with Chaucer's Prioress.[22]

The imperfect text begins at the moment when Joseph of Arimathea is released from forty-two years of captivity in Jerusalem. The lost opening probably consisted of a short account of the cure and conversion of Joseph's liberator, Vespasian. The eucharistic themes of the *Queste* and the *Estoire* are minimized in *Joseph* whose author consistently stresses the precious Blood itself rather than the Grail, its receptacle.[23] Arthurian allusions present in the analogues disappear from *Joseph* and only a perfunctory reference survives to Joseph's begetting of his second son, Galahad, who seems to be confused with the Grail knight without, however, the author showing any interest in the future of Arthurian Britain which that Galahad signifies.

The role of Joseph's celibate son, Josephes, is systematically reduced, apparently with the aim of heightening Joseph's own part in the story, and such episodes as Josephes's vision of his ordination by Christ (258-312) are drastically cut in the interest of a similar single-minded focus on the status and missionary activities of the eponymous hero. The hagiographic tone is additionally enhanced by the relative concentration on the miraculous or marvellous elements of the inherited narrative: Evelac's dreams of the tripartite tree and the child (181-211), Josephes's vision of Christ within the ark enclosing the Holy Blood (called in the English text the 'whucche') (258-78), the prophecy of King Tholomer's invasion (353-8) and the sensational comeuppance of Evelac's clerk (359-62). This 'determined and unpretentious conversion of spiritual mysteries into showcase miracles' (*Lawton*, p.33), involving radical and skilful restructuring of the source, also has the effect of conferring artistic unity on the poem.[24] The more expanded portions of narrative just referred to tend to be closely translated from the French, as is the Queen's narrative of her girlhood conversion to Christianity (631-62). In this she tells Joseph how she confused the holy hermit who had converted her mother with the Redeemer in whom she has been asked to believe:

> 'And I wepte water warm and wette my wonges   *cheeks*
> And seide his bert was so hor I bad not on him leeve.' (647-8)   *white*

This is not only a neat literal translation, but also one in which the alliteration of the English version adds a human concreteness to the girl's response, while the gentle directness of the hermit's reply ' "douȝter, he is feirore þen I or þou or out þat is formed" ' (649-51) is better judged than the French source or Lovelich's more complete, but heavy handed rendering of it:

> 'Thanne anon lowgh this good old man   *laughed*
> For that I seyde of him than,
> Nay, faire dowghter, it nam not I.' (*Furnivall*, §15, 279-81).

The queen has an important role in all the versions of the story, further emphasized by *Joseph of Arimathie*'s relative brevity. Her faith in Joseph results in essential reinforcements, under the command of her brother Seraphe, being sent to Evelac during the struggle against Tholomer, King of Egypt. If the heroic figure of Seraphe does arrive 'as if by overnight express' (*Lawton*, p.38), the lack of realism is nevertheless consistent with the overall atmosphere of marvels.[25]

Frequent transpositions of indirect narrative into direct speech add to the liveliness and accessibility of *Joseph of Arimathie*: for example a passage in the French which consists of extensive instructions from the deity (Sommer, I, 19) is rendered as a brief exchange between God and Joseph concluding:

> 'Lord, I was neuer clerk – what and I ne cunne?'   *what if I cannot?*
> 'Louse þe lyppes atwynne and let þe gost worche   *part, spirit*
> Spech, grace and vois schul sprynge of þi tonge,
> And alle turne to þi mouþe holliche at enes.' (48-51)   *entirely at once*

The intimate tones of alternate humility and benevolence are reminiscent of such dramatic encounters between God and patriarch as those in the Mystery Cycles, or of female visionary and revealed deity,[26] and make their appeal perhaps to a similarly broad and not necessarily educated audience.   **Karen Hodder**

Henry Lovelich's *History of the Holy Grail*

Henry Lovelich's translation of the *Estoire* into 23,794 octosyllabic couplets (*c.* 1430) demonstrates the late medieval takeover of romance dissemination by laymen for lay audiences (Barron 1987, 56). It is the only English rendition of the complete early history and, as such, of great interest for the study of the Joseph legend.[27]

Lovelich's *Grail*, together with his *Merlin*, is preserved uniquely as Corpus Christi College Cambridge MS 80. Having lost the beginning, the *Grail* starts with the destruction of Evelach's idols, prior to Tholomes's invasion.[28] Lovelich names himself in both his *Grail* (*Furnivall*, §56, 533) and his *Merlin* (*Kock*, 10251). A marginal note on f.127^r says that 'henry louelich skynner' made the translation 'at þe instance of harry barton'. Other documents confirm both Lovelich's profession and his business relationship with Barton, who was also a member of the Skinners' Company as well as twice Lord Mayor of London during 1417-29.[29] These tantalizing facts, however, actually give little unambiguous information about Lovelich or his relationship with Barton which might account for his literary activities. The identity of the scribe is unknown, though the marginal annotator has been identified as a clerical copyist called John Cok who was acquainted with the famous scribe John Shirley. Together with the professional appearance of the manuscript and the possibly commercial terminology of Cok's note, this association may imply that Lovelich's work aimed at a wider circulation than has previously been assumed (Meale 1994, 217-19). It certainly raises interesting questions about the demand for Arthurian romances among the fifteenth-century urban mercantile class, as well as why a prominent 'citizen and skinner', who evidently found the act of translating an onerous and thirsty task (*Kock*, 21579-88), should ever have embarked on it.[30]

At the end of the *Grail* Lovelich says he has chosen,

> Into owre modris tonge for to endite
> The swettere to sowne to more and lyte; *greater and lesser*
> And more cler to your vndirstondyng
> Thanne owther Frensch oþer Latyn. (*Furnivall*, §56, 527-30)

A consequence of the thoroughness of Lovelich's rendering of the *Estoire* is that, unlike *Joseph of Arimathie*, it includes the narrative of Joseph's evangelization of Britain and, furthermore, in an important departure from his source, refers to

Joseph's supposed burial at Glastonbury (*Furnivall*, §54, 141-56). In doing this, Lovelich may have been influenced by the contemporaneous John of Glastonbury's *Chronicle*, while slightly later John Hardyng's *Chronicle* (*c* .1450) and a fifteenth-century interpolation in Robert of Gloucester's *Chronicle* also emphasize these aspects of the legend.[31]

It is slightly puzzling that Lovelich's ability to translate French deteriorates as he progresses from the Vulgate *Estoire del Saint Grail* to the *Estoire de Merlin*. But a poor exemplar and a waning interest in the immense project, as well as greater familiarity with the Grail story and its biblical characters, besides, possibly, more external supervision, may account for the difference between the two translations.[32] Lovelich's universal reputation among literary historians for tediousness and ineptitude has yet to be modified by a broader appraisal based on good modern editions of his work with adequate commentaries; and Ackerman's plea for a fuller study of adaptation and translation, which concerns the Prose *Merlin* as well as Lovelich, has still been largely ignored. Further study of Lovelich's French exemplars, for example, might suggest whether they were responsible for some of his apparently unsystematic omissions from the source of the *Grail*, such as the history of the 'Turning Isle'.

A few distinctive traits of Lovelich's narrative can nevertheless be identified, despite its evident general adherence to source. He seems to have expected his audience to take considerable interest in military detail, both in the *Merlin* and here, where it chiefly involves the conversion of the city of Sarras. Other parts of the narrative most voluminously rendered are the confusing wanderings of Solomon's Ship, the miraculously achieved evangelization of Britain, and the history of Joseph and his descendants as Grail guardians which extends into Arthur's reign and the coming of Lancelot and Galahad. Like the author of *Joseph of Arimathie*, however, he curtails the role of Josephes in favour of Joseph, and he also enhances the reputation of Nasciens by making Mordrains responsible for breaking the sword which symbolizes sinfulness (§34, 328).[33] Lovelich gets confused, as a merchant well might, about the disposition of Evelach's battalions (§12, 469 and p.132, n.1), but no doubt the history of 'The Rock Perilous' and its occupant, the pirate Foucaire, who lured merchant ships to their doom there, interested him more (§20).

Lovelich's style has some superficial courtliness: Nasciens's wife's protector, for example, is 'an old vavasour, a full gentil knyt' (§26, 53); but more typical is the general hacking and slaying of infidels; and it is the villainous pagan Tholomes who (like Herod and Pilate in the Mystery Plays) favours gallic epithets such as 'bewfys' and 'belamy' (§12, 475, 483). The audience is not expected to relish the frenchified details of Castle Valachin's sumptuous architecture which Lovelich considerably abbreviates (§12, 343-98); and the historical setting which is evoked by Lovelich's often garbled rendering of French onomastic terms is not a realistic one: for example, 'Escoce' becomes 'Soose' (§44). However, the elimination of known locations such as Scotland may be an attempt to increase the historical validity of the reference to Glastonbury. Through its strangeness, it also creates an atmosphere of unspecific anti-infidel feeling akin to the missionary fervour of *Joseph of Arimathie*.

In common with the earlier translator, some of Lovelich's more engaging moments are found in his colloquial treatment of dialogue during passages concerning conversion, or puzzlement at mysteries,[34] and his handling of the complete *Estoire* account of the conversion of Queen Sarracynte and her mother has some potential for a gendered reading of his text, particularly in relation to the possible female component of his audience.[35] Guenevere is briefly mentioned, in favourable terms, as 'A worthy lady . . . and of good lore' (§52, 1156), and Lovelich's retention of the Arthurian references which he found in the *Estoire*[36] relates to the interest in the future of the Grail in Arthurian history which led him to promise, as he concludes his translation of the *Grail*, that he will next undertake the *Merlin* (§56, 511-20).   **Karen Hodder**

Henry Lovelich's *Merlin* and the Prose *Merlin*

The relative rarity of late Middle English prose romances makes Lovelich's 27,852 octosyllabic couplets a more predictable product of the mid-century, perhaps, than the anonymous Prose *Merlin* (*c*. 1450-60) which, like his romance, was translated from the Vulgate *Estoire de Merlin*, in its turn based on the work of Robert de Boron and his continuators. Lovelich, who acknowledges de Boron on numerous occasions, and the Prose *Merlin* author, both stick closely to the narrative of the French, but probably used different manuscript redactions of the *Estoire*;[37] and both stress Merlin's role as the prophet of the Holy Grail. The links between Merlin, Arthur and the Grail are: the dictation of the Grail book to the hermit Blaise by Merlin; the three tables of the Last Supper, Grail and Round Table; the family lineage of Arimathea which descends from Joseph down to Lancelot's son, Galahad, and other kin of Joseph of Arimathea; and finally, the Grail Quest itself. Both English romances are incomplete, lacking leaves at the ends of their respective manuscripts, Lovelich's being the earlier of the two to break off, at Arthur's victory over Claudas, while the Prose *Merlin* ends with Gawain's return to court following his discovery of the imprisoned Merlin, prior to the accounts of the births of Lancelot and Lionel.

Two independent copies of the Prose *Merlin* exist: one, a single leaf, Bodleian MS Rawlinson D.9B, f.43, includes Merlin's prophecies to Arthur, Ban and Bors, and may have been aimed at an audience not dissimilar to Lovelich's.[38] The other, Cambridge Library MS ff.3.11, contains annotations by early readers, most

notably Elyanor Guldeford. Two women of that name, living in the late fifteenth
and early sixteenth centuries, have been identified as possible owners of the MS,
both belonging to a powerful and cultivated social milieu (Meale 1994, 100-10)
which indicates the high status of Arthurian romance among this class as well as
that of the literate bourgeoisie.

Further testimony to the popularity of Merlin in English romance is provided by
his brief appearance as 'the child with no father' in the empress's sixth story in *The
Seven Sages of Rome* (*Brunner*, 2329-510). This romance, which survives in nine
MSS, including the famous Auchinleck collection, depicts a just recognizable
Merlin whose chief characteristic is the possession of second sight which enables
him to detect a hidden hoard of gold under a dunghill and to determine the reason
for the Emperor Herod's blindness, a debasement of the episode of Vortigern's
subterranean dragons which is closer to folktale than the *Estoire*.[39]

The Prose *Merlin*, though a close translation, is not a verbatim one of any of
the known French versions (*Wheatley*, IV, clxxxiv); as a result, there may be
many subtle variations between the *Estoire*, Lovelich's *Merlin* and the English
prose version, as well as between the two English translations (emphasized by
the difference in literary form between the last two), which have yet to be
examined. For example, Lovelich's version of the incestuous begetting of
Mordred (*Kock*, 12313-418) is more than twice the length of this episode in
either of the other two versions. Its diffuseness is most marked at the point where
Arthur embraces the queen, his half-sister :

> So as hit happede this kas gan gon,   *affair, occurred*
> this lady awok & hire tornede anon,
> and him embraced al in hire slepe
> that of non othir took she non kepe
> but of hire owne lord so dere,
> weneng to hire to ben hire fere.   *seeming, mate*
> And whanne that Arthewr felte this,
> thanne wiste he wel, with owten mys,
> that of hym sche took none kepe
> but as a wommen that was in slepe.
> So that he embraced hire ageyn,
> and so be hire he lay, in certeyn,
> where offen the lady ful joyful was;
> sche wende hire lord hadde ben in þat plas.
> And that nyt, in certein to say,
> was mordred begeten, with owten delay,
> in this manner, as 3e now here. (12345-61)

The Prose *Merlin*'s version says briefly:

> And it fill so that the lady awoke and turned hir toward hym, and toke hym in her armes as a woman slepynge, that wende verely it hadde ben her lorde. And that nyght was begete Mordred, as ye have herde. (§12, p.181)

In this apparently not untypical comparative example it can be seen that Lovelich's version impersonates minstrel treatment of its subject and displays many of the characteristics of a popular, orally delivered text: it is padded out with otiose expressions such as 'withowten mys' and 'in certayn' to fill out the couplet. Nevertheless, this rambling style may also be expressive of Lovelich's attitude toward his subject matter, or the reaction which he anticipates from his audience: the account of the innocent queen 'as a woman slepynge, that wende verely it hadde ben her lorde', is so fully amplified by Lovelich, especially in lines 12350-8 which include repetition of the idea that she believed Arthur to be her husband, as to suggest some anxiety to exonerate her from collusion in the incest.

The Prose *Merlin* writer, too, has been held guilty of prolixity, discontinuous narration, structural incoherence and repetitiveness (IV, ccxlii-viii). However, while we do not know whether Harry Barton, John Cok or any other reader of Lovelich's romances expressed a critical opinion about them, we do know that the Prose *Merlin* was read – indeed scrutinized – with great attention by some contemporary readers, the cultivated aristocratic owners of Cambridge Library MS ff.3.11. The sixteen passages marked by Elyanor Guldeford in her copy of *Merlin* draw attention to five narrative threads, all concerned with important female characters such as Ygrine, Gonnore, the mother of Lancelot and Nimiane, Merlin's lover, and their love-relationships. These episodes all examine questions of honour, shame and fidelity with subtle variations and suggestive contrasts and parallels. The theme of Merlin's conjurings is common, as might be expected, to several of these related narratives. Since most of her comments have been lost by cropping of the manuscript, it is only possible to guess what Elyanor thought notable about these passages, but they offer a provocative starting-point for considering the preoccupations of some late medieval readers of romance.[40]

This diverse group of texts, mostly strongly derivative from the French, displays uncomplicated patriotism or piety apparently directed at audiences who were expected to be historically and aesthetically uncritical. A dramatic ballad and a long prose romance clearly performed different social functions, so that texts like *King Ryence's Challenge* and the Prose *Merlin*, though both demonstrably aimed at aristocratic audiences and using romance material, are also very different in the seriousness and depth of their approaches to their Arthurian subject matter. Both *The Legend* and *Joseph*, on the other hand, treat legendary material with historical seriousness, despite their differences in form, while expansiveness *per se* does nothing to enhance the profundity or sensitivity of the bourgeois Lovelich's literary efforts. Nevertheless, as documents of the values and aspirations of a culture, even a poem like the much-reviled *Arthur*,[41] preserved for the use of a provincial magistrate, can help to enlarge an appreciation of the pervasive influence of national, dynastic concerns manifested in forms other than the 'great' Arthurian romances.   **Karen Hodder**

Of Arthour and of Merlin

The romance *Of Arthour and of Merlin* exists in a shorter version in three manuscripts: Lincoln's Inn Library, MS Hale 150 (*c.* 1450), Bodleian MS Douce 236 (early fifteenth century), and the seventeenth-century Percy Folio MS (BL Additional 27879). However, the fullest manuscript version – National Library of Scotland Advocates MS 19.2.1, the Auchinleck manuscript, (*c.* 1330) – is earlier in date and closer in dialect to the author's original, and in fact is the only one which takes the story beyond the birth of Arthur, the others ending with the coronation of Uther Pendragon. It is a story of the *enfances* of Arthur, covering his birth, coronation, and the establishment of his power; but, unlike the chronicle treatments, it makes Merlin almost as important a protagonist as Arthur himself. Instead of a political agent and prophet, in this romance treatment Merlin becomes a clairvoyant and a magician upon whose powers much of Arthur's military success rests.

All versions of *Arthour and Merlin* are derived primarily from the French prose romance known as the *Estoire de Merlin*, second section of the so-called Vulgate Cycle, consisting of the *Merlin* attributed to Robert de Boron, which covers the story until the coronation of Arthur, and a prose sequel.[42] But it would be misleading to call *Arthour and Merlin* a translation, since the author has not only selected and discarded material from his source, but seems in the section prior to Arthur's coronation to have had access to other source material. Parallels can be drawn both with Wace and with Laȝamon, but the resemblances are not close enough to assert the direct use of either of these texts in extant versions.[43] Since detailed dependence on any specific original is not demonstrable, it is best to regard the poem as an independent adaptation of an inherited tradition.

The chronicle versions of the Arthurian story treated in this volume purport to reveal the early history of Britain. Geoffrey of Monmouth had offered a political 'history' and an account of Merlin's prophecies, and his text was discreetly amplified by Wace as an account of early British chivalry, and rendered by Laȝamon as a record of the heroic origins of pre-Conquest Britain.[44] Although *Of Arthour and of Merlin* inherits incidents and some of its handling of the story from its source, it is modified in ways characteristic of its native genre and suited to its context. The focus is now narrowly

English, and Fortiger's (Vortigern) problems as ruler are envisaged not as international conflict, but as civil disturbance. The threatening invaders are no longer the 'historical' Saxons, but the Saracens who inhabit popular romance.

The unknown author of *Arthour and Merlin* is a skilled adaptor of French romance, whose hand has been seen also in *Richard Coer de Lion*, *Kyng Alisaunder* and *The Seven Sages of Rome* (in which he tells a variant version of the tale of Merlin's diagnosis of buried dragons).[45] But, although scholars have seen signs of individuality, his genre and the expectations of his audience impose certain characteristics on his work. His handling of the French source material follows the general pattern found in the sixty-odd English verse romances similarly derived from French originals. This can be illustrated from his handling of the story of Pendragon and Ygerne. Treatment in the chronicle tradition is minimal, but the *Estoire de Merlin* devotes several pages in Micha's edition to this event, where it extends over several days and distinct encounters. Pendragon begins by sending jewels as gifts before, eventually, the cup which Ygerne is ordered by her husband to accept. In *Arthour and Merlin* these scenes are reduced to a single encounter at Cardoel, followed by the siege of Tintagel. The jewels are removed from the story; the king's gift is the cup alone, which Ygerne refuses without permission from her lord. We are told in a couple of lines that such permission was eventually given, but the king's reflections on wifely virtue, like his lengthy consultations with advisers, are omitted. The tendency, then, is to the simplification of the story by omitting complex psychological motivation, extended speeches, and by the simplification of incident. Romance narrative 'shorthand' is used, as when the king sits Ygerne beside him and plies her with 'win and piment' (2316). Her rejection of the king echoes a mode of expression more colloquial and less elevated than the French:

> 'I nam no þef
> To breke mi treuþe oȝain mi lord
> Raþer ich wald hing bi a cord
> No schal y neuer for loue no ȝift
> Wiþ mi bodi don vnriȝt.' (2322-6)

More generally, the adaptation places emphasis upon narrative action, and although some traces of interlacing structure remain in the switches between Arthur, Merlin and Gawain's individual adventures, and also in the parallel story of Cleodalis and Leodegan, the narrative thread is much simpler. Expansions on the original are to be found in the extended accounts of battles and the descriptions of feasts, but in terms of the Middle English romance adaptation it is significant that the author, while accepting romance incidents offered by his source, declines to develop them. From the French are adopted mysterious and fabulous additions to the earlier story, such as the account of the sword in the stone, and love interest in the tale of Arthur and Guinevere, and the tale of Leodegan's adultery with Cleodalis's wife. As in French romance, Guinevere's attention is drawn to Arthur by his prowess on the battlefield,[46] and the dispute between Leodegan and Cleodalis is settled by the respect owed to chivalry and the gratitude arising from a rescue on the battlefield, but all are rendered as spare narrative. The story of Vortigern's infatuation with Hengist's daughter Ronwen had been found as a warning against diabolic suggestion in 'Nennius', but the scene is already romanticized by Geoffrey of Monmouth, and is much more so by Wace.[47] The *Estoire de Merlin*, however, contents itself with a brief mention of the fact of Vortigern's marriage to Hengest's daughter, and an uncomprehending reference to the custom of wassailing. This scene is completely omitted from *Arthour and Merlin*, where the girl is not even named. Indeed, the author has little time for discussion of love, and remarks with evident satisfaction that Fortiger who took his wife for *loue fin* was consequently accursed all his life. *Fin amour* is rather considered discreditable than to be celebrated. Although he mentions Guinevere's first sight of Arthur, the scene is not developed, and Arthur is approved because he 'tempred so his blod' (6538) in her presence.

The values of the poem are not congruent therefore with those encountered in the French romance tradition. Effectiveness and action are valued above reflection and subtlety. In the relationship between Ygerne and Pendragon, Ygerne is the honest and virtuous wife and Pendragon the lustful ruler, prepared to employ corruption, flattery or force to obtain what he desires. Sympathy in the telling seems to be with marital fidelity rather than with Pendragon, but this is easily abandoned in the face of the inevitabilities of the story. Following tradition, the author of *Arthour and Merlin* represents Ygerne as immediately happy with her new husband following the death of his predecessor. There are no emotional complications. Merlin is of course complicit in the deception of Ygerne, but no moral censure attaches to his actions. Merlin's role in Arthur's coronation may also raise questions in the mind of the modern reader, since (unlike the chronicle tradition) perfectly reasonable objections are raised against the imposition of his power, but the baronial opposition is quelled by a combination of magic and brute force. Blinkered moral values are not unusual in Middle English popular romance, and equate approximately to the position that once having established where proper loyalties lie, then might is right in support of them in disregard for natural sympathy. Such a view justifies the destruction of the honest steward or the innocent children in *Amis and Amiloun*, when the action is required by the thematic demands of friendship. In *Arthour and Merlin*, respect for *force majeure* is matched by a certain cynical realism. A scene which is handled at some length in the earlier tradition is managed with an appropriately brutal abruptness here. On being asked to assume power following Moine's defeat by Angys, Fortiger avoids the direct question 'Wiltow þat we Moyne slo?' (222), by answering that he can offer no support whilst the king is living. Later, when the regicides demand their reward, he turns on them as traitors and has them hanged and drawn. His reproach, ' "ȝe han ȝour lord yslawe; / ȝe schul ben honged and todrawe" ', echoes Godard's reply to Grim in like circumstances in *Havelok* (682-91).

This shift in emphasis away from the moral values of French romance is interesting because it represents a move towards what we might term 'popular epic' values. Many Middle English romances exhibit a similar shift, but it is especially notable here because it is accompanied by a range of stylistic devices which have been identified by G.V. Smithers as of epic origin.[48] Among these devices are:

(a) The 'seasonal head-pieces' which mark divisions in the story and are paralleled in *Kyng Alisaunder*.

(b) Epic blows incorporated into the battle scenes, which are characteristic of the French *chanson de geste*, although the idea of a similarly unrestrained blow is also found in Anglo-Saxon in *Beowulf* (1520) and *Maldon* (118).

(c) Epic similes of three types:

   i) those in which warriors are compared to wild beasts, perhaps in the hunt:

. . . sir Vter Pendragon,	
Fauȝt þer as a wode lyoun,	*raging*
And his broþer nouȝt forȝat	
He leyd on mani a sori flat	*blow*
Sum he cleue, to þe bacin,	*helmet*
Til þat he com to þe chin (1855-60);	

   ii) those in which blows are figured as the work of craftsmen: 'Ich kniȝt hewe on his per / On schide so doþ þe carpenter'(8837-8);

   iii) natural or elemental images: 'XII hundred oȝain fourti þousinde / Ferd so smoke oȝain þe winde' (7071-2).

(d) The exploitation of the *cohortatio* or pre-battle speech in which a leader exhorts his men to fight bravely to protect their homes, families and homeland, or, as in this case, a retainer reminds warriors of their loyalty:[49]

   'Listneþ me now mi lord þe king
   And ȝe oþer lordinge

What do we here, whi and warfore?
ȝif we fle þis lond is lore   *lost*
And wif and child and al our blisse
Al is forlorn mid ywis   *doomed*
Better is to sterue worþschipliche   *die*
Þan long to liuen schandfulliche,
ȝif we be desirite   *despoiled*
Our cowardschippe we may it wite;
O þing ouȝt ous comfort wel
Our newe lord ȝong naturel
Þat so wiȝtliche fiȝteþ for ous   *doughtily*
Helpe we him for Crist Ihesus,
ȝif he were hunist at þis asaut   *overthrown*
He miȝt wite it our defaut
And bot we him help at þis nede
We beþ forswore so Crist me rede,
And ȝete sle þat folk Sarraȝine
Is our soule medicine.'   (9191-210)   *remedy*

(e) The use of certain phrases which reflect particular epic perspectives, such as the corporate action of the army – 'our', 'our men', 'our kniȝtes' (*li nostre*) and 'our folk', 'our floc', 'our Cristen', 'our þede' (*li peuple*), 'our king Vter Pendragoun', 'our lond' – imitate phrases used in the *chansons de geste* to emphasize Christian solidarity in conflicts with the pagan. The device 'mani a' (from French *mainte*) is used to manipulate narrative perspective, describing the action of one weapon or man, or a single combat, and representing it as multiply repeated across the battlefield.

(f) Ironic metaphors of a somewhat grim tone, such as the statement that enemies 'maden her acord / Wiþ axes, speres, kniif and sword' (335-6).

Such devices are paralleled in the *chansons de geste*, but also in Latin epic and often in Old English verse, and here match the crusading ethos of much of the poem.

These positive stylistic choices should be noted because they defy a possible impression that the adaptation of *Arthour and Merlin* from its source is simply a debasement arrived at through authorial incompetence. They illustrate a coherent purpose and direction in the changes made, and this more positive assessment is further borne out by some indications of literary sophistication in the author. He himself does not wish to be considered an ignorant minstrel, and he regards his story as more than simply light entertainment. He claims a reputable source in the *Brut* (538, 2730, etc.), and speaks like a clerk of his 'matery' (*materia*). He shows an awareness of the technical terminology proper to dubbing and warfare, and gives his audience the benefit of the etymology of the name of the sword

Estalibore (2817-20). The accuracy of the information given is questionable, which points the limits of his learning; but what is significant is his earnest desire to inform, and especially his assumption that the destined public will value such information. The adaptation is with the interests of a particular audience in mind. *Arthour and Merlin* is offered as a work of instruction:

Childer þat ben to boke ysett	
In age hem is miche þe bett	
For þai mo witen and se	
Miche of Godes priuete	*mystery*
Hem to kepe and to ware	*protect*
Fram sinne and fram warldes care,	
And wele ysen ʒif þai willen	
Þat hem no þarf neuer spillen –	*need, perish*
Auauntages þai hauen þare	
Freynsch and Latin eueraywhare.	
Of Freynsch no Latin nil y tel more	
Ac on I[n]glisch ichil tel þerfore	
Riʒt is þat I[n]glische vnderstond	
Þat was born in Inglond. (9-22)	

An interesting contrast can be drawn between the claims of this passage and the prologue to William of Nassyngton's *Speculum Vitae*.[50] William duplicates the usual point about the use of English, but he also expresses a rather low opinion of the instructional value of romance, referring to two of the texts found in Auchinleck, and two found in similar miscellanies such as MS Cotton Caligula A.ii and the Thornton MS as examples. Nassyngton's critical viewpoint dismisses what in Auchinleck are very long romances as merely the typical performances of minstrels at a feast. Is this justifiable? Such minstrel entertainment is confirmed at a coronation feast in *Havelok* (2328), but romance-reading as household entertainment is mentioned in *Beues of Hamtoun* (3895), and in *Reinbrun*: 'Meche ʒhe kouþe of menstralcie, / Of harpe, of fiþele, of sautri, / Of romaunce reding' (142-4). Such examples of domestic entertainment are paralleled in Chaucer and in earlier French romance.[51] The Auchinleck manuscript was written by six copyists, and from the relative consistency of its layout, it seems to have been planned as a collection and purchased as a whole.[52] We may infer it might have been intended for reading in the home of a wealthy purchaser. Furthermore, the reading of *Arthour and Merlin* itself might have taken up to nine hours, and such a performance is credible only under the controlled conditions of a household. Nassyngton's criticism should not be taken literally, but points up a possible challenge to those with a taste for romance. These poems therefore seek to reassure their audience that they are reputable literary works for orderly performance – 'Þis is nouʒth romaunce of skof, /

Ac storye ymade of maistres wyse' (*Kyng Alisaunder*, 668-9) – and not fairground entertainment. Although it certainly contains works of escapist entertainment, the Auchinleck manuscript reassures its prospective owner by its assertion of educational value and by its inclusion of religious works.

What kind of purchaser was envisaged for the collection? Someone, evidently, who was expected to have interests in the origins of the aristocracy, since it contains a listing in French of the baronage of England; but the presence of the political satire, the *Simonie*, suggests also some perturbation at the established governance of England. Although the explicit derivation of stories like those of Alexander and Merlin from reputable French and Latin sources would suggest an audience with some concern for literary authority, the deliberate choice of English as the medium does not restrict the audience. It was clearly not for a learned audience, nor a purely aristocratic one. In 1513 Henry Bradshaw produced his *Life of St Werburge of Chester* in English, which he says is 'for marchaunt men hauyng litell lernyng' (2017). The words are perhaps too dismissive, but probably reflect the destination of the Auchinleck collection. The organization involved, the prosperity required in the purchaser, and the language of the manuscript, all point to the London area.[53] The first owner of the manuscript was probably a substantial merchant household, whose French did not extend much beyond that required for book-keeping, whose business connections were in the Midlands or East Anglia rather than across the Channel, who had at once an interest in aristocratic status and a critical attitude to the establishment, based on a strong sense of propriety and a taste for firm government. Whatever its place of origin, the Auchinleck MS is a miscellaneous collection of a sort later known to have been in the possession of prosperous London merchants.[54]

The Englishness of this environment is worthy of special notice, since the repeated assertion of an English perspective is a feature of Auchinleck. It is found not only in the tales of English heroes (Beues, Guy, Richard the Lion Heart) but repeated references to the deliberate selection of the English language, and even to the conscious emulation of foreign genres in English.[55] The apparently conscious attempt in the manuscript context of *Arthour and Merlin* to create a tradition of secular English literature to rival that in French, a whole generation before Chaucer, is matched by its inclusion of the *Short Metrical Chronicle*, which gives an account of the history of the English nation from its foundation to the date of the manuscript, asserting the independent English right to Normandy and Gascony. *Arthour and Merlin*, based as it claims to be on the *Brut*, may be seen in this anglophone mercantile context as a vigorous assertion of English national awareness through the medium of entertainment. As part of this role it appropriates Arthur as 'oure king', a hero of the English. **David Burnley**

The Alliterative *Morte Arthure*

'a tale þat trewe es and nobyll' (16)[56]

For the fourteenth-century chronicler Ranulph Higden, one of the less credible aspects of Geoffrey of Monmouth's *Historia Regum Britanniae* was its account of King Arthur as conqueror and colonizer of thirty kingdoms and successful opponent of the Emperor of Rome. Why, Higden wonders, is this important period of British triumphs not attested in Roman history, or in chronicles of the French and the Saxons; and why do some of the persons involved (Emperor Leo, Procurator Lucius) apparently belong to other periods of Roman history?[57] Despite the absence of such corroboration, there were, in Higden's day, many historical narratives in circulation in England – Latin, Anglo-Norman and English – which accepted and reproduced the Galfridian version of Arthurian history representing Arthur as the king who made the island of Britain a single political unit, extended his dominion overseas, and challenged the might of a Roman emperor.

Just how far Arthur advances towards Rome in his campaign of conquest varies somewhat in those narratives which follow Geoffrey of Monmouth's outline of Arthurian history. In the *Historia Regum Britanniae*, King Arthur and his forces, having successfully engaged the Roman army under the leadership of the Roman Procurator Lucius, are at Siesia when news comes of Mordred's treacherous activities in Britain, requiring Arthur's return. However, Pierre de Langtoft, in his early fourteenth-century *Chronicle*, which incorporates Geoffrey's material in a history of the kings of British and subsequently Anglo-Saxon England, recounts how Arthur and his army cross the Alps and reach Pavia before they receive news of Mordred's rebellion.[58] When Malory comes to incorporate the story of Arthur's Roman campaign in his encylopaedic collection of Arthurian narrative (completed in 1470), he tells how Arthur and his men, having defeated Lucius (the Emperor of Rome in this version) at 'Sessoyne', continue to Rome, where Arthur is then crowned Emperor 'by the Poopys hondis' (*Vinaver*, 245). The late fourteenth/early fifteenth-century alliterative poem, the *Morte Arthure*, is an important advance towards Malory's version of imperial Arthurian history, because it takes Arthur further in the direction of Rome – the king learns of Mordred's betrayal as he is camped outside Viterbo – and provides an unprecedented account of Arthur's campaign against Roman allies as he heads towards Rome: the poem is Malory's principal source for his 'Tale of Arthur and Lucius'.[59]

But the *Morte Arthure* is much more than a mere preliminary to Malory. It is a text that demands attention in its own right for, in many respects, it offers a more interesting and challenging account of this sequence of Arthurian history.[60] The poem expresses an admiration for the governance of Arthur (worthy to be 'ouerlinge ouer all oþer kynges', 289) and the martial achievements of the king and his 'ryeall renkys of the Rownnde Table' (17), at the same time as it allows recognition of the costs of such achievements: one of the most striking images in the final frames of the narrative is of Arthur in the role of a grieving widow, alone and lamenting the loss of her loved ones (4284-7).[61] The emotional pitch of this Arthurian narrative, especially in its representation of the power and strength of noble homosocial bonds, is one of its most distinctive features.[62]

Equally distinctive, however, is the way the anonymous poet has taken up the opportunities offered by this particular sequence of Arthurian history to create an anachronistic world, a composite (though not seamless conflation) of various historical epochs.[63] The result is a prismatic kind of text which allows its readers to perceive refractions of events from the more recent history of England in an account of events in the distant British past.[64] In addition, the opportunity offered by this sequence of Arthurian history for reflection upon more abstract issues concerning the definition of the political sovereignty of a kingdom, the rights of a conqueror and those of the conquered (already a feature of Geoffrey of Monmouth's narrative), has been very much developed in the alliterative *Morte Arthure*.[65] The nature of kingship, the business of governance, the justification for war, its proper conduct (should ransoms be allowed?), the achievements of military might and its terrible consequences are all matters which the audience of this poem are invited to consider.[66]

What is at stake in the campaigns which dominate the narrative is not a straightforward matter. The poem both encourages and resists the tendency to represent Arthur's campaign against the Romans in terms of a crusade (a tendency most developed in the brief poem *Arthur*, but which is also perceptible in some of the vernacular chronicle accounts).[67] In the *Morte Arthure*, the orthodox piety of Arthur and his supporters is expressed on several occasions in the course of the Roman campaign: for example, in the series of vows they make on the 'Vernicle' – a symbol of pilgrimage to Rome; and in Arthur's thanks to God for protecting his messengers to Lucius (1559-64).[68] The Roman forces mobilized against Arthur have very striking non-Christian, or non-orthodox, components (570-610), as do those of his other opponents, most notably the Duke of Lorraine (2652-7, 2889-96).[69] Nevertheless, the audience is not allowed to forget that Rome itself is a spiritual, as well as an imperial, centre.[70] Arthur himself seems to have this in mind when, rather pragmatically, he suggests to his men *en route* for Rome: '"3if we spare the spirituell, we spede bot the bettire"' (2414). However, despite Arthur's claim to '"gyffe my proteccione to all þe Pope landez"' (2410), the Papal city state of Spoleto is attacked *en route* (3161) and the representatives who come out from Rome to sue for peace at Viterbo say that the Pope is 'put at under' by the forces of the king (3180).

Such references certainly must complicate the perception of Arthur's Roman campaign as a crusade. But, in any case, the campaign is very clearly represented as being triggered by a feudal dispute: King Arthur disputes the claims made by Lucius in his official 'summons' (86-103) that he owes homage to the Emperor for the lands he governs; that he has unlawfully killed the Emperor's subjects; that he has withheld 'rentez' that properly belong to Rome.[71] Wolfgang Obst has argued that the author of the *Morte Arthure*, from the very beginning of the poem, 'accepts it as natural that Arthur should conquer the realms to which he has a rightful claim and that he should concern himself with the maintenance of law and order in his empire'.[72] However the issue of exactly which lands are rightfully Arthur's remains a rather more complex matter than Obst acknowledges here, especially in the light of the references to Uther's act of fealty to Lucius which are unique to this text.[73]

That he and his men are, in effect, engaged in a holy war, a battle for the faith, does not feature in the battle rhetoric of Arthur's side during the Roman campaign; but it does feature in the claims made by Gawain about the status of the campaign against Mordred and the fate of those on Arthur's side who die in the course of it (3029-31). On this occasion, though, there appears to be a discrepancy between the status claimed for the action by Gawain, and the way events are described by the narrator who recounts Gawain's frenzied, and ultimately fatal, attack on Mordred and his forces. Gawain's action would appear to illustrate those of an 'unwyse' man of arms in this case (see *Hamel*, note on 3991-6), even in the light of Arthur's subsequent treatment of his corpse as if it were a holy relic (note on 4095).

The *Morte Arthure* recounts the story of a golden age – 'Off the ryeall renkys of the Rownde Table / That chefe ware of cheualrye . . . / How they whanne wyth were wyrchippis many' (16-22) – and its subsequent demise with the loss of Arthur and the majority of his cherished men; but its narrator does not arbitrate on the final moral judgement the audience is expected to make on the whole sequence of Arthurian history given here. Various ways of understanding the significance of his reign are suggested in the narrative, most obviously in the episode in which the king's philosopher-companion interprets the meaning of Arthur's second dream (3394-455), a dream, recounted by the king (3227-393), which seems to address the shaping of Arthur's life, and afterlife, as a whole. However, it is only possible for the audience to extract a single 'lesson' of Arthurian history from this incident by reading selectively what the philosopher has to say.[74]

The audience is also induced to make judgements on the characters and incidents in the poem by the descriptions offered there. Identification with the 'Conqueror' Arthur and his followers is encouraged by the narrator who refers to their party as 'ours' throughout the narrative.[75] But the descriptions given in the text also allow associative connections to be made in the narrative and this may have the effect of blurring what may initially seem to be clear-cut distinctions between the good and the bad factions, between good and bad figures of authority, distinctions which at other moments the narrator seems so ready to endorse. The significance of the dragon symbol in this poem, where it refers in different contexts to King Arthur and to his Roman antagonists, offers a good example of the way in which distinctions between the antagonists may be blurred; or at least the way in which the audience may be encouraged to perceive similarities between the factions involved, as well as crucial differences.[76]

Given the way in which the poem encourages its readers to judge events and yet itself offers more than one frame of reference for assessing the significance of Arthur's achievements, it is hardly surprising that the interpretation of the poem has been a controversial matter in twentieth-century responses to the text. Arguments about if, and when, Arthur's campaign shifts from being legitimate to illegitimate, about when he commits the sins he is accused of in the philosopher's interpretation of his dream (3398-400), have been major preoccupations for modern critics, as has the related issue of the genre of this text, which necessarily involves deciding between possible frameworks of judgement.[77] I will mention some of these controversies here, but limitations of space preclude anything like a comprehensive review of its twentieth-century critical reception, let alone a full account of the poem, and its contexts of production and reception. Entire books, rightly, have been devoted to this narrative poem of 4346 lines of alliterative verse, which itself seems to be a product of a lifetime's reading and reflection on the business of diplomacy, military campaigning and governance in late fourteenth-century England (see *Hamel*, p.34).[78]

Although the controversial modern critical reception of the *Morte Arthure* may present some difficulties to readers approaching the text for the first time, there can be no doubt that twentieth-century scholarship has illuminated many aspects of this complex poem. The best single aid for modern readers of the *Morte Arthure* is the excellent edition by Mary Hamel. My discussion is indebted to her scholarship, and to that of many other medievalists who have worked on this fascinating text.[79]

'as þe Bruytte tellys' (4346)

The tradition of historical narrative mentioned in the last line of the *Morte Arthure* – a reference to the Brut chronicles – refers its audience to the most important source for the matter of the poem, although it is by no means the only literary tradition which informs this text. Though the history of Arthur's campaign against Rome ultimately derives from Geoffrey of Monmouth's *Historia Regum Britanniae*, it is clear that the composer of the *Morte Arthure* was acquainted not only with this version of events but had also read around the subject in vernacular historical narratives. Wace's *Roman de Brut*; possibly Robert of Gloucester's *Chronicle*; probably Laȝamon's *Brut*; either or both of Langtoft's *Chronicle* and Robert of Mannyng's *Chronicle* formed part of the poet's bibliography on the subject of insular history and influenced this particular telling of Arthurian history in various ways.[80] As Mary Hamel has observed:

> One has no sense that [the poet] searched these sources and compared them in any attempt to verify accuracy or historical truth, but rather that he sought for structures and details that would add narrative and dramatic effectiveness in the shaping of his own fiction. (p.37)

The episode in which Arthur encounters the giant of Mont St Michel (840-1221) offers a good example of how effectively the poet has worked up received material from his chronicle sources.[81] The giant depicted in the *Morte Arthure* is a composite figure made up not only from the figure whom Arthur encounters in the chronicles, but also from the giant (Ritho) whom Arthur briefly recalls having defeated on Mount Arvaius (1174-7) and whose distinctive trait in the chronicles was to collect the beards of kings he had killed.[82] This latter detail seems to have offered the cue for the particular ways in which the giant of Mont St Michel, a 'tyraunt' (843) who terrorizes the region, is figured in the *Morte Arthure*: his practices are described in ways which suggest they are influenced by, and hideously invert, those of powerful rulers, such as Arthur and Emperor Lucius. The giant, too, has elaborate feasts (1025-8); but his appetites are satisfied upon the populace, by consuming boy children and raping 'birdez' to death (1026-33). He, too, seeks the submission of figures of authority and power: he not only has a cloak spun in Spain, decorated in Greece, from the hair and beards of kings (998-1004), but annually receives the tribute of fresh beards from the kings of fifteen realms (1005-7) and has been demanding just such a tribute from Arthur for seven years (1009).[83]

In recasting this episode on Mont St Michel, the alliterative poet has developed the 'adventure' structure of the action, as Mary Hamel has argued: Arthur is the lone seeker here, and Bedevere does not play the mediatory role he is given in other versions of the sequence.[84] This tendency to structure episodes in the narrative around adventure can be seen elsewhere in the text. However the reworking of Arthur's encounter with the giant not only makes the action conform to an important structural pattern in the poem, it also enhances the thematic resonance of the episode so that it now not only prefigures (and refigures) Arthur's encounter with Lucius, but is further recalled at other stages in the narrative. For example, when Sir Gawain in his adventure outside Metz encounters Sir Priamus (2513-939), the issues at stake in the battle between Arthur and the giant are recast in complex ways. Here Gawain does not encounter a Saracen giant (as in the analogues at this point), but a Greek schismatic whose status derives not from a collection of royal beards, but the collection of powerful rulers from whom he claims descent, Alexander, Hector, Judas Maccabeus and Joshua (2595-611).[85] Their encounter does not conclude with the death of Sir Priamus, nor his religious conversion, but rather with his political conversion which adds to the prestige (and actual power) of Arthur's side.[86] Arthur's encounter with Sir Craddoke outside Viterbo also recalls some aspects of the meeting on Mont St Michel. Whereas Arthur had earlier represented his meeting with the giant as a pilgrimage (playing, anachronistically, on the place name and its reputation), he now encounters a pilgrim whose destination potentially throws his military ambitions into question.[87]

Here, then, we can see the alliterative poet working up a distinctive, and thematically more significant, version of events from material in the chronicle sources. But the *Morte Arthure* is not simply the product of an informed acquaintance with the Arthurian sections of these analogues; the narrative also reflects an awareness of the much broader scope of the Brut narrative tradition. For example, in elaborating Arthur's final approach to Rome, the poet has gone back to an account of the campaign against Rome by the brothers Belinus and Brennius, at an earlier stage of British history, as told by Wace in the *Roman de Brut*.[88] The significance of this borrowing may extend beyond the relatively small sections of Wace's text which are recycled in the *Morte Arthure* (see 3134-48, 3150-63, and Hamel's notes to these lines). The distinctive feature of Wace's account of the campaign of Belinus and Brennius is that he adds some geographical details (probably drawn from contemporary pilgrim itineraries)[89] which give a more precise and rather 'contemporary' impression of the brothers' route to Rome. This 'modernizing' strategy is one deployed on a much grander scale by the alliterative poet as he describes a whole series of military encounters *en route* from Val-Suzon in Burgundy to Tuscany which have no counterpart in the Brut texts (2386-3149). In the section of the narrative which recounts Arthur's progress via Luxembourg, Metz, over the Mount Gottard Pass, to Como and then into Tuscany, a series of details are built into the text which suggest the poet had an informed acquaintance with the cities and the political state of northern Italy in the late fourteenth century. It is these details which provide the most convincing evidence for dating the composition of the poem to sometime around 1399-1402.[90]

A more tentative example of how the poet may bring to bear on his text material from outside the sequence of Arthurian history – this time from much later in the history of England – can be found in the scene outside Metz where Arthur refuses to heed the advice of Sir Ferrers to protect himself better in a dangerous situation (2420-55). Arthur claims that as an anointed king he has divine protection and is not endangered by casual or accidental attack. Roy Pearcy has argued that some acquaintance with the circumstances in which Richard I died (perhaps from Robert of Gloucester's *Chronicle*) could have provided the inspiration for this scene.[91] Arthur's claims to be impervious may have had ironic reverberations for any members of the poem's audience who also knew that a later crusading King of England had been killed in very similar circumstances. This scene might, however, carry more recent reverberations still for an early fifteenth-century audience who recalled the claims and fate of Richard II (*Hamel*, p.58 and note on 2446-7).

This cameo episode involving Arthur and Ferrers outside the walls of Metz provides an example of how the audience of the *Morte Arthure* might be encouraged to perceive reflections of a more recent English past in the much more chronologically distant story of a British King. However, it also illustrates just how elusive a precise identification of any apparent 'topical allusion' might be; the interpretation of an allusion depends obviously on variables in the audience's perceptions and knowledge. That the poem does encourage its audience to perceive it as a topical text is clear. But this is not so much the result of references to specific episodes in English history being built into the poem, as an effect of the poet's consistent practice of 'translating Arthurian material into contemporary terms', as Juliet Vale has so convincingly shown.[92] By localizing the geographical backdrop of the action, by 'modernizing' the identities of protagonists and antagonists, by realizing the action in detailed descriptions in which precise and technical references are made to diplomatic, legal and military procedures of the fourteenth century, the poet is able to set 'his characters in a distinctly fourteenth century milieu without reproducing any particular historical situation'.[93] The narrator of the *Morte Arthure* does not ostensibly tell of Edward III, Richard II or Henry IV but offers a history of Arthur's campaign against Rome and subsequent campaign against Mordred which may, at the same time, remind its audience, of certain episodes and important political and military issues and practices of fourteenth-century England.

But if *Morte Arthure* encourages its audience to telescope the historical, geographical and political distance between Arthurian Britain and contemporary England, it also requires them to take a long view of Arthurian history and to stretch their historical imaginations beyond the limits of Brut chronicles and histories. In the episode of Arthur's second dream and its philosophical interpretation, the Arthurian period is placed within a pattern of heroic history that encompasses earlier classical and Jewish 'Worthies'(Alexander, Hector, Julius Caesar, Judas Maccabeus, Joshua, David (3268-323, 3405-21)) and looks forward to future Christian exemplary achievers (Charlemagne, Godfrey of Bouillon (3324-37, 3422-37)). The topoi central to the dream and its interpretation are those of the Wheel of Fortune (portending the fall of princes), and the Nine Worthies (exemplars of heroic achievement), and precedents for their use can be found in earlier texts (including the French prose *Mort Artu*).[94] But it is the attempt to coordinate these two modes of understanding the shaping of history which is the distinctive feature of their appearance in the *Morte Arthure*; and it is this attempt to synchronize that turning of Fortune's wheel with the histories of the Nine Worthies which challenges the poem's audience, once again, to consider the significance of King's Arthur's history.

In the historical vignettes given of kings positioned around Fortune's wheel we can also glimpse something of the extensive textual hinterland to this alliterative poem which ranges beyond the Brut narratives, Arthurian chronicles and romances: the poet had evidently read around the individual histories of the Nine Worthies too and incorporated motifs and references from those histories into this sequence of the poem. Whilst it may be something of an exaggeration to claim, as William Matthews has, that the poet views Arthur 'through spectacles commonly reserved for Alexander', there is no doubt that knowledge of a range of exemplary heroic narratives, most especially those involving Alexander and Charlemagne, inform the narrative of the *Morte Arthure*.[95]

> '. . . wysse me to werpe owte som worde at this tym
> That nothyre voyde be ne vayne . . .' (9-10)

Modern responses to the *Morte Arthure* have changed as we have come to understand more about the formal nature of Middle English alliterative verse and its stylistic resources. The research of scholars such as Milman Parry and Alfred Lord on the formulaic techniques of twentieth-century oral composition has been usefully applied to the analysis of formulaic expressions in the Middle English alliterative corpus, especially to those of the *Morte Arthure*.[96] However, if 'oral composition implies the use of formulas', the use of formulaic expression is not, by itself, a sign of oral composition and there now seems to be something of a consensus on the literary qualities of Middle English alliterative verse in general, and the literary qualities of the *Morte Arthure* in particular.[97] The poet of the *Morte Arthure* was evidently drawing on a tradition of composing in alliterative verse as a 'high style' medium for large-scale narratives on serious matters; but he also used this verse medium in innovative ways, developing, for example, alliterative verse clusters which extend the alliterative patterns over a number of lines and cultivating very precise word plays and puns in the text.[98]

However, all we know about this most skilful writer has to be induced from the *Morte Arthure* itself, there being no convincing evidence at this stage for the writer being responsible for any other alliterative poems, although she, or more likely he, had read and used other alliterative poems.[99] The single extant manuscript copy of the poem in Lincoln Cathedral Library MS 91 contains within it dialectal evidence of at least two earlier stages of transmission within it and, on the basis of this, Angus McIntosh has suggested that the poem was probably composed in eastern Lincolnshire.[100] The dating of the poem is still open to some debate but, if we accept Larry Benson's arguments, then the time of composition seems to be between 1399 and 1402.[101] From the various kinds of technical knowledge and textual influences built into the poem, Mary Hamel has offered the fullest sketch of the *Morte Arthure* poet that can be proposed at this stage. Her portrait is of a man of diplomatic and bureaucratic experience; someone widely travelled who had a knowledge of Latin, French and some Italian too; who may have had access to the considerable number of texts used in the poem through employment in the household of some lord (p.62). The poet also seems to have been someone engaged with the debate over the conduct and object of crusades (a matter of some concern in late fourteenth-century England); a subject also of interest to the copyist and owner of the single extant text of the *Morte Arthure*, Robert Thornton, lord of East Newton in Rydale, Yorkshire.[102]

The research of George Keiser and John J. Thompson in particular has shed considerable light on Robert Thornton, who is named as the copyist of the *Morte Arthure* in one of the three lines added at the end of the text in the Lincoln manuscript.[103] Thornton was responsible for the compilation of two large anthologies: the *Morte Arthure* is the second historical narrative in the collection, made *c.* 1420-50, of historical narratives, devotional texts and other useful material, such as a medical treatise, in English and Latin, which seems to have been used and read within Thornton's household. Phillipa Hardman has suggested that the layout of the text of the *Morte Arthure* and that of the Middle English prose *Life of Alexander* (with which the manuscript opens) may indicate something of Thornton's way of reading both texts as being, above all, about powerful earthly conquerors (rather than as moral tragedies).[104] This was, Hardman suggests, perhaps a subject of wider topical interest for Thornton:

> As English power in France dwindled in the mid-fifteenth century, Robert Thornton was perhaps looking back to the conquests of Henry V, celebrated in popular literature as a great hero, comparable to the Nine Worthies, and acclaimed 'Emperoure / And also kyng and conqueroure'.[105]

Whether we accept this proposal or not, Hardman's suggestion draws attention, once again, to the way in which the topical interpretation of this poem is obviously affected by the circumstances of its reception and reproduction.

At the end of the *Morte Arthure* a line has been added ('Hic jacet Arthurus rex q[u]ondam rexque futurus') which is not in Thornton's hand (*Hamel*, note on 4347-9). In some ways this reference to Arthur as a 'once and future king' seems oddly juxtaposed with a poem in which the death and burial of the king is recounted in some detail. There is no reference in the *Morte Arthure*, unlike some of its chronicle sources, to Arthur's retreat to a mysterious island and the hope of his return. Perhaps the sense of this insertion in the manuscript is that King Arthur is a once and future king because his history continues to be of use and interest in the present time of reading. Perhaps the writer of this line simply wanted to supplement the poem with details of Arthur's supposed epitaph. Perhaps, as Mary Hamel has suggested, the writer simply 'disagreed with the poet's ending' (note on 4347-9). There is no reason to suppose that disagreements about the meaning and interpretation of the *Morte Arthure* will decline as its circle of modern readers grows and as we are able to fill in more details of the context of the text's production and reception. And as we come to understand more about the circumstances in which the poem was composed, it may be that the figure of Geoffrey Chaucer will seem less of an exceptional literary presence in late medieval England. Chaucer was not the only skilled writer of the time interested in issues of governance, codes of élite masculine behaviour, matters of faith and the worldly engagements of crusaders, popes and of convents.[106]   **Lesley Johnson**

The Stanzaic *Morte Arthur*

The stanzaic *Morte Arthur* survives in only one copy; it occupies folios 86-133 in British Library MS Harley 2252, a miscellany compiled in the early sixteenth century by John Colyns, a London mercer and bookseller. But palaeographical and paper evidence has established an earlier date for that section of the manuscript containing the stanzaic *Morte*, revealing its previous existence as an independent, commercially produced booklet, published between 1460 and 1480.[107] The date of composition of the poem and its provenance are unknown, but it is thought to have been written some time during the fourteenth century, in the north or north-west Midlands.[108]

Like the alliterative *Morte Arthure*, apparently a product of a similar age and area though not necessarily the same social milieu, the stanzaic *Morte* is set against the close of Arthur's reign and the ending of the Arthurian world. Yet the two poems are radically different in every respect, from their dominant idealism to the verse forms in which they express it. The alliterative *Morte*, clearly influenced by the chronicle tradition, shows us an Arthur at the height of his powers, when defiance of Rome opens the way to wider imperial conquests by a military brotherhood united around a warrior-king. The stanzaic *Morte*, reminiscent of *roman courtois*, opens at a stage in Arthur's reign not recorded in the chronicle account, when the mimic warfare of tournament diverts a court divided by suspicion and malice under a king soon to be torn between public duty and personal loyalties. The dominant activity of the alliterative *Morte* is warfare, with Arthur supreme in leadership, defending faith and nation against evil forces, his personal prowess an instrument of Christian justice in single combat against emperor and ogre. The stanzaic *Morte* celebrates the chivalric ideals of love and loyalty but, while extolling their positive aspects, presents them simultaneously as divisive and destructive forces. The alliterative *Morte* looks back to the ethos and motifs of epic, with Arthur as emperor and paladin, Charlemagne and Roland in one, uniting his followers in patriotic warfare, yet vulnerable to excess when the brutality of war overwhelms judgement and self-control. It is the ethos of the chivalric world which the stanzaic *Morte* both celebrates and scrutinizes, the divisive personal loyalties set against the needs of the body politic revealing shortcomings in the ideals of *roman courtois*. In both poems Arthur and his world become vulnerable to the wilful malice of Mordred and are overwhelmed by it.

The stanza form and narrative style of the stanzaic *Morte* provide the poet with a flexible medium for his thematic design. Though criticized and neglected in the past for its affinity to minstrel composition, its use of the ballad stanza with its sparse, repetitive vocabulary, it is now generally acknowledged that the choice of narrative medium reflects the conscious decision of a highly skilled poet. The particular stanza form, apparently unique in both French and English, has been described as 'technically a marriage between the continuous octosyllabic couplets of French romance and the economical stanzas of lyric poetry', its rhyming pattern of *abababab* providing a 'unit large enough for sustained narration but flexible enough for quick and effective focusing on details'.[109] The poet varies the pace of the narrative and the perspective upon the events described by differentiating the ways in which individual stanzas relate to each other. Rapid changes of scene or speaker are effected between one stanza and the next, and consequence can follow events with dramatic swiftness in successive stanzas. Different perspectives are gained by the description or evaluation of events by more than one character in separate stanzas, while symmetry of structure and verbal repetition in blocks of stanzas confer a sense of ceremonial formality upon a sequence of events, at the same time investing such events with thematic significance. Groups of stanzas are also paralleled or contrasted with other groups elsewhere in the poem, the intertextuality of reference giving a greater depth of meaning to the simply expressed surface narrative. The sparse, formulaic and repetitive vocabulary, and the use of stock images link the stanzaic *Morte* with Middle English narrative forms such as the love lyric and the popular romance; but the stanzaic poet uses this diction deliberately, to place his narrative within a recognizable chivalric world, while manipulating the conventional diction in such a way as to scrutinize the chivalric ideals it normally conveys.

That the stanzaic *Morte* is concerned with the close of Arthur's reign is announced at the very beginning of the poem:

> In Arthur dayes, that noble kinge,
> Byfelle aunturs ferly fele,   *wondrously many adventures*
> And I shall telle of there endinge,
> That mykell wiste of wo and wele. (5-8)[110]   *knew much, joy*

The opening lines place the poem within the tradition of chivalric romance, but the tense of the verb *byfelle* is past, and it is what has led up to the *endinge* of this chivalric world which concerns the poet. In the stanzaic *Morte*'s description of the downfall of the Round Table we find, for the first time in English, that version of the Arthurian narrative in which the love between Lancelot and Guinevere has a central role to play in the unravelling of the bonds holding together both chivalric fellowship and kingdom. The last two books of Malory's *Morte Darthur* contain the much better known version of the Arthur–Guinevere–Lancelot triangle and its outcome, but Malory himself used the stanzaic *Morte* as one of his sources.[111] The other known source for the final Tales in Malory is *La Mort le Roi Artu*, closing section of the post-Chrétien Vulgate Cycle of French prose romances and itself the direct source of the stanzaic *Morte*.[112] Both the French prose and the English poem superimposed upon the fatal enmity of Arthur and Mordred, derived from Geoffrey of Monmouth's chronicle account, the destructive love affair of Lancelot and Guinevere which originated in Chrétien's chivalric narrative, *Lancelot* or *Le Chevalier de la Charrette*.

At the outset of the stanzaic *Morte* the mutual love between Lancelot and Guinevere is directly referred to as the reason for Lancelot's reluctance to join King Arthur and his knights at a tournament in Winchester:

Knightis arme them bydene	*at once*
To the turnemente to ride	
With sheldis brode and helmys shene	*shining helmets*
To wynne grete honoure and pride.	
Launcelot lefte withe the quene,	*remained*
And seke he lay that ylke tyde;	*sick, at that time*
For love þat was theym bytwene,	
He made inchessoun for to abyde. (49-56)	*an excuse*

When, however, Guinevere voices her fear that they will be betrayed by the spying Agravain, Lancelot decides to participate in the tournament, but in disguise, leaving his armour at the castle of Ascolot where the lord's daughter has fallen in love with him. Gawain, searching for Lancelot, arrives at the castle, recognizes the armour, and is led by the Maid of Ascolot to believe, mistakenly, that she and Lancelot are lovers. This sets in motion an unfortunate sequence of events: without apparent malice, Gawain passes on his misinformation to Guinevere, she believes it and reproaches Lancelot on his return. Lancelot leaves the court once again, so that when a poisoned apple, intended by a disaffected squire for Gawain, kills a Scottish knight at Guinevere's table, she is without a champion to defend her, having alienated Lancelot's fellow knights who blame her for his absence from court. Although Lancelot is alerted to the danger and returns in time to champion Guinevere and restore the status quo, the eventual revelation of their love affair leads him to kill three of Gawain's brothers, two of them unintentionally. This brings down upon Lancelot's head the undying hatred of Gawain, and Arthur, as his kinsman, is reluctantly drawn into the blood-feud. While Arthur and Gawain are absent from the kingdom, besieging Lancelot in his Breton stronghold, Mordred seizes the throne. As in the chronicle account, Mordred's usurpation leads to civil war, the outcome of which is the death of Arthur and the destruction of the Arthurian realm.

These are the events which form the narrative core of the stanzaic *Morte* and mirror, in outline, the narrative in the *Mort Artu*. But there are significant differences. The English poet condenses his French source and disentangles its complex interweaving of narrative strands, replacing the interlace with a fast-moving linear narrative focusing upon speeches and actions essential to the onward thrust of the story. Yet the most notable change is an addition by the poet, the final, poignant, encounter between the lovers at the end of the poem.[113] Guinevere, who has resisted Mordred's advances by immuring herself in the Tower of London, takes the veil upon hearing of Arthur's death, and in a chance meeting with Lancelot blames their love for the death of Arthur and his knights:

> '. . . I knowlache here   *acknowledge*
> That throw thys ylke man and me,
> For we togedyr han loved us dere,
> All thys sorowfull werre hathe be.
> My lord is slayne that had no pere,
> And many a doughty knyght and free,   *valiant, noble*
> Therefore for sorowe I dyed nere   *almost died*
> As sone as I evyr hym gan see.' (3638-45)

Guinevere begs Lancelot to leave her, to return to his kingdom and take a wife. He, however, refuses to be 'untrew' to what he sees as a lifelong bond between them:

> 'Forbede it, God, that evyr I shold
> Agaynste yow worche so grete unryght.
> Syne we togedyr upon thys mold   *earth*
> Have led owre lyffe by day and nyght,
> Unto God I yiffe a heste to holde   *give, promise*
> The same desteny that yow is dyghte.
> I will resseyve in som house bolde,   *accept*
> To plese hereafter God allmyght.' (3682-9)

Like Guinevere, Lancelot withdraws from the world and, forsaking worldly glory, leads a penitential life. In death Guinevere is restored to Arthur, her body laid to rest alongside his at Glastonbury, while we learn, through a prophetic dream of the Archbishop of Canterbury, that when Lancelot dies he is received into Heaven.

The closing stanzas of the stanzaic *Morte* demonstrate the personal consequences of the love affair in the aftermath of the political, returning us to the private world of the lovers. As they part forever – Guinevere admitting the harm occasioned by their love – the emotion between them, the kiss they dare not exchange, acknowledge that it still endures. And the emphasis upon Lancelot's redemptive end provides a fitting closure for a narrative in which he embodies all the knightly qualities, as Arthur himself declares:

> 'Welle may Launcelot holden be
> Off alle þe world the beste knight
> Off biaute and of bounte,   *beauty, knightly prowess*
> And sithe is none so moche of myght
> At every dede beste is he.' (123-7)

The Maid of Ascolot, enamoured of Lancelot at first sight, but driven to suicide by unrequited love, acknowledges him as '"the noblest knight þat may go"' (1075). Forced to face Arthur in battle, Lancelot refuses to harm '"the noble kynge that made me knyght"' (2193), and when Arthur is unhorsed in the mêlée, rescues him and mounts him on his own horse:

> Launcelot lokys he uppon,
> How corteise was in hym more
> Than evyr was in any man.
> He thought on thyngis that had bene ore,   *had previously been*
> The teres from hys y3en ranne.
> He sayde, 'Allas,' with syghynge sore,
> 'That evyr yit thys werre began.' (2199-205)[114]

This view of Lancelot as the chivalric knight *par excellence* is problematized, however, by his love affair with Guinevere, wife of his lord and king. The narrator withholds any direct comment, but Arthur, on hearing 'How Launcelot liggys by the quene' (1730), is distressed that '"any treson"' should be found in one '"off so mykylle noblyte"', yet is in no doubt that '"it is so, withouten fayle"' (1741-4). Lancelot's rescue of Guinevere from burning at the stake, when their love affair has been revealed to the king, may be in accord with the highest values of knightly chivalry in the service of a lady, yet it also sets in train the most ill-fortuned sequence of events. But then Gawain's blood-feud, undertaken for the best of chivalric motives, to avenge the killing of his unarmed brothers, also leads to disaster. Gawain is implacable in his desire for vengeance upon Lancelot, and his unwillingness to make peace has dire consequences both for himself and the Arthurian realm. He, like Lancelot, is drawn by emotional ties into actions which are both imprudent and potentially fatal. It has been said of Gawain that 'constancy so extreme that it is unchanged in a thoroughly changed situation cannot be seen as an unqualified virtue';[115] but neither can the constancy of Lancelot's love be seen as an unqualified virtue when it causes him to throw caution to the winds, visiting the queen in her bedroom by night, in reckless disregard of the spying Agravain. Sir Bors, fearing the worst, pleads with Lancelot not to go; but he, putting his desire to be with Guinevere above all other considerations, acts imprudently, and both he and the kingdom reap the consequences.

The narrator's impersonal stance avoids explicit condemnation of either Gawain or Lancelot, and when they ultimately face each other in single combat, he balances one knight's honour against the other's in succeeding stanzas, impartially voicing the claims which have brought them into conflict (2770-85). Like Lancelot, Gawain's end is seen in redemptive terms: after his death he appears to Arthur in a dream, accompanied by an angelic host who, he explains, '"byde in blysse ther I motte be"' (3207).

The narrative symmetry in the presentation of Gawain and Lancelot reflects the parallelism of approach to their respective roles in the poem. In a sense Lancelot and Gawain are mirror images of each other, each displaying both ideal and human qualities, each compelled to choose between the claims of conflicting personal loyalties. Personal loyalty is shown to be a significant determinant of behaviour in the chivalric world of the stanzaic *Morte*. An obvious example is the loyalty between the two lovers, Lancelot and Guinevere, a personal loyalty which, for Lancelot, takes precedence over all else when Guinevere is about to be burned at the stake. The depth and sincerity of Lancelot's love is never questioned, and his devotion to Guinevere is steadfast, though both his love and his loyalty have disastrous public repercussions. No less sincere is the unreciprocated love and devotion of the Maid of Ascolot who, like Guinevere, is deeply in love with Lancelot. On her first appearance in the poem she is described in language conventional to the description of the youthful beauty in medieval love lyrics: 'Hyr rode (*complexion*) was rede as blossom on brere (*briar*), / Or floure þat springith in the feld' (179-80).[116]

Given what we have been told about Lancelot's chivalric qualities (123-7), it is not at all surprising that the Maid should respond to his dynamic presence by falling in love with him. But Lancelot does not reciprocate the Maid's love – '"In another stede myne hert is sette; / It is not at myne owne wille"' (203-4), he tells her – though his treatment of her is described by the narrator as courteous and compassionate. But seen from the Maid's perspective, Lancelot's courtesy is no courtesy at all; in a letter found with her dead body she charges Lancelot with 'churlysshe maners' (1083) in that '"To be my leman he sayd evyr nay / And sayd shortely he wold have none"' (1086-7). The Maid is accusing Lancelot of acting ignobly in his seeming insensibility to her pitiful plight. Arthur's response to the letter is to sympathize with the Maid; from his point of view, Lancelot's refusal to respond to the Maid's love puts him to shame. But Arthur is not aware of Lancelot's quandary, of his commitment and loyalty to Guinevere which makes it impossible for him to respond to the Maid's entreaties. Arthur's view of Lancelot's conduct is, therefore, premised on partial knowledge and, ironically in view of the wider context, Arthur is reproaching Lancelot for the wrong reasons.

One of the striking features of the stanzaic *Morte* is the frequency with which characters act upon knowledge which the narrative shows to be limited and misleading.[117] When Gawain, searching for Lancelot, is led to believe by the Maid of Ascolot that ' "For his leman he hathe me take" ' (582), we, but not Gawain, know that Lancelot has actually rejected her advances. Challenged by the queen, Lancelot protests his innocence; but, feeling his honour impugned by her accusation, vows never to see her again. So, in the episode of the poisoned apple, Guinevere is without support. The knights who blame her for the death of the Scottish knight are acting upon what they assume, given the evidence available to them, to be true, but the narrative has already made it clear to us that they are mistaken. On this occasion the full facts, when revealed to the Arthurian court, resolve a potentially dangerous situation. But when, later in the poem, the knights assume that Mordred is the best person to take charge of the kingdom in Arthur's absence, their misreading of Mordred's character proves disastrous. Whether or not we are meant to see such misunderstanding as stemming from lack of judgement, the threat to the stability of the Arthurian world is only too real. Again and again in the course of the narrative, assumptions are made from the limited knowledge available at the time that, seen against the wider context, expose the fragile nature of the bonds holding together the fellowship of the Round Table.

Once the love affair between Lancelot and Guinevere becomes public knowledge, rifts appear between those of the king's party and Lancelot's followers, and personal loyalties dictate allegiances. After being discovered in Guinevere's bedchamber, Lancelot bids Sir Bors ' "awaken up all my knyghtis, / And loke whiche will with us holde" ' (1882-3), acknowledging that ' "We have begonne thys ilke nyght / That shall brynge many a man full colde" ' (1886-7). Group loyalty takes precedence over loyalty to the realm; in the very next stanza the personal commitment of Lancelot's knights to his cause is underscored by recognition of the cost of such loyalty:

> Bors than spake with drery mode,
> 'Syr,' he sayd, 'sithe it is so,

> We shalle be of hertis good,
> Aftyr the wele to take the wo.'
> The knyghtis sprent as they were wode, *sprang forward, crazy*
> And to there harneise gon the go. *equipment*
> At the morow armyd before hym stode,
> An hundrethe knyghtis and squyers mo. (1888-95)

Interestingly, Gawain, whose brother Agravain, a known trouble-maker, has been killed by Lancelot when surprised in the queen's bedroom, refuses at first to take sides, since he had previously warned his brother in no uncertain terms of the harm that would ensue should Agravain reveal their love affair to the king (1688-711). Gawain refuses to attend the burning of Guinevere, but two more of his brothers, reluctantly present and unarmed, are accidentally killed in the melee during her rescue, and Gawain becomes obsessed by the need to take revenge upon Lancelot. The bonds of chivalric fellowship snap as Arthur is drawn through the personal code of kin loyalty into the blood-feud against Lancelot, and open conflict ensues, endangering the stability of the realm.

Though Arthur is the third member of the Lancelot–Guinevere–Arthur triangle, critical discussion of the stanzaic *Morte* has tended to marginalize him, or to depict him as less important thematically than Lancelot or Gawain, a weak-willed king whose main function in the poem is to provide an unfavourable contrast to Lancelot, the hero.[118] But evidence for this characterization of Arthur is lacking when one considers the English poet's treatment of his French source. The outraged and irrational husband of the *Mort Artu*, betrayed by a wife he cannot stop loving, and thirsting for revenge, is replaced in the English text by a king who is seen in a more positive light.[119] Whereas the Arthur of the French source pursues a personal vendetta against Lancelot, heedless of the cost to the kingdom, the English Arthur is keenly aware of the danger to the realm when personal and political imperatives collide. His dynastic identity as ruler of England is stressed when word of his war with Lancelot reaches the Pope: 'And yit at Rome it was full couthe (*well known*) / In Ynglande was such sorowe stronge' (2248-9).[120] On pain of England being placed under a papal interdict, Arthur is commanded to take back Guinevere, be reconciled with Lancelot, 'And holde Yngland in reste and pes' (2261). Arthur's immediate response shows his concern for his kingdom:

> The kynge aȝeyne it wolde noȝte bene,
> To do the popys comaundemente,
> Blythely ayeyne to have the quene,
> Wolde he noght that Ynglonde were shente. *destroyed*

> Bot Gawayne was of herte so kene   *fierce*
> That to hym wolde he nevyr assente
> To make acorde hem bytwene
> While any lyffe were in hym lente. (2270-7)[121]   *he lived*

It is as a king who 'myght not be ageyne the right' (913, 921) that Arthur accedes to Sir Mador's demand that Guinevere face trial for having poisoned his brother 'with grete treasoun' (937) – a charge of which she is innocent, since the poisoned apple was offered at her table without her knowledge. Lancelot proves her innocence in combat against Sir Mador, and the poisoner when discovered undergoes the punishment demanded by the law for treason:

> The squyer than was done to shende, *put to a shameful death*
> As it was bothe lawe and ryght,
> Drawen and hongyd and forbrende   *burned to death*
> Before Syr Mador, the noble knyghte. (1664-7)[122]

'Treson' is the term used by Arthur to describe Lancelot's adultery with Guinevere, and it is for treachery to their king that the lovers are condemned. Arthur is acting here according to the law and not out of personal revenge; in counsel with his knights, they condemn her to be burnt, the punishment for treason in women (1921-5). Likewise, the decision to appoint Mordred Steward of England, when Arthur leaves the country to wage war on Lancelot, is not taken autocratically:

> At hys knyghtis all bydene,   *all together*
> The kynge gan hys conselle take,
> And bad hem ordeyne hem bytwene
> Who beste steward were for to make,
> The reme for to save and ʒeme, (2508-12)   *realm, govern*

It is the knights who choose Mordred as the most trustworthy man 'to save the reme in trews and pees' (2520), a decision, says the narrator, for which they will pay dearly (2523).[123]

Arthur is torn between love for Lancelot and concern for the welfare of his realm: ' "me rewis sore / That evyr was werre bytwexte us two" ' (2394-5; cf. 2442-3, 2675). When Lancelot offers a twelve-month's truce, the king and all his men 'spake to have pese, / But, hymself, Syr Gawayne' (2686-7), who vows that ' "To Yngland will I not torne agayne / Tylle he be hangid on a boughe" ' (2680-81). Only family loyalty to his nephew makes Arthur issue grim orders to his earls and barons throughout England: ' "On Launcelot landys for to ryde, / To brenne and sle and make all bare" ' (2506-7). The detailed description of Arthur's military campaign against Rome in the alliterative *Morte*, with its emphasis on the bravery of 'our' knights, is missing here. The stanzaic *Morte* sees no glory in warfare, since this is not a war against threatening external forces, but a conflict within a society at odds with itself.

Reluctant to wage war against his sovereign, Lancelot refuses to engage with Arthur's forces when they besiege him in Joyus Garde, earning Sir Bors's rebuke for seeming to act 'cowardlye' (2132). And when engagement cannot be avoided Lancelot transfers to the battlefield the chivalric code of loyalty to ' "The noble kynge that made me knyght" ' (2145), refusing to harm Arthur and rescuing him when he is in danger. But the ironic euphemism underscoring the grim reality of battle puts a different perspective upon Lancelot's 'corteise' on the battlefield:

> Off thys bataille were to telle,
> A man that it wele undyrstode,
> How knyghtis undyr sadels felle,
> And sytten downe with sory mode.
> Stedys that were bolde and snelle   *steeds, speedy*
> Amonge hem waden in the blode. (2230-5)

The battle ends, not like the ending of a chivalric tournament where there is rejoicing for the victor, but with 'wepynge sare: / Amonge hem was no chyldys playe' (2244-5). The bravery and courtesy of Lancelot are applauded, but in such a conflict cannot of themselves prevent disaster. Courtesy expects courtesy in others and Lancelot, having restored Guinevere to the king and returned to his own country, declares to his followers: ' "My lord is so corteise and hende / That yit I hope a pees to make" ' (2594-5). One of them responds: ' "Syr, cortessye and youre sufferynge / Has wakend us wo full wyde" ' (2566-7), warning of the dangers to his own realm if he does not engage Arthur's forces in battle. The battle itself is described in chivalric terms of single combat between individual knights and Gawain, in which Gawain is always the victor.

The treachery of Mordred in seizing the throne is the last in a line of actions described in the poem as treacherous – the poisoning of the Scottish knight, Lancelot and Guinevere's adultery, Agravain's public exposure of it, and the killing of Gawain's unarmed brothers[124]– all treasonable in that they threaten the stability of the Arthurian world. In their destructive effect upon the social and political cohesion of the realm, the actions of individuals of good faith are undifferentiated from those perpetrated by individuals of bad faith. Lancelot is 'grete of honoure' while Mordred is a 'fals traytor', but the deeds of both combine to bring down the kingdom.

In Arthur's absence Mordred has false documents issued announcing his death, and with the consent of the people Mordred is 'made . . . kynge with crowne' (2981). Mordred's treachery in usurping the throne forces Arthur's abandonment of the siege of Joyus Garde and his return to a country precipitated into civil war. Gawain accompanies Arthur on the homeward journey, but dies in forcing a landing on Dover beach, struck upon an old wound given him by Lancelot in single combat during the siege. Arthur's first direct encounter with Mordred ends with Mordred's withdrawal and 'many a dede beryed on a rowe' (3125), but on the eve of the third and final battle Gawain appears to Arthur in a dream and advises caution:

> 'A monthe day of trewse moste ye take,   *a month's truce*
> And than to batayle be ye bayne;   *you will be prepared*
> Yow comethe to helpe Lancelot du Lake
> With many a man mykell of mayne.   *of great strength*
> To morne the batayle ye moste forsake,
> Or ellys certis ye shall be slayne.' (3216-21) *for certain*

Unlike the French version, where the final battle begins because Arthur disregards Gawain's advice, the English poet has Arthur heed his warning and arrange a truce. But one of Mordred's followers, stung by an adder, draws his sword to kill it and so precipitates, by chance and not intent, the final, fatal battle. Whereas in the *Mort Artu* the king kills Mordred in the heat of battle and is himself mortally wounded, in the English poem he survives the battle, but afterwards rushes at Mordred in fury and, in killing him, receives his own mortal wound. This altered version makes the killing of Mordred a more deliberate and personal act of vengeance, in which the identity of Arthur the brave, reckless, chivalric hero contrasts with his more prudent political role as king.[125]

The portrayal of Arthur in the stanzaic *Morte*, like the narrative design of the poem itself, combines the dynastic perspective of the chronicle tradition with the personal and social values of the chivalric romance. But Arthur is neither as central to the narrative as he is in the chronicle accounts, nor as peripheral as he is in many of the chivalric romances. Lancelot's actions take centre stage, and it is through their effect upon others, notably Gawain and Arthur, that we are made aware of the dangers facing the Arthurian world. Misunderstanding, mishap, misjudgement and malice all have their part to play in undermining the realm, and in their interaction the possibility of avoiding a tragic outcome becomes less and less likely; the sequence of events leads ultimately and seemingly relentlessly to the destruction of the Arthurian ideal.[126]

But the narrative does not end here. Against the backdrop of the larger dynastic calamity the two lovers play out the final scene of their calamitous love affair. The link between their love and the fall of the Arthurian kingdom is acknowledged by Guinevere; yet the tender farewell scene between Arthur's wife and the best of Arthur's knights, resists, in the last resort, a simplistic moralization. The life of penance both Lancelot and Guinevere embark upon implies recognition of their responsibility and a spiritual turning away from their former earthly preoccupations, but the very anguish of their parting, expressed so movingly and realistically, recalls to mind the depth and sincerity of their love and its steadfastness. Codes of conduct which can bring out the best in personal behaviour interact with social and political contexts which doom these individuals and their world to destruction.

The theme of a great and ancient society threatened and ultimately destroyed by the power of love has had an enduring hold upon the literary imagination. Within the Arthurian world this theme owes its origin to the French *Mort Artu*, but transposed and reimagined in the English stanzaic *Morte*. In the earliest strand of the medieval English Arthurian tradition, derived from Geoffrey of Monmouth, dynastic strife was seen as a significant factor in the destruction of the Arthurian ideal, and within this tradition the very nature of kingship came under scrutiny in such texts as Laȝamon's *Brut* and the alliterative *Morte Arthure*. The unknown author of the stanzaic *Morte Arthur* clearly knew the chronicle tradition surrounding Arthur, but found in his French source a romance version of the legend, prioritizing an examination of the chivalric ideals of love and loyalty. Interrelating the two traditions, the English poet wove a poem rich in human issues and complex in theme. Though seemingly naïve in its surface presentation of the story, it reveals a subtlety of treatment which at times approaches that of a modern novel. Through its use as a significant source by Malory, often in preference to the French *Mort Artu*, the stanzaic *Morte Arthur* has played a decisive though largely unacknowledged role in the way succeeding generations have read the Arthurian legend. **Carole Weinberg**

5

CHIVALRIC ROMANCE

The distinction between the romances contained in this chapter and those in the previous one is far from clear-cut, not least because texts considered in both involve 'chivalry' in some of the most fundamental senses of the word: characters who are 'knights or horsemen equipped for battle' (OED *chivalry* n. 1), and actions that are, or should be, informed by an 'ethical code . . . comprising allegiance (honour), valour, generosity, courtly manner' (MED *chevalrie* n. 5). But what makes the 'chivalric romances' distinctive is their concern with the prowess and fortunes of individual knights, even when they also relate the activities of a large company of such knights at court (*Ywain and Gawain*), in the hunting field (*The Awntyrs off Arthure*), or on a pilgrimage (*Golagros and Gawane*). As Auerbach long ago made plain, the primary object of such an individual hero is the pursuit of 'adventure'.

Auerbach found his exemplary adventure – and with it the antithesis of the (more dynastic) concerns of the *chansons de geste* – in the first part of Chrétien de Troyes's *Yvain*, the direct, if much more extensive, source of *Ywain and Gawain*. It was a natural choice, since this particular adventure is not only complex and impressive in itself, but is described a number of times, at varying length, with different protagonists, and by different narrators; it thus becomes firmly impressed upon the reader's mind, not as 'an' adventure, but as 'the' adventure. What is more, its further development brings the hero to the experience of romantic love, another important element in the chivalric romance. It is often said that the effect of such love will be to inspire a romance hero to even greater feats of valour, but this is not always evident in the romances dealt with in this chapter. The connection is explicitly made in *Sir Launfal* and in *Lancelot of the Laik*, and – implicitly, and on a very basic level – in *The Jeaste of Syr Gawayne*. But when in *Sir Tristrem* the hero rescues his mistress from an abductor, it is by cunning and not by fighting, while the love-relationship of the hero and heroine in *Ywain* proves more at odds than in harmony with any quest for glory in the field. By resulting in the neglect of the lady, and consequent estrangement from her, this quest gives rise to a whole series of new and varied adventures. As might be expected, it is this more varied pattern that is found in most other romances of this kind. It is especially developed in *Lybeaus Desconus*, where the individual adventures are more loosely organized than in the second part of *Ywain*. Only once, when the hero's defeat of a knight in one episode provokes attacks from his kinsfolk in the next, is a link made between two of the constituent adventures.

Such use of revenge as a linking device is fairly common; it controls almost all the actions of the hero's opponents in *The Jeaste*, while love – of a sort – controls those of the hero. On a much larger scale this interweaving of the two impulses to action can be seen in *Tristrem*, another story of a compulsive lover with powerful enemies, but this time the hero is also moved by the urge to revenge outrages against his kinsfolk and himself. The hero of *Sir Percyvell of Gales* too, avenges the killing of his father on his murderer, but does so accidentally, not seeking him out as Tristrem had done. Links between the individual episodes are often much less explicit than this; in *The Awntyrs* they are so hard to find that the second component of the romance has been held to be the work of a different redactor. In *Sir Gawain and the Green Knight*, however, the parts could not be more closely and meaningfully bound together.

The principal hero of both these last romances is Gawain, and in the English corpus he fills this role more often than any other Arthurian knight. For the most part he does so with distinction, being almost always successful in combat, and both moderate in himself and a moderating influence upon others; in *Golagros* he even shows consideration for the feelings of a defeated enemy. On the other hand, some of Arthur's more ill-considered actions implicate Gawain as well (*The Awntyrs*), and the knight will sometimes discredit himself by actions that are entirely his own. His weakness for women both sets and keeps in motion the action of *The Jeaste*, and while this is a very curious romance indeed, the same tendency is also briefly apparent at the beginning of *Lybeaus*, where Gawain is said to have begotten the hero of the title upon a lady casually seduced in a forest. It is also raised in an altogether more subtle and ambiguous manner in *Sir Gawain and the Green Knight*.

Otherwise, the most interesting of the primary heroes are those who are not from the beginning established members of the Arthurian court, and who find their true fulfilment outside it. The hero of *Launfal*, while both denied proper maintenance and sexually harassed by Guenevere, finds spectacular financial support and love elsewhere. So too – despite their much better treatment at Arthur's hands – do Ywain, Lybeaus, and Perceval, even if the ladies won by the two last are not granted much personality of their own; to a very large extent their love goes with the territory. From this point of view such heroes stand at the opposite extreme from Tristrem, whose adulterous love for Ysonde can by its very nature bring him no direct territorial rewards.

Only when exiled from her and in the service of other lords than his king can he hope for such, or for the collateral (but embarrassing) offer of a wife. Lancelot, who in the stanzaic *Morte Arthur* has so much in common with Tristrem, makes a rather different impression in *Lancelot*, since this romance, while reaffirming his unchanging and inspirational love for Guenevere, allots much more space to the description of Arthur's wars with Galiot.

Also important are members of Arthur's court who are not the principal heroes of their stories, but who provide those that are with support or competition. Once again, Gawain is the dominant figure, most often as a helper. The help that he gives will usually take the form of advice on proper chivalric conduct (*Ywain*), but may also be more practical: how to remove the armour of a dead enemy, or when to dismount and fight on foot with a sword (*Percyvell*). In *Lybeaus* he is assigned the task of educating the hero in the martial aspects of chivalry, but events move too quickly for him even to begin this. At the other extreme he may find himself in combat with the principal hero after having failed to identify him (*Ywain, Percyvell*). Competition of a less taxing kind is provided by Kay, who is at once unattractive in his disparaging of his fellow knights, and unsuccessful in combat with them (or with anyone else). The difficulties created by his unchivalrous behaviour may be resolved by the antithetical conduct of Gawain (*Golagros*).

Finally, there is the king himself, less often a central figure in these works than in the dynastic romances. The major exception is *Golagros*, where, like Gawain, he is both active and decisive, unable to tolerate the refusal of Golagros to acknowledge his overlordship. The same view of the king is also conveyed – though more obliquely and at less length – in the first part of *The Awntyrs*. Usually, however, the part that he plays is more passive and less open to criticism. It is his knights who set out from court to achieve difficult undertakings and redress wrongs, while he reserves for himself the functions of decision-maker and upholder of truth and justice. The purest example of this shift of emphasis is found in *Lybeaus*, where he not only confers knighthood upon the young hero, but upholds his claim to the first adventure to present itself. This ensures a respect and devotion in Lybeaus that will underpin all the later events of the story. The antithesis to this situation is found in *Launfal* where Arthur, while initially supportive, becomes increasingly unstable and unjust in his dealings with the hero. Different again, and perhaps most extraordinary of all, is the Arthur of *Sir Gawain*. He too remains within the limits of his principal court, but while sedentary in one sense of the word he is hardly so in others: intensely lively, he assigns to himself the staggering adventure that has turned up on his doorstep, until courteously but firmly prevented from going further with it by Gawain.

Elsewhere the mixture of qualities in the king is different, in that he will appear now dynamic (and, as in the dynastic romances, potentially aggressive), now static to the point of feebleness. In *Ywain*, while introduced to the reader as a conqueror, and sufficiently energetic to make his own trial of the adventure at the spring – even if he delegates the actual fighting to Kay – he can still astonish his knights by taking, Gerontion-like, an after-dinner sleep while they indulge their fondness for tales of adventures and marvels. This is a momentary lapse, but in *Percyvell* his weaknesses of character and constitution are more persistent. From the outset, he is ineffective in dealing with overbearing intruders at court, and when he later takes to his bed, it is with every intention of staying there. He makes partial amends by journeying with a handful of knights to the siege of the Maydenlande (though he takes no active part in the fighting there), and manages at least the appearance of authority in his subsequent dealings with the hero.

Arthur and his knights generally work well together in these romances, although in *Launfal* the court shows itself more balanced and fair-minded than the king. Occasionally both may appear so deficient as to raise serious questions about the very nature of chivalry (*The Awntyrs*, *Sir Gawain*). Most subversive of all is *Sir Percyvell*, where the hero not only refuses to go back to Arthur's court once he has left it, but abandons the armour that proclaims him a knight for his original woodland costume.

With the exception of the stress placed upon the ambitions and achievements of individual knights, not all the themes noted above are present in every romance considered here. Nor is there any reason why they should be. Like any other categorization of the medieval stories of Arthur, 'Chivalric Romance' is a concept of our own time, not of the fourteenth and fifteenth centuries; an aid to our own study of these works, not a generic template to help their authors decide what incidents and topics were to be included or left out, emphasized or underplayed. Nor need the handful of texts included in this chapter communicate the full range of this romance mode. The survival of texts in a manuscript culture given to recycling its products was always precarious; a number will have been lost, and some of these, at least, would have offered fresh combinations of the major themes, and made less abrupt the gradations of those texts we still have.

Maldwyn Mills

Ywain and Gawain

Ywain and Gawain[1] was composed in the north of England in the second half of the fourteenth century and survives in a single (still more northerly)[2] copy in British Library MS Cotton Galba E.ix. Impressive in itself, it has additional interest as the only surviving romance in Middle English that was quite certainly translated directly from an original by Chrétien de Troyes: *Yvain*, or *Le Chevalier au Lion*,[3] generally seen as his masterpiece. The English version surmounts most of the constraints imposed by translation, and by abbreviation to roughly three-fifths the original length; only rarely need we consult the original to clarify obscurities in the narrative.[4] More sustained comparison of the two works has sometimes been used to emphasize other negative features in *Ywain*, most notably its relative lack of subtlety in both style and sense.[5] But its own positive qualities have increasingly been recognized; in particular its emphasis upon 'trowth' (*loyalty, constancy*) rather than upon *amour courtois* as a principle of chivalric action.[6] And what has never been in doubt is its efficiency as a piece of story-telling – which is appropriate, since this is an activity that receives a good deal of sympathetic attention within the romance itself.[7]

The medieval titles given to the English, French and Welsh versions of the story helpfully throw into relief its principal narrative concerns. *Ywain and Gawain*[8] evokes not only the scenes that celebrate the close companionship of the two knights, but the climactic episode in which they unwittingly and indecisively fight with each other. *Le Chevalier au Lion*, on the other hand, directs our attention to a sequence of episodes in which Gawain plays no direct part at all, and the hero's companion – as well as indispensable helper in combat and source of a fresh identity – is a lion, endlessly grateful to him for having saved its life. And 'Chwedyl iarlles y ffynnawn' (*The story of the lady of the fountain*), the title once assigned to *Owein*, the Welsh prose version of the story,[9] focuses attention on its first and final sections; what matters here is the testing of the hero by an adventure at a magic spring, and his winning – or regaining – of the love of the lady associated with it. Between them, these three groups of episodes not only account for nearly the whole of the action of the story, but exemplify the main concerns of chivalric romance: the search for 'adventure'; its varied nature and motivation; the balancing of love and male companionship; the knight as the active champion of those in need, and his own need of the help and counsel of others.

The events at the fountain, together with their preliminaries and sequel, cohere to provide a romance adventure at once complex and exemplary.[10] So it is appropriate that it should be introduced to the reader, not by the narrator, but by Ywain's cousin, Colgrevance, who had himself attempted it some six years earlier:

> While riding alone in search of adventures, Colgrevance had met with a gigantic herdsman of wild animals, who guided him to a marvellous spring. Here the knight raised an alarming tempest by casting water on a stone; this was followed by a massive assembling of singing birds in the tree over his head. Salados, the formidable guardian of the spring, next appeared, very quickly defeated him, and took away his horse. Deeply humiliated, Colgrevance returned home. (*Friedman and Harrington*, 154-456)

This story within a story was told to an audience of knights that included both Ywain and Gawain (60-1, 54-7), and it had earlier been made plain that the telling of such 'true'[11] stories in order to celebrate the virtues of their protagonists was a regular part of the festivities at Arthur's court (25-30). Colgrevance seems to be promising something of this kind when he prefaces his own narration with a demand for the most careful attention from his hearers (149-52), but the tale that follows proves to be exemplary only in a negative sense.[12] It chronicles failure, not success; an action left incomplete, not achieved; and the behaviour of its narrator-protagonist provides a warning, not a model – ' "I fand þe folies þat I soght" ' (456).

But this very failure makes his story a powerful spur to further action, and on two distinct levels. As a piece of Arthurian fiction, its lack of closure demands a retelling that will carry it forward to its proper conclusion; as a 'true' story for its inner audience of Arthurian knights, it demands vengeance for a humiliation that reflects upon them all.[13] In consequence, the principal hero of this romance is – for once – led to it neither by a challenger seeking an opponent, nor a messenger seeking a champion, but by a narrative generated within the court itself. And while a challenger or a messenger normally gives only a summary account of what is in store for the volunteer, Colgrevance has supplied a blueprint for adventure that, as far as it goes, is both detailed and seductively marvellous. If there is little in the narrator to encourage imitation, there is plenty in what he has narrated to encourage a fresh attempt upon the adventure.

More than one person is so encouraged. Ywain (on his own), and Arthur and Kay (jointly) make trial of it within the space of the next fortnight, while for good measure Ywain does so a second time, near the end of the romance (3837-46). His first attempt has the widest range of incident, and the narration of it, properly laconic when presenting characters already described at length by Colgrevance, becomes more expansive when it moves beyond these:

The fight lasts longer than before, but Ywain finally gives his opponent a mortal wound, and pursues him into his castle. Here the sudden descent of a portcullis bisects Ywain's horse, and makes him a prisoner. He is saved from detection and death by Lunet, the confidante of Alundyne, the dead man's widow, and then falls hopelessly in love with the latter. At first hostile, she is finally won round by Lunet and marries Ywain, who then becomes the new guardian of the spring, in time for the arrival of Arthur and his retinue there.

(635-1266)

The role of the challenger is then split in two, with Arthur casting the water on the stone, but Kay (at his own insistence) doing the fighting. He is unhorsed almost as quickly as Colgrevance had been (419-22, 1321-6); but since Arthur has not been personally defeated, his own glory remains undimmed. And if yet another of his knights has been humiliated at the spring, it was at least at the hands of one of his fellows.

Arthur's reception by Alundyne's subjects modifies two earlier (but very different) impressions given of him as a less-than-ideal king. The first was produced by his strange lethargy near the beginning of the story – 'After mete went þe kyng / Into chamber to slepeing' (47-8); the second, more insistently, by rumours that his expedition to the spring had as its aim the conquest of Alundyne's lands. These rumours are repeated by Lunet to Alundyne (943-7),[14] remain very much in her mind afterwards (1021-4), and are even more forcefully expressed to her barons by her steward: ' "Were es waxen in þir (*these*) landes" ' (1212). The effect of such misleading rhetoric is to create an Arthur who resembles the land-hungry conqueror of the alliterative *Morte Arthure*, or the first part of *The Awntyrs off Arthure*. But his actual words to Alundyne are wholly gracious – ' "Lady white so flowre, / God gif þe joy and mekil honowre, / For þou ert fayre with body gent." ' (1421-3) – even if the size of his retinue produces a rather ambivalent reaction in the onlookers: 'Þai said he was worthy to dowt (*fear, respect*), / Þat so fele (*many*) folk led obowt' (1391-2).[15]

The motives of the other challengers are diverse. For all his lack of success, Colgrevance is the one most obsessed with adventures (154-5, 180, 237, 314-15), using them to test his powers of endurance to their limits (316). The equally unsuccessful Kay is less self-aware, but views it as his right to attempt any adventure that may present itself; as Ywain had feared, he is the first to ask Arthur for the 'batayl' at the spring (539-40, 1307-8). Ywain's motivation is more complex: like Colgrevance, he likes marvels, and wants to experience for himself those of which he has so recently heard (551-62); like Kay, he wants to do this before anyone can anticipate him. But he also wishes to avenge his cousin's disgrace at the hands of Salados (461-5).

Of all the knights who accompany Arthur to the spring the most important to the subsequent development of the story is Gawain, but in the romance as a whole he appears much less often than the presence of his name in its English title might suggest.[16] No adventure in which he alone is involved is developed at any length; all that we have are two extremely brief allusions (2181-6, 2293-6) to his quest to rescue Guenevere from an abductor,[17] and the outcome of this is never disclosed. Occasionally, the esteem which he and Ywain feel for each other is mentioned,[18] or they are linked as paragons of knighthood; but his only real contributions to the story are in two widely separated episodes in which he and Ywain are equally prominent.

In the earlier of these he plays his familiar role of counsellor. This time what he advises is that Ywain should leave his newly married wife to go tourneying with him (1451-72), and his advice is taken (1561-78). But it is inappropriate, and leads to disaster. His fear was that Ywain might fall into shameful indolence if he remained apart from his companions of the Round Table: ' "Þat knyght es nothing to set by, / Þat leves al his chevalry / And ligges bekeand (*keeping warm*) in his bed, / When he haves a lady wed" ' (1457-60). But this, while reasonable under different circumstances – and a danger later acknowledged by Ywain himself (2923-4) – was improbable as long as there was the fountain to defend. Alundyne had warned him to return at the end of a year (1499-514); but he becomes too absorbed by his tourneying, is publicly repudiated by her messenger, and runs mad to the woods in the conventional *folie* tradition. (1649-54).

Gawain's failure as a counsellor contrasts with the success of Lunet in the same role (Barnes, 36-8). While his advice – however unintentionally – brings about the estrangement of Ywain and Alundyne, that of Lunet twice brings them together, and against very heavy odds. She takes the trouble to coach Ywain in some detail – 'Sho talde him al how he sold do, / When þat he come þe lady to' (1107-8), although most of her teaching is directed at the lady, whose 'maystres', 'keper', and 'cownsaylere' she is (936-7). She pleads Ywain's case so persuasively to Alundyne (938-58, 975-1010, 1049-56) that she becomes implicated in his later perjury, and is condemned as a traitor to her mistress (2133-6, 2163-5, 2558-9).

In other ways, however, Gawain proves of more help to the hero. Although the word is never applied to him in the English romance, he is Ywain's 'companion' in battle,[19] and this relationship not only helps them win enormous fame together in tournament (1563-76), but adds a new dimension to Ywain's character. Before this, he – like Colgrevance – had seemed primarily a solitary knight, ready to detach himself from the Arthurian company in order to achieve private ends. Now, for the first time, he appears in a close and reciprocal relationship with one of his fellows.

But even this mutually profitable companionship-in-arms is shattered in the second episode in which Gawain plays a major part, since here they find themselves matched against each other as the anonymous champions of two litigant sisters. The narrator underlines the absurdity of the situation – 'Ful grete luf was bitwix þam twa, / And now er aiþer oþer fa (*enemy*)' (3515-6) – but what impresses the less well-informed spectators is the phenomenal and evenly matched prowess of the combatants (3593-600). But in other respects Gawain seems the less worthy of the two. In his support of the younger sister, Ywain is, once again, championing the deserving, while the sister who has Gawain's support cannot open her mouth without alienating all who hear her. The sustained inferiority of the more famous knight is not really surprising in a work based upon a romance by Chrétien, who so often uses Gawain as a foil to his principal hero.

If Gawain is successful as a companion-in-arms but disastrous as a counsellor, and Lunet a most efficient counsellor and advocate, but powerless against armed force – '"wemen may maintene no stowre (*combat*)"' as the steward puts it (1221) – the lion combines the helpful virtues of both. Like Gawain, it is Ywain's companion,[20] and each will attack their common opponents more fiercely when the other is hard pressed (2605-7, 2631-6); like Lunet (757-60, it provides Ywain with food (2027-33), and once even manages to instruct him in the proper way to react to the loss of a loved one (2097-101).[21] Most important of all, it provides him with a new identity ('þe knight with þe lyoun') to replace the better-known name that he has discredited, and so gives him the chance to create a new reputation, rather different from the old.

He first names himself in the new way to Alundyne, the very person that, as Ywain, he had so badly betrayed (2661-2). Under this new title he soon becomes known as a knight who helps all in real need (2774-6), and is much sought after in consequence (2795-807). But the form of the title is significant. Ywain has not become 'the knight *of* the lion' (which could suggest no more than a heraldic image), but 'the knight *with* the lion', and its physical presence starkly reinforces the impact that he now makes. On the realistic level, it is at once a source of fear – 'Bot al þai fled for þe lyown' (2216) – and an index of its master's quality: '"He es of grete renowne, / For with hym dwels þe lyoun"' (2339-40). It also has a more emblematic force that is easily felt, but less easy to define, although there have been many attempts at doing so.[22]

Once he has become the Knight with the Lion, Ywain's motivation is different, and more noble, than it had been when he fought under his own name.[23] In addition, none of the adventures that he now meets with is deliberately sought out by him, so that each is essentially 'something that happens by chance' – a combination of MED *aventure* senses 2(a) and 1(a). Also noteworthy is the harsher, more 'realistic' texture of the world in which he moves. One aspect of this is the need to work to a strict timetable; Ywain, who had disastrously failed to do this in his dealings with Alundyne becomes involved in an adventure in which the life of the lady championed depends on his doing so. If he does not conclude his fight with the giant Harpyns in time, Lunet will infallibly be burnt (2373-5).

The third and most difficult of the combats in which the lion takes part is at the 'Castel of þe Hevy Sorow',[24] an episode that is close to that of the spring in its complexity and unpredictability, and would in some ways have provided a more impressive climax to the romance than the Ywain–Gawain duel that now follows it. It tells the following story:

> Once at the castle, Ywain is told by all he meets that he will suffer humiliation there. Undaunted, he goes in, and finds an enclosure in which many wretched maidens work at embroidery; an empty hall, and then a garden where a lord, a lady, and their daughter take their ease. He is told that he will not be allowed to leave without fighting with two powerful opponents; if he wins, the lord's heritage and daughter will be his. and the maidens will be set free. At first kept out of the fight, the lion finally breaks out of his prison, kills one enemy and maims the other. Ywain angers the lord by refusing both daughter and lands, but the prisoners are freed, amid general rejoicing. (2931-3358)[25]

Here the hero's opponents and their victims are alike distinctive. The first are designated '"champions"' (3017, 3066, 3146, 3156) and '"devils sons"' (3018, 3155), and both labels are justified. They are dressed and armed as the first (3157-62),[26] but prove invulnerable to normal weapons wielded by human opponents (3229-34); only the lion can get the better of them. Their female victims are captives who must work for starvation wages; the leisured accomplishment of romance heroines has become the basis of badly paid mass-production.[27] These features combine with others to draw attention to the darker sides of both the chivalric adventure and chivalry in general, and do so much more forcibly than had the earlier scenes at the spring. There the tempest generated by the questing knight is at worst a cause of annoyance to its guardian (409-12) or of fear to Alundyne and her subjects (3847-54), and the economic gains to Ywain of achieving that adventure, while solid enough, are not discreditable. His 'purchas' of lands and castles through his marriage is noted approvingly by the narrator (1445-8), and the only mildly cynical note is struck when Gawain comments, in an addition to the French:

'"Þou has inogh to þi despens (*spending*); / Now may þow wele hante (*frequent*) turnamentes"' (1469-70).

In the later episode, however, the misery of the captive ladies is said to arise directly from the folly and inadequacy of their young king, who – like Colgrevance – had been searching for adventures '"forto asay his owen body"' (3014), when he came to the castle. But once confronted with the two demi-devils ('"Geten of a woman with a ram"' (3019)), he had been forced to save his own life by promising an annual tribute of thirty maidens (3029-40). Their sweated labour could be said, retrospectively, to subsidize his adventure-seeking.

Even more suspect is the relation of the lord of the castle to the enforced combat with the champions. In 3129 and 3148 he blames this upon '"ane unsely law (*accursed regulation*)"', and a '"knawen (*acknowledged*) custum assise (*of long standing*)"', and so implies that he has no control over the champions, and may even be their prisoner. But in between these points he characterizes them as '"Grete serjantes (*servants*) of mekil myght"' (3133),[28] and his later behaviour towards Ywain is very much that of a man in authority. Most suggestive of all is the contrast between Ywain's first sight of him, lying on a cloth of gold with his wife and the daughter who reads to them 'a real (*noble*) romance' of (deliberately?) unspecified content (3088-90), and his earlier encounter with the underfed maidens in their torn smocks (2968-76). From one point of view this juxtaposition of the wretchedness of the many, and the leisured refinement of the few could be read as a metaphor for the economic basis of chivalry and even of romance itself.

The two episodes that follow, in which the lion plays no active part,[29] bring us to the end of the story, and to other aspects of the chivalric romance. In the first, the supreme valour of the two heroes is demonstrated in combat before the royal court; in the second, Ywain and Alundyne are reconciled. But even here questions are raised, and the claims of realism at least briefly acknowledged. Stupendous as it is, a bloody duel between two such noble companions is terribly wasteful, and a number of unsuccessful attempts are made to stop it (3571-4), before the combatants recognize each other; Arthur then intervenes, to give a judgement that sets a precedent for the bloodless settlement of other disputes of the same kind (*Friedman and Harrington*, pp.130-1). The last episode of all also has its unexpectedly violent side. As an act of desperation, Ywain returns to the spring and again casts water on the stone,[30] in a scene in which the emphasis shifts away from everything that had most charmed Colgrevance about the place – the precious stones and the magnificent tree with its singing birds – to the storm itself which becomes more devastating than ever. It also becomes a vital mechanism to produce a happy ending, by making it possible for Lunet – once again, and as deviously as before – to persuade Alundyne that she must secure the best of knights as her defender. And so, at long last, 'þe knyght with þe liown / Es turned . . . to Syr Ywayn' (4020-1), and he and Alundyne are able to live happily ever after. Against all the odds, love has survived, but the world of romance itself seems to have become subject to time, and grown older, more uncomfortably close to feudal reality.   **Maldwyn Mills**

Lybeaus Desconus

If the number of surviving copies of a medieval text is a reliable guide to its popularity, then the tail-rhyme *Lybeaus Desconus*[31] must have been the most popular of all the Middle English Arthurian romances;[32] no fewer than six copies of it have survived, five medieval, and one of the seventeenth century.[33] What is more, the differences between these are so pervasive and substantial that they can only be explained by supposing that there had once existed an even larger number of intermediate copies.[34] And even the best of those that have survived – British Library MS Cotton Caligula A.ii (C) – is so full of errors as to compel frequent reference to the others, in particular that of Lambeth Palace Library MS 306 (L).[35]

In structure *Lybeaus* is a classic Arthurian 'romance of adventure', with the hero of its title leaving the king's court in response to an appeal, made by a maiden accompanied by a dwarf, for a champion to release her lady of Synadowne[36] from a cruel imprisonment (C. 148-50). Not until much later does the hero learn that her gaolers are two enchanters, Maboun and Irayn, who have built a hall outside the city (1690-728). He enters this alone, to be confronted with an adventure as startling as any found in *Ywain*:

> At first only minstrels are seen and heard there; when these abruptly leave, a terrifying earthquake rocks the building. The enchanters then appear and attack Lybeaus with poisoned swords; Maboun is killed, but the wounded Irayn vanishes. After praying for help, the hero is kissed by a serpent with a woman's face, which is then transformed into the queen of Synadowne, who offers herself to him in marriage. (C. 1759-2037).

The special importance of this adventure is kept before us by allusions made to it (C. 456, 546, 996, 1444, 1464) in or between the preceding episodes. In these Lybeaus fights with a wide range of opponents: William Selebraunche, who defends a causeway; his three vengeful nephews; two gigantic abductors of a maiden; Sir Gyffroun le Fludous, who defends his mistress's claim to the prize of beauty; the huntsman-knight Sir Otes de Lyle and his vassals, and the giant Maugys who besieges a seductive enchantress, the Dame d'Amore, at the Yle d'Or. Some are known to his guides in advance, some are met with by chance; but although Lybeaus is several times described as an 'aunterous knyȝt', (1119, 1521, 1550) only the episode at the enchanters' hall is designated an 'aventure' (2070).

Near the beginning and end of the English romance the narrator cites a 'Frenssch tale' as the source of particular incidents (C. 222, 2122), and the second of these is also present at the same point in Renaut de Beaujeu's *Li Biaus Descouneüs* (*c.* 1190).[37] This romance has a great deal in common with *Lybeaus*, giving its own version of every one of the episodes there, as well as much of their detail, and about half of the names of the most important persons and places. But the differences are also striking: the order of the common episodes is as often different as not; even names and incidents identical in themselves may be reassigned, and the structure and sense of the narrative as a whole are radically altered by the absence from *Lybeaus* of two episodes that between them take up nearly the whole of the second half of *Descouneüs* (3675-5054, 5055-6092). These describe the hero's return to his real love, the lady of the Yle d'Or, and the tournament that Arthur proclaims to lure him away from her and assure his marriage to the queen of Synadowne.[38] Important in a different way is the general lack of close verbal parallels between the French and English texts, since this makes it only rarely possible to use the first to clarify any difficulties in the second, or to support a reading in one of the copies against its variants in the others.[39] If the English author[40] really did use *Descouneüs* as his primary source, he treated it with quite extraordinary freedom.

When the hero first appears at Arthur's court he admits that he is ignorant of his real name (already given as Gyngelayne by the narrator (L. 7)), and Arthur decrees that he shall be called Lybeaus Desconus, which he at once glosses as '"Þe Fayre Unknowe"' (C. 71). In its modern form this second title has served as label for a small but important group of romances in which the hero who – like Lybeaus and Descouneüs – is usually the son of Gawain, and is brought up by his mother well away from Arthur's court.[41] The French and English romances give very different accounts of this childhood; Descouneüs is educated in chivalry, but Lybeaus is not, and gets his first suit of armour by stripping it from the corpse of a knight. Appearance is turned into reality when Arthur knights him, and grants him the adventure at Synadowne (C. 73-5, 163-8). Elene, the 'lady messenger', is outraged that this '"chylde / Þat ys wytles and wylde"' should be preferred above so many knights of proven valour, but her hostility vanishes after the first of his victories on the way to Synadowne.[42]

In any case, the 'wildness' to which she had objected is not equally apparent in all the manuscript copies of *Lybeaus*, and in every one of them it coexists with more civilized behaviour. Whether intentionally or not, this mixture suggests a conflict between noble ancestry and ignoble upbringing, and brings it about that in this romance, action (or 'adventure' with a small 'a') more often exists for its own sake – or, at best, as proof of the hero's physical strength – than to exemplify any chivalric ideal; indeed, the few comments about how a knight should behave are as likely to proceed from the opponents as from the hero.[43] Only in his dealings with (and references to) Arthur is he unfailingly respectful and 'courtly', and no fewer than five of the tail-rhyme stanzas balance a polite request on his part with a matching response from the king (L. 49-60; C. 49-60, 85-96, 157-68, 241-52). The last of these comes just before their parting:

> Þe knyȝt to hors gan spryng
> And rod to Artour þe kyng
> And seyde, 'My lord hende: *gracious*
> Ȝef me þy blessynge,
> Anoon wythoute dwellynge:
> My wyll ys forto wende.'
> Artour hys hond vp haf   *raised*
> And his blessynge he hym yaf,
> As korteys kyng and hende;
> And seyde, 'God graunte þe grace
> And of spede space   *success, time*
> To brynge þe lady out of bende.'   *prison*

The two do not meet again until very near the end of the romance, when Arthur at last ventures beyond the limits of his court to escort Lybeaus and his bride back to Synadowne. More cut off from the main action than in *Ywain*, the king risks being diminished as well as upstaged by the hero. But both Lybeaus and Elene make him a significant presence in the action by frequently invoking his name: the first, as part of a challenge, or statement of intention; the second, to stiffen her companion's resolve, or shame him into action.[44] More explicit still is Lybeaus's praise of him at Synadowne as the '"man most of myȝtes, / And welle of curtesye / And flowr of chyualrye / To felle hys fon (*foes*) yn fyȝtes"' (C. 1527-30). Arthur had already done no less for him, and this reciprocity of esteem – foreshadowed with mathematical precision in the stanza quoted – finds tangible expression in Lybeaus's despatch of the falcon won from Gyffroun to the king, and the quantity of '"tresour"' that is then sent in return. And throughout the story defeated opponents – or their heads – are sent to court (C. 373-87, 523-37, 682-4,

1198-203; L. 1257-62). In marked contrast to the Arthur of *Ywain*, the Arthur of *Lybeaus* never deviates into either lethargy or (imagined) tyranny, but remains the solid as well as the still point of the turning world of the romance.

Although the king never comments on any 'wildness' in the hero, he does remark that he seems too young to fight really well; and assigns him to Gawain for training in arms. But the arrival of the messengers from Synadowne prevents this, and his father is then able to do no more than help in arming him (C. 229-31). Where Gawain is of crucial importance to Lybeaus is in their blood-relationship, since it is retrospectively claimed that only Gawain, or one of his kinsmen, had the power to restore the transformed queen to human shape. And as it happens, the lack of formal military training never really matters. Lybeaus does not have to rely solely on his firmness in the saddle to survive in combat. With William Selebraunche, his first opponent, he fights 'as a noble kny3t, / As werrour queynte (*skilful*) and scle3 (*crafty*)' (350-1) – even though he goes on to shave William's beard with his sword. This mixture of efficiency and unpredictability is sustained throughout the episodes that follow.

The behaviour of his opponents can be equally unpredictable, even when they are most concerned with the pursuits and procedures of chivalry. With both Lambard and Gyffroun le Fludous the fighting takes the form of carefully regulated jousts (904-72, 1516-638) in which lances with blunted, spreading heads ('coronals') are used; the participants charge at each other until one of them is unseated, and there is a large body of interested spectators. In the combat with Gyffroun, moreover, the individual strokes are recorded by umpires ('descouerours', 'dissoures' (C. 926; L. 955)), and the courtly tone is enhanced by earlier descriptions of the beauty of Elene and Gyffroun's lady, as they compete for the prize of the falcon (C. 832-43, 868-91). Nevertheless, not only is Gyffroun's back broken by the end of the joust, but each of these episodes begins with a preview of what defeat would have meant for Lybeaus that is quite at odds with any notion of courtly and civilized behaviour. The walls of Gyffroun's castle are fringed with the heads of previous contenders for the prize (C. 736-8), and outside the walls of Synadowne the sewage 'that men hade ere oute caste' (L. 1534) is diligently brought in again to hurl at any knight defeated by Lambard (C. 1468-73, 1498-500). In however exaggerated a form these juxtapositions suggest the disturbing paradoxes that underlie medieval chivalry.[45]

In the episodes set between these two it is the more savage and less regulated elements that prevail. The first (C. 1000-218) takes place in a forest where the theft of a marvellous hunting dog from Sir Otes de Lyle

compels Lybeaus to fight against two bands of that lord's retainers. He fights
so fiercely that they identify him with the 'fend Satan', hem him in like a wild
beast, and make the blood pour from him like a waterfall; he responds by
cutting off three horses' heads with an axe. This is so very extreme that one
is tempted to see it as a parody of the more 'heroic' mode of native romance
writing.[46] The same mode is evoked in the episode which follows (C. 1231-
398), where the enemy is Maugys, a giant 'as blak as ony pych', who
worships Termagant, and has three images of Mahomet on his shield. Rather
surprisingly, this begins – like the jousts with Gyffroun and Lambard – with a
mounted charge with lances, but it quickly turns savage, each combatant
deliberately beheading the other's horse, and after this there seem to be few
rules of any kind; even the truce agreed to allow Lybeaus to drink is broken
when Maugys knocks him into the river, prompting the hero to joke about
his 'baptism' (C. 1336-62).

None of these distinctively 'heroic' features is found in *Descouneüs*.
Malgiers li Gris, the counterpart of Maugys, is unpleasant enough for the
spectators to pray for his defeat (*Descouneüs* 2161-4; cp. C. 1297-302), and
– like Gyffroun – sets up the heads of defeated opponents on stakes,[47] but he
is certainly not a Saracen giant. And the vassals of Orgoillous de la Lande,
the counterpart of Otes, do no more than help to arm their lord. These
features are not present in any other romances of the Fair Unknown, either,
but – together with a number of others – they are to be found in a handful of
Middle English romances, almost all of which are contained in the
Auchinleck manuscript (National Library of Scotland MS Advocates 19.2.1)
of *c*. 1330-40.[48] The echoing of these romances in *Lybeaus* heightens its
'Englishness', no less than its heroic aspect, and the two that throw most
light on the combats with Otes and Maugys are *Bevis of Hamtoun* and *Guy
of Warwick*. The first contributed the idea (and some of the detail) of a
woodland battle against superior numbers; the second, the knocking of the
hero into the river by a Saracen giant.

Since Guy's lengthy combat with Amoraunt is certainly the source of this
part of Lybeaus's fight with Maugys, a comparison of the two scenes helps
us to form a notion of the *modus operandi* of our author. What it makes very
clear is that he not only greatly abbreviated his source-material – whether for
the sake of narrative economy, or to emphasize the hero's importance – but
also altered the focus of the whole, and left the occasional loose end, by
redistributing and reassigning individual details. Since these same practices
would account for some of the differences between *Descouneüs* and
Lybeaus, it becomes tempting to argue that, after all, the first of these works
was indeed the primary source of the second. But some important difficulties

remain in the way of this assumption, such as the fact that, while the early scenes at Arthur's court certainly suggest the garbling of material in the source, it is not *Descouneüs* but Wirnt von Gravenberc's *Wigalois* that provides the most likely antecedent for what we have in *Lybeaus*.[49]

The range of incident and register, and the distinctive 'Englishness', produced by this eclectic mode of composition must have contributed to the unusual popularity of *Lybeaus*. At the same time its – equally characteristic – gaps and inconsistencies puzzled some of its scribes enough to make them turn redactors themselves, by altering, deleting or adding to what they found in their copy. Such patchwork revision was made easier by the self-contained nature of the twelve-line stanza, and of the three-line units within it.

The work of the most radical of these scribe-redactors is preserved in the texts contained in Bodleian Library Oxford MS Ashmole 61 and Biblioteca Nazionale Naples MS XIII B.29. His most obvious concern was with such oddities as the amalgam of Saracen giant and knight in black armour in Maugys, or the seeming determination of Lambard to humiliate the very knight who had come to rescue his queen from the enchanters. The first problem was solved by emphasizing the gigantic nature of Maugys in an extra stanza after L. 1316, and – by altering C. 1291-3 – making him fight on foot throughout. The second was addressed by replacing the allusion to muck-gathering in C. 1471-506 with two stanzas, in the first of which Lambard in his turn became a giant keeping a lady prisoner; suspicions of his integrity were voiced and answered in a third new stanza, inserted after C. 1650.[50] The other concern of such scribe-redactors was to make good the absence in the copy of motifs thought essential to the proper conduct of the narrative. One obvious deficiency was the lack of any reunion of the hero with his father and mother at the end of the story, and the gap was filled by writing in three stanzas after the description of the wedding feast in C 2107-18.[51] The mother turns up first, recognizes her son and identifies him to Gawain, who admits his fatherhood, blesses Lybeaus and tells everyone to call him Gyngelayne in future.

More clearly than any other Middle English Arthurian romance, Lybeaus shows how such works might be treated, by the scribes who transmitted them, as anything but achieved and inviolable literary artefacts. There were undeniably some things in them that could not be altered – the main personnel, general drift of the action, conclusion – but almost everything else could be, and was. Texts were not simply recreated, as they are now often held to be, in successive acts of re-reading, but also in successive acts of rewriting, and these expressed any latent narrative possibilities more succinctly, and in more permanent form.   **Maldwyn Mills**

Sir Landevale, Sir Launfal, Sir Lambewell

Marie de France's *lai* of *Lanval*,[52] the only one in her collection to have an explicitly Arthurian setting,[53] was probably translated into English in the first half of the fourteenth century.[54] This translation is now lost but texts descended from it show that it must have been written in four-stress couplets, often rendering Marie's octosyllabic original very closely. The lost translation gave rise to two different lines of development of which the first, or mainstream, line, consists of a series of texts which retain the couplet form and are best regarded as developing revisions of the same poem, though almost all render the hero's name a little differently and therefore tend to be given different titles.[55] The earliest and best surviving exemplar in this group is the poem usually known as *Sir Landevale*.[56] Even this, however, though clearly not far from the original, is found only in a manuscript assignable, at earliest, to the last years of the fifteenth century. This late date bears witness to the enduring popularity of the couplet version, whose variant texts show a process of continuous expansion and reworking over a period of two or three centuries. One, known as *Sir Lamwell*, was printed at least twice in the sixteenth century;[57] the tradition did not end until a seventeenth-century scribe copied the last of the line into the famous Percy Folio under the title of *Sir Lambewell*.[58] These two later texts clearly stand much closer to each other than either does to *Sir Landevale*, though deriving ultimately from the same source.[59] Only *Sir Landevale* and *Sir Lambewell* survive complete, but the Percy text is almost a hundred lines longer, reflecting a tendency to verbal inflation while adding nothing of substance to the plot. *Sir Landevale* is thus the best representative of a far more crisp and succinct original, *Sir Lambewell* its last extant revision.

Popular as it evidently was, however, the couplet tradition is today largely overshadowed by a second, far more radical redaction made towards the end of the fourteenth century by a minor poet of whom nothing is known but his name, Thomas Chestre.[60] Although he adopted a large number of lines direct from his couplet source, Chestre remodelled the text in the more up-to-date tail-rhyme stanza, adding several new episodes and greatly increasing the story's length. In his hands, what had been a modest lay now became the full-blown chivalric romance of *Sir Launfal*. It is this text which has received the greatest critical attention as well as being much better served by its editors,[61] but there is no evidence that it ever gained in its own time the popularity evidently enjoyed by the couplet version.

The *Lanval* story has long been recognized as an independent folk-tale[62] with no original Arthurian connection. It tells of a noble and generous young man, undeservedly impoverished and neglected by his king. A mysterious and beautiful lady comes to his aid, offering him her love and inexhaustible wealth provided he does not speak of her. It is clearly implied that she is a magical being, who will vanish should he break his vow of silence. Returning to court he is provoked by the proud and promiscuous queen into boasting of his lady's beauty, and challenged to prove his claims by producing her at a public trial. Having broken his promise he cannot do so; but she vindicates him by appearing in the court nonetheless, and he departs with her to her own country.

Some version of this story was presumably taken over by Marie from a Breton, or even an insular British, source,[63] and attached to the court of a king whose name was just beginning to resonate excitingly in French literary circles. Other versions are known which do not mention Arthur, including the anonymous Breton *lai* of *Graelent*,[64] and some of the story's separate components, such as the fairy mistress[65] and the vengeful queen,[66] are also common narrative motifs in their own right.

Marie is one of the earliest writers to adopt the previously historical (or pseudo-historical) Arthurian setting for a romance. Her main source of information is usually thought to have been Wace,[67] from whom she could have derived her dubious portrayal of Arthur's queen[68] as well as the concept of Arthur as a real king ruling a real country. Marie calls his land *Loengre* but this is not the mysterious, unlocalized *Logres* of Chrétien de Troyes: it is England, invaded from the north by Picts and Scots whom, at the start of *Lanval*, Arthur has gone north to fight. This is why his court is located, logically enough, at Carlisle, though no previous author had placed it there.[69] Perhaps also unexpected is her portrayal of Arthur as an irascible and callous *roi fainéant*, neglecting his knights and apparently preferring the hunt to the battlefield. This is not from Wace,[70] who had portrayed a heroic king; but Marie's own life may have taught her that the court of a historically real Arthur might also be subject to the usual political realities. Though a Frenchwoman, Marie is thought to have lived and worked in England,[71] and bitter experience has been read in the poignancy with which she draws attention to her hero's plight, alone and unvalued at a foreign court.[72] This forms a genuine sub-theme of her story.

The details of Lanval's trial, though probably owing something to a literary source, have been shown to reflect the actual practices and terminology of an appeal for felony, another realistic element in what is too readily seen as an idealized tale of magic.[73] The role of Gawain is significant here. The *Graelent* analogue suggests that it was Marie who created the part of the hero's only friend at court and assigned it to Gawain, who volunteers to go bail for Lanval and alone supports him in the course of the trial. This image of chivalrous male companionship anchors the tale firmly in its new romance context. It also foreshadows the sympathetic portrayal of Gawain in later English Arthurian tradition, though Marie was presumably building on hints derived from Wace, where already Gawain is wise and courteous, a man of *mesure*,[74] countering Cador's belligerence with praise of peace.[75] Moreover, the particular pursuits of peace which Gawain advocates in Wace, the bonding of lovers and the arts of love, are precisely those which characterize the secret and enclosed world into which Lanval's mistress has drawn him, and which have led him to this crisis. Gawain's efforts on his behalf, protecting his interests and acting as his liaison with the court, therefore contrast somewhat ironically with Lanval's marked passivity, affected by events rather than initiating them, a self-absorbed lover helpless on the fringe of a politically aware society.

By the time *Lanval* was translated into English some century and a half later, the whole literary climate had changed. The English language, so long eclipsed as a literary medium, had at last begun to emerge from the shadow of French, and the chivalric romance had taken root as the dominant form of secular narrative.[76] The Arthurian legend had also become a familiar topic in the land of its origin, though English audiences seem to have preferred stories about its old-established characters, not otherwise unknown knights like Lanval. English romances also tend to be anonymous, the product of a shared culture rather than of named authors, supplying the needs of an audience with a different range of interests from Marie's: lower down the social scale, probably more mixed in background and with a literary experience based less on book-learning, more on the (originally) oral effects and structures of the traditional tale. A dramatic pattern of events, vividly conveyed, often seems preferred to subtle thematic undercurrents reflecting an author's individual bias, and characters tend to take on the clearly defined outlines of folk-tale types.

    Sir Landevale is thus a very different kind of poem from *Lanval.*[77] Though clearly reflecting a process of written composition – many lines are straight translation – its effects are often oral and dramatic: there is, for instance, far more direct utterance, the narration conveyed by the voices of the characters which often strike the ear with colloquial bluntness.[78] The poem's thematic subtlety is also changed. Almost gone is Marie's conceptual dichotomy between a historically conceived, politically manipulative Arthurian court and an enclosed, self-contained world of love, secretly inhabited by Lanval until his rash action shatters it. Arthur's court is still at Carlisle but not to fight Picts and Scots. Now it is simply an established locus of valour and delight to which young knights gravitate and where gifts are freely distributed 'to eache man of honour' (16), including Landevale, whose destitution, when it comes, is due not to his king's neglect but to his own excessive *largesse*. Far from being an isolated alien, Landevale is thus redefined as that favourite romance figure, the 'Spendthrift Knight'.[79] His reaction to his fall from affluence is expressed in two brief laments that have no parallel in Marie. They contain a passing allusion to his status as a stranger (27) but their main thrust is quite different: without money he will have lost the respect of his peers, his integration into the chivalric brotherhood. All this reveals a marked change of attitude: not only is Arthur's court too well-known to need explaining and Arthur himself too magnificent for meanness, but shame has become the major motivating factor that drives Landevale from the public gaze, not loneliness or neglect.

The 'alien' theme is similarly lost in the scenes of accusation and trial. Gawain still stands surety for Landevale, but the knightly fraternity does not reject its comrade in this court where the queen's promiscuity is an open secret. She, moreover, plays a far more prominent role in the trial scene, screaming vindictively for vengeance. The grave precision of the appeal for felony has gone and the scene is conceived in strongly theatrical terms as a climactic drama, with all characters present on stage and emotions bared.

If feelings are more explicit in *Sir Landevale*, so too is magic. The lady in *Lanval* is never called *fée* and her origins are not explored; she simply says that she has come from far away, a kind of parallel to Lanval himself, another stranger in a strange land. Even the *Avalun* to which she finally departs is no more than a very beautiful island, not manifestly magical.[80] In *Sir Landevale*, however, the concept of a mysterious Otherworld approaches objective existence. The lady's magnificent tent is identified as the work of fairies (80) and although her island home has been transmuted (probably by prosaic scribal error) into *Amylion*, it has become a fairy island (93), and she its king's daughter. More interesting than these overt statements, however, is the allusive treatment of Landevale's journey to meet the fay, which the translator has transformed, by a series of apparently casual references to noonday heat and trees, into a subtle forewarning of an imminent encounter with the Otherworld.[81] Very similar passages occur in two other English lays of the period, *Sir Orfeo* and *Sir Degaré*,[82] where again they serve as preludes to an incursion from a mysterious but clearly conceived parallel world, bright and numinous, whose denizens are able to make forays – usually sexual, often violent – into the everyday world when the sun is at its height. Whereas in *Sir Orfeo* and *Sir Degaré* a female victim is ruthlessly seized, in *Sir Landevale* the male hero falls in love willingly, indicating again his passive tendency to be borne along by events, just as in the end he is borne off to Amylion on his lady's steed.

This beautiful but ominous Otherworld, reflecting the ease with which popular belief and chivalric setting can coexist in these English lays, is almost absent in Marie's, though its characteristic ruthlessness is clearly adumbrated. Fairies, notoriously, stand rigidly by a given word, so neither Lanval nor Landevale can expect to be saved once they have broken their promise of silence; but the romance genre also portrays these fairies as ideal courtly mistresses whose perfection is expressed in their capacity for mercy, which demands a happy ending. So too do the conventions of folk-tale.[83] For Lanval however there is no word of mercy: he simply leaps upon his lady's horse and disappears, unforgiven. Sir Landevale, in contrast, pleads and, although at first rejected, is finally reconciled.[84]

A brief look at *Sir Lambewell*, last and longest of the couplet texts, reveals evident uneasiness with some aspects of its subject matter.[85] The treatment of the Arthurian material is generally respectful, but the magic, so interestingly emphasized in *Sir Landevale*, has gone. The lady, splendid and regal, is no fairy, though apparently ruthless to the last.[86] Despite the extension of the scene of pleading to include support from the king, she speaks no words of forgiveness before taking Lambewell off to the 'jolly iland' of 'Amilion' where, mundanely, both eventually die. The mystery of the Otherworld has no place in this seventeenth-century text,[87] whose redactor falls back on the language of religious hyperbole to create a sense of awe.[88]

Before the couplet text had run its course, however, a version of it had served as the basis for Chestre's much-elaborated *Sir Launfal*.[89] Noteworthy are the increased references to Arthur's court and its personnel, clearly familiar and popular, and the absence of the scene of pleading and forgiveness at the end, which suggests that Chestre may have worked from a text into which this had not yet entered.[90] The magical forewarnings implicit in the scene of noonday heat and trees are fully present, but though the lady's country is identified as 'Fayrye' (280) her tent is the work of Saracens only, exotic but not magical. Chestre, in other words, was more interested in earthly wonders, and specifically earthly action, as exemplified in the episodes he adds which allow the hitherto passive hero to show his skills in the tournament. For these chivalric additions Chestre is thought to have drawn on two analogues of the Lanval story, one of which included a joust.[91] The other was *Graelent*, in which the antipathy of the vicious queen emerges before, not after, the hero's fall from favour and is indeed the cause of it. In adopting this structure Chestre centres the focus of evil on Guinevere from the start and so distances Arthur still further from blame. This early appearance of the queen's spite has been seen as a flaw, as it seems to conflict with her later attempt to seduce Launfal, but her obsessive switch from hate to desire is not inexplicable in human terms and current criticism of *Sir Launfal* tends to be less concerned with psychological, novelistic 'realism'. The emotional polarity of chivalrous, male bonding against the vicious Queen is, however, even more marked, as is the contrast between the loyal and disloyal courtly lady.

A marked lowering of the social tone has been noted in *Sir Launfal*,[92] especially in the scenes where Launfal lodges in his disgrace with the mayor of Caerleon, mocked by the populace and unable even to find a clean shirt. The outline of this episode also comes from *Graelent*, but Chestre's treatment is far more astringent, with its portrayal of the mayor as a fair-weather friend who rejects Launfal after his fall from favour – a bourgeois transformation of his rejection by the king in *Lanval*, but one which leads in exactly the same way to his departure from the town and his meeting with the fay.

Though the succinct and well-told story in *Sir Landevale* reveals the clean bones of its folk-tale structure, some of the additions in *Sir Launfal*, far from obscuring that structure with unnecessary padding, have been shown to bring it still closer to the type: these include the fairy's gift of the horse as well as her ruthlessly logical blinding of Guinevere in fulfilment of the rash words the queen herself had uttered,[93] all related in the spare, folk-tale style which deliberately eschews indulging in the sensual or emotional dimension of the actions described. The predominance of action over characterization also recalls folk-tale, whose heroes tend, like Lanval, to move unquestioningly from event to event without attempting to control their course. From the same genre comes the principle that the good will be rewarded and that luck will turn when fortunes are at the lowest ebb. This wish-fulfilment element has long been recognized in the *Lanval* story,[94] though not always with reference to the folk-tale genre. The story, after all, does not end in the traditional way with the hero and his bride establishing themselves as a new and independent family unit in the world. Instead Lanval and his fairy mistress vanish out of this world altogether. This withdrawal may be one reason why a recent psychoanalytic approach to *Sir Launfal* in particular has been so hard on it, identifying in the story the ultimate male erotic fantasy, and Chestre's full-blooded acceptance of it an act of naïve ineptitude.[95]

Elizabeth Williams

Sir Percyvell of Gales

Sir Percyvell has survived in a single manuscript copy of the mid-fifteenth century, contained in Lincoln, Dean and Chapter Library, MS 91;[96] that the original romance was in existence by the latter part of the fourteenth century is proved by an allusion to it in Chaucer's *Sir Thopas*.[97] It is composed in tail-rhyme stanzas of sixteen lines,[98] roughly three-quarters of which are linked by repeating some or all of the words in the last line of one in the first line of the next. This emphasizes both the continuity of the narrative, and its dynamic forward impetus – 'His way rydes he. / Now on his way rydes he' (480-1).[99]

An earlier and much fuller version of the same story is the *Perceval* of Chrétien de Troyes,[100] but the relationship of the two is even less close than that of *Lybeaus* to *Descouneüs*. Not only is almost the whole of the second half of the French narrative lacking in the English one, but its first half contains episodes unknown to the latter, and lacks episodes present there. Altogether the differences between the two texts are so great as to rule out the possibility that the English romance could have been derived directly from a written copy of the French one, and it is tempting to suppose that it goes back to another, more primitive, antecedent.[101] But the possibility of a very free and intermittent use of *Perceval* remains;[102] it would, among other things, explain how detail concentrated in a single episode there is diffused through several episodes in *Percyvell*.[103]

Episodes common to both texts tell us that

> after the death of his father, the hero is brought up by his mother in a forest, away from the life of chivalry and its attendant dangers. But a chance meeting with knights determines him to become one himself, and he sets out for Arthur's court, meeting on the way a solitary lady from whom he takes a ring. Before Arthur can knight him, he dashes off in pursuit of a Red Knight who has snatched away the king's gold cup; he kills him, dons his armour, and sends the cup back to Arthur. He next goes to the help of a lady besieged by a powerful suitor, whom he defeats, and wins the lady's love. Arthur and some of his knights search for the hero, who fights with at least one of them before speaking with the king. Later he again meets the lady from whom he had taken the ring, and defeats her jealous lover in combat.[104]

The most substantial of the episodes common to both romances is the rescue of the besieged lady, but the English text lacks those that immediately precede and follow this in *Perceval*: the hero's stay at the castle of Gornemant de Gorhaut (the uncle of the lady in question), where he is instructed in both the military and moral aspects of chivalry;[105] and his visit to the Grail castle, where he fails to ask questions about what he sees there.

For this he is later reproached by no fewer than three separate characters: his female cousin, a messenger to Arthur's court, and his hermit-uncle. All three, together with the episodes in which they appear, are also lacking in the English romance.

Despite a very perfunctory ending, in which Perceval journeys to the Holy Land and is killed there, the English version of the story is not left obviously incomplete, as the French is. Since there is no Grail Castle, there are no questions to be asked, and no silence on the hero's part to blame or to rectify. The hero's mother (here named Acheflour, and the sister of Arthur), does not die when he leaves her – a further cause of reproach to the French Perceval – but survives to be reunited with him. Not found in *Perceval* are the elaborate introductory story of the hero's father (rather confusingly of the same name) that ends with his death at the hands of the Red Knight his son is later to kill; the episode involving the mother of this knight; a second uncle of the hero's (this time paternal) with nine sons; and the brother of the sultan Gollerotherame (the enemy of Lufamour, the besieged lady), who has become the rather unlikely suitor of Perceval's mother.

Whatever the source of its components, the English narrative has a very tight and satisfying structure, which underlines the importance of family relationships to the romance. Even the preliminary story of the father is less detached from what follows than might at first appear,[106] since Perceval's ignorance of it is balanced by the obsessive concern of Arthur, the dead man's brother-in-law. The climactic adventure at the Maydenlande, which takes up over a third of the whole (953-1772), is more nearly central than final, and most of the shorter episodes around it are linked, either because they involve characters who are kin to each other, or because the second of the pair is the necessary conclusion of the first. Near the end of the story, the hero meets again, in reverse order, the two ladies he had harmed near the beginning of it: the mother he had left to fend for herself in the woods (425-32), and the sleeping lady who had been ill-used by her lover, the Black Knight, after Perceval had exchanged rings with her (469-80, 1821-64). He makes amends by forcing this knight to forgive the lady (1913-44), and by finding his mother, restoring her to sanity, and bringing her back with him to his kingdom (2209-80).[107]

The extent to which the claims of kinship are compatible with the ideals and practice of chivalry varies a good deal. In the opening sections there is no problem, since the chivalric excellence of the elder Perceval was precisely what led the king to give him his own sister Acheflour in marriage (21-4). Equally, his death at the hands of the Red Knight is a blow to chivalry in general as well as a cause of grief to his family, and Perceval's reciprocal

killing of that knight is not only an act of private (if unintentional) revenge,
but eliminates a source of repeated humiliation to the king at his own table –
' "Fyftene ȝeres hase he þus gane / And my coupes fro me tane!" ' (633-4).

But when Perceval and Arthur first meet there is no such comfortable
accommodation of the two ideals. The boy's conception of chivalry is very
limited, but very insistent: ' "Bot if (*unless*) þe kyng make me knyghte, / To-
morne I sall hym sloo!" ' (383-4). Arthur, although intermittently
sympathetic, is preoccupied with familial concerns: Perceval's resemblance to
his dead brother-in-law reduces him to tears, and his obsessive mutterings
seriously try the boy's patience (574-6). Later, this combination of impotence
and grief is even more marked; the apparent loss of the younger as well as
the elder Perceval makes the king take to his sickbed, from which he gives a
dishearteningly unchivalric response to the messenger who has come from
the Maydenlande to seek help for Lufamour: ' "The mane þat es seke and
sare, / He may full ill ferre fare (*journey*), / In felde forto fyght." ' (1078-80).

In conjunction with the preceding scene – in which the same messenger
sought help from the hero's paternal uncle – this can be seen as a highly
original reworking of the familiar motif of chivalric romance in which a
messenger seeks help for a distressed lady at Arthur's court. The motif has
been split in two, with a redistribution of roles very little to the king's credit.
The necessary hero is no longer with Arthur, but with his other, paternal
uncle, where he gives the messenger a whole-hearted response to his appeal
(1005-20). But at Arthur's court no hero seems available, since the king is
not only helpless, but represents all his knights as unworthy as well (1087-8).
The news that Perceval is alive and active appears to cure both king and
knights of their debility, and they too set off for the Maydenlande (1109-20).
But – as in *Ywain* – the hero who had ridden off alone arrives at the scene of
the principal adventure before the others can get there.

Until this sudden access of vitality, Arthur's behaviour has given almost
literal force to the hero's earlier boast that ' "I am als grete a lorde als he" '
(814), and could account for the fact that Perceval never returns to his court,
even though he is related to three of its principal knights (261-4) as well as
to Arthur himself. Nor is there ever any hint that he considers himself as
Arthur's representative, as Lybeaus so notably does – that he never sends
back any prisoners to the king[108] is less significant, as he rarely leaves any of
his opponents alive. And though he is ultimately knighted by the king (1638),
he continues to resist assimilation to the court and to anything it may stand
for.

The episode at the Maydenlande contains the only scenes of large-scale
fighting in Perceval's story,[109] inviting comparison with the preliminary story

of his father, which devotes so much of its space to the description of tournaments. They certainly have points of detail in common: the lady watching from the walls (59-60; 1399-401); the splendid marriage (18-48; 1737-44); the rage of a humiliated opponent (83-96; 1609-24). But in other ways they could hardly be more different. The battle is fiercer than even the most unbridled of tournaments, with the hero single-handedly massacring hordes of the enemy on his first two days there – 'Made þe Sarezenes hedebones / Hoppe als dose hayle-stones, / Abowtte one þe gres.' (1190-2);[110] in the same part of *Perceval* the two sides are rather more evenly balanced. Within *Percyvell* the only explanation of his phenomenal success is given retrospectively, when we learn that the ring acquired before his first meeting with Arthur made its wearer invulnerable in battle (1855-64).

This central episode tells us a good deal about the hero's distinctive character, and its antecedents. His exalted parentage ('nature') but lack of the upbringing proper to it ('nurture') could have produced behaviour that was alternately courtly and gross, as in the hero of *Lybeaus*. But while some variation is detectable in his speech,[111] his actions are consistently those of a boy whose mother had taught him 'nowþer nurture ne lare' (*(book) learning*) (231-2). Lufamour who had seen him perform 'nothyng bot werkes wylde' (1570), is amazed that 'he was so styffe in stour (*battle*) / And couthe so littill of nurtour' (1566-7); Arthur explains the 'wildness' in terms of his fifteen years in the forest (1580-4), but does not mention that the boy's valour might come from his father, who had been 'a styffe body on a stede, / Wapynes to welde' (19-20). Only the mother acknowledges the force of heredity, when she sees him come riding home for the first time: 'Scho wiste wele, by þat thynge, / Þat þe kynde (*nature*) wolde oute sprynge' (354-5).

He never receives the formal training in chivalry that would make good the shortcomings of his life in the forest. He is in too much of a hurry to allow Arthur to give him the armour he has gone to fetch for him (649-54), or to allow his other uncle to do more than give him his nine sons as companions – in any case he does not want them, and soon gets rid of them (1021-44). When he is on the point of leaving her, his mother teaches him a few precepts, but these – like others given earlier[112] – are liable to be misapplied, usually with comic effect. Her injunction to be 'of mesure' makes him divide all the food he finds in the lady's hall into two exact portions (445-62); her advice to burn a broken shaft out of its metal head determines him to burn the corpse of the Red Knight out of the armour that baffles him by its complexity (741-64).[113] Only Gawain – who had encouraged him in his desire to be made a knight – gives him any practical instruction, and even this is limited and (necessarily) unsystematic. He is able to show him how to remove the Red Knight's armour without damaging it by fire (781-8); later still, he tells him how to continue the fight with the sultan once he has unhorsed him (1685-8). Between these two points, however, he actually fights with him, as the result of misunderstanding on both sides, though much more briefly than in the comparable episode in *Ywain* (1469-76).

After he has been made a knight, and Arthur and his companions have left the Maydenlande, he spends an idyllic year there: 'With Lufamour, his lemman, / He thoughte on no thyng' (1771-2). Immediately after this both the narrator and the hero remark that he has completely forgotten his mother and her privations (1773-88) – which makes Lufamour sound less like a legally married wife than an enchantress who keeps him from moving on to his proper objective – more like Lybeaus's Dame d'Amore than his Queen of Synadowne.[114] Equally unexpected is the fact that on leaving he shows signs of orthodox piety for the first time: 'A preste he made forthe bryng, / Hym a messe forto syng' (1806-7). But he returns to his old self when he meets, successively, with the lady of the hall and her Black Knight, and with the giant brother. After killing the latter, he resumes the search for his mother in a scene in which the chivalric life gives way to the claims of kinship even more impressively than in the first two appearances of Arthur in the romance.

The chief difference is that, while his king's repudiation of chivalry was passive and lachrymose, his own is dynamic and positive. Once he has learned of his mother's madness, he decides to put aside both horse and armour, and seek her out where he had first left her (2169-88); this strikingly contradicts his early view of these outward and visible signs of knighthood as indispensable. Admittedly, his present laying of them aside is a practical and temporary measure, essential if he is to get close enough to his mother to help her, but it creates a powerful visual symbol of regression – travelling on foot, dressed in a goatskin, he becomes once again what he had been when he lived with her in the forest. Of course it does not last, and he returns with his mother to receive a great welcome in the Maydenlande. But that does not last either, for he is almost immediately on his travels again, this time to the Holy Land (2281-4). In some romances, this would imply a shift of emphasis from the life of 'secular chivalry' to that of 'celestial chivalry', but the allusion is so completely militant – 'Wanne many cites full strong' (2282) – that the second concept, like the first, must here be understood in a very personal and limited sense. What the passage does bring out is the fact that Perceval is not only the most endearingly comic but the most purely energetic of Arthurian heroes. This energy is an inherited quality – once again the family asserts itself – since it had informed all the actions of his father. But while the older hero had found that his vitality could receive full expression within the limits and life-style of traditional Arthurian chivalry, the younger one is too restless to imitate him; he can only be satisfied with a life of perpetual movement, and is prepared to go anywhere to ensure its continuance.

Whatever the impulse behind this restlessness may be, it is never said to be a search for adventure; indeed – in contrast to *Perceval* – the word itself is never once used in this romance; after leaving the lady of the hall, what Perceval looks for are 'moo selles' (*more marvels*) (482), not more adventures. But explicit marvels are also in short supply; the witch-mother of the Red Knight is never given the chance to demonstrate her powers, and Lufamour is never actually said to use magic to keep the hero with her. And for all its length and complexity, and the fact that it is deliberately sought out by the hero, the fighting at the Maydenlande constitutes an 'adventure' of a radically different kind from those at the magic spring in *Ywain*, and at Synadowne in *Lybeaus*. However formidable, it quite lacks the impressive strangeness of these last, standing closer to what the hero's exploits in the Holy Land might have been like, and perhaps explaining why the author chose to dismiss these in four lines. Once was probably enough for one so concerned with narrative economy, patterns and proportions.

Maldwyn Mills

Sir Tristrem

Sir Tristrem has survived in a single copy preserved in National Library of Scotland MS 19.2.1 (the Auchinleck MS), and, like many other items of this collection, it is defective, lacking some 11 or 12 stanzas at its end.[115] But a fair idea of the missing conclusion can be obtained from the fragmentary Anglo-Norman *Tristan* of Thomas, the ultimate source of the English romance;[116] though itself very seriously defective in the earlier parts of the story, it is fortunately complete at the end.

Difficulties of another kind can be created by the unusual stanza[117] and the style of the English romance, sometimes lyrical, very often dramatic, but always exceptionally terse, with frequent omissions of linking or explanatory detail, and disruption of the linear progress of the narrative.[118] Although one soon gets used to supplying what is unexpressed, and rearranging detail that has become jumbled, it is still occasionally necessary to go over the text a second time, or even to consult the relevant part of Thomas's poem, or – where this is defective – its German or Norse derivatives.[119] Even personal names may be ambiguous:

> Tristremes loue was strong
> On swete Ysonde, þe quene;

> Of Ysonde he made a song,
> Þat song Ysonde bidene.   *sang, indeed*
> Þe maiden wende al wrong,   *supposed*
> Of hir it hadde y-bene.
> Hir wening was so long,   *(mis)understanding*
> To hir fader hye gan mene   *she, speak*
> For nede.
> Ysonde with hand schene   *white*
> Tristrem to wiue þai bede.   *offered*
> (*McNeill*, 2652-62)

It is not immediately apparent here that the lady mentioned in the fourth line is no longer Ysonde of Ireland, the wife of Mark, but – as in the tenth line – Ysonde of Brittany, with whom Tristrem will contract an experimental and frustrating marriage. But this stanza also communicates the forcefulness of the *Tristrem*-style. The short ('bob'-)line at once checks the flow of the eight that precede it, and throws into relief the special importance of the statement made in the two that follow. This effect is even more striking when the first eight lines are essentially lyrical rather than dramatic (as in 12-22 and 1728-38).

This consistently laconic style allows the poem to cover more narrative ground than any other English Arthurian romance of comparable length, and most particularly the stanzaic *Morte Arthur*, which also tells of a queen who becomes the mistress of her husband's greatest knight. In this, however, the story does not open until long after the beginning of Lancelot's affair with Guenevere, whereas *Tristrem* not only charts the progress of its hero's love for Ysonde from the fateful drinking of the love-potion, but devotes almost as much space to narrating his youth and first heroic deeds (243-1643); earlier still, it gives an account of those of his father, Rouland. Specific allusions increase our awareness of the passage of time. We are told that Tristrem spends two years in settling Ermonie (Brittany) after winning it back from Morgan, his father's murderer (903); lies for three years on his sickbed after fighting with Moraunt, the Irish oppressor of Mark (1121); spends three years at court after persuading the king of the innocence of his love (2170-71), and nearly a year in exile with Ysonde when their love is proved beyond doubt (2508). The unusually wide chronological range gives to *Tristrem* something of the aspect of a romance biography – perhaps even of a saga – as well as a chivalric romance.

Its status as chivalric romance is established both by the actions and the instincts of its hero. He prefers to fight alone rather than as part of a group,[120] and will at once engage in any adventure that presents itself: a combat with an Irish dragon (1409-85); an attack on the abductors of his namesake's lady (3296-344). His role as one of the two supreme lovers of Arthurian literature is determined by his drinking of the love-potion, at a point almost exactly mid-way through the romance – 'Her (*their*) loue miȝt no man tvin (*bring to an end*) / Til her ending day' (1671-2) – and this makes him still more likely to act on his own behalf. In the first half of the romance he had fought for Mark and his subjects against Moraunt, the giant demanding a tribute of English youths and money (984-1089), and later undertook for his king the dangerous courtship of Ysonde, Moraunt's niece (1365-75); after drinking it, he wins back Ysonde from her Irish abductor, as much for his own sake as the king's, and with his true reward coming not from anything that Mark may offer but from a week of uninterrupted love-making with the queen before they return to court (1849-925). His motives can be equally personal when he later finds himself in the service of the Breton Duke Florentin, father of Ysonde of Brittany. At first, he does this duke great service, imposing peace in his lands, and winning back territory he has lost (2643-6); but after his marriage to this second Ysonde proves a failure, he acts with greater independence. He ignores the duke's prohibition against trespassing on the giant Beliagog's lands, first through curiosity and love of adventure (2738-9), then because he likes what he sees and wants it for himself (2764-7). And his victory provides him with one reward that not only heightens his independence, but to some degree restores the first Ysonde to him. For Beliagog and his artisans create for him a hall peopled with images that include those of Ysonde, Mark, Brengwain and Meriadok (2840-44) – a convincing surrogate for Mark's court, over which Tristrem has total control.[121]

Only in the French prose romance and Malory's reworking of it,[122] do Arthur and his knights appear throughout the story; in the earlier versions of Béroul and Eilhart von Oberg, their role is largely confined to single episodes (though very elaborate ones),[123] while in Thomas, the knights play no part at all, and Arthur, though mentioned once as a giant-killer (873-935), never appears in the story in his own person. Since even this allusion is lacking in *Tristrem*, its only connections with Arthurian romance are the broader parallels offered by the story of Lancelot and Guenevere in the stanzaic *Morte*, and in a few related texts,[124] and even here there are important differences. More forgiving than Arthur, Mark more than once allows Tristrem to return to the court, and in consequence the love affair begins again, is betrayed again, and one or both of the lovers must go into exile.

The principal characters are also set apart from Lancelot, Guenevere and Arthur by distinctive features of their own. Tristrem, while undeniably heroic, is also an opportunist and a born trickster. He gives a false name (Tramtris) to Ysonde at their first meeting (1187-8), uses guile rather than force to get the better of her lover (1855-914), and prompts her to take part in a piece of play-acting to lull Mark's suspicions (2104-56). It is significant that while in *Ywain* the importance of 'trowth' is stated at the very beginning, 'treuþe' is not mentioned until near the end of *Tristrem*, and then only as a formal device to cement a relationship (2898, 2938, 3005, 3134). 'Trewe' occurs more frequently, mostly as an epithet for Tristrem, but in the second half of the romance it becomes somewhat inappropriate when Mark as well as Ysonde is present (2167, 2552, 2567). It is applied only once to Ysonde on her own, in a prophetic allusion to her quality as a lover (1331), and she soon proves anything but 'trewe' towards Brengwain – who is repeatedly characterized as being so (1775, 1793, 1803) – arranging to have her murdered, so that the secret of her own infidelity may be kept (1737-60). This goes well beyond Alundyne's consent to the burning of Lunet in *Ywain* (2126-36), and it is hardly surprising that the confidante – spared by her intended executioners – should later turn upon her mistress, if only briefly (3182-5).[125] As for Mark, he has some features in common with Arthur – often sympathetic and supportive, but both rash and helpless in his dealings with outsiders. But, with the exception of Tristrem, his knights have no positive virtues; like Agravain and Mordred in the stanzaic *Morte*, Meriadok and Canados are good for nothing but making trouble for the lovers with the king, or with each other (1959-69; 3037-47). And both the king and these other knights are deeply unadventurous; none ever travels far to seek for marvels, or to undertake the defence of the oppressed. We are a long way from the Round Table of chivalric romance.[126]

The first section of the romance does, however, evoke the same part of *Percyvell*; both tell of the love of the hero's father for his king's sister, and death in combat with a treacherous enemy; and of his son's secluded upbringing until his fifteenth year, when he kills his father's murderer. But in *Tristrem*, Rouland dies fighting for his lands, not seeking glory in tournament; the boy is brought up by his father's vassal, Rohand, not his mother Blaunchflour (who hardly survives his birth), and the threat to his life is immediate, and not at some distant point in the future. And while – like the hero of *Percyvell* – he is not said to have any training in arms, the skill in hunting and music that he acquires later secures him a welcome at both the English and Irish courts (452-528, 551-61, 1224-32, 1248-54).

The same kind of introductory story is also important in such non-Arthurian 'Exile and Return' (or 'Matter of England') romances as *Bevis of Hamtoun* and *Horn Childe and Maiden Rimnild*.[127] *Guy of Warwick*, a third romance of this group, offers an especially close parallel with Tristrem's relationship with the second Ysonde in its hero's involvement with the daughter of the Greek emperor, when far removed from his first love.[128] In *Guy* this goes as far as the wedding ceremony; in *Tristrem*, as far as the wedding bed; but in both the hero is kept from being physically unfaithful to his real love by the sight of a ring (*Guy*, A. 4193-216); *Tristrem*, 2683-95). But while Guy's lapse is the result of something like amnesia, Tristrem's is the result of deliberate policy. He undertakes the marriage, partly because his wife-to-be is also called Ysonde (2672-73), but also as a desperate attempt to escape from an intolerable situation. Of course the experiment does not work and – helped by the recreation of Ysonde of Ireland in the hall of images – is soon abandoned; but it outrages Lancelot in the prose versions of the story (see *Vinaver*, 435, 467).

Doublings of other situations and events that characterize the Matter of England are also present in *Tristrem*. In its first half, he fights with two monstrous opponents, Moraunt and the fiery dragon, and each of them gives him a poisonous wound (1112-26, 1486-91) which is healed by Ysonde's mother (1200-10, 1519-29). In the second half, Tristrem enters the service of King Triamour of Wales as well as of Duke Florentin of Brittany (2309-10), and here too he fights with and defeats a troublesome giant, Urgan (2322-96). Like the duke, this king has a young daughter, Blauncheflour (2302-3), although he never formally offers her to Tristrem as a reward for his services.[129]

A final link with these romances is the sustained importance of revenge as a theme. In *Tristrem* the most extended sequence begins with Morgan's slaying of Rouland, and ends with the reconciliation with Beliagog, the last of the clan of giants. But Moraunt, the second brother to be killed, also has his niece Ysonde and her mother as potential avengers, and between them they very nearly kill off Tristrem once they have discovered his true identity (1594-5). Near the end of the romance Tristrem – like the Red Knight in *Percyvell* – achieves an act of revenge of his own in a tournament that he has proclaimed for the purpose of settling accounts with Meriadok and Canados (3230-4, 3250-6, 3259-67). So that love and revenge, the two dominant themes of the romance, are appropriately kept before us in what is now the last complete episode in the Auchinleck text.

Thomas's romance and its derivatives represent what has been called the 'courtly' version of the story, in which the more primitive features of the 'popular' version represented by Béroul and Eilhart were softened, and more insight was given into the thoughts and motivation of its characters.[130] *Tristrem*, while belonging to the first group by literary derivation, often suggests the second by its characteristic emphases and tone. The lengthy self-questionings of its source are reduced to short-winded antitheses – '"Her loue, Y say, is mine, / Þe boke seyt, it is nouȝt / Wiþ riȝt!"' (2669-71); its elaborate self-reproaches, to simple assertions: '"Þe dern dede, / Do it Y no dare"' (2698-9). Action and movement predominate throughout, and so bring *Tristrem* closer to such romances as *Ywain*, *Lybeaus* or *Percyvell*, however unlike these it may be in its personnel and temporal range.

Maldwyn Mills

Lancelot of the Laik and *Sir Lancelot du Lake*

Although Sir Lancelot, with the paradoxical combination of his excellence in knighthood and his sinful love for the wife of Arthur, his king, is a major figure in Malory's *Morte Darthur*, and the stanzaic *Morte Arthur* also pays attention to his problematic status as knight and lover, Lancelot does not appear otherwise to have featured prominently in English story-telling. The only known pre-modern texts in English which take Lancelot as their primary subject are *Lancelot of the Laik,* a Scottish verse romance dating from the fifteenth century, and *Sir Lancelot du Lake,* a ballad treatment of an episode from Malory's *Morte Darthur.*

Lancelot of the Laik exists in a single copy, Cambridge University Library MS KK. 1.5., which is incomplete at 3484 lines. The outline of the intended scope of the story given in the prologue suggests that the surviving text represents at most two-thirds of the whole poem. The dialect used, while basically Scots, differs from most examples of fifteenth-century Scots in showing a number of English features, and this may well be a sign that the poet was influenced by the earlier fifteenth century poem *The Kingis Quair,* written by King James I.[131] While editors and critics have been in general agreement, on linguistic and palaeographic grounds, that the poem dates from the later fifteenth century, it is not possible to establish a precise date within this period, and dates suggested vary from before 1460 to as late as 1497.[132] It has been thought that aspects of the content give grounds for relating the text to events in the reign of James III (1460-88), but as is shown below this is by no means beyond dispute. There has been no convincing attribution of authorship. There is some reason to think that the author may be the same poet, possibly named Auchinleck or Affleck, who wrote *The Quare of Jelusy*, another late fifteenth-century Scottish text written like this poem in a language which contains elements of English influence in vocabulary and style. However, common authorship has not been proved, and the strong resemblances between the texts might be produced by two different poets writing in a common style.[133]

Essentially *Lancelot of the Laik* is a translation of a portion of the thirteenth-century French prose *Lancelot* – part of the vast Vulgate cycle – which deals with Arthur's wars with Galehaut.[134] The French romance traces the life of Lancelot from early childhood.

> After his father, King Ban, is dispossessed of his kingdom and dies, Lancelot is brought up in the care of the Lady of the Lake. On reaching adulthood he is knighted, and begins to establish his reputation by fighting as the White Knight at Dolorous Guard. His success brings him to the attention of Arthur's knights, and the discovery of his identity becomes for them the object of a quest. Having killed one of her knights, he is imprisoned by the Lady of Malohaut, who also is unaware of who Lancelot is. When Arthur's power is challenged by Galehaut, Lord of the Distant Isles, the Lady grants Lancelot leave to fight on Arthur's behalf as an unknown knight, first in red armour, and secondly in black. Lancelot's success is such that he is able to persuade Galehaut to make peace with Arthur, thus preserving the king's honour. Love develops between Guinevere and the unknown knight, and after their first kiss she tells him she has guessed that he is Lancelot, son of King Ban of Benwick.

The French *Lancelot* is constructed around two major themes, that of the hero's identity and reputation, and that of the troubled love between him and Guinevere.[135] The Scottish poet selects as the source for his work the parts of *Lancelot* which treat Lancelot's imprisonment by the Lady of Melyhalt (Malohaut) and his participation in Arthur's battles with Galiot (Galehaut). His poem is introduced by a prologue, for which there is no source in the French text, in which the narrator presents himself as an unhappy lover, receiving in a dream an instruction from the God of Love to write something as an expression of his love. Lancelot's love for Guinevere, and also the ill-fated passion which the Lady of Melyhalt develops for Lancelot, are thus connected to the narrator's own situation. The prologue indicates that the focus of *Lancelot of the Laik* was to be on Lancelot's achievements as Arthur's champion, and architect of the peace between him and Galiot, and on Venus rewarding him for this with success in love (*Gray*, 299-312). As it is, the manuscript breaks off at a point where Lancelot as the Black Knight is engaged in the second battle against Galiot, and so the poem lacks the culminating section which should treat Lancelot's negotiation with Galehaut and his later dealings with Guinevere.

In the source, the narration of Lancelot's story alternates with long discussions of monarchy and the behaviour required of a king, generated by dreams which disturb Arthur and for which he demands interpretation from learned clerks. These discussions are part of an exploration of values such as honour and justice, which emerges from the representation of Arthur, and from the comparison between the king and his opponent, Galehaut. The interaction between Arthur and Lancelot is thematically important. A wise man who comes to the court to advise Arthur significantly reproaches the king for his failure to avenge the death of Ban, Lancelot's father. This draws attention to the irony that Arthur depends for the defence of his kingdom on the knightly prowess of a man to whose father he failed in his obligations as sovereign and overlord, and who is also his own wife's lover.[136]

Arguments have been advanced that the poet's choice of a source which includes an element of reproach to a monarch, and his expansion of this aspect of the material, point to a specific connection with the discontent produced in Scotland by the behaviour of King James III. These theories are based on evidence of the king's unpopularity during the 1480s, disaffection among some of his nobles, and difficulties in the relations between Scotland and England at this time. It has been suggested that the poem's dreams and prophecies, and comments on the evil of listening to flatterers, as well as its concern with justice and good government, and the idea that the kingdom is endangered, are indications that the poet must have been writing with James's inadequacies as a monarch in mind. There have been further suggestions that the treatment of Arthur's war with Galiot should be related to the historical conflict between James III and John, Lord of the Isles – a member of a family which traditionally had bad relations with the Stuart monarchs.[137] Tempting as these hypotheses are, it has not been shown conclusively that the poem can be linked to any particular historical persons or events. Recent scholarship urges scepticism on this point, and notes that the advice given by the clerk in the Scottish text does not in fact differ very much from that in the source, and further, that much of what the clerk has to say is fairly conventional material drawn from the *speculum principis* tradition, rather than advice pointing specifically to weaknesses characteristic of James III.[138] One aspect of the adaptation of the source which might, however, relate to the conduct of James III is a passage in which the clerk gives advice to Arthur about his treatment of the poor. Where in the French text the clerk urges him to make a point of associating with the poor and talking with them, the Scottish poem modifies this to include advice not to be over-familiar with them, which could reflect contemporary disapproval of King James's habits of associating with friends of common birth (1697-700).[139] Otherwise, although the poet is certainly much concerned about good government, his arguments about justice do not appear to refer exclusively to the reign of one particular king.

This poet, like the author of the other late Scottish romance *Golagros and Gawane*, sees in Arthurian materials a vehicle for examination of ideas of feudal and chivalric behaviour. In *Golagros and Gawane* Arthur's imperious behaviour is exposed to criticism by being contrasted with the noble resistance of Golagros, and the magnanimity of Gawain. *Lancelot of the Laik* draws, as does *Golagros and Gawane*, on the interest in the theme of resistance to aggression produced in Scotland by the national struggle, dating from the late thirteenth century, to preserve independence from England. Arthur's refusal in this poem to pay homage to Galiot, insisting that he will hold his kingdom from none but God, is couched in language very similar to that in which Golagros refuses to submit to Arthur as overlord. Here Arthur's desire for independence attracts sympathy, but at the same time the conflict with Galiot in *Lancelot of the Laik* is used to reveal the king's faults: Galiot's attack is connected with Arthur's bad dream, the rebuke from the clerk Amytans, and the king's neglect of his obligations to King Ban, Lancelot's father. In both of these Scottish poems, as also in the alliterative *Morte Arthure*, King Arthur is a figure whose strength is balanced by a certain weakness, allowing opportunities for critical scrutiny.

Although some alterations are necessarily made to the source in the process of producing a verse adaptation, *Lancelot of the Laik* is for the most part a close rendering of *Lancelot do Lac*. Some changes are made in the arrangement of material, for example in the placing of the discussions of kingship, in relation to the story of Lancelot and Galiot, but these changes do not appear to have any thematic significance. The narration of events is to some extent simplified, appropriately since the poet is writing a work conceived on a more limited scale than his source. In the French romance the sense of a complex world in which the characters live is built up slowly over a series of adventures. In *Lancelot of the Laik* the poet selects from this world material which he can focus on the central questions of Lancelot's identity and his love, the virtues of heroic brotherhood between knights, and the behaviour of a just monarch. Although on the whole he writes economically, he expands on his source occasionally when he is dealing with the achievements of Gawain and Lancelot, and the powerful bond that exists between them. He is especially eloquent in the address in which Gawain encourages his troops to fight (794-804), in the account of Gawain's heroic performance in battle (865-71, 878-81), and the description of Lancelot's prowess which culminates in words of praise for Lancelot uttered by Gawain (1090-127). When Gawain is wounded and his life is despaired of, a lament uttered by Arthur increases the emotional intensity of the narrative:

> 'Far well,' he sais, 'my gladnes, and my delyt,
> Apone knychthed far well myne appetit,
> Fare well of manhed al the gret curage,

Yow flour of armys and of vassolage,
Gif yow be lost!'   (*Gray*, 2719-23)

Cumulatively these additions to the source help to create a fuller sense of the bonds and shared values that link the two knights at the centre of the narrative. The poem is announced in the prologue as a story of love and arms (200), and the poet elaborates on Lancelot's love in an inner monologue (1010-27), and a lament in four stanzas in which the hero dwells on the pain of being a lover and in prison (698-717). The decasyllabic couplets used throughout the poem are usually adequate for their purpose, and sometimes impressive in their simple economy.

Sir Lancelot du Lake is a ballad of 31 four-line stanzas, collected in Thomas Percy's *Reliques of Ancient English Poetry* (Series 1, Book 2, no.9). It tells in ballad style, and so in simplified terms, the story from Malory's *Tale of Sir Launcelot du Lake* (*Vinaver*, 264-8) of the encounter in which Lancelot slays Sir Tarquin. Lancelot demonstrates his excellence as a knight of the Round Table by releasing three score and four of Arthur's knights whom Sir Tarquin had been holding as prisoners.   **Flora Alexander**

The Awntyrs off Arthure

The Awntyrs off Arthure is an early fifteenth-century poem in two distinct and nearly equal parts. In the first section, while Guinevere ('Gaynor/ Waynor') and her escort Gawain are watching Arthur's court hunting deer near Carlisle, they are accosted by the ghost of her mother rising from Tarn Wadling in a snow storm. The ghost urges Guinevere to have a trental of masses said to release her guilty soul from torment, while briefly warning her against pride and counselling charity to the poor. More poignant is the ghost's warning to Gawain that Arthur's territorial acquisitiveness will lead to treachery and downfall. The ghost leaves and the court goes to supper, which is interrupted by the arrival of an unnamed lady leading Sir Galeron of Galloway, who claims that lands taken from him by Arthur were given to Gawain and demands combat as a means of regaining his rights. Gawain takes up Galeron's challenge, but they are nearly equally matched, and Guinevere, prompted by Galeron's lady, has the contest halted. Galeron does homage to Gawain, Arthur gives Gawain compensatory land elsewhere on condition he relinquish Galeron's, and re-enfeoffs Galeron with his own territory provided he joins the Round Table. Galeron marries his lady, and a concluding stanza records Guinevere's payment for a 'million masses' for her mother.

There are four extant manuscripts of *The Awntyrs*.[140] Three of the manuscripts were edited in the eighteenth and nineteenth centuries, one of them twice and one three times.[141] Four further editions have been published since 1974, sustaining an interest in the poem's literary qualities which contrasts with earlier adverse judgement of its structure.[142] The title *The Awntyrs off Arthure* is found only in MS Lincoln 91, written by Robert Thornton of Ryedale in North Yorkshire. Thornton may have constructed the title from the first line of the poem, but it is not unapt. Although both *awntyrs* (*adventures*) in the poem have Gawain as chief protagonist, in each he is Arthur's surrogate, receiving a dire warning of the king's downfall through over-ambitious annexation of lands and responding on his behalf to a local challenge to his territorial policy.[143] The two incidents are thematically linked, if divergent in genre and tone.[144]

Since the 1960s scholarly interest has focused on three aspects of *The Awntyrs* in particular: the textual problems posed by its four manuscripts, its literary form and prosody, and the message the text constructs. The divergence of the extant manuscripts challenges the audacity of even the boldest editor's capacity for reconstructing the textual tradition. Establishment of the text inevitably precedes literary assessment, and the edition published by Hanna (1974) is usually regarded by literary critics as definitive; yet each recent edition differs significantly from the others,[145] both in selection of copy text and choice between different but equally possible readings. Meanwhile, critics are divided in their interpretation by the differing tones they identify in the work: is it a critique of court culture and aristocratic appropriation of wealth and power, or an exemplum of salvation through self-restraint and compassion for others?

Until the 1970s critics regarded the poem, despite its complex rhyme-scheme and verse form, as a poor imitation of the best alliterative texts, like *Morte Arthure* and *Sir Gawain and the Green Knight*, which it patently echoes, and considered it a composite written by two poets with divergent aims. The plot was reckoned 'weak and meagre', sense and narrative momentum being retarded by the prosodic virtuosity and verbal resource.[146] In the late twentieth century, however, the poem is thought structurally unified with a single message: the need for disregard of self and generosity to others. Klausner reads the poem as a dual moral exemplum, and Hardman points to the Ireland scribe's reading of the poem as a positive exemplum of the reinvestment of the knightly code by Christian principles,[147] though Hanna thinks Guinevere ignores the ghost's plea for personal reform.[148] Opinion on the structure sharpened after Hanna's 1974 edition. Spearing points to the centrality of the crowned king Arthur in the mid-point of the extant text, Matsuda and Lowe emphasize the hunt as a frame, and Phillips identifies the unifying theme of 'changed states'.[149]

Date and audience have recently been reconsidered: 1424-5 has been suggested from probable allusions in the poem to the Triple Alliance of 1423-6 between England, Brittany and Burgundy, and to the heavy losses of France and her ally Scotland in the 1420s; its audience may have included the affinity of the Nevilles, who were connected by marriage with James I of Scotland, Earl of Carrick – Sir Galeron names Carrick as his territory.[150]

Formerly *The Awntyrs* was praised mainly for its prosody. Its 714 extant lines are organized in fifty-five thirteen-line stanzas,[151] with nine four-stress lines, usually with four alliterative staves, and four concluding two-stress lines.[152] Alliteration often runs on for two lines. As in *Sir Gawain and the Green Knight*, *Pearl* and *Patience* the final line echoes the first. The prosody is eminently constructed for oral recitation and sound-patterns create both structure and meaning.[153]

As David Lawton has shown, the surviving Middle English poems in thirteen-line stanzas were composed in the north Midlands from the late fourteenth century, and focus on the themes of mortality and Marian devotion.[154] One of these, *De Tribus Regibus*, recorded (but not composed) by the blind Shropshire cleric Awdelay, must have provided inspiration for *The Awntyrs*: three kings out hunting a boar confront three speaking skeletons of their own fathers.[155] *Summer Sunday* also begins with a hunt,[156] and exploits the motif of Fortune's Wheel, which is present in *The Awntyrs*[157] though probably drawn from the alliterative *Morte Arthure*.[158] Two other extant Middle English texts are discernible in the poem. One is *The Trental of Gregory*, propaganda for the recital of masses for the dead.[159] There is also almost certain reference to *Sir Gawain and the Green Knight*.[160]

The correspondence of public and private worlds is prominent in *The Awntyrs*, where Gawain, as in romance, demonstrates personal responsibility, while the ghost's prophecy (261-312) reflects the chronicle tradition of Arthur's political fortune. The poem presents the enhanced Gawain of the English tradition,[161] and probably refers to but subverts a folk-tale linking Gawain with a Loathly Lady. This legend has four extant derivatives: *The Weddynge of Sir Gawen and Dame Ragnell*, set in Inglewood Forest, and the Percy Folio *Marriage of Sir Gawaine* located at 'Tearne Wadling', on the one hand, and Chaucer's *Wife of Bath's Tale* and Gower's *Tale of Florent* on the other.[162] *The Awntyrs* reverses the type narrative, transposing descriptions of the loathly and beautiful ladies, allowing the challenger for his territory to gain rather than lose land through her intervention, and framing her 'answer' as 'mekenesse and mercy' (250) rather than sovereignty, which is instead invested (temporarily) in a male figure, Arthur 'þe soueraynest sir sitting in sete' (358; *most dominant lord sitting enthroned*).

The Awntyrs has to be read as an intertextual work. Its meaning is constructed from at least five late medieval cultural motifs, which must have been known to the poet's audience in written/oral, painted and embroidered representations.[163] These are: the exemplum of the dead relative returning from hell to request masses;[164] the loathly lady who has a beautiful counterpart;[165] the mysterious place in the wildwood where personal values are tested; the intruder in the hall;[166] the contest voluntarily lost.[167] The first three are closely associated with the first half of the poem, and the remaining two with the second half. But each section of the poem constructs its meaning from all the areas of intertextual reference, and it would be wrong to limit their relevance to authorial 'source material'. They form a base chord with which other themes throughout the work resonate but without a common key, as in early polyphonic music.[168] Guinevere's mother, who disrupts the hunt, is an intruder with a demand on her interlocutor, and there are two further intruders: another nameless female and a male with a challenge. Both sets of alien intruders provide tests: Galeron challenges Gawain's prowess, the ghost challenges Guinevere's personal standards of conduct and Galeron's lady tests her further. The male leading a female (14, 31) disturbed by an intruder in the first section is balanced by a female leading a male who are the disturbers in the second (344).[169] Indeed, both intrusions are invasions of private space referred to as a 'hall' (*lefesale* 70; *sale* 339). Aristocratic ideals are challenged in the disbanded hunt in the first part, and by the declined victory in the second.

Other commonplaces set up similar resonances throughout the poem; it is not merely that the first part sets up a proposition demonstrated in the second.[170] The hag transformed, traditionally associated with Tarn Wadling and Sir Gawain, who tests the relative values of self esteem and public image, has counterparts in the Celtic sovereignty emblem and Fortune who has hair on her forehead and is bald behind.[171] Lady Fortune was certainly known to the audience from the alliterative *Morte Arthure* (and perhaps the French *Mort Artu* as well). The plot structure echoes this duality. In the first half of the poem a beautiful lady, Guinevere, is described at length and in such splendour as to justify the ghost's warning of the danger of 'pride with þe appurtenaunce' (*attendant evils*) (239). Her description is followed by that of the ghost who is 'Naxté and nedeful, naked on night' (185) (*filthy, desitute and naked in darkness*): by a reverse transformation the lady has become loathly. The audience is invited to see the ghost as both Fortune, harbinger of the Round Table's collapse, and Loathly Lady seeking empowerment – but in the next life not this. Yet in Part Two the hag as intruder is indeed replaced by a beautiful woman, the unnamed lady whose attire is 'glorious' (366).[172] It looks very much as though *The Awntyrs* parodies the 'hag transformed' plot by showing that personal and social reform (Guinevere's and Arthur's) are never final and cannot subvert the ultimate degeneration of the human form, a chilling message for a politically prominent audience – especially in old age.[173]

Gawain, Arthur's surrogate in Tarn Wadling legends,[174] is the appropriate recipient of the ghost's warning about Arthur's coming misfortunes. But, in the location where his own reputation is traditionally tested, he is not heroic.[175] Indeed, the implications of his remaining with Guinevere while the rest of the Round Table are hunting may well be sinister, and the ghost's admonition against lechery all too apt.[176] Tarn Wadling, where Gawain traditionally braves dangers (see also *The Avowynge of King Arthur)*[177] has its counterpart in *Sir Gawain*'s Hautdesert and the woodland where the three kings meet their dead fathers in *De Tribus Regibus Mortuis*.[178] 'Wood' is distinguished in *The Awntyrs* from 'forest', the former designating a wilderness outside human habitation, the latter a source of income and food.[179] Though the hunt is conducted in the royal forest of Inglewood, the Tarn within it is otherworldly, an Avernus from which the dead parent comes to foretell the future. In English tradition, the hunt is more an encounter with personal death than an emblem of sexual pursuit,[180] but (like the hag whose question transforms both her and her bridegroom) it presents an opportunity for self-revaluation and new life. Like Guinevere and the three kings of *De Tribus Regibus*, Gawain learns of his own death, is temporarily restored by mock-decapitation,[181] renounces lands and is compensated with others; he and Galeron are dubbed dukes at the close (695). Bodies and property are divested and restored in this re-presentation of the 'removable head' motif. The allusions are more profound than imitation or travesty. The second part restates the elemental themes of disruption and isolation in the romance format of challenge and combat. This section may be by the same poet, or by another who recognized the implications in part one: the extant poem works as a whole. Arthur sits as crowned sovereign at its midmost point, but by the second half of that mid-line, 'sittand in sete' (*sitting enthroned*), Arthur on Fortune's wheel has already passed the mid-point and is declining to a conclusion. Arthur is going to lose – but if the audience knew a version of his death besides that in the alliterative *Morte Arthure*, they would know of his expected return; at its close the poem revolves back to its first line, and to Arthur.[182]

Was the poem performed as a semi-dramatic monologue or with speakers (perhaps nobles) reciting the dialogue?[183] The audience is highly significant in *The Awntyrs*. They negotiate the intertextual references, which to a great extent establish the tone. Critics have long ceased to criticize as lack of inspiration quotations in the poem from other alliterative texts and allusions to commonplaces of romance and folk tradition. These features signal to a highly sophisticated audience an ironic or parodic reading of the text.[184] For instance, the ghost parodies the traditional loathly lady of Tarn Wadling, but in a more sinister way since she follows rather than precedes the beautiful Guinevere; like the 'auncien lady' in *Sir Gawain* she reminds us not merely of age but of the dissolution which succeeds it. Gawain has more than a 'nirt' in his neck: he will carry his wound in the collar-bone 'to his deþday' (515) and is later nearly decapitated (583); his famous strength, which traditionally waxes until noon, as he is aware (437) will now leave him: midday is past (565), as his opponent reminds him.[185] Gawain again acts as emblem for the Round Table and, like his departure to seek the Green Knight, his 'bargan' (*undertaking*) to fight Galeron is lamented by his fellow knights (592, cf. *Sir Gawain* 672-686), while Guinevere mourns him (597-600, 629-37) just as Arthur laments over his corpse in *Morte Arthure* (3947-69). Gawain is already dead in the ghost's prophecy (298) and is almost a 'revenant' himself after it. Intertextuality reinforces the elegiac commonplace of the downfall of the Round Table. By relocating its contrastive topoi, male–female bonding drawn from romance and the divorce of soul and body from debate, within a precisely localized area known to its first audience as a financial resource to the crown and playground for the nobility, the poem creates sophisticated amusement at its own glittering reflection of literary allusion, fashionable cultural artefacts and refined social entertainment.[186] *The Awntyrs* invites close scrutiny by its parallelism and verbal echoes; its prosodic riches provide a reflex of the cultural wealth it depicts. But this urbane surface suddenly ruptures as we recognize those interactive temporal allusions. In her mother's past Guinevere sees mirrored her own future: 'muse on my mirour' (MS D).[187] A perceptive audience would realize that as they themselves were playing where the Round Table once sported, they were being invited to view their political situation reflected in Arthur's disastrous foreign policy, and to see mirrored in the ghost's physical disintegration the deterioration of the very culture being commodified in the poem itself.   **Rosamund Allen**

Golagros and Gawane

Chivalric romance having entered the English language comparatively late, there was some danger of over-dependence upon the dominant French tradition, of mechanical manipulation of established conventions, or parody, conscious or unconscious, of classic models. But even late examples show understanding of chivalric values, employ conventions creatively, and treat source material with radical independence. One of the latest was written in Lowland Scots towards the end of the fifteenth century and printed in 1508 among the first productions of the Scottish Press.[188] That was, comparatively at least, a golden age in the troubled history of Scotland, the reign of James IV (1488-1513), when a royal marriage brought a temporary truce in the perpetual conflict with England. Long-standing relations with France, the reflex of that old enmity, had encouraged political independence and cultural awareness, resulting in a functional parliament, three universities, a lively if tiny capital, and a king who aspired to emulate ancient chivalry.[189]

The Knightly Tale of Golagros and Gawane reflects an eclectic and self-confident culture, using a sophisticated variant of the English alliterative tradition in reinterpreting a French text so radically that it was long assumed to be an original composition.[190] The source has been identified in a section of the First Continuation of Chrétien's *Perceval*, the *Livre du Chastel Orguelleus*. The First Continuation, which largely abandons Chrétien's hero and his Grail quest in favour of conventional romance adventures of Gawain, survives in eleven verse manuscripts, and a prose version printed in 1530. Analysis suggests that the source of the Scots version is most nearly represented by the 1530 print, though precise judgement is inhibited by the radical nature of the redaction.[191]

The redactive process might, indeed, be judged by comparison with any text of the Long Redaction, to which the prose print belongs, since all surviving copies contain the same major sections and, with minor variations, the same sequence of episodes in each. Of the sixteen episodes editorially distinguished in the fourth section, *Le Livre du Chastel Orguelleus*, the first three and numbers eight to fifteen feature in *Golagros and Gawane*. The Scots redactor rejected a mass of romance incident in the rest of the First Continuation, much of it centred upon Gawain, and even within his selected book omitted one of the three component adventures, reducing some thirty-six closely printed pages to 1362 lines of verse in stanzas of thirteen lines tightly rhymed and heavily alliterated.[192]

The stylistic demands of such a complex medium made literal translation of the French prose, with its easy, fluent narrative and eloquent colloquial exchanges, technically impossible. The difficulty of finding alliteratively variable synonyms for common verbs of action restricted direct narration in favour of the rhetorical elaboration of speeches, descriptions, combats by accumulating detail in substantival and adjectival phrases. The author of

Golagros and Gawane has made full use of all the devices appropriate to his medium, detailing emphatically the violence of combat, matching the splendour of feasts and ceremonies with the verbal elaboration of his descriptions, and substituting dramatically effective speech for much of the original narration.

Clearly his choice of a medium rooted in native tradition was fundamental; but he has exploited to the full the freedom which it compels in radically re-handling the context, structure, characterization, thematic balance and meaning of the original. The adventure of the Chastel Orguelleus, originally undertaken by Arthur to rescue his follower Girflet, taken prisoner during an earlier siege of the castle, part of the *Perceval* proper (4721-3), has been freed from its context. The rescue mission is replaced by a pilgrimage to the Holy Land, readily abandoned when adventures arise *en route*. In one (40-221 : ff.103ᵛb-105a)[193] Gawain, by behaving courteously, secures hospitality for his companions in a wayside castle, where Kay, making a more peremptory approach, had earned himself a beating; in another (222-1362 : ff.113a-115ᵛa; ff.116ᵛb-119a) his magnanimity in feigning defeat by the lord of Chastel Orgelleus, when he has actually won the encounter between them, ultimately brings his opponent's surrender to Arthur. Between them comes an episode representing unfinished business from the earlier *Livre de Brun de Branlant* in which Gawain seduces the Damoisele de Lis and kills her father and brother. He now encounters another brother, Bran de Lis, and fights him until they are separated by a tiny child – Gawain's son, Bran's nephew – who catches at their flashing swords. They are reconciled and Bran joins the court in its mission to Chastel Orguelleus. This episode, with its reminder of the darker side of Gawain's traditional reputation, his heart-free, love-them-and-leave-them attitude to women and his ruthless pursuit of personal prowess, has left no trace in the Scots redaction (: ff.105b-113a). Without it, what is left of the *Livre du Chastel Orguelleus* might seem no more than a conventional chapter in the hagiology of Gawain – the other Gawain celebrated in northern tradition for old-fashioned, uncomplicated chivalry, courtesy, generosity of nature. But the radical character of the redaction has produced something very different.

The initial episode has been thematically concentrated by elimination of the incidentals which flesh out the French narrative realistically: the wayside hut where an old woman directs Kay, in search of supplies, to a *manoir* nearby; the peacock being roasted by the dwarf he finds in the hall; the greyhounds accompanying the castellan who ejects him for mistreating his servant. With them go more material details which underscore the theme: the blow with the spit which marks Kay for life, Arthur's ironic comment on the greyhounds still eating the peacock when the hungry court enters, the humorous queries by which Gawain deflates Kay's deceptive account of his mission. The English Gawain attacks Kay as ' "crabbit of kynde" ' (119), and it is Arthur's name rather than his own, as in the French, which wins them hospitality and an offer of thirty thousand troops. The familiar chivalric contrast has been economically re-established – a contrast in which the Scots poet has associated Arthur, who promises recompense for hospitality, ' "As I am trew knight" ' (169), with Gawain. In the process the subtlety and humour of the French have been somewhat blunted, promising a rather conventional redaction.

But with the second, much longer, episode, comes a radically different redaction, omitting much, adding even more, altering events, motives, meaning. And with it comes a new Arthur who, on sighting the Chastel Orguelleus and learning that its lord owes allegiance to no one, vows to compel him to homage. The violence of his language – ' "Sall neuer my likame (*body*) be laid vnlaissit (*disarmed*) to sleip, / Quhill I haue gart (*made*) yone berne bow" ' (294-5) – and the haste with which his pilgrimage is despatched in eleven lines so that he can begin the siege, evoke the tradition of the imperious Arthur. His will becomes the driving force of the Scots romance, a substitute for the mission to rescue Girflet. The Riche Souldoier, lord of Chastel Orguelleus, derives his status from holding him prisoner; the role of his Scots counterpart, the unknown Golagros, has to be created from nothing.

Typically, the redactor has converted for that purpose a device provided in the original for a different function. There, Bran de Lis accompanies the court as a detached commentator on the usages of Chastel Orguelleus. His English counterpart, Sir Spynagros,[194] becomes, without explanation, an ardent partisan of Golagros. It is he who warns Arthur not to challenge the independence of one from whose ancestors not even ' "The myghty king of Massidone" ' (282) had won homage (261-98 :   ), and comments on his impressive preparations to resist a siege, for which the French supplies only a few details (480-544 : f.113b). When, in an invented episode (320-457 :   ), emissaries are sent to the castle, he warns them to approach with respect one meek as a maid but ' "wondir staluart and strang, to striue in ane stour" ' (353); Gawain, smoothly diplomatic, speaks of Arthur's power and the generosity with which he will reward friendship; Golagros, calmly courteous, refuses to surrender his ancestral independence.

Conflict begins: in the French a series of formal jousts, one against one, within defined limits, which in thc English develops into a mêlée where rising numbers on both sides engage with all the violence of emphatic alliteration, resulting in capture, injury, and death (545-768 : ff.113b-115a). In the French a truce is signalled, during which Arthur's party goes hunting; Gawain comes upon an unknown knight in a swoon under a tree and then meets a distressed lady who, arriving late for an assignation with her lover, had found him apparently dead of grief; later he learns that the knight was the Riche Souldoier, lord of Chastel Orguelleus, and the lady his *amie*. The hunting interval is entirely absent from the Scots redaction, (: ff.115^{v}a-116^{v}b) which continues the sequence of engagements with an encounter between Gawain and Golagros (769-1024 : ff.116^{v}b-117^{v}a).[195] As Gawain is arming, Kay, in pique, dashes out into the field – we anticipate his humiliation, the conventional contrast with Gawain, as in the French where he is mocked by his comrades for claiming victory though, unhorsed, he has been driven out of the lists. Instead, the English has him bring his defeated opponent to submit to Arthur (836-83 : f.115a-115^{v}a).[196] Spynagros has already repeated his familiar function by warning Gawain not to risk an encounter with an opponent of outstanding courage and skill (795-833:   ); now the redactor exploits the convention by which the prowess of a knight is reflected in the splendour of his equipment, replacing the original account of the arming of Gawain by a similar description of Golagros (884-902 : f.117a).

When the two meet, the struggle is long, many times longer than in the French, (903-1024 : f.117b-117^{v}a) and full of alliterative violence. Defeated, the Riche Souldoier refuses to surrender since his humiliation would kill his *amie* – unless Gawain will go with him to the castle in pretended defeat until she can be reassured. In the Scots version, which knows nothing of the lady, Golagros refuses to dishonour his ancestors by surrender, and to the offer of ducal rank in Arthur's court replies that his honour is not to be bought; but, if Gawain will spare him public disgrace by riding to the castle in seeming defeat, he will promise that his reputation shall not suffer (1025-1141 : f.117^{v}a-118a). In the French romance, what Gawain has seen, during the hunt, of the extremes to which passion has brought both knight and lady justifies the claim made upon him by such a love. His English counterpart, knowing nothing of it, is forced to weigh his opponent's reputation against his own honour and that of the Round Table: ' "To leif (*trust*) in thi laute, and thow war vnlele, / Than had I cassin in cair mony kene knight" ' (1107-8). His decision is made in three lines, justified in the reader's mind by all he has learnt of Golagros from the redactor's inventions: the inflexible resolve with which he rejects Arthur's embassy, the magnificence of his armour, the loyalty of his lieges flocking to his support, their impassioned prayers at his fall (1051-63), the laudatory commentary of Sir Spynagros throughout. The

duel is briefly resumed, Gawain pretends defeat and, to the laments of the
Round Table, accompanies Golagros to the castle as his prisoner.

Within the fortress, in the original version, Gawain surrenders his sword
to the lady; then her lover persuades her to withdraw, releases Girflet, and
leads his followers to do homage to Arthur. The redactor, not content merely
to round off the narrative, creates new episodes to complete his thematic
scheme. Feasting with his followers, Golagros asks in hypothetical terms
whether they would prefer him to admit defeat in the field or lose his life by
refusing to surrender. They reply that they would remain loyal to him in
defeat; he confesses the truth and praises Gawain's self-sacrifice (1194-
1206).[197] Together they ride to Arthur's camp, Golagros makes his
submission to the king and praises Gawain's magnanimity before his
companions. Arthur matches it, as the poem ends, by freeing Golagros from
his sworn allegiance:

> 'I mak releisching of thin allegiance;
> But dreid I sall the warand,   *certainly, guarantee*
> Baith be sey and be land,
> Fre as I the first fand,
> With outin distance.' (1358-62)[198]   *without dispute*

The close structure and strict economy of the Scots romance – limited
episodes intensively treated, violent action alternating with static, formal
speeches – concentrate and emphasize theme. At one level the theme seems
entirely conventional: a tacit lesson in magnanimity and respect for the
identity of others delivered by Gawain to his royal uncle, emphasized by the
familiar contrast with the unchivalrous Kay and implicitly acknowledged by
Arthur in his final act of generosity. Gawain's self-sacrifice in his uncle's
service is already established in the chronicle tradition. Both the prowess he
displays there and the courtesy he embodies in the romance tradition serve
Arthur's interests in the twin episodes of *Golagros*. The susceptibility to
women which so often proves his Achilles heel might well have made
concern for the distressed lady seem an appropriate cause of Gawain's
magnanimity to her lover. But though the Damoisele de Lis episode may
have been omitted for the sake of Gawain's honour, it is his opponent's
reputation which gains by the excision of the lady. The claims which his
French counterpart makes upon Gawain for his *amie*'s sake, Golagros must
make for his own sake. The values of courtly love are replaced by older
values: the mutual respect of chivalric equals, trust justified by integrity,
rewarded by fidelity. By the self-abnegation with which he sacrifices his
victory in arms and the trust he places in his opponent's good faith, Gawain's
known reputation becomes the guarantor of the unknown Golagros,

establishing tacitly but powerfully what Spynagros spells out at such length.[199]

Two features distinguish the unknown hero from the known: at the feast where Golagros confesses his defeat, he seats Gawain by his wife and daughter (1150-4) – inventions of the redactor – tacitly recalling the victor's ambivalent reputation with women; his own status as the sovereign leader of an independent society is confirmed by his followers, who respond to his confession with: ' "Your lordschip we may noght forga, alse lang as we leif; / Ye sal be our gouernour, / Quhil your dais may endure" ' (1189-91). His feudal status equates him with the leader of the Round Table; Arthur's reaction, imperiously demanding what is another's by right, equates *him* with the greedy Kay of the first episode. His lust for absolute power has been interpreted nationalistically: an English Arthur demanding the fealty of an independent ruler, seen as reminiscent of the persistent attempts of the English crown to exert its suzerainty over Scotland.[200] But an imperious nature is a constant of Arthur's role, from his imperial ambitions in the chronicles to his ruthless determination to maintain the integrity and pre-eminence of the Round Table in romance. What is exceptional here is not his behaviour but the nature of his antagonist: noble, inflexible, heir to an ancestral tradition which he refuses to dishonour:

> 'I will noght bow me ane bak for berne that is borne; *submit*
> Quhill I may my wit wald,
> I think my fredome to hald,
> As my eldaris of ald
> Has done me beforne.' (449-53)

Golagros might speak for any vassal struggling for independence within the feudal system, for a border chieftain caught between the competing claims of Scots and English overlords, or for a Scottish king rejecting English suzerainty.[201]

If there is a nationalistic perspective in the poem, its focus is Golagros. He is the moral and emotional core of what might have seemed to English readers a strangely old-fashioned text, combining the feudal realities of chronicle with the chivalric idealism of romance. That it was widely read in the Scotland of James IV may do something to explain the quixotic chivalry of Flodden in which national independence foundered five years after its publication.[202]

W. R. J. Barron

The Jeaste of Syr Gawayne

Although the *Jeaste of Syr Gawayne* was certainly in existence in the later fifteenth century,[203] it has survived only in four sixteenth-century copies, all to varying degrees fragmentary. Three are from printed originals;[204] the fourth and most substantial is the close transcript of such an original, that is contained in Bodleian Library Oxford, MS Douce 261, a densely illustrated[205] collection of short romances of which *The Jeaste* is the only one that is Arthurian in its subject matter,[206] and is composed almost entirely in tail-rhyme stanzas of six lines. It tells of Gawain's seduction of a maiden found in a tent, and his subsequent combats with her father and three brothers when they find him there. It lacks its opening pages, and begins abruptly with the hero's response to the maiden's warnings of danger to come:

> And sayde, 'I dreede no threte;
> I haue founde youe here in my chase':
> And in hys armes he gan her brace,
> With kyssynge of mowthes sweete.
>
> There Syr Gawayne made suche chere
> That greate frendeshyp he founde there
> With that fayre lady so gaye;
> Suche chere he made and suche semblaunce
> That longed to loue – he had her countenaunce   *favour*
> Withoute any more delaye. (*Hahn*, 1-10)[207]

Comparison of the format of the Douce text with that of the printed fragments suggests that only about 70 lines have been lost from the former.[208] A small part of their content can be inferred from later allusions in the text; a potentially greater one, from the version of the same events presented in the First Continuation of the *Perceval* of Chrétien de Troyes, the 1530 print of which has been noted as the most likely source of the Scottish *Golagros and Gawane*. And here again the self-contained English narrative corresponds to two widely separated episodes in the French[209] – those omitted by the Scots redactor – but now the second not only completes the first, but includes a fresh account of the events in it. This is supplied, not by the narrator, but by Gawain, and in a way that presents him in a much less favourable light than before; where the narrator's version had been a story of seduction, Gawain's own is an admission of rape.[210]

The *Jeaste* combines features of both these accounts. As in the second, Gawain remains with the lady in the tent until the last of her kinsfolk has appeared there (392-406); as in the first, he never has to force himself upon her. This eclecticism makes it impossible to assume that any specific detail in the early part of either of the French accounts of events was also present in the missing section of Douce. In what is now its third stanza, the girl's father, Gylbert, finds the couple making love, refuses Gawain's offer of reparation, fights with him, and is overcome. This pattern is then twice repeated with her brothers Gyamoure and Terry as the hero's opponents, but is modified when Brandles, the much more formidable third brother, appears. This time the combat is indecisive, although both knights promise to resume it when they next meet. Gawain hobbles away ingloriously on foot; Brandles reviles and beats his sister: '"Fye on the, harlot stronge! / Yt ys pyttie thou lyvest so longe: / Strypes harde I wyll the sette."' (506-8), and both knights are said by the narrator to be glad that they never met again.[211]

Such a concentration of uncourtly and unheroic detail at the end of the romance, together with the use of 'Jeaste' in its title,[212] suggests at least a partial burlesque of Arthurian chivalry. This is also implied at some earlier points. The reduction of a knight to a mere footsoldier by the loss of his horse – that outward and visible sign of chivalry – is something that is experienced not only by Gawain, but by the first three of his opponents (83-5, 179-80 and 301).[213] On the other hand, there is little in the detail or phrasing that is obviously grotesque;[214] what is more striking is the relative sameness of the individual combats. This is not to be found in any of the other short romances with Gawain as hero, but – as the relevant parts of the First Continuation remind us – is not uncommon in romances on a larger scale.[215]

The uneasy response *The Jeaste* provokes in the reader is closely bound up with its characterization of Gawain, which unites a number of the diverse qualities ascribed to him in Arthurian romance as a whole. He is at once a formidable fighter (53-5, 155-7, 264-8, 449-54), and a knight who prefers to make reparation to an injured party than to fight with him (32-7, 131-6, 242-4, 422-30); a lover who is obsessive in his own pursuit of pleasure – '"I am nowe here in my playnge – / I wyll not go awaye for no threatynge, / Or that I will feele more woo"' (80-2) – but is considerate enough to try to shield his mistress from any harm: '"Syr knyght be frende to that gentle woman, / As ye be gentle knyght."' (486-7). His attitude towards his opponents varies from the contemptuous – '"ys that youre boast greate? / I wende youe woulde have foughten tyll ye had sweate! / Ys youre strenght all done?"' (275-7) – to the generous: '"I sawe not or nowe thys yeares thre / A man more lyke a man to be"' (410-11). In much the same way, while the father Gylbert – like his sons – reviles Gawain (18), he also concedes that no man had ever before won his daughter's love (20-2), and later gives him an unexpected testimonial:

> 'The knyght ys stronge and well fight can,
> And when he hathe at hande a man,
> He wyll do hym none yll;
> But gentle wordes speake agayne   *in reply*
> And do hym no harm ne mayne: *violence*
> Thus gentyll he ys in skyll.' (383-8)   *self-control*

One of the more surprising features is that, while the reader is constantly reminded of the identity of the hero, the other characters never seem to be aware of it; the nearest that any of them gets to being so is when Gyamoure surmises that he must be one of Arthur's knights of the Round Table (193-4). This is in marked contrast to what we find in both French versions of the story.[216]

Apart from its own interest as a stripped-down chivalric narrative, with a characterization of its hero that is more complex than has sometimes been held, *The Jeaste* provides a fascinating contrast with *Golagros and Gawane*, that other fusion of episodes originally treated separately, and at considerable narrative distance in the First Continuation. For all his redeeming features, the hero of *Jeaste* remains very different from the epitome of chivalric virtue who dominates the Scottish romance, and the differences between the two texts – and possibly between the audiences for which they were intended – are pointed by the contrasting stanza-forms used: weightily elaborate in *Golagros*, simplistically loose-limbed in *The Jeaste*. The one is perfectly adapted to a complex and traditional ideal of knightly behaviour; the other to a more flexible, 'modern' and opportunistic approach to living, conduct which, while not sexually aggressive, is very much of the kind that earned Gawain his dubious reputation as a womanizer.   **Maldwyn Mills**

Sir Gawain and the Green Knight

Texts such as *The Awntyrs* and *Golagros and Gawane* have, until recently, been critically undervalued in a way which has deprived *Sir Gawain and the Green Knight*, perhaps the most subtle and complex of all medieval romances, of an important part of its creative context. Largely disassociated from the northern alliterative tradition, despite the evidence of its dialect and metre, it was initially related to, and unfavourably compared with, the French tradition of courtly romance.[217] Some early commentators rejected any idea of a French source, judging the construction too clumsy, the motivation too inept to derive from *roman courtois*; for later critics it was precisely the structural complexity and unique interrelation of structure and theme which ruled out redaction from any integral source.[218] No such source has emerged from the detailed study of plot analogues;[219] and plot is, in any case, no more than the skeleton of the poem. The fabric in which it is clothed combines themes, motifs, conventions found in the most sophisticated French romances, notably those of Chrétien de Troyes and his continuators and contemporaries, deployed with a structured ambivalence, humour, irony and verbal dialectic reminiscent of the expressive techniques of Chrétien himself.[220]

Both literary analogues and expressive means imply an audience of social sophisticates and an author familiar with courtly values and clerical disciplines. But the text is rooted in the West Midlands by its alliterative affiliations, its dialectal and stylistic integrity, its vocabulary rich in regional words of Scandinavian origin, even by certain geographical references which suggest the local landscape.[221] The modest manuscript, crudely illustrated, where *Gawain* is associated with three complex, intellectually demanding, religious poems, hardly implies a courtly readership. But the manuscript is not the author's original; his idiom is eclectic, including many French words in general literary use; and he shows intimate knowledge of law, theology and dialectic, of chivalric armour, castle architecture, aristocratic dress, and the refined etiquette of court and hunting field. The enigma of author and audience remains unresolved.[222]

But it is perhaps more apparent than real: the infinite subtlety of the poet's art suggests a genius equalled only by Chaucer, the complexity of his poems projects an audience exceptional anywhere. If, as most recently suggested (Putter, 191-7), the London of Richard II could have furnished an audience of his Cheshire courtiers whose chivalry had been refined by the civility, introspection and moral deliberation taught by clerics and the personal honesty and contractual integrity of metropolitan merchants, there seems no reason why they should not have been equally alert to this admixture of values when at home in their provincial base. In an age when the royal administration was peripatetic and nobles of all ranks maintained great households upon their estates, provincial residence need not imply provinciality. The respect shown by the poet for such a provincial court at Hautdesert, equated with Arthur's Camelot, and his persistent irony suggest a degree of detachment from metropolitan values.[223] Whether the detachment is that of a provincial with an outsider's fleeting experience of court and commerce or of a court poet with an unconventional mind is, in the last analysis, less significant that the capacity he anticipated in his audience. That he could conceive an audience capable of the poem which, after over a hundred years of study, we still inadequately understand, is perhaps the greatest mystery about the *Gawain*-poet.

Any judgement on the make-up of the audience must take into account the multiple levels on which the poem may be read and the wide variety of materials on which it draws. Among the latter are many types of folk-lore, from major plot motifs, such as the Beheading Game, to trifling but significant details like the flint-fire which springs from the hooves of their horses as the Green Knight rides away from Camelot, no man knows whither (459-61), and Gawain sets out to follow him into the unknown (670-71). *Sir Gawain* shares such knowledge with the courtly romance of Chrétien and his contemporaries, with its Middle English counterpart, and with folk-memory across the ages. It is ageless, classless, the core of common humanity on which rest the multiple layers of meaning in the poem.

The narrative relationships of romance and folk-tale are problematic: common motifs, common patterns of incident cannot establish direct derivation. But it is nonetheless striking that similar life-patterns often underlie their contrasting social surfaces, notably the experience of a youthful protagonist who leaves family and friends to endure trial and danger and returns mature and confident.[224] It was perhaps Gawain's reputation as the embodiment of basic manly virtues rather than the more esoteric codes of chivalry which attracted the English to him as the potential hero of such rite-of-passage episodes, the subject of many of their Arthurian romances.[225] In them he is subjected to a test imposed by a magical figure, antagonistic to Arthur's court, an opposition which may be interpreted at many levels: civilized man opposed to nature, Christianity to the ritual of pagan cults, the known and ordered to the mysterious and powerful; or – with the folk-tale focus on the hero – Gawain torn between the duty owed to his uncle Arthur and the temptation to self-interest offered by an agent of his aunt, Morgan le Fay, between the chivalric code of honour and the basic instinct for self-preservation. To declare any of these aspects of its folk-tale core the 'true' meaning of the poem would be to privilege the subtext, the latent value of the myth above what the poet chose to make of it in a complex, conscious literary creation. Related texts, rooted in the same rite-of-passage myth, demonstrate the variety of form and meaning derived from it.[226]

In the evolution of the *roman courtois*, where the fundamental human concerns of folk-tale often underlie a specific cultural idealism, courtly and chivalric, a repertoire of appropriate expressive motifs was developed: the court gathered round an archetypal feudal monarch in embodiment of chivalric values; a challenge to those values provoked by its reputation; the solitary quest of its representative through the wilderness to answer that challenge; adventures *en route* and temptations which beset him in welcoming wayside castles; the eventual encounter with the challenger and triumphant return to court. *Sir Gawain* makes use of all – but none, seemingly, in purely traditional form or with merely conventional significance. Most strikingly the anticipated outcome seems undermined by the hero's conviction of failure (2379-88), the confession of fault in which he persists to the end (2505-12), despite his companions' bland determination to interpret the outcome to the honour of the Round Table (2513-21). The nature of his fault, the moment of its occurrence, and its thematic import have stimulated a torrent of commentary and exegesis, a degree of consensus, but no absolute interpretative agreement.[227]

The natural tendency has been to read the romance in traditional terms, guided in the search for clues to meaning by the apparently conventional procedure, the clarity of the action and vividness of the verbal surface. But the conventions are confusingly deployed: the chivalric court is engaged in mimic games of love (66-70) and war (41-2), their king in honouring a custom to be fulfilled either by idealized fiction or by deadly reality (85-99); the expected challenger portends both, combining in his person the knight-challenger of romance and a mysterious emanation of nature bearing symbols of peace and war (206-20), and proposing 'a Crystemas gomen' (283), a pluck-buffet exchange which promises to be fatal. The challenge is accepted, but in general shock, royal anger and, on Gawain's part, self-abnegation (301-65); the arming ceremony confirming his heroic status as representative of the Round Table is undercut by the obvious futility of arms against an undefended blow and by the muffled laments of his comrades (672-86); the anticipated wayside adventures flash past in a catalogue parodying romance convention (715-25), while the hero contends with the bitter realities of winter and spiritual isolation (691-7, 726-39).

The reader, alternately reassured by familiar procedures of romance and frustrated in the expectations they raise, may also be puzzled by the pace of the narrative, where action develops slowly among much that seems of merely incidental interest. Yet the incidentals are so vividly presented, the action so sharply visualized that they grip the attention equally. For contemporaries the clarity and detail with which the Arthurian world is pictured may – initially at least – have fulfilled their expectation of seeing their society and their values given ideal embodiment. But even for us, cynically suspicious of romance as an idealizing mode, the writing evokes settings (natural rather than architectural), social situations, human reactions, emotions, turns of phrase which we recognize from personal experience as 'real'. Yet expectations raised by both romantic and realist readings continue to be frustrated. The knight errant's heartfelt prayer for a Christian refuge seems instantly answered by the vision of Hautdesert (753-66), part insubstantial fantasy, part contemporary fortress (763-806) (Davenport, 149-50), part Camelot, a place of ceremonious procedure, religious observance, festivities, and games involving a contract for an equal exchange; but also a place of boisterous mirth with ominous undertones, interwoven (perhaps interlinked) games of love and death, a hyper-active host like a force of nature, a seductive hostess rhetorically linked with a rebarbative hag, for each of whom romance tradition provides conflicting models which inhibit judgement (Barron 1980, 4-12).

But there are similar inhibitions in a 'realist' reading based on the thoughts and actions of the hero. Presented initially as an exemplar of chivalric courtesy and self-control, silent after the beheading while Arthur tries to dismiss it as a Christmas spectacle (462-90), then as a romance stereotype, the knight in shining armour, tight-lipped among the laments of his comrades (539-65), Gawain the man is gradually exposed through his suffering, loneliness and instinctive piety in the wintry wilderness (691-762), his pleasure in the warmth and admiration of Hautdesert (807-900), embarrassment at the Lady's intrusion into his bedroom (1179-1207), wit and verbal skill in keeping her courteously at arm's length, despite moments when sexual attraction threatens to throw him off balance (1760-9). But fellow-feeling for, identification with, the hero does not give access to his motives and intentions. His assessment of the ambiguous adventure in which he is involved, obscured by his silence, is queried by the poet's direct address to him at the end of the first fitt:

> Now þenk wel, Sir Gawan,
> For woþe þat þou ne wonde   *danger, shrink*
> Þis auenture for to frayn   *pursue*
> Þat þou hatz tan on honde. (487-90)[228]   *undertaken*

Stasis in the action follows until Gawain leaves Camelot, 'He wende (*thought*) for euermore' (669), implying a gloomy assessment in contrast with the poet's interim statement that 'Gawan watz glad to begynne þose gomnez in halle' (495), for which we have no objective evidence, itself undercut by his warning: 'Bot þaȝ þe ende be heuy (*grave*) haf ȝe no wonder' (496). Again, Gawain's judgement of his hostess is queried by his reaction to her entrance to his bedroom: initial caution (1184-6), embarrassment, avoided by feigned sleep (1189-90), concealing emotional unease and social uncertainty (1195-9) and ending eventually in an elaborate and self-conscious 'awakening' whose artifice is underlined by the poet's ponderous syntax (1200-3). Recognizably human conduct minutely observed, but motivation unclear: momentary shock, social tact, genuine suspicion of the Lady's intentions? The sign of the cross with which he greets her ends the stasis in personal action which began when he crossed himself in praying for help in the wood, its manifest sincerity there querying its sincerity in his play-acting.

This selective mimesis proves crucial at the moment when the Lady urges on Gawain the life-preserving properties of her girdle which he has already refused (1846-67). As before, we are made privy to a mental process, incomplete, leading to action and a commitment to the Lady seemingly irreconcilable with a prior commitment to her husband – all apparently in the interest of a yet earlier commitment to the Green Knight. This will later prove to be the moral core of the poem, but it is rooted in intention, implied but not manifest. Thereafter there is no direct access to Gawain's mind until, daunted by the ominous appearance of the Green Chapel, he debates with himself the demonic nature of the adversary he is to meet there (2168-211). But he struggles for self-control under his opponent's axe (2250-330), and then collapses in shame, bitterness and persistent self-accusation when the Green Knight claims the girdle as his by right of the Exchange-of-Winnings agreement (2331-438).

Convention may have prepared the original audience for some inter-connection between the two games, the two contracts, but romance tradition offers little guidance to the cause of Gawain's collapse in apparent victory, the source of his self-accusation. They will, however, have been instinctively alert to sources of meaning beyond convention and narrative incident, not least in many passages which seem to modern readers incidental, ornamental or merely rhetorical. Even the modern mind accepts that there may be elements of symbolism in the arming of the hero (566-669), a rhetorical set-piece characterizing both military exterior and moral core, rooted in St Paul's symbolic itemization of the Christian virtues as parts of 'the whole armour of God' (Ephesians VI, 10-17), and the widespread epic tradition of the hero's arms as embodying both the man and his mission (Burrow 1965, 37-40). Here the focus is on the shield, Paul's 'shield of faith', and its heraldic charge, emblem of Gawain's chivalric identity, the pentangle, a perfect figure, balanced, unbroken, yet a composite of five fives, 'In bytoknyng of trawþe' (626). This diversity in unity and the potential meanings of 'trawþe', whose complex semantic range is rooted in the concept 'truth', have troubled commentators, many of whom stress the underlying quality of integrity.[229]

Recent study of medieval symbolism has revealed the roots of such complexity, varying symbolic meaning being attached to objects, animals, etc. according to context, interpreted now favourably, now pejoratively. The result, after centuries of evolution, was a flexible vocabulary of signs whose multivalence poets could exploit with deliberate ambiguity to convey multiple levels of meaning (Arthur, 3-9). R.G. Arthur, noting that the pentangle is known among the English as 'þe endeles knot' (630), distinguishes related functions: as a perfect figure symbolising absolute *veritas* represented by God and, as a composite, the relative human values to which Gawain seeks to be true, not in emulation but, by grace, in *imitatio christi*[230] – his aspiration to perfection in thought and deed, in faith in Christ the Redeemer and devotion to Mary the Intercessor, and in the practice of five chivalric virtues.

Even to an age more alert to ambiguous symbols than our own, the itemization of the pentangle may, at first reading, have seemed as conventional as the rest of his armour, as formally pious as the religious ceremonies in which he is involved at Camelot and Hautdesert, devoid of ambiguity. Yet other items in his equipment, emblematic rather than formally symbolic, foreshadow ambiguity, suggesting the possibility of one element in his integrated code being privileged above others, distorting the unity of the pentangle.[231] The image of the Virgin on the inner side of his shield (644-50) may imply a special devotion to one of the five pentads. Similarly, the embroidery on the 'vrysoun', the band securing his helmet, the handiwork of many Camelot maidens (607-14), may allude through its paired motifs to two types of love, sacred and profane, and the eloquence used to express both.[232] The diamonds on the circlet about his helmet (615-8), credited in the lapidaries with protective properties, may suggest a magic talisman, such as that 'juel for þe jopardé' (1856) which Gawain later sees in the girdle.[233]

Contemporary readers would not have been surprised to detect ambiguities underlying the code of the Pentangle Knight. In French tradition, Gawain had long been a notorious philanderer, the skilled seducer who loves and leaves (Benson 1965, 104-5), while the English went on celebrating the old, uncomplicated, heart-free Gawain for his physical prowess and manly virtues until Malory introduced his amorous counterpart. The poet's intention to play upon his ambivalent reputation is openly apparent from Gawain's reception at Hautdesert, where his name brings instant recognition as one esteemed for 'prys (*worth*) and prowes and pured þewes (*refined chivalry*)' (912), skilled in 'þe teccheles (*polished*) termes of talkyng noble' (917). This narrowing of focus isolates the social virtues of the fifth pentad, in particular 'cortaysye', the refinement of conduct appropriate to courts: the protective service which knighthood owes to the weak, women among them; the deference and courtesy due to ladies; the elegant wooing and verbal, if not physical, seduction to which such devotion leads (Spearing 1970, 199-201). And there are signs that the renowned seducer is susceptible to his hostess: in his sensual awareness of her at first meeting (970-6), their privy conversation in the presence of her husband (1010-19), and his panic at her entrance to his bedroom (1182-1203).

The inversion of conventional norms (the notorious seducer trapped, naked in his bed, by a beautiful woman) and the uneasy moral atmosphere (laughter at the Pentangle Knight's questionable use of a sacred sign) set the tone for the remainder of Gawain's stay at Hautdesert. The situation seems familiar: a new adventure beginning, presumably to be interwoven with, perhaps to supply a solution to, the Beheading Game; a new game, a new exchange, possibly a new test. But a female testing agent, a wayside hostess for whom tradition suggests many different roles: a self-interested sexual fly-trap, an agent of entrapment acting for some jealous male, the wife of some generous host whose sexual hospitality permits kisses but nothing more – what is her real aim in the courtly love badinage in which Gawain, skilled in 'luf-talkyng', keeps her courteously at arm's length? In such uncertainty a contemporary reader might fall back upon romance convention and look for an emblematic or metaphorical relationship between the Lady's wooing and her lord's hunting.

Where modern commentators first saw incidental celebrations of contemporary idealisms – the courtly art of amorous badinage, literature made life, and hunting raised to a noble art, life made literature – they now see a bewildering variety of interpretative possibilities. Given the complex structure of Fitt III, the repetitive patterning of events on all three days, the meticulous indication of time implying that hunting and wooing occur simultaneously, it seems natural to identify Gawain with the hunted prey.[234] But, noting the ease with which, overcoming his initial embarrassment, he defends himself against the Lady's advances with wit and courtesy, Burrow (1965, 78-89) rejects parallelism in favour of contrast, in keeping with the general contrast of healthy, natural, outdoor activity against the cloistered, static, vaguely unnatural pursuit of male by female in the bedroom, the one ending – initially at least – in substantial winnings to be exchanged against kisses whose worth is problematic.

For the medieval audience, judgement on the interrelation of hunting and wooing was complicated by the complex tradition of the metaphorical hunt, rooted in the imagery of the chase exploited by classical love poets and developed over centuries in multiple literary forms and interpretations: the hunt of love, its obverse the mortal hunt in which the hunter falls victim to his quarry, the sacred chase in which the quarry is the emissary of a deity, benign or vengeful, sent to aid or punish the hunter, whose pursuit may lead him from ignorance to knowledge in the instructive chase (Thiébaux). In the alliterative tradition there are texts, including *The Awntyrs off Arthure*, in which the hunt is used as a figure for the Pride of Life, pleasure in worldly pursuits represented both by the seductive Lady and her hunting lord (Rooney, 188-9). Anne Rooney suggests that the function of this combination of motifs is not to alert the audience to the real nature of the action in Fitt III, the relation of the games being played to the anticipated outcome of the Beheading Game, but rather to mask it, inducing complacent expectations of a traditional outcome to the amorous hunt as merely an interlude in the main action, licensing supposition that the worldly hunter foreshadows Gawain's deadly opponent there.

The literary situation seems, however, to be even more complex. The simultaneity of action suggests to Burrow (1965, 74-7) a basic technique of fabliau, bringing something of its bedroom atmosphere and the question of how the returning husband will react to tokens of sexual favour exchanged against material goods as so often in fabliau. If fabliau is to be the dominant mode it promises laughter. But the vivid mimesis with which both bedroom and hunting field are evoked makes it difficult to forget the real world and the likely response of a husband to a kiss gained during a day spent in the company of his wife. By feudal usage, the proper recourse for him, should he interpret the kiss as evidence of sexual impropriety, is either to execute summary justice upon a seducer taken *in flagrante* or to arraign Gawain before his seigniorial court on a charge of sexual treason, as one owing temporary allegiance to him while his guest (1039-41, 1089-92). And when, after the bedroom interlude, we find the lord still in the field (1319-64), presiding among his followers in the solemn ceremony of the 'asay' – 'examination of the venison for quality and condition' but also 'a testing of character or personal traits (such as faithfulness, friendship, faith, fortitude); trial, ordeal' (MED *assai* n., 2(a)) – followed by the disembowelling, beheading and quartering of the deer, the metaphorical hunt may seem to end in the contemporary death of traitors. So the Lady might indirectly achieve the death of her prey, the amorous hunt fusing with the mortal – as in similar texts (Thiébaux, 105-43).

The idea is, of course, ridiculous, to be dismissed as untenable, alien to romance – though not, perhaps, more improbable than a Christmas game at Camelot which ended in decapitation. The proper balance of game and earnest is restored in the good-humoured Exchange-of-Winnings (1372-97); the suspect kiss is received with jokes about its value and its source, and the compact renewed (1398-411), both in strangely mingled terms of game, commerce and law. But when, on the second day, the narrative leaves the bedroom for the hunting field, Bertilak brings to bay a solitary boar, so often the emblem of heroic valour, in an epic duel perhaps intended as a metaphor for the judicial process known as trial by combat under which a charge of treason within the Court of Chivalry was resolved in single combat. The defeated accused, if still living, immediately suffered a traitor's death, as the boar is beheaded, disembowelled and dismembered, and his head set up upon a stake (1560-614). The parallels with contemporary justice are stronger and the verbal duel in the bedroom is conducted in terms of chivalric literature, but the implications of the metaphorical hunt are no less exaggerated, unacceptable.

The third morning must bring uncertainty, since by the thrcefold narrative pattern which romance inherited from folk-tale, the pattern of events established on the first day and confirmed on the second is varied on the third. And the lord's quarry is a fox, inedible vermin, ignoble game, unknown elsewhere in romance but notorious in fable as wily, malicious, greedy and, above all, a thief (Rooney, 190-1). An unthinkable metaphorical model for the Pentangle Knight? Some critics suggest that the hunted beasts typify the role which Gawain is *invited* to play;[235] but, though his momentary alarm at the Lady's first entrance to his bedroom may suggest the panic of the driven deer, he rapidly recovers his social poise and when, on the second day, she implies that he could overcome by force any resistance she might offer, he rejects the implied parallel with the violence of the boar (1489-500). The relationship of hunting and wooing, on these two days, is primarily one of contrast rather than parallelism (Burrow 1965, 87); yet Gawain's resemblance to the fox is widely accepted (Burrow 1965, 98). What has passed in the bedroom to justify such a parallel?

Though the pattern of each day there is subtly varied to sustain tension, Gawain's evident concern throughout has been to maintain 'cortaysye' towards the Lady by responding to her advances and 'felaȝschyp' towards her husband by confining his response to 'luf-talkyng'. Both social virtues are part of the indivisible unity of the pentangle and, as such, breach of either is a breach of 'trawþe'. On the third morning, when the danger of a physical response is heightened by Gawain's sensual reaction to the Lady's decolletage (1760-5), the poet comments 'Gret perile bitwene hem stod, / Nif (*unless*) Maré of hir knyȝt mynne' (*be mindful*) (1768-9) – evoking the protective power of divine love – and summarizes the multiple threat to his 'trawþe' should he

> Oþer lach þer hir luf, oþer lodly refuse.   *accept, offensively*
> He cared for his cortaysye, lest craþayn he were,   *boor*
> And more for his meschef ȝif he schulde make synne,
> And be traytor to þat tolke þat þat telde aȝt. (1772-5) *castle, owned*

The use of 'traytor' seems exact, a technical term for one who breaks his feudal troth and, if by adultery with his lord's wife, doubly a sinner, both against 'clannes' and against the Christian basis of the feudal oath. But there is to be no adultery; Gawain maintains his courtesy, refuses to give a love-token too trifling to be worthy of the Lady (1798-812), or to accept one of great worth from her – because, she suggests, it would impose too great an obligation, offering instead her silken girdle. That too is refused – because of its trifling worth, she suggests, adding: ' "But who-so knew þe costes (*qualities*) þat knit ar þerinne, / He wolde hit prayse (*value*) at more prys (*worth*), parauenture" ' (1849-50). It has, she says, the power to protect from violent attack. Suddenly, as at the moment of her first entrance to the bedroom, we are admitted behind the verbal facade to share Gawain's thoughts and, as on that occasion, they seem entirely human and natural, calculating the value of the life-saving girdle: 'Hit were a juel for þe jopardé (*perilous adventure*) þat hym iugged (*assigned*) were: / When he acheued (*arrived*) to þe chapel his chek for to fech (*meet his doom*)' (1856-7). As before, they lead to impulsive action, his acceptance of the girdle interjected into the Lady's offering speech before the governing condition of concealment from her husband is mentioned (1859-65).[236] As with the sign of the cross, motive and intention remain unclear; but Gawain's consciousness expresses itself in the language of the fox-hunt – 'kest', 'chek', 'slypped'. Yet when he rises, and has carefully concealed the girdle, he passes the day with even greater contentment than usual.

Meanwhile, in the hunting field, the fox is still running well, dodging and doubling back, when suddenly, finding the lord in his path, he starts back from the drawn sword, falls into the mouths of the hounds, and is stripped of his skin. If the metaphorical hunt is still felt to be operative, the implications for Gawain are ominous: that, shrinking from fear of death under the Green Knight's axe, he has turned thief by taking the girdle, and may suffer a felon's fate as one who stole covertly. The fox-hunt (1697-730, 1893-921), presented in terms of the sounds of pursuit by a 'rabel' (MED *rabil* n. (a) A crowd of people, ? a noisy crowd; also, a pack of hounds), with hallooing and sounding of horns, like villagers pursuing a common thief by the legal process of hue and cry whereby, if taken with the stolen goods upon him, he is tried by a kangaroo court and executed immediately, the owner of the goods perhaps acting as executioner (Barron 1980, 73). Even those who accept a metaphorical relationship between Gawain and the fox could not countenance the idea that he may die the death of a common thief, still less by flaying, that rare but notorious penalty for treason more likely to result from mob violence than due legal process.[237] And so far the metaphorical hunt has been used, not to predict narrative developments, but to draw attention to inherent moral and thematic possibilities. What felony on Gawain's part might merit the fate of the fox? Sexual treason? – since the girdle, a typical *gage d'amour*, the first garment to be removed in a seduction, may seem to Bertilak weightier evidence than the mounting toll of kisses. Theft? – since, should he retain the girdle, either for his own protection or that of the Lady's reputation, he will be beholding what properly belongs to her lord. Breach of 'trawþe'? – towards his host, should he retain the girdle; towards his hostess, should he surrender it. Talk of treason must seem grossly exaggerated in what amounts to no more than a case of petty theft, devious avoidance of a merely social commitment. But what treason does breach of the pentangle constitute? Treason to self, by falling short of self-imposed aspirations? To man, in neglecting those chivalric obligations which govern social relations in a feudal society? To God, in sinning against the fundamental Christian bond between man and his creator on which feudalism, chivalry and Gawain's pentangle ultimately rest?

That bond is evoked when, on rising, Gawain goes to confession (1872-84) 'þere he schrof hym (*confessed*) schyrly (*completely*) and schewed his mysdedez' (1880) and was fully absolved and made as pure as if Doomsday were to fall upon the morrow. The reader, excluded from the confessional relationship between Gawain's conscience and his God, must accept the impenetrable candour and verbal precision of the narrative. What the poet allows him to observe is Gawain's eagerness for the final exchange of winnings with his host (1924-59), and sleeplessness during a stormy New Year's night (1991-2008). Then, in a pendant to the arming at Camelot, he openly dons the girdle he had so carefully concealed (2025-42) and, rejecting his guide's warning to avoid the ruthless guardian of the Green Chapel (2089-159), rides off with every appearance of Christian confidence to meet his doom.

As Gawain wraps the green and gold of the girdle over the golden pentangle emblazoned on the red of his surcoat (2025-42) it is evident that a new symbol has emerged, the obverse of the old in physical form and symbolic potential. Its oblique introduction and the complexity of the associated tradition might well disorientate the reader: offered and refused as a love-token (1827-45), offered again as a protective talisman (1846-54), accepted and worn by Gawain in a way which suggests confidence in its magic powers, it continues to mutate throughout the poem, referred to variously as 'girdle', 'belt', 'lace', 'luf-lace', 'drurye', 'saynt', challenging the reader's judgement of its significance in each new situation.[238] So Gawain sets out to meet the Green Knight already wearing his green livery, no longer wholly the Pentangle Knight yet still wearing his badge of 'trawþe' juxtaposed with 'his drurye (*love token*)' which he values 'for to sauen hymself' (2040) – symbol of his love of life or of self-love? He bows his head under the Green Knight's axe openly wearing the kind of protective charm forbidden to knights in single combat – but this is no equal combat and the adversary no natural opponent. We cannot tell, as he flinches from the first feint, what faith he puts in the girdle, whether he is conscious of any breach of contract in having retained it, of any incompatibility between retention and a valid confession, but the very openness with which he wears it suggests either moral blindness or shamelessness.

When the axe finally descends, doing no more than graze Gawain's neck, leaving a drop of blood on the snow at his feet, he falls immediately into a defensive posture, shouting defiance in a speech incoherent with jumbled emotions (2315-30) – 'Neuer syn þat he watz burne borne of his moder / Watz he neuer in þis worlde wyʒe (*man*) half so blyþe' (2320-1). Natural feelings in one who has escaped from death, but the blood on the snow, potentially an image of punishment for sin and of the source of redemption for sinners, coupled with that of the new-born child, a reminder of the shriven soul as a soul reborn (Burrow 1965, 132), may query their source: the justified confidence of the sanctified; the triumph of one who relies solely on his own prowess at the failure of an adversary; instinctive relief of one who, offered the girdle, reflected that 'Myʒt he haf slypped to be vnslayn, þe sleʒt (*device, trick*) were noble' (1858), at the success of his protective talisman? The conventional reader can relax; somehow or other the hero has survived as romance tradition anticipates, seemingly confirmed by the Green Knight's laughter as he mocks Gawain's over-reaction (2331-68).

But the ambivalence of laughter throughout the poem, the frequency with which it has been undercut by the threat of aggression, the uneasy parallelism between the Green Knight's grim game and the social sports at Hautdesert with their undertones of violence, undermines complacency as the interdependence of the two exchange compacts is revealed and the *personae* of the two instigators fuse together. As this composite personality claims the girdle as his own, reminding Gawain that ' "Trwe mon trwe restore" ' (2354), and so ' "here yow lakked a lyttel, sir, and lewté yow wonted" ' (2366), we may wonder what he knows of the circumstances of its retention. His comment may be a legal one on the breach of the Exchange-of-Winnings compact, but some of the terms he uses evoke echoes of treason and restitution, implying the wider moral issues involved in Gawain's fault.

Gawain's response (2369-88) is stunned silence, inner mortification, violent physical symptoms of shame, then an impulsive ejaculation: ' "Corsed worth (*be*) cowarddyse and couetyse boþe! / In yow is vylany and vyse þat vertue disstryez" ' (2374-5). It seems an accurate, if impersonal, acknowledgement of his fault – that cowardice in the face of death made him covet another's property, which he now returns, tossing it to the Green Knight with ' "Lo! þer þe falssyng" ' (2378). His perception of the girdle has changed: what he once saw as 'a juel for þe jopardé' has become a token of broken faith, as if he confounds his devious behaviour (MED *falsing* ger., (a) 'deceitful or treacherous dealing') with the innocent agent of his downfall ('also something that deceives or misleads'). The forms are those of penance – contrition, restitution – but without the spirit of *caritas*, the sorrow for sins which should inform them. There follows confession of mouth, beginning with personal admission of the faults already recognized, cowardice and covetousness, but in chivalric rather than moral terms, as failings in knightly integrity, offences against 'larges' and 'lewté', the 'fraunchyse' and 'felaȝschyp' of the pentangle, culminating in:

> 'Now am I fawty and falce, and ferde haf ben euer   *afraid*
> Of trecherye and vntrawþe: boþe bityde sorȝe   *befall*
>   and care!
> I biknowe yow, knyȝt, here stylle,   *confess, humbly*
> Al fawty is my fare;   *sinful, behaviour*
> Letez me ouertake your wylle,   *understand, wishes*
> And efte I schal be ware.' (2382-8)   *henceforth*

Gawain accuses himself, by implication, of 'untrawþe' – but is his offence against the social values of the pentangle or its Christian basis? – and of 'trecherye' – but treason to man or to God? It is as if, in shock, he realizes that theft and retention of the girdle must mean his confession at Hautdesert was, consciously or unconsciously, incomplete, and his first coherent impulse is to claim the cleansing power of the sacrament he has abused, an act as instinctive and unreflecting as his use of the sign of the cross, acceptance of the girdle, even, perhaps, his first confession. In each case his behaviour must be judged on the intention behind his act – since, according to Aquinas, 'there is no sin unless the act is ultimately controlled by the will' – which the reader cannot determine from the limited access afforded him to Gawain's consciousness.[239] In retrospect it is possible to imagine that, overwhelmed by inordinate desire for the protective girdle – a 'gust of passion' in Aquinas's terms – he was unconscious of the nature and consequences of his act. Yet the taking of the girdle – as, in a lesser sense, the sign of the cross – was in defence of the values of the pentangle and the reputation it represents, that the Pentangle Knight might not prove 'a knyȝt kowarde'. If we doubted Gawain's sincerity in defence of his reputation, can we doubt it now when he exposes it to the judgement of the man he has offended, as to a new confessor?

Laughingly, the Green Knight accepts the role, acknowledges completeness of confession along with the penance received from his axe, and pronounces an absolution as blandly absolute as that at Hautdesert (2391-4), reminding us that both confessors are merely intermediaries; only God knows the penitent's heart and forgiveness is His. Conscious intention to retain the girdle would have invalidated Gawain's confession, preparation for which should have involved ordered recollection of sinful acts and intentions. Withholding the girdle from Bertilak equalled him with the fox as a sneak-thief; failing to recognize that he put greater faith in it than in God, an act of spiritual treason, would associate him with the fox as the type of covetousness, pride and hypocrisy. If the flaying of the fox implies that Gawain has been guilty of spiritual treason, the metaphorical hunt may suggest that form in which the quarry is driven by a deity to salvation or destruction – a possibility readily dismissed by those who know less of Gawain's heart than he who confesses 'trecherye and vntrawþe'.

Penance should restore the state of *caritas* between the sinner and God on one hand and the fellow man he has offended on the other, but there seems to be something wrong with Gawain's post-confessional state (2395-428). Urged to return to Hautdesert and be reconciled with the Lady, he bursts into a bitter catalogue of famous men brought to grief by the wiles of women – Adam, Solomon, Samson, David – exemplary types used in the Middle Ages to illustrate both the possibilities and limitations of human virtue. The echo of Adam's accusation against Eve in Gawain's '"hit were a wynne (*gain*) huge / To luf hom wel, and leue (*believe*) hem not"' (2420-21) associates him with the type of those who, by blaming others for misleading them, attempt to throw their sin upon God and their lack of free will. The irrelevance of his antifeminism – since it was not love for the Lady but covetous desire for her girdle which led him to credit her account of its powers – underscores his uncharitable bitterness. The modern reader's sympathies for him are roused by the revelation of Bertilak's dual identity, his role as the agent of Morgan le Fay in challenging the arrogance of the Round Table (2439-70), which seems to some critics late and inadequate motivation (Benson 1965, 32-4). The contemporary reader may well have found it purely conventional, a sop to the rational mind; the moral sense recognizes that no chivalric hero can justly complain of lack of fair play in his testing. Romance demonstrates that the very existence of chivalry is a challenge to the forces of evil which lie in wait for knights-errant on every forest path, in every wayside castle – that is why they don 'the whole armour of God'.

Nevertheless Gawain parts from his testing agent in charity, exchanging the kiss of peace, and returns to Camelot wearing the girdle, permanent badge of his penitential wound, slung baldric-wise across the pentangle on his surcoat as a bend sinister modifying his claim to 'trawþe', and in formal public confession before the Round Table proclaims: ' "Þis is þe token of vntrawþe þat I am tan (*detected*) inne" ' (2509). For him the shape-shifting girdle has become a badge of perpetual penitence to be worn throughout life: ' "For mon may hyden his harme, bot vnhap ne may hit, / For þer hit onez is tachched twynne wil hit neuer" ' (2511-12; *'for one may conceal one's offence, but cannot undo it, for once it has become fixed it will never leave one'*). The rejection of any remedy for sin suggests despair of salvation, itself a mortal sin. The gravity of Gawain's self-condemnation is immediately undercut by the laughter of his Round Table comrades, who adopt the green girdle as a badge of honour to be worn by all (2513-21). Theirs is the third judgement on Gawain, the Green Knight having already judged his failing entirely human – ' "For ȝe lufed your lyf; þe lasse I yow blame" ' (2368), and his worth by comparison with other knights that of a pearl among dried peas, to be honoured ' "for þy grete trauþe" '(2470). A rational and comparative judgement to be contrasted with the court's glib response; but what do they or Bertilak know of Gawain's heart?

He does not speak again and his self-condemnation stands, suggesting at best attrition but not yet perfect contrition. 'In strictly theological terms Gawain is still in a state of sin at the end of the poem – for he has made no sacramental atonement' (Burrow 1965, 156); a dangerous condition, but not necessarily a permanent one.[240] So the action ends not with resolution but implication, not with a pat solution confirming chivalric values, in the manner of conventional romance, but in an enigma challenging reconsideration of their validity in relation to human instinct on one hand and God's will for his creation on the other – as in the other works attributed to the *Gawain*-poet.[241] The three judgements passed upon the hero's conduct challenge our own. The moral arena of the poem is located in his heart to which our access is limited; but our knowledge of his acts is intimate enough to make us participants, challenged to weigh their outcome in the light of our own moral perception. As readers of romance we accept that literature should express human idealism in its most exalted form. But when the issue becomes one of life and death, we find it natural if not excusable, recognizing our own humanity in the hero, that absolute values should give way to pragmatic ones, concern for reputation to love of life, the sense of honour to the instinct for self-preservation (Davenport, 151-2). Our own failure to identify the precise nature of Gawain's fault, the moment of its occurrence, its complex moral implications, all the elements which have exercised critics, involves us in his humiliation. In response we can complacently agree with Bertilak/Green Knight that comparative virtue is the best of which our humanity is capable, smile with Arthur's court at the intemperance of a disappointed idealist, or, recognizing signs of dawning contrition, accept that the Pentangle Knight's aspiration to *imitatio christi* has been modified rather than abandoned, that the metaphorical hunt has ended in self-knowledge, and that Gawain's fault may prove a *felix culpa* bringing greater awareness of the nature of Christian chivalry as an ideal conditioned by human fallibility, of romance as an idealizing mode illuminating the limitations of reality (Arthur, 151-8, Haines, 74-105).

The literary category of the poem is evoked and its theme generalized when, at the last moment, as Arthur's court relegates its representative's bitter experience to the perspective of romance (and the word is mentioned for the first time), the linear record of western chivalry runs back through 'þe Brutus bokez' to the moment when, 'After þe segge and þe asaute watz sesed at Troye' (2525; cf. 1), the archetypal hero 'þat þe trammes of tresoun (*web of treason*) þer wroȝt' (3), tested under a double obligation, redeems his betrayal of one by an admirable deception, 'þe trewest on erthe', in the other, and survives to father the race which founded that New Troy where 'blysse and blunder' have alternated ever since. By echoing the opening line at line 2525, multiple reminder of the five pentads of the symbol of 'trawþe', the poem connects the founding father with the Pentangle Knight who, through a petty deception for the preservation of his chivalric values, fell into a spiritual treason as yet unpurged. But it does not end there; its 101 stanzas, completing one cycle and beginning another (Turville-Petre 1977, 68), suggest that the history of man has its steady cycles like the seasons (Tristram, 112), that 'blunder' may turn to 'blysse', that, as readily as he turned from 'trawþe' to 'vntrawþe', the traitor may become the truest on earth. And the lines which extend beyond the historical circularity of the poem, with its evocation of the dynastic tradition and the eventual downfall of the Round Table, offer, in the tritest of terminal conventions, an escape from the inevitability of human error, a redeeming power forged by trial and suffering from man's most monstrous sin: 'Now þat bere þe croun of þorne, / He bryng vus to his blysse! AMEN' (2529-30).

As time, the past, British history encapsulates the experience of the poem, so its complex, manifold structure frames, focuses, directs, deceives, compelling constant interpretation and reinterpretation. The conventional reader, early identifying the linear structure of quest, follows it complacently – despite a distracting profusion of parallels and contrasts and the apparent interlude at Hautdesert, protracted and hermetically structured – until Fitt IV repeats in reverse order narrative motifs which preceded the interlude, revealing a circularity of structure completed by the reversed repetition of the dynastic framework. This fusion of the linear structure of romance with the ring structure of oral literature, folk-tale, ballad, disorientates, confusing expectation of where the crisis of the action may lie and compelling reinterpretation of parallels earlier perceived.[242]

Other elements of romance convention are similarly varied, juxtaposed, combined with extraneous motifs in a way which queries their conventional significance and the values they traditionally express. In his antifeminist outburst (2411-28), for example, Gawain falls back in self-justification upon an established rhetorical convention, inviting consideration of its relevance to his observed conduct but also reconsideration of the validity of the topos itself, reassuring in its banality. His reliance on such a commonplace implies the limitation of Gawain's self-awareness; his literary persona is often evoked in terms of similar topoi which – like his reputation for 'cortaysye' in his response to the Lady – constrain his freedom of action and moral choice.[243] By continually arousing predictable expectations only deliberately to disappoint them, the poet queries the nature and procedures of romance. Evoking in turn the various sub-types of the genre, he passes from the dynastic romance of the opening to the courtly romance evoked by Camelot, where Arthur's custom raises expectations of adventure romance, apparently fulfilled by the Green Knight's proposal of a typical Challenger-Tryst, whose presentation as game seems to undermine its heroic potential. The ritual arming of Fitt II evokes the Gawain of courtly tradition and, through the moral itemization of the pentangle, a Christian warrior, suggesting two potential heroes, two contrasting types of romance. Fitt III promises *entrelacement* of love with adventure but proves apparently self-contained; eventual proof of its thematic significance outrages the normal expectations of romance, as much of a shock to the audience as to Gawain, since it reverses the usual function of interlace by proving the hero's *unfitness* to achieve the overall adventure. Fitt IV returns to the adventure paradigm and the atmosphere of conventional romance heightened by concentration on the hero's expectations as, exposed to humiliation rather than saved by the girdle, he finds his chivalric integrity flawed. The linking of romance with history in the closing frame suggests its ambiguous relation to reality; self-conscious manipulation of its conventions and the expectations of both audience and characters focuses critical attention not only upon chivalric values but upon chivalric fiction.[244]

The evocation of various types of romance is part of the dialectic of opposites which pervades all levels of the text, from the opening opposition of 'blysse' and 'blunder', through contrasting pairs of symbols, structurally juxtaposed episodes, to the underlying contrast between civilized and natural values leading to Gawain's ultimate choice between chivalric 'trawþe' and the instinct for self-preservation, and consequently to the issue of his moral status. The poet is apparently exploiting his audience's familiarity with contemporary debate poetry; if so, it seems significant that such debates so often avoid formal conclusions and leave thematic resolution to the individual reader. In an age of orthodoxies, such literary games allowed the free play of ideas, recognition of the bewildering complexity of the human condition, perhaps a freshened appreciation of established dogma.[245] The multiple perspective which such techniques permit seems characteristic of contemporary art and literature, particularly the romance, where several levels of meaning operate side by side, creating irony and ambiguity. Where normally emblematic values are embodied in Arthur's court and alternatives in courts elsewhere, *Gawain* presents Camelot in utopian terms (yet unprepared for the challenge it expects) and Hautdesert as superficially similar (yet a place of concealed identities, ambiguous behaviour, unexpressed truths) – where, nonetheless, the weaknesses of the Arthurian court are exposed. Yet for the potential audience, provincial knights or courtly nobles, Camelot represented the norm by which all courts were to be judged.[246]

As presented, the two courts are not opposed; both are elaborated as models of civilization, but in a way which disguises or subverts the underlying reality compelling readers to interpret. Yet the very ambiguity that requires interpretation contributes to thwart interpretation: Arthur's urbane gloss on the events of Fitt I (467-80) (assimilation or trivialization?), the court's *volte face* on acceptance of the challenge (692-86) (prudence or cowardice?), Hautdesert's reception of Gawain (901-27) (flattery or sincerity?) epitomizing the poet's vision of the ambiguities inherent in the civilization he portrays, courtly, Christian, chivalric and heroic.[247] Interpretation is complicated by the varying viewpoint provided by a narrator who assumes at times the omniscient perspective of romance, at others the limited perspective characteristic of dream vision (Benson 1965, 172), and elsewhere allows characters to express their own point of view. The irony which results from fluent changes of perspective ultimately distances the audience from the action until they see their own predicament mirrored in

Gawain's disorientation. Having won the audience's attention to a distanced chivalric fiction, the narrator establishes numerous parallels between fiction and contemporary reality, leading them to accept the fictional moral as applicable to themselves.[248] The fact that there is no clear, definitive statement of that moral has troubled some critics, but others see the poet's refusal to approve any of the judgements passed upon Gawain, not least his own, as a rejection of any form of emphatic closure. The poet's awareness of the humanity of his chivalric hero and the irony it produces suggests the foolishness of all spiritual grandeur in a man. The conclusion is tacit, defined by what is not, cannot be, said.[249]

Sir Gawain posits an absolute ideal of spiritual, chivalric, personal and social values in perfect harmony, but acknowledges the restraints of reality, the forces of evil at work in a fallen world, the imperfections of human nature, demonstrating how the instinctive, impulsive nature of fallen man can undermine idealism, an assault upon one of the pentangle virtues through an aspect of the hero's reputation – his amorousness – leading through love of life to self-love and a flaw which, however grave or trifling, his offended idealism cannot accept. The critique of chivalric values is exploratory rather than destructive, the literary method oblique, a game played with familiar conventions often ambivalently employed, leaving the audience to determine whether they carry their familiar significance or, expectations deceived, to note the irony of their novel use. The common expressive means condition the reaction of the audience through the relationship formed with the poet who, by sharing with them narrative facts, insights into situations and judgements on values to which the characters are not privy, encourages them to maintain a certain detachment, ironic, amused and alert to judge. The detached persona of the narrator acts as the catalyst in that process, at times undercutting the narrative by the perspective he offers upon it, at others undermining the characters by commentary and innuendo. Forced to determine whom to trust, what to believe, the individual reader is drawn into the creative process at his own level of perception. By his trust in the narrator or his sympathy with the characters, later proved misplaced, he is exposed to ironies which increase awareness and understanding, guided in his appreciation of meaning by evolving patterns of key terms which pinpoint and contrast the values between which he must learn to discriminate.[250] The final balance struck in a literary method which offers so many and such complex perspectives can only be personal, frustrating the instinct of modern critics to resolve the tension created by the coexistence of an idealistic and a critical spirit in the romance.[251]   **W. R. J. Barron**

ARTHUR IN ENGLISH SOCIETY

Juliet Vale

There is a certain paradox in writing about social manifestations of Arthurianism in an English context, for – at least initially – they found their predominant expression in a noble and courtly society which was by no means confined to England. It formed part of a network of feudal and dynastic ties that stretched across north-western Europe and beyond to cover the whole of western Christendom. Ironically, this same supra-nationalism may also be seen as ultimately limiting such development in England. While a whole range of medieval social characteristics might be seen as being held in common with the knights of Arthurian romance (most obviously, displays of prowess, largesse, loyalty to lord and lady), few can be isolated as exclusively 'Arthurian', rather than characteristic also of the values propounded in other narrative forms, whether *chanson de geste* or other types of romance. This discussion must, therefore, focus – perhaps somewhat artificially – on unambiguously 'Arthurian' elements.

The image of Arthur and the knights of the Round Table was a crucial paradigm that operated at a number of levels. It was in the reign of Edward I (1272-1307) that its potency was first substantially realized in England.[1] The image of a large number of knights, chosen only for their chivalric excellence, sitting with the king around a fundamentally non-hierarchical round table was powerful; a monarch with Edward's vivid youthful memories of the unruly period of baronial rebellion under his father neglected it at his peril. Arthur is *primus inter pares* among his knights; but he is also sovereign among rulers of the British Isles and Europe. This was another important, and potentially 'propagandizing', aspect of the image of Arthur for Edward I: as his reign lengthened, and military and diplomatic successes swelled his personal prestige, so he was increasingly able to fill the power vacuum that appeared with the death of Louis IX and the fall of the Hohenstaufen. Edward became the chivalric arbiter of the West (Vale 1996, 177-8), called upon to settle disputes and in enormous demand from young bachelors eager for him to knight them; parallels might be drawn in both areas with the established Arthur of the romances.

The flow of requests from Aragon, Gascony, Savoy and northern Italy for knighthood at his hands,[2] coupled with a remarkable eagerness to fight beside him in time of war (Vale 1996, 202-3), no doubt owe something to the image of both valorous knight and chivalrous king, propagated (for example) at the 'round table' at Oloron-Sainte-Marie in southern Gascony (1287) as part of the protracted (and ultimately futile) negotiations for the proposed marriage of Edward's daughter, Eleanor, to Alfonso III of Aragon.[3] The political role of chivalric assemblies held in imitation of Arthur's Round Table in strengthening Edward's chivalric image should not be underestimated.

Such round tables were perhaps the most distinctive expression of the cult of Arthur and his knights, but they were by no means confined to England.[4] The earliest recorded round table seems to have been held by the Lusignans in Cyprus in 1223;[5] they seem to have become current in England in the second quarter of the century. In 1252 the chronicler Matthew Paris felt he had to explain the expression.[6] Such festivals enjoyed huge popularity in the later thirteenth century in England, northern France and the Low Countries. They were chivalric occasions where knights and nobles drawn from all these regions might attend, probably at least in part, in an attempt to side-step the papal ban on tournaments,[7] but also because opportunities for participation were open equally to jousters and non-jousters – significantly including women. A verse narrative of the Arthurian *feste* held at Le Hem in Picardy in 1278 (where the participants assumed roles from the story of *Yvain* and acted out episodes as interludes between bouts of combat) is perhaps our best guide as to the combination of activities which might characterize a round table.[8]

It would be tempting to describe round tables, which lasted several days, as combining jousting with blunted weapons with enactments of scenes from Arthurian romance; on some occasions, at least, participants adopted Arthurian names and personae, together with equally fictitious coats of arms. Though they must have changed over time, the cardinal features seem to have been a combination of 'hastiludes' (armed encounters with blunted weapons), singing and dancing – one chronicler describes the participants as 'entertaining themselves with hastiludes and singing in turn'[9] – together with magnificent feasting. This was such an important element that, in one source, the round table is identified as the feast itself, rather than the accompanying *armorum exercitio*.[10] An explicit role for women can also be inferred, for example, from the reference to Roger Mortimer's invitation to 100 knights and 100 ladies to attend the Kenilworth round table of 1279,[11] and similarly in Edward III's refoundation of the Round Table at Windsor in 1344 – and by this date the wives of London burgesses were included, as well as noble ladies.[12] Lavish expenditure and gift-giving were other salient characteristics.[13]

In England, and in his other possessions, Edward I was responsible for a series of round tables. They were certainly not an exclusively royal prerogative, but there is some evidence to suggest that they were increasingly associated with the figure of the monarch and viewed as an expression of sovereign power. Edward I's round table at Nefyn (Gwynedd) in 1284 celebrated his victorious campaign in Wales.[14] The prose *Brut* roundly criticizes Roger Mortimer for his presumption in holding one in 1328,[15] while in the alliterative *Morte Arthure* Arthur's round table seems often to be synonymous with sovereign power.[16]

The obliqueness of the laconic English sources of the period is a constant problem. Drawing upon archaeological techniques, however, we can claim the round table hanging on the wall of the Great Hall in Winchester Castle and traditionally associated with Arthur for the reign of Edward I, since dendrochronology now dates it to 1275 plus or minus fifteen years.[17] This massive circular table, 18 feet in diameter and originally made from 121 separate pieces of oak, weighing 1 ton 4 cwt, was supported by a huge central column and by twelve outer legs.[18] The innovative technology employed suggests that the man who commissioned it must also have been breaking new ground in the representation of the Arthurian Round Table on such a scale.[19] It was probably constructed for a 'tournament' at Winchester attended by the king and doubtless featured at such festivities. Originally covered with cloth attached by nails, its massive size and weight would have made transport to another site impractical in the extreme. It is only the irrefutable existence of the Winchester round table itself which suggests that a round table must have taken place there, for there is no explicit chronicle reference and documentary sources are inconclusive. This nexus underlines the problems encountered when discussing Arthurianism in an English medieval context and the dangers of delineating too sharply categories such as 'round table', 'tournament' and 'hastilude' which may well not have been used consistently at the time (Vale 1982, 57-8).

In 1278 Edward I explicitly associated himself with the 'matter of Arthur' by holding his Easter court at Glastonbury, where the monks purported to have discovered the tombs of Arthur and Guinevere. The chests were solemnly opened and their contents reburied the following day with equal ceremony and in full view of the court and nobles – to say nothing of the visiting count of Savoy.[20] The episode is in many ways typical, revealing Edward I involving himself wholeheartedly in the 'Arthurian' proceedings (and thereby binding closely to himself any associated prestige) and also arranging matters so that the maximum political propaganda advantage could be derived from them – in this case, a tangible refutation of Arthur's legendary survival that was highly pertinent in the context of his continuing conflict with Llwellyn, prince of Wales. Similarly he was to make use of (entirely spurious) Arthurian 'evidence' taken from the *Prophecies of Merlin* and Geoffrey of Monmouth's *Historia Regum Britanniae* in prosecuting his claim to the Scottish throne.[21]

The same approach can be seen after Edward's defeat of the Welsh, with the removal from Wales of the much-revered Croes Neyd (*Y Groes Naid*) – believed to be part of the True Cross – and the equally potent secular relic, 'Arthur's crown', which, like the Stone of Scone of the Scottish kings, were presented to the shrine of St Edward in Westminster Abbey. As one monastic chronicler put it:

> corona famosi regis Arthuri, qui apud Wallenses a longo tempore in maxime honore habebatur . . . domini regi est oblata . . . sic Wallensium gloria ad Anglos, licet invite, est translata.

> (*the famous crown of King Arthur, which had been held in the greatest honour by the Welsh for a long time . . . was presented to the king. . . thus the glory of the Welsh passed, although unwillingly, to the English.*)[22]

Edward ensured that the relics were presented to the shrine of the English king, St Edward the Confessor, at Westminster with great ceremony, and news of the act was well disseminated.[23] The description of the crown by the author of the *Flores Historiarum* simply as 'quandam aureolam, quae fuerat quondam principis Walliae Leolini' (*a certain golden coronet, which once belonged to Llwellyn, prince of Wales*),[24] with no reference to Arthur, is a reflection of the way in which control of the theme of Arthur could be intertwined with the issue of sovereignty.[25]

Clearly it was not merely details concerning the transfer of Arthur's crown to the shrine of the Confessor that were reported in such detail by English chroniclers. Accounts of the spectacular round table held by Edward I at the culmination of this successful Welsh campaign (1284) were also in circulation. The few striking phrases used by the Dunstable chronicler, 'infra Walliam in ultimis finibus de Snowedune, supra mare' (*in Wales, at the farthest boundaries of Snowdon, above the sea*),[26] communicate something of the drama of the setting, which cannot have been lost on Edward I and his contemporaries as they imitated the court of King Arthur. Although the exigencies of supply and location largely dictated the site, Edward could surely not have held a round table at this wild coastal site beside Nefyn (a small fishing-town and 'one of the most important courts . . . of the former house of Gwynedd'),[27] on the northern side of the Lleyn Peninsula, without recollecting the sites of Arthur's combats. Journeying to the site of the round table through wild and unfamiliar country must have been an *aventure* in itself.

Specifically evocative of Arthurian romance is the practice, which seems to have become more frequent under Edward I, of the king knighting squires at the feast of Pentecost. Thus, for example, four visiting squires in the retinue of Count Amadeus of Savoy were knighted by the king after formal bath and vigil at Pentecost 1292, in the collegiate church of St Cuthbert at Darlington.[28] At

Pentecost 1306, with still greater ceremony, the ageing king knighted his own son, the future Edward II, at Westminster, and he in turn knighted nearly 300 further aspirants.[29] At the feast that followed the king swore a solemn vow (*votum*) on a pair of decorated swans to avenge the death of John Comyn at the hand of Robert Bruce, and had all the new knights follow him in this public vow. The extent to which the vow and its setting reflect any specifically Arthurian content is unresolved,[30] but the greater resonance which Arthurian romance had given the feast of Pentecost can scarcely be denied.

The Nefyn setting on the north Wales coast would perhaps have been most strongly evocative of Arthur's last battle, characterized by treachery, discord and the king's own death, and so pointing to the limitations of Arthur as an *exemplum* of kingship. Ambiguities such as these might have guided Edward in his choice of scenes of kingship from the life of Judas Maccabaeus rather than Arthur for the decoration of the Painted Chamber at Westminster.[31]

Furthermore, in the lamentation on his death (*Commendatio lamentabilis in transitu magni Regis Edwardi*) by John of London,[32] Edward I is compared with a range of biblical and secular heroes – Saul, David, Brutus and Alexander, the English kings Edward the Confessor and Richard I – but the reference to Arthur does not flinch from the legendary king's shortcomings:

> Patricius Arthurus rex Orcadas, Norwagicas, Aquitannicas, Scoticas et Hybernicas insulas populis semiplenas constituit sub tributo. Porro tribum Saxonum quae subdole Britannicam intrarat omnino delere non potuit, a quibus denique per Mordredum cognatum suum salva pace Britonum evanuit sauciatus.

> (*The noble King Arthur placed under tribute the sparsely populated islands of the Orkneys, Norway, Aquitaine [sic], Scotland and Ireland. Then he was by no means able to destroy the Saxon tribe, which had craftily entered Britain, by means of whom, at last mortally wounded by his kinsman, Mordred, he passed away, together with the secure peace of the Britons.*)[33]

A resounding denial of any parallel follows: 'Non sic succubit Edwardus rex noster' (*Our King Edward did not surrender thus*).[34]

Arthur the king was an ambivalent role model; Arthur at the head of the knights of the Round Table much less so. In the *Commendatio* (probably composed soon after Edward I's death)[35] there is an interesting and striking change of key when it is the turn of the knights ('Commendatio lamentabilis militum').[36] They alone, of all social groups and not excluding the queen, address the king directly in the intimate second person singular: 'O magnanime rex Edwarde, tu primicerius noster in bello, tu dux in castris et bravium cursus nostri' (*O great King Edward, our chief in war, our leader in the camps, and the reward of our efforts*).[37] The repeated use of the first person plural in the lines that follow underscores their collective loyalty as they list the struggles they have endured with and for him in France, Gascony, Wales and Scotland. There is in fact considerable evidence to suggest that Edward I deliberately fostered his relations with the knightly classes (Prestwich, 147-53)

Already, St George and figures from the Alexander tradition, Alexander and Judas Maccabaeus, were emerging as chivalric models coexistent with Arthur.[38] This tendency became still more marked in the reign of Edward III, with the increasing popularity of the Alexander romances and growing devotion to the cult of St George. Something of the plurality of secular chivalric role models available at the beginning of this reign is reflected in the decoration of a ewer given by Queen Philippa to the king as a New Year's present in 1333 (Vale 1982, 45). It was enamelled with figures derived from the Nine Worthies grouping (Caesar, Judas Maccabaeus, Charlemagne, Arthur), *chanson de geste* (Roland and Oliver) and Arthurian romance (Gawain and Lancelot). The fact that Arthur can both be paired with Charlemagne as one of the triad of Christian Worthies and grouped with Gawain and Lancelot in a romance context reflects something of his double-faceted image, as king and knight. Nevertheless, the paradigm of Arthur and the knights of the Round Table was still hugely potent.

English sources are oblique on such topics as tournament and chivalric spectacle in the thirteenth and fourteenth centuries and this makes the subject of Arthurianism exceptionally difficult for the historian. The gossipy John of Reading, the mid-fourteenth-century Westminster chronicler who recorded a number of tournaments fought (often in disguise) by members of the court, was the exception:[39] most chroniclers did not consider it any part of their brief to record what was often in effect street entertainment. References in other sources are purely incidental. In this respect the problems involved in documenting ephemeral court culture are not unlike those encountered by historians of popular culture.

Thus it is a jigsaw of interlocking fragments of information that tell us how Edward III participated incognito at a tournament held at Dunstable in 1334 in the arms of 'Mons[r] Lyonel': argent a canton gules.[40] This enthusiasm seems not to have been a passing fancy: four years later the king's third son was called 'Lionel' – an unusual choice – after the Arthurian knight of the Round Table (Vale 1982, 68). The same red-and-white shield on a green ground was an important decorative motif in the celebrations of the four-year-old Lionel's betrothal in 1342; eagle crests supplied for the occasion had green silk mantling decorated with three crowns.[41] It is possible that this was a variant on the three crowns often associated with Arthur.

In fact the arms and crest chosen by Edward for Lionel are those usually ascribed to Gawain in an Arthurian heraldic tradition stretching from the thirteenth to the fifteenth century.[42] There seem to have been a number of different heraldic traditions rather than any consistent and universal practice. They coexisted alongside continued awareness of the shield with the image of the Virgin traditionally ascribed to Arthur since Geoffrey of Monmouth.[43] The *Gesta Edwardi Tertii* by the 'Canon of Bridlington', for example, makes an interesting comparison between the youthful coronations of both Arthur and Edward III, and links Edward's devotion to the Virgin to that of Arthur expressed on his shield.[44] The coats of arms of living individuals might also be incorporated: an author who hoped to impress gave the hero and his friends the arms of his patron and associates[45] – a practice that spread into manuscript illumination and applied arts – expressing in a textual context the participation-integration also manifest in the assumption of Arthurian identities in the various activities that characterized round tables.

One such Arthurian source incorporating contemporary coats of arms is Girart of Amiens's *Escanor*, composed *c.* 1280 for Eleanor of Castile, wife of Edward I.[46] With other texts (notably *Durmart le Galois* of *c.* 1200 and an interpolation – probably dating from the second half of the thirteenth century – in the Second Continuation of Chrétien's *Perceval*), it represents 'an earlier [pre-fifteenth-century] and distinct phase to Arthurian heraldry'.[47] The evidence strongly suggests that this tradition of Arthurian heraldry remained a living resource at the English court in the late thirteenth and early fourteenth centuries. The material might of course have been disseminated through text – the same arms are ascribed to Gawain by Adenet le Roi, another northern French poet-minstrel connected with the court of Edward I.[48] However, the fact that Gawain's coat of arms is found without any corresponding textual reference in the illuminations of several early fourteenth-century romance manuscripts[49] points to an independent Arthurian heraldic tradition which could be drawn upon for chivalric occasions such as Edward III's 1334 Dunstable tournament, and presumably for any occasion (especially round tables?) for which Arthurian identities were required in an armigerous context. The relatively consistent treatment of the differencing of the coats of Gawain and his brothers[50] suggests that this heraldic tradition was communicated in a roll of fictitious arms rather than purely orally. At this period the roles of herald and minstrel were still closely linked; unduly rigid distinctions between literary text, heraldic record, and tournament practice and spectacle are anachronistic. What seems clear is that there was an Arthurian continuum which could also be drawn upon for essentially ephemeral occasions, few of which were thought to merit specific record.

This is one of the striking aspects of Edward III's planned refoundation of Arthur's Round Table in January 1344. In contrast to most events with an Arthurian or other secular chivalric colouring, generally accorded an annalistic chronicle entry of varying detail, the exceptional nature of the ceremony at which the project was announced is underlined by the surprising length at which it was recorded. The chronicle (*Continuatio Chronicarum*) of Adam of Murimuth, civil lawyer, cosmopolitan diplomat and canon of St Paul's, London, generally accords the occasional tournament no more than a passing mention. The fact that he records in some detail the ceremonial context in which Edward made this declaration is significant – and the fact that the mere announcement of the Round Table scheme was made with such pomp and ceremony is a gauge of the much greater solemnity with which the king presumably intended to cloak the foundation itself.[51]

Firstly, Edward held a splendid feast at Windsor castle attended by the two queens (Philippa and Isabella), the prince of Wales, and all the earls, barons, knights and other nobles of the kingdom. There were three days of continual hastiludes for the knights, with prizes for the best knight each day, accompanied by much music and dancing – thus far, magnificent but unremarkable. The morning after the close of these activities witnessed the exceptional, Edward vesting himself and his queen in full regalia – with cope and crown – before proceeding to mass; afterwards he left the chapel holding the royal sceptre in his hand and preceded by the seneschal and marshal with their rods of office.[52] The king had personally commanded that 'a crown of his of gold and precious stones' was to be brought expressly to Windsor Castle for the occasion, and it arrived two days before the commencement of the jousts and hastiludes.[53] The solemnity of any occasion when the king appeared in full regalia cannot be sufficiently stressed, and it is reflected in the chronicler's telling observation of the court procession followed by 'omni populo, hujusmodi spectaculum visuri insolitum' (*all the people, unaccustomed to seeing a spectacle of this kind*).[54] The sense of spectacle continued as, at a prearranged location, the king and all those with him halted, and the king swore a sacred oath that

> mensam rotundam inciperet, eodem modo et statu quo eam dimisit dominus Arthurus quondam rex Angliae, scilicet ad numerum trecentorum militum, et eam foveret et manuteneret pro viribus, numerum semper inaugendo.
>
> (*he would institute the round table, in the same form and condition in which Arthur, once king of England, left it, namely to the number of 300 knights, and that he would foster and maintain it with all his might, by always maintaining their number.*)[55]

Upon which, all the nobles and knights present followed him in taking the same oath. There are two versions of this episode: one as quoted, the other placing the announcement of the Round Table and the oaths at the final banquet, but it is clear that those whom the king wished to participate in the Round Table swore solemn oaths (*juramenta*) of a specific (unrecorded) form.[56] Following closely the pattern of Arthurian romance, the date on which the Round Table was to be formally initiated was fixed for Pentecost.[57]

Royal accounts demonstrate that Edward III did indeed, just as Murimuth's chronicle tells us, set in hand works for a building to house the Round Table at Windsor Castle. The authors of *The King's Works* think it most likely that the materials were for a 200-foot-wide circular structure in the outer bailey, probably with an open central area surrounded by a ring-shaped building roofed with tiles (H.M. Colvin in Brown, 871-2). It is difficult to reconcile these details with a solid circular table such as that at Winchester: we should perhaps rather envisage participants sitting with their backs against the outer wall of a circular building (rather as in an ecclesiastical chapter-house), with a table in front of them running round the edge of the building in an almost complete circle. Doors at the break would provide access for participants and service, and the opposite point a natural 'high seat'.[58] If the inner wall were open, rather like a circular cloister, all participants would have an excellent view of any entertainment in the central open space.

Although financial and diplomatic pressures brought Edward III's building schemes for the Windsor Round Table to a halt in 1344,[59] there was no reason why they should not have been resumed later. Very substantial rebuilding and redecorating were undertaken mid-century at St Stephen's, Westminster, and at Windsor (H.M. Colvin in Brown, 873-81; Binski, 182-3). Instead, Edward III chose to abandon formal links with Arthur's Round Table and founded the Order of the Garter with its collegiate church of St George in Windsor Castle. Why? What was different about the chivalric order he established?

The Garter was very exclusive (with only twenty-four members); the Round Table was not[60] – although the criteria for membership (unswerving loyalty, personal honour, prowess in arms) are ideals whose origins may of course be sought in Arthurian romance (Vale 1982, 87-91) It also had a formal ecclesiastical institution, overt liturgical content and saintly patron. The Garter's focus was on the soldier-saint George, who had been the patron of fighting English kings and English forces since the previous century.[61] Speculation as to his personal reasons for the adoption of St George is boundless – perhaps in fulfilment of a vow, or from a sharper realization of his own mortality – but it is worth noting, firstly, the growing popularity of soldier-saints as a focus for secular devotion throughout Europe. Edward III's wall-paintings at St Stephen's, Westminster, included Eustace and Mercurius, apparently part of a whole series of soldier-saints, while St George and the Virgin appear as dual patrons in a manner comparable to the Garter.[62] A chivalric order with its own ecclesiastical-liturgical institution was inevitably an infinitely more solemn phenomenon than a re-created Round Table, however magnificently established.

Second, this focus on a legendary saint closely identified with a conflict – dynastic in origin but acquiring an increasingly 'national' dimension[63] – to some extent expressed the aspirations of a more consciously English knighthood. St George and the Garter thus offered what Arthur and the Round Table could not: an exclusive loyalty to the sovereign and an effectively binding dependence of his subjects upon him, from which Arthurianism, by its very internationalism, was barred. Unlike, for example, the Burgundian Order of the Golden Fleece (founded in the next century), where the Old Testament figure of Gideon provided an alternative biblical framework,[64] King Arthur and his Round Table presented few unproblematic links and parallels which could ease their translation into contemporary liturgical and devotional practice.

This is not to say that Edward III and his court turned their backs on Arthur as a source of chivalric inspiration. Significantly, the association of Arthur with Windsor seems to appear only after the mid-fourteenth century, featuring first in accounts of the 1344 Round Table 'foundation', a number of which had court connections, notably that of Froissart (who arrived in England in the 1360s) and of the St Alban's chroniclers.[65] In the second recension of the *Chroniques* Froissart describes Edward III's magnificent building projects at Windsor castle, but also notes the survival of older buildings, including the keep and 'le grande sale où li rois Artus faisoit . . . son tinel et tenoit son estat de chevaliers aventureus, de dames et de damoiselles' (*the great hall where King Arthur had his banqueting-hall and maintained his court of adventure-seeking knights, ladies and damsels*).[66] It is unlikely to be coincidental that his (erroneous) account of the Garter foundation, conflating the 1344 plans with the Order's foundation later in the decade, retains the Arthurian element.[67] The magnificent annual Garter celebrations lasted several days and involved the entire court; apart from the liturgical duties of the Garter knights, considerable periods remained for other activities, whether armed encounter, music, dance or feasting. It has been convincingly argued that the motet *Sub Arturo*, in which the king is identified with Arthur, was composed for the Garter celebrations of 1358.[68] Edward III relished ludic activity (Vale 1982, ch.4), and it is possible that secular and informal aspects of the Garter celebrations may have had an Arthurian theme.

Later fourteenth-century evidence sheds some light on such activities. One of the young Richard II's banquets (1378), for example, was interrupted, Arthurian-style, by a knight disguised as a damsel bearing a challenge (Barker, 92). A series of fictitious letters of challenge (1400) addressed to the eight-year-old Blanche, daughter of Henry IV, is significant, not simply for the continuing use of an Arthurian-inspired challenge structure and the inclusion of knightly Arthurian, or Arthurian-derived, characters (Palamades, 'Lancelot de Libie') in a galaxy of mythical and allegorical personages. It also presents an allegorical and fictional framework with a considerable proportion of female protagonists, and one which demonstrates the potential for joust framed in, and initiated by, dramatic interlude.[69] With roles for specific members of the court and a topical eastern colour (the Eastern Emperor was visiting the English court), we have an indication here of the elusive dramatic content of Arthurian hastiludes that is recorded in the very earliest documented round table[70] and elusively glimpsed in the interim.[71] Unsurprisingly, there is a considerable element of fantasy in this – Henry IV is 'seigneur des pays de merveilles' (*lord of the Wonderlands*) and 'roy de lisle des geans' (*king of the Island of the Giants*)[72] – but the king also seized the opportunity to use the Arthurian legend to bolster his claim to the throne: he is king of Britain and France and 'vray successeur du puissant empereur Arthur' (*true successor to the powerful Emperor Arthur*).[73] Arthur himself became a desirable ancestor appearing, for example, in the genealogies of the Mortimers in the late fourteenth and the earls of Warwick in the fifteenth centuries, as well as of Edward IV.[74] Henry VII and his first son, Arthur, were identified with him in pageants, and he featured in Henry's wall-paintings of the kings of England at Richmond Palace.[75]

The 'companionate' knighthood which has its origins in the knights of Arthur's court, and which can be traced from Edward I's good relations with the knightly classes through Edward III's exceptional ties with his knights who were committed to the pursuit of honour at his court, seems to have resurfaced in the reign of Edward IV.[76] He was probably inspired by the Arthurian enthusiasm of the court of Burgundy, together with the example, expressed both in arms and books, of the lord of Gruthuyse at Bruges where the king was exiled in the winter of 1470-1.[77] This led him, for example, to rebuild St George's chapel, Windsor (H.M. Colvin in Brown, 884-7). At the end of the century, Henry VII's choice of 'Arthur' for the name of his eldest son was not only to bury the old rivalries of York and Lancaster, but also to '[promise] England a new Arthurian reign'.[78] The image of 'King Arthur riding a golden triumphal chariot through the sphere of the sun . . . was to have enormous significance for the development of the Tudor Arthurian myth' (Kipling, 79, 83-90).

The extent to which political goals were served by the virtues promoted in Arthurian literature is germane to the whole question of the fostering of knighthood and chivalric values by successive English kings. By the mid-fourteenth century the virtues of knighthood were concentrated to a much smaller degree in the figure of Arthur and the knights of the Round Table; the chivalric values and ideals on which Edward III set such great value – and which he undoubtedly shared – reflected a shifting focus, but they also served changed political goals. Arthur's profile was thus highest in medieval England when the ideals of Arthurian chivalry coincided most closely with the political aims and personal practice of the monarch, but the spotlight was always upon Arthur as founder of the Round Table and at the head of a splendid court rather than upon Arthur as king. These were also periods when greatest fusion was possible between personal knightly ideals and those attributed to the knight in Arthurian literature.

6

FOLK ROMANCE

Edited by *Gillian Rogers*

The texts grouped together in Chapter Five as chivalric romances share a narrative preoccupation with adventure and a thematic concern with chivalrous conduct. But they show a general tendency for narrative to dominate theme, and for theme to concentrate upon personal behaviour and social interaction rather than that demonstration and analysis of codes which constitutes the art of the *roman courtois*. The consequent exposure of narrative patterns highlights the extent to which the English romances share the structures, motifs and expressive means of folk-tale. Its narrative circularity, tripartite structures and formulaic characters feature in French romance also, but there such stereotypes are disguised by art and rhetoric. Art is not lacking in the exploitation of folk elements in English romances, from *Sir Gawain and the Green Knight* where their power to evoke basic human experiences and values provides the foil to an aspiring idealism undermined by human fallibility, to *Lybeaus Desconus* where characteristic episodes from the career of a folk-hero are given no more than a veneer of chivalry.

The texts treated here are distinguished from the chivalric romances not by any absolute difference of components but by a shift in the balance between them, a balance which varies from one text to the next. The two groups are linked by the prominence of Gawain, most apparent here where he is the hero of six of the ten tales. Their plots revolve obsessively around tests, vows, quests, hostile challengers with a beheading game or an exchange of buffets to propose, Imperious and Hospitable Hosts with marriageable daughters, bespelled people who require the hero's help to disenchant them, Helpful Attendants who assist him. In an Arthurian context Gawain was the obvious hero, not only because of his habitual involvement with folk-tale themes, but also because of the way he evolved as a character. From Chrétien onwards he served as a universal foil, as a model of chivalry against whom aspiring romance heroes had to prove themselves worthy of a place at Arthur's court, and so was himself condemned to stasis, in tale after tale – with a few notable exceptions. Such a simplified static character was a gift to traditional story-tellers and ballad-makers, lending itself easily to repeated appearances in formulaic roles where character development was irrelevant.

Rejecting for the most part the 'epic degeneration' that overtook Gawain in later French romance, English poets enthusiastically embraced the traditional image of him as the loyal supportive vassal, the perfectly courteous knight, upholder of the reputation of the Round Table and reconciler, *par excellence*, of hostile elements in society with the law and order embodied in the Arthurian court. Only the merest hint of the amorous reputation he had acquired in the French tradition remained to haunt him; presented subtly and amusingly in *Sir Gawain*, and crudely in *The Jeaste*, it appears more straightforwardly in the two Carl of Carlisle texts[1] and in *King Arthur and King Cornwall (Cornwall)*. Gawain was thus open to an almost iconographic treatment as the embodiment of certain social values. As such, he seems to have touched a nerve deep in the English psyche, as the representative man, at home in all levels of society, successfully undertaking tests and trials to enhance the reputation of his king. Casting him as hero signalled to audiences the reassurance that all would be well, since no harm could possibly come to the chief knight of the Round Table. Yet, despite his martial reputation in both French and English tradition, his prowess is displayed in only one of these tales (*The Avowynge of King Arthur*). In seven of the eight in which he appears, it is his moral qualities which are of importance, notably his courtesy, social skills and status as Arthur's active right-hand man.

On the sliding scale between chivalric romance and folk romance operative here, the largely chivalric *Avowynge* lies at one extreme, *The Turke and Gowin (Turke)*, a virtual folk-tale, at the other. In the latter, Gawain steps out of his Arthurian milieu into the folk-tale world of the Turk, exchanging his traditional persona for the role of a folk-hero such as the miller's youngest son in *Puss-in-Boots*, whose resourceful cat helps him to vast estates without the naïve youth having to lift a finger. Uncharacteristically, he complains bitterly of the weather, becomes almost querulous when denied food, proves utterly incapable of performing the tests set for him and has to rely entirely on the competent Turk. But, once back at court, he reverts to his Arthurian persona, refusing the kingship of Man in favour of the transformed Turk, '"for he it wan"' (325), so subverting folk-tale expectations, where it is the hero who gains the kingdom, but remaining true to Arthurian tradition, in which Gawain is known for his reluctance to take kingship upon him.

Though the composition of such popular texts is impossible to date with precision, the accepted chronological range is from *c.* 1400 to *c.* 1500.[2] The manuscripts range from the late fifteenth century to *c.* 1650, the accepted date of the Percy Folio manuscript, in which six of these poems appear, three of them, unfortunately, in the mutilated early part of the manuscript.[3] Both texts and manuscripts are predominantly Northern or Midlands – west, south and east; the locality in which the action takes place, even in *The Boy and the Mantle* (*Boy*) in which Gawain plays no part, is almost invariably the area around Carlisle and Inglewood Forest, with which he seems to have been traditionally associated.[4]

The predominance of Gawain in this group suggests that the fifteenth century saw the height of his popularity in English literature, with Robin Hood his only rival as a folk-hero. But, despite his democratic adaptability, his fame was not to endure much beyond the sixteenth century. Although in that century he continues to be mentioned among the figures of romance, there are few references to his courtesy, the one quality which might have been expected to endure. For instance, Laneham's well-known comparison of Captain Cox to him celebrates his courage – 'and hardy az Gawin' – not his courtesy.[5] With one very late exception known to me, there are no Gawain chapbooks, no Gawain Garlands.[6] His appearance as hero in four of the six Percy Folio poems in this group is evidently an isolated instance of one collector's antiquarian interest rather than an indication of continued popularity.   **Gillian Rogers**

The Grene Knight

The Grene Knight, probably dating from the late fifteenth century, is a poem of 516 lines in tail-rhyme stanzas of six lines preserved only in the Percy Folio manuscript (ff.101^v-105^r). It tells essentially the same story as *Sir Gawain and the Green Knight*, about a beheading game played out by the Green Knight and Gawain, modified by the inclusion of Gawain's agreement with the lord of a wayside castle (the Knight in another guise) and temptation by the wiles of his lady.

The Grene Knight shares features with other Gawain poems in the Percy Folio: the beheading game with *Turke*, and the Green Knight's name 'Bredbeddle' with *Cornwall*. It also has structural similarities with other medieval English poems centred on Gawain.[7] Inevitably, however, it is most often discussed in relation to *Sir Gawain*. Whether *Sir Gawain* was the actual source of *The Grene Knight* remains a moot point, though verbal correspondences and details of narrative variation suggest that the later poem was derived at least from a text very like the *Sir Gawain* we have.[8] Close relationship in terms of plot does not, of course, mean that the two had the same social or literary rationale, as past critics seem often to have assumed.

The Grene Knight is much shorter than *Sir Gawain*. Its formal division into two parts may reflect the similarly formal division of the latter into four fitts, but, whereas the first section of each covers more or less the same material, the second section of *The Grene Knight* covers events that occupy three fitts of *Sir Gawain*, four-fifths of the whole. Both incident and description are much briefer; the three days of hunting and tempting in *Sir Gawain*, for example, fit into one day here. The apparent abbreviation of such a complex, searching episode, in fact, brings into focus this poem's concern to entertain and reassure its audience, rather than problematize its values and assumptions. One obvious difference between the two narratives is that, whereas in *Sir Gawain* the action unfolds through the eyes of the Arthurian court and Gawain in particular, so that the audience is positioned with them and questioned in the same way, in *The Grene Knight* the background of the Knight is explained before he ever arrives at Arthur's court (*Speed*, 37–84), allowing the audience to share the omniscience of the narratorial voice and remain ultimately undisturbed.

The world of this poem is altogether more familiar than that of *Sir Gawain*. The name 'Bredbeddle' (40) is not élite like 'Bertilak'. The motive for the challenge is unconnected with larger patterns in Arthurian literature: Bredbeddle's mother-in-law just wants to help her daughter meet Gawain, the man she yearns for (46–66), and Bredbeddle himself only wants to see if Gawain is as fine a knight as he is reputed to be (472–80). He has a green horse and armour (80), but is not himself green. At Arthur's court, the Green Knight has two new encounters common in romance, first with the conventional porter (91–105), then with Kay, acting in his usual self-promoting manner by rushing to take up the challenge (154–62). Arthur is presented as unambiguously dignified, and his guest is sufficiently ordinary to dismount and accept a meal before the game proceeds (175–80). His challenge itself is specifically directed to the bravest among the knights present (120), not including the king; Gawain takes up the challenge, not as a caring and responsible substitute for his uncle and king, but rather as the winner of a contest for the opportunity to do so (163–70). Only his personal honour is henceforward at stake; he does not represent king and court. They and their world are not under scrutiny – indeed, at the end of the poem, Bredbeddle wants only to return with Gawain and become part of the court (490–92), a conventional romance ending for antagonists who are still alive.

Gawain's winter journey is a hunting trip amongst waterfowl, wolves, and wild beasts (280–5), not the dangerous passage amongst wolves, wild beasts, and supernatural beings of *Sir Gawain*; the landscape of the wild here does not extend far from civilization. When Gawain leaves the castle for the Green

Chapel, he is alone, as usual on an individual quest, without a mysterious guide who may not be all he seems, and the whetting of the axe awaiting him is preceded by the sound of a hunting horn (447), irrelevant to the plot, but confirming the wild as a semi-domestic region known to a hunting party. The chapel itself, difficult as it has been to find, proves to be an ordinary chapel, green because it is covered with ivy (450), not a fairy mound, green because it is covered with grass.

The narrative is bounded by identifications of Arthur and Guinevere as 'our' king and 'our' queen (17, 516), and the Round Table is an order of knighthood (23) that generates, through the actions of its leading knight, the present-day Order of the Bath (503). The Golden Age of chivalry and security evoked in the poem, and brought into the everyday world by such touches, would have offered reassurance, even direction, in the troubled years of the late fifteenth century

It is sobering to reflect that, had the unique manuscript of *Sir Gawain* gone up in flames in the Cotton fire of 1731, *The Grene Knight* would be our only version of this tale. Would it have been possible to imagine that so richly textured, inventive and memorable a poem lay behind the bald utilitarian recital of the bare bones of the story, where plot is foregrounded at the expense of theme, and moral significance becomes, for Gawain, as for the folk-tale hero, a matter of simple choices between right and wrong, unencumbered by any of the doubts and uncertainties that beset the Gawain of the alliterative romance on his painful journey towards self-knowledge?

Diane Speed

The Turke and Gowin

The Turke and Gowin, dated *c*. 1500, is a fragmentary romance of north or north-west Midlands provenance, possibly localized to Cheshire, the unique copy of which is preserved on half-torn leaves in the Percy Folio manuscript. Its six-line tail-rhyme stanzas, as close to the form and mode of ballad as to the earlier tail-rhyme romances, may indicate oral delivery by a popular entertainer (Pearsall 1977, 260). Even so, despite considerable metrical deficiencies and missing passages that can be plausibly but not definitively reconstructed, its combination of romance and folk-tale materials is marked by sufficient intelligence and vigour to suggest that its significance is greater than the mechanical arrangement of disparate episodes with tenuous Arthurian associations.

Central to the poem's appeal is the unlikely pairing of the flower of English chivalry and a mysterious 'Turk' or dwarf, the Marvellous or Helpful Attendant common to folk-tale, but actually the spellbound Sir Gromer, who helps Gawain through a series of tests and is then rewarded with freedom from enchantment.[9] The basic impulse is that of the knightly quest, and it displays its romance allegiance in a concern for the chivalric estate and the sovereignty of Arthur, figuring these issues through images of hierarchy and natural order. As in other Arthurian romances, the principal themes are introduced through an opening challenge to the court.[10] Though the Turk's invitation ' "to giue a buffett & take another" ' (*Hales and Furnivall*, 17) is less hostile than other attacks on Arthurian morality, there is genuine indignation at Arthur's attempts to ' "try mastery" ' (65), personified here by the habitually arrogant Sir Kay (19-27). Gawain's silencing of Kay and his acceptance of the contract with the Turk, apparently inferior in status but approaching the court as a 'brother' (16), establish the importance of courtesy, discretion and service.

As in *Sir Gawain*, and its Percy Folio derivative *The Grene Knight*, the agreement between Gawain and the challenger provides the basic frame for the narrative, eventually leading to the concluding disenchantment by decapitation that returns the Turk to his true identity, a transformation comparable to that in the Percy Folio *Carle*.[11] Having accepted the bargain and landed the first blow, Gawain vows to follow the Turk until the stroke is repaid (42-7). Their initial journey to the Otherworld is signalled in purely conventional terms: passage northward, entry into a fairy mound through a hole in a hill as in *Sir Orfeo*, preternatural weather conditions, and a deserted castle with echoes of the mysterious Grail castles and a taboo on eating food that is a customary precaution against enchantment.[12] The controlling theme is Gawain's deference to his guide, despite extreme hunger (95-7) and the Turk's mockery of his reduced circumstances.[13] For Gawain this restraint seems to be the culmination of the test but it is merely confirmation of his suitability for the task ahead, as the Turk's refusal to strike the return buffet indicates.

Once this oblique test of character has been negotiated, movement to the chief arena of adventure follows immediately by means of a supernaturally rapid sea voyage to the Isle of Man (116-20). This is a magical realm inhabited by giants, unnatural figures of Manx folklore,[14] and ruled over by a 'heathen soldan' (130), a standard image of otherness in romance. His hostility to Arthur is predictable, but the attack upon Bishop Bodwine (154-9) is remarkable for its similarity to the anti-clerical outburst by the equally alien figure of the Carl in *Carle*. It is more probably an attack upon the rule of orthodoxy than evidence of contemporary anxieties about the Church's infringement of temporal power, but it does imply a general endorsement of aristocratic privilege.

In his attempts to bring about the destruction of Arthur's chivalry (226-31) the king of Man sets Gawain three tasks: throwing a massive brass 'tennisse ball' (173), wielding an 'axeltree' (190-2), and lifting a fireplace or 'chimney' (199); these are followed by an encounter with a particularly hideous giant who stirs a cauldron of boiling lead (238-43). There are numerous analogues for these tests in French romance and Scandinavian myth and saga,[15] but the influence of folk-tale is equally marked (Gillian Rogers in Mills, 56). Here, the romance hero, passive in the face of these seemingly impossible tasks, is displaced by his 'boy' (253), the Turk, who defeats the Manx giants with a combination of brute strength, cunning and the aid of a magic cloak of invisibility.[16] When the king refuses to accept Arthurian overlordship he is summarily killed by the Turk, who thereby secures the release of female captives and the occasion for Gawain to behead him. The Turk's decapitation is clearly a kind of rejuvenation, achieved by means of Gawain's virtue and focused by the Grail-like imagery of the blood being caught in a 'bason of gold' (268).

Magic and enchantment are throughout metaphors for social and political alienation, and like most popular romances *Turke* ends with the control and encompassing of all external threats. This validation of the dominant order is apparent in the series of dependent relationships that fill the concluding scenes, in contrast to earlier inversions: man to God, subject to king, servant to master, wife to husband.[17] Gromer's transformation and elevation to king of Man establishes him as a Christian monarch under Arthurian jurisdiction, just as Gawain's refusal of land confirms him as the faithful vassal always ready to act in the service of his king.[18] Even so, it is not merely a victory for an imaginary and abstract version of chivalry. As in those Gawain romances centred on Inglewood Forest and Carlisle, meaning is located in the bridging of real and fictional worlds.[19] During the early fifteenth century the strategically important Isle of Man had finally come under English control, effected by one of the most powerful families in the north-west of England, the Stanleys. As 'Kings' and later Lords, of Man the Stanleys were heavily involved in counteracting Scottish influence in Man and across the North of England.[20] Such tales of Arthurian expansion model and authorize this extension of English sovereignty, suggesting that even unsophisticated pieces such as *The Turke and Gowin* are more than merely entertaining diversions for undiscerning audiences.   **David Griffith**

Syre Gawene and the Carle of Carelyle and
The Carle off Carlile

The two versions of the Carl of Carlisle story present a very interesting case-study of the different ways in which two redactors can treat a common source, for that the two go back to the same basic original, at whatever remove, cannot be doubted. The version in NLW Aberystwyth MS Porkington 10 (*Carelyle*), dating from *c.* 1400, was composed in the north or the north-west Midlands, is written in twelve-line tail-rhyme stanzas, and runs to 660 lines; the other, in the Percy Folio manuscript (*Carle*), was composed around 1500, somewhere in the north, in couplets, and is 500 lines in length.[21] Although both texts are corrupt, with much disruption of the order of events, and neither of them is an accurate copy of their common ancestor,[22] the two share many couplets, differing sometimes only in spelling. That the original was in tail-rhyme, rather than couplets, however, is suggested by the fact that the *Carle*-redactor on occasion uses a tail-line appearing in *Carelyle* and provides a second line, unrepresented in *Carelyle*, to make up his rhyming couplet.[23]

The basic plot is that of the visit to the Imperious Host, a very widespread tale, in which the benighted guest (occasionally accompanied by two others), seeking a night's shelter at the Host's castle, is warned in advance that he will not escape without a beating but is not usually told why, or how he might avoid this outcome. He accepts hospitality nonetheless, and is offered the Host's wife as a bed-companion. The next morning he departs, but, remembering the warning, turns back to ask why he has escaped without harm. He is told that it is because he has obeyed his Host in everything, has allowed him to be master in his own hall.[24] In the story of the Carl of Carlisle, there is also a strong element of the 'King and Beggar' tale-type, in which a king, benighted while out hunting, is given lodging by a host of apparently lowly station, and is taught a salutary lesson in how a guest should behave.[25] This basic plot is here augmented by a series of tests which the hero must pass in order to achieve the Host's hidden purpose.

The Imperious Host theme is one in which Gawain features on several occasions, usually encountering this autocratic personage while on a quest concerned with other matters.[26] In the Carl of Carlisle story-type, however, the Arthurian world, which he normally leaves behind him in such tales, accompanies him. Both Kay and Baldwin, here a bishop, play a prominent part. Arthur not only initiates the action by announcing a hunt, but also, by attending the Carl's feast at the end and creating him an earl and a knight of the Round Table, validates Gawain's actions in bringing about this reconciliation between a hostile opponent and the Arthurian court; he also, of course, ennobles, retrospectively and conveniently, Gawain's bride.

In *Carelyle,* this hostile opponent, the eponymous Carl, although evidently not a carl in the sense of 'low-born' (he possesses a castle, great wealth, and a beautiful wife and daughter), implies a deliberate contrast between his own apparently lowly social status and the higher social standing of his guests, to the detriment of the latter. He does this by distinguishing sharply between his own brand of courtesy, 'Carl's Courtesy' and the presumed courtesy of Arthur's court. The former embraces on the one hand the principle of strict obedience to one's host, thereby making him 'lord of his own', and on the other, summary justice meted out to those guests who do not adhere to this principle and challenge his authority, both aspects logically working out the implications of the Imperious Host theme. But as long as his guests perform their proper function *as* guests, they receive the courtesy due to guests. This is true courtesy as the Carl sees it, and he underlines the point in his instruction to Arthur to enjoy the feast he has prepared for him: '"Dothe gladly. / Here get ye no noþir curtesy . . ."' (*Kurvinen,* 619-20).

His counterpart in *Carle* on the other hand, emphasizes the *vilain/courtois* dichotomy of the host–guest relationship. However, in piquant contrast to the attitude of Kay and Baldwin, he sees himself as the *courtois* host and his guests, even Gawain, as potential *vilains.*[27] He is, of course, right about Kay and Baldwin, who are not, in either version, concerned with courtesy in any of its aspects. Kay's motiveless malice before the Carl's gates, threatening to beat him up if he refuses them lodging, and his arrogant treatment of the porter indicate clearly his view that a carl's stronghold is no place for a knight of Arthur's court to lodge in. Baldwin who, mysteriously, alone of the three, knows of the Carl's reputation in advance, is more propitiatory at first, only lapsing into arrogance of rank during his encounter with the Carl and his foal.[28]

Only Gawain seems to understand the principle involved; his abiding virtue of courtesy uniquely equips him to succeed where Kay and Baldwin fail in the series of tests which follows their admittance to the Carl's castle. Gawain's survival depends, essentially, upon obedience, upon a passive acceptance of every situation his host devises to test him without demur, no matter how extreme it may seem.[29] The Carl's tests are all designed to separate out the one guest who will, by reason of his implicit obedience to his every command, be able to release him, from a self-imposed vow in *Carelyle* and from enchantment in *Carle*, and, with the exception of the first, the 'foal' test, he achieves his aim by placing that guest in situations which seem to contravene the very idea of guesthood. Thus, in the apparently pointless 'spear' test, he asks Gawain to try to hit him in the face with this weapon; in the 'wife' test, he commands him to get into bed with his wife, and – in the *Carle* only – he asks him to behead him with a sword, the Disenchantment by Decapitation motif.

The 'foal' test, the only one undergone by all three knights when they go out, one by one, to tend their horses, is a private test of inner worth, the 'eliminating round'. In true English fashion, it hinges on the treatment of animals. Kay and Baldwin eject the Carl's 'foal' with blows when they find it next to their own proud beasts in the stable, and are consequently punished with blows by the mysteriously appearing Carl; Gawain covers it up and gives it food, and, having triumphantly proved himself a true Englishman, he alone is deemed fit to undergo the other tests.[30]

The presence of both the Carl's wife *and* his daughter introduces a *fabliau* element into the proceedings, which undermines the basic premise of the plot.[31] In both versions, Gawain is commanded to kiss the wife while the Carl looks on. And although he somewhat oversteps the mark in both, he is deemed to have passed the test, and is given the Carl's daughter to spend the night with, almost, it would seem, as a reward for good behaviour. '"Now, Gawen"', says his host in *Carelyle*, '"holst þe well payde?"' (481), and on Gawain's enthusiastic agreement, he leaves them with the injunction to '"play togeydor all þis ny3t"' (486).

The often contradictory figure of the Carl himself has many resonances. Indeed, the source-hunter is overwhelmed with the profusion of sources from which his creator seems to have drawn. Thus, the Carl has affinities with such characters as Curoi, in *Bricriu's Feast*, and the giant Yspaddaden Pen Kawr in *Culhwch and Olwen*. The King of Man in *Turke*, King Cornwall in *Cornwall*, and the hosts in *Le Chevalier à l'Epée* and *Hunbaut* are likewise brothers under the skin. The most intriguing parallels, however, lie with that other Imperious but Hospitable Host, Bertilak, in *Sir Gawain*. Both have castles with strong Otherworld overtones, both have designs on Gawain, and both employ an ironic, epigrammatic mode of speech when addressing him. Both have alternative personalities. But, whereas Bertilak's Mr. Hyde personality is neatly stowed in the figure of the Green Knight, the Carl has to suffer his good and bad aspects within the same body. His 'dede menn bonys' (533) are real, and at the end of the tale they remain. He becomes in consequence a grotesque Bluebeard figure, whose repentance, however sincere, fails to appease the reader's sense of justice.

The denouement differs radically in each version. *Carelyle* introduces the motif of the Breaking of the Evil Custom of the Castle; Gawain's obedience to his every whim releases the Carl from his self-imposed vow to kill all who lodge with him if they do not obey him to the letter, a logical enough resolution to an Imperious Host tale. *Carle* introduces the motif of Disenchantment by Decapitation, a motif possibly borrowed from its Percy Folio companion, *Turke,* by a redactor unhappy with the idea of such bloodshed ensuing from a mere vow.[32]

The tale ends with the reconciliation between the Arthurian ethos and that of the Carl (which turn out to be not so very different after all). This reconciliation, as so often in Arthurian romance, is symbolized by a great feast. But it is the Carl who takes the initiative and invites Arthur and his court to his castle. The very splendour of his arrangements and the magnitude of his hospitality confirm the impression that the rest of the tale has fostered despite his insistence on his lowly status, that this so-called carl is a very comfortably-off, not to say rich, land-owner. The Carl is a folk-tale ogre, and an exemplum Imperious Host, and a typical Arthurian antagonist, who ends up being accepted into the world of the Round Table. This makes the tale underlying both versions in some ways the most complex composite of all this group – in it one has the sense of eclecticism run riot.

It is probable that contemporary audiences would have perceived a strong element of burlesque in the spectacle of the famous Sir Gawain being ordered about by a hideous rough churl who addresses him with a certain kindly contempt (' "Fellowe, anoun, / Loke my byddynge be well idoun" ' (*Carelyle*, 382-3)), who reads his thoughts, particularly those pertaining to his own wife, and who has complete control over him. They would certainly have seen it in the rough and ready treatment of Kay and Baldwin. The tale is a comedy with a serious moral underlay, with the two noblemen, Kay and Baldwin, in violent social opposition to the supposedly lower-class Carl who gives them a hard lesson in true courtesy. Gawain's innate courtesy allied with his acute social sense sees him through the trials to a successful conclusion, where he reconciles both sides and fortuitously ends up, in true folk-tale style, with a beautiful, and very rich, bride.   **Gillian Rogers**

The Weddynge of Sir Gawen and Dame Ragnell and *The Marriage of Sir Gawaine*

Alongside Chaucer's 'Wife of Bath's Tale', both the romance *The Weddynge of Sir Gawen and Dame Ragnell* (*Weddynge*) and the ballad *The Marriage of Sir Gawaine* (*Marriage*) employ the folk-tale motif of the 'Loathly Lady transformed'. These three texts all place the motif in an Arthurian context, unlike the remaining analogues, the ballads *King Henry* and *The Knight and Shepherd's Daughter*, and Gower's 'Tale of Florent'.[33] In 1299 one of

Edward I's 'round tables'(see above, pp.187-91) featured a loathly lady as part of a staged interlude – on this occasion the hag rode into the hall and demanded of those men playing the roles of Sir Perceval and Sir Gawain that they assist in the recovery of a castle, and end strife between lords and commons[34]– although the yoking together of the themes of transformation and the voluntary abdication of sovereignty by man to hag seems ultimately to have been Celtic in origin.[35]

Of all versions employing this motif Chaucer's is the best known, but it is also the most unusual in that the riddle and subsequent transformation take place in the context of a punitive and educative process: the anonymous knight must pay for the crime of rape by answering correctly the question 'What is it that women most desire?' To provide the wrong answer means death. The Loathly Lady's price for his salvation is marriage, but uniquely the wedding night is used as an opportunity to lecture the knight on the virtues of 'gentilesse', and the 'fair or foul by day' dilemma hinges instead upon 'ugly but faithful' or 'fair but take your chances'. However, what makes *Weddynge* and *Marriage* especially interesting is that, besides providing analogues to one of the *Canterbury Tales*, they show themselves also to be part of particular literary groupings. Both texts feature Gawain as their central hero, placing him in a position where, as in *Sir Gawain*, his courtesy is tested rigorously. Moreover, both texts have as their setting Inglewood Forest in the north-west of England.

Weddynge survives uniquely in Oxford, Bodleian Library MS Rawlinson C. 86.[36] The manuscript containing the poem can be dated to London in or about the year 1500.[37] The text runs to 852 lines of verse, and was probably conceived originally as a tail-rhyme romance rhyming *aabccb*, with four stresses to the couplet line and three to the tail, although the text is transcribed as one single narrative block. One leaf is missing, and the poem as we have it is plainly defective: on occasion the metrical structure collapses completely, and simple copying errors as well as evidence of attempts to 'improve' upon the original during the course of transmission make it impossible to assess how close the Rawlinson text is to the poet's intentions. However, it has been argued on dialectical grounds that the author of *Weddynge* came from the Midlands, while the Rawlinson scribe may have come from the south Staffordshire region.[38] Previous criticism of the poem has been almost uniformly dismissive and unsympathetic.[39]

The poem itself, however, is less concerned with the theme of sovereignty than with portraying Arthur as a hapless and helpless king and Gawain as his cheerfully courteous and loyal friend. Arthur is out hunting in Inglewood Forest when he is threatened by Sir Gromer Somer Joure.[40] As in *The

Awntyrs off Arthure, disputed territory provides the cause of grievance against Arthur and his court, and Arthur is faced with the familiar task of answering a riddle at the end of the year, with death as the penalty for failure. The hideous Dame Ragnell subsequently offers to provide Arthur with the answer required on condition that she marry Gawain.[41] To Arthur's evident relief, Gawain does not hesitate, and as a result Gromer is frustrated and Gawain doomed to wed the frightful hag. It is Gawain's willingness to grant his wife her conjugal rights that prompts Ragnell's transformation into a beautiful woman, and his willingness to cede sovereignty by letting her have the choice on the fair/foul, night/day issue that ensures that the transformation is permanent. Unusually, the poem does not end happily, as Ragnell dies within five years of the wedding itself.

Weddynge is not without its own sly humour. Arthur's unheroic anxiety when confronted by Gromer, his evident glee when insisting that Gromer plod through two large books containing possible answers to the riddle before springing on him the correct answer, Ragnell's cheerful insistence on a public wedding while Guinevere tries her best to hush the whole thing up, her demure teasing in bed when Gawain fails to rise to the challenge of a beautiful woman next to him (her ' "Why are ye so unkynde?" ' (646)) hints at unusual male reticence and literally unkind behaviour from her husband, and may even be a mischievous allusion to Gawain's reputation as a ladies' man) – these represent a refreshing and highly entertaining look at the traditional chivalric romance. Indeed, part of the poem's charm arises from a deliberate intention on the part of the author to subvert the genre by use of allusion, hyperbole and frustrated expectation.[42] The poet's use of 'false endings' to delay the conclusion seems a deliberate ploy, and the decision to 'kill off' the heroine undermines the pathos one might otherwise have expected. As Stephen Shepherd has observed: 'To feel sad or perturbed here at the death of Ragnell risks missing the joke.'[43]

While the poem is generally held to have been written *c.* 1450, the plaintive reference at its conclusion to an imprisoned author has led to the suggestion that the poet was none other than Sir Thomas Malory.[44] It seems more likely however that the poem's effect relies upon an awareness of Malory's status as a 'knight prisoner': the penitential nature of the poem's final lines is in itself part of the referential humour.[45] Moreover, given the omission from Caxton's edition of *Le Morte Darthur* of references to Malory's captivity, such awareness could only arise from knowledge of a text other than that printed by Caxton in 1485. Such an argument raises interesting questions concerning the poem's audience, and the circulation of the Winchester Malory manuscript and other Arthurian texts in late fifteenth-century London. Accordingly, *Weddynge* may represent less a surviving example of a folk-tale than a conscious attempt to mimic the romance genre with satiric effect. The location of the poem, for example, is in keeping with a number of other Gawain-poems. Rosamund Allen has argued convincingly that events in *Awntyrs* could reflect political activity in England in 1424-5, and that the detailed topographical references could indicate that the poem was composed in honour of the powerful Neville family, possibly by someone from St Mary's Priory in Carlisle.[46] The setting by a non-native author of *Weddynge* in this region could simply have been to provide the poem with a sense of authenticity. The use of alliteration and concatenation may even have been designed to recall the poem's northern cousins, such as *Sir Gawain and the Green Knight.*[47]

The Marriage of Sir Gawaine is found uniquely in the mutilated part of the Percy Folio manuscript. The surviving text consists of 217 lines, just over half the original number, and is written as a ballad in four-line stanzas rhyming *xaxa*. The ballad clearly has much in common with the romance in terms of narrative, as Arthur meets with a 'bold barron' at Tarn Wadling (here named), and is confronted by the usual riddle and manner of its solution. However, this is a less subtle version in style and sentiment: Arthur volunteers Gawain unbidden in payment for the riddle's answer; on being told the correct answer, the baron denounces his sister as a 'misshappen hore' (111); and when faced with the fair/foul dilemma in bed, Gawain chooses the option that will yield him most sexual pleasure. Sovereignty is only granted to the lady when it is obvious that his own choice has upset her. Sir Frederic Madden argued in 1839 that the ballad was derived from the romance, a view that Garbáty more recently believes beyond much doubt, but Child was less sure, and Laura Sumner believed quite the opposite. Lucia Glanville has, however, convincingly concluded that Madden was probably right, although a common source cannot be ruled out.[48]

Whether or not *Weddynge* and *Marriage* represent fragmentary evidence of long-standing folkloric themes, handed down over the generations, is impossible to say. For example, it should be remembered that the Arthurian ballad *King Arthur's Death*, also found in the Percy Folio manuscript, is less traditional than it may seem, having been shown by Robert Wilson to be not medieval in origin, but a continuation of *The Legend of King Arthur* (published in 1584), based upon Thomas East's 1578 [?] edition of Malory's *Le Morte Darthur.*[49] Notwithstanding the possibility that both romance and ballad could be more imitative than original in their use of these well-known motifs, they testify nonetheless to a long-standing interest in Gawain, that most English of heroes, an interest which exists to the present day.

John Withrington

The Avowynge of King Arthur, Sir Gawan, Sir Kaye, and Sir Bawdewyn of Bretan

The Avowynge of King Arthur, until recently rather neglected, was composed by a northern poet between 1375 and 1475. It survives only in the Ireland Blackburne manuscript, so-called from its nineteenth-century owner, who lived at Hale in south Lancashire, where, on the linguistic evidence, it was probably copied, sometime in the mid-fifteenth century.[50] It relates the fulfilling of certain vows made by the young King Arthur and his companions, Gawain, Kay and Baldwin, in Inglewood Forest in the presence of a monstrous demonic boar which is despoiling his hunting grounds. Arthur vows to kill it single-handed, a feat he achieves after a heroic fight, Gawain to keep watch at Tarn Wadling all night, and Kay to ride through the forest till dawn, killing anyone who denies him passage. Baldwin, older than his companions and somewhat impatient with such childish goings-on, makes not one vow, but three, which are, as Greenlaw pointed out, not really vows, but 'maxims of life'.[51] He vows never to be jealous of his wife, to dispense hospitality to all, provided he is in a position to do so, and never to fear death.

Avowynge has long been recognized as a bi-partite romance, in which the more purely 'Arthurian' vows of the first three characters are carried out in part one, while Baldwin's testing and his explanations of why he came to hold his 'maxims of life' occupy the second part, itself broken into two unequal parts, containing the three tests and the three explanations.[52] It was for long dismissed as a somewhat incoherent and miscellaneous ragbag of motifs and episodes. Greenlaw, for instance, whose study of the sources underlying Baldwin's vows is still the standard work on the subject, observed that the poet made a sharp distinction between the characters of Arthur and Baldwin, Kay and Gawain, but he did not develop this idea in terms of structural coherence, and the poem remained for him 'a curious jumble of materials drawn from conventional chivalric romances'.[53]

Since then, however, the structure and the themes of the romance have been examined more closely in a series of studies. Stephany saw its structure in terms of a conflict between two fundamentally opposed views of life, represented by Arthur's court in part one, and Baldwin's castle in part two, the one compared unfavourably with the other. He further saw the contrast between the four main characters as being both structural and thematic, with Kay set against Gawain in part one, and Arthur against Baldwin in part two. Hardman saw Baldwin's vows as constituting a 'summary code of knightly virtue', and Baldwin himself as 'a representative of ideal knightly values' which complement rather than oppose the traditional ideal of knighthood represented by Gawain, and 'relate the knightly code to social situations other than the conventional fictions of chivalric adventure'.[54]

Dahood, whose full and useful edition seems to have stimulated renewed interest in the romance, reverted to the idea of the poem as 'a series of discrete adventures unified by the device of the vows' (*Dahood*, p.36), but two recent articles by Burrow and Johnson again examine it in more positive terms as a conscious construct of the poet. Burrow emphasizes the symmetry of the poem, and picks up the idea, developed by Spearing in relation to *Awntyrs*, of the diptych, in which the meaning of the whole emerges from the juxtaposition of the two seemingly disparate parts, which are here 'firmly hinged' by the fact that the incidents in part two have been prepared for by Baldwin's three vows in the first part. Johnson, like Burrow, sees the connection between the parts as one of juxtaposition, and as an expression of 'the poet's awareness of the dichotomy between the theory and practice of chivalry', part one deriving from the 'literary, fantasy world of Arthurian romance', part two being 'an expression of a view grounded in a more practical, real-world experience of the values treated in both'.[55]

It is thus now possible to see *Avowynge* as a much more complex and thought-provoking romance than was previously held to be the case, and its author as a poet of considerable breadth of knowledge of both Arthurian themes and more widely dispersed traditional tales. Furthermore, he has a fresh and unusual approach to these themes and tales, and on occasion produces a twist in the tail, a surprise variation on the 'received' version. So, for example, in the vowing scene, where the expectation is that each character in turn will make one vow which he will then fulfil, the poet suddenly presents us with a character who not only makes three vows instead, but who is obviously bored by the whole proceeding and who has no intention of fulfilling them, since he then goes off to bed leaving the others to get on with their self-imposed labours.

Again, in the traditional Gawain–Kay opposition, which, often simply a brief excuse for a little comic by-play, is here expanded into a thematically significant episode, the expectation is that Kay will behave in a boastful aggressive manner and will receive either his come-uppance at the hands of the antagonist or a courteous reproof from Gawain, or both. This does, of course, happen. But there are unsettling elements in this portrayal of Kay. First of all, he goes far beyond his 'normal' behaviour in English Arthurian romance in vowing not only to fight anyone who denies him passage while he patrols the forest near the 'anturis hoke', but to *kill* him. Then, apparently contradicting this viciousness, he becomes, albeit briefly, the champion of the weak against the strong, and challenges the knight he meets, Menealfe of the

Mountain, not simply for the sake of his vow, but to save the damsel Menealfe has abducted with much bloodshed from her family. This he does in impeccably chivalric terms. Later, he displays a most unusual degree of self-knowledge when, challenged by Gawain in the night, he answers: '"I, Kay, þat þou knawes, / Þat owte of tyme bostus and blawus"' (353-4).

He quickly reverts to his accustomed behaviour, however, demanding that Gawain ransom him, and then directing a stream of abuse at his erstwhile opponent when Gawain overthrows Menealfe efficiently and without fuss, not once but twice, the second time to ransom the damsel. Gawain meanwhile, quite unruffled by Kay's behaviour, picks Menealfe up after each bout and puts him to rights, thus demonstrating by his courteous action how true chivalry works. Menealfe himself underlines the correctness of Gawain's conduct towards him: '"And þou was aye curtase / And prins of ich play"' (407-8).[56]

Perhaps the most striking example of the poet taking a traditional theme and producing a twist is the scene in part two in which Arthur tests Baldwin's vow never to be jealous of his wife. The very widespread motif of the 'Wife falsely accused' is here used adroitly to subvert expectations of the usual outcome of such a tale, and to point up the contrast between the two men.[57] Arthur sets up his trap for Baldwin without the least regard for his hostess's feelings, or indeed for those of either Baldwin or his own fearful young knight. Baldwin's extreme self-control in allowing his wife to regulate her own behaviour underlines the crassness of Arthur's act, and is the counterpart of the scene in the forest in part one, where Gawain's self-control similarly highlights Kay's lack of it and his insensitivity towards the feelings of others.

The two parts of the romance are connected by a 'bridge passage', where the various combatants of the night return to Carlisle, bearing with them the carcase of the boar and the rescued damsel. Gawain then drops out of the proceedings, and the focus of interest shifts to Baldwin and his testing, instigated, very much in character, by Kay, the 'gadfly', never one to let a situation rest. It takes very little persuasion to get Arthur to agree to let him test Baldwin's claim that he does not fear death. Kay's attempt inevitably fails and, with this, his part in the tale ends. His presence here at the beginning of part two may perhaps be seen as the other flap of Burrow's 'hinge' joining the two parts together.

The realism of Baldwin's explanation to the mystified Arthur of how he came to hold his philosophy of life creates a sharp contrast to the 'romance' world of the rest of the poem. Nonetheless, each of Baldwin's 'real-world' experiences is based upon a traditional tale with numerous analogues, which the poet economically weaves into the one set of circumstances, the siege of the Spanish castle of which Baldwin is the castellan. The explanations, in reverse order to that of the testing of the vows themselves, consist of the motifs of 'the Murderous Women', explaining why Baldwin is not jealous of his wife; 'the coward who loses his life trying to save it', explaining why he is not afraid to die; and 'the raising of the siege', explaining his extraordinary hospitality.[58]

The first of these explanations raises the question of literary 'tact', in that it seems quite alien to the spirit of the rest of the romance. It is made quite clear that the besieged Baldwin, equally with his men, makes use of the three washerwomen's sexual favours, and he recounts the murder of two of them by the third without any obvious emotion.[59] The uneasy juxtaposition of the romance and the everyday worlds here poses a real problem for the modern reader. The two worlds do not really mix, and Baldwin comes across as a stiff, slightly arid and unemotional figure, rather than the epitome of knightly conduct in the 'real' world as opposed to the 'romance' world (where Gawain reigns supreme) that he is intended to be.

The treatment of Arthur, particularly in the second part of the poem, relates to that critical strain running through Arthurian romance from its beginnings. He is portrayed as an impetuous, somewhat heedless young man, and his youthfulness is clearly seen to be reprehensible in a king. The fact that he has to bring out the book of laws in order to determine the criteria for creating a knight of the Round Table, may also suggest a novice king, who relies heavily upon Gawain's judgement, a habit which is deeply ingrained in him throughout the whole course of Arthurian romance.[60]

Although Gawain's part in the proceedings may seem slight, and no different from many another brush with Kay, it is in fact extraordinarily rich, both in terms of its meaning within the romance itself and in terms of its links with other Gawain-romances. His role here, as so often, is that of the 'yardstick', the standard by which other knights' behaviour may be measured, and as such, he is a completely appropriate figure to carry the burden of the 'romance' ideal of chivalric practice as distinct from the 'real' ideal that Baldwin represents. Both demonstrate the right way to behave in their given set of circumstances. Lightly touched in by the poet are Gawain's associations with magic and the supernatural: he evidently expects to encounter a supernatural being at the Tarn Wadling as he does in *Awntyrs*, and, according to Dahood, actually does so, in the person of Menealfe of the Mountain;[61] his unstated relationship with Guinevere, another echo of *Awntyrs*; his role as the *chevalier as demoiseles*, pledged to aid women in distress; his position at court as the king's counsellor; his habit of bringing his erstwhile opponent back to the court to be reconciled with it and take his place among the king's knights – all these are present in the brief compass of a few stanzas of part one.

A different pairing of characters from that suggested by Greenlaw and Stephany becomes apparent by the end of the tale, namely, Arthur and Kay, Baldwin and Gawain, where Arthur's reprehensible and insensitive treatment of Baldwin's wife can be seen to echo Kay's equally insensitive treatment of the defeated Menealfe, and Gawain's habitual courtesy and competence can be seen as a parallel to Baldwin's assured way of handling himself in all the emergencies that life throws at him.

Despite Burrow's comment that *Avowynge* 'could have been a masterly creation – if only the *Gawain*-poet had written it', it is by no means negligible as a work of literature.[62] The poet has a strong sense of structure and symmetry, and his seventy-two sixteen-line stanzas, rhyming *aaabcccbddddbeeeb* and making considerable use of alliteration, move along at a brisk pace, creating a spare, sinewy narrative, which relies heavily on dialogue as a means of characterization.[63] Like most of the other tales discussed in this chapter, it has a highly individual, slightly quirky approach to its subject matter, showing a creative mind at work on traditional materials, both Arthurian and non-Arthurian, to create a particular moral vision, setting the romance world of idealistic chivalry against the everyday world of down-to-earth pragmatism.   **Gillian Rogers**

King Arthur and King Cornwall

The mutilated and fragmentary ballad *King Arthur and King Cornwall*[64] is a loose, idiosyncratic and quite witty adaptation, through some intermediary version, of the main features of Charlemagne's visit to King Hugo of Constantinople, as recounted in the twelfth-century Old French burlesque *chanson de geste*, *Le Pèlerinage de Charlemagne*, with Arthur and his chosen companions replacing Charlemagne and his paladins as the chief actors.[65] The mutilated state of the text means that we have to proceed by inference in piecing together the details of the plot, but, although its unknown author had a quite different purpose and wished to create a very different effect, using the original tale more as a springboard than as a blueprint, the main features are unmistakable: the queen's reply to her husband's boastfulness, that she knows of a more magnificent king than he; her husband's instant resolve to seek this unknown king; his journey, ostensibly a pilgrimage, with his favoured companions; his impressive reception by his rival and the marvels he sees at his court; the 'gabs' or vows he and his companions make; the spy set to report on their conversation; and at least two of the vows themselves – all proclaim the author's familiarity with the events depicted in the *chanson*. The ingenuity with which he has matched the deeds of the Carolingian heroes to his Arthurian protagonists is considerable and demonstrates a respectably wide knowledge of the Arthurian world.

The poet's choice of Tristram and Gawain as two of Arthur's four companions on his journey is particularly apt. Tristram, who might otherwise seem an odd addition to the company, is in fact an excellent choice to take on the part played by Roland, who vows to blow a horn so hard that the walls of Hugo's palace will come tumbling down, for Tristram was well-known in Arthurian tradition for his skill at hunting. His actual vow is missing, but from subsequent events it is clear that he too vowed to blow the horn unusually hard.

Gawain's propensity for visiting hostile Imperious Hosts with supernatural associations and beautiful daughters is likewise well-attested, and fits him perfectly for the role of Oliver, who, having fallen in love with Hugo's daughter at supper and wished to take her home to France with him, then 'gabs' that he will lie with her 'a hundred times during the night'. Although in the popular tradition of Arthurian romance Gawain tends to marry the women he falls in love with rather than to rape them, he too vows to take 'yonder faire lady', King Cornwall's daughter, back to Little Britain with him when he goes, and in the meantime he will '"hose (*clasp*) her homly (*closely*) to my hurt, / & with her Ile worke my will"' (*Hales and Furnivall*, 154-5).

Although the fulfilment of Gawain's vow is missing, in the course of his two brief extant appearances we find several other features that suggest the poet's familiarity with the character's past history: his position as Arthur's favoured nephew, his customary epithet, 'Gawaine the gay', a hang-over from the alliterative tradition, and, perhaps most interestingly, his opposition to a proposal of Arthur's, a very common motif that goes back to Chrétien's *Erec et Enide*, where he rebukes Arthur for proposing to reward the victor in the forthcoming hunt with the opportunity to kiss the most beautiful lady at court. Here, he objects to Arthur's vow to be Cornwall's 'bane' on the grounds that it ill-becomes him, as a Christian, to talk of killing an '"anoynted King"' (140). Less familiar is Arthur's instant imputation of cowardice, taunting Gawain to '"goe home, and drinke wine in thine owne country"' (145), which in fact spurs Gawain on to make his own vow.

Again, the travellers' arrival at Cornwall's unnamed castle, while loosely paralleling that of Charlemagne at Hugo's court, has its roots firmly in Arthurian soil, echoing other such arrivals, both by Gawain and by Arthur himself. Most obviously, it echoes the arrival of Gawain, Kay and Baldwin at the Carl's castle in the Carl of Carlisle versions, with the ubiquitous figure of the porter, here dressed in gold to underline King Cornwall's wealth, who tells the travellers about his master and goes to kneel at the latter's feet to express his amazement at the visitors, although the overtones of class warfare found in the Carl of Carlisle texts are absent from *Cornwall*. More strikingly, Arthur's request for lodging strongly echoes Gawain's to the porter in *Carle*, particularly the two lines: ' "& in the morning that we may scape away, / either without scath or scorne" ' (70-71).

There are other strong indications of the balladeer's extensive acquaintance with Arthurian matters. The appearance of Sir Bredbeddle, explicitly called 'the greene knight' in the later part of the poem, as one of Arthur's companions, can only be the result of his acquaintance with some version of *The Grene Knight*, where Bredbeddle, at first opposed to Arthur's court, eventually becomes a knight of the Round Table. It is not clear, in *Cornwall*, whether he too makes a vow,[66] but he becomes, in effect, the controller of events once he has undertaken to overcome the 'spy', Burlow-Beanie. This he does, after a fierce, but inconclusive, combat with 'Collen brand', 'Millaine knife' and 'Danish axe', by means of a mysterious 'litle booke' that he had found by the sea, 'wrucked upp in a floode' (*thrown up on shore by the tide*), written by 'Our Lord' and sealed with his blood.[67] The fact that in *The Grene Knight*, Bredbeddle is the son-in-law of the witch Agostes, who effects his transformation into the green knight, may have suggested to the *Cornwall*-poet his role here as a controller of necromantic forces with similar powers. Nothing in his character or function resembles that of any character in *Pèlerinage*.

At the same time, the poet includes features and draws in characters previously unknown to English Arthurian romance. Sir Marramiles, for instance, the fourth of Arthur's companions, is entirely unknown outside this poem; thus, his relevance to the test of riding Cornwall's magic horse, which presumably formed his now missing 'gab', is unclear. It is possible that this 'gab' formed a very rough equivalent to that of Turpin in *Pèlerinage*.[68]

The *Cornwall*-poet's substitute for King Hugo, the rich, powerful and hostile necromancer, King Cornwall, is similarly unknown outside this ballad, and the part he plays bears little resemblance to that of Hugo, except in its broad general outlines. He it is who provides the *Cornwall*-poet's most intriguing divergence from tradition – his boast that he was ' "clad & fed" ' in Little Britain for seven years and had a daughter by Guinevere, thereby making Arthur a ' "kindly Cockward" ' (90-5).[69] We shall meet Arthur as cuckold later, but there is, I think, no other instance of Guinevere having a child as a result of her extra-marital affairs. The incident may perhaps be seen as part of the 'anti-Guinevere' tradition, the strong moral condemnation of her as adulteress, that surfaces in such romances as Thomas Chestre's *Sir Launfal*, where she is portrayed as a spiteful mischief-maker.[70]

Cornwall's possession of a round table which, Guinevere claims, is more splendid than Arthur's, and a daughter, suggests some confusion in the poet's mind with Guinevere's father Leodegrance, the original owner of the Round Table, made for him by Merlin, and given by him to Arthur as a wedding gift. As a host he has much in common with the Carl of Carlisle in addition to his porter. He has wild creatures at his command – the magic horse and the 'spy' Burlow-Beanie; he has a daughter; his behaviour is threatening; and, eventually, like the Percy Carl, he is beheaded, although, unlike him, he does not survive his beheading.[71]

The exuberantly flamboyant fiend, Burlow-Beanie, the *Cornwall*-poet's version of the sober, disapproving spy of *Pèlerinage*, is another newcomer to Arthurian romance, although what must surely be his close relative, Billie Blin, plays the part of a friendly household spirit in no fewer than four Child ballads.[72] Burlow-Beanie is also a household spirit, though hardly a friendly one until subdued, but, appropriately for a necromancer's attendant, he is a fire-spirit, who has to be tamed by a more powerful magic than that of King Cornwall, that of the little book found by Bredbeddle on the seashore. As a Helpful Attendant, his role can be seen as, in some sense, a witty subversion of the supernatural aid afforded by the angel in *Pèlerinage*, with whose help alone the paladins are able to carry out their impossible vows.

In the fulfilment of the vows, it is hard to resist the idea that the *Cornwall*-poet was having a little teasing fun at the expense of Arthur and his famous knights. Marramiles, who so confidently undertakes to ride Cornwall's magic steed, is quite unable to make it stir an inch until Bredbeddle has commanded Burlow-Beanie to tell them the secret of how it works. Tristram cannot blow the horn until Burlow-Beanie has fetched some alchemical powder from his master's store, which he instructs Tristram to mix with milk (surely an unheroic liquid in this context) and 'swill' it about. Tristram does so, but then blows so hard that he splits the horn up the middle, not, one supposes, quite the intended result.

Arthur cannot fulfil his vow until Bredbeddle orders Burlow-Beanie to fetch Cornwall's own sword.[73] Having received it from the fiend, he then hands it over to Arthur who rushes off to behead Cornwall – who is asleep in his bed. No heroic combat against evil forces here. Bredbeddle is the controlling spirit, the 'master of ceremonies'; all dance to his tune. Burlow-Beanie changes from a malicious fiend to a Helpful Attendant, without whom none of the vows could have been achieved, except Gawain's, which, like

Oliver's, needs no supernatural agency to ensure its success. In this, *Cornwall* follows a familiar folk-tale pattern, in which the passivity of the hero is a necessary corollary to the services of a Helpful Attendant. *Puss-in-Boots* and *Jack the Giant-Killer* are notable folk-tale examples of this theme; as we have seen (p.203 above), it also plays a significant part in *Turke*, the most folk-like of all these poems.

Stylistically, the poem falls into the category of 'romance ballad', consisting mainly of four-line stanzas rhyming *xaxa*, but with some six-line stanzas, rhyming *abcbdb*. The pace shifts between a fast-moving ballad rhythm and a more leisurely romance rhythm. The former is particularly noticeable during both the vowing and the vow-fulfilling scenes, where the poet falls into an incantatory style, employing incremental repetition to create an almost ritualistic effect. Because of the stylized patterning that results from this, it is possible to reconstruct at least some of the missing stanzas in the vow-fulfilling section, where Marramiles presumably rides the horse, and Burlow-Beanie fetches the powder for Tristram's horn. There are signs of a northern origin; the word 'tranckled' (i.e. 'trauchled', *trudged wearily*; 34) for instance is Scottish, but, as with so many of the Percy Folio texts, modernization has made it difficult to be precise about its place of origin.

In spite of its fragmentary state, *Cornwall* is a work of considerable resonance and mystery, with an extraordinarily rich range of reference to other Arthurian romances and indeed to other literary and non-literary works. It is not great literature, but it has a certain robust charm, and, as is the case with so many of the popular folk romances, it testifies to a wide and continuing interest in matters Arthurian, by both poets and audiences, whether reading or listening; audiences who, moreover, could be expected to take the Arthurian references and appreciate its author's burlesque treatment of the famous hero-king and his knights, playing roles at once familiar and strange.

Gillian Rogers

The Boy and the Mantle and *Sir Corneus*

These two short poems,[74] one a ballad, the other in six-line tail-rhyme stanzas, are the only English language representatives of a very widespread folk-tale motif, the testing of women's chastity by means of a magic object, usually either a drinking horn or a mantle. Although there are many Arthurian analogues, chief among which are the *Carados* episode from the First Continuation of Chrétien de Troyes's *Perceval* (horn), Robert Biket's *Le Lai du Cor* (horn), the anonymous *Le Lai du Cort Mantel*, all written at about the turn of the twelfth century, and Heinrich von dem Türlin's *Diu Crône*, written in the first half of the thirteenth century, no direct source has been found for either poem.[75] The author of *Corneus* has a unique approach to his subject matter, but it is clear that the poet of *The Boy and the Mantle* was extensively acquainted with other versions.

The basic elements of the Arthurian versions of the story remain fairly constant throughout its long history: a young messenger, either a squire or a damsel, serving an enchanter, brings the magic testing object to Arthur's court. If the object is a horn, all the men of the court have to drink from it, including Arthur, who usually begins the test; the drink spills over him, and his reactions range from murderous rage to tolerant acceptance. If the object is a mantle, all the women of the court have to try it on, usually beginning with Guinevere.[76] She fails, sometimes completely, sometimes only slightly (perhaps depending on the bias of the poet). Arthur's reaction again ranges from rage to tolerance. In the 'stand-alone' tales, among the men drinking from the horn, only Carados succeeds; among the women trying on the mantle, only his wife passes the test. In those versions incorporated into a longer narrative, the virtuous one is the heroine of the moment. Harmony is usually restored at the end.

It is noticeable that, with the exception of *Diu Crône*, there is no test for a man's infidelity in any of these tales; horn or mantle, both reveal the woman's guilt, not the man's. Consequently they may be seen as part of a long tradition of antifeminist tales, in which Guinevere is frequently the unfortunate chief victim.[77] We have seen in *Cornwall* traces of the censorious tradition concerning Guinevere's infidelity to Arthur, there possibly stemming from the tradition related in both *Diu Crône* and *Lanzelet* of her previous association with another powerful king before she became Arthur's wife. In *Boy,* this tradition is shockingly reinforced by the poet's characterization of her, when, furious at losing face, she shrieks insults at Craddock's wife, claiming she has seen no fewer than fifteen men taken from her bed. The Boy, in confining himself to calling her "'a bitch and a witch / and a whore bold'" (*Furrow*, 148) and telling Arthur to chasten his wife, is kinder than Launfal's fairy mistress in Chestre's *Sir Launfal*, who takes a dreadful revenge on Guinevere by blinding her.

The Boy and the Mantle is unique in presenting not one, but three testing objects to the harassed court: the mantle, the horn, and the boar's head which can only be carved by a man whose wife is perfectly faithful to him. This last is the only extant example of this motif, but that it was at one time a popular tale, with Caradoc as its hero, is suggested by a reference to it in one of the thirteenth-century Harley lyrics, *Annot and John,* where Annot's virtues are compared by her lover to those of famous heroines and heroes: she 'cud ase Cradoc in court carf þe brede' (47).

However, only the mantle test is described at any length, taking up thirty-six stanzas of the forty-five. It is told with pace and verve. The cast of characters is kept to a minimum; with two exceptions, only those essential to the development of the theme are actively involved: Arthur and Guinevere as the chief victims, Kay – as ever, 'crabbed' and disagreeable, with his wife – and Craddock and *his* nameless wife. It ends abruptly, without any reaction from Arthur or the court to the Boy's condemnation of the queen and his stern and scornful pronouncement that Arthur is a cuckold in his own hall, and is followed by the boar's head test, somewhat arbitrarily introduced and dealt with in six perfunctory stanzas. No personalities save Craddock are singled out for treatment here. Arthur stands with the Boy, watching his knights' antics in detached fashion, suddenly an onlooker, not a participant. The atmosphere in this section is distinctly more primitive than in the first part. We seem suddenly to be in a chieftain's hall surrounded by forest rather than in a king's palace in a city, for the Boy, looking over a half-door in the hall, sees a wild boar and rushes out to kill it, returning immediately with the head. The women are not mentioned.

A mere two stanzas are given to the horn test, and a single six-line stanza sums up very concisely Craddock's success in all three tests. This strongly suggests that the original intention of the poet was simply to tell the tale of the mantle, but that, while he was working on it, he came across two other examples of the same theme and decided to use them as well. The effect is distinctly 'antiquarian' and disjointed, as of someone determined to include all the tales he had collected on the subject of magic testing objects, but not adept at making smooth transitions from one version to another.[78]

Boy is, like *Marriage* and *Cornwall*, an example of a 'romance ballad'. It is predominantly in the four-line 'ballad' stanza, *xaxa*, but there are also seven six-line stanzas, rhyming *abcbdb*, one relating the failure of the old knight's wife, two relating the success of Craddock's wife, and a run of four concluding the poem; that is, the last stanza of the boar's head test, the whole of the horn test and the summary. There are certain features which we now associate with traditional ballads: the effective use of repetition as each wife, scarlet-faced, flings down the mantle and flees to her room, and one instance of incremental repetition, in Craddock's wife's explanation of why the mantle crinkled very slightly when she first put it on.

Furrow (298-9), using the vocabulary as evidence, suggests the second half of the fifteenth century as the date of composition of the original, and a northern, or north Midland provenance for both the original and the Percy Folio version. She also notes the influence of the alliterative long line and the presence of inexact rhymes, suggesting corruption of the text.

Sir Corneus, which relates the horn test, is described by the poet as a 'bowrd', or jest, and stands apart from the mainstream tradition in that Arthur himself owns the horn and drinking from it gives him the power to see the truth. Oddly, he does not learn of his own cuckoldry from it, until the Duke of Gloucester comes to visit him and wonders aloud why so many men sit together at a special table wearing willow garlands, this being Arthur's way of genially tormenting the cuckold-knights. Arthur sends minstrels to their table to cheer them, and tells them they must dance together after the meal. He sends for his 'bugyll' so that he can test them with it. His joke misfires however, when the courteous duke refuses to drink before he does.[79] This time, as a result of a 'gyle' or trick, the horn spills its liquid all over him. The cuckolds rejoice; the queen blushes for shame, and Arthur with a dry comment to her, declares himself their brother. He is now cheerfully ready to join the cuckolds' dance.[80] The narrator and author of the tale names himself as Sir Corneus, presumably, from his name, himself also a cuckold.[81]

The tale is rather laboriously narrated, with much repetition and heavy underlining of the point. Arthur's behaviour seems entirely heartless as he enjoys the cuckolds' discomfiture night after night, but to do him justice, once the horn has played its trick on him too, he is quick to see that the joke is on him. Guinevere's reaction is confined to a blush of shame, and Arthur is not at all put out by this evidence of her guilt, indeed, he blesses the man who comforted her during his absence. The whole tone of the piece is burlesque, and the atmosphere is that of a jolly after-dinner tale told among men.

The only extant manuscript version of the poem (Bodleian Library, Oxford, MS Ashmole 61) is dated from the watermarks to between 1479 and 1488.[82] *Furrow* (275-7) suggests that, like *Boy,* it too originated in the second half of the fifteenth century. Her analysis of the language of the manuscript suggests a northern provenance for it, with the original being written in the area around Essex or London. Blanchfield, however, supports McIntosh's localization of Rate, the scribe of MS Ashmole 61, in Leicestershire.[83]

The two poems are minor additions to the English Arthurian canon, and by no means show as wide a knowledge of Arthurian matters as do the other poems discussed in this chapter, their range of reference seemingly confined to the one motif of the testing of the women of Arthur's court by means of a magic object. Both partake of that strain of satire running through Arthurian romance from its very beginnings, that tendency to regard the figure of Arthur not quite seriously; he seldom sinks, however, to such depths as in *Sir*

Corneus, an extreme example of how a once charismatic king descends, in the popular imagination, to an 'Old King Cole' figure of fun. **Gillian Rogers**

Among the many challengers in these texts, some significantly threaten the stability of the Round Table or the life of Arthur. The values of the court are repeatedly questioned, and on occasion found wanting. Interestingly, however, there are challengers who seek and gain membership of the court, suggesting that some poets felt that Arthur's fellowship, in spite of its shortcomings, represented the best that could be achieved – or perhaps that the pattern inherited from French romance, of conquered knights being sent back to join the court, was too potent to ignore.

Few of the familiar Arthurian characters feature in these tales; the most prominent of them are Arthur himself and Kay, and both are repeatedly played off against Gawain, neither to his own credit. Arthur is seen in a variety of roles and from a variety of viewpoints: in general, he is depicted as the sovereign lord, to whom all defer, and the final arbiter in all disputes, though the giant reputation which made him synonymous with Britain in the dynastic tradition has dwindled to that of an ancient worthy beyond time and place. But in two tales, *Turke*, and *Carle*, there is also a contrasting view, that of the king of Man and the Carl, who both see him as the aggressor. Apart from when he is hunting, his place is at court, the centre of his world. On occasion, when he steps out of this world, the results are disastrous. His ambitious attempt to hunt the white stag by himself in *Weddynge* leads to Gawain having to marry the Loathly Lady. He cuts a most unheroic figure: Gromer Somer Joure bullies him, Dame Ragnell handles him with tolerant scorn, and Gawain treats him like a small boy who has got himself into a terrible scrape. Irresponsibility and a certain heartlessness characterize his behaviour in *Avowynge*. In *Cornwall* he goes off on his headlong quest to seek the unknown owner of the rival round table in a fit of pique against Guinevere, and the idea of the cuckolded king begins to emerge, an idea which becomes central in *Boy* and *Corneus*. By and large, the treatment of Arthur in these tales perpetuates the critical attitude towards him that had existed since Chrétien's time.

Kay, Arthur's left-hand lieutenant, was as early set in his disagreeable role – in romance as opposed to chronicle – as Gawain in his exemplary one. Codified as icons, the two are used to set the parameters of chivalric behaviour, Gawain as the best, Kay as the worst exemplar. The interplay between them has, in these poems, a range of uses, from the merely iconographic telegraphese of *The Grene Knight* and *Turke*, to thematic exegesis in *Avowynge* and the Carl of Carlisle texts, playing off one set of values against another. Only in *Avowynge*, however, is there any attempt at subtlety in the depiction of this most contradictory of Arthur's knights. His degradation was to go further in the centuries ahead, to judge from the ballad of *Kempy Kay* (several versions of which were collected in Scotland from the late eighteenth century onwards) in which he woos and weds a sluttish, louse-ridden bride as grotesque as he himself has become.

These late romances and ballads reveal an intriguing duality of attitudes towards Arthur and his court, for side by side with the still flourishing chronicle tradition, portraying Arthur as the all-conquering hero who created a golden age in Britain, we find in these late poems distinct signs that he and his Round Table company were gradually receding into a once-upon-a-time never-never land in which they could be depicted in a variety of undignified but comic situations, simply because they were no longer taken seriously. Though the contrast might be explained in terms of different audiences from different social milieux, it is worth noting that among the earliest Celtic texts there are traces of a burlesque tradition, a foolish, ignorant Arthur engaged with his rumbustious comrades as supernumeraries in the adventures of some questing folk-hero (see above, pp.1-9). Coexistence rather than progressive degeneration may better explain the survival of these texts, contemporaneous with Malory's *Morte Darthur* and Lord Berners' *Arthur of Little Britain* (early sixteenth century) translated from a fourteenth-century French fantasy of adventures and wonders which, though it owes nothing to Arthur except its hero's name, testifies to his enduring charisma. This dual tradition was to lead ultimately to the situation in which, despite Spenser's recreation of him as prince Arthur, symbol of Magnificence, in *The Faerie Queene*, folk-tale heroes such as Tom Thumb could be recruited to lend lustre to Arthur's court; newly created characters such as Tom a Lincoln and Chinon of England could take precedence over such established knights as Lancelot and Tristram; and Mistress Quickly could describe Falstaff as sleeping in Arthur's bosom – which, in a speech not intended to be comic, perhaps accurately reflects the contemporary 'groundling's' perception of Arthur.

Gillian Rogers

7

SIR THOMAS MALORY'S *LE MORTE DARTHUR*

P. J. C. Field

Malory's *Le Morte Darthur* is probably the most influential of all Arthurian texts.[1] It brought together a great deal of what the Middle Ages accepted as the authentic story of King Arthur, and transmitted it to future centuries in what turned out to be the most acceptable of many potentially competing forms. Nevertheless, it is very much the product of its time. For instance, we know, as we do not with most earlier Arthurian texts, the name of its author, and even something of his life,[2] although, as with the civil servant Geoffrey Chaucer and the businessman William Shakespeare, Malory's life is not what one would have predicted from his book, or his book from his life.

All that is known for certain about Malory comes from his own writings. The most important passage is the book's closing words, which identify the author as a knight and prisoner called Thomas Malory, and say that he completed the book during the ninth year of the reign of King Edward IV (4 March 1469 to 3 March 1470). The rest of the book reveals that he loved hunting, tournaments and chivalry, that he had read a good deal of Arthurian romance, and that he had access to what must have been one of the best collections of such romances in Europe. His English, in so far as it can be made out through that of his various scribes, seems to have been that of the Midlands. Occasional more northerly elements may have been deliberately adopted from Arthurian poems of northerly origin because he felt they were appropriate to his material. He was proud of his French, though it was far from perfect, and he could understand at least a few phrases in Latin, but he was no intellectual as it was understood then or now. A particularly sympathetic description of how one of his characters was made suicidally depressed by a prison illness suggests he himself may have suffered something similar. A passage near the end of the book, presumably written under the Yorkist King Edward IV, reproaches the English for their ingratitude to good kings. This has often been felt to show sympathy with Edward's rival, the ousted Lancastrian Henry VI; but the totality of the book's possible contemporary allusions suggests that Malory could sympathize with chivalrous actions whoever performed them.

Of the dozen recorded fifteenth-century Thomas Malorys, only two are known to have been knights, and one of them had died by 1412. That necessarily makes the other, Sir Thomas Malory of Newbold Revel in Warwickshire, who died in 1471, the favourite for authorship. He also came from the right area linguistically, but his life seems to be at odds with the chivalric ideals that the *Morte Darthur* has been taken to embody, and partly for this reason there have been several attempts to show that the *Morte Darthur* might have been written by another man of the same name. However, neither of the plausible alternatives was a knight at the right time, and a group of pardons and related documents issued near to the time when the *Morte Darthur* was written implies that there was no unknown knight of that name either. Scholarship therefore has to make what it can of Sir Thomas Malory of Newbold Revel.

He was born about 1416 and begins to appear in local affairs in 1439. For some years he seems to been a respectable country land-owner; he was knighted by 1441 and represented Warwickshire in the parliament of 1445-6. In 1450, however, according to later accusations, he began a spectacular career of crime, ranging from the attempted murder of the most important magnate in the area to rape, extortion, theft of livestock, sacrilegious robbery of a local abbey, and miscellaneous vandalism. The accusations were certainly politically motivated, but that does not mean they were false. By 1452 he was in prison in London awaiting trial, but the authorities for their own purposes made sure no trial took place. As the country drifted into civil war, the dissatisfied Yorkists began taking an interest in him, which made the Lancastrian authorities even more determined to keep him behind bars.

He was apparently freed when the Yorkists seized power in the 1460s, and in the winter of 1462-3 took part in a Yorkist campaign in the north. In the mid-1460s, he again looks briefly like a respectable country landowner, but in 1468 and again in 1470 he was one of a small group excluded by name from pardons offered by King Edward, probably because he was involved in a Lancastrian plot discovered in July 1468. Others involved in the plot were promptly arrested and imprisoned, and although there is no direct evidence of what happened to Malory, the *Morte Darthur* reveals that he was in prison at about that time. The political nature of his presumed offence, his surprising importance in the 1450s, and the disturbed state of south-eastern England suggest that he is most likely to have been imprisoned in the Tower of London, as he had been briefly during the worst unrest in the 1450s. He completed the *Morte Darthur* during his imprisonment, but probably remained in captivity until, in September 1470, a Lancastrian invasion freed that party's sympathizers from London gaols and sanctuaries. The Lancastrian 'readeption' also brought him prosperity. When he died, six months later, on 14 March 1471, he was buried under a marble tombstone in the fashionable church of Greyfriars, Newgate.

Although it was the *Morte Darthur* that made Malory famous, he may also have written another English Arthurian romance.[3] *The Wedding of Sir Gawain and Dame Ragnell* is a vigorous reworking in stanzas of the traditional folktale theme of What Women Most Desire.[4] There are notable similarities between the two works in language, the handling of narrative, and authorial comment. The similarities are strongest at the end of the poem, where its author reveals that he is in prison and prays for his release in terms strikingly reminiscent of those Malory uses at the end of various sections of the *Morte Darthur*. However, even if *The Wedding* is by Malory, it is an achievement of a much lower order than the *Morte Darthur*: the versification, for instance, is little better than doggerel. Nevertheless, it is easy to see it as an early effort from the same hand, valuable for the light it sheds both on the undemanding popular fiction of its period and on the literary development of a major author.

Although the *Morte Darthur* is in prose, it is more ambitious than *The Wedding* in almost every way, as well as more successful. The author's own manuscript is lost, but happily two early texts survive. If, as seems likely, Malory completed the *Morte Darthur* late in the ninth year of Edward IV,[5] both texts were in existence within sixteen years of his laying down his pen. One of them, the printed edition completed by William Caxton at Westminster on 31 July 1485, is known in a perfect copy in the Pierpont Morgan Library in New York, and in one lacking eleven leaves in the John Rylands Library in Manchester.[6] Caxton's edition is a literary monument in its own right: until the mid-twentieth century, it was the only known version of the *Morte Darthur*, and it was therefore in editions derived from it that Malory's book became an English literary classic in the sixteenth century and re-established itself as one in the nineteenth.

It was Caxton's edition that gave Malory's book its striking and inaccurate title.[7] In his closing words Malory calls what he had written 'the hoole book of Kyng Arthur and of his noble knyghtes of the Rounde Table'. Caxton failed to recognize that for what it was,[8] and took as the title of Malory's 'hoole book' the much crisper title of its last section, 'The Deth of Arthur', which occurs a few words later. He turned this into a sort of French, no doubt influenced by his sense of what buyers liked, and perhaps by the variant title given at the beginning of the section, 'The Moste Pyteuous Tale of the Morte Arthure Saunz Gwerdon' (1154). The result is at cross purposes with what the author intended, and so inaccurate that Caxton, who invented it, devoted half his own closing words to explaining it away; it has also been repeatedly criticized for its grammar, punctuation, and use of capitals. Despite that, every attempt to displace it has failed, and it remains the accepted title of Malory's book. The verdict of time has shown it to be magnificently appropriate (*Vinaver*, xliii-xliv); even its linguistic short-comings say something about the nature of Malory's achievement.

The second text of the *Morte Darthur* is a manuscript discovered in Winchester College in 1934, and still usually called the Winchester Manuscript, although it is now in the British Library in London, as Additional MS. 59678.[9] It has lost its first and last quires and suffered minor damage elsewhere, leaving the Caxton text as the only source for (among other things) the biographical information about Malory at the end of the book, the book's most quoted single passage, Ector's lament for his dead brother Launcelot, and its best-known episode, the story of the sword in the stone. Despite these shortcomings, a manuscript-based edition by Eugène Vinaver published in 1947 established itself immediately as the standard edition.[10]

For the reader who wants what Malory wrote, the most important fact about the two texts is that they derive independently from a lost original. This is surprising, since traces of printer's ink on some 60 pages of the manuscript show that it was being carefully read in Caxton's printing shop at some time during the years 1480-3, when he was preparing his edition.[11] Nevertheless, Caxton certainly based his edition on a different manuscript, now lost. Perhaps, since the Winchester manuscript is a handsome and expensive product, its owner would not allow it to be marked up as printing required.[12] Caxton may have used it as a consultation copy, to correct a base manuscript that was illegible or damaged at some points. He produced his second edition of Chaucer's *Canterbury Tales* (in 1484) by a rather similar process of conflation.[13] The Winchester manuscript remained in his printing house until 1489, when it was repaired with a piece of waste from his press, and perhaps until 1498, when his successor Wynkyn de Worde may have used it to correct an edition of his own. How it found its way from Caxton's or de Worde's print-shop to Winchester is still a matter of speculation.[14]

The independent derivation of the two surviving texts makes it possible to correct each from the other. Both certainly need correction: both contain not only scribal errors but also deliberate alterations to their originals. Caxton admitted making one set of alterations: his Prologue says he divided his edition into 21 books and 507 chapters. However, he also drastically shortened and rewrote Malory's story of Arthur's Roman War to make it more like the rest of the book, tinkered with the wording of his original to make it fit the printed page, and 'translated' its Midland English into

something more south-easterly.[15] He may also have toned down a few
passages he thought irreligious.[16] Overall, his text is often a little clearer and
more modern in idiom than that of the manuscript, and slightly less vivid. On
the other hand, although it is tempting to ascribe all apparent conscious
changes to Caxton, the scribes who copied the manuscript had made
deliberate changes too. They also – being notably less concerned with
accuracy than with a handsome page – made a good many accidental errors.
On balance, though, the Winchester text seems to be appreciably closer to
what Malory wrote than the Caxton,[17] and a reader who wants the *Morte
Darthur* that Malory intended will therefore look for a well-edited
manuscript-based edition.

Vinaver's edition was immediately accepted as providing just what was
needed, but his introduction and notes provoked a controversy that
dominated Malory studies for a generation. It had been widely accepted that
Malory's greatest achievement had been to make 'one story and one book'
out of the miscellany of previously existing Arthurian tales, and that that
marked an important stage in the evolution of the novel, the dominant
literary form of our time.[18] Vinaver argued that Malory's part in the
evolution of the novel was negligible, and that far from being a primaeval
novel what he wrote was not even a single book, the contrary view having
been created by changes Caxton had introduced to make his edition sell.
What Malory had written was 'a series of eight separate romances'.[19] That
view was implied in the provocative title of Vinaver's edition, *The Works of
Sir Thomas Malory*.

In support of his view, Vinaver pointed principally to the newly
discovered manuscript. He argued that the manuscript showed that Malory
had divided his work into eight major sections, which Vinaver called 'tales'.
That is what Malory calls most of them, and scholars have generally adopted
the term, which conveniently distinguishes these eight sections from Caxton's
twenty-one 'books', although Malory sometimes uses 'tale' (and 'book' too,
for that matter) in other senses.

Vinaver pointed out that his eight tales end with short authorial
postscripts, often giving information about the author in the first person, of a
kind commonly used in the Middle Ages to provide formal endings for
books, and usually called 'explicits'. All but one of Malory's contain either
the Latin word *explicit* itself or an English equivalent such as 'here endyth'.
The seventh has no such phrase, but may create the strongest sense of an
ending of all: it contains a long passage in which Malory as narrator
confesses that he has lost part of his story, and is therefore going on to the
next tale. Caxton retained the final explicit, presumably to give his entire

volume an emphatic ending of the kind readers expected from a single work, but reworked the rest into briefer and more impersonal indications of his book-and-chapter scheme. Vinaver argued that it was above all that scheme and Caxton's title, *Le Morte Darthur*, which had made readers think Malory had written one literary work rather than eight.

Vinaver offered a second reason for seeing the eight tales as separate works: that there were discrepancies between them but not within them (*Vinaver*, xxxvii-xxxviii). He pointed out that Sir Tristram appears as an important knight in the Fourth Tale, but that the Fifth begins with the story of his birth, and Sir Tarquin appears in full vigour in a tournament in the Fourth Tale although he has been killed by Sir Launcelot in the Third.

Scholarly scrutiny left this last argument looking distinctly battered, revealing discrepancies within tales as striking as any between them: the Fourth Tale, for instance, has the Red Knight of the Red Lands make *two* first appearances at King Arthur's court, and the Fifth Tale announces that it will relate the death of Sir Keyhydyns, but never does.[20] As stated, that particular argument was simply untenable: whatever readers made of the discrepancies in the *Morte Darthur*, they had no place in arguments about the unity of the book. The discrepancies can, however, help in other ways to define the nature of Malory's work, so we shall have to return to them.

The argument from the explicits was stronger in itself – there could be no doubt that an explicit implied some kind of ending – and could be strengthened by another factor: that, with a single apparent exception, the eight tales were based on different major sources. The exception is that the seventh and eighth tales are based on two sources in parallel rather than one apiece; the 'apparent' is necessary because the Fourth Tale has no known source, although, wherever Malory got it from, it was not from the source of the tale before or the one after it. Despite these qualifications, it was clear that an author who took his tales so consistently from different sources might well have seen them as independent stories.

However, even if Malory's explicits implied breaks in literary continuity, those breaks did not seem to be total. Three of the eight explicits, for instance, not only complete a tale but announce the next one. The Third Tale ends:

> Explicit a Noble Tale of Sir Launcelot du Lake Here folowyth Sir Garethis tale of Orkeney that was callyd Bewmaynes By Sir Kay.[21]

All twenty-three words are part of the explicit. The first nine look back, the remaining fourteen forward to the elaborately decorated initial over the page that begins the next tale, yet the two parts are not separated by so much as a punctuation mark or a line-break.[22] The explicits to the fifth and seventh tales are similar.

This suggests that the break implied by explicits in the *Morte Darthur* is not complete. That is confirmed by the fact that Malory uses explicits not only for the eight tales, but also for subsections within them. In the First Tale, the second subsection ends 'thus endith the Tale of Balyn and Balan . . . Explicit', and the third 'Explicit the Weddyng of Kyng Arthur' (92, 120). Vinaver's theory could be modified to make these two subsections into tales,[23] which, with the subsections before and after them, would increase the number of tales to eleven. That, however, would be incompatible with the explicit to the First Tale, which says that tale begins with the marriage of King Uther, the first episode in the *Morte Darthur* (*Vinaver*, p.180). It is clear that, despite their explicits, 'The Tale of Balyn and Balan' and 'The Wedding of King Arthur' are component parts of a single tale. If so, the eight tales, despite their explicits, may be component parts of a single larger work.

Moreover, Malory's own words show that he thought he had produced one book, not eight. He calls what he has written

> the hoole book of Kyng Arthur and of his noble knyghtes of the Rounde Table, that whan they were holé togyders there was ever an hondred and forty. (1260.16-19)

If a work has wholeness, its parts cannot be autonomous. It must be said that the idea of wholeness may need clarification: a fifteenth-century book will not necessarily have the same kind of wholeness as a twentieth-century one. However, wholeness must imply completeness and coherence of some kind; and in the passage quoted, Malory as narrator is clearly claiming those attributes for the *Morte Darthur*.

The book certainly exhibits one kind of completeness in beginning with the events leading up to Arthur's conception and ending with the consequences of his death, and one kind of coherence in presenting the events in the story in what looks broadly like a chronological order. Both things were Malory's doing. None of his known sources had his kind of completeness: some related only part of Arthur's story, others set it in a larger context. The native 'Brut' tradition derived from Geoffrey of Monmouth, which provided the standard history of Britain in Malory's time,[24] made Arthur's reign the high point in that history; and the hugely popular French Vulgate Cycle of Arthurian romances made Arthur's reign the culmination of a Grail history beginning in the time of Christ and ending with Arthur's death. Malory followed neither of these traditions, although he knew both of them; he used the Vulgate Cycle in four of his tales, and he seems to have used a version of the Brut story, John Hardyng's *Chronicle*, as a minor source throughout the *Morte Darthur*.

The wide diffusion of these legendary histories across Europe invited authors to rework other Arthurian stories into new combinations,[25] an urge that seems to have been particularly strong in Europe in the century before Caxton's *Morte Darthur*, when there were reworkings in French, Welsh, Italian and German.[26] None of them integrated its source materials fully, but all show a wish to put events into an order that makes sense in itself, or in relation to the pre-existing legendary history of Britain, or both. They are much more tolerant of other kinds of inconsistency, such as variation of ethos or style. Malory similarly seems to have aimed above all to make a coherent story, and in pursuit of this, although he proclaimed his use of 'authorized' books (1260.8), he rough-hewed them to a shape of his own devising.

Malory's independence shows from the very beginning, in his choice of source and starting point. He knew two accounts of Arthur's early years, both of them French prose romances named after the enchanter Merlin: one was the second romance in the Vulgate Cycle, the other the corresponding romance in a less popular rival called the Post-Vulgate Cycle. Malory thought well enough of the Vulgate *Merlin* to use it in his Second Tale,[27] but he based his First Tale on its Post-Vulgate cousin. The original component of the Post-Vulgate romance, the *Merlin* proper, ends with Arthur's coronation and is followed by a long continuation called the *Suite de Merlin*, which describes Arthur's early wars and the adventures of his first Knights of the Round Table. Malory began his story with the marriage of Uther Pendragon, late in the *Merlin* proper, and continued almost to the end of the *Suite*, so turning a long story about Merlin into a much shorter one about Arthur and his knights.

The First Tale begins as a kind of history of court life, dynastic politics, international alliances, and military campaigns, interwoven with supernatural events, mostly brought about by the magician Merlin. After Arthur has come to the throne, he has to fight a brutal civil war, from which he emerges victorious a third of the way through the tale as king of all Britain, Guenivere's husband, and sovereign of the Round Table (78.11). He has also begotten a son in incest, Mordred, who is destined to kill him (41.12-25, 44.16-30). Although he is still sometimes threatened by invasion from abroad and treachery from within his own household, the rest of the tale modulates into the familiar chivalric world of individual quests and adventures which are to dominate the middle part of the *Morte Darthur*. Some of the events in this tale already prepare the way for the greatest of all quests, the quest for the Holy Grail.

The ending of the First Tale also shows Malory's independence. He abandoned the *Suite* just before Gaheriet, brother of Gauvain, is knighted by Artus and undertakes his first series of adventures.[28] Gaheriet's English counterpart Sir Gareth is the protagonist of Malory's Fourth Tale, which tells how he arrives at Arthur's court, is knighted by Launcelot and undertakes his first adventures. Malory's practice elsewhere suggests he omitted Gaheriet's adventures because he saw a double set of first adventures for the same knight as an undesirable duplication, even though the sets had few similarities and would have appeared in different tales. The source of the Fourth Tale offered more possibilities than the *Suite* for increasing coherence between tales, which may be why Malory chose it as the one to keep.

The tale ends instead with an explicit that dates the ending 'when Sir Launcelot and Sir Tristram come to court' (180.18-19). That implies a first arrival in Camelot for the two knights at more or less the same time, an event that Malory presumably invented, since it is unknown elsewhere in Arthurian romance. He never relates it in full, so it exists in the narrative background, providing verisimilitude, like the adventures referred to in the Sherlock Holmes stories. The explicit also creates a point of temporal reference. The popularity of stories about Launcelot and Tristram meant that medieval audiences 'knew' that the two knights' adventures occurred in the heyday of Arthur's reign. Their arrival at Arthur's court therefore marks the end of the beginning of the Arthurian story. Malory also ties the beginning of his Second Tale to that moment: its opening explicitly sets it soon after Launcelot and Tristram come to court (185.3-6). That relates the Second Tale chronologically both to its predecessor and to an 'objective' Arthurian time-scheme.

The Second Tale is based on *Morte Arthure*, a fourteenth- or fifteenth-century English alliterative poem that tells the story of Arthur's war against the Roman Empire, which Malory used in a version perhaps rather longer than the one known today.[29] The epic tale of conflict between empires is occasionally relieved by individual exploits, as when Arthur himself seeks out a predatory giant, and when Gawain finds himself involved in single combat on a foraging expedition.

Malory generally follows the English poem closely, but with one important exception. As the opening reference to Launcelot and Tristram shows, he moved the story back in time to the early years of Arthur's reign. In *Morte Arthure*, as in almost all comprehensive accounts of Arthur's life, this story is the climactic final episode in Arthur's reign, the foreign war that leaves him open to betrayal by Mordred and brings about his death.[30] Malory's change makes the tale revive and develop the theme of war from the early part of the First Tale. Consequential changes fit the story to the rest of his book. He cut the tragic ending of the poem, and ended the war with a victory that brings Arthur to the height of his power: he is crowned as Emperor of Rome and returns home in triumph. Malory also changed the deaths of characters needed later into mere woundings, and increased Launcelot's part from six passing mentions to that of a minor principal, the rising star of chivalry. He did not, however, suggest any relationship between Launcelot and Guenivere: when Arthur leaves Tristram behind for Isode's sake, Launcelot, far from showing sympathy towards another lover, is said to be 'passyng wrothe' (195.8-10).

The Third Tale is said to begin soon after Arthur returns from Rome (253.1). That ties it to the Second Tale rather as the second is tied to the first, but more loosely. In this tale Malory set a number of stories about Launcelot in a frame of his own making. He took most of them from the French Prose *Lancelot*, the third romance in the Vulgate Cycle, although one comes from another French prose romance called *Perlesvaus*, and another may be his own invention.[31] In the section of the *Lancelot* that Malory used, Lancelot has long been known as the best knight in the world and as Guenivere's lover. Malory, however, put his selected episodes together to show a younger Launcelot achieving a reputation, friends and followers for the first time. The tale ends with Launcelot's return to Camelot, where his fellow knights acclaim him as the best knight in the world.

Malory also drastically changes the presentation of Guenivere. Although we are constantly reminded of her, what is happening between her and Launcelot remains obscure. The narrator says that Launcelot's prowess made her love him, which made him love her, and rescue her from being burnt at the stake (253.15-19). The narrator seems to suggest that their love has not yet begun, and may never be more than Platonic. The former is plausible enough, but a medieval audience would have seen the latter as distinctly economical with the truth. In Arthurian 'history', the rescue from the stake that the narrator mentions revealed Launcelot's adultery with the queen, and began the process that destroys Arthur's kingdom and the fellowship of the Round Table. Readers who knew that would have heard in the narrator's voice the bland discretion of an obituary.

We have little basis on which to draw conclusions of our own. Guenivere appears once, very much as queen, delivering a competent judgement on a prisoner Launcelot sent her (296.1-18). Some characters say confidently that the two are lovers, even that she has bewitched him (257-8, 270.1), but none of them sounds like a credible witness. On the other hand, Launcelot's vehement denials are entirely opaque. He could be a young idealist devoted to chivalry, who has taken the queen as his lady *ex officio*, and will not allow malicious gossip to stop him serving her. He could be fleeing from temptation or actual sin to the untainted perils of knightly adventure, his closely argued outburst against 'paramours' representing the voice of his conscience; or he could be already a habitual adulterer trying to compound for his sins by good works elsewhere, as he does in the last two tales.[32] This uncertainty makes us aware by contrast of the lovers' part in the coming destruction of Arthur's kingdom, an awareness that hangs ominously over Launcelot's exhilarating chivalric achievements.

The Fourth Tale is most naturally taken as occurring after the Third, although, just as the chronological links between the second and third tales are looser than those between the first and second, so the links between third and fourth tales are looser than those between the second and third. The Fourth Tale is simply set when Arthur is at the height of his power (293.3-4), but Launcelot is the king's close friend, and the most famous knight at his court. Guenivere makes two brief appearances as a member of Arthur's court.

The tale itself is devoted, as we have seen, to the first adventures of Sir Gareth. It is apparently based on a lost English poem featuring his brother Gawain, Arthur's principal knight in English Arthurian tradition, which in turn will be a reworking of a younger-brother story from the world of traditional oral story-telling.[33] (*The Wedding of Sir Gawain and Dame Ragnell* will be a similar adaptation of a traditional story.) The logic of the younger brother story is that the hero should come anonymously to a court where his elder brother is held in the highest regard and prove himself his brother's equal, first at court, then in adventures in the wider world, reaching a narrative climax when the two fight each other to a standstill. In the course of doing these things, Gareth also achieves reputation, love, marriage, friends, a fief and barons who do him homage.

However, although the elder brother's role should be Gawain's, much of it is actually either shared with Launcelot or given to Launcelot alone; and at the end of the tale the narrator says that Gareth and Launcelot become close friends, and that Gareth begins to avoid Gawain because of his vindictiveness (360.29-36). These things must be Malory's changes to his source, presumably to harmonize this tale with the others. Nothing in the Fourth Tale shows Gawain as vindictive, but in the first he conspires to kill a man he believes has killed his father, and in the eighth his obsessive pursuit of Launcelot, who accidentally kills Gareth, leads to his own death and the extermination of his family.[34] Relationships established in this tale play an important part in the final one, where the tragedy is so finely balanced as to suggest that any significant change might avert it. One factor preventing that is Gawain's resentment at Gareth's love for Launcelot (1189.1-25), whose origins we see in this tale.

The Fifth Tale is much the longest, longer than the total length of the four that precede it or the three that follow it. It is based not, as might have been expected, on the Prose *Lancelot*, but on the French Prose *Tristan*, a companion romance that makes Tristan, the lover of Iseult, the central character in an extensive complex of chivalric adventures. Lancelot's adventures and relationship with Guenivere have a secondary place. Malory apparently used a hybrid version of the *Tristan* descending from three different traditions.[35] His most important change was to trim his source at both ends. He cut a long account of Tristan's ancestors without replacing it with any chronological link to the previous tale, and began with the hero's birth (1443). That, as Vinaver noticed, apparently subverts the progression established by the previous tales, because the First Tale tells of Tristram's arrival at Arthur's court, the second implies he is Isode's lover, and the fourth shows him competing in a tournament.

The contradiction, however, is only apparent. After three sentences on Tristram's parents, the narrator observes that

> at that tyme kynge Arthure regned, and he was hole kynge of Ingelonde, Walys, and Scotlonde, and of many other realmys.[36]

Arthur could be said to have reigned at any time after his coronation, but he could only properly be called king of the whole of England, Wales and Scotland after the final battle in the civil war, when he defeats Rions of North Wales and Lot of Orkney. The passage above echoes the opening of the part of the First Tale which relates that battle:

> After the deth of Uther regned Arthure, hys son, which had grete warre in hys dyes for to gete all Ingelonde into hys honde; for there were many kyngis within the realme of Ingelonde and of Scotlonde, Walys and Cornuwayle.
>
> (61.1-5)

The beginning of the Fifth Tale seems to be what the twentieth century calls a flashback, implying that Tristram's birth took place about the time of Arthur's victory over Lot, and his early adventures were concurrent with the remainder of the early tales.

The body of the Fifth Tale is a mass of chivalric adventure. Tristram is the most prominent character, but hundreds of others are involved too. Some themes emerge, such as Tristram's relationship with Arthur's knights and his rivalry with Palomides the Saracen; the first culminates in his becoming a Knight of the Round Table and the second in Palomides becoming his friend and a Christian, whose baptism ends the tale. There are hints of other themes. There seem, for instance, to be fewer oppressive barons for the Round Table to keep in order, but ominous factions gather within the Round Table itself. As suspicion of Launcelot's relationship with the queen increases, his devoted supporters become a potential danger. Towards the end of the tale, he is tricked into bed with the destined mother of the Grail-winner, believing she is Guenivere; so Galahad is conceived by the act that tells us, almost with certainty, that the rumours of adultery are true.[37]

Despite these themes and the hints of underlying purpose suggested by anticipations of the Grail-quest, most of the episodes seem simply to be 'adventure' in the fullest sense, the chance products of events outside our knowledge. The tale has little plot, as that is usually understood: individual adventures, sometimes alternating in the narrative style called *entrelacement*, often have no bearing on what comes before and after. Characters appear and disappear without explanation. Explanations may be late, partial or even contradictory, and *entrelacement* and various kinds of narrative displacement may make connections hard to follow: important parts of some stories only become known when characters refer to them or tell each other about them. The narrative context created by the other seven tales suggests that the apparent main theme, what happens between Tristram and Isode and King Mark, is less important than what happens between Launcelot and Guenivere and King Arthur, of which we see very little. As a result the tale has a profusion, depth, and disorderliness like life itself, which is hardly to be judged by criteria developed for the tight causality typical of modern fiction. The same factors create an impression of comprehensiveness: the lack of apparent pattern in the narrative makes the tale's length and extensive cast of characters appear even longer and more extensive.

The Fifth Tale hardly promotes the coherence of Malory's 'whole book': it simply stands as its centre, the place where the chivalric world of quests and tournaments exists in its purest form. It is the *royaulme aventureux*, where questing Knights of the Round Table, particularly Launcelot and Gareth and Tristram, deal with overmighty barons, but where adventures of many other kinds happen too. At the end, however, Malory notably reduced one potential incoherence by cutting the last section of his source, a Grail story adapted from the Vulgate Cycle to include Prose *Tristan* characters.[38] He presumably cut it because he knew he would base his next tale on the Vulgate Grail-story itself. However, late in the Fifth Tale, as we have seen, he kept the *Tristan* episode that relates the begetting of Galahad. That provided him with a strong introduction to his own Grail story, whose fitness for the purpose is no accident, since it was composed for that very purpose in the Vulgate Cycle, from which the *Tristan* borrowed it with very few changes. The decision to keep it locks Malory's Fifth Tale firmly to his sixth. The two tales also fit together because the mass of adventures in the Fifth Tale finds a natural culmination in a sixth tale about the greatest of all quests, that for the Holy Grail.

Malory took his Sixth Tale from the Vulgate *Queste del Saint Graal*, the fourth romance in the cycle. He ends his tale by saying as narrator that the story is 'chronicled as one of the truest and holiest in the world' (1037.8-11), which suggests that he rated the *Queste* highest among the 'authorized' Arthurian books that he had set himself to turn into English.[39] It is the only source where he begins at the beginning and relates all the episodes in the same order through to the end, sometimes word for word. One result of following his source so closely is a narrative style very different from that of the Fifth Tale. Although the adventures are much interlaced, they make a highly coherent story. Not only are there none of the conspicuous loose ends of the Fifth Tale, but the meaning of many events is explained in great detail by hermits and other privileged figures. This is appropriate to the theme of divine providence, the most important theme in this tale.

The tale begins with the opening words of the *Queste*, translated with no introductory link to the preceding tale.[40] Links, however, might be thought superfluous when the whole tale fulfils anticipations generated by Grail episodes in earlier tales. The tale relates how Galahad comes to Arthur's court, how the Grail appears there and vanishes, and how the Knights of the Round Table set out to search for it. They find a strenuously spiritual quest: there is no advantage in worldly skill in arms, nor in the bonds of natural affection, which have been almost equally important in previous tales. One of Launcelot's cousins comes to resent his brother's dedication to the Grail so much that he tries to murder him. He and many others fail in the quest and are disgraced. Galahad and two others succeed, and Launcelot sees a limited vision of the Grail, but is told that his adultery, which he has only partly repented, prevents him from seeing more.

However, although Malory followed the story of the *Queste* closely, he changed its mystical and severely ascetic ethos into a more humane spirituality. Among other things, Launcelot becomes a would-be-repentant sinner suffering from instability of purpose.[41] Malory also added to the ending what amounts to a new link to the next tale: the only surviving Grail-knight, Launcelot's cousin Bors, gives him a last message from Galahad, a warning not to put his trust in this world.[42]

The Seventh Tale, like the Third, is based on a variety of sources. Its first two episodes come from an English poem, the stanzaic *Morte Arthur* and its source, the *Mort Artu*, the last romance in the Vulgate Cycle; the fourth from the Prose *Lancelot* (or perhaps from one of its sources, Chrétien de Troyes's *Chevalier de la Charette*); the other two may be Malory's invention. After an opening chronological link setting the tale after the Grail quest, the narrative immediately relates how Launcelot, disregarding Galahad's warning, returns to his affair with Guenivere. Each of the five episodes shows them in danger of discovery.

Compared with earlier tales, the world of this one is naturalistic, even familiar. Time is measured by the church calendar: the second episode begins at the Assumption (15 August), the third at Candlemas (2 February), the fourth in May, and the fifth at Pentecost. The action takes place not in Sorelois or the Forest Perilous, but in London, Guildford and Winchester. There seem to be no overmighty subjects left for the Round Table knights to put down, and mysterious strangers no longer appear in Arthur's court to challenge them to quests: when a foreign knight appears, he is a Hungarian who has come from Spain by way of Scotland. It even contributes to this effect that the dangers to Arthur's court are from within. In the first episode, for instance, Gawain's brother Aggravain is shown spying on the lovers, and a member of another faction tries to poison Gawain at a dinner given by Guenivere. In the fourth, Guenivere is abducted by a knight of the Round Table.

The most obvious danger in this situation, which we see in each episode, is the lovers' inability to control their own emotions. They are profoundly understood: the first episode opens with a bitter quarrel, because Guenivere cannot bear Launcelot's inconsistent efforts to placate his conscience by staying away from her. Rather than wait to be rejected, she banishes him from the court, so leaving herself defenceless when she is wrongly accused of the poisoning. In the second episode Launcelot, perhaps in subconscious resentment, allows a younger woman to fall in love with him, causing her death; and in the third, Guenivere, perhaps from similar motives, makes Launcelot wear a conspicuous token of hers at a tournament.

The story creates a strong sense of impending disaster, which is increased by the narrowness of the repeated escapes and by a sparer narrative – this tale has a stronger main theme than its predecessors, fewer events irrelevant to that theme, and no interlacing. The steady succession of events, with four episodes taking place in nine months,[43] increases this effect, as do memories of predictions in earlier tales, external knowledge of Arthurian 'history', and the final sentence of the narrative, which looks ominously both back and forwards:

> But every nyght and day sir Aggravayne, sir Gawaynes brother, awayted quene Gwenyver and sir Launcelot to put hem bothe to a rebuke and a shame.

That recalls Aggravain's plotting at the beginning of this tale, and looks forward to the last tale, which opens:

> And all was longe uppon two unhappy knyghtis whych were named sir Aggravayne and sir Mordred, that were brethirn unto sir Gawayne. For thys sir Aggravayne and sir Mordred had ever a prevy hate unto the quene, dame Gwenyver, and to sir Launcelot; and dayly and nyghtly they ever wacched uppon sir Launcelot. (1161.9-14)

The last two tales are tied tightly together by that echo, the impetus of the previous tale, and its explicit chronology. An awkward time-reference at the end of the Seventh Tale also suggests that the Pentecost with which it ends is the one immediately before the May that begins the Eighth Tale,[44] making the final tale follow a matter of months after its predecessor, like a sixth episode. Aggravain and Mordred's plotting precipitates yet another crisis for the lovers, like those in the previous tale. This time, however, they are discovered.

The Eighth Tale tells the story of the final downfall of Arthur's kingdom. It is based on the stanzaic *Morte Arthur* and the *Mort Artu*, but, like the English poem, Malory's tale omits a number of subsidiary stories in the *Mort Artu*, including a version of the Roman War story. That simplifies and clarifies the narrative, making it less like his Fifth Tale. So do the identifiable places and dates, although in this case the dates do not provide a uniform sequence.[45] So above all does the plot, which has a strong complicated causal articulation. Unlike the Fifth Tale, with its seemingly autonomous separate adventures, this tale is driven not by chance but by cause and effect, or fate, or both. When Aggravain and Mordred, against Gawain's vehement urging, denounce the lovers to Arthur, everything else follows with a seeming tragic necessity.

Aggravain himself is one of the first to die, but the process he sets in motion continues inexorably until the Round Table as an institution is destroyed, and all the major characters who have become familiar in the previous seven tales are dead. It is part of the tragedy that in this tale chivalry works against itself. As king, Arthur must allow Aggravain and Mordred to set a trap for his wife and his friend. Escaping from that trap by killing all but one of those involved is Launcelot's greatest feat of single combat; but that very achievement suggests that he and Guenivere are guilty. That in turn drives Arthur to condemn Guenivere to death, and Launcelot to rescue her. The rescue is a second astonishing feat of prowess, but it splits the Round Table fellowship, and in the course of it Launcelot kills his friend Gareth. That provokes the furious enmity of Gawain, whose thirst for revenge, unaffected by a reconciliation between Arthur and Guenivere, drives him to make Arthur pursue Launcelot to his continental lands. That gives Mordred his chance to usurp his father's throne and marriage-bed. On Arthur's return, Gawain is killed, and then Arthur and Mordred and almost all the remaining Knights of the Round Table are killed in a huge battle on Salisbury Plain. The tale ends on a note of expiation: Guenivere enters a convent and Arthur's last knight, Bedivere, a monastery, where Launcelot and his kinsmen join him.[46] After Launcelot's death, his kinsmen, the last survivors of the Round Table, are killed on crusade in the Holy Land.

The *Morte Darthur*, then, is not a life of Arthur, although the narrative is defined by his birth and death. Rather, it is precisely what Malory called it: the story of Arthur *and* his noble Knights of the Round Table. That is the story that Malory tried to unify, and he largely succeeded. Creating its parts in their present order made a story with completeness and coherence. The coherence extends to a satisfying symmetry in the plot: the rise, supremacy, and fall of Arthur's world is counterpointed against a focus that shifts between the king and his knights. The opening and closing tales are primarily about what the king does or may do, the middle four about the knights. Coherence, however, is preserved because the narrative interest is in him as their king and them as his knights.

The completeness and coherence were achieved both positively and negatively. We have seen something of the larger-scale positive achievements, but, if only to show the comprehensiveness of Malory's aims as compared with other authors who combined Arthurian stories in his period, it is worth noting that there were many smaller-scale achievements too. For instance, Malory repeatedly introduced minor characters from one source into stories derived from others.[47] Across the whole book, these new minor characters create a social background more fully realized than in any of Malory's sources. In particular, it is the introduction of these characters that creates the slow growth of factions among Arthur's knights across Malory's whole book. In the Eighth Tale, Launcelot's followers from the Third Tale and Gareth's from the Fourth and Tristram's from the Fifth have to choose individually between Launcelot and Arthur, much as Malory's own contemporaries had to choose in the England of the Wars of the Roses.

Negatively, Malory resolved many discrepancies created by the interaction of material from different sources. However, he also created some new ones.

For instance, two knights who are killed early in the First Tale, Harleuse and Peryne, appear in good health late in the Fifth,[48] and well before Gareth becomes a kitchen boy at Arthur's court in the Fourth Tale, he is said to capture a fortress in the Alps for Arthur in the Second (242.24). There are related oddities that do not quite amount to contradictions. For instance, the sword Arthur draws from the stone is called Excalibur, but when he breaks it on a quest the Lady of the Lake gives him a replacement with the same name. Again, in the Second Tale, Arthur fights a war with a Roman Empire that stretches from the Caspian Sea to Portugal, a huge swathe of territory, even bigger than the one that Arthur rules. Arthur's victory makes him Emperor; yet we never hear later of his doing anything for or with this extended empire.

As with plot, so with characterization: Malory was faced with contradictory sources, which he tried to harmonize. Again he was largely successful, particularly with the principal characters, as we have seen with Launcelot,[49] but there are significant minor discrepancies. These include Arthur's Herod-like attempt in the First Tale to murder all the boys born on Mayday, and Bors's attempt to salvage his cousin Launcelot's adulterous affair in the seventh and eighth tales, in contrast to his heroic dedication to moral principle in the Sixth Tale.[50]

Although these discrepancies are small in proportion to the overall scheme of Malory's book, scholars have tried hard to resolve them, and particularly the ones implying chronological inconsistency. The fullest attempt proposed a complex of implied flashbacks and anticipations that could only be grasped with the help of a complicated diagram.[51] The scheme, however, did not work, nor did any alternative.[52] Moving events out of sequence to resolve discrepancies too often created new discrepancies somewhere else. There seemed to be no alternative but to accept that Malory's attempt at consistency had failed on a significant number of occasions. It was easy enough to offer biographical explanations, in Malory's psychological make-up or in the difficulties of writing in prison or both, but explaining a weakness does not turn it into a strength.

Although the overall effect of the contradictions and anomalies was small, they were a problem for the modern reader, accustomed to assuming that a major work of literature will be aesthetically totally integrated. If they could not be explained away, perhaps it could be said that, since the book is big and they are small, it might be able, like Whitman, to contain them. It might even be argued that, if a work of art should be interpreted in the light of the effect it will have on the audience for whom it was intended, then, since ordinary readers rarely notice the discrepancies (which had only been brought to light by the detailed scrutiny of professional scholars), they are no proper part of the *Morte Darthur* as a work of art.

It may, however, be possible to do more for the book than that. The discrepancies may be positively useful in at least two ways. In the first place, the discrepancies in the *Morte Darthur* help to characterize the narrator who relates the story to us. For the most part he is very unobtrusive. His paratactic narration and the limited number of mostly conventional observations he makes in the first person, in contrast to the often vivid dialogue, make the story seem simply to happen before our eyes.[53] When we are aware of him, it is as someone whose attention is almost exclusively on Arthur and his knights, rather than on us, or himself, the world of his own time. Yet even his silences can have an effect, particularly when, as with his reluctance to speak of Launcelot's adultery, they are consistent across the whole of Malory's book (1165.10-13).

The discrepancies can be understood as errors committed by the narrator. 'Error', of course, means distortion of the totality of the work: in fiction, 'truth' cannot be a correspondence with an external reality.[54] In any contradiction, what harmonizes best with the rest of the book will be 'true', and the rest will be 'false'. So, since more damage is done to the story by discounting Gareth's conspicuous appearance at the beginning of the Fourth Tale than the brief mention of his name in the Second, the former is 'true' and the latter is 'false'.

Such an approach can help us to cope (in some sense) not only with inconsistencies in plot and characterization, but, for instance, with the stylistic oddities of the Second Tale. It has a further advantage in that it 'shadows' the probable real cause of most of the anomalies, carelessness by Malory as author. Sometimes, the best response to the anomalies may be to read in something like their real causes. The probable cause of the 'false' appearance of Gareth in the Second Tale is authorial distraction. The corresponding passage in the alliterative *Morte Arthure* says that when Arthur crosses the Alps by the St Gothard Pass: 'the garett he wynnys' (3104) The word *garett* means 'watch-tower'. Its similarity to the name of one of his favourite characters presumably made Malory misread it, and the grammar of the rest of the clause with it. Since the narrator tells us he is taking his story from a 'romance' (216.10) we may attribute exactly the same mistake to him.

We may contrast the situation here with that in the Prologue to Chaucer's *Canterbury Tales*, where Chaucer as author provides signals that his narrator is a character with limitations that the author is using to entertain and inform us. In the absence of such signals, modern readers normally assume by default the omniscient narrator conventional in western literature, and particularly in the novel. Malory's narrator, however, seems to be genuinely fallible.[55] He is attempting to tell the authentic history of Arthur and his knights, and at times he seems to have considerable success. He can give us (as his sources could not) the names of all fourteen of Gawain's kinsmen and 'well-willers' who trap Launcelot in Guenivere's bedchamber. At other times, however, he may have to confess that he has lost part of a source, or put forward something his source has told him but which he seems unable to endorse, as if he was dubious about it but could do no better. He may stress how conscientiously he has searched for the true story, but raise, by his very emphasis, the possibility that he might have failed to find it. Occasionally he may even seem, as we have seen, to be trying to suppress part of the story that he finds distasteful.

It is entirely in keeping that such a person should sometimes make mistakes; and in someone like that, readers can tolerate errors that they could not in an omniscient narrator, provided that, as is clearly the case here, the errors do not damage the main thrust of the book. We can understand these errors as having been committed by someone who cares about fact, who has tried to find the 'auctorysed' version of his story, who, if he had noticed an error in his story would normally have put it right, not merely (as Thackeray did in comparable circumstances) apologized for it. In the last analysis, however, Malory is writing about something other than factual consistency. His subject is the nobility of King Arthur and his knights of the Round Table, that when they were together there was ever an hundred and fifty. It is significant that the last words of the *Morte Darthur* get that number wrong: against the consistent testimony of the rest of the book, they say that the number was a hundred and *forty*. The error may well be scribal, but even if it is not, the attentive reader will not be much disturbed, because Malory gets the nobility right.

The discrepancies in Malory's narrative also serve a second purpose: they help to remind us what kind of book the *Morte Darthur* is. Vinaver may have been wrong over the unity of the book, but he was right to insist that it is not a novel but romance. Romance has had a bad press as 'escapist': it has associations of self-indulgence and day-dreaming. Since there is a real analogy between romance and dreams, there are many romances like that, but there are other kinds too.[56] Where the novel gives us the world of the probable, the world reported by physical science and individual pyschological experience, romance gives us worlds of the possible, sometimes worlds only capable of existing in the imagination. They may be escapist, or nightmarish, or quite different from either of those things. The exact kind of possibility on offer has to be identified from the work in each case.

All Malory's tales are generically romance. The kinds of romance vary from tale to tale, but they have features in common, which readers become aware of as the world of the *Morte Darthur*.[57] There are things that it generally ignores, such as money (for the most part), estate management, lawsuits, and social classes below the gentry.[58] There are things of which it makes much less of than most novels, such as physical causality, psychological individuality, and realistic time-schemes: they can be vividly realized at one point, sketched in casually at another, and ignored at a third. And there are things that are consistent and continuing parts of the book, such as its castles and forests, quests and strange customs, and the obligations of knightly behaviour. In their origins, these components vary from idealized elements of the gentry life of Malory's time to scraps of long-dead pagan mythology, transformed by generations of oral story-telling into integral parts of the strangeness of Arthur's kingdom.

Taken as a whole, however, Malory's romance does not (except perhaps briefly in the Fourth Tale) display the characteristic simplifications and evasions of day-dreams. His world is often radically different from our own, but it is no easier to understand, or to live in. Heroism is frequent, but it does not guarantee life, happiness or dignity. Great purposes may move some or even all of the events, but even in the face of occasional intrusions of the supernatural, it may be hard to make out whether an event was brought about by chance, or fate, or providence. Some of the participants seem to have a special understanding of some events, but it brings them little comfort, at least in this life, as we see from Merlin in the first tale, who foreknows his own death but cannot avert it, and Arthur in the last, who knows that Excalibur must be returned to the element from which it came, even at the cost of his own life, but who, to bring that about, has to threaten to kill his last surviving knight with his own hands.

In these respects the *Morte Darthur* is broadly consistent, but in others there are real differences between its component parts. Vinaver could have made a better case for the eight tales being distinct works if he had argued from genre rather than from plot and *explicits*.[59] The Second Tale is conspicuously anomalous in this respect, having carried over from its source both an epic and masculine ethos and a half-alliterative style. There are, however, notable discrepancies elsewhere too, for instance between the spirit of the Fifth Tale, where there seems to be a large tolerance of the adulterous affair between Tristram and La Beale Isode, and that of the uncompromisingly religious Grail story which follows it.

This variety can, however, be seen in another light. I would suggest that the sequence of tales makes a varied generic pattern as appropriate and satisfying as the movements of a great symphony. Readers work their way from the almost-history of the first two tales into worlds of chivalric adventure in the third, fourth and fifth, through the supreme challenge of the Grail quest, and back in the last two tales to a world more like that of the novel, and therefore more like the everyday world of our senses. In the final tales, as often in great tragedy, the major characters seem simultaneously to be reacting freely, out of their own natures, and acting out a destiny imposed by external necessity. That tragedy is variously qualified by Arthur's mysterious end, by the lovers' life of penance, and by Launcelot's kinsmen's deaths on crusade; but those things cannot entirely negate the sense of loss created by the sight of a potentially ideal society built up and then destroyed. This tragedy is yet another form of romance, as we are reminded by the many continuities with earlier tales, as well as by occasional supernatural events.

In these things we find some of the reasons why a book that is so much of its own age has appealed so often to others. Malory's fictional world presents a great variety of events and characters in a generic pattern that moves from almost-history into quintessential romance and back again. It does not reproduce the real world of his own time, still less that of ours, but that distancing makes its dominant symbols more powerful. They are his knights' quests, which are apt symbols for individual endeavour by any human being, of whatever age or sex or social class, and the rise and fall of Arthur's kingdom, which is a similarly apt symbol for collective endeavour. The narrating voice that puts the story before us allows us to share its often painful attempts to discover truth, and in its vision we find what Malory's most sympathetic modern expositor has called 'a civilisation of the heart'.[60]

8

THE ARTHURIAN LEGACY

Chris Brooks and *Inga Bryden*

The enduring English cultural fascination with Arthur can be located in a process of myth-making whereby medieval Arthurian literature is reinvented as part of a historicist impulse. Writers inherited medieval texts in which Arthur 'appears in more than one form - as a historical figure, as an exemplar of chivalry, and as a Christian member of the Nine Worthies' (Dean, 163). Yet these 'Protean appearances' (Merriman, 5) always engage issues of historical, national and political identity. The Arthurian legacy reveals contradictory social and cultural attitudes towards kingship, and to the relationship between personal and political ideologies.

Despite increasing scholarly scepticism concerning Arthur's historicity, English acceptance of the historical Arthur was, until the nineteenth century, largely based on Geoffrey of Monmouth's *Historia Regum Britanniae*. Indeed the *Historia* was the earliest appropriation of Arthurian material in the conscious creation of a national epic. It was translated into English in 1718 by Aaron Thompson (three more editions were published in the eighteenth century). Thompson included a preface on the *Historia*'s authority, acknowledging the continuing importance of chronicling the nation's legendary kings.

Moreover, Arthur's historical existence as a Christian worthy, a matter of 'common imagination' (Lewis, 181), had been reaffirmed in the preface to the 1485 edition of Malory's *Le Morte d'Arthur*. Arthur's reputation as 'one of the nine worthies' persisted into the post-medieval period, though it was Nathanial Crouch's *History of the Nine Worthies* – which went through at least five editions between 1687 and 1759[1] – rather than Malory's text which ensured the literary continuity of the tradition.

The Tudor emphasis on Arthur's political and historical dimensions problematized 'disbelieving' the Arthurian legends. However, the figure of Arthur was consistently the focus of debates about the status of history itself: how could the past be simultaneously real and fabulous? This question was closely related to the ongoing quest for a literary epic to consolidate the emerging sense of English and – by colonial extension – British nationhood. Yet, despite numerous literary appearances of Arthur in the period from Malory to the early Victorians,[2] no epic based in the medieval tradition was written. This was due partly to the conception of Arthurian material as fantastical, and partly to its being seen as a vehicle for political propaganda.[3]

Edmund Spenser's Arthur in *The Faerie Queene* (1596) has 'no literary successor' (Dean, 168) and indeed Spenser largely regarded Arthur's story as mythical. Even so, though there is no attempt to reconstruct Arthur within a historical landscape, *The Faerie Queene* does use 'signposts' from chronicle tradition: Spenser needed to take Arthur's historicity seriously if he was to glorify the monarchy by depicting Arthur allegorically as a perfect courtier.[4] John Milton contemplated writing an Arthurian epic, further placing Arthur at the centre of critical debate concerning the function of native history in literature. In *Mansus* he describes his hope to:

> . . . recall hereafter into rhyme
> The kings and heroes of my native clime
> Arthur the chief, who even now prepares
> In subterraneous being, future wars. (Haywood, 49)

Yet Milton eventually omitted Arthur from notes of historical figures and projects, privileging Alfred instead.[5] Haywood speculates that Milton 'had doubts about Arthur's reality' (50), although the rejection of a legend which had bolstered Tudor absolutism, and which carried the mystique of divine kingship, was surely linked to Milton's growing support for English constitutional liberty.[6]

In *A Discourse Concerning the Original and Progress of Satire* (1693) the Restoration poet John Dryden announced his intention of writing 'for the honour of my native country', wondering 'whether I should choose. . . King Arthur, conquering the Saxons' (Haywood, 50) – a subject he ultimately rejected as matter for epic poetry. Dryden did, however, stage, with Henry Purcell, the dramatic opera *King Arthur*, or, *The British Worthy* (1691) in which Arthur is seen pitted against the Saxon Oswald in a struggle for possession of Britain. Dryden's Arthur has a vision of future political and racial unity – although the whole text was diplomatically rewritten in the aftermath of James II's deposition. This episode exemplifies the difficulties English poets faced in negotiating the tangled relationships of the legendary past, the political present and the literary epic. Writers such as Alexander Pope and the poetaster Richard Blackmore aimed to 'abate the nationalist thirst' (Haywood, 51): Pope by considering writing an epic based on the founding of Britain by Brutus, and Blackmore by producing the poems *Prince Arthur* (1695) and *King Arthur* (1697) which paralleled Arthur with William III. Blackmore's works were certainly epics, and drew historical material from Geoffrey of Monmouth. But their detailed modelling on Virgilian precedent ('I sing the *Briton* and his Righteous Arms', says the opening line of *Prince Arthur*), their elaborate political allegories, and their long discussions of contemporary philosophical and scientific issues, take them well away from any medieval tradition.[7]

In the eighteenth century, as any survey of Arthurian tradition will reveal, Arthur 'fell out of literary fashion' (Lagorio, II, 149). Simpson, even after taking account of the pseudo-historical, topographical and burlesque Arthurian traditions that were reworked in late eighteenth-century periodicals and literary magazines, concludes 'it is only after 1800 that a widespread interest in Arthurian literature becomes apparent' (3). In cultural terms the marginal currency of the legends was arguably enshrined in the neo-Gothic Merlin's Cave, a much-satirized hermitage commissioned by Queen Caroline to house the Thresher Poet Stephen Duck, along with various wax models of historical and Arthurian figures.[8] The relative lack of enthusiasm for the Arthurian legends was evident at least as late as 1790. In the wake of the Rowley controversy (1777-82), Horace Walpole, writing to a friend, compared Arthur's marginalization to the discrediting of Rowley: 'As to Rowley, when Dr. Glynn is gone, he will be as much abandoned as King Arthur.'[9] Chatterton's forgeries, however, had exposed the dilemma in fictionally representing Arthur: what were the dynamics between the historical, romantic and mythical traditions? During the eighteenth century interest in the romantic Arthur was in one sense eclipsed as scholarly work on the Anglo-Saxon period strengthened. Whitaker's *History of Manchester* (1771-5) is cited by Simpson as evidence that a historical Arthur did continue to be vindicated (6).

Yet cultural anxiety that native history had yet to be glorified in epic form remained strong. 'Historical' fiction was deemed preferable to literature marked by improbability and fancy, and Arthurianism was central to this literary debate. The Arthurian 'mythologists' were attacked, for example, by David Hume in *The History of England* (1763). Hume argued that history *was* largely fictional, but that poets make matters worse because they 'disfigure the most certain history by their fictions'.[10] In *Essay on the Writings and Genius of Pope* (1756) Joseph Warton defined history in specifically nationalistic terms, and for Samuel Johnson (*Life of Pope*, 1779) ideal literature combined history and invention, almost rendering the latter invisible. None of these formulations favoured the use of explicitly legendary material, which helps to explain why the problems of writing an Arthuriad were so intractable.

The cultural desire for a nationalist reinvention of Arthurian legend was also parodied in the eighteenth century – notably in Henry Fielding's dramatic burlesque *Tom Thumb, A Tragedy* (1730). Here, Arthur is one hero among many, elevated only in that he is the last of the cast to die.[11] Furthermore, within the terms of the century's antiquarian revival, Arthur could be seen as belonging to earlier constructions of national identity, with only dubious relevance for the historically based identity of the present. The lines from Thomas Gray's poem 'The Bard' (1757), 'No more our long-lost Arthur we bewail / All hail, ye genuine Kings, Britannia's Issue, hail!', remind us that 'Britannia's Issue' is the 'genuine' dynastic line of monarchs, though it also rests ambiguously upon literary tradition.[12] On the other hand, if the figure of Arthur was perceived to have declined in its historical role, a different kind of relevance could be asserted through allegorical or mythological means: a resurgent interest in comparative mythology found expression in studies such as Jacob Bryant's *A New System, or, An Analysis of Ancient Mythology* (1774).

The emphasis on the Arthur of chronicle tradition was also balanced by the reinvention of Arthurian legend through the study of medieval romance (which was partly indebted to the work of French scholars). The manuscripts of English Metrical Romances known to such antiquarians as Thomas Percy, Thomas Warton, Joseph Ritson and George Ellis, included *Arthour and Merlin*, *Sir Tristrem*, *Awntyrs off Arthure*, the alliterative *Morte Arthure* and the stanzaic *Morte Arthur*.[13] It was, however, in the ballad sheets and chapbooks of popular tradition that Arthur was mainly kept alive. Evidence that the tales of Arthur, Merlin and Taliesin existed in oral culture at the end of the seventeenth century can be found among the correspondents of Edward Lhuyd in the 1690s.[14] William Nicolson noted that 'King Arthur's story in English' was 'often sold by the Ballad-singers, with the like Authentic Records of *Guy of Warwick* and *Bevis of Southampton*'.[15]

Within this context the Arthurian romances were frequently associated with childhood nostalgia and 'fancy'. This contributed to Wordsworth's and Coleridge's ultimate rejection of Arthur as unsuitable for 'adult' poetry. Wordsworth, rehearsing possible themes for *The Prelude* (1805; 1850), refers to 'Some old / Romantic tale by Milton left unsung', while Coleridge remarks in *Table Talk* (1833): ' "As to Arthur, you could not by any means make a poem on him national to Englishmen. What have we to do with him?" ' (Johnston, 37). Increasingly though, Englishmen were demonstrating that they had, in fact, a great deal to do with Arthur. Eighteenth-century antiquarianism, together with Romanticism, the Gothic Revival, and Medievalism, set the conditions for a major Arthurian Revival in the nineteenth century.

Arthurian material was committed to print in Warton's *History of English Poetry* (1774-81) and in Ritson's *Ancient English Metrical Romances*

(1802). Walter Scott's edition of *Sir Tristrem* (1804), reprinted five times by 1848, was influential in textual dissemination of the legends. Yet within the scholarly context which contributed to the Victorian Arthurian Revival key texts stand out. Thomas Percy's *Reliques of Ancient English Poetry* (1765), which included six Arthurian ballads, relegitimated the Arthurian legends as historical artefacts.[16] Renewed interest in Malory can be traced to Thomas Warton's *Observations on the Faerie Queene of Spenser* (1754), which described Spenser's debt to *Le Morte d'Arthur*.[17] The *Observations* is significant as a historical approach to Spenser. Although Warton discounts Spenser's 'fiction of Fairies', he is keen to trace the origin of such romantic histories, explaining terms such as 'quest' and 'recreant knight' by reference to Malory (Johnston, 103). Increasingly scholars and antiquarians regarded the medieval past as a text of human and social relations. What interests Warton in his Arthurian poems, suggests Merriman, are 'not the themes of medieval romance, but the physical vestiges of medieval times' (102). Such a response to the medieval past anticipates the nineteenth-century quests to locate Arthur in archaeological, architectural, literary and visual terms.

Although most of the major Romantic writers ignored Arthur as a specific subject, poems like Coleridge's 'Christabel' (1797-1800), Wordsworth's 'The White Doe of Rylstone' (1807) and Keats's 'The Eve of St Agnes' (1819), promoted an evocative medievalism that provided the general imaginative context for later Arthurianism. The one Romantic to make direct use of Arthurian material was Sir Walter Scott, whose narrative poem 'The Bridal of Triermain' appeared anonymously in 1809. The tale, Scott's own invention, is a hybrid effort that incorporates ballad traditions and folkloric elements. This is odd given Scott's scholarly interest in Arthurian sources: as we saw earlier, he produced an edition of the Middle English romance *Sir Tristrem* in 1804,[18] and the notes to the opening section of *Marmion* (1808), his long poem about Flodden Field, show an extensive acquaintance with Malory and with post-medieval attempts to re-write Arthur. It seems likely that Scott felt more at home when reinventing a medieval past he could ground in history rather than legend: his medieval novels, *Ivanhoe* (1819) in particular,[19] had a pervasive effect on English constructions of the medieval past well into the twentieth century, and provided much of the chivalric backdrop against which the Victorians would envisage the doings of Arthur and his court at Camelot.[20]

Cultural medievalism was thrown into sharp relief by the prodigious economic and social upheavals of the Agrarian and Industrial Revolutions, and by the political agitation they engendered – agitation that a frightened ruling class frequently traced back to the fiery ideals of revolutionary France.

In the countryside and, even more, in the towns the social relations of the old economic order, structured by the vertical ties of responsibility and deference, were replaced by the horizontal divisions of class. Hierarchical and paternalist social models, that their supporters liked to trace back to a mythologized Olde England, had to confront a new society built on *laissez-faire* and the Carlylean cash-nexus. The pace and the extent of change were alike unprecedented, driven on by population growth, and intensified by the startling, often savage, consequences of rapid urbanization. The power of commerce and industry began to eclipse the landed interest, and new money as well as old built Gothic houses and Romantic castles as if to compete for the favours of an inherited, or imagined, past. The physical environment was transformed, most obviously in the great manufacturing districts and in ever-spreading London, but also in cathedral cities, market towns, and coastal resorts. Nostalgia for a rural past, frequently cast in medievalist form, grew as countryside was swallowed up or 'cockneyfied' – to use a favourite term of cultural élitists. From the 1830s the railway system, product and agent of change, pulled the whole country more closely together, helping to create in the process a new national culture that was urban in origin and increasingly configured around the demands of a mass market. And that market stretched ever further overseas, along the trade routes policed by the British fleet, beyond Europe to the Americas, to Africa, to India and the Pacific, to all the domains of a greedy and growing Empire. Economically, politically, physically, and not least psychologically, the modern Matter of Britain was being wrought.

In such a turbulent context medievalism in all its forms, including Arthurianism, could become a site of cultural reassurance,[21] as in the Gothic of the new Palace of Westminster, designed by Charles Barry after the old Palace burnt down in 1834. Through style and decoration it affirmed a particular continuity, a history of free institutions and representative government at home, defended by martial triumph abroad.[22] In the iconography of the new building this heavily mythologized history begins with the set of Arthurian paintings and carvings in the Royal Robing Room:[23] just as the procession of the monarch to open parliament begins in the Robing Room, so also the succession of the English crown starts with Arthur. Frescoes by William Dyce,[24] started in 1851 and finished after his death by Charles West Cope in 1866, illustrate Religion and a range of social virtues – Courtesy, Mercy, Generosity, Hospitality – by scenes from Malory. In 1870 these paintings were complemented by narrative bas-reliefs carved by Henry Hugh Armstead,[25] showing scenes from the life of Arthur and from the history of the Grail. Arthurian material thus functions not only to establish a myth of dynastic origin, but also to provide moral exemplification, and both are recruited ideologically to the service of the British crown.[26]

Something of the same cluster of concerns had found literary form in the late 1840s, as the Westminster decorative schemes were being publicly discussed,[27] in the twelve-book epic *King Arthur*, by Edward Bulwer-Lytton.[28] One of the most popular novelists of his day, Bulwer-Lytton was regarded as the successor to Scott. His voluminous, highly varied output included a successful line in historical tales, among them *The Last of the Barons* (1843), a story of king-making in the Wars of the Roses, and *Harold: The Last of the Saxon Kings*, published in the same year as *King Arthur*. All three works share a central concern with the historical constitution – political and cultural – of England, with the construction and disintegration of the state, and with the cohesive role of the crown; and Bulwer-Lytton's Arthur, like the characters who populate the two novels, is very much the creature of history rather than legend. As a consequence, the poem largely avoids the traditional matter of the Arthurian cycle,[29] resting instead upon a 'historical' narrative of Bulwer-Lytton's own devising. Arthur is located as a warrior-king of the Dark Ages who successfully leads the Cymrians – the Welsh or British – against the incursions of the Saxons, who are identified as Teutons. Arthur is both a national hero and a champion of Christianity, and is claimed by Bulwer-Lytton as the founder of the royal line that descends to Queen Victoria.

King Arthur's ethnographic basis is important, for Bulwer-Lytton had to confront the difficulty that the much-vaunted inheritance of English liberty, with the historical creation of a constitutional monarchy at its core, was held to derive from the Gothic polities of the Saxon tribes[30] – a position promoted through the style and iconography of the Palace of Westminster and endorsed in *Harold*. As Dryden and Blackmore knew at the end of the seventeenth century, Arthur had to appear both as the saviour of the Britons and, somehow, as the supporter of the free polities that originated with the Saxons. Bulwer-Lytton manages this by conflating Cymrians and Teutons into the broader category of 'northern' peoples, an ethnic group supposed to have a common passion for freedom and a common instinct for 'the deep mysteries of the Christian faith' (p.3). Britons and Saxons, Arthurian monarchy and Gothic liberty, combine conveniently with religious purpose to lay the grounds of national destiny. Beyond the conflicts of the Dark Ages the future offers an empire 'broader than the Caesar won' (p.36), with English as a world language, and Arthur himself 'Not the faint memory of some mouldering page, / But by the hearths of men a household name' (p.37).

King Arthur deploys a reinvented past to validate the present of Victorian Britain – its claim to being a Christian society, its imperial domain, above all its political institutions.[31] Other writers' constructions of the medieval past were less reassuring, using versions of the Middle Ages to critique contemporary society.[32] Perhaps the first writer to recruit Arthur to this medievalist attack was John Walker Ord in *England: A Historical Poem*, which appeared in 1834-5.[33] In his 'Preface' Ord essays a parallel between King Arthur and his namesake Arthur Wellesley, Duke of Wellington, the poem's dedicatee and the modern-day saviour of the nation. Wellington, however, is condemned to heroism in an age characterized by 'dissatisfaction' and 'insubordination', at the service of a state debauched by 'seditious and revolutionary measures' and of ministers 'bred in the school of French and anti-national politics'. Accordingly, throughout the poem, a medieval and mythic past, of which Arthur is both the origin and the exemplar, is paraded to the detriment of a present that has abandoned 'ancient dignity, strength, loyalty, and patriotism'.

Although many medievalist evocations of the past, from Scott onwards, implicitly contrast a glamorous lost world with drab modernity, Ord's *England* is somewhat unusual in having an overtly political target – specifically the Whig reforms of the 1830s. Where painful disjunctions between past and present were explicit, a more familiar focus was religion. Henry Alford's 'The Ballad of Glastonbury' (1835)[34] recounts the coming of Joseph of Arimathea and the legendary founding of English Christianity, locates Glastonbury as the Avalon of Arthur's passing, and tells the story of the great abbey's rise and fall, ending amidst the ruins with a plea for restoration and spiritual revival: 'let . . . England's towers that lowly lie / Lift upward to the skies'.[35] F.W. Faber's introverted *Sir Lancelot: A Legend of the Middle Ages* (1842)[36] tracks its protagonist through a penitential progress that relates both to the poet's own spiritual journey and to that of the English Church in the modern world. The most obvious Arthurian context for exploring faith and doubt, however, was the Grail Legend: Thomas Westwood, in 1868, and Sebastian Evans, in 1898, both produced versions of the Quest based more or less closely on medieval sources.[37]

Perhaps the most original of the Victorian Grail poems, and certainly one of the most intense, is *The Quest of the Sangraal* (1864),[38] by Robert Stephen Hawker. Hawker's troubled life as a priest in the isolated Cornish parish of Morwenstow was itself the stuff of legend,[39] as he gathered tales of the remote Celtic past, brooded over a wrecking coast with its freight of drowned mariners, and fought the nightmares of opium addiction. Much of this is evident in *The Quest of the Sangraal*, of which he completed only the first of the four sections, or 'Chants', that he planned. Opening with the cry 'Ho! for the Sangraal! vanish'd Vase of Heaven!', the poem launches immediately into the dramatic moment of the start of the Quest, which Hawker places in the double context of the primitive Cornish landscape and the early British Church. The Grail heroes, 'the bounding men / Of the siege perilous, and the granite ring' (p.172), seem to rise spontaneously from the terrain of Dundagel. Celtic Christianity is to redeem the land, recovering what the bard Merlin calls ' "The link that bound it to the silent grasp / Of thrilling worlds" ' (p.176). The Quest has been called by Arthur himself, who understands it not as the end of ' "our land / Of noble name, high deed, and famous men" ' (p.177), but as its fulfilment. Lancelot, Perceval, Tristan, and Galahad set out to quarter the world between them, and Arthur embraces his destiny to ' "tarry by the cruel sea . . . 'Mid all things fierce, and wild, and strange, alone!" ', for ' "The lonely one is, evermore, the King" ' (p.185). The poem, in what remains of its first 'Chant', does not follow the questers, but remains focused on Cornwall and the King. It finishes with three visions in which Merlin shows Arthur his own last battle, Galahad's achievement of the Grail, and, last of all, the emergence of modern England. Secular, militaristic, industrial, ignorant alike of the Celtic past and the Quest, England's power is as terrible as it is transitory.

> 'Ah! haughty England! lady of the wave! . . .
> What is thy glory in the world of stars?
> To scorch and slay: to win demoniac fame,
> In arts and arms; and then to flash and die!' (p.190)

The constitution of the Arthurian past as an epoch of faith also lies at the core of the greatest nineteenth-century reworking of the Matter of Britain, Alfred Tennyson's *Idylls of the King* – though religious belief in the *Idylls* is shot through with an ironic perplexity that is foreign to the passion of Hawker's poem. From the very beginning of his career, Tennyson was drawn to the Arthurian stories, finding in them a means both of reflecting upon the central concerns of his own society and of imaging an alternative social order. Integral to his engagement was a search for the role of the poet in a time of unprecedented change, one result of which had been the very dislocation between past and present that cultural medievalism was at once premised upon and sought to repair. Thus, the central figure of Tennyson's first complete Arthurian poem,[40] 'The Lady of Shalott', written in 1832, is an isolated artist, ' "half sick of shadows" ',[41] impelled to a confrontation with the real world that she can neither encompass in her art nor survive.

Issues of poetic purpose and contemporary relevance are debated even more directly in the frame poem to the substantial 'Morte d'Arthur' fragment that Tennyson wrote in 1834 and that was published in 1842 under the title 'The Epic'.[42] In the setting of a Christmas Eve discussion – not wholly serious – about the decay of tradition and declining faith, 'the poet Everard Hall' is prompted to read his 'Morte d'Arthur', part of ' "His epic, his King Arthur, some twelve books" ' (II, 2), most of which he has destroyed. As Hall says:

> 'Why take the style of those forgotten times?
> For nature brings not back the Mastodon,
> Nor we those times; and why should any man
> Remodel models? these twelve books of mine
> Were faint Homeric echoes, nothing-worth,
> Mere chaff and draff, much better burnt.' (II, 2-3)

Everard Hall's doubts allow Tennyson – and the reader – to confront the task of nineteenth-century Arthurianism: to remodel the cultural models inherited from a forgotten past, so that they may be liberated from the constraints of historical determination and redeployed in terms of the present. Such a formulation is affirmative: the historical/mythical is to be redeemed from oblivion; the present reconnected to its past; the poet has found a role. But Tennyson acknowledges the paradoxical nature of this position: perhaps there is no truth to be rescued from the past, or, if there is, perhaps it will not be recognizable to the present. And if cultural transmission is impossible then the effort is pointless, and there is no purpose to being a poet. The existence of Hall's – or Tennyson's – 'Morte d'Arthur' is itself an assertion of at least the possibility of the project, and its main narrative matter – Bedivere's reluctance to relinquish the material evidence of the past by throwing away Excalibur – courageously engages the very stuff of Tennyson's misgivings. But Arthur's final words to Bedivere re-establish a paradoxically assured uncertainty.

> 'But now farewell. I am going a long way
> With these thou seëst – if indeed I go –
> (For all my mind is clouded with a doubt)
> To the island-valley of Avilion . . . (II, 18)

Emanating from the King, Arthur's doubt resonates through 'The Epic', just as a feeling for the final elusiveness of truth, and an increasingly vertiginous sense of instability come to characterize *Idylls of the King*. For Tennyson's 1834 'Morte d'Arthur' proved to be the starting-point for the *Idylls*, eventually reappearing as 'The Passing of Arthur', the final book of the cycle.[43] Writing ' "His epic, his King Arthur" ' took Tennyson the rest of his life, and – given the perplexities from which it was spun – there is a peculiar appropriateness in its beginning becoming its ending, and in its inception being premised on the destruction of the work as a whole.

Unsurprisingly, the composition and publication history of the *Idylls* is involved.[44] In 1857 Tennyson published two thematically linked Arthurian poems under the joint title *Enid and Nimuë: The True and the False*, setting Enid's long-suffering fidelity to Geraint against the story of Merlin's corruption by Nimuë, or Vivien. 'Enid' and 'Vivien', as the second of the two was renamed, then reappeared in 1859 along with two further poems focused on Arthurian women, 'Guinevere' and 'Elaine' (subsequently 'Lancelot and Elaine'), the collection of four being entitled *Idylls of the King* for the first time. It seems probable that Tennyson became committed to writing a complete epic cycle from this moment. Progress was delayed, however, by difficulties in knowing how to incorporate the Grail story, and it was not until 1867 that he started work on 'The Holy Grail', using the spotless Galahad and the cynically corrupt Gawain as defining moral poles – much as he had used Enid and Vivien a decade before. Needing a starting-point for what was now clearly an Arthurian series, he next wrote 'The Coming of Arthur', following that with 'Pelleas and Ettarre', which takes up the story of the Round Table in the aftermath of the Grail Quest. With some preliminary linking narrative and an extended ending, 'Morte d'Arthur' was already on hand as a final book, and duly re-emerged as 'The Passing of Arthur'. This made up a second batch of four, first appearing at the end of 1869 as *The Holy Grail and Other Poems*, then republished in 1870 along with the four poems of 1859 as an eight-book *Idylls of the King*. Two more idylls were added in the next two years: 'The Last Tournament' in 1871, grimly retelling the story of Tristram and Isolt; and in 1872, contrasting totally in mood, 'Gareth and Lynette', which became the first book after 'The Coming of Arthur'. In 1873, both were incorporated in an expanded *Idylls*, which also divided 'Enid' into two books, 'The Marriage of Geraint' and 'Geraint and Enid'. One more book was needed for the epic twelve, and this came in 1885 with 'Balin and Balan', its story of brother killing brother set pivotally between 'Geraint and Enid' and 'Merlin and Vivien' – as the original 'Vivien' had now become. With a 'Dedication' to the memory of Prince Albert and an epilogue 'To the Queen', both of which had first appeared in the early 1870s, the complete cycle was published as *Idylls of the King in Twelve Books* in 1886, more than half a century since the writing of 'Morte d'Arthur' and six years before Tennyson's death.[45]

The epic cycle occupied by the *Idylls* is coextensively a single cultural cycle. In 'The Coming of Arthur', at the start of his reign, the king dismisses imperial Rome's demand for tribute from Britain with the words ' "The old order changeth, yielding place to new" ' (III, 281); he uses the same phrase, this time with reference to the order he has created, in his final speech to Bedivere in 'The Passing of Arthur' (III, 559). It is Arthur who generates the cycle: as the victor in the twelve wars against paganism, he is the bringer of Christian order, and it ends with him. But within the cycle he functions primarily as a centre of moral and religious values. His martial achievements take place outside the poem: within it they are remembered, imaged, turned into the stuff of story and legend. Arthur himself is set apart, distanced from the poem's narrative action. Crucially, however, the king and his wars form the atmosphere in which, and because of which, that action happens. Even in destroying itself, Arthur's world moves, and can only move, in terms of the social and religious regimen he has established: ' "My house are . . . they who sware my vows, / Yea, even while they brake them, own'd me King" ' (III, 553). This regimen constructs the relationship between the individual and the state as both continuous and reciprocal, for upon the ethical health of the one depends the ethical health of the other.

Thus it is that the stories in the ten books of the *Idylls* between Arthur's coming and passing are personal, psychological – frequently indeed, for all their medievalist exoticism, domestic. And they form an overall narrative which is one of defeat. The youthful idealism and selflessness of 'Gareth and Lynette' and the 'Enid' books, are corroded by Vivien's seductive cynicism in 'Balin and Balan' and 'Merlin and Vivien'; unrequited love in 'Lancelot and Elaine' and unachievable spiritual aspirations in 'The Holy Grail' both lead to the destruction of the self; disillusion provokes the murderousness of 'Pelleas and Ettarre' and the deathliness of 'The Last Tournament'; in 'Guinevere' remorse and absolution come too late to avert the ruin of the state, and in 'The Passing of Arthur' the Arthurian world goes down in the 'last, dim, weird battle of the west' (III, 551).

At the core of the *Idylls'* tragedy is the illicit passion of Guinevere and Lancelot, the betrayal that Vivien can exploit to bring about the destruction of Camelot from within. Consonant with this, the *Idylls* is built between the defining moral polarities of purity, exemplified by Arthur, and impurity, represented by Vivien and the shadowy King Mark, and its dominant process is that of internal corruption. But the whole structure is premised upon a central irony that Tennyson never loses sight of. Arthur, ' "selfless man and stainless gentleman" ', as Merlin says, ' "wouldst against [his] own eye-witness fain / Have all men true and leal, all women pure" ' (III, 417). That is, Arthur's Christian order is founded upon a willed disregard for the basic Christian tenet of original sin. The more that Arthur wills selflessness and purity, the greater becomes the desolating gap between human aspiration and human achievement. The result is a prescriptive impossibility, which Merlin presents to the youthful Gareth as an ethical paradox:

> '. . . the King
> Will bind thee by such vows, as is a shame
> A man should not be bound by, yet the which
> No man can keep . . .' (III, 289)

Tennyson's sense of the idealism Arthur can inspire is always accompanied by an equivalent consciousness of the inevitability of failure. For Vivien's lesson, learnt of Mark, that ' "There is no being pure" ' is also a truth, albeit ' "That old true filth, and bottom of the well, / Where Truth is hidden" ' (III, 397). There is Arthur's truth and there is Vivien's truth, and in the perplexed ground between, as Merlin knows ' "truth is this to me, and that to thee" ' (III, 278). The two twine together throughout the *Idylls* as also do past and present – the past of Arthur's wars and the Christian society triumphant, the present of moral compromise, betrayal and defeat. All this is symbolized by the gate into Camelot, where Merlin warns Gareth of the impossibility of Arthur's vows. The gate's sculpture shows 'New things and old co-twisted, as if Time / Were nothing', and the 'dragon-boughts and elvish emblemings . . . move, seethe, twine and curl', so that Gareth's companions cry out ' "Lord, the gateway is alive" ' (III, 287-8).

Camelot's gateway is indeed alive, happening *now* in a multiplicity of presents: in the narrative present of the *Idylls*, in Tennyson's present as he writes the poem, and in the audience's present as the poem is read. Here, in effect, is Tennyson's answer to the problems of relevance that Arthurian material raised for him at the beginning of his career. Like Bedivere with Excalibur, Tennyson learns to trust mythic matter to the inherent nature of myth itself, for it is precisely myth's open-endedness, its peculiar resistance to closure, that allows it to be perenially remade. Permanence resides not in the fixity of having been, but in the fluidity of becoming, of being permanently now. Inevitably it is the riddling Merlin who understands this.

> 'For an ye heard a music, like enow
> They are building still, seeing the city is built
> To music, therefore never built at all,
> And therefore built for ever.' (III, 289)

The music to which Camelot is built is, of course, Tennyson's own.

For all their ambiguities and artful elaborations, Tennyson's *Idylls* drew largely upon the narrative matter of Malory. Robert Southey's 1817 edition of *Le Morte d'Arthur* proved particularly important, not only for Tennyson but also for other Victorian builders of Camelot. For Edward Burne-Jones, painter of the Tennysonian *Merlin and Vivien* (1870-4)[46] and the elegiac *Last Sleep of Arthur in Avalon* (1881-98),[47] the appeal of Southey's edition was its 'strength and beauty, its mystical religion and noble chivalry of action, the world of lost history and romance'.[48] Indeed, nostalgia for this chivalric world to a large extent characterized Arthurian literature and art from the 1850s onwards, particularly the work produced by the Pre-Raphaelites. Pre-Raphaelitism, as it expanded beyond the membership of the original Brotherhood (formed 1848) to include friends and associates, profoundly affected Victorian cultural responses to the Arthurian legends.[49] From the outset Pre-Raphaelitism was entangled in debates about historical realism and the efficacy of historical revivalism – and this implicated the reinvention of Arthur.[50]

Turning to the medieval past involved both a leap of the imagination and a sense of historical realism, a point picked up by David Masson in one of the first extended reviews of Pre-Raphaelitism in literature and art. Significantly, he made a comparison between the Brotherhood and the renowned Eglinton Tournament (1839), a cultural event testifying to the general revivalist mood which blurred Arthurianism with medievalism. Would Pre-Raphaelitism, Masson asked, become an 'artistic anachronism' like the Tournament?[51] The influence of the Arthurian legends extended to the formation of the Brotherhood itself: the model recalled the fellowship of the Round Table, representing masculine comradeship and the chivalric loyalty of a 'medieval' community. On Millais' election as Associate of the Royal Academy in 1853 the Pre-Raphaelite painter and poet Dante Gabriel Rossetti commented: ' "So now the whole Round Table is dissolved" ' – echoing Bedivere in Tennyson's *Morte d'Arthur*.[52]

An important catalyst in the confluence of Pre-Raphaelitism and Arthurianism was the creation, in 1857, of a second 'brotherhood' or 'set' of Oxford friends which included William Morris and Burne-Jones. They were enlisted, among others, by Rossetti to decorate the walls of the Oxford Union Society debating chamber: the chosen theme was *Le Morte d'Arthur*.[53] The form of romantic medievalism espoused by this group was in effect a kind of 'Rossetti-ism'.[54] Other Oxford friends included Algernon Swinburne and the poet-painter Elizabeth Siddal, both of whom produced reworkings of Arthurian stories.[55]

By the time of the Oxford murals, the Arthurian legends were familiar material to Victorian audiences – though now the stories took on 'a more tragic, doom-laden atmosphere' (Simpson, 225). Simpson's assessment could apply to the prominence of the theme of guilty love, or passion, since a number of major contributions to Victorian Arthurian literature post-1850 are reworkings of the stories of Tristram and Iseult, and Lancelot and Guinevere. In contrast to the emphasis on the historical Arthur in the 1830s and 1840s, poets and critics such as Matthew Arnold, 'Owen Meredith' (Robert Lytton, son of Edward Bulwer-Lytton), Morris, and Swinburne were interested in the domestic ideologies at work in Arthur's kingdom.[56] Intrigued by the contradictions in Malory's text between social and private conceptions of adultery, the poets investigated social debate concerning the claims of state-legitimated marriage and romantic love.[57] Furthermore, 'one of the great discoveries of the nineteenth-century writers on these themes' (Brewer and Taylor, 134) was a 'psychological' approach to reinventing Arthurian love stories. Insistence on a particular 'moment' from a legend, coupled with experimental narrative techniques, allowed psychological analysis of character. For example, medieval literary devices, such as colour-symbolism to represent emotional states, were employed by Morris in his early poetry and adopted in Pre-Raphaelite art.

Matthew Arnold's three-part poem 'Tristram and Iseult' was published in *Empedocles on Etna and Other Poems* (1852). Arnold was inspired by a French prose summary of the Tristram and Iseult legend in a scholarly article published in the *Revue de Paris* of 1841. The details and background information he took from Southey's notes and preface to Malory. Although 'Tristram and Iseult' emerged as part of the quest for a national epic, it also grew from the same debate about the contemporaneity of poetry that engaged Tennyson. The poem's focus was very much on 'lawless love' and 'unhappy passions', as its reviewers highlighted.[58] Arnold challenged readers' expectations and created psychological portraits of his characters by using experimental narrative techniques such as flashbacks. In part one, for instance, the dying Tristram is nursed by his wife, Iseult of Brittany, but recalls his past with Iseult of Ireland. In introducing readers to the less familiar Iseult of Brittany, and portraying her as both wife and mother, Arnold made a distinctive contribution to the Arthurian corpus, and to a degree domesticated the legend.[59] In part three of 'Tristram and Iseult' Iseult of Brittany (and Arnold) retells the story of Merlin's seduction by Vivien. In telescoping and revalidating the Arthurian legends for a modern readership, Arnold dealt with the difficult transition from a heroic past in which Arthur conquered Europe, to a fragmented, industrialized present.

The story of Tristram and Iseult appeared to have a more personal relevance for William Morris, especially in relation to his visual rendering of Arthurian legend, as critics have commented (Whitaker, 195). The models for the figures of La Belle Iseult, Tristram and Sir Palomydes in Morris's contribution to the 1857 Oxford Union murals were Jane Burden (the 'stunner' whom he married), Morris himself and Swinburne. In addition, Morris's design for a series of thirteen stained glass panels commissioned by Walter Dunlop in 1862 tell the story of Tristram and Iseult.

Morris's literary Arthurianism comprises fragments written in the early 1850s and the poems in *The Defence of Guenevere* (1858), some of which were printed initially in the *Oxford and Cambridge Magazine* (1856). Published five years after the Pre-Raphaelite Brotherhood had disbanded, *The Defence of Guenevere* was nevertheless reviewed as 'Pre-Raphaelite', partly due to its 'conscientious rendering of the actual'.[60] Morris took Froissart's chronicles as a source and was influenced by Malory, and the volume was dedicated to Rossetti.[61] The resulting Arthurian world is peopled by anti-heroic figures and invites anatomization of what 'love' signifies. Following on from Arnold, Morris also achieves in these poems a 'psychological realism'.[62] Literary critics have focused particularly on the title poem, its 'narrative, chronological and spatial dislocations of consciousness', and the nature of its 'defence'.[63] Morris's 'Guenevere' is one of a number of literary representations of the same subject produced in the 1850s and 1860s,[64] but is unique in having the Queen speak her own defence against charges of adultery. No clear judgement is offered, and Morris's invented scenario questions any tendency for writers to give definitive versions of the medieval past.[65] Indeed, Morris is above all preoccupied with history's relation to the present, radically exploiting the conservative tradition of Arthurian legend which saw Arthur as upholder of establishment values.[66]

Algernon Swinburne, in *Tristram of Lyonesse* (1882), exploded any sense of Arthurian legend as representative of a reassuringly ordered feudal community. Initially influenced by Morris and the Pre-Raphaelites, Swinburne produced the experimental Arthurian fragments 'Queen Yseult', 'Lancelot', and 'Joyeuse Garde'.[67] In writing *Tristram* he used Walter Scott's edition of the Middle English *Sir Tristrem* and was familiar with Béroul's *Tristan*. Throughout the nine-section *Tristram*, Swinburne redefines adulterous passion as a virtue – the lovers are exempt from social blame, unaware that fate has determined the drinking of the love-potion.[68] Reacting against Arnold's avoidance of direct passion, and Tennyson's endorsement of an Arthurian socio-moral system, Swinburne presented the Victorian reading public with a politically, socially and theologically subversive medievalism. For example, the passage describing the terrible moment of transformation when the potion is drunk – Tristram is taking Iseult from Ireland to Cornwall to wed Mark – has a clear sadomasochistic dimension.[69]

Reviewing Victorian literary reinventions of the Arthurian legends, Edward Russell commented on the marginalization of King Arthur as a driving ideal: the King was perceived as 'too seriously occupied to worry himself about the precise complexion and temperature' of Guinevere's love.[70] In this reading, Swinburne's Arthurian text, like Arnold's and Morris's, is no exception. The Arthurian court is remote and Arthur's youthful, incestuous sin is referred to as an analogue for Tristram and Iseult's own story. Nonetheless, fame and immortality still beckon: Arthur's 'name shall be one name with knightliness' and, though Swinburne's poem is a record, the lovers will find peace after death in a static existence which obliterates history.[71]

In the last decades of the nineteenth century Arthurian literature frequently linked Arthur with social and dynastic collapse, or exhibited a loss of faith in Arthur's role as manly hero. Sebastian Evans's poem 'The Eve of Morte Arthur' (1875), for example, does not allow Arthur to save a morally decaying nation from destruction.[72] The theme of the decline of Camelot, related to cultural fears concerning the nature of Britishness, continued to fascinate writers in the early twentieth century. A 'new trend' (Brewer and Taylor, 204) for dramatic productions of Arthurian legend coincided with a renewed interest in the story of Tristram and Iseult and a penchant for poignant death scenes. Arthurian plays included Henry Irving's staging of Joseph Comyns Carr's *King Arthur* (1895), Carr's *Tristram and Iseult* (1906), Martha Kinross's *Tristram and Isoult* (1913) and Thomas Hardy's *The Famous Tragedy of the Queen of Cornwall* (1923).

In 'To the Queen', the poem that forms the epilogue of the *Idylls*, Tennyson foresaw the possibility of national decline and glimpsed the signs of a 'battle in the West / Where all of high and holy dies away' (III, 563). In 1914 his most apocalyptic fears were realized. Young men, trained by their public schools into Arthurian chivalry and self-sacrifice, fell before the machine guns of the Western Front. In 'Hospital Barge at Cérisy' (1917), Wilfred Owen saw the remnants of Arthur's knights amidst the carnage and recognized, in the screaming funnel of a hospital barge, the tragic truth of Tennyson's prediction: 'And that long lamentation made him wise / How unto Avalon, in agony, / Kings passed in the dark barge, which Merlin dreamed.'[73] Ironically, in the aftermath of war, the same young men were frequently memorialized in stained glass and statues that used Arthurian iconography to mythologize the slaughter.[74]

The association of brothers-in-arms, front-line fighting, and Arthurian legend is clearly apparent in post- and inter-war Arthurian literature, for example the work of the artist and writer David Jones.[75] Jones's long poem

In Parenthesis (1937) employs Arthurian legend as one among an array of literary, religious and cultural myths. In this sense it uses myth to make shape out of chaos (both an inner, psychological chaos and a social, spiritual chaos) and belongs to a group of post-war texts interested in a 'history of consciousness' approach to Arthurian legend, using its symbolic potential. Some writers, situating themselves in the Arthurian literary tradition, felt that Victorian Arthurians such as Tennyson, Morris and Hawker did not possess 'the full capacity of the mythical imagination' which the modern world allowed.[76]

In part four of *In Parenthesis*, 'King Pellam's Launde', Jones makes a direct link between the land laid waste by war and the blasted terrain of the maimed King Pellam of Malory's Grail story: a flooded shell hole, for example, recalls a twisted, half-submerged Excalibur. Indeed, the waste land and the Grail are dominant elements in earlier twentieth-century Arthurian literature, a move away from the theme of romantic love.[77] Writers emphasized the symbolic significance of the Grail which allowed exploration of different forms of mystical, as opposed to orthodox Christian, and scientific, experience.[78] In the second half of the twentieth century, shaped by the processes of capitalism, technological developments and the 'heritage' industry, Arthur has been re-represented in diverse forms, from fantasy literature and role-playing games to film.[79]

Some literary texts still relied on Malory, such as T. H. White's *The Once and Future King* (1958). White's book, and more particularly, the film *Camelot* based on it, helped popularize a romanticized version of Arthurian legend, as Tennyson's poetry had done in the nineteenth century.[80] A contrasting development in Arthurian literature, however, has been a shift away from Malory as source text, and an emphasis on historical realism, in works such as Rosemary Sutcliff's *Sword at Sunset* (1963) and Mary Stewart's trilogy.[81] Finally, recent postmodern novels, such as Donald Barthelme's *The King* (1992) and Paul Briars's *In a Pig's Ear* (1996), shed Arthur's medieval associations, or rather, recontextualize Arthurian legend in a multi-textual world. *The King*, a series of conversational sketches, shows an ineffectual Arthur fighting not the Saxons, but the Nazis, while Guinevere's adultery is broadcast on radio. It is the media system which in the end challenges us to think whether 'England, as an idea, is through, finished' (69).

NOTES

Abbreviations

ALMA	*Arthurian Literature in the Middle Ages*, ed. R.S. Loomis (Oxford, 1959)
Archiv	*Archiv für das Studium der Neueren Sprachen und Literaturen*
AL	*Arthurian Literature*
AUMLA	*Journal of Australasian Universities Modern Language and Literature Association*
AY	*The Arthurian Yearbook*
BBIAS	*Bibliographical Bulletin of the International Arthurian Society*
BL	British Library
BN	Bibliothèque Nationale
CFMA	Classiques Français du Moyen Age
Chau. Rev.	*The Chaucer Review*
CL	*Comparative Literature*
EC	*Essays in Criticism*
EETS	Early English Text Society; ES: Extra Series; SS: Supplementary Series
EHR	*English Historical Review*
ELH	*Journal of English Literary History*
ES	*English Studies: A Journal of English Letters and Philology*
FMLS	*Forum for Modern Language Studies*
JEGP	*Journal of English and Germanic Philology*
LSE	*Leeds Studies in English*
MÆ	*Medium Aevum*
MED	*Middle English Dictionary*, ed. H. Kurath, S.M. Kuhn and J. Reidy (Ann Arbor, Mich., 1952-)
MLN	*Modern Language Notes*
MLQ	*Modern Language Quarterly*
MLR	*Modern Language Review*
MA	*Moyen Age*
MP	*Modern Philology*
NM	*Neuphilologische Mitteilungen.*
NMS	*Nottingham Medieval Studies*
N&Q	*Notes and Queries*
OED	*The Oxford English Dictionary*, ed. Sir J.A.H. Murray, H. Bradley, Sir W. Craigie, and C.T. Onions (Oxford, 1933); 2nd. edn., ed. J.A. Simpson and E.S.C. Weiner (1989)
PMLA	*Publications of the Modern Language Association of America*
PQ	*Philological Quarterly*
RES	*Review of English Studies*
RMS	*Reading Medieval Studies*
Rom.	*Romania*
RS	Rolls Series
SATF	Société des Anciens Textes Français
STS	Scottish Text Society
YES	*Yearbook of English Studies*

1: The Celtic Tradition

1. See Ann Dooley, 'Arthur in Ireland: The Earliest Citation in Native Irish Literature', *AL,* 12 (1993), 165-72.

2. Ed. Sheila Falconer (Dublin,1953). Falconer argues that the Irish version was probably based on a fourteenth-century English text, but Dooley, ('Arthur in Ireland', 165), casts doubts on this conclusion, which she is currently reassessing.

3. For editions see R.A. Stewart Macalister, *Two Irish Arthurian Romances,* Irish Texts Society 10 (London, 1908), and M. Mac an tSaoi, *Dhá Sgéal Arturaíochta Mar atá Eachtra Mhelóra agus Orlando agus Céilidhe Iosgaide Léithe* (Dublin, 1946). See also J.E. Caerwyn Williams and P.K. Ford, *The Irish Literary Tradition* (Cardiff and Belmont, Mass., 1992), 137-8.

4. In both Ireland and Scotland, however, the Arthurian legend has left some traces in modern popular tradition. See e.g., Alan Bruford, *Gaelic Folk-Tales and Medieval Romances* (Dublin, 1966), and Linda Gowans, *An bròn binn: An Arthurian ballad in Scottish Gaelic* (Eastbourne, 1992).

5. On Cornwall see O.J. Padel, 'The Cornish Background of the Tristan Stories', *Cambridge Medieval Celtic Studies,* 1 (1981), 53-81, ibid., 'Geoffrey of Monmouth and Cornwall', *Cambridge Medieval Celtic Studies,* 8 (1984), 1-28, and *idem,* 'Some South-Western Sites with Arthurian Associations' in Bromwich, 229-48; on Brittany see J.E. Caerwyn Williams, 'Brittany and the Arthurian Legend' in Bromwich, 249-72.

6. Kenneth Jackson, *The Gododdin: The Oldest Scottish Poem* (Edinburgh, 1969). For the text see also Ifor Williams (ed.), *Canu Aneirin* (Cardiff, 1961); for a modernized text and English translation see A.O.H. Jarman, *Aneirin: Y Gododdin* (Llandysul, 1989).

7. *Godolei o heit meirch e gayaf / Gochore brein du ar uur / caer ceni bei ef arthur* ('He gave gifts of horses from the herd in winter / he fed black ravens on the rampart of a fortress / though he was no Arthur'), ed. Williams, ll. 1240-2; cf. Jarman, ll. 970-2.

8. See Marged Haycock, '*Preiddeu Annwn* and the Figure of Taliesin', *Studia Celtica,* 18-19 (1983-4), 52-78; cf. Patrick Sims-Williams, 'The Early Welsh Arthurian Poems' in Bromwich, 33-71, esp. 54-7.

9. A.O.H. Jarman (ed.), *Llyfr Du Caerfyrddin* (Cardiff, 1982), 66-8; for discussion see e.g. Patrick Sims-Williams in Bromwich, 38-46.

10. See Rachel Bromwich (ed.), *Trioedd Ynys Prydein,* 2nd edn., (Cardiff, 1978), 291, 417-18, 555, and Keith Busby, 'The Enigma of Loholt' in Varty, 28-36.

11. See A.O.H. Jarman, *Llyfr Du Caerfyrddin,* 36-44; for discussion see Patrick Sims-Williams in Bromwich, 49-51.

12. See Patrick Sims-Williams in Bromwich, 58-9.

13. For text and discussion see Marged Haycock, *Blodeugerdd Barddas o Gerddi Crefyddol Cynnar* (Llandybïe, 1994), 297-312; also Patrick Sims-Williams in Bromwich, 57-8.

14. Rachel Bromwich and D.S. Evans (eds.), *Culhwch ac Olwen* (Cardiff, 1992). For discussion of the date see lxxvii-lxxxiii.

15. These correspondences, and similarities in the language, raise the possibility that in its present form *Culhwch ac Olwen* had been influenced by the 'Pa gur' poem in the Black Book of Carmarthen, and, like that manuscript, may itself be associated with a scriptorium at

Carmarthen. See Bromwich and Evans, lxxxiii.

16. See Bromwich, *Trioedd Ynys Prydein*, cvii-cxxi.

17. This tradition was, of course, later developed by Geoffrey of Monmouth and his successors, and later triads are often based on, or ultimately derived from, the *Historia*.

18. See Bromwich, *Trioedd Ynys Prydein*, 145-6.

19. For texts see Henry Lewis (ed.), *Brut Dingestow* (Cardiff, 1942), and B.F. Roberts (ed.), *Brut y Brenhinedd* (Dublin, 1971); for discussion see also B.F. Roberts, 'Testunau Hanes Cymraeg Canol' in Geraint Bowen (ed.), *Y Traddodiad Rhyddiaith yn yr Oesau Canol* (Llandysul, 1975), 274-302, and *idem*, *Studies on Middle Welsh Literature* (Lewiston, Queenston and Lampeter, 1992), 25-40.

20. The most notable example is the collection of triadic material put together to form the list of the *Pedwar Marchog ar Hugain a farnwyd yn gadarnaf* ('The twenty-four chief knights at Arthur's court'). See P.C. Bartrum, 'Y Pedwar Marchog ar Hugain', *Études Celtiques*, 12 (1968-9), 157-94, and Bromwich, *Trioedd Ynys Prydein*, 250-5.

21. See A. O. H. Jarman, 'The Merlin Legend and the Welsh Tradition of Prophecy' in Bromwich, 117-45.

22. The earliest vernacular poems celebrating such classical heroes as Hercules and Alexander are in the Welsh language, preserved in the Book of Taliesin, and reveal that the earliest known native poets were familiar with narratives from continental Europe. See Marged Haycock, '"Some Talk of Alexander and some of Hercules": Three Early Medieval Poems from the Book of Taliesin', *Cambridge Medieval Celtic Studies*, 13 (1987), 7-38.

23. Ceridwen Lloyd-Morgan, '*Breuddwyd Rhonabwy* and Later Arthurian Literature' in Bromwich, 183-208, esp. 183-93.

24. All three are included in the diplomatic edition of J. Gwenogvryn Evans and R. M. Jones, *Llyfr Gwyn Rhydderch* (Cardiff, 1973); the only modern editions at present are R. L. Thomson, *Owein or Chwedyl Iarlles y Ffynnawn* (Dublin, 1968) and Glenys W. Goetinck (ed.), *Historia Peredur vab Efrawc* (Cardiff, 1976). See also the chapters on each in Bromwich, 147-82. *Peredur* will be reassessed in a volume of studies in preparation, edited by Sioned Davies and Peter Wynn Thomas.

25. For the first part of the text, see Thomas Jones (ed.), *Ystoryaeu Seint Greal. Rhan 1: Y Keis* (Cardiff, 1992); for the complete text see Robert Williams (ed.), *Y Seint Greal* (London, 1876, repr. 1987).

26. There is no complete edition of Elis Gruffydd's Chronicle; extracts have been published and an edition of the Arthurian section, by Ceridwen Lloyd-Morgan, is in preparation.

27. See Ceridwen Lloyd-Morgan, 'Elis Gruffydd a Thraddodiad Cymraeg Calais a Chlwyd', *Cof Cenedl*, 11 (Llandysul, 1996), 29-58, and 'Oral et écrit dans la chronique d'Elis Gruffydd', *Kreiz: Études sur la Bretagne et les Pays Celtiques*, 5 (1995), 179-86.

28. Ed. G.H. Hughes (Cardiff, 1961).

29. See B.F. Roberts, *Studies on Middle Welsh Literature*, 37, 40, note.

30. See Ceridwen Lloyd-Morgan, 'Qui était l'Arthur des Gallois?', *Pris-Ma*, 11 (1995), 149-58. The identification of Owain Glyndŵr, in particular, as the 'national redeemer' and the persistence of that tradition to the present day is discussed in E. R. Henken, *National Redeemer: Owain Glyndwr in Welsh Tradition* (Cardiff, 1996).

2: Dynastic Chronicles

Geoffrey of Monmouth's *Historia Regum Britanniae*

1. Geoffrey's *Historia*, having been treated in relation to the Arthurian tradition in Welsh in the first volume of this series (Bromwich, 97-116; 130-37) and to be included in a later volume dealing with texts in Latin, is here briefly presented as an introduction to English texts which stem from it. I am grateful to my colleague Julia Crick for helpful advice on this abbreviated treatment

2. Announcing his discovery in a letter to a friend, Henry commented: 'Warinus Brito, my urbane friend, you ask me why I began my account of the deeds of our nation from the time of Julius Caesar and omitted the dynasties which so flourished from Brutus to Caesar. In reply I tell you that, despite a most diligent search, I was unable to discover a record of that period, either oral or written. Such is the deadly oblivion which with the passing of ages over-shadows and snuffs out the glory of mortals.' The drastically abbreviated outline of the *Historia* given in this *Epistola ad Warinum* has been modified to avoid disagreements with Bede, the *Historia Brittonum* and Henry's own *Historia Anglorum*, where he appended the letter rather than try to reconcile his account with Geoffrey's, suggesting that his initial enthusiasm had given way to doubts about its authenticity, doubts of a kind openly expressed by other medieval historians which were eventually to undermine its credibility in the sixteenth century. See Neil Wright, 'The Place of Henry of Huntingdon's *Epistola ad Warinum* in the Text-history of Geoffrey of Monmouth's *Historia Regum Britannie*: A Preliminary Investigation' in Jondorf, 71-113, which incorporates an edition and translation from which the above quotation is taken (106).

3. The ambivalence of the chroniclers, academic rectitude in conflict with patriotic imagination, is perfectly typified by William of Malmesbury's comment – on the legend rather than the book, since he wrote (1125) before the *Historia* appeared: 'He is that Arthur about whom the trifles of the Bretons (*nugae Britonum*) rave even today, a man worthy not to be dreamed about in false fables but proclaimed in veracious histories, for he long upheld his sinking fatherland and quickened the failing spirits of his countrymen to war' (*Gesta Regum Anglorum*, p.55). William of Newburgh denounced Geoffrey's book as full of falsehoods but accepted the incorporated prophecies as genuine translations from the Welsh; Giraldus Cambrensis told scabrous stories of how the *Historia* attracted crowds of evil spirits which could distinguish false passages in a book – yet he cited it in his own work. Nevertheless, 'there are few medieval historians after 1150, Giraldus Cambrensis included, who do not show extensive traces of Geoffrey's influence' (M.B. Shichtman and L.A. Finke, 'Profiting from the Past: History as Symbolic Capital in the *Historia Regum Britanniae*', *AL*, 12 (1993), 1-35 (7))

4. One measure of the cultural importance of the *Historia* is the list of over 210 extant manuscripts given by J.C. Crick, *The* Historia Regum Britannie *of Geoffrey of Monmouth*, III: *A Summary Catalogue of the Manuscripts* (Cambridge,1989). A long-term project for a critical edition has so far produced two volumes: a text of the basic Vulgate version, *Historia Regum Britannie*, I: *Bern Burgerbibliothek MS 568*, ed. Neil Wright (Cambridge, 1985), and *Historia Regum Britannie, II: The First Variant Version*, ed. Neil Wright (Cambridge, 1988).

5. Bretons formed a significant element among the forces of the Conqueror, many settled in south-east Wales, and by 1075 the castle and lordship of Monmouth were in the possession of Wihenoc, from Dol in Brittany, who established a priory under the jurisdiction of the Abbey of St Florent de Saumur. In referring to himself as Galfridus Monemutensis (*of Monmouth*), Geoffrey may have been indicating a family connection with the region with which he shows familiarity, in particular Caerleon whose impressive Roman remains may have suggested to him the location of Arthur's court. He shows marked interest in Brittany: 'The greatest of all the kings of Britain has a Breton ancestry and Arthur's most glorious soldiers are the Bretons. . . . throughout the latter part of the *Historia* Brittany is portrayed as a refuge where is to be found the true essence of Britain's former glory' (B.F. Roberts in Bromwich, 98). But Cornwall also figures prominently in his work; see O.J. Padel, 'Geoffrey of Monmouth and Cornwall', *Cambridge Medieval Celtic Studies*, 8 (1984), 1-27. 'It seems justified to conclude that Geoffrey was a Normanised Celt, perhaps of Breton descent, although we cannot be sure of his exact racial extraction.' (N. Wright (ed.), *Historia Regum Britannie*, I (Cambridge, 1985), x.)

6. For fuller biographical details see: J.E Lloyd, 'Geoffrey of Monmouth', *EHR*, 57 (1942), 460-8, Tatlock, 438-48, and Lewis Thorpe (trans.), *Geoffrey of Monmouth: The History of the Kings of Britain* (Harmondsworth, 1966), 10-14.

7. The prophetic tradition in Welsh and Merlin's connection with it is helpfully outlined by A.O.H. Jarman in Bromwich, 117-45. 'The medieval Welsh tradition of prophecy sprang from memories of the struggle of the Britons and the English for supremacy in the fifth and sixth centuries.' 'More specifically, however, the roots of later Welsh prophecy are to be associated with the tradition of the struggle of the red and white dragons recorded in the *Historia Brittonum*. In that work the boy Ambrosius tells Vortigern that the white dragon represents "the people who have seized many peoples and countries in Britain, and will reach almost from sea to sea; but later our people will arise, and valiantly throw the English people across the sea".' 'On the whole, however, what Geoffrey received from Welsh tradition was a general concept of the nature and purpose of vaticination, rather than specific prophecies related to particular events. He then deployed the concept with the aid of the inexhaustible resources of his imagination . . . ' (136-7).

8. References are to the chapter numbers of the edition of the Vulgate version of the *Historia* by Neil Wright, I (Cambridge, 1985).

9. On the forms of the various dedications and their bearing on the date of completion of the *Historia*, see the edition by Neil Wright, I, xii-xvi.

10. See J.C. Crick, *The* Historia Regum Britannie *of Geoffrey of Monmouth*, IV: *Dissemination and Reception in the Later Middle Ages* (Woodbridge, 1991), 153-7.

11. One eminent authority accepts Geoffrey's claim: R.W. Southern, 'Aspects of the European Tradition of Historical Writing, 1: The Classical Tradition from Einhard to Geoffrey of Monmouth', *Transactions of the Royal Historical Society*, 5S, 20 (1970), 173-96. Others suggest the possibility of a partial source: '. . . there is nothing inherently impossible in the suggestion that Walter should have brought from Brittany a manuscript which contained native historical material relating to Brittany and south-west Britain' (B.F. Roberts in Bromwich, 101). Two texts of Breton origin, the *Vita Goeznouii* and the *Livre des faits d'Arthur*, reflect a narrative tradition similar to Geoffrey's, but they are in Latin and their dating is still uncertain (see N. Wright (ed.), *Historia*, I, xvii).

12. Neil Wright ('Geoffrey of Monmouth and Gildas', *AL*, 2 (1982), 1-40) notes that, though Geoffrey incorporated large sections of Gildas's work into the *Historia* he only once acknowledges his debt, while elsewhere attributing to him incidents of his own invention. By contrast with this use of Gildas's reputation to lend credibility to his fictions, he freely alters and contradicts Bede's accepted version of national history (see N. Wright, 'Geoffrey of Monmouth and Bede', *AL*, 6 (1986), 27-59).

13. The issue of the historical existence and identity of Arthur, reassessed by the editors and by Thomas Charles-Edwards in Bromwich, 2-7, 15-32, cannot be reopened in the limited space available here.

14. Geoffrey's knowledge of Welsh, written or spoken, is uncertain. Tatlock (445) sees signs of some knowledge in his use of place and personal names; T.D. Crawford ('On the Linguistic Competence of Geoffrey of Monmouth', *MÆ*, 51 (1982), 152-62) suggests that he had a better knowledge of spoken than of written Welsh.

15. Text from the edition of the *Historia* by Neil Wright, I (Cambridge, 1985), translation by Lewis Thorpe (Harmondsworth, 1966), 54.

16. It was precisely such ambiguous elements which immediately attracted the interest of redactors. Neil Wright ((ed.), *Historia*, I, lvi-lix) attributes to scribal revision verbal modifications in Bern MS 568 which, as well as presenting the Saxon invaders in a somewhat more favourable light, resolve the ambivalence of Arthur's departure to Avalon by adding 'Anima eius in pace quiescat' (§178), so ending the hope of his return and justifying to some degree the English succession.

17. It is perhaps a tribute to Geoffrey's skill in shaping his narrative in a way which might appeal to various elements in his potential audience that modern analysts differ as to where his real sympathies lay. For an outline of the debate see J. Gillingham, 'The Context and Purposes of Geoffrey of Monmouth's *History of the Kings of England*', *Anglo-Norman Studies*, 13 (1991), 99-118.

18. On the remarkably rapid and widespread dissemination of the *Historia*, see J.C. Crick, *The* Historia Regum Britannie *of Geoffrey of Monmouth*, IV, and on the Welsh versions, B.F. Roberts in Bromwich, 110-13.

19. The process of extrapolating romance from 'history' had perhaps already begun with the verse translation of the *Historia* by the Anglo-Norman Gaimar, now lost, but discrimination is evident in the version by Wace (1155) which superseded his, the poet making use of the twelve-year interval of peace following Arthur's establishment of his authority over the whole of Britain (§153) to allude sceptically to fabulous accounts of adventures attributed to him, rejecting them as historically unreliable. Other vernacular authors, notably Chrétien, can be seen as implying that the action of their full-blown romances occurred during the same interval, and one scribe actually inserted Chrétien's texts into Wace's narrative at that point. (See Ad Putter, 'Finding Time for Romance: Mediaeval Arthurian Literary History', *MÆ*, 63 (1994), 1-16.) The potential conflict between edification and entertainment was thus resolved by fitting *aventure* within the framework of chronicle, with Arthur as presiding genius in both spheres. The *Historia* itself was similarly adapted to changing tastes: a version in Latin hexameters (see N. Wright (ed. and trans.), *The* Historia Regum Britannie *of Geoffrey of Monmouth*, V: *Gesta Regum Britannie* (Woodbridge, 1991)), composed by a Breton poet between 1236 and 1254, exploits the parallels between Arthur's Britain and contemporary Brittany, and

heightens the epic tone by constant intertextual echoes of Latin poets, classical and medieval, extending Geoffrey's cultural myth-making into a new age.

Wace's *Roman de Brut*

20. Wace was not the only, nor even the first, translator of Geoffrey's *Historia* into French, but the popularity of his work was such that previous translations quickly fell into oblivion. Among those that we know of, Geffrei Gaimar's *Estoire des Bretuns* (probably written in the 1140s) is completely lost, while others, such as the so-called Munich *Brut*, are extant only as fragments. For a discussion of these fragments, see Tatlock, 451-62, and the Introduction to I.D.O. Arnold's edition of the *Roman de Brut,* 2 vols, SATF (Paris, 1938, 1940).

21. The political unity of England and Normandy came to an end in 1204, following a dispute between the rulers of England and France. On Wace's Caen, see U.T. Holmes, Jr., 'Norman Literature and Wace', in William Matthews (ed.), *Medieval Secular Literature: Four Essays* (Berkeley, Cal., 1967), 47-67. The links between Caen and England are underlined by Marie-Claude Blanchet in her 'Maistre Wace, trouvère Normand', *Marche Romane,* 9 (1959), 149-58; two Caen monasteries owned estates in Gloucestershire, Hampshire and Dorsetshire.

22. On Wace's life, see Tatlock, 463-82, and Marie-Claude Blanchet, 'Maistre Wace'. The date of birth, 'about 1100', is that suggested by Charles Foulon in ALMA, 95; however, U.T. Holmes, 'Norman Literature', 64-7, warns that this may be on the early side, since it would imply that Wace was still an active professional writer when he was over 70 – a ripe old age in the twelfth century. The most important autobiographical passage is in the *Roman de Rou* (ed. A.J. Holden, 3 vols., SATF (Paris, 1970-73)), III, 5299-316.

23. See Margaret Houck, 'The Sources of the *Roman de Brut* of Wace', University of California Publications in English, 5.2 (Berkeley, Cal., 1941), 161-356, esp. 226-8 and 275-87, and Foulon, ALMA, 97.

24. The highly self-conscious nature of Wace's art, and his desire to please, is noted by W.R.J. Barron and S.C. Weinberg in the Introduction to their *Laȝamon's 'Arthur': The Arthurian Section of Laȝamon's* Brut (Harlow, 1989), xxvii; see also I.D.O. Arnold and M.M. Pelan (eds.), *La Partie Arthurienne du* Roman de Brut *de Wace* (Paris, 1962), 31-5. For a detailed analysis of Wace's style, see M. Jirmounsky, 'Essai d'analyse des procédés littéraires de Wace', *Revue des Langues Romanes,* 63 (1928), 261-96.

25. Wace's indebtedness to the Variant version was discovered only in 1951, with Jacob Hammer's edition of the Variant text (Cambridge, Mass., 1951). As a result, much that has been written on Wace's use of his sources is outdated.

26. All quotations from the *Roman de Brut* are taken from I.D.O. Arnold's edition of the poem (Paris, 1938, 1940); the translations are mine.

27.   Maistre Wace, ki fist cest livre,
                             Ne volt plus dire de sa fin
                             Qu'en dist li prophetes Merlin;
                             Merlin dist d'Arthur, si ot dreit,
                             Que sa mort dutuse serreit.
                             Li prophetes dist verité;
                             Tut tens en ad l'um puis duté
                             Et dutera, ço crei, tut dis,
                             Se il est morz u il est vis. (13282-90)

(*Master Wace, who wrote this book, does not wish to say any more about his* [i.e. Arthur's] *end than did the prophet Merlin; Merlin said about Arthur, and he was right, that his death would be uncertain. The prophet spoke the truth; ever since it has always been a matter of doubt, and I think it will always be questioned whether he is alive or dead.*)

28. This aspect of the characterization of Arthur is stressed by Tatlock, 311, 318-20, and Arnold and Pelan (n.24 above).

29. The figures for the *Historia* are somewhat tentative, inasmuch as we have to take into account the varying length of the two versions of it used by Wace. Arthur's reign covers 35 of the 207 chapters of the Vulgate version.-

30. On the subject of politics and prophecies, see Rupert Taylor, *The Political Prophecy in England* (New York, 1911).

31. See *Roman de Brut*, 10765-72. This passage seems to have been suggested by the fact that, in the Variant version of the *Historia*, the outburst by Cador of Cornwall which brings Gawain's rejoinder condemns *inter alia* the time wasted in womanizing by men during periods of peace. On courtly themes in Wace, see Barron and Weinberg (n.24 above), xxvii-xxviii. Despite the title under which the poem is now known (i.e., *Roman*), it can in no way be considered a romance in the contemporary sense of the term.

Laȝamon's *Brut*

32. For a brief description of the verse-form of the *Brut*, see Tatlock, 486.

33. The fire which partially destroyed MS Otho C xiii took place in 1731; the manuscript originally comprised some 155 leaves, of which 145 are now bound in the same volume. For a description of the two manuscripts, see *Brook and Leslie* I, ix, Le Saux 1989, 1, and Jane Roberts, 'A Preliminary Note on British Library, Cotton MS Caligula A ix', in Le Saux 1994, 1-14. For an analysis of the characteristics of the Otho text, see Christopher Cannon, 'The Style and Authorship of the Otho Revision of Laȝamon's *Brut*', *MÆ*, 62 (1993), 187-209. Sir Frederic Madden, the first editor of the poem, came across further, loose leaves of the Otho manuscript after the publication in 1847 of his edition of Laȝamon's *Brut*, and transcribed them in his notebook. Those MS leaves are now lost, and the notebook was not known to Brook and Leslie. For the 'missing' text, see E.J. Bryan, 'Sir Frederic Madden's Annotations on Layamon's *Brut*', in Pilch, 21-69.

34. For a discussion of the dating of the work, see Le Saux 1989, 1-10; also Rosamund Allen in the Introduction to her translation, *Lawman*: Brut (London, 1992), xvi-xviii.

35. On the subject, see A.W. Glowka, 'The Poetics of Laȝamon's *Brut*', in Le Saux 1994, 57-63, and S.K. Brehe, '"Rhythmical Alliteration": Ælfric's Prose and the Origins of Laȝamon's Meter', ibid., 65-87.

36. The most plausible explanation for this feature is probably that Laȝamon's audience was not 'bilingual' enough for him merely to 'adopt' French terms, rather than translating the concepts into English equivalents. See Le Saux 1989, 59-62 and 189-92; also W.R.J. Barron and Françoise Le Saux, 'Two Aspects of Laȝamon's Narrative Art', *AL*, 9 (1989), 25-56.

37. Quoted from Rosamund Allen, 'The Implied Audience of Laȝamon's *Brut*', in Le Saux 1994, 121-39, (122). On the issue of the wider community in which Laȝamon wrote and possible cultural and linguistic influences upon him, see S.C. Weinberg, '"By a noble church on the bank of the Severn": A Regional View of Laȝamon's *Brut*', *LSE*, n.s. 26 (1995), 49-62.

38. For a description of the church of Areley Kings, see Tatlock, 507-9.

39. The Otho text of the *Brut* states that the poet lived 'wid þan gode cniþte' (4). If this is not due to scribal misreading, it could indicate that Laȝamon was indeed a household priest. From 1200 to 1233, the Manor of Martley (to which Areley Kings belonged) was in the hands of the de Frise family. For a good presentation of what is known on the subject, see R. Allen (n.34 above), xviii. Allen suggests that Laȝamon may have written the *Brut* during the Papal Interdict (1208-14), which would have left him (like the other clergy) with time on his hands.

40. Quotations from and translations of the *Brut* are from *Barron and Weinberg*. The reading of books reminds one of Wace, who also describes himself in his prologue as a 'clerc lisant'.

41. On the 'book of St Albin and Austin', see Le Saux 1989, 11-23.

42. For a discussion of Laȝamon's possible indebtedness to Geoffrey of Monmouth, see Le Saux 1989, 94-117. Further borrowings from the *Historia Regum Britanniae* are noted by Neil Wright in his review of Le Saux 1989, *YES*, 22 (1992), 260-61.

43. See I.J. Kirby, 'Angles and Saxons in Laȝamon's *Brut*', *Studia Neophilologica*, 36 (1964), 51-62.

44. For an analysis of the character of Gawain, see M.B. Shichtman, 'Gawain in Wace and Laȝamon: A Case of Metahistorical Evolution', in L.A. Finke (ed.), *Medieval Texts and Contemporary Readers* (Ithaca, N.Y., 1987), 103-19.

45. For the corresponding relationship of Wace's *Brut* to Geoffrey's *Historia*, see above p.21.

46. The point is explicitly made at the beginning of the poem: King Ebrauc, we are told, is the first British monarch to wage war on France, and he does so under pressure from his knights: 'heo wilneden after worre – for heom wes heora drihten wroð' (1314; *they were eager for war – for which their god was angry with them*).

47. The fact that these long-tailed similes (as opposed to the shorter, simpler ones we find throughout the *Brut*, and indeed in its French source) are concentrated in one episode led H.S. Davies ('Laȝamon's Similes', *RES*, 11 (1960), 129-42) to postulate the influence of an additional, lost source which would account for this feature. There is, however, little evidence to support this hypothesis; see Le Saux 1989, 206-11.

48. The ringleader is to be strangled and thrust into a bog, his kinsmen exterminated, and his womenfolk are to have their noses cut off (11390-406).

49. For a discussion of this trait and the necessity to avoid an anachronistic, twentieth-century reading of such passages, see W.R.J. Barron and S.C. Weinberg in the Introduction to their *Laȝamon's 'Arthur'* (n.24 above), xlv-xlix. Other scholars, however, have argued that Arthur's extreme forcefulness is to be seen as a tragic flaw in his character. See Marie-Françoise Alamichel, 'King Arthur's Dual Personality in Layamon's *Brut*', *Neophilologus*, 77 (1993), 303-19, and D.P. Donahue, *Lawman's* Brut, *An Early Arthurian Poem: A Study of Middle English Formulaic Composition* (Lewiston, N.Y., 1991).

50. This is the translation of *Barron and Weinberg*; *Madden*, in his glossary (III, 647), defines 'wiȝe-fulle' as 'cunning', 'guileful', though he glosses the related 'wigeling' as 'magic' (III, 644).

51. These prayers, as pointed out by Barron and Weinberg (n.24 above), xlix-l, are all said in public. This is in keeping with the public nature of the royal function; the king cannot have a private life, as is clearly demonstrated by the example of King Locrin at the beginning of the poem, whose illicit liaison leads to civil war.

52. Other medieval historians, on the contrary, see Arthur as the exception in a predominantly undistinguished line of monarchs. See R.W. Leckie, Jr., *The Passage of Dominion: Geoffrey of Monmouth and the Periodization of Insular History in the Twelfth Century* (Toronto, 1984), and Lesley Johnson, 'Reading the Past in Laȝamon's *Brut*', in Le Saux 1994, 141-60.

53. There are a number of features in the *Brut* which appear to have been derived from Welsh sources; four passages (3594-5, 13716-17, 14263-5, 14380-1) display triple groupings which suggest an influence of the Welsh triadic genre, and there are cases of clear borrowings from the tenth-century prophetic poem *Armes Prydein* (*The Prophecy of Britain*). For a discussion of the Welsh elements in the *Brut*, and the possible routes of transmission of such material, see Le Saux 1989, 118-54. Moreover, the Caligula text of the *Brut* displays traits that suggest that an earlier exemplar may have been copied by a scribe trained in Wales. See Le Saux, 'Listening to the Manuscript: Editing Laȝamon's *Brut*' in Pilch, 11-20. Bilingualism appears to have been relatively common in the Welsh borderlands, at least in certain circles. See, for example, Bullock-Davies, and Melville Richards, 'The Population of the Welsh Border', *Transactions of the Honourable Society of Cymmrodorion*, 20 (1976), 29-40.

54. *Roman de Brut*, ed. Arnold (n.26 above).

55. This would go a long way towards explaining the 'ambivalence' detected by some critics (see D. Donoghue, 'Laȝamon's Ambivalence', *Speculum*, 65 (1990), 537-63) in a poem which celebrates the hereditary enemy of Laȝamon's putative Saxon ancestors.

56. This description is comparable to that given by Giraldus Cambrensis of the Welsh *awenyddion*, who also composed 'inspired' verse in a trance-like state. See Gerald of Wales, *The Journey Through Wales and the Description of Wales*, trans. Lewis Thorpe (Harmondsworth, 1966), 246-7.

57. Merlin's foreknowledge of even apparently trivial events comes to the fore in the Uther episode, where he can tell his hermit friend where he has secretly been, and why – to Uther's court to claim the reward offered for anyone who could reveal the prophet's whereabouts. He then goes on to reveal the reason for Uther's desire to see him (his passion for Ygerne), and prophesies about Arthur.

58. On the indebtedness of Laȝamon to Geoffrey's *Vita Merlini*, see Le Saux 1989, 110-17. The passages where Merlin refuses the gifts of Aurelius or Uther (*Brut* 8509-11 and 9444-6) echo the prophet's refusal of King Rodarch's presents, *Vita Merlini*, 272-7.

59. The prophecy is a variation of the Prophecies of Merlin section of the *Historia Regum Britanniae*, §112, which states that the walls of Rome will crumble before Arthur. The passage is also echoed (but much more closely) in *Brut* 13530-2 and 13964-5.

60. In all, there are five passages in the *Brut* echoing sayings from the Prophecies of Merlin. These passages are discussed by Tatlock, 490-1, and Le Saux 1989, 95-117.

61. The potentially distracting monster-killer side to Arthur's character is underplayed, Laȝamon omitting the grotesque story of the giant Ritho's collection of royal beards. Moreover, Ritho becomes a *king* Riun; the monstrous quality of Arthur's earlier adversary therefore disappears completely.

62. The character of Modred is consistently demonized in the *Brut*. Whereas Wace attempts to analyse Modred's motivations and feelings (he is shown grappling with inner conflict, his awareness of his own crime preventing him from seeking reconciliation with Arthur), Laȝamon stresses the traitor's evil nature. By contrast, Arthur's Queen Wenhauer is less shadowy than in

Wace. She is depicted as a woman in love (with Modred), who eventually takes the veil out of despair at her lover's defeat, rather than out of shame, as in Wace.

63. This passage, which turns Arthur's 'near miss' into total success, is proper to the *Brut*; neither Geoffrey nor Wace makes such a statement.

Prose Chronicles

64. Felicity Riddy ('Reading for England: Arthurian Literature and National Consciousness', *BBIAS*, 43 (1991), 314-32), modifying the view of Laȝamon's *Brut* as 'a massive erratic in the history of English poetry' (Pearsall 1977, 112), sees it as an attempt to restore the English language to serious literary use, even though, on the evidence of the two surviving copies, it may have circulated only among knightly families in the West Midlands (323-4). Something similar might be said of its use of alliterative verse, even though its idiosyncratic medium has no exact counterpart either in the Anglo-Saxon heyday of the medium or its fourteenth-century revival. Perhaps the most significant feature about Laȝamon is his persistence in a massive task without apparent prospect of gain or fame; the survival of a distinctively English literature may owe much to such forlorn-hope efforts, even though the process cannot be traced from text to text.

65. This explanation of the aboriginal state of Britain, queried by Geoffrey's account of Albion and its giant inhabitants, was supplied by an Anglo-Norman poem, *Des Grantz Geanz*, and its Latin prose derivative, *De origine gigantum*, produced – probably at Glastonbury – in the 1330s, and frequently prefixed to *Brut* texts, including both the Anglo-Norman and the English versions. For editions of both forms of proem see J.P. Carley and J. Crick, *AL*, 13 (1995), 41-114.

66. The Anglo-Norman chronicle, as yet unpublished, survives in some fifty manuscripts, representing a long and a short recension (Taylor, 110-27); the English prose *Brut* derives from the former.

67. A second translation of the basic Anglo-Norman, attributed to John Maundevyle, rector of Burnham Thorpe in Norfolk from 1427 to 1441, survives in two manuscripts (see L.M. Matheson in A.S.G. Edwards (ed.), *Middle English Prose: A Critical Guide to Major Authors and Genres* (New Brunswick, N.J., 1984), 210.

68. The complexity of the textual tradition is such that no comprehensive classification has so far been made. The classification of F.W.D. Brie (*Geschichte und Quellen der mittelenglischen Prosachronik* The Brut of England *oder* The Chronicles of England (Marburg, 1905, repr. 1960) was limited to the 120 manuscripts known to him, not all of which he had been able to examine. The preliminary results of a survey by L.M. Matheson ('The Middle English Prose *Brut*: A Location List of the Manuscripts and Early Printed Editions', *Analytical and Enumerative Bibliography*, 3 (1979-80)) suggest classification in four main categories incorporating sub-groupings but without assigning existing texts to groups. A brief illustration of the variety and complexity of the tradition is provided by the description of some notable texts by E.D. Kennedy in Hartung *Manual*, VIII, 2632-4.

69. The Latin version survives in at least fifteen manuscripts, some incorporating genealogical tables, including those of the kings of England (Taylor, 131). C.L. Kingsford (*English Historical Literature in the Fifteenth Century* (Oxford, 1913), 113-39) interprets them as representing at least three or four different chronicles, all deriving from the English *Brut*.

70. Merlin's role as sage and seer continues throughout the chronicle: his prophesies of Henry III as a lamb '"wiþ trew lippis, and holynesse wryten in his hert"' (§160), of Edward I as a dragon that '"shulde ben mellede wiþ mercy & also wiþ sternesse, þat shulde kepe Engeland fram colde and fram hete"' (§186), of Edward II as a goat, since 'to miche he ȝaf him vnto realte and folie' (§211), are recalled at their death or deposition.

71. References are to the chapter numbers of *Brie*, from which quotations are taken. The third volume of the edition, which was to discuss the manuscripts, sources and literary influence of the *Brut*, never appeared. Though it made available a basic text and parts of some of the continuations, other versions and continuations remain unpublished.

72. 'Contemporary England, therefore, is understood as the aftermath of Arthurian England. The genealogy of fourteenth- and fifteenth-century English kings extends back via Arthur to Brutus and so Arthurian genealogies themselves are used as political propaganda in the dynastic quarrels of the period' (Riddy, 'Reading for England', 326). On the political exploitation of the Arthurian legend, see below, Interchapter A, *passim*.

73. John Taylor (113-14, 146-7) suggests an office attached to the Chancery which travelled north with the administration in the early 1330s when the *Brut* continuations have detailed accounts of northern events.

74. F. Riddy, 'Reading for England', 326-7; cf. L.M. Matheson in Lagorio, I, 254: 'The *Brut* had a wide appeal: copies were owned by secular and religious of all ranks and the surviving manuscripts range in quality from the sumptuous to the shoddy. One group of Abbreviated Version texts shows signs of having been mass-produced to meet public demand.'

75. On Higden's sources and the basis of the *Polychronicon*'s appeal to his contemporaries, see Taylor, 96-8.

76. Two brief essays on translation, prefixed to some copies of Trevisa, are apparently his work (A.S.G. Edwards, in *Middle English Prose*, 134). He takes issue with Higden's comments (I, §59) on the dialectal variety of English compared with the uniformity of Anglo-Norman, as, in part, a consequence of children being taught to construe their school Latin into French. Trevisa interjects that by 1385 children in grammar schools were being taught to construe into English, with the result that they knew no more French than their left heel, a drawback in foreign travel.

77. See L.M. Matheson in Lagorio, I, 255-6. From the evidence of monastic library catalogues and from wills we know of yet more copies of the Latin text, now lost; copies of the English chronicle were less likely to survive the centuries in the hands of laymen (Taylor 1987, 263).

78. See A.S.G. Edwards, 'The Influence and Audience of the *Polychronicon*: Some Observations', *Proceedings of the Leeds Philosophical and Literary Society*, 17, 6 (1980), 114-15.

79. References are to the edition of the *Polychronicon* by C. Babington and J.R. Lumby, 9 vols, RS 41 (London, 1865-86), quotations from Trevisa's translation given there in parallel.

80. On the similarity of Higden's ambivalence to that of Henry of Huntingdon and William of Malmesbury, see notes 2 and 3 above. Even as late as the second decade of the sixteenth century, when the Italian Polydore Vergil, long resident in England, attempted to

undermine Geoffrey's *Historia* in his *Anglica Historia*, dismissing Brutus outright and reducing Arthur to Uther's successor who reigned too briefly to reunite Britain, the patriotic reaction was vitriolic and he was vilified as 'that most rascall dogge knave in the worlde'. (See J.P. Carley, 'Polydore Vergil and John Leyland on King Arthur: The Battle of the Books', *Interpretations*, 15 (1984), 86-100.)

81. When the concept of nine pre-eminent historical figures, models for the modern world, was evolved early in the fourteenth century, Arthur was included among the Christian trio as an exemplar of military glory, but fated eventually to join the others upon Fortune's fickle wheel.

82. Arthur's historical reputation was first challenged by those least susceptible to the spirit of English nationalism. The Italian Polydore Vergil, long resident in England (1502-53), who in his *Anglica Historia* used the new humanist rationalism to undermine Geoffrey's *Historia*, provoked a xenophobic reaction which demonstrated the enduring power of the national myth. The Scottish chroniclers who initially seemed to accept Geoffrey's account of Arthur's victories over Scots and Picts (among whom he also had important allies), when the Plantagenets claimed him as their dynastic predecessor, began to portray him as the embodiment of aggressive, imperialistic England. The chroniclers (especially John of Fordun in his *Chronica Gentis Scotorum* (*c.* 1385) and his continuator Walter Bower, Abbot of Inchcolm in the mid-fifteenth century) show increasing scepticism about his foreign conquests, stressing his illegitimacy and claiming that the true heirs to his throne were his nephews Gawain and Mordred, Scots through their father, Lot of Lothian. The anonymous *Chronicle of Scotland in a Part* (*c.* 1460) presents Arthur as a tyrant, a 'huris sone' made king by the 'devilry of Merlin' and justly slain by Mordred 'in his rychtwyse querele' (Lacy, 1991, 92-3). This ambivalence towards Arthur is apparent in some Scots romances; see below pp.148-9 and p.161, and associated references.

Metrical Chronicles

83. Thomas Wright (ed.), *The Chronicle of Pierre de Langtoft*, RS 47, 2 vols. (London, 1866-8), II, 296-7. For further discussion of Langtoft's narrative see Thea Summerfield, 'Context and Genesis of Pierre de Langtoft's *Chronicle*' in Donald Maddox and Sara Sturm Maddox (eds.), *Literary Aspects of Courtly Culture* (Cambridge, 1994), 321-32. It is worth noting, as Summerfield does (n.25) that Langtoft describes William the Conqueror as having been crowned with Arthur's crown and Richard I as owner of Excalibur – the latter reference is not unique to Langtoft. Thea Summerfield discusses the function of the Arthurian references in Langtoft's *Chronicle* in more detail in Lacy 1996, 187-208.

84. See Edward Kennedy's very helpful survey of the English metrical chronicles in Hartung *Manual* VIII for summaries of the contents, details of the extant manuscripts and further bibliographical information. R.H. Fletcher (1958) discusses the treatment of Arthurian history in this group of texts (though the reader will notice some difference of emphasis in my discussion of this topic here).

85. For more detailed discussion of the attempts to assimilate British history within the contours of English historiography (and the problems this posed) by Latin and vernacular chroniclers following the appearance of the *Historia Regum Britanniae*, see R.W. Leckie, *The Passage of Dominion* (Toronto, 1981), especially 73-119.

86. See D.B. Tyson, 'King Arthur as a Literary Device in French Vernacular History Writing of the Fourteenth Century', *BBIAS*, 33 (1981), 237-57, for a discussion of Arthur's wider exemplary function in this corpus of historical narrative. The various 'fronts' of Arthur's colonizing campaigns (such as his achievement of dominion over Scotland, or his achievements in France and further afield on the Continent) no doubt attracted variant levels of interest from the producers and audiences of the chronicles I am discussing here, according to the contemporary policies and ambitions of the English crown.

87. For Gaimar see A. Bell (ed.), *L'estoire des Engleis by Geffrei Gaimar*, Anglo-Norman Text Society (Oxford, 1960); I. Short, 'Gaimar et les débuts de l'historiographie en langue française', in Danielle Buschinger (ed.), *Chroniques nationales et chroniques universelles* (Göppingen, 1990), 155-63; I. Short, 'Patrons and Polyglots: French Literature in Twelfth-century England', *Anglo-Norman Studies*, 14 (1991), 229-49. For an early and important short chronicle tradition in Anglo-Norman prose see D.B. Tyson, 'An Early French Prose History of the Kings of England', *Rom.*, 96 (1975), 1-26. For the translation of the Short Metrical Chronicle into Anglo-Norman prose see *Zettl*, 92-107. Lister Matheson (n.67 above) has observed that '[w]ith the cessation in the mid-twelfth century of continuations to the *Anglo-Saxon Chronicle*, the writing of historical prose in English lapsed until the late fourteenth century' (209).

88. The nomenclature of these chronicles varies considerably in modern discussions: I have chosen the simplest forms of reference.

89. For further discussion of this learned/lewd distinction and its partly rhetorical, rather than sociological, value see Turville-Petre, 1996, 28-31.

90. Regional factors may have played a part in determining the decision to use English verse as a literary medium: Laȝamon, for example, seems to be aware of long-standing learned uses of English as a medium of historical narration; no doubts are expressed in Robert of Gloucester's *Chronicle* about the value of the chosen mode of expression. The copy of the *Short Metrical Chronicle* in London BL MS Royal 12 C xii (which shares a compiler and copyist with the more famous trilingual collection, London BL MS Harley 2253) is the most obvious example of a Middle English chronicle being found in a trilingual manuscript compilation.

91. For discussions of the evidence for 'Robert of Gloucester' see Kennedy, Hartung *Manual* VIII, 2618-19. Anne Hudson notes that the *Chronicle*'s first editor, Thomas Hearne (whose edition was published in 1724), 'was quite explicit about the absence of evidence for the title 'of Gloucester', and shows a knowledge and appraisal of the evidence beyond that of many later writers' ('Robert of Gloucester and the Antiquaries, 1550-1800', *N&Q*, 214 (1969), 322-33, (322)). For a less sceptical review of the possibility that a Robert of Gloucester was responsible for the chronicle, see Turville-Petre 1996, 73-4. Although I am persuaded that there is evidence of a shaping design in this *Chronicle*, it is important to recognize, nevertheless that the work survives in multiple versions (see the comments on the longer, shorter and prose versions below) and the title, Robert of Gloucester's *Chronicle*, is thus a convenient shorthand form of reference for a group of texts.

92. The so-called 'longer' version of the narrative (*c.* 12,000 lines) spans the period from the foundation of the island to the last years of Henry III's reign and includes a reference to the 'maker' of the work who witnessed an ominous darkness descend on the land at the

time of the battle of Evesham: 'þis isei roberd / þat verst þis boc made' (*Wright* II, 748-9). This reference is not found in the so-called shorter version (*c*.10,000 lines) which spans the period from the foundation of Britain to the accession of Edward I. This shorter version provides an account of British and English history up to 1135 which corresponds to that of the longer version (with some supplementary material on the kings of Britain totalling *c*. 800 lines drawn from Laȝamon's Brut and the *Short Metrical Chronicle* and possibly another Geoffrey of Monmouth-influenced source), but then offers a different version of the reign of Stephen and much briefer accounts of subsequent events, in comparison with the longer version. Wright prints the additional British material, none of which concerns Arthur, in the appendix to his edition. For the use of the *Short Metrical Chronicle* as a supplementary source for the account of British history in the shorter version, see Turville-Petre 1996, 105, n.22. For the evidence for the probable date of composition see *Wright*, ix-xi, Kennedy, Hartung *Mannual* VIII, 2618; Turville-Petre 1996, 74. For a list of the manuscripts see Kennedy, Hartung *Manual*, VIII, 2798; Anne Hudson, 'Tradition and Innovation in some Middle English Manuscripts', *RES*, n.s. 17 (1966), 359-72, n.1 and n.2.

93. See Kennedy, Hartung *Manual* VIII, 2621-2 for an account of the prose adaptations and 2620 for a review of the post-medieval responses to this chronicle (the latter subject is tackled in more detail in Anne Hudson's article cited above, n.91). Kennedy observes that Robert of Gloucester 'followed the lead of twelfth and thirteenth-century Latin chroniclers and produced the first vernacular chronicle that incorporated . . .[the Galfredian history of Britain] into the whole history of Britain and England' (2621). But this is true only if we discount the very strong possibility that Gaimar's *Estoire des Engleis* originally had this scope too.

94. Although there is no developed portrait of an authorial persona in this narrative (for the single reference to the 'maker' of the book, see n.92 above) to compare with those provided by Laȝamon and Robert Mannyng in their respective prologues, the audience is made aware, nevertheless, of a mediating presence throughout: the narrator on occasions, for example, draws his audience's attention to the organization of his work (see, for example, his reference to the earlier account of Arthur's reign, *Wright*, 4737-8) and sometimes adds comments which reflect 'a point of view' (see for example the narrator's comments on Arthur's 'rightful' trust of Mordred (4135), and the comment on the 'proud' tone of the letter sent to Arthur from Rome, (4011), or anticipates the outcome of events (see, for example, the narrator's comment about the 'uerste truage' that Arthur sends to Rome (4013-14), or the reference to the discovery of Arthur's bones at Glastonbury, (4592-4). For the narrator's single direction to another narrative (a 'romance' about King Richard), see 9987.

95. The topic of the sources used in this chronicle awaits further detailed investigation which might build on the work of Wright and W. Ellmer, 'Über die Quellen der Reimchronik Robert's von Gloucester', *Anglia*, 10 (1887), 1-37. For some discussion of the range of Latin sources deployed (and also the *Anglo-Saxon Chronicle*), see *Wright*, xv-xxxiii, and Kennedy, Hartung *Manual* VIII, 2619. On the use of the *South English Legendary* see Turville-Petre 1996, 76.

96. For the stress on Arthur's piety see, for example, Arthur's oath to revenge the Saxons' betrayal (*Wright*, 3585), his 'þoȝte' on the battlefield (3619), his gesture before fighting the giant of St Michael's Mount (4217). In general, there is a greater concern in the

Middle English narrative to stress that Arthur's cause and actions are 'riȝt' and there is much less equivocation in the episode in which Arthur hears and responds to the charges brought by the Roman ambassadors about the rightfulness of Arthur's case (in comparison with Geoffrey of Monmouth's version in which there seems little to distinguish the British and Roman claims to rightful conquest and tribute). Arthur's defence of his rightful, chivalric, use of force in conquering France (4032-58) has a wider resonance for the thematic interests of this metrical chronicle in the relationship between 'might' and 'right'. The narrator appears to approve of Arthur's plan to conquer Rome, describing it as a 'noble dede' (4499). The heathenness of some of Arthur's antagonists on the Roman side is brought into focus at one point in his campaign (4462) and the wickedness of his later antagonist, Mordred, is also stressed by the repeated use of the epithet 'luþer'. The part Guinevere plays in the last stages of Arthur's reign is also rendered less equivocal in this text: she colludes with the 'luþer trycherye' (4505).

97. Although the detail of the military engagement is generally reduced, it is worth noting the scope of Arthur's intended conquest in the *Chronicle* (he aims to win 'al europe', *Wright*, 3760). The scale of Arthur's engagement with the Roman forces is also emphasized through a comparison with the Trojan war (4991-2). See Fletcher, 195-8 for further discussion of some of the distinctive details of Arthurian history in this chronicle.

98. It is difficult to suggest a precise source for this reference to the Round Table (as a distinctive gathering of Arthur's entourage). Kennedy (n.95 above) suggests that some of the additional details in the *Chronicle* 'suggest knowledge of Arthurian romances' and cites the reference to Gawain as the 'flour of corteysye' as evidence. This is certainly possible. Robert's use of the abstract vocabulary of chivalry in Arthur's reign is striking.

99. The account of Arthur's final confrontation with Mordred is not to be found in Henry of Huntingdon's *Historia Anglorum*, but in the letter, *Epistola ad Warinum*, in which he records the outline of the Geoffrey of Monmouth's *Historia Regum Britanniae* after being shown a copy by Robert of Torigni at Le Bec in 1139. See above n.2.

100. Later in his narrative, the narrator returns to the subject of Arthur's grave when he notes that Arthur's bones were first discovered after the great fire at Glastonbury (*Wright*, 9849-53). Robert of Gloucester clearly had access to more information about Glastonbury and the Arthurian connections the community promoted from the end of the twelfth century onwards, though the precise source of this information is difficult to trace from its abbreviated form in his *Chronicle*. The political significance of this identification of Avalon with Glastonbury and the location of Arthur's grave there, for an English chronicler writing after 1284 (when Wales was annexed to England), is obvious enough from the narrator's remarks in Robert of Gloucester's chronicle about the (here 'false') prospects of a Welsh revival under the leadership of a returned Arthur (4589-91). I owe thanks to Sarah Mitchell for answering some queries on Robert of Gloucester.

101. At the moment when Robert of Gloucester traces the passage of dominion from the British people to the English, however, he does give some credit to the possibility of a British revival (not an Arthurian one however) as predicted by the angel and Merlin (*Wright*, 5132-6). The attitude towards Merlin's prophecies in the narrative as a whole is an interesting one: although the narrator refuses to tell any more of them beyond the point when Merlin talks of the removal of the bishopric from London to Canterbury (2795-814), he does endorse the predictive value of the prophecies up to that point – 'Al þis biuel afterward as ȝe ssolleþ ihure' (2815) – and identifies Arthur with the figure of the boar of

Cornwall here (2816) and later (3849-51). The reason given for not providing any more of Merlin's prophecies is that the subject requires learning beyond the powers of this narrator (it is 'so derc to simplemen' (2820). This 'excuse' is rather like Wace's in the *Roman de Brut* but, unlike Wace, Robert does offer an account of the first part of Merlin's prophecies (including a reference to Arthur's status as a 'suete mete' to those who tell of him).

102. The *Short Metrical Chronicle* has attracted very little critical attention; the account in Fletcher (see n.84 above) is not very clear or helpful. In addition to the introduction to *Zettl* and Kennedy's overview (Hartung *Manual* VIII, 2622-4), see Turville-Petre 1996, 108-12 for the most recent critical assessment.

103. For an account of these manuscripts, the two fragmentary copies (or more precisely extracts from the narrative), and the translation into Anglo-Norman prose extant in one copy, see *Zettl*, xi-xxxiv. It is worth noting that one of the extracts of the *Short Metrical Chronicle* (MS C – containing further information on Bath) has been used to supplement one copy of Robert of Gloucester's *Chronicle*, and one copy of the text as a whole (MS B) follows that of Robert of Gloucester's *Chronicle*. The dates of the extant manuscripts range from *c*. 1320 to the first half of the fifteenth century. The sources of the text are not easy to identify because of the relative brevity of the narrative, and the issue is anyway complicated by the existence of variant versions of the text. *Zettl* (cxxxii-cxxxiii) provides an overview of likely sources (though his comments about the use of Robert of Gloucester's *Chronicle* need modifying – see n.95 above). References to bookish sources are found in the various versions (see, for example, *Zettl*, 6) and the texts seem to orientate themselves more specifically to the *Brut* tradition of narratives: MS A opens with a reference which emphasizes that the 'Brut' material is now available in English; the majority of the other versions have a reference to the 'Brut' in line 32; MS F recalls the 'Brut' in line 747.

104. The tradition of the 'abridged' *Brut* narratives in Latin, Anglo-Norman and English awaits much more detailed analysis and research. One such 'abridged' Anglo-Norman narrative is copied in the Caligula MS of Laȝamon's *Brut*. For the best account of this tradition narrative and a text of an Anglo-Norman prose version, see D.B. Tyson, 'An early French prose history' (n.87 above).

105. The variation in the extant versions and the variety of contexts in which the *Short Metrical Chronicle* is found (see *Zettl*, xlvi-ci) itself testifies to the usefulness and adaptability of this kind of narrative history. For the continuation of the version in MS D up to the reign of Henry VI see *Zettl*, xix-xxi, and for the subsequent influence of the *Short Metrical Chronicle* on the later *Verses on the Kings of England* see *Zettl*, cxxxiv. See Turville-Petre 1996, 108-112, for a discussion of the function of its specific form and place in the Auchinleck MS as a whole.

106. Zettl suggests that the 'original' version of the text assigned Arthur a reign of only ten years (as is the case in the version of MS F which also contains a reference to Arthur conquering 'al to þe ȝates of Rome', l.260). The foundation stories of Brutus and Ynge attract comparatively more attention than the reign of Arthur here. Merlin appears only in the versions in MS F (as Dunval's clerk and founder of Stonehenge, F. 209-16) and in the Anglo-Norman prose translation (as the maker of Stonehenge and other marvels, 139-40).

107. For a detailed discussion of the contents of this manuscript and further bibliographical information see Turville-Petre 1996, 108-41.

108. For further discussion of the broader tradition to which this version of the Albion story belongs, see Lesley Johnson, 'Return to Albion', *AL*, 12 (1995), 19-40.

109. The attitude towards Lancelot in this incident is not a pejorative one (contrary to Kennedy's description in Hartung *Manual* VIII, 2623). It may be that this incident also contains an echo of that involving Locrine and Estrildis from the Galfridian tradition of British history. In Thorlac Turville-Petre's view, the Auchinleck version of the *Short Metrical Chronicle* serves an important structural function in this manuscript compilation as a whole: it provides a chronological backbone which enables its audience to see how the central protagonists of some of the other narratives copied in the manuscript (such as Arthur, Guy of Warwick, Richard the Lionheart) fit into the overall scheme of insular history and suggests that the audience should regard these other narratives 'not just as entertainments but as sources of historical knowledge' (Turville-Petre 1996, 112).

110. The elliptic reference to the mantle that 'To no cokkewold wiif nas it nouʒt' brought by Cradoc recalls events related in the *Manteau Mautaillé*.

111. The new edition of the *Chronicle* by Idelle Sullens offers the most comprehensive introduction to date to Mannyng's work, its sources, the extant manuscripts, and scholarship on the *Chronicle* (see *Sullens*, 1-89). For further overviews of these matters see Kennedy Hartung *Manual* VIII, 2625-8 and Turville-Petre 1996, 14-18, 28-31, 34-40, 75-80 (the latter being too recent to be included in Sullens's edition).

112. The prologue to Mannyng's *Chronicle* represents an extensive effort to contextualize the work, not only in terms of the broader historiographical traditions on which it draws, but also in terms of the narrative as an exercise in writing in English verse; in this latter context Mannyng mentions the poor transmission of 'Sir Tristem', said to have been composed by 'Thomas' (*Sullens*, 97-114). For more detailed analysis of Mannyng's statements about the circulation of Arthurian literature later in the *Chronicle* see Lesley Johnson, 'Robert Mannyng's History of Arthurian Literature' in I. Wood and G. Loud (eds.), *Church and Chronicle in the Middle Ages* (London, 1991), 129-47 and Ad Putter, 'Finding Time for Romance' (n.19 above).

113. However, the cameo portrait of Yvain having resisted Mordred's treachery whilst Arthur was fighting in Italy appears to be original to Mannyng's narrative (*Sullens*, MS L 13641).

114. The topic of Geoffrey of Monmouth's contribution to the field of Arthurian historiography comes up again in this discussion; his work had been mentioned previously in Mannyng's prologue (*Sullens*, 163-76).

115. The point made by Turville-Petre about the way in which the *Short Metrical Chronicle* in the Auchinleck Manuscript encourages its readers to view other 'romances' in the compilation as offering historical information on the history of the land (see n.109, above) could be extended to Mannyng's *Chronicle*: he locates a historical place for not only French Arthurian romance but other narratives which tell of insular heroes, such as Havelok. Unlike the compiler of the *Short Metrical Chronicle*, however, Mannyng is not prepared to countenance the historical value of the origin story of Ynge (*Sullens*, 7427-9, 14215-18).

116. In opposing any suggestion of Arthur's return, Mannyng's stance might be compared to that of the narrator of Robert of Gloucester's *Chronicle*. However, unlike Robert of Gloucester (and the compilers of the *Short Metrical Chronicle* and Thomas Castleford's

Chronicle), there is no suggestion in Mannyng's text that Avalon is to be identified with Glastonbury.

117. Caroline Eckhardt provides a brief introduction to the *Chronicle* in the first volume of her edition but promises a much more extensive introduction to the work, its sources and context, which will appear as a third volume. Until that time, surveys of the contents and interest of the narrative (heavily dependant on an 1889 dissertation on the Chronicle by M.L. Perrin) can be found in Fletcher, 202-3 and Kennedy Hartung *Manual* VIII, 2624-5. For a suggestion that this Chronicle dates from later in the fourteenth century , see Turville-Petre 1996, 75.

118. This version is not, as Kennedy suggests (Hartung *Manual* VIII, 2625), similar to the one found in London BL MS Cotton Cleopatra D.ix; the version in Castleford's *Chronicle* retells the form of the story in which the sisters are daughters of a Syrian king. See 'Return to Albion' (n.108 above) for an overview of the two major traditions of the Albion foundation story.

119. For Robert of Gloucester's partial translation/interpretation see n.101 above. For a brief overview of the treatment of Merlin's prophecies in English see Caroline Eckhardt, *The* Prophetia Merlini *of Geoffrey of Monmouth: A Fifteenth-Century English Commentary* (Cambridge, Mass., 1982), 17-19. There is evidence to show that translations of the prophecies in French were in circulation long before Castleford's *Chronicle*, however, both as 'independent texts' and as part of 'Brut' narratives. Although Wace, for example, refuses to offer a translation of Merlin's words, a translation of Merlin's prophecies (which appears to derive from an independent translation of the prophecy sequence alone by one 'Helias') is inserted into a copy of Wace's *Roman de Brut* at the appropriate point in the text in Durham Cathedral Library MS C IV 27 (and it follows a copy of the *Roman de Brut* in Geneve-Cologny Codex Bodmer 67). Traces of an independent translation of the prophecies survive in London BL MS Arundel 220 where the narrator provides a metrical introduction to a promised prose translation (which is not copied out in the manuscript).

120. Other small details which appear to distinguish Castleford's version of Arthurian history from that of Geoffrey of Monmouth, and perhaps reflect the subsequent versions of Arthurian history, include an interesting attempt to clear up the confusion surrounding Arthur's antagonists in his Roman wars by positing the existence of two emperors of Rome at this time (Lucius and Leo – see *Eckhardt* 22752-57) and a more pejorative attitude towards Guinevere's complicity with Mordred (23576-82). The emotive quality of the nurse's lament over the tomb of Helen, reminiscent of the affective techniques of some Middle English devotional lyrics, is very striking too (22076-99).

A: Arthur in English History

1. See Thomas Charles-Edwards, 'The Arthur of History' in Bromwich, 15-32; O.J. Padel, 'The Nature of Arthur', *Cambridge Medieval Celtic Studies*, 27 (1994), 1-31; also J.T. Koch, 'The Celtic Lands', in Lacy 1996, 239-322. I am grateful to E.D. Kennedy, Lister Matheson, Oliver Padel and Charles Wood for their helpful comments on earlier drafts of this chapter

2. See Padel, 'The Nature of Arthur', 14: 'The overall picture is of the leader of a band of heroes who live outside society, whose main world is one of magical animals, giants, and other wonderful happenings, located in the wild parts of the landscape . . . There was a belief that Arthur was not dead; this could have been connected with the idea that he would come again to save the island from its oppressors, but that is not clear in the scanty materials available. The final feature to be noted is that Arthur was a pan-Brittonic hero. Wherever a Brittonic language was or had lately been spoken, the legend of Arthur can be shown to have been current in the pre-Geoffrey period – in southern Scotland, southern Wales, the Welsh borders, south-west England, and Brittany. In most of these areas its main manifestation was his presence in the landscape in the form of place-names and legends.'

3. For Arthur's role in medieval Welsh culture see Ceridwen Lloyd-Morgan, 'Qui était l'Arthur des Gallois', *Pris-Ma*, 11 (1995), 149-58, and Chapter 1 above.

4. On Geoffrey and the Celts see B.F. Roberts, 'Geoffrey of Monmouth', in Bromwich, 97-116. He observes (98) that 'Geoffrey's subject was the early history of the Britons who were the ancestors not only of the Welsh but also of Cornishmen and Bretons'.

5. Much has been written about contemporary reception of Geoffrey's Arthur and in particular the hostile response of William of Newburgh, who in his *Historia Rerum Anglicarum* referred to Geoffrey's ridiculous fictions, decrying both the lack of earlier substantiating accounts and the obvious anachronisms. For a summary of critical response see Dean, 15-19. Unlike most critics Dean argues that Henry of Huntingdon may have been negative in his assessment of Geoffrey; Antonia Gransden takes a more typical position (*Historical Writing in England c.550 to c.1307* (Ithaca, N.Y., 1974), 200-1) when she states: 'Henry liked Geoffrey's work partly because he found it amusing . . . Like Geoffrey of Monmouth, Henry was interested in King Arthur, giving an account of his battles (derived from Nennius).' She concludes: 'Geoffrey of Monmouth did not create the appetite in his contemporaries for romance history: he fed and sharpened an existing appetite.' This, of course, explains why Geoffrey was so quickly assimilated. Subsequent to William of Newburgh the first real voice of dissent was Ranulph Higden, who in his *Polychronicon* rejected much of Geoffrey's Arthuriad, although not the essential premise of Arthur's existence. L.M. Matheson, 'King Arthur and the Medieval English Chronicles', in Lagorio, I, 248-74 (255-7) discusses Higden in detail, observing that Higden's own views evolved from version to version. Not surprisingly, Higden's English translator, John Trevisa, attempted to answer Higden's criticisms.

6. *Willelmi Malmesbiriensis Monachi de gestis regum Anglorum* . . . (ed.), W. Stubbs, 2 vols, RS 90 (London, 1887-9), I, 11.

7. See B.N. Sargent-Baur, '*Dux Bellorum / Rex Militum / Roi Faineant*: The Transformation of Arthur in the Twelfth Century', in Kennedy 1996, 29-43 (29): 'The

change occurred rather abruptly during the twelfth century and at the same time as the works concerning Arthur's life, era, and companions evolved from pseudo-history to the obviously fictional genre of romance. Arthur at this point was shifted to the background and changed from a leading actor at the center of events to a supporting player, almost a decoration, while others moved forward to claim our attention.'

8. For reference to the texts and a discussion of modern scholarship see J.P. Carley, 'England', in Lacy 1996, 1-82. Felicity Riddy observes ('Reading for England: Arthurian Literature and National Consciousness', *BBIAS* 43 (1991), 314-32 (330-1)) that those French romances which were translated into English were inevitably texts 'sanctioned' by Geoffrey. The French, on the other hand, did not generally include Arthur in their chronicle accounts: Rosemary Morris ('King Arthur and the Growth of French Nationalism' in Jondorf, 115-29 (121)), has made the point that Arthur's conquest of Gaul may have been a 'political irritant' to the French.

9. See Riddy ('Reading for England', 320), who argues that all later versions must be seen in the context of Geoffrey's canonical text; he is the *auctor* and his *Historia* the *auctoritas*: '. . there are, of course, texts which have radically different accounts of Arthur's life and death from Geoffrey's, like *Perlesvaus* or the *Vera Historia de Morte Arthurii*, or at the humbler level the *Short Metrical Chronicle* . . . but all of these seem to be reading against Geoffrey, against the canon. Or if any of these do represent alternative oral traditions, they do not win out against Geoffrey; they flare momentarily into textual life and then die out.' Concerning the historical texts as such Matheson points out ('King Arthur and the Medieval English Chronicles', 248-9): 'Accounts of King Arthur and his reign are included in the majority of historical chronicles dealing with the general history of England that were written in England between the twelfth and the fifteenth centuries. Ultimately, such accounts are based on Geoffrey of Monmouth's *Historia Regum Britanniae*, often through intermediate versions or translations.' Individual chroniclers, nevertheless, do introduce regional variations. The Auchinleck recension of the *Short English Metrical Chronicle*, for example, adds information not found elsewhere, asserting that Uther Pendragon was buried at Glastonbury, that Lancelot built a castle at Nottingham for Guenevere and offered to defend her honour at Glastonbury. Lambeth Palace Library MS 84 contains material relating to Merlin as well as 'King Arthur and the Wildcats' (on which see L.M. Matheson, 'The Arthurian Stories of Lambeth Palace Library MS 84', *AL*, 5 (1985), 70-91).

10. See Riddy 1987; Riddy sees the 'hoole book' in the context of other similar manuscript compilations of the period. She also observes ('Reading for England', 331) that Malory is the first 'if not to dispense with, at least radically to alter the contours of Geoffrey's framework, and the reason for this might be that by the time he wrote, about two and half centuries after the *Historia Regum Britanniae*, that framework had been too widely criticised to continue to command assent. Whatever the reason, Malory provides the era of print in England with a new canonical Arthur.' It is, of course, Caxton's Malory which became generally known and used.

11. As Dean observes (p.10), giving key examples, this was 'the medieval historians' most fundamental belief about Arthur. The finding of his remains proved beyond any doubt that he really had existed at some point in the past.'

12. 'Arthur est vivant! Jalons pour une enquête sur le messianisme royal au moyen âge', *Cahiers de civilisation médiévale*, 32 (1989), 135-46 (143).

13. On dating see C.N.L. Brooke, *The Church and the Welsh Border in the Central Middle Ages* (Woodbridge, 1986), 42. The story of Guenevere's abduction by Melwas has strong resonances with the story of Guenevere's abduction by Kay in Chrétien's *Knight of the Cart*. Roberts ('Geoffrey of Monmouth', 112) sees a conflation between Melwas the abductor of Guenevere in Caradog and Medrawd (Mordred) as her abductor elsewhere. The primary function of the story in Caradog's version is to explain why Glastonbury received great estates in ancient times.

14. The identification first appears in Giraldus Cambrensis; see Antonia Gransden, 'The Growth of the Glastonbury Traditions and Legends in the Twelfth Century', *The Journal of Ecclesiastical History*, 27 (1976), 337-58 (353-4). For further elaborations, bringing in Glasteing as eponymous founder, see 356-7.

15. The main accounts – by Giraldus Cambrensis in his *De principis instructione* and *Speculum ecclesiae*, by Ralph of Coggeshall in his *Chronicon Anglicanum* – differ in crucial details; see Richard Barber, 'Was Mordred Buried at Glastonbury? An Arthurian Tradition at Glastonbury in the Middle Ages', *AL*, 4 (1985), 37-69. Barber considers the lesser-known *Annales de Margan* to be another important witness. His transcription of the different versions (52-63) is used in my quotations. See also Gransden, 'The Growth of the Glastonbury Traditions', 349-54.

16. The Celtic sleeping king tradition was not, in fact, extinguished with the exhumation and was variously reported by English chroniclers, generally with contemptuous dismissal, throughout the Middle Ages; see Dean, 26-7.

17. For a brief summary of scholarly hypotheses on this topic see J.C. Parsons, 'The Second Exhumation of King Arthur's Remains at Glastonbury, 19 April 1278', *AL*, 12 (1993), 173-7 (173).

18. In a forthcoming paper, to appear in *AL*, 16 (1998), C.T. Wood charts the course of events leading up to the exhumation.

19. There was, however, an epitaph, including a reference to Guenevere, composed for the mausoleum; see M.P. Brown and J.P. Carley, 'A Fifteenth-Century Revison of the Glastonbury Epitaph to King Arthur', *AL*, 12 (1993), 179-91 (180):

> Hic iacet Arturus, flos regum, gloria regni
> Quem mores, probitas, commendant laude perhenni.
> Arturi iacet hic coniux tumulata secunda,
> Que meruit celos uirtutum prole fecunda.

For possible meanings of 'secunda' see Neil Wright, 'A New Arthurian Epitaph?', *AL*, 13 (1994), 149.

20. 'Was Mordred Buried at Glastonbury?', 47-9.

21. Matheson ('King Arthur and the Medieval English Chronicles', 265) makes the point that 'the person and story of Arthur were eminently adaptable to ideological purposes. They could, for example, be used to provide moral justification or explanation of the Norman Conquest by Wace or Laȝamon. Later, Arthur gave the English a national hero, one of the Nine Worthies, and the type of the ideal Christian monarch. In the fourteenth and fifteenth centuries the record of Arthur's foreign victories and conquests had obvious contemporary implications with regard to Scotland and France. Skeptics were few, and the political advantages of royal identification with Arthur and his military prowess ensured that offical disapproval or skepticism would not occur.' On the political

ramifications of the verse romances see Schmolke-Hasselmann, 232-44; she considers, for example, that *Erec et Enide* was conceived for the court of Henry II. Elsewhere ('King Arthur as Villain in the Thirteenth-century Romance *Yder*', *RMS*, 6 (1980), 31-44) she argues that *Yder* must be seen in the light of King John's conflict with the barons and that it was written in the sphere of Glastonbury Abbey.

22. Roberts maintains ('Geoffrey of Monmouth's *Historia*', 101-2) that the themes of *Historia Regum Britanniae* are 'the unity of the Island of Britain, symbolized by the Crown of London, the sign of a single kingship, of the loss of sovereignty to the English, and of the national renewal and the restoration of British hegemony, expressed in prophetic terms'.

23. On the English identification of *Anglia* with *Britannia* see F. Liebermann, *Über die Leges Anglorum saeculo XIII. ineunte* (Halle 1896), 6-9.

24. By creating his son Prince of Wales, moreover, Edward I coopted the Welsh royal line into the English one.

25. The most useful general summaries of Arthurian materials in medieval English historical writings remain Fletcher 1966, and Laura Keeler, *Geoffrey of Monmouth and the Late Latin Chroniclers 1300-1500* (Berkeley, Cal., 1946). For English texts see Matheson, 'King Arthur and the Medieval English Chronicles'; also E.D. Kennedy, 'Chronicles and Other Historical Writings', in Hartung *Manual*, VIII.

26. See Parsons, 'The Second Exhumation', 173.

27. *Adami de Domerham Historia de Rebus Gestis Glastoniensibus*, ed. T. Hearne, 2 vols (Oxford, 1727), II, 587-9.

28. Parsons, 'The Second Exhumation', 176.

29. See R.S. Loomis, 'Edward I, Arthurian Enthusiast', *Speculum*, 28 (1953), 114-27. For a cautionary note concerning Edward's supposed identification of himself as Arthur, however, see M. Prestwich, *Edward I* (Berkeley and Los Angeles, 1988), 120-2; also T. Summerfield, 'The Arthurian References in Pierre de Langtoft's *Chronicle*', in Lacy 1996b, 187-208 (197): 'In Langtoft's *Chronicle* the point is made that the king of England is justified in his territorial ambitions, that he is part of a long line of legitimate rulers, stretching beyond the Norman Conquest, but that his ambitions can be realized only by using generosity and reconciliation to avoid discord.'

30. 'Reading for England', 324-5. For references to different versions of the *Brut* – as Matheson points out, one of the most popular and influential 'Arthurian' narratives of the Middle Ages – see J.P. Carley and J. Crick, 'Constructing Albion's Past: An Annotated Edition of *De Origine Gigantum*', *AL*, 13 (1995), 41-114 (44-50) and references cited therein.

31. See Carley and Crick, 'Constructing Albion's Past', 54-69.

32. For example, the 1291 return from Glastonbury, a copy of which survives in the documents prefacing the monastery's Great Cartulary (written *c*. 1340), notes that:

> In historiis Britonum inuenitur quod rex Arthurus regem Scocie interfecit in bello, et precipue in uita Sancte Gilde capitulo secundo, qui Gildas Britonum historiographus magnus fuit et precipuus, et frater Hoelis regis Scocie quem occidit Arthurus, et Scocia subiugata rediit cum triumpho.

(*In the histories of the Britons it is recorded that King Arthur killed the king of Scotland in battle; see in particular the second chapter of the Life of Gildas. And this Gildas was a great and distinguished historian of the Britons and brother of Hoel, King of Scotland, whom Arthur killed, and by this means having subjugated Scotland returned home in triumph.*)

For the Latin original see *The Great Chartulary of Glastonbury*, ed. A. Watkin, Somerset Record Society 59, 63-4, 3 vols (Frome, 1947-56), I, i-ii. In his *Descriptio Cambriae* Giraldus had earlier used this episode in a different context; that is to explain away Gildas's silence about Arthur:

De Gilda uero, qui adeo in gentem suam acriter inuehitur, dicunt Britones, quod propter fratrem suum Albaniae principem, quem rex Arthurus occiderat, offensus haec scripsit. Unde et libros egregios, quos de gestis Arthuri, et gentis suae laudibus, multos scripserat, audita fratris sui nece, omnes, ut asserunt, in mare proiecit. Cuius rei causa, nihil de tanto principe in scriptis authenticis expressum inuenies.

(*Concerning Gildas, indeed, who bitterly inveighed against his people, the Britons say that he wrote these things in a fit of rage on account of his brother, a ruler of Scotland whom Arthur had killed. Moreover, they assert, when he heard of the murder of his brother, he threw all the excellent books about the deeds of Arthur and the praises of his people, of which he had written many, into the sea. For this reason you will find nothing specific about this great prince in Gildas's authentic writings.*)

For the Latin original see *Descriptio Kambriae*, ed. J.F. Dimock, in *Giraldi Cambrensis Opera*, ed. J.S. Brewer *et al.*, RS 21, 8 vols. (1861-91), VI, 209.

33. Printed in *Anglo-Scottish Relations 1174-1328: Some Selected Documents*, ed. and trans. E.L.G. Stones (Edinburgh and London, 1965), no.30. See also P. Johanek, 'König Arthur und die Plantagenets: Über den Zusammenhang von Historiographie und höfischer Epik in mittelalterlicher Propaganda', *Frühmittelalterliche Studien*, 21 (1987), 346-89 (364-6).

34. See the *Instructiones* and *Processus* of Baldred Bisset; printed in *Anglo-Scottish Relations*, ed. and trans. Stones, no.31. On Scottish portrayals of Arthur see Flora Alexander, 'Late Medieval Scottish Attitudes to the Figure of King Arthur: A Reassessment', *Anglia*, 93 (1975), 17-34; also K.-H. Göller, 'King Arthur in the Scottish Chronicles', in Kennedy 1996, 173-84.

35. See Carley and Crick, 'Constructing Albion's Past', 61.

36. Once again the ploy seems to have succeeded: among the chroniclers Froissart, for example, made explicit comparisons between Edward III and Arthur. Some scholars would, moreover, interpret episodes in the alliterative *Morte Arthure* in the context of Edward's reign.

37. At some point in the second half of the thirteenth century the Glastonbury community had designated Joseph as the founder of the Old Church and the evangelizer of Britain, but there is no evidence that the story had an early currency outside Glastonbury. Valerie Lagorio has posited that Edward's visit in 1331 rekindled Glastonbury's interest both in King Arthur and in Joseph of Arimathea; see 'The Evolving Legend of St Joseph of Glastonbury', *Speculum*, 46 (1971), 209-31 (217).

38. See Johanek, 'König Arthur und die Plantagenets', 363, who has observed that Edward's pilgrimage to Glastonbury might have connections with his Scottish problems.

39. When the Scottish barons wrote to Boniface they claimed that 'Truly the Scots first received the firmness of the faith before the Saxons and Angles received the same faith by four hundred years and more through the revered relics of the apostle St Andrew, carried through a miracle from Greece to Scotland by ship'. See G.W.S. Barrow, *Robert Bruce and the Community of the Realm of Scotland*, rev. 3rd edn. (Edinburgh, 1988), 306; also E.D. Kennedy, 'John Hardyng and the Holy Grail', *AL*, 8 (1989), 185-206 (195).

40. On Arthur's descent from Joseph see *The Chronicle of Glastonbury Abbey : An Edition, Translation and Study of John of Glastonbury's* Cronica siue Antiquitates Glastoniensis Ecclesie, ed. J.P. Carley, trans. D. Townsend (Woodbridge, 1985), 54-5. The same genealogy is found in the marginal note to the earliest surviving copy (s.xiv/xv) of Robert of Avesbury's *De Gestis Mirabilibus Regis Edwardi Tertii* and is copied into the text of subsequent versions.

41. On the former see J.P. Carley, 'A Glastonbury Translator at Work: *Quedam narracio de nobili rege Arthuro* and *De origine gigantum* in their Earliest Manuscript Contexts', *Nottingham French Studies*, 30.2 (1991), 5-12; on the latter Carley and Crick, 'Constructing Albion's Past'.

42. Although there is no specific feature which conclusively ties one translation to the other, their general style as well as their physical proximity suggest that they were prepared by the same individual. They also show strong similarities with John of Glastonbury's *Chronicle* in the use of vernacular source text and in method of dealing with source.

43. For a useful discussion of the attitude of medieval historians towards romance see J.M. Levine, *Humanism and History: Origins of Modern English Historiography* (Ithaca and London, 1987), ch.1. At the most basic level, by Levine's reckoning, the general exegetical frame of mind mitigated against a historical approach: 'a reflex which (whether one accepted the literal level of the text or not) sought always to uncover a hidden meaning, and this was an outlook that was bound to distract from any need to establish the simple facts about the past' (36-7). Matheson, 'King Arthur and the Medieval English Chronicles', notes that although distinctions do blur, the romances tend to examine individual characters from a moral perspective and the chronicles provide a historical framework. See also Rosalind Field, 'Romance as History, History as Romance', in Mills, 163-73, who maintains that the quality of the Matter of Britain romances derives precisely from their conscious historicity, their blurring of the distinction between fiction and history.

44. Charles Wood has argued that the genealogical claims put forward at the start of the Hundred Years War in 1337 acted as a stimulus to Edward's Arthurian interests; see *The Chronicle of Glastonbury Abbey*, ed. Carley, xxvii, n.11. On Edward's proposed Round Table see M. McKisack, *The Fourteenth Century, 1307-99* (Oxford, 1959), 251; also Vale 1982, 67-8.

45. Wood posits that Edward distanced himself from the Glastonbury/Arthur/Joseph tradition in part because of the heterodox aspects of the Grail story; see *The Chronicle of Glastonbury Abbey*, ed. Carley, xxviii.

46. See *The Chronicle of Iohn Hardyng*, ed. H. Ellis (London, 1812), chs. 48, 50, 77, 78.

47. See Kennedy, 'John Hardyng and the Holy Grail', 206, on Hardyng's attitude to the Scots: 'To Hardyng the legend of Joseph of Arimathea and the Holy Grail were of interest because he found them applicable to his basic political theme, the right of England to rule Scotland.'

48. See Felicity Riddy, 'Glastonbury, Joseph of Arimathea and the Grail in John Hardyng's Chronicle' in *The Archaeology and History of Glastonbury Abbey*, (ed.) L. Abrams and J.P. Carley (Woodbridge, 1991), 317-31. Riddy observes (324): 'It seems, then, that the five passages in which "Mewynus" is cited as the authority derive from different sources: from Hardyng's own fertile imagination, from a Scottish chronicler and from a conflation of the *Queste del Saint Graal* and *Prophetie Merlini*.'

49. See *The Chronicle of Glastonbury Abbey*, ed. Carley, p. 52. The material, which is taken from the Vulgate Cycle, is found in a thirteenth-century marginal note to William of Malmesbury's *De Antiquitate Glastoniensis Ecclesie*.

50. If this speculation is accurate, then Galahad's putative Order of the Grail should be seen in the context of Edward's proposed Round Table. Hardyng or the scribe of the manuscript, moreover, attributed to Melkin's authority the information that Galahad's heart was buried at Glastonbury. Kennedy ('John Hardyng and the Holy Grail', 204-5) points out that the inspiration for this episode was probably the events leading up to the burial of Robert Bruce's heart at Melrose Abbey after his death in 1329. The fabrication of the story of the burial of Galahad's heart at Glastonbury makes better sense, of course, in the context of the 1330s than in the second half of the fifteenth century.

51. In the sixteenth century John Bale – admitttedly an unreliable witness – alleged that Melkin wrote a work entitled *De Arthurii mensa rotunda*. John Leland gave Melkin's *Historiae* (a fragment of which he found at Glastonbury among other manuscripts 'admirandae uetustatis') as the source for information about Gawain and Arthur which does not appear in Melkin's prophecy itself and Leland, who spent considerable time examining the Glastonbury library, did not fabricate evidence, no matter how naïvely he did on occasion interpret it.

52. See J.P. Carley, 'A Grave Event: Henry V, Glastonbury Abbey, and Joseph of Arimathea's Bones', in Shichtman, 129-48.

53. It should be noted, however, that at the Council of Siena in 1424, Richard Fleming did announce that Joseph's body had been found at Glastonbury with a leaden plaque identifying it; see Carley, 'A Grave Event', 134-5.

54. On the linking of Joseph's and Arthur's burials see William Worcestre, *Itineraries*, ed. and trans. J.H. Harvey (Oxford, 1969), 296.

55. The first version of Hardyng's chronicle was, for example, written for presentation to Henry VI; the second was intended for Richard, Duke of York and it was then revised for Edward IV.

56. In 'Malory's *Le Morte Darthur* and Court Culture under Edward IV', *AL*, 12 (1993), 133-55, Richard Barber argues that Malory's choice of materials must be seen in the context of tournaments and other chivalric activities at Edward's court. In his epilogue to the translation of Lull's *Book of the Order of Chivalry*, Caxton looked back to the golden age of Arthur and urged Richard III to hold jousts and revive the noble order of chivalry.

57. Lloyd-Morgan ('Qui était l'Arthur des Gallois', 155) argues that Henry chose the name Arthur to be assured of the loyalty of the Welsh.

58. It is quite possible that the sceptics represent a kind of straw man, as N.F. Blake and other critics have argued. Moreover, as Matheson points out ('King Arthur and the Medieval English Chronicles', 264-5) it is the context of almost universal belief in Arthur's historicity which makes the preface so startling.

59. Levine, *Humanism and History*, 45.

60. In their encomia on Prince Arthur's birth, for example, the humanist poets turned to classical models rather than the medieval legend: see D. Carlson, 'King Arthur and Court Poems for the Birth of Arthur Tudor in 1486', *Humanistica Lovaniensia*, 36 (1987), 147-83. See also S. Anglo, 'The British History in Early Tudor Propaganda', *Bulletin of the John Rylands Library*, 44 (1961-2), 17-48 (40): 'But after this first efflorescence there followed a marked decline in every aspect of the British History theme. The Trojan descent, the prophecy to Cadwalader, and Arthurianism were not abandoned; they were simply no longer emphasized.'

61. See J.P. Carley, 'Polydore Vergil and John Leland on King Arthur: the Battle of the Books' in Kennedy 1996, 185-204.

62. See also the comments of John Rastell in *The Pastime of People* (printed London, 1811), 107: 'I wyl nother denye the seyd story of Arthur, nor exort no man presysly to affyrme it; but to let euery man be at his lyberte to beleue ther in what he lyste.'

63. For the Latin original see Leland's *Codrus sive Laus et Defensio Gallofridi Monumetensis Arturii contra Polydorum Vergilium*, ed. T. Hearne in *Joannis Lelandi Antiquarii de rebus Britannicis Collectanea*, 6 vols. (Oxford, 1715; London, 1770, 1774), V, 2-10 (5).

64. *Humanism and History*, 49.

65. Actually, this phrase was found on an 'old' wax seal at Westminster Abbey; see Carley, 'Polydore Vergil and John Leland', 187.

66. Quoted in Carley, 'Polydore Vergil and John Leland', 199, n.13; see C.T. Wood, 'At the Tomb of King Arthur', *Essays in Medieval History: Proceedings of the Illinois Medieval Association*, 8 (1991), 11-12 (14).

67. Interestingly, *c.* 1602, when an 'Academye for the studye of Antiquity and History' was proposed to Elizabeth I, she was reminded that historical precedents had been used by Edward I when he wished to show the legitimacy of his claim to rule Scotland and Henry VIII when he rejected papal authority; see K. Sharpe, *Sir Robert Cotton 1586-1631: History and Politics in Early Modern England* (Oxford, 1979), 27.

3: The Romance Tradition

1. Wace's comment on the veracity of Arthurian legend is from his *Roman de Brut*, l.9793. French texts referred to in this chapter are available in the following editions and translations:

L'Atre Périlleux, ed. Brian Woledge (Paris, 1936); trans. R.G. Arthur in *Three Arthurian Romances: Poems from Medieval France* (London, 1996).

Benoît de Sainte-Maure, *Roman de Troie*, ed. Léopold Constans, 6 vols. (Paris, 1904-12).

Beroul, *The Romance of Tristan*, ed. and trans. N.J. Lacy (New York, 1989).

Jehan Bodel, *La Chanson des Saisnes*, ed. Annette Brasseur, 2 vols. (Geneva, 1989).

Le Chevalier à l'épée, in *Two Old French Gauvain Romances*, ed. R.C. Johnston and D.D.R. Owen (Edinburgh, 1972); trans. R.G. Arthur in *Three Arthurian Romances: Poems from Medieval France*, (London, 1996).

Les Romans de Chrétien de Troyes: I. Erec et Enide, ed. Mario Roques (Paris, 1978); *II. Cligés*, ed. Alexandre Micha (Paris, 1957); *III. Le Chevalier de la charrete*, ed. Mario Roques (Paris, 1958); *Chrétien de Troyes, Yvain*, ed. T.W.B. Reid (Manchester, 1942); *Chrétien de Troyes: le Roman de Perceval ou le Conte du Graal*, ed. William Roach, 2nd edn. (Paris, 1959); trans. D.D.R. Owen, *Chrétien de Troyes: Arthurian Romances* with revd. introduction and bibliography (London, 1993).

Eneas, ed. J.J. Salverda de Grave, 2 vols. (Paris, 1925-9).

La Folie Tristan d'Oxford, ed. Ian Short, Anglo-Norman Texts Society, Plain Texts Series 10 (London, 1993); trans. Judith Weiss in *The Birth of Romance: An Anthology* (London, 1992).

Gui de Warewic: roman du XIIIe siècle, ed. A. Ewert (Paris, 1932-3).

Guillaume le Clerc, *Romance of Fergus* ed. Wilson Frescoln (Philadelphia, 1983); trans. D.D.R. Owen as *Fergus of Galloway* (London, 1991).

Hue de Roteland, *Ipomedon*, ed. A.J. Holden (Paris, 1979).

Lancelot do Lac: The Non-Cyclic Old French Prose Romance, ed. Elspeth Kennedy, 2 vols. (Oxford, 1980).

Marie de France, *Lanval* and *Chevrefoil*, in *Marie de France: Lais*, ed. Alfred Ewert (Oxford, 1960); trans. G.S. Burgess and Keith Busby in *The Lais of Marie de France* (Harmondsworth, 1986).

Payen de Maisières, *La Mule sans frein*, ed. R.C. Johnston and D.D.R. Owen in *Two Old French Gauvain Romances* (New York, 1973).

Robert de Boron, *Le Roman de l'Estoire du Graal*, ed. William Nitze (Paris, 1927).

—— *Merlin, roman du XIIIe siècle*, ed. Alexandre Micha (Geneva, 1980).

—— *The Didot-Perceval*, ed. William Roach (Philadelphia, 1941).

Le Roman de Thèbes, ed. Guy Raynaud de Lage, 2 vols. (Paris, 1966-68).

Le Roman de Tristan en prose, ed. Philippe Menard, vols. 1-8, (Geneve, 1987-95).

Thomas: Les Fragments du roman de Tristan, ed. B.H. Wind, 2nd edn. (Geneva, 1960).

La Version Post-Vulgate de la 'Queste del Saint Graal' et de la 'Mort Artu', Troisième Partie du 'Roman du Graal', ed. Fanni Bogdanow, vols. 1, 2, 4 (Paris, 1991-).

The Vulgate Version of the Arthurian Romances, ed. H.O. Sommer, 8 vols. (Washington, 1908-16).

Lancelot-Grail: The Old French Arthurian Vulgate and Post-Vulgate in Translation, gen. ed. N.J. Lacy (New York, 1992-).

L'Estoire del saint Graal, ed. J.-P. Ponceau, 2 vols. (Paris, 1997).

Lancelot: roman en prose du XIIIe siècle, ed. Alexandre Micha, 9 vols. (Geneva, 1978-83).

La Queste del saint Graal: roman du XIII siècle, ed. Albert Pauphilet (Paris, 1923); trans. P.M. Matarasso (Harmondsworth, 1969).

La Mort le roi Artu: roman du XIII siècle, ed. Jean Frappier (Geneva, 1964); trans. James Cable (Harmondsworth, 1971).

Le Roman de Brut de Wace, ed. Ivor Arnold, 2 vols. (Paris, 1938-40); ed. and trans. Judith Weiss (Exeter, 1998).

2. This is after all the era of Ailred's complaint (*Speculum Caritatis, PL*, vol.190, 565), that his monks preferred Arthurian to sacred story. For a survey of other Latin Arthurian material, see M.L. Day in Lagorio, I, 44-55.

3. John Ganim, 'The Myth of Medieval Romance' in H.R. Bloch and S.G. Nichols (eds.), *Medievalism and the Modernist Temper* (Baltimore and London, 1995), 148-68.

4. Tony Hunt, 'Chrétien de Troyes' Arthurian romance, *Yvain*', in Boris Ford (ed.), *Medieval Literature, II: The European Inheritance* (Harmondsworth, 1983), 126-41 (129).

5. Sarah Kay, *The Chansons de geste in the Age of Romance: Political Fictions* (Oxford, 1995).

6. Felicity Riddy, 'Reading for England: Arthurian Literature and National Consciousness', *BBIAS*, 43 (1991), 314-32.

7. Jean Bodel, *La Chanson des Saisnes*, discussed in R. Guiette, 'Li Conte de Bretaigne sont si vain et plaisant', *Rom.*, 88 (1967), 1-12.

8. Rita Copeland, 'Between Romans and Romantics', *Texas Studies in Literature and Language*, 33 (1991), 215-24, points out the ambivalence of the term 'romance', to designate the vernacular, with its echo of the classical Latin against which it sets itself (216). See Michel Zink, 'Une Mutation de la conscience littéraire: Le langage romanesque à travers des exemples français du XIIe siècle', *Cahiers de civilisation médiévale*, 24 (1981) 3-37, on the possibilities for literary self-justification offered by romance, and Gabrielle Spiegel, *Romancing the Past: The Rise of Vernacular Prose Historiography in Thirteenth-Century France* (Berkeley, Cal., 1993), for useful background to the development of vernacular writings in France during the twelfth and thirteenth centuries.

9. See the discussion in Barbara Nolan, *Chaucer and the Tradition of the 'Roman Antique'* (Cambridge, 1992), Renate Blumenfeld-Kosinski, 'Old French Narrative Genres: Towards the Definition of the *Roman Antique*', *Romance Philology*, 34 (1980), 143-59.

10. Ad Putter, 'Finding Time for Romance: Mediaeval Arthurian Literary History', *MÆ*, 63 (1994), 1-16.

11. Jean Frappier, 'Structure et sens du *Tristan*: version commune, version populaire', *Cahiers de civilisation médiévale*, 6 (1963), 255-86.

12. The best case for the identity of Bledri/Bleheri is made in Bullock-Davies. For a recent claim that Bledri is 'the key to the diffusion of Arthurian tales on the continent' see Keith Busby, 'The Characters and the Setting' in Lacy 1987, 60-1.

13. See Keith Busby in Lacy 1987, 66, and Karl Uitti in Uitti, 126-8, who reads *Perceval* as 'Chrétien's . . . most profound response to the *matière* of Tristan and Iseut'.

14. See Michelle Freeman, 'Marie de France's Poetics of Silence', *PMLA*, 99 (1984), 860-83, Sharon Kinoshita, 'Cherchez la Femme: Feminist Criticism and Marie de France's *Lai de Lanval*', *Romance Notes*, 35 (1994), 273-83, A. C. Spearing, *The Medieval Poet as Voyeur*

(Cambridge, 1994), ch.5, Elizabeth Williams in Fellows, 155-70.

15. See Lacy 1991, 88-9, for a concise discussion of Chrétien's dates. Also Claude Luttrell, *The Creation of the First Arthurian Romance* (London and Evanston, Ill., 1974), for the argument that Chrétien's writing is mainly concentrated in the 1180s, and Tony Hunt's review of Luttrell's work, *BBIAS*, 30 (1978), 209-37.

16. M.-L. Ollier, 'The Author in the Text: The Prologues of Chrétien de Troyes', *Yale French Studies*, 51 (1974), 26-41 (27-9).

17. Tony Hunt in 'Chrétien's Prologues Reconsidered', in Busby 1994, 153-68, notes that in the prologues we see a 'playful, critical and detached manipulator of literary techniques who is not committed to any single or systematic point of view', though one might add that determining 'Chrétien's' perspective is part of his challenge to the reader.

18. Lee Patterson, 157-95, reads the echoes of Troy and the *roman antique* in *Erec* as constituting a critical inquiry into ways of narrating and accounting for historical causation.

19. Roberta Krueger in 'Love, Honor, and the Exchange of Women in *Yvain*: Some Remarks on the Female Reader', *Romance Notes*, 25 (1985), 302-17, examines how Chrétien engineers 'a *mise en question* of the gender relationships embodied in marriage and chivalry'.

20. Chrétien adapts Wace's account of Mordred's final war against Arthur in the episode of Arthur's campaign against Angres; Maddox, 9-12, discusses in detail the treatment of the siege of Windsor.

21. Roberta Krueger, 'Desire, Meaning, and the Female Reader: The Problem in Chrétien's *Charrete*' in Baswell, 31-51.

22. David Hult wittily interprets Godefroi as Chrétien's fiction, 'Author/Narrator/Speaker: The Voice of Authority in Chrétien's *Charrete*', in Kevin Brownlee and Walter Stephens (eds.), *Discourses of Authority in Medieval and Renaissance Literature* (Hanover, 1989), 76-96.

23. Patricia Parker, *Inescapable Romance: Studies in the Poetics of a Mode* (Princeton, 1979), notes deferral as a typical characteristic of romance: ' "Romance" is characterized primarily as a form which simultaneously quests for and postpones a particular end, objective, or object . . .' (4).

24. On the custom see Maddox, 36-48. Simon Gaunt considers the custom further in gender terms in *Gender and Genre in Medieval French Literature* (Cambridge, 1995), 94-5.

25. Stephen Knight, 'From Jerusalem to Camelot: King Arthur and the Crusades' in P.R. Monks and D.D.R. Owen (eds.), *Medieval Codicology, Iconography, Literature, and Translation: Studies for Keith Val Sinclair* (Leiden, 1994), 223-32 (225).

26. For evidence of widespread knowledge across western Europe of the adventures of at least one of Chrétien's heroes, see J.A. Rushing, *Images of Adventure: Ywain in the Visual Arts* (Philadelphia, 1995).

27. See Spiegel's account of medieval thinking on distinctions between prose and verse, *Romancing the Past*, 54-8.

28. Valerie Lagorio, 'The Apocalyptic Mode in the Vulgate Cycle of Arthurian romances', *PQ*, 57 (1978), 1-22; M.V. Guerin, *Fall of Kings and Princes: Structure and Destruction in Arthurian Tragedy* (Stanford, Cal., 1995), 19-86.

29. Spiegel, *Romancing the Past*; J.H.M. Taylor, 'Order from Accident: Cyclic Consciousness at the End of the Middle Ages', in Bart Besamusca, W.P. Gerritsen, Corry Hogetoorn and O.S.H.

Lie (eds.), *Cyclification: The Development of Narrative Cycles in the Chansons de Geste and the Arthurian Romances* (Amsterdam, 1994), 59-73. This fiction may be a knowing comment on Henry II's own political reasons for being interested in hearing from Map of the deaths of Arthur and his knights about whose deeds of arms he has written, as the opening of the *Mort Artu* states. See also M.L. Day's account of 'The Letter from King Arthur to Henry II: Political Use of the Arthurian Legend in *Draco Normannicus*', in Burgess 1985, 153-7.

30. As Fanni Bogdanow, *The Romance of the Grail: A Study of the Structure and Genesis of a Thirteenth-Century Arthurian French Prose Romance* (Manchester, 1966), reconstructs this cycle, it consists of an *Estoire del saint Graal*, a modified version of the Merlin legend which includes the account of Arthur's begetting of Mordred, and the tale of Balain, and, in place of the Lancelot material, a series of adventures leading into a reworked *Queste del saint Graal* and *La Mort le roi Artu*. See further the Introduction to her edition of the latter part of this Arthuriad (n.1 above).

31. On the Continent, an example of the impulse to encyclopaedize the Arthurian world finds full realization in Micheau Gonnot's 1470 compilation, the dominant subject of C.E. Pickford's *L'Évolution du roman arthurien en prose vers la fin du moyen âge* (Paris, 1960)

32. White provides a wide range of Arthurian chronicle material in translation.

33. Scotland apparently provides the exception to this in the *Romance of Fergus*, written in continental French by 'Guillaume le clerc', but given an authentic setting in Galloway. For Anglo-Norman romance see Crane 1986. On the absence of Arthurian subjects in Anglo-Norman romance see Rosalind Field in Lawton. Alison Stones, 'Aspects of Arthur's Death in Medieval Illumination' in Baswell, 52-86, discusses possible political reasons for the lack of English Arthurian manuscripts (71-2).

34. *Canterbury Tales*, VII, 3212. For a range of references see Dean, ch.7.

35. Thomas of Woodstock owned a romance on Arthur, two on Merlin and a 'Launcelot', Margaret, Countess of Devon, left three romances, on Tristan, Merlin and 'Arthur de Britaigne', Elizabeth la Zouche left a 'Launcelot' and a 'Tristrem' and Isabel, Duchess of York, a 'Launcelot'. Guy of Warwick's famous bequest to Bordesley Abbey numbered 'le premer levere de Lancelot' among its contents. See Scattergood 1983, 32; C.M. Meale, '". . . alle the bokes that I haue of latyn,englisch, and frensch"; laywomen and their books in late medieval England' in Meale 1993, 128-58 (139); Madeleine Blaess, 'L'Abbaye de Bordesley et les livres de Guy de Beauchamp', *Rom.*, 78 (1957), 511-8.

36. Scattergood, ibid.

37. See Terry Nixon in Keith Busby, Terry Nixon, Alison Stones, Lori Walters (eds.), *Les Manuscrits de Chrétien de Troyes / The Manuscripts of Chrétien de Troyes*, 2 vols. (Amsterdam and Atlanta, Ga., 1993), I (31), and Stones, 'Aspects', 63. The MS contains Benoît, Wace and all of Chrétien's romances placed at the mention of 'aventures' in the time of Arthur and followed by the conclusion of Wace's *Brut*.

38. Lacy 1987, I, appx.

39. The *Perceval* is placed in a manuscript anthology of chronicles of British history, the mid-fourteenth century College of Arms Arundel XIV: a list of knights from Chrétien's *Erec et Enide* has been found in the margin of MS BL Harley 4971, copied in a fourteenth-century Anglo-Norman hand, indicating an interest in this information separate from its narrative context. See also the discussion of the relation between French and English material at this date in Calin, 138-40.

40. The civil war context of both Geoffrey of Monmouth and Malory is to be echoed in the nineteenth century by Mark Twain's *Connecticut Yankee at the Court of King Arthur.*

41. Compare Lacy, 1987, I, ch.2 with Joerg Fichte, 'Grappling with Arthur or Is There an English Arthurian Verse Romance?', in *Poetics: Theory and Practice in Medieval Engish Literature*, ed. Piero Boitani and Anna Torti (Cambridge, 1991), 149-64. See also Anita Guerreau-Jalabert, *Index des motifs dans les romans arthuriens français en vers (XIIe-XIIIe siècles)*, (Geneva, 1992), E. H. Ruck, *An Index of Themes and Motifs in Twelfth-Century French Arthurian Poetry* (Cambridge, 1991).

42. See D. Matthews, 'Translation and Ideology: The Case of *Ywain and Gawain*', *NM*, 76 (1992), 452-63, also Busby's discussion of English versions of Chrétien, 'Chrétien de Troyes English'd', *NM*, 71 (1987), 596-613, and Barron's of the alliterative poets' treatment of French material in Lawton, 70-87. It could be added that the ideological context of academic disciplines has itself institutionalized anachronistic barriers between the study of French- and English-language medieval literatures.

43. See Fichte , 'Grappling with Arthur', for a discussion of the applicability of Jauss's concept of 'horizon of expectation' to Arthurian romance (151).

4: Dynastic Romance

1. The complete edition of the Vulgate Cycle by H.O. Sommer, 8 vols. (Washington, D.C., 1908-16, repr. New York, 1969) is supplemented by partial editions and translations listed in Barron 1987, 270 and in Ch. 3, n.1 above. In its evolution over the first third of the thirteenth century various hands were involved, much of the Vulgate's structure and some of its thematic complexity being prefigured in the work of Robert de Boron, a Burgundian poet who, at the turn of the century, produced a *Joseph d'Arimathie* recasting the history of the Grail from biblical origins, a *Merlin* following its arrival in Britain up to the birth of Arthur, and a *Perceval* in which the quest for the Grail becomes the goal of a society doomed to eventual disaster, which survive partially in their original verse forms as well as the prose adaptations which helped to shape the Vulgate (Lacy 1991, 115-6, 285-6, 373).

Arthur, The Legend of King Arthur, King Arthur's Death

2. See R.W. Ackerman in Loomis 1959, 481, 484 and John Finlayson, 'The Source of *Arthur*: An Early Fifteenth-Century Verse Chronicle', *N&Q*, 7 (1960), 46-7.

3. See Derek Pearsall, 'The Development of Middle English Romance', *Medieval Studies*, 27 (1965), 91-116 (94-5).

4. See John Finlayson, 'The Source of *Arthur*', 47.

5. Assonantal rhyme is used in 81-2; 89-92 and 105-8 use alternate rhyme *abab* in lieu of couplets, perhaps implying that there may have been a stanzaic source for this section.

6. See R.H. Wilson, 'Malory and the Ballad *King Arthur's Death*', *Medievalia et Humanistica*, 6, (1975), 139-49 (139); Valerie Lagorio 'The Glastonbury Legends and the English Arthurian Grail Romances', *NM*, 79 (1978), 359-66 (360). On Percy's subdivision, accepted in Severs *Manual* (nos.17, 24), see C.B. Millican, 'The Original of the Ballad *King Arthur's Death* in the Percy Folio MS', *PMLA*, 46 (1931), 1020-24 (1020).

7. See C.B. Millican (n.6 above), whose comparison of the two texts also incidentally demonstrates the corrupt state of the Percy Folio version.

8. See D.C. Fowler, *A Literary History of the Popular Ballad* (Durham, N. C., 1968), 133.

9. See R.H. Wilson, 'Malory and the Ballad', 144-5. In the course of popular transmission the names and roles of Bedevere and Lucan (Lukin) have been reversed, and it is the latter who disposes of Excalibur (Escalberd) in *The Death*.

10. A contemporary recorded what he ironically referred to as this 'sollem' song, noting 'more of the song is thear, but I gatt it not' (*Wheatley*, III, 24-5).

11. Malory uses the name Ryence for the King of Wales, but the beard-trimmed mantle belongs to the Giant of St Michael's Mount (*Vinaver*, 120-1). However, 'Kyng Ryown of jeawntez' and his bearded cloak feature in Lovelich's *Merlin* (*Kock*, 8205-18) and in the English Prose *Merlin* (*Wheatley*, §VII, 114-15) where Kay is also a chivalrous character. The romance story of 'the beard toll' transmitted in this ballad is also alluded to by Spenser in *The Faerie Queene*; see A.B. Friedman, 'Percy's Folio Manuscript Revalued', *JEGP*, 53 (1954), 524-31 (527).

12. See Richard Barber, *King Arthur in Legend and History* (London 1961), ch.9.

Joseph of Arimathie

13. That the French *Joseph d'Arimathie* might also sometimes be perceived by contemporaries primarily as a Passion narrative is suggested by a scribal colophon in a recently discovered MS of Robert de Boron's *Joseph*. See A.E. Knight, 'A Previously Unknown Prose *Joseph d'Arimathie*', *Romance Philology*, 21 (1967), 174-83.

14. See V.M. Lagorio, 'The Evolving Legend of St Joseph of Glastonbury', *Speculum*, 46.2 (1971), 209-31; 'The Glastonbury Legends' (n.6 above), 359-66.

15. See M.L. Samuels 'Some Applications of Middle English Dialectology', *ES*, 44 (1963), 81-94 and K. Sajavaara 'The Relationship of the Vernon and Simeon Manuscripts', *NM*, 68 (1967), 428-40.

16. See *Skeat*, xiv-xv, J.N.L. O'Loughlin in Loomis 1959, 520-8, W.R.J. Barron, '*Joseph of Arimathie* and the *Estoire del Saint Graal*', *MÆ*, 33 (1964), 184-94 (184), V.M. Lagorio, 'The *Joseph of Arimathie*: English Hagiography in Transition', *Medievalia et Humanistica*, 6 (1975), 91-101 (92-3), and James Noble, Review of *Lawton* in *Speculum*, 60 (1985), 428. Barron's study offers a useful methodological model for exploring redaction techniques, but warns of 'the dangers involved in identifying the source of *Joseph . . .* in specific texts of the *Estoire*' (193).

17. See the reviews of *Lawton* by V.M. Lagorio in *Quondam et Futurus*, 2 (1984), 1-2 and James Noble in *Speculum*, 60 (1985), 427-8 (428).

18. See Barron (n.16 above), 194 and Lagorio (ibid.), 92ff.

19. See respectively V.M. Lagorio 'St. Joseph of Arimathea and Glastonbury: A 'New' Pan-Brittonic Saint', *Trivium*, 6 (1971), 59-69 (60) and K. Sajavaara (n.15 above), 428-40.

20. The definitions are respectively those of J.P. Oakden, *Alliterative Poetry in Middle English*, single vol. reprint (Manchester, 1968), II, 41; Mehl, 277, n.5; *Lawton*, xli; and James Noble, Abstract in *BBIAS*, 45 (1993), no.508.

21. See James Noble 'The Grail and its Guardian: Evidence of Authorial Intent in the Middle English *Joseph of Arimathea*', *Quondam et Futurus*, 1 (1991), 1-14.

22. Cf. the punishment of Joseph's Jewish captors, designated 'gruesome sarcasm' (*Lawton*, p.22, notes to 12-20). If Chaucer wrote his *Prioress's Tale* with satirical intent, perhaps it was directed against a particular class of militant Christian reader rather than an individual.

23. See *Lawton*, xxxiv and p.31, notes to 258-312. Lagorio (n.16 above) suggests that this may be because of a lack of ecclesiastical sanction for the Grail 'concerning which the English were more scrupulous than the French' (95).

24. See Noble, 'The Grail and its Guardian', 2, 10.

25. While comparisons with sources are immensely informative, excessive familiarity with them can create a kind of editorial 'grid' through which the modern reader has the sensation of peering at the medieval English text. For example, Evelac, who is not named by the English poet until line 214, and his queen who remains permanently anonymous, are both alluded to by their *Estoire* names throughout Lawton's edition. But it is perhaps significant that Evelac's name is reserved by the English poet until after the king has seen his visions, momentous steps toward his understanding of the Christian mysteries. Naming and renaming constitute an important motif in this narrative where Evelac and Seraphe are climactically transformed into Mordreins and Naciens at baptism (683-4; 694-5). A contemporary medieval audience being initiated into these stories in English because their French was rudimentary or non-existent (and why else were they translated?) would have been free of a modern editor's assumptions. We need

not always read these romances from the point of view of the medieval translator (who would, of course, have been aware of making changes) or of a modern scholar deciphering the artist's method.

26. Cf. Noah and God in 'The Building of the Ark' in *York Mystery Plays* ed. Richard Beadle and Pamela King (Oxford 1984), lines 148-56; and Julian of Norwich *A Revelation of Love*, ed. Marion Glasscoe (Exeter 1976), ch.29, 30.

Henry Lovelich's *History of the Holy Grail*

27. The title of this work, *The History of the Holy Grail by Henry Lovelich*, is that of the nineteenth-century editor, Furnivall, who also divided it into 'chapters' according to scribal divisions noted in the manuscript which were derived in turn from divisions in the source.

28. For a comparison with the complete narrative of the *Estoire*, see Sommer, I. Lovelich's surviving text begins at chapter XII.

29. See R.W. Ackerman 'Henry Lovelich's *Merlin*, *PMLA* 67 (1952), 473-84 (476).

30. Ibid, 476, citing the description of Lovelich as 'Civis et pelliparius' in Harry Barton's will (1435). Perhaps the guild to which Lovelich and Barton belonged had a special interest in literature which linked the history of Jerusalem with that of England via a saint associated with the Virgin Mary and the Holy Blood: in York and Beverley, for example, in the fifteenth century the Skinners were responsible for presenting the pageant of 'The Entry into Jerusalem'. See P.J.P. Goldberg, 'Craft Guilds, the Corpus Christi Play and Civic Government' in *York 600, the Government of Medieval York: Essays in Commemoration of the 1396 Royal Charter*, ed. Sarah Rees Jones, (York, 1997), 141-63. Another skinner, William Gregory, had a copy of *The Seven Sages of Rome*, which includes a Merlin story, in his commonplace book, MS Egerton 1995 (see Pearsall 1977, 300).

31. See V.M. Lagorio 'The Glastonbury Legends' (n.6 above), 361. We need not necessarily assume, of course, that Lovelich's work was completed before Barton's death in 1434.

32. See R.W. Ackerman 'Henry Lovelich's *Merlin*', 478-83

33. Consequently, he also omits Celidoyne's reproaches to his father, a passage from the *Estoire* which may have influenced Malory's treatment of the relationship between Lancelot and Galahad.

34. Examples are Naciens's reaction to the miraculous sword and scabbard, proverbially expressed as 'ʒit cowde he not putten the ex in þe helve' (*fit the axe in the helve*, i.e. solve the problem) (§28, 410); or the pagan Mathegrans's relieved response to Josephes's lecture on the Trinity: 'In three goddis thou belevest also?' (§49). A similar instance of ingenuous but enlivening dialogue occurs in Lovelich's *Merlin* when the midwives question Merlin's mother about his precocious speech (*Kock*, 1047-54), a passage which is related much more briefly and decorously in the French and the English Prose *Merlins* (Sommer, II, 13-14; *Wheatley*, §1, pp.15-16).

35. Lovelich's wife Margaret is also mentioned in Harry Barton's will (Ackerman (n.29 above), 476).

36. For example, *Furnivall*, §49, 395-6; §50, 227-9; §52, 1114-15; §53, 192-8, 274-84.

Henry Lovelich's *Merlin* and the prose *Merlin*

37. See R.W. Ackerman in Loomis 1959, 488 and *Wheatley*, IV, lxii-lxix, cxii.

38. See C.M. Meale 'The Manuscripts and Early Audience of the Middle English Prose *Merlin*' in Adams, 92-111 (93-4). Cf. *Wheatley*, pp.315, 15-317, 24.

39. Any comprehensive comparison of all the English *Merlins* is hampered at present by the lack of good modern editions of Lovelich and the Prose *Merlin* establishing criteria by which they can be appreciated as distinct linguistic versions of narrative as well as a peculiarly insular style of writing. Cf. Pearsall 1977, 224. Lovelich acknowledges his French source in his *Merlin* (*Kock*, 10245-52), as he did in his *Grail*, but the poor quality of his text, including 'more than half a dozen errors which must be regarded as serious' (R.W. Ackerman, 'Henry Lovelich's *Merlin*', 483), suggests that he was negligent as well as baffled by a poor exemplar.

40. See C.M. Meale (n.38 above), 98-9 and K. Stern (Hodder), 'The Middle English Prose *Merlin*' in Adams, 112-22 (120-1).

41. Pearsall's (n.3 above) devastating judgement 'grotesquely inept' is fairly typical of those based on purely literary criteria.

Of Arthour and of Merlin

42. The work attributed to Robert de Boron has been edited by A. Micha, *Merlin: Roman du xiiie siècle*, Textes Littéraires Français, 281 (Geneva and Paris, 1979). The remainder may be found in H.O. Sommer (n.1 above), II, *Lestoire de Merlin*.

43. See *Macrae-Gibson*, II, 19-32.

44. Laȝamon's nationalistic purpose is reviewed in the introductory essay to *Laȝamon's 'Arthur': The Arthurian Section of Laȝamon's Brut*, ed. and trans. W.R.J. Barron and S.C. Weinberg (Harlow, 1989), li-lvi.

45. See *Macrae-Gibson*, II, 65-75.

46. J. Frappier ('Vues sur les conceptions courtoises dans la littératures d'oc et d'oil au xiie siècle', *Cahiers de civilisation médiévale*, 2 (1959), 135-56) regards the connection between love and chivalric prowess as characteristically Arthurian..

47. Geoffrey's *Historia* (§100) makes human infatuation more believable than diabolic suggestion, and Wace's *Roman de Brut* (6947-80) treats the whole scene with courtly elegance and romantic motivation.

48. See G. V. Smithers (ed.), *Kyng Alisaunder*, 2 vols., EETS 227, 237 (London, 1952, 1957), II, 28-40.

49. See J.D. Burnley, 'Comforting the Troops: An Epic Moment in Popular Romance', in Mills, 175-86.

50. Transcribed here from the version in Cambridge University Library MS Ff.4.9:

I warne ȝow at the begynnyng	And many other gestes
I wylle make no vayn carpyng	And namely whan they come to festes,
Off dedys of armes ne off armours,	Ne off the lyf off Beuys of Hamtoun
As don these mynstralles and gestours	That was a knyght off grete renown,
That makyn carpyng in many place	Ne off Sir Gy of Warwyke.
Off Octouian and off Isambrace	

51. See Michael Chesnutt, 'Minstrel Reciters and the Enigma of the Middle English Romance', *Culture and History*, 2 (1987), 48-67.

52. See T.A. Shonk, 'A Study of the Auchinleck Manuscript: Bookmen and Bookmaking in the Early Fourteenth Century', *Speculum*, 60 (1985), 71-91 and I.C. Cunningham and

J.E.C. Mordkoff, 'New Light on the Signatures in the Auchinleck Manuscript', *Scriptorium*, 36, no. 2 (1982), 280-92.

53. Linguistic evidence alone is not conclusive. K.A. Rand Schmidt, *The Authorship of the Equatorie of the Planetis* (Cambridge, 1993), 43. Dr Rand Schmidt points out that Samuels Type II language (of which Auchinleck has been cited as an exemplar) extends beyond the city proper into Essex. The *Linguistic Atlas of Later Middle English* (Angus McIntosh, M.L. Samuels, Michael Benskin, 5 vols (Aberdeen, 1985)) considers the main hand of the manuscript to be from Middlesex, and cites only Hand 3 as of London origin.

54. See Carol Meale, 'The Compiler at Work: John Colyns and BL MS Harley 2252', in Pearsall 1983, 82-103.

55. This is made clear in the opening lines of the poem in Auchinleck, quoted from G.V. Smithers, 'Two Newly-Discovered Fragments from the Auchinleck Manuscript', *MÆ*, 18 (1949), 1-11:

> Lord Ihesu, kyng of glorie,
> Swiche auentour and swiche victorie
> Þou sentest king Richard,
> Miri it is to heren his stori
> And of him to han in memorie,
> Þat neuer no was couward
> Bokes men makeþ of Latyn,
> Clerkes witen what is þerin,
> Boþe Almaundes and Pikard;
> Romaunce make folk of Fraunce
> Of kniჳtes þat were in destaunce,
> Þat dyed þurth dint of sward:
> 　Of Rouland, and of Oliuer,
> And of þe oþer dusse per,
> Of Alisander, and Charlmeyn,
> And Ector, þe gret werrer,
>
> And of Danys le fiz Oger,
> Of Arthour, and of Gaweyn.
> As þis romaunce of Freyns wrouჳt,
> Þat mani lewed no knowe nouჳt,
> In gest as so we seyn;
> Þis lewed no can Freyns non,
> Among an hundred vnneþe on;
> In lede is nouჳt to leyn
> 　Noþeles, wiþ gode chere
> Fele of hem wald y-here
> Noble gestes, ich vnderstond,
> Of douჳti kniჳtes of Inglond.
> Þerfore now ichil ჳou rede
> Of a king douhti of dede,
> King Richard, þe werrour best
> Þat men findeþ in ani gest.
>
> 　　　　　(Auchinleck MS f.326ʳa)

On the Englishness of Auchinleck, see further Turville-Petre 1996, 108-41.

The Alliterative *Morte Arthure*

56. All quotations from this text will be from the excellent edition by Mary Hamel (*Hamel 1984*) cited by line number here.

57. See Ranulph Higden, *Polychronicon*, ed. C. Babington and J. R. Lumsby, 9 vols., RS, 41, 9 vols. (London, 1865-86), V, 332-9. John Trevisa, who translated Hidgen's work into English prose (*c.* 1385-7) is very much less sceptical about the historicity of Geoffrey's King Arthur and appends a comment in his translation (also reproduced in this edition of the *Polychronicon*) defending the imperial figure of King Arthur and justifying possibile disparities in the naming of personnel in historical narratives. Boccaccio also expresses some scepticism in his epitome of Arthurian history in *De Casibus Virorum Illustrium*: see E. Kennedy, 'Generic Intertextuality in the English Alliterative *Morte Arthure*' (Lacy 1996, 41-56). J.S.P. Tatlock discusses the anachronistic representation of the Roman Empire in Arthur's time in the *Historia Regum Britanniae* (Arthur's Roman antagonists

appear to represent the Roman empire at the height of its power) in 'Contemporaneous Matters in Geoffrey of Monmouth', *Speculum*, 6 (1931), 206-24.

58. For Langtoft's account, see Thomas Wright (ed.), *The Chronicle of Pierre de Langtoft*, RS, 47, 2 vols. (London, 1866-8), I, 216, here compared with the Vulgate version of the *Historia*, ed. N. Wright (Cambridge, 1985), §§157-76. See *Hamel*, pp.34-8 for further discussion of the variations and Lesley Johnson, 'King Arthur at the Crossroads to Rome', in Ni Cuilleanain, 87-112 (95-7). There is also some variation, if not confusion, in the vernacular narratives which follow Geoffrey of Monmouth's text on the identity of the Emperor of Rome who summons Arthur to his court: see *Hamel*, note on 86-7. In Thomas of Castleford's *Chronicle* there are two emperors of Rome at this time (Eckhardt 1996, 22752-7).

59. See *Hamel*, pp.4-14, 79-80 for further discussion of the relationship between the *Morte Arthure* and Malory's 'Tale of Arthur and Lucius' (Winchester MS).

60. In Malory the campaign is a success and is not interrupted by news of Mordred's rebellion; it is a strenuous, but relatively uncomplicated, colonizing episode in the history of Arthur's reign. Obviously Malory has to alter some important plot details in his version and thereby eliminates some of the ambivalences about how to judge the actions of Arthur and his men which distinguish the narrative of the *Morte Arthure*.

61. The pointless loss of children, especially the 'foster sons' of Arthur's chamber, is a leitmotiv of the narrative. It first appears in the depiction of the grotesque tyrant, the Giant of Mont St Michel who feasts on children, mainly boys (842-51, 1025-8); for references to the killing of Arthur's 'foster sons', see 1821-3, 2952, 2957, 2962-5. The actions of Mordred, 'a childe of [the king's] chambyre' (690) complicate the motif (3776); Arthur's final action is to order the killing of Mordred's children (4320-2). The figure of the grieving widow first appears, literally, in the episode on Mont St Michel (950-3); see *Hamel*, note on 4322 for further comments on the use of this figure in the poem. That Arthur's emotional response to the death of Gawain is (pejoratively) too 'feminine' has previously been suggested by his men (3977-8); with the death of so many of his knights in the last battle, Arthur takes this image of the grieving woman upon himself and thus extends the notion of his 'foster sons' to include all his best (dead) knights. See *Hamel*, note on 4143 for further comments on the handling of father/son relationships in the final battle.

62. Because the poem focuses so intensely on relations between élite men, as expressed through the code of knighthood, it has been identified by some modern critics as working in the heroic/epic mode, or as belonging to the *chanson de geste* genre (see *Hamel*, p.38 and references therein). However, the use of such terms is helpful only if they do not carry the implication, at the same time, that the poet is working in an archaic literary mode that predates the development of romance. Many of the problems of determining the genre of the *Morte Arthure* arise from modern misunderstandings of the capacious category of medieval feudal narratives set in the past, in circulation in fourteenth-century England, which resists tidy classification. For a discussion of the notion of 'homosocial relations' in more general terms, see E. K. Sedgwick, *Between Men: English Literature and Male Homosocial Desire* (New York, 1985). The élite women who feature in the text, for example Queen Guinevere, Duchess of Lorraine, Duchess of Brittany, are viewed primarily in terms of how they affect relations between men of power. The normative relationship between noble males and females seems to be signalled by the image used in

2857-8; its abusive form is figured as rape (most graphically in the violent account of the death of the duchess of Britanny). The female form is also used to figure forces beyond men's control (the 'Duchess' of Fortune). These aspects of the poem await further detailed discussion.

63. For discussion of the anachronistic features already built in to Geoffrey of Monmouth's narrative see J. S. P. Tatlock, 'Contemporaneous Matters in Geoffrey of Monmouth' and for an analysis of the topical representation of Arthur's antagonists, see Mary Hamel, 'The "Christening" of Sir Priamus in the Alliterative *Morte Arthure*', *Viator*, 13 (1982), 295-307. On the way in which the poem brings together two levels of time in the representation of the Roman Empire as if it were also the Holy Roman Empire, see *Hamel*, note on 3210. The issues of anachronism and topicality will feature again in my discussion. There seems to me little doubt that the composer of the *Morte Arthure* was very self-conscious about the syncretisms of the world he creates in the poem, choosing at times to conflate epochs, to conflate Britain and England, at other times to remind his English audience of the 'otherness' of this past world. For an opposite view, see Britton J. Harwood, 'The Alliterative *Morte Arthure* as a Witness to Epic' in M. C. Amodio (ed.), *Oral Poetics in Middle English Poetry* (New York, 1994), 241-86.

64. This point will be developed and exemplified later in my discussion. Lee Patterson makes a persuasive case for the composer of the *Morte Arthure* being a sophisticated thinker about the making of history in 'The Romance of History and the Alliterative *Morte Arthure*' in Patterson, 197-230.

65. Occasions for more abstract discussions about rights of sovereignty, the rights of a conqueror, etc. are to be found in the *Historia Regum Britanniae* (*Wright* 1985, 157-76) in, for example, the exchanges of letters between the Roman Emperor and Arthur in which both cite historical precedents to support their claims over the other; in the discussions in the council scene in the Giant's Tower; in the speeches that take place on the battlefield as the leaders of both sides encourage their men to fight in a righteous cause.

66. That Arthur here possesses two named swords, Excalibur and Clarent, which have very different functions, might be taken as symptomatic of the developed interest in the poem in the theory and practice of kingship. See *Hamel*, note on 4193. For the developed interest in the 'laws of war' in this poem, see Elizabeth Porter, 'Chaucer's Knight, the Alliterative *Morte Arthure* and Medieval Laws of War: a Reconsideration', *NMS*, 27 (1983), 56-78.

67. For *Arthur* (*Furnivall* 1864), see pp.74-5 above. *Arthur* gives special emphasis to Arthur's campaign against Rome and provides an unambiguous representation of the righteousness of Arthur's cause, for which its narrator solicits prayers from the audience. The strategies and interests of this narrative offer interesting comparisons and contrasts with those of the *Morte Arthure*. See *Arthur*, 433-42 for King Arthur's prayer that God should protect Christian people against the 'heþen men'. For examples of how the Saracen component of Lucius's allies may be given added emphasis in Middle English chronicle accounts, see Robert of Gloucester's *Chronicle* (*Wright* 1887, 4462); Robert Mannyng's *Chronicle* (*Sullens*, MS L only, 11693). For the special interest in the subject of crusades in England in the 1390s, which forms part of the background to the composition of the *Morte Arthure* (and other vernacular texts), see Mary Hamel, 'The Siege of Jerusalem as a Crusading Poem', in B. N. Sargent-Bauer (ed.), *Journeys Towards God: Pilgrimage and Crusade* (Michigan, 1992), 177-94.

68. For the avowing structure, introduced into the council scene in the *Morte Arthure*, see *Hamel*, pp.44-6 and note on 296-7.

69. See Hamel, 'The "Christening" of Sir Priamus', 299-300.

70. That the Roman senators and knights are Christians is brought into focus for the audience, for example, at 502; 1506-7; 2314-19. But Lucius's speech of encouragement to his men, 2032-43, refers equally to Roman conquests in Christendom and those in 'Sarazenes' lands. The ambivalent representation of the Roman side is part of the legacy of the *Historia Regum Britanniae*, but the *Morte Arthure* poet may also be influenced by the role of the Romans in one of his sources, *The Siege of Jerusalem*, where they play the role of crusaders. See *Hamel*, pp.46-51.

71. On the technical precision of this summons, see Juliet Vale, 'Law and Diplomacy in the Alliterative *Morte Arthure*', *NMS* 23 (1979), 31-46 (33-6) and Britton Harwood, 'The Alliterative *Morte Arthure* as a Witness to Epic', 265-6.

72. Wolfgang Obst, 'The Gawain-Priamus Episode in the Alliterative *Morte Arthure*', *Studia Neophilogica*, 57 (1985), 9-18 (13); Obst also underestimates the complication of the spiritual allegiances involved in the battle between Arthur and Lucius; it is not just a struggle of 'Arthur's christian empire against the heathen empire of Lucius' (11).

73. The emperor claims Uther made 'fewtee' (*fealty*; 112). Arthur does not explicitly reply to this charge (repeated by the senator in his report to Lucius, 521), but later Gawain seems to concede that Uther's holdings were exceptional (1310).

74. For detailed analyses of this dream and its interpretation, see Mary Hamel, 'The Dream of a King: The Alliterative *Morte Arthure* and Dante', *Chau. Rev.*, 14 (1980), 298-312; Lee Patterson, 'The Romance of History and the Alliterative *Morte Arthure*'; L. Johnson, 'King Arthur and the Roads to Rome' (100-5).

75. See for example 'oure cheualrous knyghtez' (1362); 'oure men' (3785); 'oure prynce' – a reference to Arthur (4224). Wolfgang Obst comments on this feature in 'The Gawain-Priamus Episode', 12-13.

76. For the significance and uses of the dragon symbol, see *Hamel*, pp.46-50, the further references therein, and her notes on 816-17, 1252, 2057. There are many possible small-scale examples of associative connections being set up between separate characters and incidents; see for example, the description of the people being tormented by the display of military might (842, 3153); the recall of the beard-shaving habits of the giant (998) in Arthur's treatment of the defeated Romans (2330); Arthur's gathering up the blood of Gawain and bloodying his beard in kissing the corpse (3970-2) may evoke a resonance of the Giant's blood-smeared mouth (1090). How to interpret these associative connections, though, remains an issue for the poem's audience.

77. For further discussions of the (controversial) evidence on turning points in Arthur's history see the essays cited in n.74 above, Elizabeth Porter, 'Chaucer's Knight, the Alliterative *Morte Arthure* and the Medieval Laws of War'; Wolfgang Obst, 'The Gawain-Priamus Episode'; J. Finlayson, 'The Concept of the Hero in the *Morte Arthure*' in Arno Esch (ed.), *Chaucer und seine Zeit: Symposium für Walter C. Schirmer* (Tübingen, 1967), 249-74; J. Eadie, 'The Alliterative *Morte Arthure*: Structure and Meaning', *ES* 63 (1982), 1-12. On the issue of genre, see E. Kennedy, 'Generic Intertextuality in the English Alliterative *Morte Arthure*'.

78. For the book-length studies, see Matthews, Göller 1981. Matthews and the contributors to Göller's collection share the view that Arthur's sin is the most important causal factor in the sequence of history recounted in the *Morte Arthure*; a view which has been challenged by many since.

79. I am indebted particularly to the work of Larry Benson and John Finlayson.

80. Given the similarity between the various chronicle versions of Arthurian history, as well as their respective variants, it is not always possible to be definite about which particular version the poet is using at any one point in his text. For a detailed consideration of the evidence of particular borrowings from Geoffrey of Monmouth, Wace, Laȝamon and Mannyng, see *Hamel*, pp.34-8. Hamel does not seem to have considered the possible influence of other Middle English chronicles on the *Morte Arthure*, most especially Robert of Gloucester's *Chronicle*, but also Thomas of Castleford's *Chronicle*; this topic awaits further detailed investigation.

81. See John Finlayson, 'Arthur and the Giant of St. Michael's Mount', *MÆ*, 33 (1964), 112-20, for further discussion and the suggestion that the development of the giant figure in the alliterative poem owes something to Chrétien de Troyes's *Yvain*. The recasting of Arthur's Whitsun coronation feast in the opening frames of the *Morte Arthure* narrative would offer another good example of the way this writer so effectively redeploys his chronicle material. See Britton Harwood, 'The Alliterative *Morte Arthure* as a Witness to Epic', 263-71.

82. See the *Historia Regum Britanniae* (*Wright* 1985, 165) for the account of Ritho. Arthur's reminiscence opens up a historical gap for the audience of the narrative who have had no information about Arthur's earlier adventures on Mount Arvaius. This may be the reason why some later redactors omit any mention of Ritho; there is no mention of him, for example, in Robert of Gloucester's *Chronicle*.

83. The duration of the giant's oppressions – he has been present in the area for seven years according to the Templar who first reports the outrages to Arthur – casts a critical shadow over the image of Arthur as an ideal governor; see Robert Warm, 'King Arthur and the Giant of Mont St Michel', *NMS* (forthcoming). For the Templar's involvement in this scene, see *Hamel*, note on 841. For a interesting reading of the giant as a grotesque embodiment of the peasantry, which rather underestimates the degree of regnal imitation involved in the figure, see Britton Harwood, 'The Alliterative *Morte Arthure* as a Witness to Epic', 275-8.

84. Mary Hamel, 'Adventure as Structure in the Alliterative *Morte Arthure*', *Arthurian Interpretations*, 3 (1988), 37-48.

85. For the sources of Gawain's adventure here, see *Hamel*, pp.38-42, and for a detailed analysis of the complex figure of Sir Priamus see Mary Hamel, 'The "Christening" of Sir Priamus'. Wolfgang Obst comments on the structural parallels between this episode and that on Mont St Michel in 'The Gawain- Priamus Episode'.

86. Typically, however, for this poem, the symbolic dimension of this conversion is modified by a gesture towards the material factors which may determine allegiance breaking. When Priamus leads his men from the side of the Duke of Lorraine to fight for 'the ryall rowte of þe Rownde Table' (2919), the men make their case for changing sides on the grounds that the Duke has not paid them (2925-33).

87. See especially, Mary Hamel 'Adventure as Structure in the Alliterative *Morte Arthure*'; George Keiser, 'The Theme of Justice in the Alliterative *Morte Arthure*', *Annuale Mediaevale*, 16 (1975), 94-109. The play on the identity of the protagonists involved in all three episodes (Mont St Michel, Gawain/Priamus, Arthur and Craddoke) is another connecting feature.

88. George Parks, 'King Arthur and the Roads to Rome', *JEGP*, 45 (1946), 164-70. See also *Hamel*, pp.36-7 for a further discussion of the reworking involved here and, for another example of the transfer of material from the Belinus section to that of Arthur, see her note on 60-3.

89. See R. Blenner-Hassett and F. P. Magoun, 'The Italian Campaign of Belin and Brenne in the *Bruts* of Wace and Lawman', *PQ*, 21 (1942), 385-90.

90. See L. D. Benson, 'The Date of the Alliterative *Morte Arthure*', in J. B. Bessinger and R. K. Raymo (eds.), *Medieval Studies Presented to Lillian Herlands Hornstein* (New York, 1969), 19-40; *Hamel*, notes on 150 and 3140-1. But it is not only in these sections that such allusions to contemporary north Italian politics are to be found, as Benson and Hamel point out: see the comments on the figure of the viscount of Rome in *Hamel*, p.54.

91. Roy Pearcy, 'The Alliterative *Morte Arthure* vv. 2420-2447 and the Death of Richard I', *English Language Notes*, 22 (1985), 16-27.

92. Juliet Vale, 'Law and Diplomacy' (n.71 above), 35.

93. Ibid., 36.

94. For a helpful overview of the range of source material combined in this second dream of Arthur's, see *Hamel*, pp.42-4. Hamel concludes that in the making of this sequence 'we see the *Morte Arthure* poet most independent of his sources even while he brings together the greatest number and variety of them within a short space' (44). As I have already indicated, the dream has been the subject of extensive modern commentary (see above n.74). The dream sequence introduces the possibility of reading the narrative as a 'tragedy' (although the whole narrative cannot be accommodated within this genre, in my view). For further discussion of the medieval genre of tragedy and the *Morte Arthure*, see R. M. Lumiansky, 'The Alliterative *Morte Arthure*, the Concept of Tragedy, and the Cardinal Virtue Fortitude', in J. M. Headley (ed.), *Medieval and Renaissance Studies: Proceedings of the Southern Institute of Medieval and Renaissance Studies, Summer 1967* (Chapel Hill, N.C., 1968), 95-118; R. Peck, ' "Willfulness and Wonders": Boethian Tragedy in the Alliterative *Morte Arthure*', in Levy, 153-82 and Edward Kennedy, 'Generic Intertextuality in the Alliterative *Morte Arthure*'. Kennedy observes that 'Arthur's being punished for sin was . . . unusual in a work based upon the chronicles' (45). It is worth noting that this mode of explaining historical action is not in itself foreign to the Galfridian chronicle tradition. It features in later stages of British history when King Cadwallo, and later king Cadwallader, lament the loss of British dominion over the island and consider it a punishment for the sins of the people.

95. William Matthews has explored the Alexandrian connections in particular, see Matthews, 33-93 (the quotation is from p.66). For a more balanced overview of the *Morte Arthure*'s debts to narratives concerning Alexander and Charlemagne, see *Hamel*, pp.38-46. R. A. Shoaf has argued that Arthur's career is modelled on another of the 'Nine Worthies', King David, see 'The Alliterative *Morte Arthure*: the Story of Britain's David', *JEGP*, 81 (1982), 204-26.

96. For an overview of the studies which have applied oral-formulaic analysis to the *Morte Arthure*, see Ward Parks, 'The Flyting Contract and Adversarial Patterning in the Alliterative *Morte Arthure*', in D. A. Allen and R. A. White (eds.), *Traditions and Innovations: Essays on British Literature of the Middle Ages* and (Newark, N.J., 1990), 59-74 (especially 59-60).

97. See Britton Harwood, 'The Alliterative *Morte Arthure* as a Witness to Epic', particularly 241-8, for an interesting variant view. Harwood argues that part of the purpose of the *Morte Arthure* poet 'was *trompe oreille* – giving his work the sound of the orally composed, orally transmitted poem that he was reshaping his written sources to imitate' and that the poet 'simulates orality in writing' (247).

98. Hamel concludes that 'this poet's stylistic individuality is shown not in his anachronistic reversion to the practices of an earlier day, but rather in his self-generated modifications of the established conventions of his own day' (*Hamel*, p.33). For a detailed analysis of the distinctive poetic style of the *Morte Arthure*, see *Hamel*, pp.14-33.

99. Certainly *The Siege of Jerusalem* and possibly *The Parlement of the Thre Ages* (*Hamel*, pp.44-52).

100. Angus McIntosh, 'The Textual Transmission of the Alliterative *Morte Arthure*' in N. Davis and C. E. Wrenn (eds.), *English and Medieval Studies Presented to J. R. R. Tolkien* (London, 1962), 231-40. For the facsimile see, *The Thornton Manuscript (Lincoln Cathedral MS 91)*, introd. D. S. Brewer and A. E. B. Owen (London, 1975).

101. See n.90 above. John Finlayson has convincingly refuted W. Matthews's argument for a mid-fourteenth century date of composition in '*Morte Arthure*: The Date and a Source for Contemporary References', *Speculum*, 42 (1967), 624-38.

102. See Mary Hamel, '*The Siege of Jerusalem* as a Crusading Poem' for suggestive comments about the revival of interest in crusading projects in late fourteenth-century England and the critical effect of the disaster of 1396 at Nicopolis on the viability of such ventures.

103. See George Keiser, 'Lincoln Cathedral Library MS. 91: Life and Milieu of the Scribe', *Studies in Bibliography*, 32 (1979), 158-79; 'More Light on the Life and Milieu of Robert Thornton', *Studies in Bibliography*, 36 (1983), 111-19; John J. Thompson, *Robert Thornton and the London Thornton Manuscript* (Cambridge, 1987); Ralph Hanna III, 'The Growth of Robert Thornton's Books', *Studies in Bibliography*, 40 (1987), 51-61.

104. Phillipa Hardman, 'Reading the Spaces: Pictorial Intentions in the Thornton MSS, Lincoln Cathedral MS 91, and BL MS Add. 31042', *MÆ*, 63 (1994), 250-74 (250-6). Hardman goes on to argue that Thornton's second manuscript anthology, BL MS Additional 31042, is organized so as to recount a 'Christocentric sequence of history' (268); the collection of crusading narratives in this mansucript is part of the continuing story of 'Christian champions taking vengance on the enemies of Christ' (268).

105. Hardman, 'Reading the Spaces', 256.

106. As Hamel observes, 'Although Guinevere retreats into a convent in Caerleon in all chronicle versions, only [in the *Morte Arthure*] is she accused of "falsehood and fraud and fear of her husband" as primary motivation' (*Hamel*, note on 3918).

The Stanzaic *Morte Arthur*

107. For a detailed description of the *Morte Arthur* manuscript and its contents, see C.M. Meale, 'The Compiler at Work: John Colyns and BL MS Harley 2252', in Pearsall 1983, 82-103.

108. On provenance, see *Hissiger*, p.5, *Benson*, xviii. The date of composition is variously given as 'the fourteenth century' (*Hissiger*, p.3), 'around the middle of the century' (*Benson*, xviii), and '*c.* 1400' (Barron 1987, 240). Terence McCarthy, however, in discussing Malory's sources (in Archibald, 76), describes the *Morte* as 'the fifteenth-century stanzaic English poem'.

109. S.E. Knopp, 'Artistic Design in the Stanzaic *Morte Arthur*', *ELH*, 45 (1978), 563-82 (567).

110. All citations from the text are from *Hissiger*.

111. See E.T. Donaldson, 'Malory and the Stanzaic *Le Morte Arthur*', *Studies in Philology*, 47 (1950), 460-72, E.D. Kennedy, 'Malory and his English Sources', in Takamiya, 27-56 (48-56), and Terence McCarthy, 'Malory and His Sources' in Archibald, 75-96.

112. Quotations from *La Mort le Roi Artu* are from the edition by Jean Frappier (Geneva and Paris, 1964). There is a translation by James Cable, *The Death of Arthur* (Penguin, 1971).

113. A.V.C. Schmidt and Nicolas Jacobs (eds.), *Medieval English Romances*, Part 2 (London, 1980), draw attention to a final meeting between Lancelot and Guinevere in one of the fifty extant manuscripts of the French text, and claim that 'the version of the *Mort Artu* containing this scene must have enjoyed some degree of popularity in the 14th century in order to have been known to the author of the stanzaic *Morte Arthur*' (266). J. Beston and R.M. Beston, 'The Parting of Lancelot and Guinevere in the stanzaic *Le Morte Arthur*', *AUMLA*, 39-42 (1973-4), 249-59, make a detailed study of the French and English versions of the parting scene and come to the conclusion that the French version 'was not known to the author of the stanzaic *Le Morte Arthur*' (256). E.D. Kennedy, 'The Stanzaic *Morte Arthur*: The Adaptation of a French Romance for an English Audience', in Shichtman, 91-112, also compares the two farewell scenes and concludes that 'the similarities between the scene in the French *Mort* and the stanzaic *Morte* could be coincidental and the contrasts suggest that they could have no direct relationship to one another' (103).

114. Lancelot's rescue of Arthur is in the finest chivalric tradition, but this is not the first reference in the poem to Lancelot's horse. At the beginning of the poem Guinevere expresses her fear that the love between her and Lancelot is in danger of being revealed, and to allay suspicion Lancelot decides to quit the court. He arms himself to leave, 'And horsyd hym on a grey stede / Kyng Arthur had hym yeve byfore' (87-8). In the *Mort Artu* we are simply told that 'Li escuiers fet son commandement; si s'apareille au plus tost que il puet et enmeinne le meilleur cheval que Lancelot eüst, car il s'aperçoit bien que ses sires voudra porter armes a ce tornoiement' (6). Flora Alexander, '*The Treson of Launcelote du Lake*: Irony in the Stanzaic *Morte Arthur*' in Grout, 15-27, notes the effect of the poet's use of earlier episodes to reflect ironically on later ones (18).

115. Ibid., 19.

116. Schmidt and Jacobs (*Medieval English Romances*, Part 2, 21-23) discuss the poet's use of stock formulae in the description of the Maid and the language in which she expresses her feelings for Lancelot.

117. For Flora Alexander ('*The Treson of Launcelote*', 21) such episodes display, through their ironies, 'how fragile peace and goodwill are, and how easily simple misunderstandings can shatter them'.

118. R.A. Wertime, 'The Theme and Structure of the Stanzaic *Morte Arthur*', *PMLA*, 87 (1972), 1075-82, sees Arthur's primary function as 'his part in the conflict between Launcelot and Gawayne. He becomes a shifting foil, first opposed to Launcelot and aligned with Gawayne, subsequently changing until his position is the reverse' (1076). For Barron (1987, 143) the English poet is deliberately shifting the thematic focus 'from Arthur, representative of the nation, to Lancelot the embodiment of knighthood'. Korrel (227-8) argues that the English poet 'presents Arthur throughout as a weak-willed monarch', and that 'the most important part Arthur is allowed to play in this romance is acting as a foil to Lancelot to bring out the best in the poet's favourite'.

119. Kennedy ('The Stanzaic *Morte Arthur*', 91-112) gives numerous instances where the English version presents Arthur in a more positive light than the French source. Kennedy argues that some of the differences 'indicate that the English author had read Arthurian chronicles' (92), and that 'in the chronicles of Geoffrey of Monmouth, Wace, and Layamon, Arthur is too much an idealized nationalist figure to be portrayed as one punished for his sins' (104). He concludes that, influenced by the chronicle accounts, the English poet wished to present an Arthur who is not responsible for the destruction of his kingdom. Though one may agree with Kennedy that the chronicle accounts of Arthur may indeed have influenced the English poet, and that the presentation of Arthur is more positive in the stanzaic *Morte*, the active support Arthur gives Gawain (however reluctantly) cannot be disregarded in an appraisal of the factors contributing to the downfall of the Arthurian kingdom.

120. Whereas the poet of the stanzaic *Morte* frequently uses the term 'Ynglande' in referring to Arthur's realm, the usual descriptive term in the *Mort Artu* is 'le roiaume de Logres' (165, 171, 192, 210, etc.). See further, below, under n.123.

121. In the *Mort Artu* Arthur agrees to take Guinevere back because his love for her is so great, but he makes it clear that he will not end his war against Lancelot: 'mes il dist que, se la reïne revenoit, que ja por ce là guerre ne remeindra entre li et Lancelot, puis qu'il l'avoit emprise' (153).

122. In the French source the guilty party is identified by the narrator as a knight called Avarlan (76), but after Lancelot has proved Guinevere's innocence there is no further reference to Avarlan. All we are told is that 'la reïne fu clamee quite de l'apel que Mador avoit fet seur li' (107).

123. This is another instance where the French and English versions differ quite significantly. In the *Mort Artu* Mordred offers to stay and look after Guinevere in Arthur's absence, and Arthur, in response, puts Mordred in charge of both Guinevere and the kingdom, ordering the people to swear an oath of obedience to him. It is made clear at this point in the narrative that it is as a result of this oath of obedience to Mordred that Arthur will ultimately be defeated and die in battle: 'et cil firent le serement dont li rois se repenti puis si douleureusement qu'il en dut estre vaincuz en champ en la plaigne de Salesbieres ou

la bataille mortex fu, si come ceste estoire meïsmes le devisera apertement' (166-7). Korrel (227) interprets Arthur's reliance on advice in the stanzaic *Morte* as a failing, contributing to his characterization as a weak-willed king 'who never makes up his mind, and who, even in matters of little importance, asks people for their advice and acts upon it'. Kennedy (n.119 above) points out, however, that in the late Middle Ages, kings were expected to seek advice, and that 'by presenting an Arthur who consistently seeks advice, the English author was presenting a king who was acting as one might expect an English king to act' (99). The emphasis in the stanzaic *Morte* on an Arthur rooted in a model of English kingship, and the repeated references to Arthur's kingdom as England, suggest a contextualization of the Arthurian world within a recognizable English past, and at the same time identifiable with an English present.

124. The repeated use of the word 'treson' is noted by Flora Alexander ('*The Treson of Launcelote*', 17) in the part of the poem which deals with the disclosure of the love affair, and she makes the point that 'the language of the poem is repetitive in its nature, but it is not poverty-stricken or careless'. The use of the term 'treson' is, thus, deliberate on the part of the poet, signifying that the actions so described are treacherous in nature, threatening the welfare both of individuals and of the very kingdom itself.

125. Kennedy (n.113 above,101), regards Arthur's action here as 'immoderate, but unlike the Arthur of the French source who acts immoderately earlier, it is the final, desperate act of one who has little to lose. By this time there was little point in heeding Gawain's warning to wait for Lancelot.' It is interesting to note that in Malory's *Morte Darthur*, as in the stanzaic *Morte*, Arthur survives the final battle with Mordred, but Malory has one of Arthur's surviving knights, Sir Lucan, advise against the killing of Mordred: ' "Sir, latte hym be", seyde sir Lucan, "for he ys unhappy. And yf ye passe this unhappy day ye shall be ryght well revenged. . . . And for Goddes sake, my lorde, leve of thys, for, blyssed be God, ye have won the fylde: for yet we ben here three on lyve, and with sir Mordred ys nat one on lyve. And therefore if ye leve of now, thys wycked day of Desteny ys paste!" ' (*Vinaver*, 1236-7). Arthur, however, does not heed Lucan's advice and, in killing Mordred, ' "the traytoure that all thys woo hath wrought" ', is himself fatally wounded. Kennedy's view (n.111 above, 51) on the episode as presented in Malory is that 'an Arthur who at this point followed Lucan's advice would have been moderate and practical, but not heroic'.

126. Wertime ('Theme and Structure', 1075) describes the poem as 'a tragedy of consequence', arguing that 'the forces of destiny are imbedded in the structure of the chivalric society and in the natures of its individual members', and that it is the actions of these individuals within the limitations imposed by the chivalric code which lead inevitably to the downfall of the Arthurian world. For Alexander ('*The Treson of Launcelote*') the poet's thematic preoccupation is with 'the way that not only the unmistakable evil of malicious knights, but also the weaknesses and misjudgements of basically good characters, combine with misfortune in a deadly process' (27).

5: Chivalric Romance

Ywain and Gawain

1. For a comprehensive list of editions and critical studies, see B.-E.S. Calf, 'The Middle English *Ywain and Gawain*: A Bibliography, 1777-1995', *Parergon*, n.s.13 (1995), 1-24.

2. See B.v. Lindheim, *Studien zur Sprache des Manuskriptes Cotton Galba E IX* (Vienna and Leipzig, 1937).

3. Line-references will be to the edition of *Yvain* by T.B.W. Reid (Manchester, 1942).

4. See *Friedman and Harrington*, notes to 601-4, 2815ff..

5. For the greater flexibility of Chrétien's handling of the rhymed couplet, see Maldwyn Mills (ed.), *Ywain and Gawain, Sir Percyvell of Gales, The Anturs of Arther* (London, 1992), 184-5.

6. See for example, Tony Hunt, 'Beginnings, Middles, and Ends: Some Interpretative Problems in Chretien's *Yvain* and its Medieval Adaptations' in L.A. Arrathoon (ed.), *The Craft of Fiction: Essays in Medieval Poetics* (Rochester, N.Y.,1984), 83-117, Ulrike Dirscherl, *Ritterliche Ideale in Chrétiens* Yvain *und im mittelenglischen* Ywain and Gawain (Frankfurt, 1991), 113ff., and David Matthews, 'Translation and Ideology: The Case of *Ywain and Gawain*', *Neophilologus*, 76 (1992), 452-63. For a study of the text in terms of reception-theory, see Keith Busby, 'Chrétien de Troyes English'd', *Neophilologus*, 71 (1987), 596-613.

7. Although his motives are suspect, Kay is much annoyed by Guenevere's interruption of the story that Colgrevance had begun to tell (104-11, 117-24), and when it is resumed it proves a most elaborate performance.

8. This title appears at the beginning and end of the manuscript copy, and in the fourth line of the text.

9. The longer title appears as part of the final colophon to the Red Book copy, but at no other point in any medieval copy; see R.L. Thomson (ed.), *Owein* (Dublin, 1968), xi. The relation of the Welsh version to the French has never been decisively established. The principal variants in *Owein* are that the duel with Gawain is placed after the defeat of Kay at the spring; the episode of the two sisters is lacking; Owein returns to his lady before the adventure corresponding to that at the Castle of the Hevy Sorow (which then concludes the romance).

10. See John Finlayson, '*Ywain and Gawain* and the Meaning of Adventure', *Anglia* 87 (1969), 312-37, and D.E. Faris, 'The Art of Adventure in the Middle English Romance: *Ywain and Gawain, Eger and Grime*', *Studia Neophilologica*, 53 (1981), 91-100.

11. This 'truthfulness' is also suggested by the use of 'tithandes' (*news, report*) in 140 to denote the story he is about to tell, but in *Ywain* 3013 'aventures' is substituted for 'noveles' in *Yvain* 5258.

12. In *Yvain*, 60 (not reproduced in *Ywain*), the narrator comments that Calogrenant's tale was 'Non de s'enor (*honour*) mes de sa honte (*shame*)'. The use of romance narratives to provide negative as well as positive exemplars of conduct is considered by Hanspeter Schelp, in *Exemplarische Romanzen im Mittelenglischen*, Palaestra 246 (Göttingen, 1967), *passim.*.

13. Ywain's promise that he will avenge Colgrevance's shame (463-5) underlines the fact that the story just narrated is in function akin to those told of the parents of Percyvell and Tristrem. This time, however, only one generation is involved, and what must be avenged is a humiliation, not a killing.

14. She cites the mysterious Damysel Savage as her informant. This is the first step in her campaign to get Alundyne to accept Ywain as her next husband; without a guardian for the spring, her mistress is without defence against aggression. Surprisingly, Ywain agrees to defend Alundyne's lands against 'King Arthure and his knyghtes' (1169-74). The king is not mentioned at the same point in *Yvain* (2033-5), but the dilemma is in any case averted by having Kay undertake the combat that Arthur has provoked (*Ywain*, 1291-310).

15. His conquest of Britain had been described in more neutral terms in lines 7-10. His own reason for leading his expedition to the spring had been simply to 'se þat ilk syght' (523), but he is much more formidable at the same point in *Owein*; upset by the three-year absence of the hero from court – and on Gawain's advice – he departs for the spring with a host of three thousand warriors (455-70); see G. Jones and T. Jones (eds.), *The Mabinogion* (London, 1992), 170.

16. In *Friedman and Harrington* it is suggested that Gawain's name may have been included in the title 'to help the popularity of the work' (p.108).

17. A third allusion to the queen's abduction in *Yvain* 4740-2 is not taken over into the English romance. In the best-known examples of such a story, Lancelot is the knight who rescues the queen, but in the version of the scene depicted on the Modena Archivolt of the early twelfth century, Gawain is the first of three knights attacking the castle in which she is confined; see the frontispiece to R.S. Loomis's *Celtic Myth and Arthurian Romance* (London, 1926, repr. 1993).

18. Gawain defends him against the sneers of Kay in 1281-8, and says that no other knight is half so dear to him in 1355-6; Gawain's name is successfully evoked by his brother-in-law to persuade Ywain to fight with the giant Harpyns in 2361-2.

19. In *Yvain* 2422 Gawain refers to the hero as 'son conpaignon et son ami', and 2685-91 tells us that 'li dui conpaignon ansanble' lodge not with the king in the town, but hold a court of their own outside it. There is no parallel to this in *Ywain*. For the range of help that one companion might expect from another, see Barnes, 72-5.

20. Though it never regards him as anything but its 'lord' (2020, etc.) or 'maister' (2046, etc.), and acts accordingly. On the one occasion when it does not obey his explicit orders (to keep out of the fight with the steward and his accomplices) it is because it is convinced that it is really doing what Ywain wants (2627-8).

21. When in its grief at its master's supposed death, it prepares to kill itself with his sword (2079-82, 2097-102). Despite its lack of language, it can thus provide its master with 'consilium' as well as 'auxilium' (for which terms see Barnes, x).

22. A number of these are surveyed by Tony Hunt, in Grout, 86-7, 237.

23. Ibid., 91.

24. In *Yvain* 5109 this was named 'Le chastel de Pesme (*evil*) Avanture', a title appropriate to the young king who had so rashly sought out adventures. But it also suggests other senses of the word: 'fortune, chance', and 'danger, jeopardy'.

25. R.S. Loomis (*Arthurian Tradition and Chrétien de Troyes* (New York, 1949), 321-3) noted three other versions of the same adventure in the *Prose Lancelot* and in Malory, and suggested that they were its cognates rather than its derivatives.

26. Ibid., 323-5. They carry round shields and clubs, and are well armed except for their heads (3157-62). It is odd however that there should be two of them, and fighting on the same side; see MED *champioun* n. 2(a) 'one who engages in combat for another's sake'. In a less professional sense, Ywain refers to himself as a 'champion' in 2690.

27. The resemblance of the working conditions here to those in Muslim workshops using slave-labour was pointed out by R.A. Hall in 'The Silk Factory in Chrestien de Troyes' *Yvain*', *MLN*, 56 (1941), 418-22.

28. In *Yvain* 5471 he explicitly calls them 'Deus miens (*two of my*) serjanz'; the French narrator also expresses doubts about the good faith of the host and his companions, that are not taken over by the English one (5407, 5424-5).

29. It does accompany him to the spring (3839-40), but had been deliberately left behind by Ywain when he set out to fight the judicial duel (3455-6).

30. Yvain is determined to go on doing this until the tempests that he produces force the lady to take him back again (6517-26); Ywain is much less explicit ('He rides right unto þe well, / And þare he thinkes forto dwell' (3837-8)), but the effects of his actions are equally devastating and – with Lunet's help – achieve the same result.

Lybeaus Desconus

31. In the *Mills* edition cited here the two best copies (see note 33 below) are given in parallel; the earlier edition of Max Kaluza (Altenglische Bibliothek, 5 (Leipzig, 1890)) offered a composite text. The romance is composed in the twelve-line tail-rhyme stanza, rhyming *aabaabccbddb*, and with the tail- and couplet-lines of mostly equivalent weight.

32. Otherwise the best-represented are *The Awntyrs off Arthure* (four copies), and *Arthour and Merlin* (five, two of them post-medieval; a 'sixth' is a transcript made for Walter Scott from the Auchinleck copy).

33. The two most significant are those of British Library London MS Cotton Caligula A.ii (C.) and Lambeth Palace Library London MS 306 (L.), the first of the middle, the second of the late fifteenth century. The others are Lincoln's Inn Library London MS 150 (early fifteenth century; only about half of the text has survived); Biblioteca Nazionale Naples MS xiii B 29 (dated 1457); Bodleian Libary Oxford MS Ashmole 61 (late fifteenth century), and British Library London MS Additional 27879 (The Percy Folio MS; mid-seventeenth century). These last four copies are all much more closely related to L. than to C.

34. Six lost copies – including the original, and the version from which all the surviving copies derive – are noted on Kaluza's stemma (see *Mills*, p.14); there must certainly have been others.

35. Since these belong to distinct manuscript traditions, any readings common to both should represent the archetype from which all surviving copies descend, though not necessarily the author's original. Each also contains stanzas lacking in the other, all of which follow the basic four-rhyme stanza pattern noted above (those found only in the other four texts exemplify the five-rhyme pattern: *aabccbdddbeeb*). Kaluza accepted all stanzas of the first type into his composite text, but some of those found in L. (and other

texts of the same group) but not in C. are awkward in both form and sense, and are more probably insertions made into the archetypal text to emphasize particular features of the story. Kaluza's text is an ingenious construct, but it remains a late nineteenth-century hypothesis, not a mid-fourteenth-century reality.

36. Identified with Segontium within the limits of present-day Caernarvon; see D.D.R. Owen, *The Evolution of the Grail Legend* (Edinburgh, 1968), ch.3 and plates I and II. In *Lybeaus*, Synadowne is the castle of the steward-host Lambard, and the enchanters Maboun and Yrayn occupy a hall outside its walls; but in Renaut de Beaujeu's *Li Biaus Descouneüs*, Lanpart is steward of the fortified city of Galigan, and the journey from this to Senaudoun – here a Cité Gaste – takes several hours (2749-75).

37. Ed. G.P. Williams (Oxford, 1915; rev. edn. CFMA 38 (Paris, 1929, repr. 1967). The detail common to both is the return of Lybeaus and his bride to Synadowne (C. 2123-4; *Descouneüs* 6217-22). But nothing in the French romance corresponds to the account of the arming of the hero by four of Arthur's knights in C. 232-40, or to a third allusion of the same kind ('In Frensshe as it is j-ffounde') that appears in L. 673 (at the end of the fight with the giants). Renaut – like Chrétien in *Erec* 13 – describes the source of his romance as '[un] conte d'aventure' (5).

38. In *Lybeaus* the restoration of the queen of Synadowne is almost immediately followed by her journey to Arthur with the hero (C. 2080-91, 2098-100); there was never any question of a return to the Yle d'Or, as the lady deserted there was presented very unsympathetically (C. 1414-46), and the hero's marriage is an enduring one ('Fele (*many*) ȝer þey leuede yn same (*remained together*)' (C. 2125)). But Renaut, who links his hero's fortunes in love with his own, alleges that if favoured by his own lady, he will even allow his hero to stay with his beloved a third time (6255-8). The relative linearity of the English narrative is also seen in the sequence of the first three episodes after the departure from court; here the defeat of William Selebraunche is at once followed by the encounter with his three would-be avengers; in *Descouneüs* these are separàted by the fight with the two giants, the final episode in the sequence in *Lybeaus* (547-705).

39. See *Mills*, 238-40, notes to C. 1700-1, 1747-52, 1821-4.

40. Very probably Thomas Chestre, the author of *Sir Launfal*; see Maldwyn Mills, 'The Composition and Style of the "Southern" *Octavian*, *Sir Launfal*, and *Libeaus Desconus*', *MÆ*, 31 (1962), 88-109 and Frances McSparran (ed.), *Octovian Imperator*, Middle English Texts 11 (Heidelberg, 1979), 55-8.

41. The most important studies of romances belonging to the Fair Unknown cycle are listed in Claude Luttrell, *The Creation of the First Arthurian Romance: A Quest* (London, 1974), 269. For the author's own study of them and their relationships see 80-126; also the review by Maldwyn Mills, *MÆ*, 44 (1977), 300-6.

42. To such an extent that she then becomes his lover ('He and þat mayde bryȝt / Togydere made all nyȝt / Game and greet solas' (C. 445-7)). In *Descouneüs* and in the C-text of *Lybeaus* the dwarf never criticizes the hero, but in L. and the other texts he does so vigorously after Arthur has granted him the adventure (L. 190-201), and reproaches him constantly over the first stage of their journey (L. 279-81); contrast C. 256-8, where it is Elene who does this.

43. Most particularly in the early parts of the story; after the loss of his steed, William Selebraunche comments that it would be proper for Lybeaus to dismount and fight on foot

(C. 328-33); a little later, that it would be 'greet vylanye' to kill him when he is without a sword (C. 361-6).

44. See her representation of his year-long servitude to the magically-gifted Dame d'Amore both as a cause of hardship to the lady he is supposed to be rescuing, and making him ' "fals of fay / Ayens þe kyng Artour" ' (C. 1439-46).

45. See, for example, Keen, 83-101 ('The Rise of the Tournament'). An interpretation of the later events in *Lybeaus* as 'a euphemistic cover' for brutality is attempted by Stephen Knight, 'The Social Function of the Middle English Romances' in David Aers (ed.), *Medieval Literature: Criticism, Ideology and History* (Brighton, 1986), 105-8.

46. As exemplified in several non-Arthurian romances in which Saracens figure largely; see, for example, Frances McSparran (ed.), *Octovian*, EETS 289 (London, 1986), MS C. 1261-350.

47. This motif is also a feature of the climactic 'Joie de la Cort' episode in Chrétien's *Erec et Enide* ed. M. Roques (Paris, 1955), 5724-64. Together with the cognate Welsh *Gereint vab Erbin* this text is closely related to the romances of the Fair Unknown, even though it has a very different kind of hero; see Luttrell (n.41 above), *passim*.

48. See Kaluza (n.31 above), cxlv-clviii.

49. In *Descouneüs* the hero's armour is removed soon after he arrives at court (91-2), and is later brought back to him by Gawain (262-5), who also provides him with a squire, Robert (270-8). There is no mention of any training, actual or potential. Contrast Wirnt von Gravenberc's *Wigalois* (ed. J.M.N. Kapteyn (Bonn, 1926)), where quite long periods separate Arthur's handing over of the hero to Gawain for training (1593-6), his knighting (1627-30), and the arrival of the lady messenger and the dwarf (1717-22).

50. See Maldwyn Mills, 'A Mediæval Reviser at Work', *MÆ*, 32 (1963), 11-23.

51. Ibid., 17-18. Matters are complicated by the fact that the second and third of these stanzas (in which Gawain is the central figure) are also found in the Lincoln's Inn MS, and so derive from an earlier lost version than does the first stanza (in which the mother appears).

Sir Landevale, Sir Launfal, Sir Lambewell

52. A. Ewert (ed.), *Marie de France: Lais* (Oxford, 1952), 58-74; see also *The Lais of Marie de France*, trans. G.S. Burgess and Keith Busby (Harmondsworth, 1986), 73-81.

53. *Chevrefoil*, which treats the Tristan and Isolde story, does not link the material with the Arthurian legend.

54. *Bliss*, 15; Severs *Manual*, 139. The only other surviving Middle English translation of one of Marie's *lais*, *Lai le Freine*, also belongs to this period, as do *Sir Orfeo* and *Sir Degaré* which have no known French source. All three are found in the important Auchinleck manuscript dated 1330-40; see *The Auchinleck Manuscript*, facsimile with an introduction by Derek Pearsall and I.C. Cunningham (London, 1977), vii. These three, with *Sir Landevale*, all in couplets, have been seen as forming a separate early group of 'Breton Lays', distinct from the later, mainly tail-rhyme lays, including *Sir Launfal* and Chaucer's *Franklin's Tale*; see Mehl, 41ff., and G. Johnston, 'Chaucer and the Breton Lays', in *Proceedings and Papers of the Fourteenth Congress of the Australasian Universities Language and Literature Association* (Dunedin, 1972), 230-41.

55. On forms of the name and a possible French derivation see A.J. Bliss, 'The Hero's Name in the Middle English Versions of *Lanval*', *MÆ*, 27 (1958), 80-5; for a possible Celtic derivation, Constance Bullock-Davies, 'Lanval and Avalon', *Bulletin of the Board of Celtic Studies*, 23 (1969), 128-42, esp. 130-3; and for its suggested origin as a near anagram of *Avalun*, Michèle Koubichkine, 'A propos du *Lai de Lanval*', *MA*, 78 (1972), 481.

56. The most common, though not the only, spelling of the name in Bodleian MS Rawlinson C. 86. As originally written (on ff.119ᵛ-128ʳ) the poem had no title in this MS, the heading *landavall* being squeezed in later. Severs *Manual* (139-40, 296) refers to the Rawlinson text as *Sir Landeval*. For editions see *Bliss*; *Laskaya and Salisbury*.

57. *Hales and Furnivall*; Severs *Manual*, 296. A few remnants of the two editions are preserved in Bodleian, Malone 941 and Douce e. 40; a further manuscript fragment closely related to the prints is found in Cambridge University Library MS Kk. 5. 30. (f.11) and printed in *Furnivall*.

58. British Library Additional 27879, ff.28ᵛ-33ᵛ; *Hales and Furnivall*; Severs *Manual*, 296.

59. *Sir Lamwell* and *Sir Lambewell* may therefore be regarded as close variants of the same text, but are together sufficiently distinct to stand a little apart from the earlier *Sir Landevale*. Opinions are divided as to whether the *Lam(be)well* text should be regarded as a distinct version or, as suggested here, simply an expanded revision of a text related to *Sir Landevale*; my position is in general that of *Bliss* (4-5); D. Carlson advocates the distinctness of *Sir Lambewell* in 'The Middle English *Lanval*, the Corporal Works of Mercy, and Bibliothèque Nationale, Nouv. Acq. Fr. 1104', *Neophilologus*, 72 (1988), 105, n.4. Detailed discussions and stemmata showing textual relationships may be found in G.L. Kittredge's edition of *Sir Landevale* in *American Journal of Philology*, 10 (1889), 1-33; and, with texts in parallel, in M.C. Edwards, 'An Edition of the Early English Versions of the *Lai de Lanval*', University of London MA thesis, 1954.

60. *Bliss*; Severs *Manual*, 138, 295-6. Unlike the couplet text, *Sir Launfal* is found in only a single MS, British Library Cotton Caligula A2, ff.35ᶜ-42ᶜ.

61. The genuine quality of *Sir Landevale* would be better appreciated if it were available in a good critical edition and not, as usually happens, relegated to an appendix in editions of *Sir Launfal*.

62. Identifiable as Type 400 (Aarne 1961), 'The Man on a Quest for his Lost Wife'. Critical discussions of folk tale elements in the English versions tend to focus on *Sir Launfal*; see B.K. Martin, '*Sir Launfal* and the folktale', *MÆ*, 35 (1966), 199-210, and B.A. Rosenberg, 'Medieval popular literature: folkloric sources', in Heffernan, 61-84, esp. 68-9.

63. For insular origin, see Bullock-Davies, 'Lanval and Avalon'; and for exhaustive treatment of analogues, Celtic and Germanic, see W.H. Schofield, 'The Lays of *Graelent* and *Lanval*, and the Story of Wayland', *PMLA*, 15 (1900), 121-80, and T.P. Cross, 'The Celtic elements in the lays of *Lanval* and *Graelent*', *MP*, 12 (1915), 585-644.

64. Conveniently consulted in R. Weingartner (ed. and trans.), *Graelent and Guingamor: Two Breton Lays* (New York and London, 1985), which contains an annotated bibliography. For the background and relationship of the poems see Schofield, Cross, (both

n.63 above), and W.C. Stokoe, Jr., 'The Sources of *Sir Launfal: Lanval* and *Graelent*', *PMLA*, 63 (1948), 392-404.

65. For the Celtic origins of fairy mistresses see T.P. Cross, 'The Celtic *Fée* in *Launfal*' in *Anniversary Papers by Colleagues and Pupils of G.L. Kittredge* (Boston and London, 1913), 377-87, and R.S. Loomis, 'Morgain la Fée and the Celtic Goddesses', *Speculum*, 20 (1945), 183-203. For the view that fairies are a largely literary invention of the twelfth century, see L. Harf-Lancner, *Les Fées au Moyen Age. Morgane et Mèlusine: La Naissance de Fées* (Paris, 1984), and for a counter-argument, citing evidence from Aarne 1961, Type 400, Pierre Gallais, 'Les fées seraient-elles nées au XIIe siècle?', *Cahiers de Civilisation Mediévale*, 29 (1986), 355-71.

66. Usually known as the 'Potiphar's Wife' motif; for the Biblical type-story see F.E. Faverty, 'Legends of Joseph in Old and Middle English', *PMLA*, 43 (1928), esp. 87-92, and for examples of the motif in Old Irish see T.P. Cross, *Motif-Index of Early Irish Literature* (Bloomington, Ind., 1952), 382: K2111.

67. Ernest Hoepffner, 'Pour la chronologie des lais de Marie de France', *Rom.*, 59 (1933), esp. 353-7; see also G.S. Burgess, *The Lais of Marie de France: Text and Context* (Athens, Ga., 1987), 18-19.

68. Marie does not actually name this queen, but major characters in her lays frequently go unnamed and we have no reason to suppose that she withheld the name from any sense that the promiscuous role was inappropriate; she presumably absorbed Guinevere into her position in the *lai* because the cap (or mantle) fitted.

69. Unless it occurred in an early Tristan text; see Hoepffner, 'Pour la chronologie', 357. For the possibility that Marie found the location in a lost north British source see Bullock-Davies, 'Lanval and Avalon', and Burgess, *The Lais of Marie de France*, 18-19. It also occurs in Chrétien, whose work *Lanval* is usually thought to predate; but for the (somewhat aberrant) suggestion that Chrétien was in fact Marie's source see W.T.H. Jackson, 'The Arthuricity of Marie de France', *Romanic Review*, 70 (1979), 1-18.

70. It is of course a well-established convention in the lives of Welsh and Breton saints (see B.F. Roberts, '*Culhwch ac Olwen*, the Triads, Saints' Lives', in Bromwich, 82-4), but it does not seem likely that Marie knew these. It was more fully developed by Chrétien de Troyes; but see n.69 above.

71. Almost nothing is known for certain about Marie's biography, but this seems to be generally accepted; see Burgess, *The Lais of Marie de France*, 18-20, and the Introduction to Burgess and Busby, *The Lais of Marie de France*, esp. 14-19.

72. E.g. by Burgess, *The Lais of Marie de France*, 19-20.

73. E.A. Francis, 'The trial in *Lanval*' in *Studies in French Language and Mediæval Literature presented to Professor Mildred K. Pope* (Manchester, 1939), 115-24.

74. See Keith Busby, *Gauvain in Old French Literature* (Amsterdam, 1980), 36-42.

75. I.D.O. Arnold and M.M. Pelan (eds.), *La Partie arthurienne du Roman de Brut* (Paris, 1962), 2185-224.

76. For a cogent analysis of the impact of the different language, time and culture on the translation of Marie's *lais* into English see A.C. Spearing, 'Marie de France and her Middle English Adapters', *Studies in the Age of Chaucer*, 12 (1990), 117-56.

77. For comparisons of *Lanval* with one or more of the Middle English texts see T. Stemmler, 'Die mittelenglischen Bearbeitungen zweier Lais der Marie de France', *Anglia*, 80 (1962), 243-63, Elizabeth Williams, '*Lanval* and *Sir Landevale*: A Medieval Translator and his Methods', *LSE*, n.s. 3 (1969), 85-99, B. McCreesh, 'The Use of Conversation in Medieval Literature: The Case of Marie de France and her First Redactor', *Revue de l'Université d'Ottawa*, 53 (1983), 189-97, and A.C. Spearing, 'Marie de France and her Middle English adapters'.

78. E.g., 'He bad her not, but she bad hym!' (484), the fay declares in the courtroom, ruthlessly exposing the cruder side of the queen's actions which Marie's legal niceties had pushed into the background.

79. Such figures are generally more admired than condemned, embodying as they do a selfless and chivalric charity from which others benefit, and are often seen as receiving earthly reward from non-earthly sources for their excessive generosity; Landevale is thus very close to such heroes as Sir Cliges or Sir Amadas.

80. In Marie's time this is probably all that Avalun was, at least in French literature. Her allusion is little different from that of Wace, from whom she probably got it (Arnold and Pelan (n.75 above), 4707). For a more prosaic view see Bullock-Davies, 'Lanval and Avalon' (n.55 above). Earlier scholars were much concerned to see the 'forth-putting fay' as a literary descendant of a Celtic goddess; see the references given in n.65 above, especially Loomis, who recognizes Lanval's mistress as Morgan la Fay whom Geoffrey of Monmouth located in Avalon in the *Vita Merlini*. The more literary analysis of Harf-Lancner differentiates the 'Morganian' union of the *fée* who takes a mortal lover back to her own world from the 'Melusinian' one in which the *fée* remains in this world and has children from the liaison. For a Jungian approach to fairy mistresses see J.-C. Aubailly, *La fée et le chevalier* (Paris, 1986), and for a useful overview, K.S. Westoby, 'A New Look at the Role of the *Fée* in Medieval French Arthurian Romance', in Burgess 1985, 373-85.

81. The only comparable detail in the French *lai* is Marie's statement that Lanval's horse trembled as he approached a river. For further discussion see Williams, '*Lanval* and *Sir Landevale*', 87, and 'Hunting the Deer', in Mills, 190-2.

82. Identified by Mehl and by Johnston (n.54 above) as forming, with *Le Freine* and *Sir Landevale*, a distinct group of early couplet lays. This shared convention of magical warning signals perhaps constitutes another link between three of them.

83. See the examples cited under Aarne, 400.

84. An even greater degree of ruthlessness is found in *Graelent*, where the fairy relents only when the hero nearly drowns in his pursuit of her.

85. Copied in the middle of the seventeenth century, a time when the Arthurian legend was in the doldrums, it seems astonishing that this story was chosen for preservation at all. The modern fairy-tale, however, was on the verge of emergence as a genteel literary form; the tales of Charles Perrault and Madame Daulnoy began to appear in France in the 1690's. It is perhaps worth noting that the Percy Folio also contains a text of *Sir Degaré* as well as a number of other Arthurian poems.

86. For further comment on the treatment of the lady in the Percy text see my 'A Damsell by Herselfe Alone': Images of Magic and Femininity from *Lanval* to *Sir Lambewell*' in Fellows, 155-70.

87. Though the 'approach' machinery of sun and trees is at least partially preserved – the MS is damaged at this point – its significance is evidently forgotten. The scene also concludes with Lambewell falling asleep and seeing the maidens on waking, possibly conceived as a naturalistic effect of the heat. Clearly Lambewell does not dream here; but contacts with the Otherworld do sometimes have a dream aspect, e.g. in *Sir Orfeo*.

88. For a rare article which takes account of the Percy text and makes this point, see E.B. Lyle, '*Sir Landevale* and the Fairy-Mistress Theme in *Thomas of Erceldoune*', *MÆ*, 42 (1973), 244-50.

89. As indicated above (see n.60), though the single surviving manuscript of this is earlier than any we have of *Sir Landevale* it represents a later fourteenth-century reworking of the originally much simpler Breton Lay. Criticism of *Sir Launfal* is much more copious than of *Sir Landevale*; brief accounts may be found in Barron 1987, 190-4, and Mehl, 44-8, as well as in the Introduction to *Bliss*.

90. Or perhaps, as Martin suggests ('*Sir Launfal* and the Folktale', 210), Chestre simply took the forgiveness as read and omitted the dialogue in accordance with his general preference for actions over words.

91. See the account of Chestre's sources in *Bliss*, 24-31.

92. E.g. by *Bliss*, 42-3; Calin, 449, seems to disagree.

93. See Martin, '*Sir Launfal* and the Folktale', 208-9.

94. See A.C. Spearing, *The Medieval Poet as Voyeur* (Cambridge, 1993), 98ff.

95. Ibid., ch.5.

Sir Percyvell of Gales

96. There *Sir Percyvell* immediately follows a text of *The Awntyrs off Arthure*; for an account of this manuscript, see J.J. Thompson, 'The Compiler in Action: Robert Thornton and the "Thornton Romances"' in Pearsall 1983, 113-24.

97. In *The Canterbury Tales*, VII.915-6: 'Hymself drank water of the well, / As dide the knyght sire Percyvell.' This couplet represents *Percyvell* 5 and 7, in reverse order.

98. A rare form of the tail-rhyme stanza, that is also used in *Sir Degrevant*, and in the *Avowynge of King Arthur* (although the metrical structure is different in this last).

99. See M.P. Medary, 'Stanza-Linking in Middle English Verse', *The Romanic Review*, 7.3 (1916), 243-70.

100. *Le Roman de Perceval ou Le Conte du Graal*, ed. William Roach (Geneva, Lille, 1956). For a detailed comparison of the content of these romances, together with the Welsh *Peredur*, and the *Parzival* of Wolfram von Eschenbach, see Glenys Goetinck, *Peredur: A Study of Welsh Tradition in the Grail Legends* (Cardiff, 1975), 41-128. A summary comparison of these four texts is given in Wilson 1988, 98-105.

101. For the view that the revenge elements in *Percyvell* could not have been derived from 'the indications of Chrétien', see R.S. Loomis, *Arthurian Tradition and Chrétien de Troyes* (New York, 1949), 398-9.

102. See D.C. Fowler, '*Le Conte du Graal* and *Sir Perceval of Galles*', *Comparative Literature Studies*, 12 (1975), 5-20; Keith Busby, 'Chrétien de Troyes English'd', *Neophilologus*, 71 (1987), 596-613, and J.O. Fichte, 'Arthurische und nicht-arthurische Texte im Gespräch, dargestellt am Beispiel der mittelenglischen Romance *Sir Perceval of*

Galles' in Friedrich Wolfzettel (ed.), *Artusroman und Intertextualität* (Giessen 1990), 19-34.

103. In particular, detail from the scene in which the sight of blood drops on the snow throws Perceval into a deep love-meditation. He cannot be forced away from the spot – as Sagremor and Kay discover – but is finally won over by Gawain's courtesy, and goes with him to Arthur (4194-500). In its original form this episode could hardly have been taken over into *Percyvell*, but no fewer than four distinct scenes in *Percyvell* contain traces of it: (1) the hero's meditation is suggested by the 'study' into which he falls during his fight with the sultan (1695-716); (2) his combat with one of Arthur's knights, by the combat with Gawain at the Maydenlande (1417-532); (3) Kay's rudeness and Gawain's courtesy, by his first meeting with the knights in the forest (285-312); (4) Gawain's persuasion of the hero to go with him, by the similar success of Lufamour's steward, Hende (*Courteous*) Hatlayne (said in 1261-84 to be as courteous as Gawain).

104. With the exception of the hero, Arthur, and the best-known of his knights, all the characters in the English romance have different names from their French counterparts, and some of the common motifs take quite different forms: in *Percyvell* 161-2, for example, the hero's father is killed in tournament; in *Perceval* 481 he dies of grief on hearing of the death of his other sons in battle.

105. See especially *Perceval* 1427-529 and 1639-70. At roughly the same point in the *Percyvell* story the hero stays with his paternal uncle, who might have been expected to fulfil the same role as Gornemant. But – as in *Lybeaus* – the messenger from the oppressed lady arrives while they are still eating (953-1004), so that no training can take place. Gornemant, while duplicating some of the mother's maxims in his own teaching, becomes impatient when the hero cites her as an authority (1675-88); such masculine and exclusive professionalism is alien to *Percyvell*, where the hero's mother-fixation survives to the end.

106. For a demonstration of the content of this kind of introductory section, and its narrative consequences, see Wittig, 112-16.

107. For the further significance of this return, see Jenny Fellows, 'Mothers in Middle English Romance', in Meale 1996, 51.

108. In marked contrast to *Perceval*, where the enemies of Blancheflor, and the jealous knight are all sent back to Arthur (2313-23, 2692-9, 3954-80). The action is more functional here than it would have been in *Percyvell*, since the defeated knights convey the hero's warnings to Kay; the difference also reflects the less chivalric status of most of the English hero's opponents.

109. It is essentially a battle in open country, with no details of the active besieging of the city; contrast the account given of the siege of Metz in the alliterative *Morte Arthure*, that is discussed in Hebron, 56-65. Such details are also missing in the corresponding episode located at Biaurepaire in *Perceval*, despite signs of damage and privation there (1708-84); see Claude Luttrell, *Le Conte del Graal* and Precursors of Perceval' *BBIAS*, 46 (1994), 300-4.

110. Compare 'Hedys hopped vndur hors fete, / As haylestones done in þe strete', in *Le Bone Florence of Rome*, 640-1. But here two armies are involved, while Perceval fights on his own. As at some other points in the romance, it is difficult not to suspect parody here.

111. For all that his 'wordis so wylde' finally persuade Gawain of this identity at the Maydenlande (1497-500), his request there that Arthur should knight him is less abrupt than before: ' "ȝif I be noghte ȝitt knyghte, / Þou sall halde þat þou highte (*promised*), / Forto make me ane" ' (1590-2). At much the same time his previous misuse of the terms 'mere' (*mare*) and 'sowdane' (*sultan*) – which he had applied to any horse (369-72), and any powerful opponent (1481-4) – is set right by Gawain (1687-92; 1501-4).

112. Notably the injunction to pray to God for virtue and long life (235-40). Her instructions are more numerous in the French romance, but at least two of them (547-55), while not present in the English list, are implied by his later actions of kissing and taking a ring from the sleeping lady of the hall (473-4). This supports the view that part at least of the English romance came from imperfect memories of the French one.

113. The idea occurs to him again when he fails to penetrate the armour of the sultan with his spear ('So ill was he kende (*taught*)' (1676)).

114. The French Perceval wishes to return to his mother both before and after his rescue of Blancheflor (1699-702, 2980-4); she is opposed to this, but he promises to return and take over the land, bringing his mother back with him if she is still alive (2922-32). This last actually happens in *Percyvell* 2273-80.

Sir Tristrem

115. This results from the loss of all but a stub (f.299a) of an entire leaf. Elsewhere the amount of text lost is relatively small: 12 lines between 123 and 136 (the result of cutting out a miniature on the recto of the leaf), and lines 80-1 and 874-5 (through careless copying).

116. The most comprehensive edition of these fragments, and the only one to number them consecutively is contained in Christiane Marchello-Nizia (ed.), *Tristan et Yseut: Les premières versions européennes* (Paris, 1995), 123-212 and 1208-87; here it is surmised that the 3298 lines preserved represent about a quarter of the original poem. In *Tristrem* a 'Tomas' is a number of times cited as a source (lines 2, 10, 397, 412, 2787), and his identity has been the subject of much conjecture, especially in view of the 'Erceldoun' mentioned in the first line of the romance; see *McNeill*, xli-xliv, C.E. Pickford, 'Sir Tristrem, Sir Walter Scott and Thomas', in W. Rothwell *et al.* (eds.), *Studies in Medieval Literature and Languages in Memory of Frederick Whitehead* (Manchester, 1973), 219-28, and Crane, 188-98.

117. This stanza is not used in any other Middle English romance, Arthurian or otherwise, but three examples of it turn up at the end of the sixth of Minot's political poems; see T.B. James and John Simons (eds.), *The Poems of Laurence Minot, 1333-1352* (Exeter, 1989), 40-3.

118. A sustained example of this last is offered by the four stanzas between lines 2025 and 2068, which have been variously arranged by successive editors to provide the best consecutive sense.

119. Friedrich Ranke's text of Gottfried von Strassburg's *Tristan* is reprinted with a facing page translation into modern German, in Philipp Reclam Jr. (Stuttgart, 1980); *Tristrams Saga ok Ísöndar* – important as the one derivative of Thomas that has survived without textual loss – is supplied together with a German translation (and an edition of *Sir Tristrem*) in Eugen Kölbing (ed.), *Die nordische und die englische Version der Tristan-*

Saga (Heilbronn, 1878, 1882). French translations of both works are given in Marcello-Nizia, *Tristan and Yseut* (see n.116), 389-635, and 783-920; for translations in English, see A.T. Hatto (Harmondsworth and Baltimore, 1960), for the poems of Gottfried and Thomas, and Paul Schach, *The Saga of Tristram and Isönd* (Lincoln, Neb., 1973).

120. Only when he fights against Morgan and his vassals in Ermonie (Brittany) is Tristrem accompanied by forces provided by Mark (773-96), and he takes only fourteen of these with him when he enters the usurper's court (816-8); their number is augmented by support brought by Rohand (876-8).

121. It is much less clear in *Tristrem* 2971-81 than in lines 1095-144 of Thomas's poem that the hero converses with the image of Ysonde as if it were a living person.

122. 'It brought the story of Tristan and Iseult, as it had been told by twelfth-century poets, within the framework of the thirteenth-century Arthurian Cycle; and while it thus added to the poetical tradition of Tristan a vast amount of fresh material, it also shifted the emphasis from the original story of tragic love to the protagonist's adventures in the service of the Round Table.' (*Vinaver*, 1443).

123. See Marcello-Nizia, *Tristan et Yseut*, 89-116 and 329-35; in both of these episodes, though in very different ways, Arthur's knights give positive support to the lovers against their enemies. In other Middle English Arthurian texts, Tristrem makes only brief (and uncharacteristic) appearances: see *The Marriage of Sir Gawaine*, 122 and *King Arthur and King Cornwall*, 26 and 276.

124. Notably in the French prose *La Mort le Roi Artu*, and Malory's 'Launcelot and Guinevere' and 'The Morte Arthur'.

125. Although Brengwain does not in *Tristrem* – as in both the French and Norse versions – actually remind Ysonde of her attempt at having her murdered; the immediate cause of her anger is the apparent cowardice of Tristrem and Ganhardin in the face of an attack by Canados and his supporters (3140-68).

126. Mark's court is most nearly comparable with Arthur's near the beginning of the English romance. In the introductory section Rouland distinguishes himself at a tournament held there (65-77).

127. Ed. Eugen Kölbing, EETS, ES 46, 48, 65 (London, 1885, 1886, 1894), A. 1-514; and ed. Maldwyn Mills, Middle English Texts 20 (Heidelberg, 1988), 1-252. Mark is throughout associated with England, not Cornwall, and during the combat with Moraunt the narrator exclaims: 'God help Tristrem, þe kniȝt! / He fauȝt for Ingland!' (1033-4).

128. Ed. Julius Zupitza, EETS, ES 42, 49, 59 (London, 1883, 1887, 1891). For the theme of the 'second lady' in these and other romances, see G.S. Loomis, *Tristan and Isolt: A Study of the Sources of the Romance* (New York, 1963), 158-77.

129. In the Norse version, the Polish duke who corresponds to Triamour offers his sister to the hero as a reward for killing Urgan (Schach (n.119), 99).

130. Although the difficulties of making a clear-cut distinction between the two have often been recognized: see, for example, Bartina Wind, 'Eléments courtois dans Béroul et dans Thomas', *Romance Philology*, 14 (1960), 1-13.

Lancelot of the Laik and Sir Lancelot du Lake

131. *The Kingis Quair*, written by King James I at some date between his return to Scotland from captivity in England (1424), and his death in 1437, is a Chaucerian love poem in a language which shows a mixture of northern and southern words and forms. The language and the literary affinities of the poem are discussed by Gregory Kratzmann in *Anglo-Scottish Literary Relations 1430-1550* (Cambridge, 1980), 33-62.

132. The difficulty of establishing a date for the poem is noted by R.J. Lyall, 'Politics and Poetry in Fifteenth and Sixteenth Century Scotland', *Scottish Literary Journal*, 3 (1976), 13-14.

133. The suggestion of common authorship of *Lancelot of the Laik* and *The Quare of Jelusy* is made in the Introduction to the edition of *Lancelot of the Laik* (*Gray*, xxxv). The possibility is discussed further by M.P. McDiarmid in the Introduction to his edition of *The Kingis Quair* (London, 1973), 31, and by John MacQueen in *History of Scottish Literature*, I, ed. R. D. S. Jack (Aberdeen, 1988), 55-72. MacQueen writes about the possible author: '*The Quare of Jelusy* has a colophon which was read by David Laing as "Quod Auchen . . ", and the poem has therefore been attributed to the Afflek (Auchinleck) mentioned as a poet in line 58 of Dunbar's "Timor Mortis Conturbat Me", who in turn has been identified with James Auchlek, who graduated at St Andrews in 1471, who in 1494 was secretary to the Earl of Ross and Precentor of Caithness, and who died in September, 1497. If this is so, we have a considerable body of verse attributable to him, verse which also displays some literary ambitions.' (60-1).

134. The part of the French romance used by the Scottish poet corresponds to *Lancelot do Lac: The Non-cyclic Old French Prose Romance*, ed. Elspeth Kennedy, 2 vols. (Oxford, 1980), I, 275-319.

135. Elspeth Kennedy discusses the themes of *Lancelot do Lac* in *Lancelot and the Grail: A Study of the Prose Lancelot* (Oxford, 1986), 31, and subsequently ch. II, 'The Making of a Mame or Quest for Identity', 10-48, and ch. III, 'The Love Theme', 49-78.

136. Kennedy (1986, 31) comments on the connection made between the death of King Ban and the King's present troubles, and the element of irony thus introduced into Arthur's situation.

137. B.J. Vogel argues that the attack on Arthur's kingdom is a reference to the threat of an English invasion of Scotland in 1482, and that the criticism of Arthur's faults reflects disapproval of the behaviour of James III and his friends ('Secular Politics and the Date of *Lancelot of the Laik*', *Studies in Philology*, 40 (1943), 1-13). K.-H. Göller, 130; 137ff.) discusses possible connections between the narrative and the conflict between James III and the Lord of the Isles.

138. R.J. Lyall ('Politics and Poetry', 5-29) points out that most of the advice given by Amytans to Arthur is already present in the French romance, and that the political thinking tends to be general and conventional.

139. James III's habit of consorting with 'familiar' friends of low rank provoked dissatisfaction among his nobles, and in 1482 a number of these courtiers were hanged by a group of lords at Lauder Bridge (Ranald Nicholson, *Scotland: The Later Middle Ages* (Edinburgh, 1974), 501-5).

The Awntyrs off Arthure

140. The earliest manuscript (second quarter of the fifteenth century) is the south-east Midland or London version in Lambeth Palace MS 491. Chapter Library of Lincoln Cathedral MS. 91 (the 'Lincoln Thornton' manuscript) was copied by Robert Thornton between 1422 and 1454, probably in the 1440s; for facsimile see D.S. Brewer and A.E.B. Owen, intro., *The Thornton Manuscript (Lincoln Cathedral MS 91)* (London, 1975, rev. 1977). The Ireland-Blackburne MS belonged to the family of that name at Hale in Lancashire until 1945 and was copied, perhaps at Hale, in the third quarter of the fifteenth century; it is now in the Robert H. Taylor Collection in Princeton. Lincoln 91 and Ireland-Blackburne contain other romances and Lincoln 91 and Lambeth 491 also have devotional and alliterative texts; the fourth manuscript, Bodleian Library MS Douce 324, now contains only *Awntyrs* but with six other fragments in the Bodleian Library once formed part of a miscellany of nearly 300 folios probably dismembered by Thomas Rawlinson. For more detailed information on the manuscripts, see *Hanna*, 1-11, and footnotes. For general discussion of scribal mark-up in romances, including *Awntyrs*, to facilitate performance and to emphasize narrative structure, see Phillipa Hardman, 'Fitt Divisions in Middle English Romances: A Consideration of the Evidence', *YES*, 22 (1992), 63-80, esp. 76-7, 80. A.I Doyle gives an overview of the four manuscripts in Lawton, 94, 96 (MS L), 96-7 ([MSS T, Ir, D]).

141. A pirated edition of Douce was printed by Pinkerton in Volume Three of *Scotish Poems Reprinted from Scarce Sources*, 3 vols. (London, 1792). The Thornton MS was edited by David Laing, *Select Remains of the Ancient Popular Poetry of Scotland and the Northern Border*, 2 vols. (London, 1822), revised and corrected by John Small (London and Edinburgh, 1885), by Sir Frederic Madden in *Syr Gawayne: A Collection of Ancient Romance-Poems* (London, 1839) with variants from Douce, and again by J.O Halliwell, *The Thornton Romances* (Camden Society 30 (London, 1844)). The Ireland MS was edited by John Robson, *Three Early English Metrical Romances from a MS. in the Possession of J.T. Blackburne* (Camden Society 18 (London, 1842)), and variant readings from Ireland are printed in F.J. Amours's edition of Thornton and Douce on facing pages in *Scottish Alliterative Poems in Riming Stanzas*, STS, 27, 38 (Edinburgh, 1897), though he makes no mention of the Lambeth MS, discovered seven years earlier by Bülbring.

142. The earliest modern edition, *Gates*, purports to follow the editorial principles of George Kane, *Piers Plowman: The A Version* (London, 1960: Introduction, 115-72). The *Hanna* edition, from which citations from *Awntyrs* in this article are taken, also utilizes Kane's editorial method. Maldwyn Mills's edition (in *Ywain and Gawain, Sir Percyvell of Gales, The Anturs of Arther* (London, 1992)) is based on the Ireland-Blackburne MS and emended from Thornton. Variant readings are recorded in the critical *Gates* edition; a selective *apparatus criticus* is provided in *Hanna*, and selected variants to Ireland-Blackburne in Mills (1992), 205-10.

143. As in *Golagros and Gawane*, Gawain is prepared to renounce victory, here just before the moment of conquest, so setting the 'covetous' Arthur an example. *Golagros* is strongly influenced by *Awntyrs* (see below, n.201).

144. *Hanna* prints *Awntyrs* in bipartite form (designated '*Awntyrs* A', stanzas 1-26, 55, and '*Awntyrs* B', stanzas 27-54) on the basis of relative incidence of rhymes and iteration (*Hanna*, 17-24). This has been disputed: e.g. Helen Phillips ('*The Awntyrs off Arthure*:

Structure and Meaning, A Reassessment', *AL*, 12 (1993), 63-88) questions Hanna's statistics and criteria.

145. Hanna supplies a list of amendments to his 1974 edition in 'A la Recherche du Temps bien Perdu: The Text of *The Awntyrs off Arthure*', *Text*, 4 (1988), 189-205.

146. Kane, 52-3. *Hahn* rightly associates the 'lapidary brilliance' of the poem's language with its 'profligate consumption of formulaic phrases and type scenes' and 'nearly fetished objects' (173).

147. D.N. Klausner , 'Exempla and *The Awntyrs off Arthure*', *Medieval Studies*, 34 (1972), 307-25.

148. Ralph Hanna, '*The Awntyrs off Arthure*: An Interpretation', *MLQ*, 31 (1970) 275-97, (290). Turville-Petre (1977) also thinks that the ghost's message is ignored by both Guinevere (Gaynor) and the court, and 'perhaps the poet's message lies in the very lack of connection between the two episodes' (65). Maureen Fries ('The Characterization of Women in the Alliterative Tradition' in Levy, 25-45 (32-3)) sees Guinevere's role as central to the theme and a unifying element in the plot: she is 'an archetype of combined courtly and spiritual significance' and her example prompts Arthur and Gawain to generosity in the Galeron episode. *Hahn* (218).explains helpfully that *Awntyrs* 'creates a showcase for the display of chivalric honor, even as it raises questions . . . about the self-evident rightness of traditional aristocratic values'.

149. A.C. Spearing, '*The Awntyrs off Arthure* in Levy, 183-202; 'Central and Displaced Sovereignty in Three Medieval Poems', *RES*, n.s. 33 (1982), 247-52; *Medieval to Renaissance in English Poetry* (Cambridge, 1985), 122-42, 162; Takami Matsuda, 'The *Awntyrs off Arthure* and the Arthurian History', *Poetica* 19 (1984), 48-62; V.A.P. Lowe, 'Folklore as a Unifying Factor in *The Awntyrs off Arthure*', *Folklore-Forum*, 13 (1980), 199-223. For Spearing the theme is kingship, extended by Helen Phillips ('The Ghost's Baptism in *The Awntyrs off Arthure*', *MÆ*, 58 (1989), 49-58) to the kingship of the baptized and the contrastive changed states of descent through misfortune and spiritual ascent and ('Structure', 81, 85) 'lordship'.

150. Rosamund Allen, '*The Awntyrs off Arthure*: jests and jousts' in Fellows, 129-42. These allusions only date the second episode and the ghost's prophecy; if the whole poem was not composed by a single poet, or at the same time, then the hunt and ghost's arrival could have been composed earlier, but almost certainly not later. *Gates* (41) dates *Awntyrs* to the late fourteenth century. David Williams (in Bolton, 144-5), who terms it a courtly poem, hints that the topographical detail in *Awntyrs* and *Golagros* may be 'complimentary to the houses of local nobles'. On dialect, see A.G. Hooper, '*The Awntyrs off Arthure*: Dialect and Authorship', *LSE*, 4 (1935) 62-74. Critics now seem agreed that the author was a cleric, but no longer try to name him.

151. Common opinion is that line 48 is missing in all four manuscripts. Perhaps we have half of line 47 and half of 48. A conjectured emendation is: *With fressh houndes and fe[l]le [in fritthes they fare] / [With fele fressh houndes] þei folo[w] her fare.*

152. James I/VI termed this verse-form 'rouncefallis' (*The Essayes of a Prentise in the Divine Art of Poesie*, ed. Edward Arber (London, 1879), cited in *Hanna*, 16, n.1). Each stanza is linked to the preceding by *concatenatio*, a verbal or phrasal echo of the last lines of the preceding stanza in the opening line(s) of that following; additionally, a similar device, iteration, binds the eighth and ninth lines of many stanzas. The first eight lines

have alternating rhymes, the ninth line, which often echoes the eighth, rhymes with the thirteenth, while the inner three lines of the four-line 'wheel' are monorhymed: $ababababc^4dddc^3$.

153. With less artistry than the poet of *Sir Gawain*, but with a nevertheless keen ear, the *Awntyrs* poet exploits the change of momentum from the body of the verse to the wheel, deploying the short lines to encapsulate horror (114-17), to summarize foregoing or ensuing matter (192-5; 283-6) and to construct climax (582-5). Where iteration exists between stanza lines 8 and 9, this 'reverse thrust' operates as a brake on the narrative flow of the long alliterating lines before the brisk contrasting wheel (cf. 633-4); this may be a deliberate attempt to echo such effects as *Sir Gawain*, lines 145-50. See M.P. Medary, 'Stanza-linking in Middle English Verse', *Romanic Review*, 7 (1916), 243-70.

154. 'The Diversity of Middle English Alliterative Poetry', *LSE*, n.s. 20 (1989), 143-72. See also Thorlac Turville-Petre, '*Summer Sunday, de Tribus Regibus Mortuis* and *The Awntyrs off Arthure*: Three Poems in the Thirteen-Line Stanza', *RES*, n.s. 25 (1974), 1-14; the Appendix supplements Amours's list (*Scottish Alliterative Poems*, lxxxii-lxxxix). The thirteen-line stanza poems, many in debate form, come from both north-east and north-west Midlands, and do not form a 'school'; see Thorlac Turville-Petre (ed.), *Alliterative Poetry of the Later Middle Ages: An Anthology* (London, 1989), 'The Three Dead Kings', 3, 148-57; Angus McIntosh, 'Some Notes on the Text of the Middle English Poem *De Tribus Regibus Mortuis*', *RES* 28 (1977), 385-92. For *Summer Sunday* see Turville-Petre, *Alliterative Poetry*, 140-7. Plays 36 and 45 of the York Cycle, Christ's death and the Assumption of the Virgin, are also in 13-line stanzas, Play 36 with a bob, and both having three stresses in line 13.

155. For a suggestion that both Awdelay and Robert Thornton had access to the same kind of material used in the Vernon MS, see Lawton ('Diversity'), 159, 163. Awdelay, chaplain to the Strange family, probably retired to Haughmond Abbey, where he died about 1426. Pearsall (1977, 249-50) suggests he may actually have used the Vernon manuscript. If manuscripts of alliterative rhyming texts were circulating (in monastic circles?) in the early 1420s, both Awdelay and the *Awntyrs* poet might indeed have shared access to a text of *De Tribus Regibus*.

156. Hunting has both spiritual and cultural significance in *Awntyrs*. Matsuda ('Arthurian History', 53-4) indicates the parallel between the terrified does at the water (lines 53-6) and the fiends (164, 186) harrying the ghost in purgatory, and Phillips ('Ghost's Baptism', 55) shows the typological importance of the hunt in *Awntyrs* to the liturgy of both baptism and requiem. Turville-Petre says ('Thirteen-Line Stanza', 10-11) that the hunt in *Somer Sunday, De Tribus Regibus* and *Awntyrs* has the same function of showing vain delight in courtly pleasures which the following contrastive vision reproves, but Matsuda thinks the 'this-worldly' Round Table nevertheless has merits. For Lowe ('Folklore', 218-19) the hunt is secular and spiritual: Arthur's chase for honour ends in death.

157. See T.M. Smallwood, 'The Interpretation of *Summer Sunday*', *MÆ*, 42, 238-43. Most Gawain narratives begin with or focus on hunting, e.g. *Sir Gawain, Avowing, Awntyrs, Jeaste of Syr Gawayne, Carle off Carlile, Weddynge, Marriage*.

158. Alliterative *Morte Arthure*, lines 3220-455; cf. *Awntyrs* 266, 270-3. In addition to these lines there are five further echoes of *AMA*; see *Hanna*, 40-3, 47 for detail on allusion and lexis, and Matthews, 156-8, and esp. 209. Galeron himself seems to have come from

AMA 3636, while other names in *Awntyrs* 654-5 echo *AMA* 4075-7, 4262-7. *Hanna* concludes, surely rightly, that the *Awntyrs* poet was 'a reader of *Morte Arthure*' (47).

159. See D.N. Klausner, ('Exempla'), 309-17, and *Hanna*, 24-5. In the *Trental* the damned spirit of Gregory's mother appears as he says mass, and says that a trental of masses would save her soul from its punishment for her unconfessed sin of murdering two illegitimate children. Gregory recites the trental, three masses on each of the ten main liturgical feasts of the Church year, and the mother reappears transformed into such beauty that he mistakes her for the Virgin Mary. The ghost in *Awntyrs* asks for thirty trentals (218), nine hundred masses, and the 'mylion' (706) she is accorded may stand for the highest possible number, or for 1,000 (*mille*).

160. Discussed in *Hanna*, 38, 44-7. *Awntyrs* 82 is clearly an allusion to *Sir Gawain* 2003, and it is very likely that the audience were meant to recognize the line. Galeron twice aims at Gawain's neck (514, 583), the first blow imparting a wound which 'greued Sir Gawayn to his deþ day' (515), in imitation of *Sir Gawain* 2264, 2510 (cf. Lacy, 1991, p.36). Galeron's arrival is modelled on the tradition which shapes Bertilak's; both address Arthur as 'thou' and both discourteously do not reveal their names until pressed to do so.

161. On which see, for example, R.W. Ackerman in ALMA, 493.

162. Tarn Wadling also features as a perilous location in *The Avowyng of Arthure*, another exposition of personal integrity. It is probably 'Laikibrait' (perhaps 'lac ki brait', *lake which cries out*) where bells were said to ring daily at noon (R.C. Cox, 'Tarn Wadling and Gervase of Tilbury's "Laikibrait"', *Folklore*, 85 (1974), 128-31). For details of Middle English texts set at Carlisle, see *Hahn*, 4, n.6, 29-33. John Withrington discusses the area, and the sovereignty theme, in his edition of *The Wedding of Sir Gawain and Dame Ragnell: A Modern Spelling Edition of a Middle English Romance* (Lancaster, 1991), 10-19.

163. For example, the 'Three Dead Kings' was frequently painted on church and domestic walls and *Trental* must have formed a popular item in many household books. The diptych motif of living juxtaposed with dead was everywhere apparent in fifteenth-century transi-tombs (see Stephen Shepherd (ed.), *Middle English Romances* (New York and London, 1995), 367). The audience must be both literate and versed in oral narratives and visual icons to appreciate this reworking of a 'what do women want most' tale into a presentation of what two women in particular want (salvation of one's soul and the other's partner's life).

164. The eleven thirteenth- to fifteenth-century Latin and vernacular exempla which deal with the related themes of adulterous mother and petition for masses are identified by Klausner ('Exempla'). Importantly, Klausner observes (316) that the audience must have had a wider knowledge of Guinevere than is presented in *Awntyrs*; it is equally likely they had a similar knowledge of the related exempla, which include the detail that the serpents sucking her breasts are the murdered children. In *Awntyrs* the ghost's sin is obliquely referred to as lust, adultery and the breaking of a solemn vow (213; 205) and knowledge of the exemplary context is necessary to appreciate Guinevere's horror of the beasts biting the ghost (211). *Gates* (20-2) claims that the ghost's sin is incest, cited without question by M.V. Guerin, *The Fall of Kings and Princes: Structure and Destruction in Arthurian Tragedy*, Figurae: Reading Medieval Culture (Stanford, 1995), 213.

165. Guerin, *Fall of Kings*, 212f.

166. Spearing in Levy, 185-6.

167. This theme reappears in *Golagros and Gawane*, where it is probably imitated from *Awntyrs*, together with the stanza form. See Gillian Rogers, ' "Illuminat with lawte, and with lufe lasit": Gawain Gives Arthur a Lesson in Magnanimity', in Fellows, 94-111.

168. *Hahn* (173) comments aptly on the ways in which phrasal and episodic repetitions 'resonate with what the audience brings to the poem, at the level of conscious memory and of a cultural unconscious'.

169. This pattern is reminiscent of the traditional 'Hocktide' ceremonies for the Monday and Tuesday of Low week, in which on successive days women and men waylaid or seized members of the opposite sex who paid a small fee for release. Hocktide was also a day for settlement of rents.

170. See Matthews, 160f. S.O. Andrew ('Huchoun's Works', *RES*, 5 (1929), 12-21 (17)) was the first to see the connection between the two parts, though, like Amours, he still calls the poem 'episodic', as does Klausner ('Exempla', 325). For Benson (1965, 161) the structure shows 'juxtaposition of parallel, opposing elements without an explicit statement of their relation'; but see *Hanna*, 277, n.6 for further critical references to the structure. Jörg Fichte ('*The Awntyrs off Arthure*: An Unconscious Change of the Paradigm of Adventure', in U. Böker *et al.* (eds.), *The Living Middle Ages: Studies in Mediaeval English Literature and Its Tradition* (Regensburg, 1989), 129-36) reverts to a 'binary' view of the structure and theme, reinforcing Göller's censure (1963, 127) and Gillian Rogers (' "Illuminat with lawte" ', 110) also thinks Gawain learns nothing from the ghost and that 'the *conjointure* is awkward and ungainly'.

171. The territories over which sovereignty is claimed in *Awntyrs* are modern Cumbria and S.-W. Scotland, which formed the ancient kingdom of the 'Strathclyde Welsh', in the Middle Ages called 'Galloway'; William of Malmesbury in *Gesta Regum* terms it 'the kingdom of the greatest Gawain'.

172. As the poem is currently constructed, the final stanza then reverts to the recital of masses for the ghost, without, however, mentioning her.

173. This is a more extreme version of the 'gay' and 'auncian' ladies of *Sir Gawain* (941-70), the former of whom John Burrow (1965, 99) has associated with Life. *The Awntyrs* reverses the plot structure of challenge/loathly lady/transformation to beauty in *Weddynge*, presumably thus parodying the original legend, which S.A. Shepherd thinks must have had Tarn Wadling as setting and Gawain as hero, and very likely used stanza-linking and presented the answer 'sovereignty' at the sovereign mid-point ('No Poet has his Travesty Alone: *The Weddynge of Sir Gawen and Dame Ragnell*' in Fellows, 112-28). In *Awntyrs* Arthur has usurped this sovereign mid-point as well as Galleron's territory.

174. As both Gillian Rogers ('The Percy Folio Manuscript revisited' in Mills, 56) and Elizabeth Williams ('Hunting the Deer: Some Uses of a Motif-Complex in Middle English Romance and Saint's Life', ibid., 198) complain, the source text from which both *Weddynge* and *Marriage* independently derive has spoiled the type-narrative of the loathly old lady in which huntsman and bridegroom are identical. In preserving the identity of the knight challenged over misappropriated lands and confronted by a loathly lady, *Awntyrs* reverts to the type form, while reversing the elements and subverting both.

175. Hanna is right to detect an element of 'inadequacy' in the colloquy with the ghost and comic frivolity in Gawain ('Interpretation', 285, 283, 291). Klausner ('Exempla', 319)

rightly sees 'lightness of tone' in Gawain's reaction to the apparition. Gawain is trying, inadequately, to accommodate two hysterical women.

176. Critics have suggested that Gawain and Guinevere are indulging in 'something not altogether innocent' in their secluded hunting lodge woven from evergreen box and thorny berberis beneath a bay-tree (Bennett 1986, 179-81 (181)); see also Klausner ('Exempla'), 317, Spearing ('Central and Displaced Sovereignty') 251. Turville-Petre (surely rightly) says 'the suggestion of immoral dalliance is clear' ('Thirteen-Line Stanza', 10), but *Hanna* (35, n.2) suggests that to contemporary readers who knew *The Weddynge* the Gawain of *Awntyrs* 'would seem far nobler and more disinterestedly loyal to Arthur than might at first appear'. *Gates* (19), on the other hand, relates the setting under a tree beside a lake to the motif of fairy visitation, as in *Sir Gowther*, *Degaré* and *Orfeo* .

177. *The Avowing of King Arthur*, lines 129-32. There are verbal and metrical similarities between *Awntyrs* and *Avowing*, which begins with a (boar) hunt. *Avowing*, like *Awntyrs*, has been dated to 'about 1425' (H. Newstead, in Severs, *Manual*, 63)

178. Phillips ('Structure', 80) notes that the poet 'harnesses . . . local legends about ghostly apparitions at Tarn Wadling'.

179. *Wode(s)*, *holte(s)*, *frithe(s)*, *greues*: Awntyrs 9, 136, 315, 434; 43, 124, 710-11; 8, 50, 331; 60-1, 69, 688, contrast *forest*: Awntyrs 7, 80, 712. For a similar observation on the contrast of greenwood and 'fre forest' in *Gamelyn* see Barnes, 49 and n.52.

180. Marcelle Thiébaux (105) identifies 'a small number of poems where the love chase fuses with one of three other symbolic types of pursuits: the sacred or supernatural chase, the moral chase (*sic*, ? for 'mortal', as on 115-27) and the instructive chase'. As in *Sir Gawain* and *Summer Sunday*, however, this is a deer-drive, a hunt of barren hinds in the close season by the 'English' bow-and-stable method. Despite Phillips's insistence ('Structure', 75) that Guinevere is a representative of all members of her ruling class, the winter hunt of barren females must be a critique of female spiritual sterility (slanted at Joan Neville?).

181. Reinforced for the reader by the intertextual allusions to the alliterative *Morte Arthure*.

182. As Fewster, 20-21 aptly notes, 'diptych is a balanced inward-looking structure, whose meaning is created within its own highly-structured literary frame'; unlike visual diptych, comprehensible at a glance, 'diptych is a literary structure that refers to other texts in the romance genre' referring to itself and to 'analogous literary structures'.

183. Where 'he/she said' precedes speeches it is mostly scribal; distinction of characters by impersonation is easy since three are women (one aged), Galeron has a Scottish accent, Gawain a northern one, and Arthur could have a 'southern tooth'. *Awntyrs* by no means meets J.O. Fichte's proposal ('The Middle English Arthurian Romance: the Popular Tradition in the Fourteenth Century', in P. Boitani and A. Torti (eds.), *Literature in Fourteenth-Century England* (Cambridge and Tübingen, 1983), 137-53 (150)) of 1100-1200 lines for a one-hour session of oral performance (but contrast Hardman ('Fitt Divisions', 69, 71, 74); MS 'fitt' divisions are 350-450 lines). Fichte is sympathetic to the view that many more texts were privately read than has been realized. Andrew Taylor stresses the function of 'pseudo-minstrelsy' in offering the solitary reader the 'pleasures and consolations of an imaginary community' ('Fragmentation, Corruption, and Minstrel Narration: The Question of the Middle English Romances', *YES* 22 (1992), 38-62 (62)).

Hahn (10-23, esp. 21-3) has, however, outlined the implications of social bonding through actual performance and the importance of public self-presentation in the shame/honour culture of popular texts.

184. I believe *Awntyrs* was initially composed for public recitation; that it was subsequently frequently copied into household miscellanies and read by gentry and merchant households is evident from the extant manuscripts. For example, MS L and its readership (a family of merchants, based in Essex from the early sixteenth century) are discussed in Julia Boffey and Carol Meale, 'Selecting the Text: Rawlinson C. 86 and Some Other Books for London Readers', in *Regionalism in Late Medieval Manuscripts and Texts*, ed. F. Riddy (Cambridge, 1991), 143-69 (162, n.63).

185. Significantly, the ghost arrives just before noon ('fast byfore vndre', 72). See Lowe, 'Folklore', 215. Hanna notes the double allusion to 'the devil that walks at noonday' (Ps. 91:6) and fairy abductions in medieval romance (1974, p.104), and Lowe the collapse of Arthur at midday on Fortune's Wheel in *Morte Arthure* 3382 ('Folklore', p.212). After the reappropriations, all-too-familiar death will claim all. That this is silently presented for a percipient audience is to the poem's credit, and not to its detriment.

186. Spearing, *Medieval to Renaissance*, 139.

187. The same line occurs in *De Tribus Regibus*, 120a, and is a fifteenth-century commonplace: cf. e.g. *Testament of Cresseid*, 457. As Speirs (257) points out, in *Awntyrs* 'each is confronted with herself in the other – the daughter as she will be, the mother as she once was'. Phillips ('Ghost's Baptism', p.56, and 'Structure', pp.86-7) notes the unlinear and 'dizzying' presentation of time in *Awntyrs*.

Golagros and Gawane

188. The linguistic forms provide the main basis for its late fifteenth-century date. The *terminus ad quem* is provided by its appearance in the Chepman and Myllar Prints, issued at Edinburgh in 1508 as the first product of the Scottish Press. Chepman was a merchant, Myllar had previously been involved with the book trade as supplier of foreign books to the king and publisher of two works probably printed at Rouen. The royal patent, intended to give them a monopoly, was for the printing of lawbooks, chronicles, massbooks and brevaries; the vernacular Prints, including popular romances and poems by Lydgate, Henryson and Dunbar, may have been by-products suggested by their commercial sense, disseminating established works whose appeal was not exclusively courtly. On the work of Chepman and Myllar, see R. Dickson and J.P. Edmond, *Annals of Scottish Printing* (Cambridge, 1890), William Beattie, 'Some Early Scottish Books' in G.W.S. Barrow (ed.), *The Scottish Tradition* (Edinburgh, 1974), 107-20, and Priscilla Bawcutt, 'The Earliest Texts of Dunbar', in Felicity Riddy (ed.), *Regionalism in Late Medieval Manuscripts and Texts* (Cambridge, 1991), 183-98.

189. In jousting incognito against French knights at Edinburgh, James announced himself as 'the wyld knycht' or 'a knycht of King Arthuris brocht vp in the wodis' – according to Bishop Leslie's Latin History of Scotland, translated into Scots by the Benedictine monk James Dalrymple (ed. E.G. Cody and W. Murison, STS 5, 14, 19, 34 (Edinburgh, 1888, 1895), II, 128) – as if to identify himself with Perceval in aspiring to belong to the Round Table. James also planned to lead a crusade against the Turks (see Denton Fox in Scattergood 1983, 118).

190. Sir Walter Scott, in his edition of *Sir Tristrem* (Edinburgh, 1804, lvi), thought it a composite of native Celtic traditions; David Laing, in his facsimile edition of the 1508 print (Edinburgh, 1827, 8), called it an original composition.

191. The provisional grouping of texts established by P.J. Ketrick (*The Relation of Golagros and Gawane to the Old French Perceval of Chrétien de Troyes* (Washington, D.C., 1931)), solely on the basis of the comparatively brief sections involved in the Scots redaction, is confirmed by the overall analysis of William Roach, editor of the *Perceval Continuations* (First Continuation, 3 vols. (Philadelphia, 1949-52), I, xiii-xli), who classifies the 1530 print as a text of the Long Redaction. Ketrick noted the surviving rhymes and obvious rhyme substitutions which indicate its derivation from the verse versions (79-80), and a limited number of readings found in none of the verse texts – mainly rhetorical and verbal changes necessitated by prosification – which have left traces in the Scots redaction (119-20). He assumed that the latter derived, not directly from the 1530 print, but from a related prose recension of the *Perceval* Continuations for whose existence in late fifteenth-century England there is some evidence (120-1).

192. Within the stanzas, the first nine lines alliterate on three or, more commonly, four stressed syllables, while the remaining lines, of three syllables, alliterate less regularly, the whole rhyming *ab, ab, ab, ab, c, ddd, c*. The effect of elaboration and concentration is increased by additional ornamental alliteration, the inclusion of the end-rhymes in the alliterative patterns, and occasional linking of pairs of lines by running the same alliterating letter through both. The corpus of poems in the thirteen-line stanza is described in Turville-Petre 1977, 115-21. *Golagros*, with other Scottish poems in the thirteen-line stanza, uses a distinctive form of the ninth line, equal in length to the opening eight rather than the shorter final quatrain, of which *The Awntyrs off Arthure*, written in the Carlisle region early in the fifteenth century, provides the only English example. The assumption that the English poem provided the model for the Scottish examples remains hypothetical, given our incomplete knowledge of both English and Scottish canons. On the strengths and limitations of the stanza as a narrative medium, see Felicity Riddy in *The History of Scottish Literature*, I, ed. R.D.S. Jack (Aberdeen, 1988), 39-48.

193. References are to the line-numbers of the English text in the *Amours* edition, and to the folio and column numbering of the *Tresplaisante et Recreative Hystoire du Trespreulx et Vaillant Chevallier Perceval le Galloys* in the British Library copy (C. 7b. 10) of the 1530 prose print.

194. Sir Spynagros appears elsewhere in romance, both French and English, as a minor member of the Round Table, Malory's Espynogrys. His name may have been borrowed because it alliterates with various parts of the verb 'to speak', since that is his principal function in the romance. Alliterative convenience probably also dictated the names of minor characters, such as the combatants in the jousting where Gaudifeir is matched with Galiot, Rannald with Rigal, Lyonel with Louys, and so on. These are, for the most part, substitutes for the names in the original, and the list of Arthur's chosen companions on his mission, given there, is naturally omitted. Many of the substitutes – Lyonel, Evin, Bedwar, Cador – are familiar from the Matter of Britain. Golagros, too, a necessary substitute for the alliteratively clumsy 'le Riche Souldoier', was no doubt partly determined by the need to alliterate with 'Gawain' in their frequent exchanges. The name has been variously explained: as related to that Galagars who appears in Malory (Sir Frederic Madden (ed.),

Sir Gawayne: A Collection of Ancient Romance Poems (London, 1839), 341), as derived by corruption of Chastel Orguelleus (Moritz Trautmann, *Anglia*, 2 (1879), 403), or originating in a descriptive phrase *'li gales gros'* or *'li galois gros'* for a powerful knight whose castle stands, according to the Scots poet, 'on the riche riuer of Rone' (1345) (Ketrick, *Relation,* 114). Of the various forms of his name in the text, that used here is the one given in the colophon of the 1508 print.

195. All known texts of the First *Perceval* Continuation agree with the 1530 print in including the hunting episode. That it was also in the exemplar used by the Scots redactor is suggested by the fact that he gives as the signal for Golagros's entry into the combat the ringing of bells (774-82) which in the French (f.115^{v}a) signal the cessation of hostilities from Saturday noon to Monday morning, spent by Arthur's companions in hunting. Elsewhere he reproduces the sounding of a horn (519-39) which is the signal for engagement in the French text.

196. Kay's victory, evoking the valiant seneschal of the chronicle tradition, in which his role as Arthur's loyal lieutenant parallels Gawain's, is made plausible by his dual reputation – see Gowans, *passim*, and Christopher Dean 'Sir Kay in Medieval English Romances: An Alternative Tradition', *English Studies in Canada*, 9 (1983), 125-35. But under the heroic surface there are details which ironize the contrast with Gawain's 'defeat'. The members of the Round Table watching his capitulation in uncomprehending horror cannot know, as the reader does, that Kay lay in ambush for *his* opponent (840) and offered his act of mercy because he was himself exhausted (869-72). Both opponents blame their defeat on Fortune, making the comparative valour of the traditional rivals seem irrelevant. By ironically undermining the conventional contrast between them, the Scots redactor presumably intended to stress the need to discriminate between appearance and reality in judging chivalric conduct, a basic theme in his romance.

197. Golagros, who had slipped in struggling with Gawain (1021-4), attributes his defeat to Fortune, under divine control: ' "Quhare Criste cachis *(directs)* the cours, it rynnis quently *(easily)*; / May nowthir power nor pith *(strength)* put him to prise" ' (1223-4). There is, perhaps, a dual implication: for his followers, that he is worthy still to be their 'gouernour', since his surrender was in obedience to God's will; for Gawain, as Arthur's representative, a reminder of the instability of all human enterprise – ' "Quhan on-fortone quhelmys *(turns)* the quheil, thair gais grace by" ' (1225), exemplified by reference to eight of the Nine Worthies, the missing name being Arthur's, for whom the ominous implications of the turning of Fortune's wheel would be familiar to readers of, among other texts, the alliterative *Morte Arthure* – see K.-J. Höltgen, 'König Arthur und Fortuna', *Anglia*, 75 (1957), 35-54. The implicit moral commentary is characteristic of the Scots redaction.

198 Arthur's final *volte face*, though benign, illustrates again that instability of temperament whose moral implications are hinted at in Golagros's commentary on the role of Fortune in human affairs (see n.197 above). Returning in haste from his pilgrimage to the city of Christ, 'that saiklese *(guiltless)* wes sald, / The syre that sendis all seill *(good fortune)*' (3-4), vowing to exact homage from Golagros ' "Or ellis mony wedou / Ful wraithly sal weip" ' (297-8), he nonetheless cries in distress for his embattled knights (693-4), calls out to Christ in fear when he sees Gawain hard pressed (953-9), prays for an outcome which will preserve both combatants' honour (1004-11), moans and weeps when he thinks his nephew defeated (1129-41), and is fearful of attack when he sees the

procession of submission approaching (1259-71). By the form of his submission (1316-23), Golagros makes clear that it is due not to Arthur's compulsion but the magnanimity of Gawain, ' "yone bald berne, that broght me of bandis" ' (1316). The reader is able to observe the contrast between Gawain and Arthur, and his intemperance in the use of power against which Spynagros warned at the beginning of the episode (274-92): ' "Your mycht and your maisete mesure (*use with moderation*) but mys (*without offence*)" '.

199. For a more detailed analysis of the redaction emphasising thematic change, see W.R.J. Barron, '*Golagrus and Gawain*; A Creative Redaction', *BBIAS*, 26 (1974), 173-85; and for one concentrating on the nationalistic perspective, see R.D.S. Jack, 'Arthur's Pilgrimage: A Study of *Golagros and Gawane*', *Studies in Scottish Literature*, 12 (1974-5), 3-20.

200. The background to 'political' readings of *Golagros and Gawane* is the Scottish tradition of national origin from Athens, at variance with the myth perpetuated by Geoffrey of Monmouth of British origin from Troy – see William Matthews, 'The Egyptians in Scotland: The Political History of a Myth', *Viator*, 1 (1970), 288-306. The ancestral enmity of Greeks and Trojans is developed in the Scottish chronicles where, from the fourteenth century onwards, Modred is treated as a Scottish hero, lawful heir to the British throne, fighting for his birthright against the illegitimate Arthur (Fletcher, 241). Such 'history' was cited in diplomatic disputes, the English boasting that Arthur had subjugated the Scots, while they cited his adulterous siring as undermining his claim to the British throne. Against this background Arthur's wars were seen as imperialistic, an embodiment of the contemporary threat from English kings to Scottish independence, justifying the generally pejorative characterization of him in Scottish romances – see G.W.S. Barrow, *The Anglo-Norman Era in Scottish History* (Oxford, 1980), 145-6, and S. Reynolds, 'Medieval "Origines Gentium" and the Community of the Realm', *History*, 68 (1983), 375-90.

Opinions differ on how severely Arthur is criticized in *Golagros*: Göller (1963, 123) sees the adverse effects of the poet's evident sympathy for Golagros as modified by the likelihood that his aristocratic audience would be familiar with the Arthur of French and English romance. But in Matthews (168-71) Arthur is accused of covetousness, vainglory, wilfulness and ruthless cruelty, a poltroon avoiding personal engagement in the fighting, hypocritical and deaf to advice – a hostile portrait seen as voicing 'Scottish political feeling toward England arising from Plantangenet claims to Scottish sovereignty and the ensuing wars' (170).

But there is nothing uniquely Scottish in such pejorative characterization of Arthur. In the *Livre du Chastel Orguelleus* itself he is petulant and querulous, sitting silent at a banquet, carelessly wounding his hand with a knife, bursting into tears and accusing his knights of disloyalty for their failure to rescue Girflet – though the tactical responsibility is surely his. In *Hunbaut* (c. 1250), learning that the King of the Isles maintains the independence of his ancestral domain, he sends Gawain to demand his submission. His decline from the benign and just chivalric leader of Chrétien's romances to the imperious, aggressive, often unjust ruler of many thirteenth-century texts is chronicled in Schmolke-Hasselmann, 61-7. Flora Alexander ('Late Medieval Scottish Attitudes to the Figure of King Arthur: A Reassessment', *Anglia*, 93 (1975), 17-34) argues that, by comparison, the Scottish texts are not more uniformly pejorative: the Chronicles are not openly hostile to Arthur until late in the Middle Ages, he is often cited as a heroic exemplar, and his failings as exposed in Scottish romances are less prominent than in the alliterative *Morte Arthure*.

201. In embodying the spirit of Scottish independence, Golagros forms part of the literary tradition which produced Barbour's *Bruce* (1376), Harry's *Wallace* (*c.* 1470), the Border ballads whose heroes resist the dominance of both Scottish and English monarchs, even *Rauf Coilyear* (late fifteenth century) who proves to Charlemagne that a humble charcoal-seller is nonetheless master in his own house and to Roland that inherent manliness can equal chivalric prowess in combat against the Saracens. 'The precariousness of Scotland's existence as an independent nation appears to have exerted a profound influence on her literature' (Walter Scheps, 'Chaucer and the Middle Scots Poets', *Studies in Scottish Literature*, 22 (1987), 44-59 (48)). Scheps attributes the democratic spirit of such literature and its preoccupation with events of daily life to the fact that escape into the mythic past had been barred by the remoteness of Troy and Thebes and the English associations of Arthurian matter (49). But *Golagros and Gawane* demonstrates what contemporary relevance Scots could find in outdated romance matter, even if the embodiment of national spirit had to be created out of resistance to imperious Arthur in emulation of chivalric Gawain.

Congruity of theme has even led to the suggestion (by Matthew McDiarmid, '*Rauf Colyear, Golagros and Gawane*, Hary's *Wallace*: Their Themes of Independence and Religion', *Studies in Scottish Literature*, 26 (1991), 328-33) that all three poems are by the same author, the blind minstrel Harry, supported (in the Introduction to McDiarmid's edition of the *Wallace* (STS, 4th Series, 4, 5 (Edinburgh 1968-69), I, cviii-cxxxii) by technical arguments on common use of alliterative phrases, plainness of diction and sharpness of visualization, preference for a manly man as hero rather than romance stereotypes, and allusion to the same non-Arthurian sources.

Technical details apart, the literary relations of *Golagros* are too complex to attribute it with confidence to the author of any other existing text. Use of the alliterative medium, with its common heritage of set phrases, links it to such texts as the alliterative *Morte Arthure*, its distinctive form of the 13-line stanza to *The Awntyrs off Arthure* (see n.192 above). It also has thematic links with both: with the *Morte Arthure,* in their ambiguous judgement of an imperious Arthur, and with the *Awntyrs* in bi-partite structure, episodes unified by thematic parallels, underlying consciousness of Anglo-Scottish conflict, and involvement of Gawain in Arthur's abuse of power, assisting yet tacitly criticizing him. (On these and other parallels between the three poems see Gillian Rogers and Rosamund Allen in Fellows, 94-111, 129-42.) Much work remains to be done on the relation of *Golagros* to the literature of Scotland and the Borders

202. Since Chepman and Myllar set up their Edinburgh press at James IV's request, it is reasonable to assume that *Golagros and Gawane* was meant for his eyes. But some of the Chepman and Myllar texts also appeared in the Asloan Manuscript, an anthology of prose and verse compiled between 1513 and 1530 by John Asloan, scribe and notary: 'a man of no very advanced tastes or ideas, [who] seems, in his selections of verse, to be copying out what other people read, and printed, not to be following any recherché interests of his own' (Denton Fox in Scattergood 1983, 120). Many items are now missing from the mutilated manuscript, but the Table of Contents shows that *Golagros* was once among them. (See W.A. Craigie (ed.), *The Asloan Manuscript*, STS, 2nd Series 14, 16 (Edinburgh, 1923-5), xiii-xv, and Catherine van Buuren (ed.), *The Buke of the Sevyn Sages* (Leiden, 1982), 1-41).

That such a text was widely read in sixteenth-century Scotland might well suggest that chivalric values were still subtly appreciated there, not in a petrified, archaic form but with critical awareness of tensions within Scottish feudalism, such as that rebellion which dethroned and killed James IV's father, in which he himself was complicit. If it was open to lesser men to cast James as the imperious Arthur, he may well have seen himself as Golagros, a patriot in gallant resistance to an invading power: 'in him . . . all that is bright, reckless, and fantastical in the late medieval tradition finds superb expression. He was primarily a knight, only secondarily and disastrously a king' (C.S. Lewis, *English Literature in the Sixteenth Century* (Oxford, 1954), 66). His quixotic chivalry cost Scotland dear when, before Flodden, he refused his master-gunner permission to fire on the English crossing a bridge – ' "for I am determinate to have them all before me on ane plain field and essay them what they can do"; and so it came about that in later times men could point to no great house in Scotland that had not a grave on Brankstone Moor' (ibid., 67). And in death, according to Bishop Leslie's History (n.189 above), he was joined with Arthur in romantic myth as a national hero vanished from sight but surviving still; the English carried off the body from the battlefield but 'our king was seine that nycht in Kelso hail and sound' (II, 146).

The Jeaste of Syr Gawayne

203. The most important evidence for this is the allusion to 'sir Florens . . . that was gotyn of sir Brandyles systir uppon a mountayne' in Malory's 'King Arthur and the Emperor Lucius' (*Vinaver*, 224). The phrase 'Aboue on the mountayne' is used as a tail-line at *The Jeaste* 52, 151 and 217; see also Terence McCarthy, 'Malory and his Sources' in Archibald, 81.

204. Lambeth Palace Library, fragment 23 (Z. 240 1.23); Westminster Abbey Library, fragment box 10; British Library, MS Harley 5927/32. In the revised Pollard and Redgrave, *Short Title Catalogue 1475-1640*, I-Z, 1986, they are listed as items 11691a.3, 5 and 7, and dated *c*. 1528, *c*. 1530 and *c*. 1540, respectively. Only the last of the three is taken into account in the editions of *Madden* and *Hahn*; an edition of MS Douce 261 as a whole is being prepared for Middle English Texts by Maldwyn Mills.

205. See Maldwyn Mills, 'The Illustrations of British Library MS. Egerton 3132A and Bodleian Library MS. Douce 261' in *Essays and Poems presented to Daniel Huws*, ed. T. Jones and E.B. Fryde (Aberystwyth, 1994), 307-27). The manuscript is dated 1564 on its final page; it has recently been redesignated as MS Bodley 21835.

206. The others are *Syr Isenbras*, *Syr Degore* and *Syr Eglamoure of Artoys*.

207. The reference to 'chase' here, and the example of some other short romances of Gawain, convinced *Hahn* (p.393 and p.414) that *The Jeaste* began with a scene of hunting. But since Gawain is armed and dressed for fighting (47, 147, 450, 500) it may be that the allusion is metaphorical, with the 'hunting ground' lying within the compass of his arms.

208. None of these fragments, however, contains any of the lines missing from the transcript: the Lambeth fragment begins at line 291 of that copy; the Westmister fragment at line 299; the Harley fragment at line 489.

209. This time the gap is larger, corresponding to no fewer than sixty pages of the prose text; the second component is set between the two sections from which *Golagros and Gawane* is derived. On the *Perceval* Continuations see the edition by William Roach

(n.191 above), here especially II, E. 6057-609 and E. 13611-5181 of the Long Redaction (to which the prose text is most closely related).

210. For the differences between the two accounts, see R.E. Bennett, 'The Sources of *The Jeaste of Syr Gawayne*', *JEGP*, 33 (1934), 57-63, and Pierre Gallais, *L'imaginaire d'un romancier français de la fin du XIIe siècle* (Amsterdam, 1988-9), 26-31, 63-70, 2259-83.

211. Since this occurs in the only three-line stanza in the entire poem, it may either be a late insertion, or the garbling of what was a stanza of six lines in the original.

212. This title is now preserved only in the colophon; there is also an allusion to 'thys lyttell Jeste' in the final stanza (537). Among other things, the word could suggest, in part ironically, 'a poem or song about heroic deeds, a chivalric romance' (MED *gest(e* n. 1(a)), or, more neutrally, 'an exploit' (MED 2(a)). MED 2(c) '? a disreputable prank' is too uncertain and simplistic to be a plausible gloss.

213. Although Gawain loudly laments his lack of a horse in 492-6, it is never explicitly said to run away like those of Gylberte and Gyamoure (84 and 158), nor are there any explicit references to fighting on horseback in the preceding combat with Brandles (the illustration on f.23ᵛ of the Douce copy reflects this by depicting, uniquely, a fight on foot).

214. A possible exception is the comment that, when Terry was knocked off his horse by Gawayne, 'in the earth hys helme stack' (267). Almost the same detail follows the unhorsing of Kay in *Ywain and Gawain* (1325-6).

215. In *Lybeaus Desconus* the hero is obliged to fight – although not in separate episodes – with the three nephews of the knight he had defeated in the immediately preceding episode (C. 454-519). This part of *Lybeaus* also offers some parallels of detail and wording with *The Jeaste*.

216. In these Gawain names himself to the lady, but is each time disbelieved – in the first account until she has checked his features against those of a portrait of him (E. 6277-318); in the second, because of his ignoble and discourteous behaviour (E. 13827-37).

Sir Gawain and the Green Knight

217. *Sir Gawain* and the three religious poems found with it in BL MS Cotton Nero A.x., Art.3, written during the latter half of the fourteenth century in the north-west Midlands dialect of the Staffordshire Cheshire border, are generally accepted as the work of one poet still unidentified. For some technical support for the unity of authorship, see R.A. Cooper and Derek Pearsall, 'The *Gawain*-Poet: A Statistical Approach to the Question of Common Authorship', *RES*, 39 (1988), 365-85. The alliterative medium is common to them all, *Gawain* employing a demanding variation in which unrhymed long lines are grouped in paragraphs of varying length, punctuated, often at a narrative crisis, by a single-stress line rhyming with a concluding quatrain of three-stress lines. Combining the ease of blank verse narration with the periodic pat summation of tail-rhyme, and exploiting structural alliteration for everything from descriptive accumulation to the word association of witty conversation, the poet exploits traditional elements in a unique way.

218. As examples of the former view, see Otto Löhmann, *Die Sage von Gawain und dem Grünen Ritter* (Königsberg, 1938) and Else von Schaubert, 'Der englische Ursprung von *SGGK*', *Englische Studien*, 57 (1923), 330-446, of whom the second compared what she saw as the unintegrated structure of *Gawain* with the juxtaposing of episodes, one moral and one chivalric, in *The Awntyrs off Arthure*, *The Avowynge of King Arthur* and

Golagros and Gawane. On the latter view, see W.R.J. Barron, 'French Romance and the Structure of *SGGK*' in W. Rothwell *et al.* (eds.), *Studies in Medieval Literature and Languages in Memory of Frederick Whitehead* (Manchester 1973), 7-25, and J. Gardner, *The Complete Works of the* Gawain-*Poet* (Chicago, 1965): '. . . to the extent that all elements in the poem are interrelated to form a coherent and balanced whole – both literal and symbolic – from which no part can be removed without serious damage to the poem on both levels, we can be absolutely certain that the interrelationship, together with the resulting aesthetic effect, is to be credited to the *Gawain*-poet himself' (26).

219. Elizabeth Brewer, SGGK: *Sources and Analogues*, 2nd edn. (Cambridge, 1992), demonstrates the variety of analogues to the poem's plot components, none of which give any hint of its structural complexity and thematic subtlety.

220. For an outline of related literary techniques, see W.R.J. Barron, 'Chrétien and the *Gawain*-Poet: Master and Pupil or Twin Temperaments?' in Lacy 1987-8, II, 255-84, where it is suggested that the similarities reflect not imitation but a common approach to romance in which irony and ambivalence invite the reader to determine the balance between chivalric idealism and human imperfection. For an exhaustive survey of literary influences, see Putter, who identifies not passive dependence but a common purpose, 'to discipline and refine chivalric behaviour by laicizing clerical ideals of courtliness and *conscientia*' (250), drawing mutually upon a common stock of literary themes and motifs and exploiting established conventions to manipulate audience expectations, create suspense and achieve psychological depth.

221. On the linguistic localisation of the text see H.N. Duggan (in Brewer 1997, 240-42) who, distinguishing between the poet's dialect and the scribe's, suggests Staffordshire as the area of composition. On its geographical setting, see R.W.V. Elliott, *The Gawain Country* (Leeds, 1984).

222. It has been variously suggested that the audience may have included the country gentry who were benefactors of monastic houses in the north-west Midlands and profited from their considerable libraries, great nobles who maintained households on and periodically visited their local estates, or men of the region who sought advancement in the court of Richard II and found there others to whom the provincial alliterative medium was an acceptable vehicle for complex moral and social ideals. (See Turville-Petre 1977, 40-47, Salter 1988, 105-10, and Bennett 1983, 231-5.) Though there is general reluctance to believe that such a sophisticated text could have been produced for provincial gentry, it seems increasingly accepted that they and the rising bourgeoisie were the audience for romance in English. For an assessment of the scanty evidence, including relevant bibliography, see P.R. Coss, 'Aspects of Cultural Diffusion in Medieval England: The Early Romances, Local Society and Robin Hood', *Past and Present*, 108 (1985), 35-79, Barron 1987, 231-5, and Rosalind Field in Lawton, 54-69, 136-40.

223. Various attempts to name the poet or to identify probable patrons among the nobility and gentry of the north-west Midlands have not solved the basic enigma. Rosalind Field, however, points out (in Lawton, 54-69) the parallel coexistence of provinciality with courtliness in the Anglo-Norman romances of the late twelfth and thirteenth centuries which 'provided a body of courtly and independent provincial literature, serving the needs and reflecting the interest of an audience which, while separate from the London court, was far from unsophisticated, and which appreciated lengthy well-structured romances with a conservative, insular and often local flavour' (58). The formation, social and

educational, of such a mind as the *Gawain*-poet's, so affectionately familiar with yet critically detached from chivalric values, cannot have been merely conventional, whether as court poet or provincial chaplain.

224. The interpretative problems raised by narrative patterns common to romance and folk-tale are helpfully explored by B.A. Rosenberg in Heffernan, 61-84.

225. 'No member of the Round Table appealed more strongly to the English imagination than Sir Gawain, perhaps because he could be most readily identified with the archetypal folk-hero seeking self-knowledge through adventure.' '. . . with them he remains the loyal lieutenant of dynastic romance, the embodiment of the basic knightly virtues in accounts of his own chivalric adventures, but also as the most prominent protagonist in a group of folk romances in which Arthur and his companions are subjected to the kind of test by which popular heroes establish their identity' (Barron 1987, 158-9).

226. The analysis of this group of Gawain romances – including, among others, *Syre Gawene and the Carle of Carelyle*, *The Turke and Gowin*, *The Marriage of Sir Gawaine* – (by Clinton Machann, 'A Structural Study of the English Gawain Romances', *Neophilologus*, 66 (1982), 629-37) on principles akin to those applied to folk-tale by Vladimir Propp, stresses the limitations of structural analysis which, though revealing the pattern of the underlying myth, does not exhaust the interpretative possibilities of a text such as *Sir Gawain*, 'the product of the complex but coherent relationship among many levels of codes, which together give it "full meaning"' (636). Derek Brewer (1988, 1-9) sees the folk-tale as offering the key to understanding the romance, the latent content which controls the manifest content expressed by characterization, description, authorial comment, with the ego as the true hero and the centre of conflict within the nuclear family in which he struggles to free himself from parental control to achieve independence, and maturity in relation to the opposite sex. In his interpretation (1980, 72-91) the rite-of-passage test is imposed on Gawain by the Green Knight/Bertilak as father-figure and his wife as mother-figure – ' "split" into her aged and authoritative and consequently (as the protagonist feels) malevolent aspects, as Morgan le Fay, and correspondingly into her affectionate and cuddly aspects, with her bare breasts, maternally and erotically attractive and kind, as the young lady' (84). A.V.C. Schmidt ('"Latent Content" and "The Testimony in the Text": Symbolic Meaning in *SGGK*', *RES*, 38 (1987), 145-68) finds the testimony of the text somewhat strained – *are* the Lady's breasts bare, does Gawain show *filial* feeling towards her? – in support of a Freudian reading which undervalues the moral, religious and theological dimensions of the poem (165). He agrees, however, with Brewer in recognizing that *Sir Gawain* ' "recapitulates not only the history of the individual's struggle through a crucial stage of life but also something of the history of the race, or at least a very general psychic struggle" (p.89)' (167).

227. Under restrictions of space, I have concentrated here on advances of the last twenty years, much earlier scholarship having been absorbed into the growing consensus. For a wider range of publications see the specialist bibliographies on the works of the *Gawain*-poet: Malcolm Andrew (New York and London, 1979); R.J. Blanch (Troy, N.Y., 1983), plus supplements in *Chau. Rev.*, 23.3 (1989), 251-82 and 25.4 (1991); 363-86; Meg Stainsby (New York, 1992). For a summary review of recent, mainly American, publications, see J.T. Mathewson in Lagorio, I, 209-33.

228. The edition referred to and quoted from throughout is *Tolkien and Gordon*.

229. See, for example, G.T. Engelhardt ('The Predicament of Gawain', *MLQ*, 16 (1955), 218-25): 'As the pentangle may be drawn in one continuous movement, so it becomes the symbol of the complete man, whose integrity admits no imperfection' (218), and Burrow (1965): 'Just as a broken pentangle loses its magical power, so "truth" loses its moral power if it is "sundered" in any of its parts; for it is an ideal of *integrity* or oneness' (50).

230. See Arthur (53-105), who summarizes: 'The pentangle, like the word *trawþe*, is therefore ambiguous . . . When it is attributed to God, it means Truth, and when it is attributed to a man, it means faith.' 'The pentangle is best seen as a sacramental badge, a visible indication of the inward spiritual grace granted to Gawain before his departure on the quest. It is also, because of its ambiguous meaning, an excellent focus for meditation on the relationship between the limited and fragile faith that may be our possession temporarily in this life and the endless Truth in which we may participate in the life to come' (104-5)

231. Within the itemization of the pentangle itself there seems to be some discrimination between the five chivalric virtues practised by Gawain: 'fraunchyse and felaȝschyp *forbe al byng*, / . . . And pité, *þat passez alle poyntez* . . .' (652-4). The emphasis (italics mine) is perhaps merely rhetorical, but significant in a context so balanced and precise.

232. E.P. Watson ('The Arming of Gawain: *Vrysoun* and *Cercle*', *LSE*, n.s. 18 (1987), 31-45) notes how the mating of ambivalent symbols – of parrots, betokening *luf-talkyng* and divine eloquence, with periwinkle, a herb associated with Courtly Love and with the Virgin, of turtle-doves, representing fidelity in love, with *trulofez* (herb-paris) – implies an aspect of Gawain's chivalric personality whose ambiguity may prove relevant to his verbal fencing with the Lady in Fitt III.

233. See Barron 1980, 71-2; cf. E.P. Watson ('Arming of Gawain', 35-6). R.J. Blanch ('Games Poets Play: The Ambiguous Use of Colour Symbolism', *NMS*, 20 (1976), 64-85) suggests the diamonds 'þat boþe were bryȝt and broun' (618) might imply malign as well as benign qualities (75).

234. H.L. Savage (*The* Gawain-*Poet* (Chapel Hill, N. C., 1956), 41-8) sees Gawain's tactful behaviour on the first day as resembling the timidity of the driven deer, his curtness on the second day the resistance of the boar at bay, and his duplicity on the third the wily deviousness of the fox. Others developed the identification in symbolic terms: John Speirs (236-7) interprets the animals as representing the qualities in natural man – cowardice, aggression, deceit – which Gawain must resist in the bedroom, and others as symbolizing sins which he is tempted to commit there (Anne Rooney in Brewer 1997, 159). Hans Schnyder (SGGK: *An Essay in Interpretation* (Berne, 1961)) develops a full-blown allegory of Gawain, representing the human soul, struggling against such temptations in parallel to the hunt by the Green Knight, embodying the word of God, for the sources of evil.

235. See, for example, Gerald Gallant, 'The Three Beasts: Symbols of Temptation in *SGGK*', *Annuale Mediaevale*, 11 (1970), 35-50 (36), Peter McClure, 'Gawain's *mesure* and the Significance of the Three Hunts in *SGGK*', *Neophilologus*, 57 (1973), 375-87 (378), Barron 1980, 57.

236. The issues in this key passage (1859-65) are stylistically underscored: the complacency of 'he þulged with hir þrepe and þoled hir to speke' (*he bore with her insistence and allowed her to speak*) after the brusqueness with which he had earlier

silenced the Lady (cf. 1840-1); the formality of *granted*, echoing the pompous refusal of lines 1836-8 and undermined by the over-eager acceptance while the Lady is still speaking; the over-ready agreement to her requirement of concealment echoing in its double negative the earlier emphatic refusal (cf. 1836); Gawain's promise to 'lelly layne' (*loyally conceal*) the girdle (1874; 'luf-lace') from her husband seems inconsistent with his rejection of the Lady's 'lel layk of luf' (1513; *the faithful practice of love*) as an act of treason against Bertilak (1775), underscoring the nature of his surrender and the impossibility of continuing to be loyal to both husband and wife.

237. It is difficult to see how those who identify Gawain with the fox, commenting that 'on the day of the fox-hunt Gawain cunningly and wrongfully keeps possession of what is Bercilak's by right' (Burrow 1965, 98), can ignore the fact and the form of the animal's death in relation to what seems – superficially – an act of petty theft. Equally, given the strict economy of the poem, it seems improbable that any metaphorical interpretation of the earlier hunts can safely ignore the detailed description of the deaths in which they end.

238. L.L. Besserman ('Gawain's Green Girdle', *Annuale Mediaevale*, 22 (1982), 84-101), reviewing the legacy of symbolic associations acquired by girdles through the ages, concludes: 'The *Gawain*-poet chose a girdle as the instrument of Gawain's testing and fall precisely because its associations were so manifold . . . : martial valour, chastity, purity, a love-token, troth, eroticism, austerity, inconstancy in love, magical binding, spiritual preparedness, magical healing. The green girdle evokes all these and more.'(100).

239. The interiority of the essential action precludes determination of its outcome, the nature of Gawain's fault, its implications for chivalric idealism, merely by accumulation of textual clues on a detective story basis. But the *Summa Theologiae* of Aquinas, as disseminated among laymen by penitential manuals, allegorical treatises, popular preaching (see Barron 1980, 88-90), represents one strand of the network of codes – of law, chivalry, courtesy, hospitality – within which hero (and audience) operate, all consciously entertained, all vulnerable to vagaries of instinct and impulse.

240. Gawain's spiritual state – attrition or contrition, boldness or despair – after his 'confessions' to Bertilak and to the Round Table, since it concerns his relationship to God, a matter of conscience, cannot be determined by external signs. R.G. Arthur (106-27), noting that Gawain's attempt to establish the girdle as a sign of permanent 'vntrawþe' fails with the court's laughing rejection of his self-condemnation, points out that the healed wound in his neck symbolizes the correct relationship between sin and forgiveness. The girdle is rather the symbol of his *wanhope*, despair of that salvation which is his to claim at any moment. Arthur sees it as no more appropriate to his condition than the pentangle of permanent 'trawþe'.

241. On the thematic community between the four poems, see D.S. Brewer 'The *Gawain*-Poet: A General Appreciation of the Four Poems', *EC*, 17 (1967), 130-42. A.D. Horgan ('Gawain's *Pure Pentangle* and the "Virtue of Faith" ', *MÆ*, 56 (1987), 310-16) defines the common theme as aspiration to a high moral ideal undermined by mere thoughtlessness, demonstrating the futility of human effort without reliance on the grace of God (314-15).

242. The analysis abbreviated here is that of Martin Camargo ('Oral Traditional Structure in *SGGK*' in J.M. Foley (ed.), *Comparative Research on Oral Traditions* (Columbus, Ohio, 1987), 121-37). Ian Bishop ('Time and Tempo in *SGGK*', *Neophilologus*, 69

(1985), 611-19) notes how the various patterns of time in the poem serve to prevent identification of the moment at which the crisis occurs.

243. See Catherine Batt, 'Gawain's Antifeminist Rant, the Pentangle and Narrative Space', *YES*, 22 (1992), 116-39, who suggests that the hero's attempt to impose an unsatisfactory rhetorical pattern upon experience undermines the operation of rhetoric throughout, leading the reader to reassess its components in an attempt to establish the poem's 'moral centre', firm ground on which to make judgements (137-8).

244. John Finlayson, ('The Expectations of Romance in *SGGK*', *Genre*, 12 (1979), 1-24) sees the poem's final admission of its status as a romance as a belated acknowledgement of its 'self-conscious parading of the conventions of the genre and a view of society in such a way as to appear to conform to those conventions and, at the same time, suggest their artificial nature' (22).

245. On the operation of antithesis, reflecting the doctrine of the dual nature of Christ, in the poem, see Lawrence Besserman, 'The Idea of the Green Knight', *ELH*, 53 (1986), 219-39, and on the influence of contemporary dialectic, with its use of oppositions, juxtapositions, paradoxes, see T.L. Reed, Jr., ' "Boþe blysse and blunder": *SGGK* and the Debate Tradition', *Chau. Rev.*, 23 (1988), 140-61.

246. See Heinz Bergner, 'Two Modes of Existence in *SGGK*', *ES*, 67 (1986), 401-16.

247. R.W. Hanning ('Sir Gawain and the Red Herring: The Perils of Interpretation' in *Acts of Interpretation: The Text in its Contexts, 700-1100*, ed., M.J. Carruthers and E.D. Kirk (Norman, Okla., 1982), 5-23), examining the way in which the elaboration of decorative detail in the poem compels yet frustrates interpretation, concludes: '*Sir Gawain* argues that we can understand human experience only in the context of civilization's processes and values yet demonstrates that civilization chronically disguises the significance of its most characteristic manifestations, thereby eluding precise evaluation of its meaning and worth. As a result of this paradox the difficulty, or perhaps impossibility, of interpretation becomes not only a hallmark but a main theme of the poem' (5).

248. See A.W. Astell, '*SGGK*: A Study in the Rhetoric of Romance', *JEGP*, 84 (1985), 188-202 and Michael Flint, '*SGGK*: Modality in Description', *Studia Neophilologica*, 61 (1989), 157-60.

249. See C.S. Finley, ' "Endeles Knot": Closure and Indeterminacy in *SGGK*', *Papers in Language and Literature*, 26 (1990), 445-58 and Lois Bragg, '*SGGK* and the Elusion of Clarity', *NM*, 86 (1985), 482-8.

250. 'By presenting the adventures of his romance as a complex of interrelated games, by using the key term *auenture* in a variety of ambiguous contexts and linking it with others which compound rather than resolve the ambiguity, the *Gawain*-poet would seem to be stimulating the reader's scrutiny of the events he narrates: conventional quest confirming the values of chivalry, or conflict with supernatural powers bent on undermining them? The technique has an obvious functional value in restoring narrative tension to a traditional form in which the hero's survival is normally assured. But it also has a thematic function, querying the relationship between appearance and reality (the hero's bodily survival and his spiritual peril) within the narrative and, by using *auenture* to refer to narrative as well as event, the relationship between romance and reality' (W.R.J. Barron in Grout, 38).

251. Critics have noted the similarity to Chaucer's literary method, particularly in the *Canterbury Tales*, of imaginative fragmentation affording many partial and limited perspectives, often conflicting, emphasizing the misperceptions and misreadings of experience to which man is prone without compelling interpretation in the absence of any authorial commentary. See Ralph Hanna III, 'Unlocking What's Locked: Gawain's Green Girdle', *Viator*, 14 (1983), 289-302 (299-301).

B: Arthur in English Society

1. See R.S. Loomis, 'Edward I, Arthurian Enthusiast', *Speculum*, 28 (1953), 114-27. For a sceptical perspective, see Prestwich, 119-22. See also Binski, 197-8.

2. See Vale 1982, 16 and refs cit. n.153.

3. See R.S. Loomis in ALMA, 54; Vale 1996, 178; S. Selzer, *Artushöfe im Ostseeraum: Ritterlich-höfische Kultur in den Städten des Preußenlandes im 14. und 15. Jahrhundert* (Frankfurt am Main, 1996), 53. For the diplomatic background, see F.M. Powicke, *The Thirteenth Century* (Oxford, 1954), 256-63. The presence of Charles of Salerno, titular king of Sicily and a figure of some chivalric renown, may have been a particular spur.

4. Instances of 'round tables' have been rehearsed endlessly, analysed somewhat less. See, seminally, R.S. Loomis in ALMA, 553-9; for a thematic approach to English material, see Barker; for a comprehensive European outline, see Selzer, *Artushöfe im Ostseeraum*, 46-63.

5. See Philippe de Novare, *Mémoires, 1218-1243*, ed. C. Kohler, CFMA (Paris, 1913), 7.

6. Matthew Paris, *Chronica majora*, ed. H.R. Luard, 7 vols, RS 57 (1872-83), V, 318.

7. See, for example, references in bulls of Clement V, Sept. 1314, to 'justis predictis que tabule rotunde in aliquibus partibus vulgariter nuncupantur': *Registrum Clementis Papae V*, ed. Monachi Ordinis S. Benedicti (Rome, 1888), 452, 462-3 (nos. 10,023, 10,043).

8. See Vale 1982, 12-14. The English knights' reputation was clearly enhanced by their country's Arthurian associations (ibid., 15).

9. Waverley Annals, in *Annales Monastici*, ed. H.R. Luard, 5 vols., RS 36 (1864-9), II, 402.

10. See Osney Annals, in *Annales Monastici*, IV, 281.

11. See W. Rishanger, *quondam monachi S. Albani . . . Chronica et Annales, 1259-1307*, ed. H.T. Riley, RS 28 (1865), 94-5.

12. See Adam Murimuth, *Continuatio chronicarum*, ed. E.M. Thompson, RS 93 (1889), 155. The filtering-down through society of Arthurian images and forms of expression cannot be treated here.

13. See, for example, *Annales Monastici*, IV, 281: Mortimer's 'round table' at Kenilworth; ibid. III, 313: Edward I's 'round table' at Nefyn, 1284 ('ubi fecerat dominus rex apparatum maximum et expensas'); Robert de Avesbury, *De gestis mirabilibus Regis Edwardi Tertii*, ed. E.M. Thompson, RS 93 (1889), 284: Mortimer's 'round table' at Wigmore, 1328; *Continuatio chronicarum* 155, 231: Edward III's Windsor 'round table', 1344.

14. The Waverley annalist states that the round table was held 'in signum triumphi contra Wallensium': *Annales Monastici*, II, 402.

15. See *Brie*, I, 262, ll.4-14.

16. See especially Arthur's denunciation of the Duke of Lorraine in the alliterative *Morte Arthure (Hamel)*: ' "The renke rebell has bene vnto my Rownde Table" ' (2402). After his initial conquests and his coronation at Rome 'as soueraynge and lorde' (3184), Arthur announces his intention to ' "Ryngne in my ryalltés and holde my Rownde Table" ' (3214). The identification with kingship is further stressed in the association of the Round Table

with the concept of 'realty': ' "the most reale place of þe Rounde Table" ' (524); ' "The araye and the ryalltez of þe Rounde Table" ' (1665).

17. *Ex inf.* Martin Biddle, Feb. 1988.

18. See M. Biddle and B. Clayre, *Winchester Castle and the Great Hall* (Winchester, 1983), 37.

19. Ibid., 37.

20. See Adam of Domerham, *Historia de rebus gestis Glastoniensibus*, ed. T. Hearne, (Oxford, 1727), II, 587-9; Vale 1982, 17.

21. See *Edward I and the Throne of Scotland, 1290-1296*, ed. E.L.G. Stones and G.G. Simpson, II, 299. An interpolation of 1301 tells how the mythical Scots king 'Anguselus' supposedly bore King Arthur's sword in front of him (ibid., 300). See also Binski, 138.

22. Waverley Annals in *Annales Monastici*, II, 401. Recorded in similar terms in *Flores historiarum*, ed. H.R. Luard, 3 vols., RS 95 (1890), III, 59; *Annales Monastici*, IV, 489; 'Annales Londonienses de tempore Edwardi Primi', in *Chronicles of the Reigns of Edward I and Edward II*, ed. W. Stubbs, 2 vols., RS 76 (1882-3), II, 91; *W. Rishanger, . . . Chronica et Annales, 1259-1307*, 107. These near-identical statements, introducing a fleeting rhetorical cast into annalistic narratives (note also the *oblata/translata* rhyme in the Waverley Annals), suggest a common source, possibly from a declaration associated with a presentation ceremony and/or expressed in a subsequent letter.

23. Recorded in monastic chronicles at Waverley, Worcester and Westminster: *Annales Monastici*, II, 401; IV, 490; *Flores historiarum*, III, 61; also 'Annales Londonienses de tempore Edwardi Primi', 92. See Vale 1982, 17-18, nn.166, 167.

24. *Flores historiarum*, III, 61.

25. See Binski, 135, 138 (Westminster context); R.R. Davies, *Conquest, Coexistence and Change: Wales, 1063-1415* (Oxford, 1987), 355-6 (fate of other insignia from Gwynedd). The identity of what was presented is unclear: no crown appears to feature among Arthur's regalia in earlier Welsh texts; on the other hand when Dafydd, prince of Gwynedd, was knighted by Henry III and paid homage to him, at Gloucester in 1240, he wore 'diadema minus, quod dicitur garlande, insigne principatus Northwallie' (*a small diadem, which is called 'garlande', the insignia of the prince of North Wales*): *Annales Monastici*, I, 115. I am grateful to Professor R.R. Davies for this reference and discussion of the question.

26. Dunstable Annals in *Annales monastici*, III, 313.

27. R.R. Davies, *Conquest, Coexistence and Change*, 355.

28. See Arnold Taylor, 'Count Amadeus of Savoy's Visit to England in 1292', in his *Studies in Castle-Building* (London, 1985), 55 (originally printed in *Archaeologia*, 106 (1979)).

29. See Constance Bullock-Davies, *Menestrellorum multitudo: Minstrels at a Royal Feast* (Cardiff, 1978), *passim.*

30. See, for example, R.S. Loomis, 'Edward I, Arthurian Enthusiast', 114-27; Bullock-Davies, *Menestrellorum multitudo*, xxxvii-xxxviii; Prestwich, 121; Felicity Riddy, 'Reading for England: Arthurian Literature and National Consciousness', *BBIAS*, 43 (1991), 121.

31. See Paul Binski, *The Painted Chamber at Westminster*, Society of Antiquaries, Occasional Paper, n.s. 9 (London, 1986), 95-103; cf. the same author's perceptive comments on Edward III's tomb epitaph: Binski, 1995, 197.

32. John of London, 'Commendatio lamentabilis in transitu magni Regis Edwardi' in *Chronicles of the Reigns of Edward I and Edward II*, ed. W. Stubbs, 2 vols., RS 76 (1882-3), II, 3-21.

33. Ibid., 15.

34. Ibid., 15. Cf., for example, Langtoft's references to Arthur's death and Mordred's treachery among allusions to various disasters in relation to the lack of English success in Aquitaine in 1297: Pierre de Langtoft, *Chronicle*, ed. T. Wright, 2 vols., RS 47 (London, 1866-8), II, 284.

35. See *Chronicles of the Reigns of Edward I and Edward II*, II, xiv. Prestwich plausibly suggests (558) that the *Commendatio* includes 'material from the funeral oration'.

36. See *Commendatio lamentabilis*, 14-16.

37. Ibid., 14.

38. For the increasing use of the arms of St George, see Prestwich, 199 (archers' bracers, 1282-4); Bullock-Davies, *Menestrellorum multitudo*, xxv (six banners, 1306); cf. also Paul Binski, *The Painted Chamber*, 44 (image of St George over the king's entrance to the Hall at Winchester, 1256). For discussion of the figure of Alexander, see David d'Avray, *Death and the Prince: Memorial Preaching before 1350* (Oxford, 1994), 70-5, 196-7; for Judas Maccabaeus, ibid. 193-6.

39. See John of Reading, *Chronica*, ed. James Tait (Manchester, 1914), 129, 130, 131. For the chronicler's characterization of his work and sources, ibid., 9.

40. Vale 1982, 68 and n.164 (royal accounts); copies of other sources recording the occasion indicate that the reference is to a single quarter, that is, a canton: BL MS. Cotton Otho D. IV, f.190^r (with marginal sketch); BL MS. Sloane 301, f.259^r.

41. Vale 1982, 69 and n.169; 36 and refs cit. at n.137.

42. G.J. Brault, *Early Blazon* (Oxford, 1972), 37-54, esp. 37-40; Michel Pastoureau, *Armorial des chevaliers de la table ronde* (Paris, 1983), 17, 69-70; Lisa Jefferson, 'Tournaments, Heraldry and the Knights of the Round Table: A Fifteenth-Century Armorial with Two Accompanying Texts', *AL*, 14 (1996), 75-6.

43. Felicity Riddy, 'Reading for England', 318-19; Brault, *Early Blazon*, 24-5.

44. See 'Gesta Regis Edwardi Tertii', in *Chronicles of the Reigns of Edward I and Edward II*, II, 95.

45. G. J. Brault, building on the earlier work of R.S. Loomis, assembled a number of twelfth- and thirteenth-century instances where the English royal family were apparently complimented in this way. See Brault, *Early Blazon*, 19-23.

46. *Escanor: Roman arthurien en vers de la fin du XIIIe siècle*, ed. R. Trachsler, Textes littéraires françaises (Geneva, 1994), 27-9; G.J. Brault, 'Arthurian Heraldry and the Date of *Escano*', *BBIAS*, 11 (1959), 81-8. For links between *Escanor* and other Arthurian romances, see P.S. Noble, 'Chrétien de Troyes and Girard d'Amiens', in Lacy 1987-8, II, 143-50.

47. Brault, *Early Blazon*, 37-40 (37). The *Perceval* interpolation occurs in the Tournament at Chastel Orguellous episode (*The Continuations of the Old French Perceval of Chrétien de Troyes*, ed. William Roach, vol. IV (Philadelphia, 1971), Appendix VII, 563-87; cf. 533-4). Descriptions of the arms of Gawain and his brother are interwoven in the verse narrative (Appendix VII, ll. 25-32, 37-52).

48. See Brault, *Early Blazon*, 40, 211 and refs. cit.

49. Ibid., 40.

50. Ibid., 38-40.

51. See *Continuatio chronicarum*, 155-6, 231-2.

52. Ibid., 232.

53. See *Calendar of Patent Rolls, 1343-1345* (London, 1902), 160. For dating, see the issue of safe-conducts for attendance in Thomas Rymer, *Foedera*, vol.2, pt. 2, Record Commission (London, 1821), 1, 242; *Calendar of Patent Rolls, 1343-45* (London, 1902), 159.

54. *Continuatio chronicarum*, 232.

55. Ibid., 232.

56. Ibid., 155-6, 232.

57. Ibid., 156.

58. The romance *Perceforest* (printed by Galiot du Pré, Paris, 1528, chs.123-4) has been suggested as a source (Keen 1984, 190-1); Barker, 93-4; Yves Renouard, 'L'ordre de la Jarretière et l'ordre de l'Étoile', in his *Études médiévales* (Paris, 1968, 93-106; originally printed in *Le Moyen Age*, 1949), but there are fundamental differences in building structure (*Perceforest*, chs.123-4) and it is unclear whether the alleged fourteenth-century English source is not entirely fictitious (ibid. fos. 3^r, 3^v-4^v, 136^v).

59. See H.M. Colvin in Brown 1963, 871. The reduction in expenditure may have been one result of William Eddington's pro-active treasurership from April 1344: E.B. Fryde, *William de la Pole, Merchant and King's Banker (†1366)* (London, 1988), 185-6, 191-2.

60. In 1344 alone Philip VI of France initiated a Round Table of his own: *Chronicon Angliae, 1328-88 auctore monacho quodam Sancti Albani*, ed. E.M. Thompson, RS 64 (1874), 17; *Chronique de Jean Le Bel*, ed. Jules Viard and Eugène Déprez, vol.2, Société de l'Histoire de France (Paris, 1905), II, 25-7, 34-5; Edward III's brother-in-law, the count of Hainault, staged a *groter taffelronde* at The Hague during the week preceding May Day at a cost of over 2,000 *livres hollandaises*: *De rekeningen der grafelijkheid van Holland oder het Henegowsche huis*, ed. H.G. Hamaker, vol.2 (Utrecht, 1876), 85-7, 91, 207; vol. 3 (1878), 282-3 *(ex inf.* M.G.A. Vale; independently noted, in part, in Selzer, *Artushöfe im Ostseeraum* (see n.3 above), 52).

61. See above, p.192. For Edward III using 'George' as a battle-cry, see Robert de Avesbury, *De gestis mirabilibus Regis Edwardi Tertii*, ed. E.M. Thompson, RS 93 (1889), 410.

62 See John Cherry and Neil Stratford, *Westminster Kings and the Medieval Palace of Westminster*, British Museum Occasional Paper, 115 (London, 1995), 39; Binski, 183. Cf. also the figures of St George and the Virgin and Child on the obverse of Edward III's

seventh great seal (1360-77): W. de B. Birch, *Catalogue of Seals in the Department of Manuscripts in the British Museum*, vol.1 (London, 1867), 26-7 (no.210).

63. For the gradually emerging consciousness of national identity, see John Barnie, *War in Medieval Society: Social Values and the Hundred Years War* (London, 1974), ch.4.

64. See Vale 1981, 39-40; Keen 1984, 192.

65. Described as 'castrum illud vernantissimum', unparalleled in Europe, after Henry III's works (cit. H.M. Colvin in Brown, 866, n.12). Le Bel, Froissart and the St Alban's chronicles all refer to the tradition: *Chronique de Jean Le Bel*, 26; Jean Froissart, *Oeuvres*, ed. K. de Lettenhove (Brussels, 1867-77), IV, 203, 204; *Chronicon Angliae*, 17. The more contemporary Murimuth confines himself to describing Windsor as Edward III's birthplace: *Continuatio chronicarum* (see n.12 above), 155. For earlier literary references to the location, see P. Rickard, *Britain in Medieval French Literature, 1100-1500* (Cambridge, 1956), 111, 138. For Froissart, see Peter Ainsworth, *Jean Froissart and the Fabric of History: Truth, Myth, and Fiction in the 'Chroniques'* (Oxford, 1990), 44. For St Albans abbey's links with the court, esp. under Abbot Thomas, see Thomas Walsingham, *Gesta abbatum . . . S. Albani*, ed. H.T. Riley, 2 vols., RS 28 (1867), II. One manuscript of the *Chronicon Angliae* was made for Edward III's youngest son, Thomas of Woodstock, lending further credence to the acceptance of the association in court circles: see *Chronicon Angliae*, xxvi.

66. Froissart, *Chroniques* in *Oeuvres*, ed. K. de Lettenhove (Brussels, 1867-77), IV, 205.

67. Ibid., IV, 203-6.

68. See Brian Trowell, 'A Fourteenth-Century Ceremonial Motet and its Composer', *Acta Musicologica*, 29 (1957), 65-75, esp. 66-8. Note also his comment that 'the commanding virtuosity of *Sub Arturo* can hardly have grown out of a musical desert' (ibid., 14).

69. The text's significance was first noted in Sydney Anglo, 'Financial and Heraldic Records of the English Tournament', *Journal of the Society of Archivists*, 2 (1960-4), 188-9; it is printed, with some discussion of dating, in Heiner Gillmeister, 'Challenge Letters from a Medieval Tournament and the Ball-Game of Gotland: A Typological Comparison', *Stadion*, 16 (1990), 184-222.

70. The participants 'contrefait les aventures de Bretaigne et de la Table ronde': Philippe de Novare, *Mémoires, 1218-1243*, CFMA (Paris, 1913), 7.

71. The episode at Kenilworth (1279), where Blanche, sister-in-law of Edward I, presents kegs of wine which, it transpires, are full of gold suggests a mimetic element: Mary E. Giffin, 'Cadwalader, Arthur and Brutus in the Wigmore Manuscript', *Speculum*, 16 (1941), 111. The northern French *feste* at Le Hem (1278) suggests how such events might be structured: above, p.188; Vale 1982, 12-14.

72. Bodleian Library MS Douce 271, ff.40ʳ, 43ʳ.

73. Ibid. f.40ʳ.

74. See Giffin, 'Cadwalader, Arthur and Brutus', 111. For the Arthurian ancestor ascribed to the Beauchamps, see *The Rous Roll*, facsimile of 1859 edn. (ed. W. Courthope), with historical introduction by Charles Ross (Gloucester, 1980), para. 7; Kipling, 15.

75. Kipling, 59, 61; Sydney Anglo, *Spectacle, Pageantry and Early Tudor Policy* (Oxford, 1969), 30-1, 54-6

76. For an overview, see Richard Barber, 'Malory's *Le Morte Darthur* and Court Culture under Edward IV', *AL*, 12 (1993), 133-55.

77. See, for example, the comment of John Paston III in a letter from Bruges: 'asfor the Dwkys coort . . . I herd neuer of non lyk to it saue Kyng Artourys cort'; quoted in *Sir John Paston's 'Grete Boke': A Descriptive Catalogue with an Introduction, of British Library MS Lansdowne 285*, ed. G.A. Lester (Cambridge, 1984), 121. Cf. Kipling, 11-12.

78. Kipling, 5. For Henry VII's choice of Winchester as the birthplace of his heir, and the impact of increased interest in its legendary history in the second half of the fifteenth century, see Derek Keene, *Survey of Medieval Winchester*, vol.1 (Oxford, 1985), 104 and n.10; Sydney Anglo, *Spectacle*, 46-7. For a more sceptical interpretation of the role of Arthur, see ibid., 55-6.

6: Folk Romance

1. The two versions of the tale are here distinguished by the use of *Carelyle* for the NLW Porkington 10 version (now Brogyntyn II.1), and *Carle* for the Percy Folio manuscript version.

2. Severs, *Manual*, 15-16, gives *c*. 1400 for the date of composition of *Carelyle*, and *c*. 1500 for *Turke*. *Kurvinen* (p.53) dates *Carelyle* to the 'end of the fourteenth or the beginning of the fifteenth century', and gives *c*. 1500 as the earliest possible date of composition for *Carle* but, noting that 'Metrical and linguistic evidence shows . . . that part of the romance probably belongs to the [Middle English] period', suggests that 'an older romance was rehandled about 1500 or in the course of the sixteenth century', before 1550 rather than after (p.63). *Dahood* (p.29) considers that *Avowynge* could have been written as early as the last quarter of the fourteenth century or as late as the last quarter of the fifteenth century. See the relevant sections below for datings of the other texts.

3. See Guddat-Figge (151-9) for a description of the Percy Folio manuscript; and Gillian Rogers in Mills, 39-64 and Joseph Donatelli, 'The Percy Folio Manuscript: A Seventeenth-Century Context for Medieval Poetry', in *English Manuscript Studies 1100-1700*, 4 (1993), 114-133, for discussions of it.

4. See R.C. Cox, 'Tarn Wadling and Gervase of Tilbury's "Laikibrait"', *Folklore*, 85 (1974), 128-31, for traditions about the Tarn, and Rosamund Allen, '*The Awntyrs off Arthure*: Jests and Jousts', in Fellows, 129-42, for the Arthurian associations of the area.

5. See *Robert Laneham's Letter*, ed. F.J. Furnivall (London, 1890), 29.

6. The exception is a strange chapbook printed by J.O. Halliwell in his *Illustrations of the Fairy Mythology of* A Midsummer Night's Dream (London, 1845), 77-90, entitled 'The Singular Adventures of Sir Gawen, and the Enchanted Castle, a Fairy Tale', printed at Glasgow by J. and M. Robertson, which includes many motifs associated with Gawain in earlier Arthurian literature: a northern setting, a hideous hag, a great storm, a deserted castle, Gawain's transportation in a trance from the castle to the countryside outside, and an encounter with the queen of the fairies. By contrast, Robin Hood broadside ballads were being produced throughout the seventeenth century, and Robin Hood Garlands began to appear in the 1650s. Furthermore, both the Percy Folio manuscript and the recently discovered Forresters' manuscript, dated to the 1670s, show that variant versions were still being transcribed by individual collectors of popular material concurrently with the printed versions.

The Grene Knight

7. See Clinton Machann, 'A Structural Study of the English Gawain Romances', *Neophilologus*, 66 (1982), 629-37.

8. A range of correspondences is considered, to different ends, in G. L. Kittredge, *A Study of* Sir Gawain and the Green Knight (Cambridge, Mass., 1916, repr. 1960), 282-9; Benson 1965, 28, 34-5, 98, 169-72, 214-15; *Speed*, II, 321-30, and D. O. Matthews, '"A Shadow of itself" ?: Narrative and Ideology in *The Grene Knight*', *Neophilologus*, 78 (1994), 301-14. Matthews discounts the possibility of direct use (302), but close comparison lends more support to the opposite view, summarized by Gillian Rogers in Mills, 39-64 (54-5), and discussed by her in more detail in Brewer, 1997, 365-72.

The Turke and Gowin

9. 'Turk' here is not an indication of nationality but of being alien or other. The figure of the Turk is common to folk plays that originated in the Middle Ages and also appears in civic pageants of the sixteenth century. See *Hahn*, 352, n.10ff.

10. See R. H. Thompson, '"Muse on þi mirrour . . .": The Challenge of the Outlandish Stranger in the English Arthurian Verse Romances', *Folklore*, 87 (1976), 201-8.

11. The ultimate origin of the numerous English and continental versions of the Beheading Game may lie in the tales of the Irish hero Cuchulainn, as in the Middle Irish prose narrative *Fled Bricrend*, extant in a manuscript of *c*. 1100 but probably of a much earlier date. See Elisabeth Brewer, *Sir Gawain and the Green Knight: Sources and Analogues* (Cambridge, 1992), 18-60. For possible instances of cross-fertilization within the Percy Folio see Gillian Rogers in Mills, 53-4.

12. There are particularly close links between this passage and similar events in the fourteenth-century romance of *Thomas of Erceldoune* and the later ballad *Thomas Rymer* (F. J. Child (ed.), *The English and Scottish Popular Ballads* (Boston, 1882-98), no.37). See E.B. Lyle, 'The Turk and Gawain as Source of *Thomas of Erceldoune*', *FMLS*, 6 (1970), 98-102.

13. For a less positive view of Gawain's behaviour see R. H. Thompson, 'The Perils of Good Advice: The Effect of the Wise Counsellor upon the Conduct of Gawain', *Folklore*, 90 (1979), 71-6 (73-4).

14. See *Hales and Furnivall*, I, 88-9, and A. W. Moore, *The Folk-Lore of the Isle of Man* (Douglas, 1891), 63-7.

15. Notably the twelfth-century French *Le Pèlerinage de Charlemagne* (Loomis 1959, 496) and the fourteenth-century *Þorsteins saga boejarmagns* which derives from Thor's adventures in the Land of Giants (Jacqueline Simpson, 'Otherworld Adventures in an Icelandic Saga', *Folklore*, 77 (1966), 1-20).

16. See J. E. Jost, 'The Role of Violence in *Aventure*: The Ballad of King Arthur and *The Turke and Gowin*', *Arthurian Interpretations*, 2 (1988), 47-57.

17. In *Turke*, as in other romances, notions of hierarchy and the exercise of authority are here expressed in terms of the consumption and distribution of food. The events are bracketed by Arthur feasting (10-12), and Gromer and Gawain eating together as brother knights (301-3); the Turk, rather unjustly, accuses Gawain of offering violence rather than food (57-60), and his testing of Gawain turns upon the hungry knight's obedience in the face of severe temptation; Gawain refuses to eat with the king of Man (166-71), and threatens him with loss of power in similar terms, '"with-out thou wilt agree vnto our law, / eatein is all thy bread"' (260-1).

18. Sir Gromer appears in different incarnations in *Weddynge* (62) and Malory (*Vinaver*, 1164). See n.40.

19. See *Hahn*, 29-33.

20. The status, if not the patronage, of the Stanleys is implicit in the nature of literary production in the north-west in the sixteenth century. John Stanley, the fifth Earl of Derby, and his forces played a crucial part in the victory at Flodden Field in 1513. A near-contemporary alliterative poetic record of this encounter, *Scotish Ffeilde*, is extant in the Percy Folio, as is the late sixteenth-century, overtly pro-Stanley, ballad *Fflodden Ffeilde*

(*Hales and Furnivall*, I, 199-234, 313-40). Lexically, *Turke* can be linked to the survival of interest in alliterative poetry in the north-west in the early sixteenth century (Turville-Petre 1977, 123-5).

Syre Gawene and the Carle of Carelyle and The Carle off Carlile.

21. The section of MS Porkington 10 in which *Carelyle* appears is dated by *Kurvinen* (p.28), to between 1453, the *terminus a quo*, established by a reference to the Fall of Constantinople in that year, and 1500. *Hahn* (p.83) dates it to about 1460 or a little later, and localizes it in Shropshire. Daniel Huws, 'MS Porkington 10 and its scribes', in Fellows, 202, concludes that 'The watermarks, hesitantly but in unison, direct us to the late 1460s' and considers that 'a date *c.* 1470 for the whole book would be unexceptionable.' All quotations are taken from *Kurvinen*.

22. Both versions also misunderstand the underlying implications of the story from time to time, although the *Carelyle*-redactor in general preserves a more logical order of events, has a firmer grasp of the tale's underlying meaning than has the *Carle*-redactor, and is much less inclined to add details which sabotage that meaning for the sake of the immediate effect. See particularly Gawain's pert replies to the mind-reading Carl, e.g.: '"Sir", said Gawaine, "I sayd nought."' (*Carle*, 225), after the Carl has reproved him for lascivious thoughts about his wife.

23. *Kurvinen*, pp.66ff., gives several examples of this tendency, e.g. *Carelyle* 138/*Carle* 93-4; *Carelyle* 252/*Carle* 179-80; *Carelyle* 576/*Carle* 445-6, and also concludes that the tail-rhyme form was the original (p.70). *Carelyle* 135/*Carle* 89-90, and *Carelyle* 567/*Carle* 435-6 are examples of the added couplet line preceding the tail-line. In the following examples, the tail-line has been slightly adapted by the *Carle*-poet: *Carelyle* 600/*Carle* 467-8; *Carelyle* 633/*Carle* 487-8, and *Carelyle* 648/*Carle* 491-2. See also Kurvinen's conclusions concerning the relative ancestry of the two versions (64-71).

24. See Gillian Rogers, *Themes and Variations: Studies in some English Gawain-Poems* (University of Wales unpublished Ph. D. thesis, 1978), 319-45, for discussion of some of these tales. The concept of allowing the host mastery in his own hall is expressed more clearly in *Carle* than in *Carelyle*, in Gawain's declaration of intent before the Carl's castle: '"Wee shall make him lord within his owne"' (126).

25. In the Carl of Carlisle texts the guests taught the lesson are of course Kay and Baldwin. The principle at stake is amusingly demonstrated in *Rauf Coilȝear*, where Ralph the Charcoal-burner physically chastises the bemused Charlemagne for not allowing him to be master in his own house, and in *John de Reeue*, another Percy Folio text, with many points of similarity to the *Carl of Carlisle* story-type, where John, who boasts that he comes '"of carles kinne"' (290), and his companions kick their noble guests on the shins with hob-nailed boots, trying to provoke a discourteous reaction. See *Hales and Furnivall*, II, 550-94, for the text, and Rogers (*Themes and Variations*, 324-6; 333-4), for a discussion of the similarities between the Carl of Carlisle versions and *John de Reeue*.

26. Other examples are: *Le Chevalier à l'Epée* (before 1210), *Hunbaut* (*c.* 1250) and a fourteenth-century anonymous Italian *morale*.

27. The *Carle*-poet uses the word 'courtesy' much more frequently than does his *Carelyle* counterpart, and it is almost always applied to Gawain, so that, despite the emphasis on the *vilain/courtois* antithesis, the courtesy issue is somewhat blurred. Nothing of the implied equation between 'Carl's Courtesy' and buffets comes through into his version.

28. Baldwin here has been allotted the traditional role in the Imperious Host tales of the character who warns the hero what to expect. Here, as do his counterparts in *Epée* and *Hunbaut*, he gives details about the nature of the host's expectations of his guest. Such an explicit warning is not part of the 'pure' form of the plot.

29. This is in essence the situation in *Sir Gawain*, where the hospitable Bertilak, turning himself into an Imperious Host for the nonce, similarly devises tests to which Gawain must agree without argument.

30. The structure of this test has strong affinities with the folk-tale structure of the three siblings who each undertake the same quest in turn. The two elder siblings fail in the quest because they are innately churlish and do not understand the rules of the game. The youngest succeeds because he or she is innately good and does understand the rules. It seems clear that Kay and Baldwin are present in the tale only to point up the difference between their class-ridden approach to someone they consider to be their social inferior and Gawain's refusal to make social judgements upon his strange host. He knows the rules and plays by them; Kay and Baldwin do not, and are lucky to escape with their lives.

31. This may be due to a confusion between those versions of the Imperious Host tale which feature the wife and include 'sex hospitality' and those versions, like *Epée* and *Hunbaut*, in which the daughter supplies the female interest. In *Epée*, Gawain also marries the daughter. In *Hunbaut*, he kisses the daughter not once, as her father commands, but four times, and barely escapes with his life.

32. The Disenchantment by Decapitation motif, not to be confused with the Beheading Game found in *Sir Gawain*, and in *The Grene Knight*, is usually assumed to be an integral part of the original tale, since it is thought to explain the Carl's behaviour more plausibly and to allow for his transformation back into a normal-sized man. See for example, *Kurvinen*, p.25; G.L. Kittredge, *A Study of* Sir Gawain and the Green Knight (Cambridge, Mass., 1916, repr. 1960), 88; *Hahn*, p.373. Most commentators consider that a folio was missing from the *Carelyle*-redactor's copy text at this point, and that he was thus forced to provide his own solution to the mystery of the Carl's behaviour (see, for example, *Kurvinen*, pp.71-2). However, given that the basic framework of the tale is that of the Imperious Host, in which such transformations play no part, there seems no compelling reason to insist that Disenchantment by Decapitation formed the original denouement of the story, and given the whole nexus of 'vowing' tales, of which we have two other examples in this chapter alone, we should perhaps not be too surprised to find the Carl carrying out his vow to the bitter end.

The Weddynge of Sir Gawen and Dame Ragnell and The Marriage of Sir Gawaine

33. *King Henry* and *The Knight and Shepherd's Daughter* may be found in Child, I, 297-300, and II, 457-77 respectively. For 'The Tale of Florent' see Book I, 1396-1861 of Gower's *Confessio Amantis*, in G. C. Macaulay (ed.), *The Works of John Gower*, vol. I, EETS, ES 81 (Oxford, 1900, repr. 1957).

34. The interlude is mentioned by R. S. Loomis in 'Edward I, Arthurian Enthusiast', *Speculum*, 28 (1953), 114-27 (119).

35. In Celtic folklore the hag Eriu demands a kiss from a prince, the man being rewarded for his daring when the transformed fair lady reveals herself to be none other than the personification of the sovereignty of Ireland. Accordingly he has proven himself fit to

rule. The standard work on the subject remains Sigmund Eisner, *A Tale of Wonder* (Wexford, 1957).

36. In addition to the *Sands*, *Sumner* and *Hahn* editions, see John Withrington (ed.), The Wedding of Sir Gawain and Dame Ragnell: *A Modern Spelling Edition* (Lancaster University, Department of English, 1991), and S.H.A. Shepherd (ed.), *Middle English Romances* (New York and London, 1995).

37. For the date and background to the manuscript, see Julia Boffey and Carol Meale, 'Selecting the Text: Rawlinson C. 86 and Some Other Books for London Readers' in Felicity Riddy (ed.), *Regionalism in Late Medieval Manuscripts and Texts* (Cambridge, 1991), 143-69.

38. For a discussion of textual defects, see Withrington, ed. cit., pp.19-20. Examples of possible misreadings caused by careless copying are given in the notes to lines 131, 419 and 660. On the poem's dialectical features, Lucia Glanville in 'A New Edition of the Middle English Romance *The Weddynge of Syr Gawen and Dame Ragnell*' (University of Oxford unpublished B. Litt. thesis, 1958), 38-9, noted many north or north Midlands words, while *Sumner* (vii) pronounced the poem 'almost certainly East Midland' in nature. For identification of the Rawlinson scribe's dialect, see P. J. C. Field, 'Malory and *The Wedding of Sir Gawain and Dame Ragnell*', *Archiv*, 219 (1982), 374-81 (374).

39. For example, R. W. Ackerman (in Loomis 1959, 504) described the author as having 'meagre talents both as a story-teller and as a poet', and as showing 'no subtlety or refinement of feeling' in his work. More recently, Derek Pearsall (1977, 262) referred to the poem as 'coarse enough', adding of *Marriage* that it demonstrated 'irredeemable banality'.

40. This name also appears as that of the Turk in *Turke* (see p.203 above). In Malory's *Le Morte Darthur*, Sir Gromer Somer Joure is one of the twelve knights who attempt to murder Launcelot in Guinevere's chamber in Carlisle. Significantly, only Malory's version of the story names these knights, and we are informed that they were all 'of Scotlonde, othir ellis of sir Gawaynes kynne, other [well-]wyllers to hys brothir' (*Vinaver*, 1164. 16-17). See also Withrington, ed. cit., pp.9-10.

41. This is the only example of a Loathly Lady tale in which the hag is named. See Withrington, ed. cit., p.46, and Shepherd, ed. cit., p.252, for this choice of name.

42. As for example in lines 243-4 where the poet parodies the conventional inadequacy of the romance poet to describe female beauty by a professed inability to do justice to Ragnell's hideousness. The poet's debt to 'The Wife of Bath's Tale' is apparent (see S.H.A. Shepherd, 'No Poet has his Travesty Alone: *The Weddynge of Sir Gawen and Dame Ragnell*', in Fellows, 112-28 (117-19), but Chaucer's 'Tale of Sir Thopas' would also have provided a useful model.

43. S.H.A. Shepherd (see n.42 above), 121.

44. See P. J. C. Field, 'Malory and *The Wedding*', 376-81.

45. See Shepherd, 126-7.

46. Rosamond Allen, '*The Awntyrs off Arthure*' (n.4 above), 129-42. Interestingly, Allen suggests (138) that *Awntyrs* itself contains 'black comedy', with a narrative that parodies the association between Gawain, the Loathly Lady and Tarn Wadling. Although a local tradition cannot be ruled out, since *Weddynge* succeeded *Awntyrs*, and if *Marriage* is

derived from *Weddynge*, then it is not out of the question that this particular association in fact originated with *Awntyrs*, whose author drew upon a folk-tale motif, known since the time of Chaucer and Gower, and provided it with a local setting.

47. See Shepherd, 114-6. On the popularity of Arthurian romance in London, see Boffey and Meale, 'Selecting the Text' (n.37 above), 161.

48. Sir Frederic Madden (ed.), *Syr Gawayne; A Collection of Ancient Romance-Poems* (London, 1839), lxvii; T.J. Garbáty, 'Rhyme, Romance, Ballad, Burlesque and the Confluence of Form', in R.F. Yeager (ed.), *Fifteenth-Century Studies: Recent Essays* (Hamden, Conn., 1984), 283-301 (296-7); Child, ed. cit., I, p.289; Sumner, ed. cit., xxiv; Glanville, ed. cit., pp.64-9.

49. R. H. Wilson, 'Malory and the Ballad *King Arthur's Death*', in *Medievalia et Humanistica*, n.s. 6 (1975), 139-49.

The Avowynge of King Arthur, Sir Gawan, Sir Kaye, and Sir Bawdewyn of Bretan

50. See *Dahood*, pp.11-31 for a description of the manuscript, its date and its provenance. All quotations are from this edition.

51. E.A. Greenlaw, 'The Vows of Baldwin: A Study in Mediæval Fiction', *PMLA*, 21 (1906), 575-636 (599).

52. As such, it has been linked with others of a similar structure, namely, *The Awntyrs off Arthure*, and the Scottish *Golagros and Gawane*, and as was the case with these two, it has taken a long time for the relationship between the two parts to be understood.

53. Greenlaw, 'The Vows of Baldwin', 576.

54. W.A. Stephany, *A Study of Four Middle English Arthurian Romances* (University of Delaware unpublished Ph.D. thesis, 1969), 43ff.; Philippa Hardman ('The Unity of the Ireland Manuscript', *RMS*, 2 (1976), 58-9), relates the ethos of *Avowynge* firmly to that of the other two romances in the manuscript, *The Awntyrs* and *Sir Amadace*.

55. *Dahood*, p.36. See also J.A. Burrow, 'The Avowing of King Arthur', in M. Stokes and T. L. Burton (eds.), *Medieval Literature and Antiquities: Studies in honour of Basil Cottle* (Cambridge, 1987), 99-109; D. Johnson, 'The Real and the Ideal: Attitudes to Love and Chivalry as seen in *The Avowing of King Arthur*', in Aertsen, 189-208. A. C. Spearing's analogy occurs in his article, 'The Awntyrs off Arthure', in Levy, 183-202. Spearing himself cites the discussion of the general idea of diptych structure in Ryding, 25-7, and 40ff.

56. Later, both Arthur and Guinevere also underline the exemplary nature of Gawain's conduct, but whereas Arthur sees it as bringing him ' "Loos of þer ladise" ' (530), Guinevere sees it as an integral part of his chivalrous nature, ' "That þus for wemen con fiȝte" ' (559).

57. Found in, for example, *Octavian*, *The Earl of Toulous*, *Sir Triamour*, and *Valentine and Orson*. The particular version used in *Avowynge* is that in which a false steward, whose attempts at seduction the queen has rejected, places a man in her bed and accuses her to the king, who believes him without question and banishes the queen.

58. Analogues to the 'Murderous Women' motif are found in John of Garland's *Poetria*, and in Anatole de Montaiglon and Gaston Raynaud's *Recueil Général et Complet des*

Fabliaux des XIIIe et XIVe siècles, no. 26: D'Une Seule Fame (Paris, 1872-90), I, 294-300. Analogues to the raising of the siege are found as early as Herodotus. The first and third vows have Irish counterparts (Thompson, 1958, M 137, M 161), the second an Icelandic one (M 158). The framework for all three is that of 'The Wise Counsels' or 'The Three Wise Counsels' (see Greenlaw, 'The Vows of Baldwin', 579-97, and *Dahood*, pp.31-4, for discussion of these motifs and analogues).

59. *Dahood*, p.37, suggests that the 'Murderous Women' fabliau was brought in from another source and Baldwin substituted for the original main character, which would explain Baldwin's apparent complaisance in the affair.

60. Arthur's courage is never in question, however, and his combat against the huge boar is described in entirely heroic terms as an epic contest against a satanic enemy.

61. *Dahood*, p.33.

62. Burrow, 'Avowing of King Arthur', 109.

63. The poet is particularly successful at two-line exchanges, as for example in the scene where Arthur knocks at the door of Baldwin's wife's bedchamber: 'The kyng bede, "Vndo." / Þe lady asshes, "Querto?"' (821-2); much is conveyed in little.

King Arthur and King Cornwall

64. *King Arthur and King Cornwall* is in that part of the Percy Folio manuscript used to light Sir Humphrey Pitt's fires, occupying the surviving half-pages 24-31. Consequently, the title and the opening stanzas are missing, together with the last six or seven stanzas. In addition, there are seven gaps of eight or nine stanzas within the body of the text itself. I would estimate that no more than three stanzas are missing from the beginning. The extant lines number 302 in *Hales and Furnivall*; the total number in the complete poem would have been between 560-600 lines.

65. G.S. Burgess, and A.E. Cobby (eds.), *The Pilgrimage of Charlemagne (Le Pèlerinage de Charlemagne)* (New York and London, 1988). The English quotation is taken from this edition. The relationship between *Pèlerinage* and *Cornwall* was first suggested by Madden, the latter's first editor (*Madden*, 1839, p.357). Most subsequent commentators have agreed that some kind of relationship exists between the two. J. W. Davis, whose unpublished Ph.D. thesis, 'Le *Pèlerinage de Charlemagne* and *King Arthur and King Cornwall*: A Study in the Evolution of a Tale', Indiana University, 1973, contains an extended and valuable discussion of the matter, finds, in his detailed comparison of the two, forty-nine distinct elements in common and in sequence, with a further thirty-three other common elements, not in sequence. Some of these details are slight in themselves, but together they add up to a convincing case. Davis furthermore examines the many translations of the *Pèlerinage* ñ Scandinavian, Icelandic, Faroese, French and Welsh, and tentatively concludes that the Welsh version in the White Book of Rhydderch (*c.* 1350) is most likely to have served as the channel of transmission, since it offers the greatest number of explanations for *Cornwall*'s peculiarities (pp.379-80).

66. The fact that Bredbeddle hands over Cornwall's own sword, fetched for him by Burlow-Beanie, to Arthur with the words: '"take this sword in thy hand, thou noble King arthur! / for the vowes sake that thou made Ile giue it thee"' (293-4), suggests that it was the subject of his vow.

67. In view of the Apocalyptic overtones to the seven-headed fiend, Burlow-Beanie, this may be intended to refer to the Book of Revelation, in which may be found much of the imagery of this passage. The Book of Revelation is: 'the testimony of Jesus Christ, and of all the things that he saw' (ch.1.2) ; St John sees in his vision a mighty angel who had in his hand 'a little book open: and he set his right foot upon the sea. . .' (ch.10.1); there is reference to a flood, to St John standing 'upon the sand of the sea' (ch.13.1), and to the sea giving up the dead, all very suggestive. See also Davis (n.65 above), 263, n.86, and 359-60 for further suggestions.

68. Turpin vows to leap onto the third of three galloping horses, while juggling four large apples in his hand (Burgess and Cobby (n.65 above), stanza 28). The magic steed in *Cornwall* may be compared with the 'steede of bras' in Chaucer's 'Squire's Tale', which could transport its rider anywhere he wished to go (116-20) and would not move for anyone who did not know the secret of commanding it (180-5).

69. The idea that Guenevere had a lover before she was married to Arthur is found in both Heinrich von dem Türlin's *Diu Crône* and in Ulrich von Zatzikhoven's *Lanzelet*. In the former, Gasozein de Dragoz claims that Ginover was stolen from him more than seven years before; she had been assigned to him at her birth, and he is therefore her rightful husband, to whom she had pledged her love 'as soon as she began to talk', and whom, he asserts, she still loves. Furthermore, she seems to have some mystical awareness of his presence in the neighbourhood (trans., J.W. Thomas (Lincoln, Neb. and London, 1989), 55-6). In the latter, King Valerin 'asserted that beyond a doubt he more properly than Arthur should have Ginover, for she was betrothed to him before she was of marriageable age' (trans., K.G.T. Webster (New York, 1951), 93).

70. Cf. the Boy's condemnation of her in *The Boy and the Mantle*, and the whole Mantle/Horn tradition.

71. He also has affinities with the king of Man, in *Turke*, another alien monarch hostile to Arthur, with a notably murderous disposition.

72. *Young Beichan* (Child 53C), called Belly Blin; *Willie's Lady* (Child 6), called Belly Blind; *Gil Brenton* (Child 5C), and *The Knight and Shepherd's Daughter* (Child 110D, F, G). In each he appears opportunely, to offer information that alters the course of the tale. In Child's phrase, he is a 'serviceable household demon' (ed. cit., I, p.67).

73. The idea that a man can only be killed with his own sword is found in the Ulster Cycle, where Curoi's wife, Blathnat, gives her husband's sword to her lover, Cuchulainn, who then kills him. An Arthurian example occurs in the Milocrates episode in *De Ortu Waluuanii*, where Gawain is the protagonist.

The Boy and the Mantle and *Sir Corneus*

74. The unique copy of *The Boy and the Mantle* is in the Percy Folio manuscript, ed. cit., II, 301-11. The unique copy of *Sir Corneus*, also known as *The Cokwolds Daunce*, is in Bodleian MS Ashmole 61. The most recent edition of both poems is: *Furrow*, 271-91 (*Corneus*), and 293-311 (*Boy*).

75. Among the many other analogues are: Ulrich von Zatzikhoven's *Lanzelet*, the Prose-*Tristan* and Malory's version of it, Sir Thomas Gray's *Scalacronica*, and the fifteenth-century Icelandic *Skikkjurímur* (Mantle Rhymes). See Child, ed. cit., I, pp.257-71, C. T. Erickson (ed.), *The Anglo-Norman Text of* Le Lai du Cor (Anglo-Norman Text Society,

1973 (for 1966)), pp.4-9 and Otto Warnatsch, *Der Mantel, Bruchstück eines Lanzeletromans des Heinrich von dem Türlin* (Breslau, 1883) pp.58-84, for discussion of the analogues.

76. In *Boy*, the mantle's reaction to Guinevere is unusual. Rather than shrinking, as it does for Kay's wife or lengthening, it hangs in shreds about her, as in Heinrich von dem Türlin's *Der Mantel*, and it also changes colour, from red to green to blue to black, as in the Icelandic *Skikkjurímur*, where the mantle is described as being both yellow and grey, green and black, red and blue.

77. In *Diu Crône*, where the vessel is a cup rather than a horn, all the women have to drink from it as well, before the men have their turn. Unusually, the cup reveals the deceitfulness in the men as well as in the women. Only Arthur fully succeeds in the test, although Gawein is a close runner-up. The stipulation, in *Le Lai du Cor*, that no jealous man may drink from it either, simply reinforces the message that the wives are automatically assumed to be guilty, at the very least of adulterous thoughts, if not of adultery itself.

78. *Furrow*, p.295, however, is of the opinion that in all probability there was an original version of the tale, now lost, combining all three episodes.

79. The role of the Duke of Gloucester (also referred to as Earl) appears to be that of a catalyst precipitating the horn's unusual behaviour.

80. A dance also ends a *Fastnachtspiel* of the fifteenth century on the same theme (ed. H.A. von Keller, *Fastnachtspiele aus dem fünfzehnten Jahrhundert*, Stuttgart, 1858, no. 127). The two have nothing else in common. W. C. Hazlitt (ed.), *Remains of the Early Popular Poetry of England* (London, 1864), I, p.38, links the tale to the origin of the country dance called 'Cuckolds all a-row', mentioned by Pepys in his diary under the date 31 December 1662.

81. Such particularity, relating the tale to actual people, events or artefacts, is often a feature of these chastity-testing tales. In Biket's *Le Lai du Cor*, Carados is given Cirencester as a reward and the horn is kept on show. In *Scalacronica*, Gray says that the mantle could still be seen in his own day, in Glastonbury. Caxton's preface to Malory's *Le Morte Darthur* states that Craddock's mantle may be seen in the castle at Dover (along with Gawain's skull).

82. See Lynne Blanchfield, 'The Romances in MS Ashmole 61: An Idiosyncratic Scribe', in Mills, 65-87 (79).

83. Ibid., 86; A. McIntosh, M. L. Samuels and M. Benskin, *A Linguistic Atlas of Late Mediæval English* (Aberdeen, 1986), III, 233-4. Blanchfield, in a later article: 'Rate Revisited: The Compilation of the Narrative Works in Ashmole 61', in Fellows, 208-20 (213), describes it as a 'quasi-Arthurian tale falling between romance and exemplum. Its style is that of a romance, but its nature is that of an exemplum, illustrating how cuckoldry, like death, is a great leveller of rank . . .'

7: Sir Thomas Malory's *Le Morte Darthur*

1. The best book-length introduction to Malory is McCarthy, 1988

2. For Malory's life, see Field 1993.

3. See P.J.C. Field, 'Malory and *The Wedding of Sir Gawain and Dame Ragnell*', *Archiv*, 219 (1982), 374-81.

4. See above pp.209-12.

5. Strictly, after 31 July 1469; for the probabilities, see Field 1993, 143.

6. See A.W. Pollard and G.R. Redgrave, *A Short-Title Catalogue of Books Printed in England, Scotland, and Ireland . . . 1475-1640*, 2nd edn., rev. Katherine Pantzer, 3 vols. (London, 1976-91), II, 41 (item 801); a facsimile edition of the Morgan copy was edited by Paul Needham (London, 1976).

7. See *The Works of Sir Thomas Malory*, 3 vols. (Oxford 1947, rev. 1948; 2nd edn., 1967, rev. 1973; 3rd edn., rev. P.J.C. Field, 1990), p.1260, apparatus criticus; subsequently cited as in the 3rd edn. as *Vinaver*, to which all references by page and line number refer.

8. See William Matthews, 'The Beseiged Printer', *Arthuriana*, 7.2 (1997), 63-92, at 85.

9. This helps, among other things, to distinguish it from the late sixteenth-century Malory manuscript copied by John Grinken, olim Phillipps MS. 100, now in a private collection in Japan; see Peter Beal *et al.*, *English Literary Manuscripts* (London, 1980-   ), I.2, 323. Although Grinken's manuscript is textually negligible, being derived from Caxton and drastically abbreviated, it is significant in Malory studies as showing the reaction of Shakespeare's generation to the *Morte Darthur*.

10. *Works*, 1st edn. (cf. n.7 above).

11. See P.J.C. Field, 'The Earliest Texts of Le *Morte Darthur*', *Poetica*, 37 (1993), 18-31.

12. On the possibility of identifying that owner, see C. Meale, 'Manuscripts, Readers, and Patrons in Fifteenth-Century England: Sir Thomas Malory and Arthurian Romance', *AL*, 4 (1985), 93-126.

13. See Robert Kindrick, Introduction, 'William Matthews on Caxton and Malory', *Arthuriana*, 7.1 (1997), 6-26, at 10, and cf. W. Matthews, 'Caxton and Malory: A Re-View', ibid., 31-62, *passim*.

14. The best hypothesis is that of Hilton Kelliher, 'The Early History of the Malory Manuscript', in Takamiya, 143-56, 215-18.

15. See P.J.C. Field, 'Caxton's Roman War', *Arthuriana*, 5.2 (1995) 31-73. In one respect, the Caxton text seems to be linguistically closer to Malory than the Winchester is; see Y. Nakao, 'Retention of Final *n* in the Two Versions of Malory's Arthuriad', in M. Amano *et al.* (eds.), *Inquiries into the Depth of Language* (Tokyo, 1996), 519-34. Perhaps Caxton's years abroad left his English in some ways old-fashioned.

16. See Sally Shaw, 'Caxton and Malory', in J.A.W. Bennett (ed.), *Essays on Malory*, (Oxford, 1963), 114-45, and cf. E. Kirk, ' "Clerkes, Poetes, and Historiographs": The *Morte Darthur* and Caxton's "Poetics" of Fiction', in Takamiya, 275-95.

17. The question is controversial, but the most recent research, by David R. Jones, supports this view.

18. See, for example, George Saintsbury, *The English Novel* (London, 1913), 25.

19. *Vinaver*, xxxv-li, esp. xxxix.

20. See *Vinaver*, 326.10-18, 336-7, 493.10-11.

21. Winchester manuscript, f.113^r; cf. *Vinaver*, 287-93.

22. Vinaver's edition, by giving the two parts of this explicit with five complete pages between them, notably changes what they imply, as Kevin Grimm observes: 'Editing Malory: What's at (the) Stake', *Arthuriana*, 5.2 (1995), 5-14.

23. The Tale of Balin in particular has often been considered as an autonomous tale. Compare, for instance, R.L. Kelly, 'Malory's "Tale of Balin" Reconsidered', *Speculum*, 54 (1979), 85-99, and Jill Mann, ' "Taking the Adventure": Malory and the *Suite du Merlin*', in Takamiya, 71-91.

24. See E.D. Kennedy (ed.), *King Arthur: A Casebook* (New York, 1996), editor's Introduction xiv-xx.

25. See, for instance, Ad Putter, 'Finding Time for Romance: Medieval Arthurian Literary History', *MÆ*, 63 (1994), 1-16; Frank Brandsma, 'The Suggestion of Simultaneity in Chrétien de Troyes's *Yvain*', *AL*, 13 (1995), 133-44; Lori Walters, 'Le rôle du scribe dans l'organisation des manuscrits des romans de Chrétien de Troyes', *Rom.*, 106 (1985), 303-25; and *eadem*, 'The Creation of a "Super-Romance", Paris, B.N. fr. 1433', *Arthurian Yearbook*, 1 (1991), 3-25.

26. See Richard Barber, 'Malory's *Le Morte Darthur* and Court Culture', *AL*, 12 (1993), 133-55, at 153-4, and Robert Williams (ed. and trans.), *Y Seint Greal* (London, 1876).

27. See Field, 'Caxton's Roman War', 42-3 and Appendix I.

28. For this part of the *Suite*, see *Vinaver* 1353-65, adding now Monica Longobardi, 'Frammenti di codici in antico francese dalla Biblioteca Comunale di Imola', in *Miscellanea di Studi in onore di Aurelio Roncaglia* (Modena, 1990), 727-59.

29. See P.J.C. Field, ' "Above Rubies": Malory and *Morte Arthure* 2559-61', *N&Q*, 240 (1995), 29-30; and *idem*, 'Malory's Mordred and the *Morte Arthure*', in Fellows, 77-93. On the alliterative *Morte Arthure*, see above, pp.90-100.

30. The Vulgate *Suite de Merlin* also sets the Roman War story early in Arthur's reign.

31. See P.J.C. Field, 'Malory and the French Prose *Lancelot*', *Bulletin of the John Rylands University Library*, 75 (1993), 79-102; and idem, 'Malory and *Perlesvaus*', *MÆ*, 62 (1993), 259-69.

32. Cf. *Vinaver*, 1045-7, 1197.6-31.

33. P.J.C. Field, 'The Source of Malory's "Tale of Gareth" ', in Takamiya, 57-70, which reviews previous scholarship. An important later essay is T.L. Wright, 'On the Source of Malory's "Gareth" ', *Speculum*, 57 (1982), 569-82.

34. *Vinaver*, 102.10-21 and 1231.8-23; and cf. 716.2-11.

35. See *Vinaver*, 1443-9, Emmanuelle Baumgartner, *Le Tristan en prose: essai d'interprétation* (Geneva, 1975), and P.J.C. Field, 'The French Prose *Tristan*: A Note on Some Manuscripts, a List of Printed Texts, and Two Correlations with Malory's *Morte Darthur*', *BBIAS*, 41 (1989), 269-87.

36. *Vinaver*, 371.10-12. The passage is original to Malory.

37. For a contrary view, see B. Kennedy, *Knighthood in the* Morte Darthur (Woodbridge, 1985).

38. Cf. *Vinaver*, 845.31.

39. See *Vinaver*, 1260.8.

40. See *Vinaver*, 853; cf., Albert Pauphilet (ed.), *La queste del saint Graal* (Paris, 1965), 1.

41. See Mary Hynes-Berry, 'A Tale "Breffly Drawyn oute of Freynshe" ', in Takamiya, 93-106

42. See *Vinaver*, 1036.23-1037.7; Pauphilet (ed.), *Queste*, 279-80.

43. See *Vinaver*, 1065.1-2, 1098.14-18, 1103.1-11, 1119.1-2, 1120.14-35, 1145.32, 1153.20-1, 1154.2-11. The limiting dates for Pentecost are 10 May-13 June.

44. The end of the fifth episode speaks (*Vinaver*, 1154.2-11) of a twelve-month period of quests after the end of the previous episode. That suggests that the fifth episode takes place during the period referred to. The fourth episode is set in May, the twelve-month period therefore ends in May, and the eighth tale begins in May. Given the consistency of time-references in this part of the *Morte Darthur*, the time-sequence inferred in the text seems a reasonable deduction, though one that could not be made everywhere in the book.

45. See *Vinaver*, 1161.6, 1187.15, 1231.12, 1233.3, 1255.3-5, 1257.12, 1259.27-9, 1260.15.

46. See K. Cherewautak, 'The Saint's Life of Sir Launcelot: Hagiography and the Conclusion of Malory's *Morte Darthur*', *Arthuriana*, 5 (1995), 62-78.

47. See R.H. Wilson, 'Malory's Naming of Minor Characters', *JEGP*, 42 (1943), 364-85; *idem*, 'Addenda on Malory's Minor Characters', *JEGP*, 55 (1956), 563-87.

48. See P.J.C. Field, 'Author, Scribe, and Reader: The Case of Harleuse and Peryne', in Ní Cuilleanáin, 137-55. This supplements the two essays by R.H. Wilson cited in the previous note.

49. For a full account of what Malory did to the major characters, see R.H. Wilson, *Characterization in Malory* (Chicago, 1932).

50. See P.J.C. Field, 'Malory's Mordred and the *Morte Arthure*', in Fellows, 77-93; idem, 'Four Functions of Malory's Minor Characters', *MÆ*, 37 (1968), 37-45.

51. See Charles Moorman, 'Internal Chronology in Malory's *Morte Darthur*', *JEGP*, 60 (1961), 240-9.

52. See Ellyn Olefsky, 'Chronology, Factual Consistency, and the Problem of Unity in Malory', *JEGP*, 68 (1969), 57-73.

53. On style, see Field 1971, Lambert 1975, Catherine La Farge, 'Conversation in Malory', *MÆ*, 56 (1987), 225-38, Bonnie Wheeler, 'Romance and Parataxis in Malory', *AL*, 12 (1993), 109-32, and Jeremy J. Smith, 'Language and Style in Malory', in Archibald, 97-113.

54. No fictional work can be entirely fictional, but although this is not the place to explore that principle, we should perhaps note one corollary of it: that, like all Arthurian authors, Malory was constrained to some extent by the quasi-historical status of the Arthurian legend.

55. See Field 1971, 142-59.

56. See Terence McCarthy, 'Le *Morte Darthur* and Romance', in Brewer 1988, 148-75; and more generally Barron 1987.

57. The best full account is Muriel Whitaker, *Arthur's Kingdom of Adventure* (Cambridge, 1984).

58. See Felicity Riddy, 'Contextualizing Le *Morte Darthur*: Empire and Civil War', in Archibald, 55-73, at 70-3.

59. For a case very close to the one he might have made, see Felicity Riddy's subtle study (Riddy 1987).

60. C.S. Lewis, 'The English Prose *Morte*', in *Essays on Malory*, (cf. n.16 above), 7-28, at 9.

8: The Arthurian Legacy

1. It is worth noting that the first of these editions, that of 1687, coincides with the Glorious Revolution. The deposition of James II was preceded by widespread debate about the nature of kingship and political authority.

2. Brinkley (chapter 3) and Dean (chapter 6) discuss the indirect uses made of Arthurian material in the sixteenth and seventeenth centuries.

3. For discussion of the reworking of medieval Arthurian tradition by English political prophecies see S.L. Jansen, 'Prophecy, Propaganda, and Henry VIII: Arthurian Tradition in the Sixteenth Century' in Lagorio, I, 275-91. See also Brinkley, 1-17 and Keith Thomas, *Religion and the Decline of Magic* (New York, 1971), 418-19.

4. Norman Vance, *The Sinews of the Spirit: The Ideal of Christian Manliness in Victorian Literature and Religious Thought* (Cambridge, 1985), 22. A. Kent Hieatt suggests Spenser's plan to evoke Arthur's political virtues in a second set of books would have shown him as conqueror of Rome. See 'The Passing of Arthur in Malory, Spenser, and Shakespeare: The Avoidance of Closure' in Baswell, 173-92.

5. William Camden had praised Alfred (Brinkley, 98). The eclipsing of Arthur by Alfred as an eighteenth-century hero is discussed in Howard Weinbrot, *Britannia's Issue: The Rise of British Literature from Dryden to Ossian* (Cambridge, 1993), 499; and in James Sambrook, *The Eighteenth Century: The Intellectual and Cultural Context of English Literature, 1700-1789* (London, 1986), 160, 182.

6. Merriman (56-7) provides a useful summary of the critical explanations for Milton's abandonment of Arthur.

7. For Blackmore see H.M. Solomon, *Sir Richard Blackmore* (Boston, 1980). Haywood (1986) and Geoffrey Ashe (ed.), *The Quest for Arthur's Britain* (London, 1971) agree that Blackmore had insufficient literary stature to precipitate a major Arthurian Revival.

8. For discussion see Judith Colton, 'Merlin's Cave and Queen Caroline: Garden Art as Political Propaganda', *Eighteenth-Century Studies*, 10 (1976-7), 1-20. Also, for Merlin's Cave in the broader context of eighteenth-century Gothic, see Chris Brooks, *The Gothic Revival* (London, forthcoming), chapter 4.

9. Horace Walpole to Michael Lort, 5 June 1790; W.S. Lewis (ed.), *The Correspondence of Horace Walpole*, 48 vols. (New Haven and Oxford, 1937-83), XVI, 228.

10. David Hume, *The History of England*, 8 vols. (London, 1763), I, 24.

11. Fielding had clarified for writers the options available in reworking Arthurian legend: to adapt the folk or mythical history (often as parody) or to present a straight historical dramatization (Haywood, 60).

12. See Weinbrot, *Britannia's Issue*, 14.

13. Johnston, Appendix 2, 223-33.

14. See Eric Hobsbawm and Terence Ranger (eds.), *The Invention of Tradition* (Cambridge, 1983), chapter 3.

15. William Nicolson, *The English Historical Library* (1714), 38.

16. Percy's letters to Thomas Warton and William Shenstone detail the Arthurian significance of the *Reliques*.

17. After William Stansby's corrupt 1634 version of Caxton, no new editions of Malory appeared until 1816. Robert Southey's *The Byrth, Lyf, and Actes of Kyng Arthur* (London, 1817), with scholarly introduction and notes, inspired republication of a range of medieval Arthurian material.

18. See C.E. Pickford, '*Sir Tristrem*, Sir Walter Scott and Thomas', in W. Rothwell, *et al.* (eds.), *Studies in Medieval Literature and Language in Memory of Frederick Whitehead* (Manchester, 1973), 219-28

19. The others were *Quentin Durward* (1823), *The Talisman* and *The Betrothed*, published under the title *Tales of the Crusaders* in 1825, *The Fair Maid of Perth* (1828), *Anne of Geierstein* (1829), *Count Robert of Paris* (1831) and *Castle Dangerous* (1831).

20. For an overview of the thematic concerns of the Victorians in their remaking of Arthur see Inga Bryden, *Victorian Arthurianism: Remodelling the Past* (University of Exeter Ph.D. thesis, 1993).

21. For a reading of Victorian medievalism, including Arthurianism, that sees the imaginative construction of a harmonious world as ideologically central, see Chandler.

22. In this version of the past, the Saxon *witans*, Magna Carta and English liberty had been perfected in the Reform parliament of 1832; and the glories of Crécy and Agincourt had been relived at Trafalgar and Waterloo.

23. For Westminster's Arthurian decorations, see Maurice Bond (ed.), *Works of Art in the House of Lords* (London, 1980), 44-59, and Whitaker, 176-83.

24. For which see Marcia Pointon, *William Dyce 1806-1864: A Critical Biography* (Oxford, 1979).

25. At the same time Armstead was working on the extraordinary podium frieze of the Albert Memorial; for Armstead's career see Benedict Read, *Victorian Sculpture* (New Haven and London, 1982).

26. For surveys of Victorian visual representations of Arthurian legends see Mancoff 1990 and 1995.

27. Dyce was commissioned to do the Arthurian frescoes in the Robing Room in August 1848.

28. Edward George Earle Lytton Bulwer-Lytton, *King Arthur* (London, 1848). Quotations from the poem, given below, are identified by the page numbers of this edition.

29. He also avoids the issue of Guinevere's adultery by inventing Genevieve as Arthur's queen, and a convenient sound-alike, called Genevra, to marry Lancelot.

30. For the classic account of the theory of Gothic liberty see Samuel Kliger, *The Goths in England: A Study in Seventeenth- and Eighteenth-Century Thought* (Cambridge, Mass., 1952).

31. The year of *King Arthur*'s publication, 1848, was also the Year of Revolutions across Europe, and in Britain brought the climax of the Chartist campaign. There was also a personal imperative for Bulwer-Lytton: as well as being a writer he was an active politician, with an aristocratic pedigree that could be traced back to the Conquest. A pro-Reform Whig MP in the 1830s, he became a Disraelian Tory after inheriting the Knebworth estate in 1843, and went on to become Secretary of State for the Colonies in 1858-9 – thus getting to run the empire whose myth of origin he had substantially helped to invent.

32. See, for examples: William Cobbett, *History of the Protestant 'Reformation' in England and Ireland; showing how that event has impoverished and degraded the main body of the people in those countries* (1824); Augustus Welby Pugin, *Contrasts: or, a parallel between the noble edifices of the Middle Ages, and the corresponding buildings of the present day; shewing the present decay of taste* (1836); Thomas Carlyle, *Past and Present* (1843); and the chapter 'The Nature of Gothic' in the second volume of John Ruskin's *The Stones of Venice* (1851-3).

33. John Walker Ord, *England: A Historical Poem*, 2 vols. (London, 1834-5). The quotations in this paragraph are from Ord's 'Preface'.

34. Written in 1832, the poem first appeared in *The School of the Heart and Other Poems*, 2 vols. (London and Cambridge, 1835); it was reprinted in *The Poetical Works of Henry Alford* (London, 1845), 100-10. Alford (1810-71) was in Tennyson's circle at Cambridge, and as vicar of Wymeswold in Leicestershire he employed Pugin to restore the parish church; from 1857 to his death he was Dean of Canterbury.

35. 'The Ballad of Glastonbury', verse XXXIII; *Poetical Works*, 110.

36. Frederick William Faber, *Sir Lancelot: A Legend of the Middle Ages* (London, 1842). Faber (1814-63) was a committed Tractarian and bosom friend of Newman, with whom he converted to Roman Catholicism in 1845; much of his personal struggle with Anglicanism is reflected in *Sir Lancelot*.

37. Thomas Westwood, *The Quest of the Sancgreall* (London, 1868); Sebastian Evans, *The High History of the Holy Grail*, 2 vols. (London, 1898). Evans's work included title pages and frontispieces by Edward Burne-Jones.

38. Robert Stephen Hawker, *The Quest of the Sangraal: Chant the First* (Exeter, 1864); reprinted in Alfred Wallis (ed.), *The Poetical Works of Robert Stephen Hawker, M. A.* (London, 1899), 171-90, from which the quotations in this paragraph, identified by page number, are taken.

39. Hawker's life was dramatically, though inaccurately, told by another eccentric West Country clergyman, Sabine Baring-Gould, in *The Vicar of Morwenstow* (London, 1876). For a more recent account see Piers Brendon, *Hawker of Morwenstow* (London, 1975).

40. There is an earlier unfinished poem, 'Sir Launcelot and Queen Guinevere: A Fragment', which runs to five stanzas and seems to have been written in 1830.

41. 'The Lady of Shalott', l. 71; Christopher Ricks, *The Poems of Tennyson*, 2nd edn. incorporating the Trinity College Manuscripts, 3 vols. (Harlow, 1987), I, 391. Ricks's prefatory note to the poem includes a detailed account of its genesis and sources. Further quotations from Tennyson's poetry are identified by the volume and page number of this edition.

42. The frame comprises 51 lines before, and 31 lines after the poem Tennyson entitles 'Morte d'Arthur', which itself is a faithful, though skilfully elaborated, version of Malory's account of Arthur's passing. The frame was certainly written later: Ricks (*Poems of Tennyson*, II, 1) gives it a probable date of 1837-8.

43. For Tennyson's attitude to Arthur's passing see J.D. Rosenberg, 'Tennyson and the Passing of Arthur' in Baswell, 221-34.

44. Similarly involved is Tennyson's use of medieval sources, for which see Staines. Ricks's prefatory notes to the poem as a whole (*Poems of Tennyson*, III, 255-62), and to

each of its component parts, contain much important bibliographical information and summarize relevant critical commentaries.

45. For a full-length critical reading of the *Idylls* see J.D. Rosenberg, *The Fall of Camelot: A Study of Tennyson's 'Idylls of the King'* (Cambridge, Mass., 1973). For discussion of the *Idylls'* publication sequence and its effect on Victorian readers see L.K. Hughes, 'Tennyson's Urban Arthurians: Victorian Audiences and the "City Built to Music"' in Lagorio, II, 39-61.

46. Lady Lever Art Gallery, Port Sunlight, Cheshire; the painting is also known as *The Beguiling of Merlin*. The critical literature on Burne-Jones is extensive; one of the best general accounts is Martin Harrison and Bill Waters, *Burne-Jones*, revised edn. (London, 1989).

47. This enormous painting occupied the last years of Burne-Jones's life and was unfinished at his death; extraordinarily it is now in the Museo de Arte, Ponce, Puerto Rico.

48. Georgiana Burne-Jones, *Memorials of Edward Burne-Jones*, 2 vols. (London, 1904), I, 116.

49. The term 'Pre-Raphaelite' derived from visual art, but was 'adopted and modified' to apply to literature. See Smith, 117.

50. For discussion of the Pre-Raphaelites in the context of Victorian historicism see Hilary Fraser, *The Victorians and Renaissance Italy* (London, 1992).

51. David Masson, 'Pre-Raphaelitism in Art and Literature' (1852) in James Sambrook (ed.), *Pre-Raphaelitism: A Collection of Critical Essays* (Chicago and London, 1974), 83. For an account of the Eglinton Tournament see Ian Anstruther, *The Knight and the Umbrella* (London, 1963).

52. See Alicia Faxon, 'The Pre-Raphaelite Brotherhood as Knights of the Round Table' in Cheney, 53-69.

53. For which see John Christian, *The Oxford Union Murals* (Chicago, 1981).

54. That Pre-Raphaelitism was linked with a romantic Arthurianism is evidenced in, for example, George Du Maurier's *The Legend of Camelot* (1866; 1898), which satirizes Pre-Raphaelite aesthetics.

55. Siddal's sketch *The Lady of Shalott* (1853) (the subject taken from Tennyson's 1832 poem) presents a very different version of the medieval past or 'interior' to other nineteenth-century visual representations of the same subject. Siddal studied medieval manuscripts to develop visual strategies. See Deborah Cherry, *Painting Women: Victorian Women Artists* (London, 1993), 189-91.

56. Owen Meredith, Morris, and Swinburne, together with Tennyson and Rossetti, were named in Robert Buchanan's infamous attack 'The Fleshly School of Poetry' (1871), principally aimed at the physicality and 'immorality' of Rossetti's poems.

57. See Carole Silver, 'Victorian Spellbinders: Arthurian Women and the Pre-Raphaelite Circle' in Baswell, 251.

58. See Carl Dawson (ed.), *Matthew Arnold: The Poetry, Critical Heritage*, 2 vols. (London, 1973), II, 108, 226.

59. The marriage between Tristram and Iseult of Brittany is consummated after Tristram visits his mistress, Iseult of Ireland. This version was included in John Dunlop's *History of Fiction*, 3 vols. (1814).

60. Although it was also dismissed as an absurd curiosity because of its associations with Pre-Raphaelitism. Smith (113-34) discusses the critical reception of *The Defence of Guenevere*.

61. Four of the poems in *The Defence* were inspired by Rossetti's watercolours of Arthurian subjects (1854-7). Pre-Raphaelite Arthurianism is characterized by an intertextuality that is part of the Victorian fascination with 'word-painting'. Pairs of poems and paintings on the same theme were produced: for example, Rossetti's watercolour *Arthur's Tomb: The Last Meeting of Launcelot and Guinevere* (1855) and Morris's poem 'King Arthur's Tomb' (1856). See also Lynne Pearce, *Woman, Image, Text: Readings in Pre-Raphaelite Art and Literature* (Hemel Hempstead, 1991). Pearce critiques literary and visual representations of the Lady of Shalott and Guenevere.

62. Frederick Kirchhoff, 'Heroic Disintegration: Morris' Medievalism and the Disappearance of the Self' in Carole Silver (ed.), *The Golden Chain: Essays on William Morris and Pre-Raphaelitism* (London, 1982), 93.

63. Florence Boos, 'Justice and Vindication in William Morris's *The Defence of Guenevere*' in Lagorio, II, 84.

64. For examples, Owen Meredith, 'Queen Guenevere' in *Clytemnestra, The Earl's Return and Other Poems* (1855); Alfred Tennyson, *Guinevere* (1859); Charles Bruce (trans.), Wilhelm Hertz, *The Story of Queen Guinevere and Sir Lancelot of the Lake* (1865); George Simcox, 'The Farewell of Ganore' in *Poems and Romances* (1869).

65. Morris reminds us that history is not a 'privileged set of myths'. See Jonathan Freedman, 'Ideological Battleground: Tennyson, Morris, and the Pastness of the Past' in Baswell, 244.

66. In common with his fellow contributors to the *Oxford and Cambridge Magazine*; see Amanda Hodgson, *The Romances of William Morris* (Cambridge, 1987), 14-17. Isobel Armstrong, in *Victorian Poetry: Poetry, Poetics, and Politics* (London, 1993), discusses Morris's radical aesthetics in *The Defence of Guenevere* (232, 236).

67. These were published in the *Undergraduate Papers* (1857-8) of Oxford University's Old Mortality Society. Swinburne wrote the prologue to *Tristram* in 1869 and resumed writing the poem in the 1880s. *The Tale of Balen* was published in 1896.

68. In *Under The Microscope* (1872), a reply to Buchanan's charges, Swinburne comments that Tennyson woefully neglects to take the element of fate into account in his reworkings of the Arthurian legend.

69. For discussion see Mario Praz, *The Romantic Agony*, translated by Angus Davidson, 2nd edn. (London, 1951), 215-58.

70. Edward Russell, *The Book of King Arthur* (Liverpool, 1889), 29. Whitaker (236) points out that among Arthurian art inspired by Tennyson's poetry, Galahad, Lancelot and the 'beautiful suffering woman' were preferred subjects to Arthur himself.

71. James Carley (ed.), *Arthurian Poets: A. C. Swinburne* (Woodbridge, 1990), 33.

72. This poem was written in the context of a more general sense of decline related to the Great Agrarian Depression. Other cultural factors affecting late nineteenth-century literary

representations of Arthur were decadence and an increasing secularization. For a brief survey of later nineteenth-century Arthurian literature see 'Arthur of Britain and America: Camelot Revisited', *PQ*, 56 (1977), 249-53.

73. 'Hospital Barge at Cérisy', ll.12-14; Dominic Hibberd (ed.), *Wilfred Owen: War Poems and Others* (London, 1973), 83.

74. The dead of Winchester School, for example, are commemorated in Winchester Cathedral by a set of windows on Arthurian themes made by Powell's of Whitefriars. For the use of Arthurian and chivalric imagery in the Great War see Girouard (ch.18).

75. For discussion see Xavier Baron, 'Medieval Arthurian Motifs in the Modernist Art and Poetry of David Jones', *Studies in Medievalism*, 4 (1992), 247-69.

76. See Charles Williams, 'Malory and the Grail Legend', in Anne Ridler, *Charles Williams: The Image of the City and Other Essays* (London, 1958), 186-7.

77. Brewer and Taylor cite the publication of Jessie Weston's *From Ritual to Romance* (1920) as the 'most important single literary cause' of this change of direction.

78. See, for examples, Arthur Edward Waite, *The Book of the Holy Graal* (1921); John Cowper Powys, *A Glastonbury Romance* (1932); Charles Williams, *Taliessin Through Logres* (1938) and *The Region of the Summer Stars* (1944); and C.S. Lewis, *That Hideous Strength* (1945).

79. Notably, *Excalibur* (John Boorman, 1981), in which the figure of Merlin plays a central role, and the parodic *Monty Python and the Holy Grail* (Terry Gilliam and Terry Jones, 1975). For discussion of Arthurian films see Kevin Harty, 'Film Treatments of the Legend of King Arthur' in Lagorio, II, 278-90; also Harty (1991). For a theoretical discussion of Arthur as artefact and the symbolic nature of Camelot see Inga Bryden, 'Arthur as Artefact: Concretizing the Fictions of the Past', in Nick Groom (ed.), *Angelaki*, I, 2, *Narratives of Forgery* (1994), 149-57. Among the extensive critical literature on Arthur and popular culture see Sally Slocum (ed.), *Popular Arthurian Traditions* (Bowling Green, Ohio, 1992).

80. See Elisabeth Brewer, *T. H. White's 'The Once and Future King'* (Cambridge, 1993). See also T. H. White's *The Sword in the Stone* (1938) and Disney's cartoon version *The Sword in the Stone* (1965).

81. *The Crystal Cave* (1970), *The Hollow Hills* (1973) and *The Last Enchantment* (1979). See Marion Wynne-Davies, final chapter, for a discussion of twentieth-century women writers of Arthurian literature, including Mary Stewart and Marion Zimmer Bradley.

REFERENCE BIBLIOGRAPHY

(The version of the Harvard Reference System employed throughout the book uses italic for the names of editors, roman for authors of studies, publication dates being given to distinguish between authors of multiple publications or of the same name.)

A: BIBLIOGRAPHIES

Annual Bibliography	*Annual Bibliography of English Language and Literature*, ed. for the Modern Humanities Research Association (Cambridge 1921-).
Arthurian Bibliography	*The Arthurian Bibliography*, I *Author Listing*, ed. C.E. Pickford and R. Last (Cambridge, 1981); II *Subject Index*, ed. C.E. Pickford and C.R. Baker (Cambridge, 1983).
BBIAS	*Bibliographical Bulletin of the International Arthurian Society,* (Paris, 1949-66; Nottingham, 1967-75; Paris, 1976-84; Madison, Wisc., 1985-).
Cambridge Bibliography	*New Cambridge Bibliography of English Literature*, I *(600-1600)*, ed. G. Watson (Cambridge 1974): 2.I Middle English Romances; 3.III Caxton, Malory; 3.VII Chronicles
Hartung Manual	*A Manual of the Writings in Middle English: 1050-1500*, III Malory and Caxton, ed. A.E. Hartung (New Haven, Conn., 1972); VIII Chronicles and Other Historical Writing, E.D. Kennedy (New Haven, Conn., 1989).
Last Bibliography	*The Arthurian Bibliography*, 3 vols., ed. R. Last (Cambridge, 1985).
MLA	*International Bibliography of Books and Articles on the Modern Languages and Literatures*, ed. for the Modern Language Association of America (New York, 1956-).
Reiss Bibliography,	*Arthurian Legend and Literature: An Annotated Bibliography*, I The Middle Ages, ed. E. Reiss, L.H. Reiss, and B. Taylor (New York, 1984).
Rice Bibliography	*Middle English Romance: An Annotated Bibliography, 1955-1983*, ed. J.A. Rice (New York and London, 1987).
Severs *Manual*	*A Manual of the Writings in Middle English: 1050-1500*, I Romances, ed. J.B. Severs (New Haven, Conn., 1967).
Year's Work	*The Year's Work in English Studies*, ed. for the English Association (London, 1921-).

B: *TEXTS*

Arthour and of Merlin, Of
Macrae-Gibson   ed. O.D. Macrae-Gibson, EETS 268, 279 (London, 1973, 1979).

Arthur
Furnivall   ed. F.J. Furnivall, EETS 2 (London, 1864, 1869; 1965).

Arthur of Little Britain (by John Bourchier, Lord Berners)
Utterson   *The Hystory of the Valiant Knight Arthur of Little Brtiain,*
ed. E.V. Utterson (London, 1814).

Avowynge of King Arthur, Sir Gawan, Sir Kaye, and Sir Bawdewyn of Bretan, The
Brookhouse   Sir Amadace *and* The Avowing of Arthur: *Two Romances*
from the Ireland MS, ed. Christopher Brookhouse,
Anglistica 15 (Copenhagen, 1968).
Dahood   *The Avowing of King Arthur: A Critical Edition,*
ed. Roger Dahood, Garland Medieval Texts 10 (New York, 1984).
Hahn   in *Sir Gawain: Eleven Romances and Tales,*
ed. Thomas Hahn (Kalamazoo, Mich., 1995), 113-68.

Awntyrs off Arthure at the Terne Wathelyne, The
Gates   ed. R.J. Gates (Philadelphia, Pa., 1969; London, 1970).
Hanna   ed. Ralph Hanna III, Old and Middle English Texts
(Manchester, 1974).
Hahn   in *Sir Gawain: Eleven Romances and Tales,*
ed. Thomas Hahn (Kalamazoo, Mich., 1995), 169-226.

Boy and the Mantel, The
Hales and   in *Bishop Percy's Folio Manuscript: Ballads and Romances,*
  Furnivall   3 vols., ed. J.W. Hales and F.J. Furnivall, II, 301-11
(London, 1867-8; Detroit, 1968).
Furrow   in *Ten Fifteenth-Century Comic Poems*, ed. M.A. Furrow,
Garland Medieval Texts (New York, 1985), 293-311

Brut, The (by Laʒamon)
Barron and   ed. and trans. W.R.J. Barron and S.C. Weinberg (Harlow,
  Weinberg   (1995).
Brook and Leslie   ed. G.L. Brook and R.F. Leslie, 3 vols., EETS 250, 277
(London, 1963, 1978).
Madden   ed. Sir Frederic Madden, 3 vols. (London, 1847; N.Y., 1970)

Brut, The Prose or The Chronicles of England
Brie   ed. F.W.D. Brie, 2 vols., EETS 131, 136
(London, 1906, 1908; 1960).

Carle off Carlile, The

Hales and Furnivall	in *Bishop Percy's Folio Manuscript: Ballads and Romances*, 3 vols., ed. J.W. Hales and F.J. Furnivall, III, 275-94 (London, 1867-8; Detroit, 1968).
Kurvinen	Sir Gawain and the Carl of Carlisle *in Two Versions*, ed. Auvo Kurvinen, *Annales Academiae Scientiarum Fennicae*, ser. B (Helsinki, 1951).
Hahn	in *Sir Gawain: Eleven Romances and Tales*, ed. Thomas Hahn (Kalamazoo, Mich., 1995), 373-92.

Chronicle (by Robert of Gloucester)

Wright	*The Metrical Chronicle of Robert of Gloucester*, ed. W.A. Wright, 2 vols., RS 88 (London, 1887).

Chronicle (by Robert Mannyng of Brunne)

Furnivall	*The Story of England by Robert Manning of Brunne*, ed. F.J. Furnivall, RS 87, 2 vols. (London, 1887).
Sullens	ed. Ioelle Sullens, Medieval and Renaissance Texts and Studies, 153 (Binghampton, 1996).

Chronicle of England (by Thomas Bek of Castelford)

Behre	*Thomas Castleford's Chronicle*, ed. Frank Behre, Göteborgs Högskolas Arsskrift, 46 (Göteborg, 1940).
Eckhardt	ed. C.A. Eckhardt, EETS 305, 306 (London, 1996).

Corneus, The Romance of Sir (or *The Horn of King Arthur*)

Hazlitt	in *Remains of the Early Popular Poetry of England*, ed. W.C. Hazlitt, vol. I (London, 1864-6).
Furrow	in *Ten Fifteenth-Century Comic Poems*, ed. M.A. Furrow, Garland Medieval Texts (New York, 1985), 271-91.

Gawain and the Green Knight, Sir

Andrew and Waldron	in *The Poems of the* Pearl *Manuscript*, ed., Malcolm Andrew and Ronald Waldron (London, 1978; Exeter, 1987).
Gollancz	ed. Israel Gollancz, EETS 210 (London, 1940).
Silverstein	ed. Theodore Silverstein (Chicago, 1984).
Tolkien and Gordon	ed. J.R.R. Tolkien and E.V. Gordon (Oxford, 1925; rev. Davis, 1967).

Gawene and the Carle of Carleyle, Syre

Kurvinen	Sir Gawain and the Carl of Carlisle *in Two Versions*, ed. Auvo Kurvinen, *Annales Academiae Scientiarum Fennicae*, ser. B 71.2 (Helsinki, 1951).
Sands	in *Middle English Verse Romances*, ed. D.B. Sands (New York, 1966; Exeter, 1986).
Hahn	in *Sir Gawain: Eleven Romances and Tales*, ed. Thomas Hahn (Kalamazoo, Mich., 1995), 81-112.

Golagros and Gawane

Amours	in *Scottish Alliterative Poems in Riming Stanzas*, ed. F.J. Amours, STS 27 (Edinburgh, 1897).
Hahn	in *Sir Gawain: Eleven Romances and Tales*, ed. Thomas Hahn (Kalamazoo, Mich., 1995), 227-308.

Grene Knight, The

Hales and Furnivall	in *Bishop Percy's Folio Manuscript: Ballads and Romances*, 3 vols., ed. J.W. Hales and F.J. Furnivall, II, 56-77 (London, 1867-8; Detroit, 1968).
Speed	in *Medieval English Romances*. ed., Diane Speed 3rd. edn. (Durham, 1993).

History of the Holy Grail, The (by Henry Lovelich)

Furnivall	ed. F.J. Furnivall, Parts I-IV, EETS, ES 20, 24, 28, 30 (London, 1874-8).
Kempe	ed. Dorothy Kempe, Part V, EETS, ES 95 (London, 1905).

Jeaste of Syr Gawayne, The

Madden	in *Syr Gawayne: A Collection of Ancient Romance Poems*, ed. Sir Frederic Madden (London, 1839; New York, 1971).
Hahn	in *Sir Gawain: Eleven Romances and Tales*, ed. Thomas Hahn (Kalamazoo, Mich., 1995), 393-418.

Joseph of Arimathie

Lawton	ed. D.A. Lawton, Garland Medieval Texts 5 (New York, 1983).
Skeat	ed. W.W. Skeat, EETS 44 (London, 1871; 1924).

Kempy Kay

Child	in *The English and Scottish Popular Ballads*, 5 vols., ed. F.J. Child, I, 300-6 (Cambridge, Mass., 1882-98).

King Arthur and King Cornwall

Hales and Furnivall	in *Bishop Percy's Folio Manuscript: Ballads and Romances*, 3 vols., ed. J.W. Hales and F.J. Furnivall, I, 59-73 (London, 1867-8; Detroit, 1968).
Hahn	in *Sir Gawain: Eleven Romances and Tales*, ed. Thomas Hahn (Kalamazoo, Mich., 1995), 419-35.

King Arthur's Death

Hales and Furnivall	in *Bishop Percy's Folio Manuscript: Ballads and Romances*, 3 vols., ed. J.W. Hales and F.J. Furnivall, I, 501-7 (London, 1867-8; Detroit, 1968).

King Ryence's Challenge

Child	in *English and Scottish Ballads*, ed. F.J. Child (Boston, Mass., 1857).

Lambewell, Sir

Hales and
  Furnivall
in *Bishop Percy's Folio Manuscript: Ballads and Romances*,
3 vols., ed. J.W. Hales and F.J. Furnivall, I, 142-64
(London, 1867-8; Detroit, 1968).

Lamwell, Sir

Hales and
  Furnivall
in *Bishop Percy's Folio Manuscript: Ballads and Romances*,
3 vols., ed. J.W. Hales and F.J. Furnivall, I, 521-35
(London, 1867-8; Detroit, 1968).

Furnivall
in *Captain Cox: His Ballads and Books*, ed. F.J. Furnivall,
Ballad Society 7 (London, 1871; 1907).

Lancelot du Lake, Sir

Hales and
  Furnivall
in *Bishop Percy's Folio Manuscript: Ballads and Romances*,
ed. J.W. Hales and F.J. Furnivall, I, 84-7 (London, 1867-8;
Detroit, 1968).

Lancelot of the Laik

Gray
ed. M.M. Gray, STS 2 (Edinburgh, 1912).

Landevale, Sir

Bliss
in *Sir Launfal*, ed. A.J. Bliss (London, 1960), 105-28

Laskaya and
  Salisbury
in *The Middle English Breton Lays*, ed. Anne Laskaya and
Eve Salisbury (Kalamazoo, Mich., 1995), 423-37

Launfal, Sir (by Thomas Chestre)

Bliss
ed. A.J. Bliss (London, 1960).

Legend of King Arthur, The

Hales and
  Furnivall
in *Bishop Percy's Folio Manuscript: Ballads and Romances*,
3 vols., ed. J.W. Hales and F.J. Furnivall, I, 497-501
(London, 1867-8; Detroit, 1968).

Lybeaus Desconus

Mills
ed. Maldwyn Mills, EETS 261 (London, 1969).

Marriage of Sir Gawaine, The

Hales and
  Furnivall
in *Bishop Percy's Folio Manuscript: Ballads and Romances*,
3 vols., ed. J.W. Hales and F.J. Furnivall, I, 103-18
(London, 1867-8; Detroit, 1968).

Hahn
in *Sir Gawain: Eleven Romances and Tales*,
ed. Thomas Hahn (Kalamazoo, Mich., 1995), 359-72.

Merlin (by Henry Lovelich)

Kock
ed. E.A. Kock, EETS, ES 93, 112; EETS 185
(London, 1904, 1913, 1930; 1961, 1971, 1973).

Merlin, Prose

Wheatley   ed. H.B. Wheatley, EETS 10, 21, 36, 112 (London, 1865, 1866, 1869, 1899).

Morte Arthur, Le (Stanzaic)

Benson   in *King Arthur's Death: The Middle English Stanzaic* Morte Arthur *and Alliterative* Morte Arthure, ed. L.D. Benson (Indianapolis, Ind., 1974; Exeter, 1986).

Hissiger   ed. P.F. Hissiger (The Hague and Paris, 1975).

Morte Arthure (Alliterative)

Benson   in *King Arthur's Death: The Middle English Stanzaic* Morte Arthur *and Alliterative* Morte Arthure, ed. L.D. Benson (Indianapolis, Ind., 1974; Exeter, 1986).

Hamel   ed. Mary Hamel, Garland Medieval Texts 9 (New York and London, 1984).

Krishna   ed. Valerie Krishna (New York, 1976).

Morte Darthur, Le (by Sir Thomas Malory)

Vinaver   in *The Works of Sir Thomas Malory*, 3 vols. (Oxford, 1947, 1967, rev. 1973, rev. Field, 1990).

Percyvell of Gales, Sir

French and Hale   in *Middle English Metrical Romances*, ed. W.H. French and C.B. Hale (New York, 1930; 1964).

Seven Sages of Rome, The

Brunner   ed. Karl Brunner, EETS 191 (London, 1933) (Southern Version).

van Buuren   ed. Catherine van Buuren, Germanic and Anglistic Studies 20 (Leiden, 1982) (Asloan MS.).

Short Metrical Chronicle, The

Zettl   ed. Ewald Zettl, EETS 196 (London, 1935; 1971).

Tristrem, Sir

McNeill   ed. G.P. McNeill, STS 8 (Edinburgh, 1886; New York, 1966).

Turke and Gowin, The

Hales and Furnivall   in *Bishop Percy's Folio Manuscript: Ballads and Romances*, 3 vols., ed. J.W. Hales and F.J. Furnivall, I, 88-102 (London, 1867-8; Detroit, 1968).

Hahn   in *Sir Gawain: Eleven Romances and Tales*, ed. Thomas Hahn (Kalamazoo, Mich., 1995), 337-58.

Weddynge of Sir Gawen and Dame Ragnell, The

Sands   in *Middle English Verse Romances*, ed. D.B. Sands (New York, 1966; Exeter, 1986).

Sumner   ed. Laura Sumner, Smith College Studies in Modern Languages,

5.4 (Northampton, Mass., 1924; repr. by B.J. Whiting in
Sources and Analogues of Chaucer's Canterbury Tales, ed. W.
Bryan and G. Dempster (Chicago, Ill., 1941; London and New
York, 1958).

Hahn   in *Sir Gawain: Eleven Romances and Tales,*
ed. Thomas Hahn (Kalamazoo, Mich., 1995), 41-80.

Wife of Bath's Tale, The   (from Chaucer's *Canterbury Tales*)

Robinson   in *The Works of Geoffrey Chaucer*, ed. F.N. Robinson
(Boston, 1934; 1957).

Ywain and Gawain

Friedman and   ed. A.B. Friedman and N.T. Harrington, EETS 254
  Harrington   (London, 1964, 1981).

C: *STUDIES*

Aarne, A., *The Types of the Folktale: A Classification and Bibliography*, trans. and enlarged S. Thompson (Helsinki, 1961).

Adams, A. *et al.* (eds.), *The Changing Face of Arthurian Romance: Essays on Arthurian Prose Romances in Memory of Cedric Pickford* (Cambridge, 1986).

Aertsen, H. and A.A. MacDonald (eds.), *A Companion to Middle English Romance* (Amsterdam, 1990).

Archibald, E. and A.S.G. Edwards (eds.), *A Companion to Malory* (Cambridge, 1996).

Arthur, R.G., *Medieval Sign Theory and* Sir Gawain and the Green Knight (Toronto, 1987).

Auerbach, E., *Mimesis: The Representation of Reality in Western Literature*, trans. W. Trask (New York, 1957).

Barber, R., *The Knight and Chivalry* (Ipswich, 1970).

—— 1976, *The Figure of Arthur* (London, 1972, repr. 1976).

Barker, J.R.V., *The Tournament in England, 1100-1400* (Woodbridge, 1986).

Barnes, G., *Counsel and Strategy in Middle English Romance* (Cambridge, 1993).

Barron, W.R.J., *'Trawthe' and Treason: The Sin of Gawain Reconsidered* (Manchester, 1980).

—— 1987, *English Medieval Romance* (London and New York, 1987).

Barrow, S.F., *The Medieval Society Romances* (New York, 1924).

Batty, J., *The Spirit and Influence of Chivalry* (London, 1980).

Baswell C. and W. Sharpe (eds.), *The Passing of Arthur: New Essays in Arthurian Tradition* (New York and London, 1988).

Beer, G., *The Romance* (London, 1970).

Bennett, H.S., *Chaucer and the Fifteenth Century* (Oxford, 1947).

Bennet, J.A.W., *Middle English Literature: 1100-1400*, ed. and completed D. Gray (Oxford, 1986).

Bennett, M.J., *Community, Class and Careerism: Cheshire and Lancashire Society in the Age of* Sir Gawain and the Green Knight (Cambridge, 1983).

Benson, L.D., *Art and Tradition in* Sir Gawain and the Green Knight (New Brunswick, N.J., 1965).

—— 1976, *Malory's* Morte Darthur (Cambridge, Mass., 1976).

Binski, P., *Westminster Abbey and the Plantagenets* (New Haven and London, 1995).

Boase, R., *The Origin and Meaning of Courtly Love* (Manchester 1977).

Boitani, P., *English Medieval Narrative in the Thirteenth and Fourteenth Centuries*, trans. J.K. Hall (Cambridge, 1982).

Bolton, W.F. (ed.), *The Middle Ages* (London, 1970).

Bordman, G., *Motif-Index of the English Metrical Romances* (Helsinki, 1963).

Braswell, M.F. and J. Bugge (eds.), *The Arthurian Tradition: Essays in Convergence* (Tuscaloosa, Ala., and London, 1988).

Brewer, D.S., *Symbolic Stories: Traditional Narratives of the Family Drama in English Literature* (Cambridge, 1980).

—— 1983, *English Gothic Literature* (London, 1983).

Brewer, D.S. (ed.), *Studies in Medieval English Romances: Some New Approaches* (Cambridge, 1988).

—— 1988 and J. Gibson (eds.), *A Companion to the* Gawain-*Poet* (Cambridge, 1997).

Brewer, E. and B. Taylor, *The Return of King Arthur: British and American Arthurian Literature Since 1800* (Cambridge, 1983).

Brinkley, R. *Arthurian Literature in the Seventeenth Century* (New York, 1967).

Bromwich, R., A.O.H. Jarman and B.F. Roberts (eds.), *The Arthur of the Welsh* (Cardiff, 1991).

Brown, R.A., H.M. Colvin and A.J. Taylor, *The History of the King's Works: The Middle Ages,* 2 vols. and plates (London, 1963).

Brownlee, K. and M.S. Brownlee (eds.), *Romance: Generic Transformations from Chrétien de Troyes to Cervantes* (Hanover, 1985).

Bruce, J.D., *The Evolution of Arthurian Romance: From the Beginnings down to the Year 1300* (Baltimore, Md., 1923; 2nd edn., 1928; repr., Gloucester, Mass., 1958; Geneva, 1974).

Bullock-Davies, C., *Professional Interpreters and The Matter of Britain* (Cardiff, 1966).

Burgess G. (ed.), *Court and Poet: Selected Proceedings of the Third Congress of the International Courtly Literature Society (Liverpool, 1980)* (Liverpool, 1981).

—— 1985, and R.A. Taylor (eds.), *The Spirit of the Court: Selected Proceedings of the Fourth Congress of the International Courtly Literature Society (Toronto 1983)* (Woodbridge and Dover, N.H., 1985).

Burrow, J.A., *A Reading of* Sir Gawain and the Green Knight (London, 1965).

—— 1982, *Medieval Writers and their Work: Middle English Literature and its Background 1100-1500* (Oxford, 1982).

Busby K. and E. Kooper (eds.), *Courtly Literature: Culture and Context: Selected Papers from the Fifth Triennial Congress of the International Courtly Literature Society (Dalfsen, Netherlands, 1986)* (Amsterdam and Philadelphia, 1990).

—— 1994, and N.J. Lacy (eds.), *Conjunctures: Medieval Studies in Honour of Douglas Kelly* (Amsterdam, 1994).

Calin, W., *The French Tradition and the Literature of Medieval England* (Toronto, 1994).

Chambers, E.K., *English Literature at the Close of the Middle Ages* (Oxford, 1945).

Chandler, A., *A Dream of Order: The Medieval Ideal in Nineteenth-Century Literature* (London, 1971).

Cheney, L. De Girolami (ed.), *Pre-Raphaelitism and Medievalism in the Arts* (Lampeter, Lewiston, N.Y., and Queenston, Ontario, 1992).

Clanchy, M.T., *From Memory to Written Record: England 1066-1307* (Oxford, 1993).

Clein, W., *Concepts of Chivalry in* Sir Gawain and the Green Knight (Norman, Okla., 1987).

Clifton-Everest, J.M., *The Tragedy of Knighthood* (Oxford, 1979).

Coleman, J., *English Literature in History, 1350-1400* (London, 1981).

Crane, S., *Insular Romance: Politics, Faith, and Culture in Anglo-Norman and Middle English Literature* (Berkeley, Cal., and London, 1986).

Davenport, W.A., *The Art of the* Gawain-*Poet* (London, 1978).

Dean, C., *Arthur of England: English Attitudes to King Arthur in the Middle Ages and Renaissance* (Toronto, 1987).

Dobyns, A., *The Voices of Romance: Studies in Dialogue and Character* (Newark, N.J., 1989).

Donovan, M.J., *The Breton Lay: A Guide to Varieties* (Notre Dame, Ind., 1969).

Dorfman, E., *The Narreme in the Medieval Romance Epic: An Introduction to Narrative Structures* (Toronto, 1969).

Everett, D., *Essays on Middle English Literature*, ed. P. Kean (Oxford, 1955).

Fellows, J., R. Field, G. Rogers and J. Weiss (eds.), *Romance Reading on the Book: Essays on Medieval Narrative* (Cardiff, 1996).

Ferguson, A.B., *The Indian Summer of English Chivalry: Studies in the Decline and Transformation of Chivalric Idealism* (Durham, N.C., 1960).

Fewster, C., *Traditionality and Genre in Middle English Romance* (Cambridge, 1987).

Field, P.J.C., *Romance and Chronicle* (London, 1971).

—— 1993, *The Life and Times of Sir Thomas Malory* (Cambridge, 1993).

Fletcher, R.H., *The Arthurian Material in the Chronicles* (Boston, 1906, repr. New York, 1966).

Frappier, J. and R.R. Grimm (eds.), *Le Roman jusqu'à la fin du XIIIe siècle,* Grundriss der romanischen Literaturen des Mittelalters, 4.1 (Heidelberg, 1978).

—— 1982, *Chrétien de Troyes: The Man and His Work*, trans. R.T. Cormier (Athens, Ohio, 1982).

Frye, N., *Anatomy of Criticism* (Princeton, N.J., 1957).

—— 1976, *The Secular Scripture: A Study of the Structure of Romance* (London, 1976).

Ganim, J.M., *Style and Consciousness in Middle English Narrative* (Princeton, N.J., 1983).

Girouard, M., *The Return to Camelot: Chivalry and the English Gentleman* (New Haven, Conn., and London, 1981).

Gist, M.A., *Love and War in the Middle English Romances* (Philadelphia, Pa., 1947).

Göller, K.H., *König Arthur in der englischen Literatur des späten Mittelalters* (Göttingen, 1963).

—— 1981 (ed.), *The Alliterative* Morte Arthure: *A Reassessment of the Poem* (Cambridge, 1981).

Gowans, L., *Cei and the Arthurian Legend* (Cambridge, 1988).

Gradon, P., *Form and Style in Early English Literature* (London, 1974).

Green, D., *Irony in the Medieval Romance* (Cambridge, 1979).

Green, R.F., *Poets and Princepleasers: Literature and the English Court in the Late Middle Ages* (Toronto, 1980).

Grout, P.B. *et al.* (eds.), *The Legend of Arthur in the Middle Ages: Studies Presented to A.H. Diverres* (Cambridge, 1983).

Guddat-Figge, G., *Catalogue of Manuscripts Containing Middle English Romances* (Munich, 1976).

Haines, V.Y., *The Fortunate Fall of Sir Gawain: The Typology of* Sir Gawain and the Green Knight (Washington, D.C., 1982).

Hanks, D.T. (ed.), *Sir Thomas Malory: Views and Re-Views* (New York, 1992).

Hanning, R.W., *The Vision of History in Early Britain: From Gildas to Geoffrey of Monmouth* (New York, 1966).

—— 1977, *The Individual in Twelfth-Century Romance* (New Haven, Conn., 1977).

Harty, K. (ed.), *Cinema Arthuriana: Essays on Arthurian Film* (London and New York, 1991).

Haymes, E.E. (ed.), *The Medieval Court in Europe* (Munich, 1986).

Haywood, I., *The Making of History: A Study of the Literary Forgeries of James Macpherson and Thomas Chatterton in Relation to Eighteenth-Century Ideas of History and Fiction* (London, 1986).

Hebron, M., *The Medieval Siege: Theme and Image in Middle English Romance* (Oxford, 1977).

Heffernan, T.J. (ed.), *The Popular Literature of Medieval England* (Knoxville, Tenn., 1985).

Hibbard, L.A., *Medieval Romance in England: A Study of the Sources and Analogues of the Non-cyclic Metrical Romances*, rev. edn. (New York, 1963).

Hopkins, A., *The Sinful Knights: A Study of Middle English Penitential Romance* (Oxford, 1990).

Huizinga, J., *The Waning of the Middle Ages*, trans. F. Hopman (Harmondsworth, 1965).

Ihle, S.N., *Malory's Grail Quest: Invention and Adaptaton in Medieval Prose Romance* (Madison, Wisc., 1983).

Jackson, W.H. (ed.), *Knighthood in Medieval Literature* (Woodbridge, 1981).

Johnson, L.S., *The Voice of the* Gawain-*Poet* (Madison, Wisc., and London, 1984).

Johnston, A., *Enchanted Ground: The Study of Medieval Romance in the Eighteenth Century* (London, 1964).

Jondorf, G. and D.N. Dumville (eds.), *France and the British Isles in the Middle Ages and Renaissance* (Woodbridge, 1991).

Kane, G., *Middle English Literature: A Critical Study of the Romances, the Religious Lyrics, Piers Plowman* (London, 1951, rev. edn., 1971).

Keen, M., *Chivalry* (New Haven and London, 1984).

—— 1990, *English Society in the Later Middle Ages, 1348-1500* (London, 1990).

Kennedy, B., *Knighthood in the* Morte Darthur (Woodbridge, 1985).

Kennedy, E.D., *King Arthur: A Casebook* (New York and London, 1996).

Ker, N.R., *Medieval Libraries of Great Britain*, 2nd edn. (London, 1964).

—— 1969, *Medieval Manuscripts in British Libraries* (London, 1969).

Knight, S., *The Structure of Sir Thomas Malory's Arthuriad* (Sydney, 1969).

—— 1983, *Arthurian Literature and Society* (London, 1983).

Kipling, G., *The Triumph of Honour: Burgundian Origins of the Elizabethan Renaissance* (Leiden, 1977).

Korrel, P., *An Arthurian Triangle: A Study of the Origin, Development and Characterization of Arthur, Guinevere and Modred* (Leiden, 1984).

Lacy, N.J., *The Craft of Chrétien de Troyes: An Essay in Narrative Art* (Leiden, 1980).

—— 1987-8, D. Kelly and K. Busby (eds.), *The Legacy of Chrétien de Troyes*, 2 vols. (Amsterdam, 1987-8).

Lacy, N.J. (ed.), *The New Arthurian Encyclopedia* (Chicago and London, 1991).

—— 1996 (ed.), *Medieval Arthurian Literature: A Guide to Recent Scholarship* (New York and London, 1996).

—— 1996b (ed.), *Text and Intertext in Medieval Arthurian Literature* (New York and London, 1996).

Lagorio, V.M. and M.L. Day (eds.), *King Arthur Through the Ages*, 2 vols. (New York, 1990).

Lambert, M., *Malory: Style and Vision in* Le Morte Darthur (New Haven, Conn., 1975).

Lawton, D. (ed.), *Middle English Alliterative Poetry and its Literary Background* (Cambridge, 1982).

Legge, M.D., *Anglo-Norman Literature and its Background* (Oxford, 1963).

Lenz, J.M., *The Promised End: Romance Closure in the* Gawain-*Poet, Malory, Spenser, and Shakespeare* (New York, 1986).

Le Saux, F.H.M., *Laʒamon's* Brut: *The Poem and its Sources* (Cambridge, 1989).

—— 1994 (ed.), *The Text and Tradition of Laʒamon's* Brut (Cambridge, 1994).

Levy, B.S. and P.E. Szarmach (eds.), *The Alliterative Tradition in the Fourteenth Century* (Kent, Ohio, 1981).

Lewis, C.S., *The Discarded Image: An Introduction to Medieval and Renaissance Literature* (Cambridge, 1964).

Loomis, R.S. (ed.), [ALMA] *Arthurian Literature in the Middle Ages* (Oxford, 1959).

—— 1963, *The Development of Arthurian Romance* (London, 1963).

McCarthy, T., *Reading the* Morte Darthur (Cambridge, 1988).

McGillivray, M., *Memorization in the Transmission of the Middle English Romances* (New York and London, 1990).

Maddox, D., *The Arthurian Romances of Chrétien de Troyes* (Cambridge, 1991).

Mancoff, D., *The Arthurian Revival in Victorian Art* (New York, 1990).

—— 1995, *The Return of King Arthur: The Legend Through Victorian Eyes* (London, 1995).

Matthews, W., *The Tragedy of Arthur: A Study of the Alliterative* Morte Arthure (Berkeley, Cal., 1960).

Maynadier, H., *The Arthur of the English Poets* (Boston, 1907, repr. New York, 1979).

Meale, C.M., (ed.), *Women and Literature in Britain: 1150-1500* (Cambridge, 1993, 2nd edn., 1996).

—— 1994 (ed.), *Readings in Medieval Romance* (Cambridge, 1994).

Mehl, D., *The Middle English Romances of the Thirteenth and Fourteenth Centuries* (London, 1968).

Merriman, J.D., *The Flower of Kings: A Study of the Arthurian Legend in England between 1485 and 1835* (Lawrence, Kan., 1973).

Merrill, R., *Sir Thomas Malory and the Cultural Crisis of the Late Middle Ages* (New York, 1987).

Mills, M., J. Fellows and C.M. Meale (eds.), *Romance in Medieval England* (Cambridge, 1991).

Moorman, C., *A Knyght Ther Was: The Evolution of the Knight in Literature* (Lexington, Ky, 1967).

Morris, R., *The Character of King Arthur in Medieval Literature* (Cambridge, 1982).

Ní Cuilleanáin, E. and J.D. Pheifer (eds.), *Noble and Joyous Histories: English Romance, 1375-1650* (Blackrock, 1993).

Norbert, M., *The Reflection of Religion in English Medieval Verse Romances* (Bryn Mawr, Pa., 1941).

Owen, D.D.R. (ed.), *Arthurian Romance: Seven Essays* (Edinburgh, 1970).

Owings, M.A., *The Arts in the Middle English Romances* (New York, 1952).

Patterson, L., *Negotiating the Past: The Historical Understanding of Medieval Literature* (Madison, Wisc., 1987).

Pearsall, D., *Old and Middle English Poetry* (London, 1977).

—— 1983 (ed.), *Manuscripts and Readers in Fifteenth-Century England: The Literary Implications of Manuscript Study* (Cambridge, 1983).

—— 1987 (ed.), *Manuscripts and Texts: Editorial Problems in Later Middle English Literature* (Cambridge, 1987).

Pilch, H. (ed.), *Orality and Literacy in Early Middle English* (Tübingen, 1996).

Pochoda, E.T., *Arthurian Propaganda:* Le Morte d'Arthur *as an Historical Ideal of Life* (Chapel Hill, N.C., 1971).

Prestwich, M., *Edward I* (London, 1988).

Putter, A., Sir Gawain and the Green Knight *and French Arthurian Romance* (Oxford, 1995).

Quinn, W.A. and S.H. Audley, *Jongleur: A Modified Theory of Oral Improvisation and Its Effects on the Performance and Transmission of Middle English Romance* (Washington, D.C., 1982).

Ramsey, L.C., *Chivalric Romances: Popular Literature in Medieval England* (Bloomington, Ind., 1983).

Richmond, V.B., *The Popularity of Middle English Romance* (Bowling Green, Ohio, 1975).

Riddy, F., *Sir Thomas Malory* (Leiden, 1987).

Rooney, A., *Hunting in Middle English Literature* (Cambridge, 1993).

Rouse, M.A. and R.H. Rouse, *Authentic Witnesses: Approaches to Medieval Texts and Manuscripts* (Notre Dame, 1991).

Rumble, T.C. (ed.), *The Breton Lays in Middle English* (Detroit, 1965).

Ryding, W.W., *Structure in Medieval Narrative* (The Hague, 1971).

Salter, E., *Fourteenth Century English Poetry: Contexts and Readings* (Oxford, 1983).

—— 1988, *English and International: Studies in the Literature, Art and Patronage of Medieval England*, ed. D. Pearsall and N. Zeeman (Cambridge, 1988).

Scattergood, V.J., *Politics and Poetry in the Fifteenth Century* (London, 1971).

—— 1983, and J.W. Sherborne (eds.), *English Court Culture in the Later Middle Ages* (London, 1983).

Schmolke-Hasselmann, B., *The Evolution of Arthurian Romance: The Verse Tradition from Chrétien to Froissart*, trans. M. and R. Middleton (Cambridge, 1998).

Shichtman, M.B. and J.P. Carley (eds.), *Culture and the King: The Social Implications of the Arthurian Legend* (Albany, N.Y., 1994).

Simpson, R., *Camelot Regained: The Arthurian Revival and Tennyson, 1800-1849* (Cambridge, 1990).

Smith, L., *Victorian Photography, Painting and Poetry: The Enigma of Visibility in Ruskin, Morris and the Pre-Raphelites* (Cambridge, 1995).

Southern, R.W., *The Making of the Middle Ages* (London, 1953, repr. 1959).

Southworth, J., *The English Medieval Minstrel* (Woodbridge, 1989).

Spearing, A.C., *The* Gawain-*Poet: A Critical Study* (Cambridge, 1970).

—— 1972, *Criticism and Medieval Poetry*, 2nd edn. (London, 1972).

Speirs, J., *Medieval English Poetry: The Non-Chaucerian Tradition* (London, 1957, 2nd edn., 1962).

Spisak, J.W. (ed.), *Studies in Malory* (Kalamazoo, Mich., 1985).

Staines, D. (ed.), *Tennyson's Camelot: The* Idylls of the King *and Its Medieval Sources* (Waterloo, Ont., 1983).

Stanbury, S., *Seeing the* Gawain-*Poet: Description and the Art of Perception* (Philadelphia, Pa., 1991).

Stevens, J., *Medieval Romance: Themes and Approaches* (London, 1973).

Sturges, R.S., *Medieval Interpretation: Models of Reading in Literary Narrative, 1100-1500* (Carbondale, Ill., 1991).

Summerfield, T., *The Matter of Kings' Lives* (Amsterdam, 1998).

Takamiya, T. and D. Brewer (eds.), *Aspects of Malory* (Cambridge, 1981).

Tanner, W.E. (ed.), *The Arthurian Myth of Quest and Magic: A Festschrift in Honour of Lavon B. Fulwiler* (Dallas, Tex., 1993).

Tatlock, J.S.P., *The Legendary History of Britain* (Berkeley, Cal., 1950).

Taylor, J., *English Historical Literature in the Fourteenth Century* (Oxford, 1987).

Thiébaux, M., *The Stag of Love: The Chase in Medieval Literature* (Ithaca, N.Y., 1974).

Thompson, S., *Motif-Index of Folk-Literature*, rev. edn., 6 vols. (Bloomington, Ind., 1955-8).

Topsfield, L.T., *Chrétien de Troyes: A Study of the Arthurian Romances* (Cambridge, 1981).

Tristram, P., *Figures of Life and Death in Medieval English Literature* (London, 1976).

Turvill-Petre, T., *The Alliterative Revival* (Cambridge, 1977).

—— 1996, *England the Nation: Language, Literature and National Identity, 1290-1340* (Oxford, 1996).

Uitti, K.D. and M. Freeman, *Chrétien de Troyes* (New York, 1995).

Vale, M., *War and Chivalry: Warfare and Aristocratic Culture in England, France and Burgundy at the End of the Middle Ages* (London, 1981).

—— 1996, *Origins of the Hundred Years War: The Angevin Legacy, 1250-1340* (Oxford, 1996).

Vale J., *Edward III and Chivalry: Chivalric Society and Its Context, 1270-1350* (Woodbridge, 1982).

Vance, E., *From Topic to Tale: Logic and Narrativity in the Middle Ages* (Minneapolis, 1987).

Varty, K. (ed.), *An Arthurian Tapestry: Essays in Memory of Lewis Thorpe* (Glasgow, 1981).

Vinaver, E., *The Rise of Romance* (Oxford, 1971).

Whitaker, M., *The Legends of King Arthur in Art* (Cambridge, 1990).

White, R. (ed.), *King Arthur in Legend and History* (London, 1997).

Wilson, A., *Traditional Romance and Tale: How Stories Mean* (Ipswich, 1976).

—— 1988, *The Magical Quest: The Use of Magic in Arthurian Romance* (Manchester, 1988).

Wilson, R.M., *Early Middle English Literature*, reprint (London, 1968).

Wittig, S., *Stylistic and Narrative Structures in the Middle English Romances* (Austin, Tex., 1978).

Wynne-Davies, M., *Women and Arthurian Literature: Seizing the Sword* (London, 1996).

INDEX